Lecture Notes in Artificial Intelligence   6356

Edited by R. Goebel, J. Siekmann, and W. Wahlster

Subseries of Lecture Notes in Computer Science

Jan Allbeck   Norman Badler
Timothy Bickmore   Catherine Pelachaud
Alla Safonova (Eds.)

Intelligent Virtual Agents

10th International Conference, IVA 2010
Philadelphia, PA, USA, September 20-22, 2010
Proceedings

 Springer

Series Editors

Randy Goebel, University of Alberta, Edmonton, Canada
Jörg Siekmann, University of Saarland, Saarbrücken, Germany
Wolfgang Wahlster, DFKI and University of Saarland, Saarbrücken, Germany

Volume Editors

Jan Allbeck
George Mason University, Fairfax, USA, E-mail: jallbeck@gmu.edu

Norman Badler
University of Pennsylvania, Philadelphia,USA, E-mail: badler@seas.upenn.edu

Timothy Bickmore
Northeastern University, Boston, USA, E-mail: bickmore@ccs.neu.edu

Catherine Pelachaud
CNRS-LTCI, Télécom ParisTech, Paris, France
E-mail: catherine.pelachaud@telecom-paristech.fr

Alla Safonova
University of Pennsylvania, Philadelphia, USA, E-mail:alla@seas.upenn.edu

Library of Congress Control Number: 2010934238

CR Subject Classification (1998): I.2, H.4, D.2, I.4, I.2.11, I.6

LNCS Sublibrary: SL 7 – Artificial Intelligence

ISSN	0302-9743
ISBN-10	3-642-15891-9 Springer Berlin Heidelberg New York
ISBN-13	978-3-642-15891-9 Springer Berlin Heidelberg New York

springer.com

© Springer-Verlag Berlin Heidelberg 2010
Printed in Germany

Typesetting: Camera-ready by author, data conversion by Scientific Publishing Services, Chennai, India
Printed on acid-free paper   06/3180

Preface

Welcome to the proceedings of the 10th International Conference on Intelligent Virtual Agents (IVA), held 20-22 September, 2010 in Philadelphia, Pennsylvania, USA. Intelligent Virtual Agents are interactive characters that exhibit human-like qualities and communicate with humans or with each other using natural human modalities such as behavior, gesture, and speech. IVAs are capable of real-time perception, cognition, and action that allow them to participate in a dynamic physical and social environment.

IVA 2010 is an interdisciplinary annual conference and the main forum for presenting research on modeling, developing, and evaluating Intelligent Virtual Agents with a focus on communicative abilities and social behavior. The development of IVAs requires expertise in multimodal interaction and several AI fields such as cognitive modeling, planning, vision, and natural language processing. Computational models are typically based on experimental studies and theories of human-human and human-robot interaction; conversely, IVA technology may provide interesting lessons for these fields. Visualizations of IVAs require computer graphics and animation techniques, and in turn supply significant realism problem domains for these fields. The realization of engaging IVAs is a challenging task, so reusable modules and tools are of great value. The fields of application range from robot assistants, social simulation, and tutoring to games and artistic exploration.

The enormous challenges and diversity of possible applications of IVAs have resulted in an established annual conference. It was started in 1998 as a workshop on Intelligent Virtual Environments at the European Conference on Artificial Intelligence in Brighton, UK, which was followed by a similar one in 1999 in Salford, Manchester. Then dedicated stand-alone IVA conferences took place in Madrid, Spain in 2001, Irsee, Germany in 2003, and Kos, Greece in 2005. Since 2006 IVA has become a full-fledged annual international event, which was first held in Marina del Rey, California, USA, then Paris, France, in 2007, Tokyo, Japan, in 2008, and Amsterdam, The Netherlands, in 2009. Since 2005 IVA has also hosted the Gathering of Animated Lifelike Agents (GALA), a festival to showcase state-of-the-art IVAs created by university students, academic, or industrial research groups. The current conference represents well the range of expertise, from different scientific and artistic disciplines, and the value of both theoretical and practical work needed to create IVAs which suspend our disbelief.

The special application theme of IVA 2010 was "virtual human communities." IVA achievements to date lead naturally to studies involving the formation, simulation, and understanding of ever widening social, cultural, and cognitive interactions among humans and virtual humans. Computer graphics techniques now permit the visual simulation of large collections of individual agents, offering real-time visualization platforms for expanding social units to families, co-worker teams, building inhabitants, and even an entire virtual populace. Mobile interactive devices and emergent human interests in real-time social networking provide some additional economic incentives and a growing industry presence. This special topic also builds on the special theme of IVA 2009, games, in that participants in virtual environments will need to interact not just with the space or with individual IVAs, but perhaps with a group or community of IVAs in order to achieve desired situations or goal states. IVA 2010 presented an opportunity to further interdisciplinary cross-fertilization between the IVA and virtual populace simulation fields.

IVA 2010 received altogether 93 submissions. Of these, 18 papers were accepted as long papers and 34 as short papers. The poster session comprised 26 displays. Three invited speakers presented keynote presentations, one per conference day. The conference opened with a keynote talk by Motion Picture Academy 2010 Technical Achievement Award recipient Paul Debevec titled "From 'Spider-Man' to 'Avatar': Achieving Photoreal Digital Actors"; the second morning keynote was presented by neuropsychiatrist Ruben Gur on "The Neurobiology of Emotion Processing by Humans and Computers"; and the third keynote was offered by video game writer and designer Lee Sheldon on "Virtual Agents in the Modular World."

IVA 2010 was locally organized by the SIG Center for Computer Graphics at the University of Pennsylvania, and took place in the Inn at Penn, an on-campus hotel. We would like to thank the people who contributed to the high scientific quality of the event: the members of the Program Committee for their reviews and the members of the Senior Program Committee for their advice on preparing the event and evaluating the papers. We express our appreciation to Stacy Marsella for his careful selection of the Best Paper Awards, Phil Heslop and Laura Pfeifer for organizing the GALA, and to Chris Czyzewicz and Daniel Schulman for arranging the busy poster and demo session. Special thanks go to Alla Safonova who guided and navigated the submission and selection process. We are greatful to Nop Jiarathanakul and Ashley Yuki for designing and administrating the conference web site. We express our sincere appreciation to Catherine Stocker for her thorough and adept local organization and care of many of the practical matters of the conference, to Penn Conference Services for managing the registration website and handling many financial matters, to Mark West for financial help and advice, to Jessica Marcus of Penn's Institute for Research in Cognitive Science for assisting onsite operations, and to the student volunteers for their assistance as needed. We are grateful for the support of our sponsors, which was essential to make the event happen.

Last, but not least, these proceedings represent the scientific work by the participants of IVA 2010. We thank all of them for their high-quality contributions. We hope that this volume will foster further research on IVAs, and we look forward to hearing of new work at future IVA conferences.

July 2010

Jan Allbeck
Norman Badler
Timothy Bickmore
Catherine Pelachaud

Table of Contents

Behavior Modeling

Gesture and Expression

Backchannels and Simulation

Personality

Interaction Strategies

Emotion

User Studies

Constraints-Based Complex Behavior in Rich Environments

Jan M. Allbeck[1] and Hadas Kress-Gazit[2]

[1] Volgenau School of Information, Technology and Engineering,
George Mason University, Fairfax, VA 22030
[2] Sibley School of Mechanical and Aerospace Engineering,
Cornell University, Ithaca, NY 14853

Abstract. In order to create a system capable of planning complex, constraints-based behaviors for an agent operating in a rich environment, two complementary frameworks were integrated. Linear Temporal Logic mission planning generates controllers that are guaranteed to satisfy complex requirements that describe reactive and possibly infinite behaviors. However, enumerating all the relevant information as a finite set of Boolean propositions becomes intractable in complex environments. The PAR (Parameterized Action Representation) framework provides an abstraction layer where information about actions and the state of the world is maintained; however, its planning capabilities are limited. The integration described in this paper combines the strengths of these two frameworks and allows for the creation of complex virtual agent behavior that is appropriate to environmental context and adheres to specified constraints.

Keywords: Complex Behaviors, Representations, Agent Architectures.

1   Introduction

Attempting to instruct artificial entities, be they robots or agents in a virtual environment, requires representing information about the actions, environment, and agents and being able to efficiently process this data to interpret and execute the instructions. In this paper we describe the integration of two subsystems that form a framework for instructing agents to perform *complex behaviors* in *complex environments* while adhering to dictated *constraints*. Instructions may indicate what behaviors an agent should perform, but they can also provide constraints on how they should be performed. A constraint might completely prohibit an action (e.g. *Don't run*). Other constraints may impact the timing or priority of actions (e.g. *Do your homework before playing video games*). There could also be spatial constraints (e.g. *Stay out of Room 12*). Finally, constraints may include a variety of factors that form an overall context (e.g. *Do not go into a classroom when a class is in session*).

Instructed behaviors can also come in a variety of forms. There may be simple imperatives containing a single verbs (e.g. *Pickup the pencil*) or complex

J. Allbeck et al. (Eds.): IVA 2010, LNAI 6356, pp. 1–14, 2010.

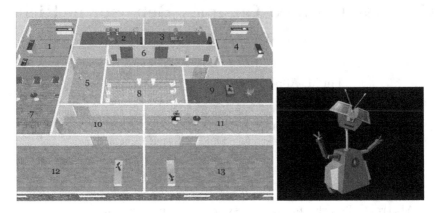

Fig. 1. (a) Virtual World with room numbers shown. (b) Murray, the virtual robot.

multi-step behaviors involving a sequence of actions or actions that should be performed in parallel (e.g. *While programming, drink coffee*). Other directives may require the agents to plan (e.g. *Search the building for weapons*). Finally instructions may include standing orders that dictate how the agents should handle scenarios they may encounter (e.g. *If you see a weapon, pick it up and move it to Room 13*). All of these behaviors can take place in a rich environment with many objects of many different types. Furthermore, these environments are dynamic. Other characters are operating within the environment, moving objects and changing their states and properties. Some instructions such as *Do not go into a classroom when a class is in session*, certainly address this dynamic nature.

In this paper, we present a framework that provides a strong representational and operational foundation for instructing virtual agents. The first component, the Parameterized Action Representation (PAR), provides a rich representation, a system for grounding the terms, and low level controllers for agents in a virtual environment. The second component, Linear Temporal Logic Mission and Motion Planning, is a framework for creating controllers such that the agent is guaranteed to satisfy high level task specifications, if they are feasible. The integration of these components provides constraints based complex planning and behaviors in rich environments. Additionally, we introduce the notion of meta-PARs. MetaPARs extend traditional, atomic PARs to provide more information about the desired behavior and constraints on it. MetaPARs aid the connection between PAR and the logic framework and will also provide a target representation for natural language parsers, semantic taggers, or pragmatic processors.

To help highlight the features of our framework and ground our discussions, we will present two example scenarios. One of the scenarios being examined involves using virtual robots in a building clearing exercise (See Figure 1). The robot searches the environment, obeying constraints, and reacting as instructed to the objects he discovers. As an example, Murray, the virtual robot, may be instructed: "*Search rooms 1, 2, 3 and 4. If you see a dead body, abandon the search and go to room 11. If you see a bomb, pick it up and take it to room 13 and then resume the search."*

To further highlight advantages of the integration, we also present examples from another scenario. This scenario involves replacing old computers with new ones. It is set in a university environment and contains instructions such as, *"Replace all of the computers. Do not enter a classroom during a class. Make sure that classrooms always have at least one computer. Replace all classroom computers before office computers. Do not remove a computer that someone is using."* Throughout the rest of this paper we will reference these two scenarios to frame examples and illustrate the advantages of our integration.

2   Parametrized Action Representation

At a finer level of detail, effective instructions may include, implicitly or explicitly, several additional elements. There are the core semantics that indicate the action or actions to be performed. There may even be an action structure composed of several sub-actions. There are also the participants of the action, including the agent being instructed to perform the action and any objects involved in the action (e.g. Pickup the *cup*). Instructions may also contain information related to the context, including path information, manner, or purpose. Initiation conditions are often implicit. Is the agent capable of performing the action? What state must the world and agent be in before the action is performed? Finally, effective instructions include either implicitly or explicitly termination conditions that indicate when an action has been completely successfully or when it cannot be. The Parameterized Action Representation (PAR) includes all of these elements and more [4].

In the PAR system, goal states are not specified and then planned for. Instead, agents are instructed to perform actions. These instructions can be sent from a high level controller [1] or from a human user [3]. The only planning included in the current PAR system is simple backward chaining done through explicitly pairing the preconditions of an action with other actions that can fulfill the conditions if required. The most common pairing is collocating the agent with an object participant of the action through locomotion. For example, if instructed to pickup an object, an agent will automatically move to the object. The location of the object is stored as a parameter of the object (initialized automatically from the environment and updated through action post-assertions). Animating the locomotion behavior and navigation is a function of the *Simulator* (See Figure 2) [12].

PAR is a rich representation that has been linked to motion generators in simulation frameworks [1,3,4]. PAR actually includes a representation of both actions and objects. Each are stored in hierarchies in a MySQL database called the *Actionary* (See Figure 2). The *Actionary* holds information about generic/uninstantiated actions and objects (e.g. what properties change as a consequence of an action or what properties are true of all chairs) as well as specific information about instantiated actions and objects (e.g. $Agent_4$ *Pickup*

Cup_0 or $Chair_6$ is RED and located in $Classroom_7$). Instantiated actions and objects are leaves in the hierarchies inheriting (or if desired overwriting) parameters from their uninstantiated parents. As actions execute, they change the state and properties of objects and agents in the simulated environment. These changes are also automatically registered in the instantiated objects in the *Actionary*, which then serves as a representational *World Model.*

Furthermore, the hierarchies provide a convenient classification system. An agent might be instructed to explore the environment and pickup all weapons and move them to a certain room. When the agent perceives an object in the environment, the agent's *Agent Process* (i.e. the PAR control process for the agent (See Figure 2)) checks to see if the perceived object is a descendant of the *Weapon* node in the object hierarchy and if so reacts accordingly. Hence instructions can use broader more general terms without explicitly enumerating predicates.

Instantiated objects also contain a lot of useful parameters including properties (e.g. color and age), postures (e.g. open or closed), states (e.g. on or off and free or in-use), and location among many others. Here *location* refers to another PAR object and not a three-dimensional coordinate, which is another parameter, namely *position*. For example, $Computer_8$ is located in $Office_2$ or Gun_9 is located in the contents of $Agent_4$. *Contents* is another PAR object parameter. It provides a list of all of the objects in a location. Many of these object parameters are updated automatically as post-assertions of actions. For example, *Pickup* Obj_0 will automatically set the *location* of Obj_0 as the agent executing the action and add Obj_0 to that agent's *contents*. In other words, successful execution of a *Pickup* action implies that the agent is now holding the object. Furthermore, the position of the object will automatically change with the position of the agent until an action, such as *Drop* is performed to release the relationship. Because all of these parameters are maintained, they can easily be referenced in conditions for modifying behaviors.

While PAR is a rich representation that includes the semantics of actions and objects and provides a level of abstraction, it is not a logic. Plan constraints such as *Do not enter $Room_7$* and *Do not remove a computer that is in use*, cannot be represented by PARs. Similarly there is no convenient way to represent general sets or quantifiers. These limitations have been overcome through integration with a logic framework.

3   Linear Temporal Logic Mission and Motion Planning

The Linear Temporal Logic mission and motion planning framework [9,10] creates continuous control inputs for a robot such that its (possibly infinite) behavior satisfies a high-level complex specification that includes temporal operators and constraints. The idea at the heart of this approach is that a continuous control problem (i.e. finding velocity commands for the robot's movement/continuous actions) is abstracted into a discrete domain where boolean propositions correspond to basic robot states. For example, a proposition $Room_1$

will be true whenever the physical location of the robot or agent is contained in the area defined as Room 1. Then, the specification is written as temporal logic formulas and synthesis techniques generate a correct-by-construction automaton that when executed activates atomic controllers that drive the robot according to the specifications. In the following we describe the different aspects of this framework.

3.1 Specification

Formulas written in a fragment of Linear Temporal Logic (LTL) are used to specify the desired agent behavior and any information about the environment in which it is operating. These formulas have specific structure [10] and are defined over a set of boolean propositions which are task and agent specific; they describe the regions in the environment, events that may be detected (such as a bomb is seen or a class is in session) and actions the agent can perform (such as pick up, drop or replace computer).

In addition to the propositions, the formulas include boolean operators ($\neg$ 'not', $\vee$ 'or', $\wedge$ 'and', $\Rightarrow$ 'imply', etc.) and temporal operators ($\Box$ 'always', $\Diamond$ 'eventually', $\bigcirc$ 'next'). Loosely speaking, the truth of an LTL formula is defined over infinite executions of a finite state machine; $\Box p$ is true if p is true in every step of every execution, $\Diamond p$ is true if for every execution there is a step in which p becomes true and $\bigcirc p$ is true if on every execution, p is true in the next step. The formula $\Box \Diamond p$ is true if p becomes true infinitely often. We refer the reader to [6] for a formal description of LTL.

The LTL formulas describe several aspects of the agent's behavior: its motion constraints, for example $\Box(Room_1 \Rightarrow (\bigcirc Room_1 \vee \bigcirc Room_5))$ states that when the agent is in room 1, it can either stay there or move to an adjacent room in the next step. This part of the LTL formula is generated automatically from a given map of the environment. Other aspects are the desired reaction to events, for example $\Box(\bigcirc bomb \Rightarrow \bigcirc PickUp)$ encodes that the agent should pick up a bomb if it encounters one, and desired motion, for example $\Box \Diamond(Room_1 \vee Room_2)$ requires the agent to go to either room 1 or room 2.

3.2 Automaton Synthesis and Execution

Once the specification is written in the logic, the formula is synthesized into an automaton such that every execution of the automaton is guaranteed to satisfy the specification, if it is feasible. If the specification cannot be guaranteed, no automaton will be generated and the user gets an error message.

The (discrete) synthesized automaton is then transformed into a hybrid controller that provides continuous control commands to the agent. This controller, based on the state of the agent and its environment, governs the execution of atomic continuous controllers whose composition induces the intended robot behavior.

4   Integration of PAR and the LTL Framework

The strength of PARs lay in providing a rich description of agents, the actions they can perform and the world around them. However, while sequential planning can be performed by backward chaining, constraint-based, temporal, complex behaviors cannot be planned by the system. Furthermore, there is no built in mechanism for remembering events that occurred in the past that influence future behavior. Integration with the LTL planning framework provides a solution to these issues.

On the other hand, the LTL planning framework naturally creates complex behaviors that are guaranteed to satisfy different constraints and temporal relations, but because it plans over a finite set of Boolean propositions, all possible information has to be enumerated, which makes the approach intractable when the environment becomes too complex. Furthermore, knowledge of the agent state (for example, it is holding a bomb) has to be captured using extra propositions whose truth values need to be reasoned about. The PAR formalism provides the LTL planning framework an abstraction layer where information about possible actions and the state of the virtual agent is maintained by PAR and only information needed for the planning is passed along. Together these two subsystems complement each other and provide a foundation for specifying and executing constraints-based complex behaviors in rich environments.

Figure 2 provides an overview of the integrated system components and their connections. Before a simulation begins, an *External Controller* is responsible for defining a scenario and hence creating the environment, objects, and agents.

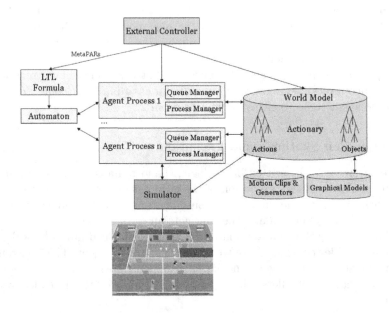

Fig. 2. Integrated System

From this information, LTL propositions are created. The information is also stored in the *Actionary* and a PAR *Agent Process* is created for each agent.

The *External Controller* also defines the behavior of the agents. The ultimate aim is to instruct virtual agents through natural language, in which case this external controller would include parsers, semantic taggers, and pragmatic processors. Currently we are using GUI forms. PARs have previously been linked to natural language processors [4] and the LTL framework receives input from structured English [9]. In order to gain the planning and reasoning capabilities of the LTL framework while maintaining the rich representation of the PAR formalism, the next section introduces the notion of *MetaPARs*. These special PARs include in addition to the standard PAR fields [4] special fields that provide information regarding desired behavior and constraints. Once these fields are defined they are converted, together with the workspace description, into LTL formulas that then get synthesized into an automaton that governs the execution of atomic PARs.

During a simulation, perceptions are passed from the *Simulator* to the *Agent Processes*. Transitions between states in the *Automaton* are based on these perceptions as well as other information stored in the *World Model* (i.e. *Actionary*). LTL propositions in the states then specify the atomic PAR actions that should be performed. These actions are processed by the *Agent Processes* resulting in updates to the *World Model* and control over the virtual agents displayed in the *Simulator*.

5 MetaPARs

MetaPARs are an integrated representation of PARs and LTL expressions. The added fields augment traditional PARs with information further detailing the desired behaviors and constraints. A PAR is considered a *MetaPAR* when it includes the following special fields:

- *Primary Action* - The main objective of the PAR. Includes behaviors such as search (area for object), explore (area), find (object), replace (area, old object, new object), goto (region), etc. These actions can be terminating or infinite.
- *Primary Action Parameters* - Parameters for the primary action such as description of the area to explore or the object to find.
- *Memory i ON Condition* - Condition for setting a memory proposition used to indicate that an event of interest occurred. For example, seeing a body needs to be remembered because it alters the future behavior of the agent.
- *Memory i OFF Condition* - Condition for resetting memory proposition i.
- *Priority i_j Condition* - Condition for behavior that is in priority i_j.
- *Priority i_j Reaction* - Behavior for the agent if the condition is true. We distinguish between two types of reactions; *liveness*, behaviors that have to eventually occur, and *safety*, behaviors the agent must always satisfy.
- *Priority i_j Condition Type* - Indicate the reaction is one of two types. For *If and only if* (iff) the action defined in the reaction field should only occur

if the condition is true. For *if* the action has to occur when the condition is true but can occur in other situations as well.

All the Condition and Reaction fields contain LTL formulas over the set of atomic propositions (atomic PARs and memory propositions). These formulas can contain, other than the Boolean operators, only the 'next' temporal operator $\bigcirc$.[1]

The priorities define which reaction takes precedence. Priority i_j is higher than k_l for $i < k$ and therefore reaction k_l will be executed only if condition i_j is not active. Reactions with priorities i_j and i_k have the same priority and the execution of one does not dependent on the status of the condition of the other. When defining these metaPARs the user needs to make sure reactions with the same priority do not contradict.

Each unique MetaPAR is automatically translated into a conjunction of LTL formulas corresponding to the MetaPAR's primary action, parameters, memory and reactions. These formulas are defined over the set of propositions that correspond to the environment of the agent, the objects in the environment, the memory propositions and a termination proposition (*done*) for primary actions that terminate. Table 1 describes LTL formulas that are generated from the primary action and parameters of several different MetaPARs. These initial parameters were created after extended discussions and preliminary corpus analysis from the robot building clearing domain. It is straight forward to extend this table to different actions as the need arises.

Table 2 describes the mapping between the rest of the MetaPAR fields (memory propositions, reactions) and their corresponding LTL formulas. There, propositions of the form M_i correspond to events that need to be remembered, that is, the proposition M_i becomes true when the 'ON' event is detected and false when the 'OFF' event is encountered. Propositions of the form C_i are used to represent conditions of required reactions. While not necessary, they simplify the formulas capturing the reactions and priorities. Note that some formulas, such as the ones defining the initial conditions of the propositions, are omitted here to maintain clarity.

Going back to our building clearing example, the MetaPAR *ExploreOnce* with parameters $Location = \{r_1, r_2, r_3, r_4\}$ contains one memory proposition (M_1) for remembering that *Dead* was true at some point in the past and four reactions. This MetaPAR translates to the following LTL formula where lines 4, 5 and 16 correspond to the primary action, 6 to the memory proposition and 7-15 to the reactions. Initial conditions of the propositions and the topology of the environment are captured in lines 1-3. The conditions of the reactions are represented using $C_1, C_{21}, C_{22}, C_{23}$. For example, C_1 becomes true when a dead person is encountered (line 7) and it is the condition for requiring the robot to go to room 11 and stay there (lines 8,9).

---

[1] For a formal description of the structure the reader is referred to [10].

Table 1. Translation of MetaPAR primary actions into corresponding LTL formulas

MetaPAR Primary Action	Parameters	Corresponding LTL Formula
Search until finding	Location $L = \{l_1, l_2, \dots\}$, Object obj	$\bigwedge_{l \in L} \neg srch_l \wedge \neg done$ {Didn't search and not done} $\bigwedge_{l \in L} \square((l \vee Srch_l) \Leftrightarrow \bigcirc Srch_l)$ {If you are in l or you searched there before, then remember you already searched l } $\wedge \square(\bigcirc obj \Rightarrow \bigwedge_i (r_i \Leftrightarrow \bigcirc r_i))$ {If you see the object, stay where you are} $\wedge \square(\bigcirc obj \Leftrightarrow \bigcirc done)$ {If you see the object you are done} $\wedge \square \Diamond((\bigwedge_{l \in L} Srch_i) \vee done \bigvee_{C \in condition} C)$ {If has to be true that infinitely often you either searched the locations, are done or a condition is true}
Explore once	Location $L = \{l_1, l_2, \dots\}$	$\bigwedge_{l \in L} \neg srch_l \wedge \neg done$ {Didn't search and not done} $\bigwedge_{l \in L} \square((l \vee Srch_l) \Leftrightarrow \bigcirc Srch_l)$ {If you are in l or you searched there before, then remember you already searched l } $\wedge \square((\bigwedge_{l \in L} \bigcirc Srch_i) \Leftrightarrow \bigcirc done)$ {If you searched all locations, you are done} $\wedge \square \Diamond(done \bigvee_{C \in condition} C)$ {If has to be true that infinitely often you either are done or a condition is true}
Explore infinitely	Location $L = \{l_1, l_2, \dots\}$	$\bigwedge_{l \in L} \square \Diamond(l \bigvee_{C \in condition} C)$ {Infinitely often go to l unless a condition is true}
Find	Object obj	$\bigwedge_i \square \Diamond(r_i \vee obj \bigvee_{C \in condition} C)$ {Infinitely often go to all regions unless you find the object or a condition is true}
Goto	location formula $\mathcal{L}$	$\neg done$ {Not done} $\wedge \square(\bigcirc \mathcal{L} \Leftrightarrow \bigcirc done)$ {If you are in $\mathcal{L}$ you are done} $\square \Diamond(done \bigvee_{C \in condition} C)$ {Infinitely often done unless a condition is true}

Table 2. Mapping between the MetaPAR fields and the corresponding LTL formulas

MetaPAR Fields	Corresponding LTL Formula
Memory i *ON Condition* (once ON stays ON)	$\Box((ON\ Condition \lor M_i) \Leftrightarrow \bigcirc M_i)$
Memory i *ON Condition, OFF Condition*	$\Box(((ON\ Condition \lor M_i) \land \neg OFF\ Condition) \Leftrightarrow \bigcirc M_i)$
Priority i_j *Condition*	$\Box(Condition \Leftrightarrow \bigcirc C_{ij})$
Priority i_j *Reaction* (safety - iff)	$\Box((\bigcirc C_{ij} \land \neg \bigvee_{k<i,\forall l} \bigcirc C_{kl}) \Leftrightarrow Reaction)$
Priority i_j *Reaction* (safety - if)	$\Box((\bigcirc C_{ij} \land \neg \bigvee_{k<i,\forall l} \bigcirc C_{kl}) \Rightarrow Reaction)$
Priority i_j *Reaction* (liveness - iff)	$\Box\Diamond((C_{ij} \land \neg \bigvee_{k<i,\forall l} C_{kl}) \Leftrightarrow Reaction)$
Priority i_j *Reaction* (liveness - if)	$\Box\Diamond((C_{ij} \land \neg \bigvee_{k<i,\forall l} C_{kl}) \Rightarrow Reaction)$

$$\bigwedge \neg M_1 \land \neg Pick \land \neg Drop \land \neg C_1 \tag{1}$$

$$\bigwedge_{i\in\{1,\dots,4\}} \neg Srch_i \land \neg C_{21} \land \neg C_{22} \land \neg C_{23} \land \neg done \tag{2}$$

$$\bigwedge \text{Topology of the environment} \tag{3}$$

$$\bigwedge_{i\in\{1,\dots,4\}} \Box((r_i \lor Srch_i) \Leftrightarrow \bigcirc Srch_i) \tag{4}$$

$$\bigwedge \Box((\bigwedge_{l\in L} \bigcirc Srch_i) \Leftrightarrow \bigcirc done) \tag{5}$$

$$\bigwedge \Box((\bigcirc Dead \lor M_1) \Leftrightarrow \bigcirc M_1) \tag{6}$$

$$\bigwedge \Box(\bigcirc M_1 \Leftrightarrow \bigcirc C_1) \tag{7}$$

$$\bigwedge \Box\Diamond(C_1 \Rightarrow r_{11}) \tag{8}$$

$$\bigwedge \Box((\bigcirc C_1 \land r_{11}) \Rightarrow \bigcirc r_{11}) \tag{9}$$

$$\bigwedge \Box((\bigcirc seeBomb \land \neg \bigcirc haveBomb) \Leftrightarrow \bigcirc C_{21}) \tag{10}$$

$$\bigwedge \Box((\bigcirc C_{21} \land \neg \bigcirc C_1) \Leftrightarrow \bigcirc Pick) \tag{11}$$

$$\bigwedge \Box((\bigcirc haveBomb \land r_{13}) \Leftrightarrow \bigcirc C_{22}) \tag{12}$$

$$\bigwedge \Box((\bigcirc C_{22} \land \neg \bigcirc C_1) \Leftrightarrow \bigcirc Drop) \tag{13}$$

$$\bigwedge \Box(\bigcirc haveBomb \Leftrightarrow \bigcirc C_{23}) \tag{14}$$

$$\bigwedge \Box\Diamond((C_{23} \land \neg C_1) \Rightarrow r_{13}) \tag{15}$$

$$\bigwedge \Box\Diamond(done \lor C_1 \lor C_{21} \lor C_{22} \lor C_{23}) \tag{16}$$

The LTL formula for the clearing example was automatically synthesized into an automaton containing 582 states. Figure 3 depicts part of the automaton; the circles (states) contain the action propositions that are true in that state.

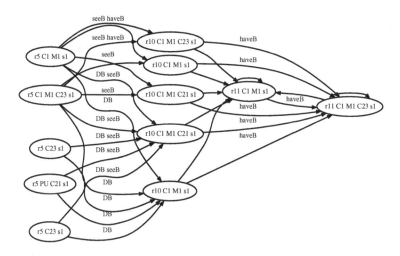

Fig. 3. Part of the automatically synthesized automaton for the clearing example. A possible execution could be starting from the top left most state: the agent is in room 5 and has searched room 1 (s_1 is true) and seen a dead body before (M_1 is true). Then, it goes to room 10. He ignores (does not pickup) bombs he sees along the way since the reaction to dead bodies has priority over bombs and then he reaches room 11, as was required.

These propositions relate to the behavior of the agent, for example, *PU* refers to the agent picking up a bomb. The arrows (transitions) are labeled with sensor propositions that must be true for that transition to take place, for example, if a dead body (*DB*) was found in room 5, the agent must go to room 10 next. These propositions are easily evaluated by PAR system. All transitions to and from other states in the automaton were omitted for clarity.

Interestingly, while executing this metaPAR Murray exhibited an unwanted, while correct, behavior. It would pick up a bomb, take it to Room 13, drop it and then begin an infinite loop of picking up the bomb and dropping it. This behavior was due to an incomplete specification; Murray was never instructed to ignore bombs in Room 13. This behavior was easily fixed by inserting a condition '$\bigcirc seeBomb \wedge r_{13}$' with reaction '$\neg \bigcirc PU$' and with priority 2 and shifting down the rest of the conditions. Figure 4 depicts snapshots of a simulation of Murray clearing a building.

Our second scenario, replacing old computers with new ones (See Figure 5), further highlights some of the capabilities of this integration. For example constraints, and therefore behaviors, can be based on dynamic conditions. Naturally, we can specify a constraint such as *Do not go into Room 12*, but the framework can also handle constraints such as *Do not enter a classroom during a class*. The applicability of this constraint changes as the simulation progresses. It is also possible to have ordering constraints, such as *Replace all classroom computers before office computers*, without strictly ordering all of the replace actions.

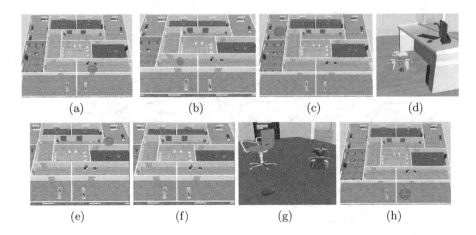

Fig. 4. Selected frames from the building clearing scenario (a) Murray begins in Room 11 and starts moving toward Room 1. (b) Murray passes through Room 10. (c) After passing through Room 5, Murray arrives at Room 1, sees a bomb, and picks it up. (d) He makes his way to Room 13 and drops off the bomb. (e) He then resumes the search and picks up a bomb in Room 4. (f) After dropping the bomb from Room 4 in Room 13, Murray picks up another bomb in Room 3. (g) Finally, he finishes his search in Room 2 where he picks up another bomb. (h) Murray drops off the bomb in Room 13 and the scenario ends.

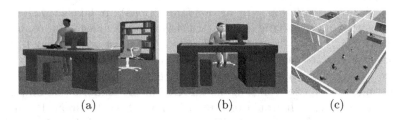

Fig. 5. Selected frames from the replacing computers scenario. (a) Replacing an office computer. (b) Office computer in use. (c) Class being held in a classroom.

6   Conclusion

While previous work on creating intelligent virtual agents (IVA's) has produced some interesting and sometimes complex behaviors [7,5,14,11], the work either did not allow users to input instructions to the characters or required them to tediously create decision and knowledge structures a priori. Many other efforts including [13] have focused on dialog planning which is beyond the scope of our current work. Like [8] and other work on IVA's, [13] also includes an element of plan recognition. The IVA's analyze user actions and recommend corrections or future actions based on stored plans for the given task domain. The focus of our framework is fulfilling complex instructions given by a user. As discussed in [2], it is important for planning to occur continuously and not be *baked* into the IVA. The LTL framework naturally provides plan flexibility since once the user changes a MetaPAR field a new plan is synthesized automatically.

The work presented in this paper was conducted as part of a large project aimed at answering the question of how robots (physical or virtual) can be instructed using natural language. In collaboration with linguists and natural language processing researchers, we have integrated the rich representation of PAR with the planning and reasoning capabilities of the LTL-based framework to create the underlaying representation and reasoning mechanism that will interface with the pragmatics and semantics of the language on one side and with the low-level robot control on the other. As a part of this project, researchers have begun collecting corpora that are being used to analyze the type of instructions that will be found in this domain so that components such as MetaPARs will be built with enough depth and robustness to meet the needs of the domain. As we learn more from these corpora, we will extend the MetaPAR representation. The ultimate analysis of the integration we have presented will come when all of the components of the entire system are joined together from the natural language parser through to a robot.

The resulting system enables complex, constrained-based behaviors for robots or virtual agents that are not possible in either framework alone. We have demonstrated the representations and frameworks through two rather different scenarios. There are, however, still limitations. We are currently using the LTL framework to determine the route an agent takes from one room to another. While the LTL framework will guarantee a successful route if one exists, the route generated is often suboptimal. Using way-point navigation, the PAR framework along with the *Simulator* does generate an optimal path. Unfortunately, constraints are not taken into account. We plan to address this by having the PAR framework generate a path that is then checked by the LTL framework to ensure that it does adhere to all constraints and when possible gives an indication of the spaces that should be avoided so that an alternative path can be obtained. As we further explore these domains and others, we may encounter other suboptimal plans that will lead to unnatural behaviors. We hope to mitigate these occurrences through the use of pragmatics and the existing semantics already available in PARs.

Furthermore, we have been testing this system on a single agent. In the future, we would like to construct teams of agents. We anticipate resource management issues as well as possible goal conflicts. The *Simulator* does include a resource manager that with extensions should handle some of these issues. Including agents statuses and referencing action priorities should help resolve some of the goal conflicts by determining which agent should take precedence, and then replanning for the others.

Acknowledgements

Partial support for this effort is gratefully acknowledged from the U.S. Army SUBTLE MURI W911NF-07-1-0216. We also appreciate donations from Autodesk and nVidia.

References

1. Allbeck, J.M.: Creating 3D Animated Human Behaviors for Virtual Worlds. Ph.D. thesis, University of Pennsylvania (2009)
2. Avradinis, N., Panayiotopoulos, T., Aylett, R.: Continuous planning for virtual environments. In: Vlahavas, I., Vrakas, D. (eds.) Intelligent Techniques for Planning, pp. 162–193 (2005)
3. Badler, N., Erignac, C., Liu, Y.: Virtual humans for validating maintenance procedures. Communications of the ACM 45(7), 56–63 (2002)
4. Bindiganavale, R., Schuler, W., Allbeck, J., Badler, N., Joshi, A., Palmer, M.: Dynamically altering agent behaviors using natural language instructions. In: Autonomous Agents, pp. 293–300. AAAI, Menlo Park (2000)
5. Cavazza, M., Charles, F., Mead, S.J.: Planning characters' behaviour in interactive storytelling. The Journal of Visualization and Computer Animation 13(2), 121–131 (2002), 10.1002/vis.285
6. Emerson, E.A.: Temporal and modal logic. In: Handbook of theoretical computer science. Formal Models and Semantics, vol. B, pp. 995–1072. MIT Press, Cambridge (1990)
7. Funge, J., Tu, X., Terzopoulos, D.: Cognitive modeling knowledge, reasoning and planning for intelligent character. In: Proceedings of ACM SIGGRAPH, pp. 29–38 (1999)
8. Johnson, W.L., Rickel, J.: Steve: An animated pedagogical agent for procedural training in virtual environments. ACM SIGART Bullentin 8(1-4), 16–21 (1997)
9. Kress-Gazit, H., Fainekos, G.E., Pappas, G.J.: Translating structured english to robot controllers. Advanced Robotics Special Issue on Selected Papers from IROS 2007 22(12), 1343–1359 (2008)
10. Kress-Gazit, H., Fainekos, G.E., Pappas, G.J.: Temporal logic based reactive mission and motion planning. IEEE Transactions on Robotics 25(6), 1370–1381 (2009)
11. Paris, S., Donikian, S.: Activity-driven populace: a cognitive approach to crowd simulation. IEEE Computer. Graphics and Applications 29(4), 34–43 (2009), 1669315
12. Pelechano, N., Allbeck, J.M., Badler, N.I.: Controlling individual agents in high-density crowd simulation. In: ACM SIGGRAPH / Eurographics Symposium on Computer Animation (SCA). ACM Press, San Diego (2007)
13. Smith, C., Cavazza, M., Charlton, D., Zhang, L., Turumen, M., Hakulinen, J.: Integrating planning and dialgue in a lifestyle agent. In: Prendinger, H., Lester, J.C., Ishizuka, M. (eds.) IVA 2008. LNCS (LNAI), vol. 5208, pp. 146–153. Springer, Heidelberg (2008)
14. Yu, Q., Terzopoulos, D.: A decision network framework for the behavioral animation of virtual humans. In: Proceedings of ACM SIGGRAPH/Eurographics symposium on Computer animation, pp. 119–128. Eurographics Association, San Diego (2007)

Smart Events and Primed Agents

Catherine Stocker[1], Libo Sun[2], Pengfei Huang[1], Wenhu Qin[3], Jan M. Allbeck[4], and Norman I. Badler[1]

[1] Department of Computer and Information Science, University of Pennsylvania, Philadelphia, PA 19104-6389
{cstocker,pengfei,badler}@seas.upenn.edu
[2] School of Computer Science and Technology, Tianjin University, Tianjin 300072, China
irisgrace@tju.edu.cn
[3] Department of Instrument Science and Engineering, Southeast University, Nanjing 210096, China
qinwenhu@seu.edu.cn
[4] Department of Computer Science, George Mason University, Fairfax, VA 22030
jallbeck@gmu.edu

Abstract. We describe a new organization for virtual human responses to dynamically occurring events. In our approach behavioral responses are enumerated in the representation of the event itself. These Smart Events inform an agent of plausible actions to undertake. We additionally introduce the notion of agent priming, which is based on psychological concepts and further restricts and simplifies action choice. Priming facilitates multi-dimensional agents and in combination with Smart Events results in reasonable, contextual action selection without requiring complex reasoning engines or decision trees. This scheme burdens events with possible behavioral outcomes, reducing agent computation to evaluation of a case expression and (possibly) a probabilistic choice. We demonstrate this approach in a small group scenario of agents reacting to a fire emergency.

Keywords: Smart events, primed agents, agent-based simulation.

1 Introduction

Real-time virtual human simulation has attracted considerable attention in recent years due to its applications in entertainment, education, architecture, training, urban engineering and virtual heritage. Often, spaces are populated with large groups of mostly homogeneous (though possibly visually differing) characters. Ideally, they would act as purposeful, functional individuals who enrich an environment, but it is difficult to keep the computational cost of intelligent agents low enough to simulate large populations. Most present simulations address scalability at the expense of expressivity by just animating walking pedestrians.

To keep the cost of agents low, simulations generally focus on emergent behaviors during collision avoidance. Alternatively, some methods center on agents with "heavy" reasoning, planning, or decision-making processers, and are too

J. Allbeck et al. (Eds.): IVA 2010, LNAI 6356, pp. 15–27, 2010.

computationally intensive to be scalable to large context-dependent groups. Our aim is to simulate groups of differentiated, functional agents with context-dependent behaviors at a low computational cost.

In this paper, we propose a new organization for virtual human responses to dynamically occurring events that embeds agent behavior options into a "Smart Event-Primed Agent" model. This model supports a simple but powerful mechanism for behavior selection. The main cost of this approach is borne in the user authoring of an event's representation. Events are then stored in a database for easy re-use in varying scenarios. The cost to each agent at run-time is simple expression evaluation. We demonstrate this approach in a small fire scenario and show that it can not only produce realistic simulation of group behaviors, but is also scalable.

The paper is organized as follows: in the next section, we briefly review related work. Section 3 focuses on the details of the Smart Event model. In Section 4, we describe the Primed Agent model. Section 5 illustrates a fire scenario where a Smart Event influences a number of Primed Agents. We discuss our conclusions and future work in Section 6.

2 Background

In order to produce behaviorally interesting agents, simulations often take one of two approaches: navigation-based motion controllers or agent-based cognitive systems. Navigation-based motion controller approaches aim at achieving real-time simulation for very large crowds, thus the behavior of each individual is not as important as long as the overall crowd movement produces realistic emergent behavior. The focus is on locomotion and collision avoidance while maintaining appropriate velocities, motions and directions. Classically [1] this was done with social force models [2] , cellular automata models [3] , or rule-based models [4] . More recently a real-time, hybrid approach was proposed [5] with a dual representation for simulating agents as both a discrete and single continuous system.

Agents must navigate in order to get to places where they are needed or should perform actions. Navigation-based models focus on fast navigation but sacrifice individuality for scalability. Agent-based approaches, on the other hand, focus on the realism of individual behavior by simulating *choice* through cognitive functions such as perception, memory, planning and emotion in every agent. The most developed of these, the SOAR (State, Operator And Result) architecture [6] , attempts to construct general intelligence systems by implementing a variety of cognitive functions, specifically memory, behavioral and learning systems. CML (Cognitive Modeling Language) [7] specifies domain knowledge and requires characters individually determine how to fulfill goals by searching a situation tree for a set of appropriate actions. PMFServ [8] aims to create culturally valid agents by using performance moderator functions (PMFs) that span the functionality of perception, biology, personality, social interactions, decision making and expression. The goal of these simulations is to cause agents to react to events in specific and individual ways that indicate internal psychological processes. The drawback is that they are generally not scalable to large groups of agents.

The agent-based systems that simulate human cognition by imposing a heavy computational load on their agents are based on the assumption that humans are logical creatures who make thoughtful and rational evaluations before acting. This assumption is often incorrect. Emotions, instincts and phobias are all well known aspects of human personality that override rationality [9] [10] [11] . A less well known phenomena, but more pervasive in the automaticity of everyday interactions, is *priming*. Priming refers to the activation of conceptual knowledge structures by the current situational context [12] . This effect is considered a result of spreading neural activation, is an automatic, unconscious process, and affects both thought and behavior. Studies have demonstrated that priming can influence a wide array of behaviors from aggressiveness [13] to walking speed [12] to test performance [14] .

There already exists a small body of work combining cognition- and navigation-based systems. Shao and Terzopolous [15] proposed a model of autonomous pedestrians, each with their own perceptual, behavioral and cognitive system. The cognitive system is needs-based and relies on each agent evaluating a potentially large set of internal variables. Although this model works for a small number of events, in our opinion it is not scalable to a complex environment with many events, because each event could require multiple new needs be added to each agent's cognitive set. Each new need would then continuously need to be monitored by every agent.

Extending the work of [15] Yu and Terzopolous [16] introduced a decision network framework. Based on a combination of probabilities of internal traits and external observations of the world, the system uses a hierarchy of decision networks to reason and choose actions. Without a centralized point of information, all agents must reason about the ambiguous world and attempt to answer questions such as "is someone else seeking help?" Instead of requiring agents to individually keep track of other agents, we centralize the heaviest cognition into the Smart Event. We could also simulate the ambiguity of incomplete information, by assigning ambiguous behaviors without the burden of requiring multiple agents to reason about them. We believe that using probabilities to assign actions at the trait group level will be as realistic as assigning them using complicated decision trees in each agent. Our justification for this belief is that a group of individuals with appropriate and plausible *collective* behaviors will appear functionally realistic.

CAROSA (Crowds with Aleatoric, Reactive, Opportunistic and Scheduled Actions) [1] is a framework for creating and simulating functional, heterogeneous populations. Its aim is to allow a user to easily create simulations that contain virtual humans with assigned roles and appropriate, contextual behaviors. CAROSA was built on top of HiDAC [1] which provides navigation and motion control. As the name suggests, CAROSA includes a variety of actions that together result in behavior rich simulations. What it does not have is an event representation. We implement Smart Events and Primed Agents on top of CAROSA-based agents.

The contributions of our framework are: a Smart Event model that acts as a resource manager, assigning agent interactions and monitoring agent participation; a Primed Agents model based on human cognition that quickly selects the behaviors provided by the Smart Event without intensive reasoning; and a virtual human simulation model that strikes a balance between individualism and scalability while simplifying scenario authoring by allowing actions to be authored for sets of agents dependent on their traits, rather than individually coded for each agent.

3 Smart Events

Our approach centers the behavioral responses of agents in the representation of the event itself, analogous to the way Smart Objects [17] inform an agent of the actions needed to accomplish manipulations on itself. Smart Objects contain interaction information of various kinds: intrinsic properties, information on how to interact with them, functionality and expected agent behaviors. Similarly, Maim [18] proposed a spatial navigation graph annotated with semantic tags that trigger specific actions of virtual characters that cross that spot, such as looking into windows or entering a shop and subsequently leaving with bread. These features inspire the Smart Event model.

For trajectory planning and a basic agent model, we extend the CAROSA system [1] to include Primed Agents reacting to Smart Events based on a primed trait. The semantics of actions and objects in CAROSA are represented in PAR (Parameterized Action Representation) [19] . A PAR may specify either single, multiple or hierarchic actions, thus {"put out the fire"} may consist of {"obtain a hose", "walk to the fire", "spray fire"}. The action types available in CAROSA are:

- **Aleatoric actions** – Random but structured by choices, distributions, or parametric variations.
- **Reactive actions** – Triggered by context.
- **Opportunistic actions** – Response to agent needs and automatically scheduled based on priorities and context.
- **Scheduled actions** – Assigned by a user and triggered by the passing of time.

We now define the Smart Event by specifying its representation, evolution and communication with Primed Agents.

3.1 Event Definition and Representation

We define an event as any scheduled or external (by environmental factors or agents other than self) assertion (fact) inserted into or deleted from the world model. A Smart Event is an event represented by the following parameters:

- **Type -** The type of event, such as emergency, social, work, etc.
- **Position** - Map coordinates of the event
- **Location** - Object (such as room) that contains the event
- **Start time** - When the event begins
- **End time** - When the event ends (may be undefined if unknown)
- **Evolution** - A Finite State Machine that alters event state variables over time and in response to internal or external triggers
- **Influence region** - The region (physical or communication) affected
- **Participants** - Lists of which agents are involved
- **Event emergency level (eEL)** - Severity of the event
- **Corresponding actions** - Set of possible actions for agents to select from

3.2 Communication between Events and Agents

The communication between Smart Events and Primed Agents is moderated by a Message Board. The Message Board is responsible for broadcasting and updating relevant information for an evolving event. The process (Fig. 1) is as follows: when the event begins, its details are posted to the relevant Message Boards according to the event's *influence region;* the *influence region* determines the location-based Message Board to post to (e.g., if there was a fire in a school building, the event would be posted to the school building's Message Board) as well as any relevant communication-based Message Boards to post to (e.g., for the same school fire, the event would be posted to the associated firehouse's Message Board, among others).

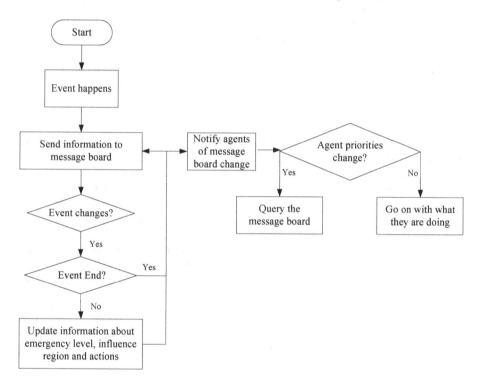

Fig. 1. Communication between the event, message board, and agent

Once an event is posted, a Message Board notifies a specified number of subscribers, according to its capacity limit, since not all agents are interested in or useful for that event. In this case, when the number of notified agents reaches the capacity threshold, the relevant message about that event is marked full. As a result, the rest of the agents do not need to see or respond to the event. Agents can be either *static* or *dynamic subscribers. Dynamic subscribers* subscribe when they enter the area overseen by the Message Board, e.g., they subscribe to the school Message Board when they enter the school or *physical radius. Static subscribers* are subscribed to a Message Board regardless of their location, e.g., a firefighter is always subscribed to the firehouse Message Board and thus event notifications on the firehouse's Message Board will be pushed out to him even if he is not at the firehouse: he is always within the *communication radius.* Using Message Boards, only relevant agents, according to *physical* and *communication radius,* are notified of events.

Agents can choose to respond, based on a very simple attention model: a comparison of their current *action's eEL* and the event's *eEL*. If agents find their current *action* to be less important than the event, they will acknowledge the event and query the Message Board for appropriate *actions* to perform. If they are "busy" (their *eEL* is > the event's *eEL*), they will ignore the event and continue what they were doing before being interrupted. When agents either run out of assigned *actions* becoming "idle", or becomes "bored" (i.e., their *eEL* falls below a threshold), or if a specified amount of time has elapsed, they will check the Message Boards they subscribe to in order to find new events. Until then, when "idle", they will perform a default *action*, as specified by their CAROSA defined roles. We see this communication system as analogous to an email/text message/voicemail system, in which people are notified of events but may not have the ability to learn about them or attend to them until they are free from obligation and can check their messages.

3.3 Event Evolution

Smart Events have the ability to change and evolve as time passes. The corresponding agent *actions* should also change to reflect their awareness and understanding of the evolving event. As shown in Fig. 2, we can use a finite state machine to model and modify event evolution based on *time* and *actions* performed by agents. In every timestep eEL is computed as a function of time and the actions of the agents involved.

As the event evolves, it will notify the Message Board of updates to its state, such as changes in the *eEL*, the *influence region* or the corresponding agent *actions*; finally when the event is over, it will notify the Message Board, which will push the information out to relevant agents before removing the event from itself. The frequency of updating information on the Message Board is a function of the evolution of the event, specifically the Δt specified in Fig. 2.

In the next section we discuss the final efficiency gain of this Smart Event-Primed Agent architecture: agent priming.

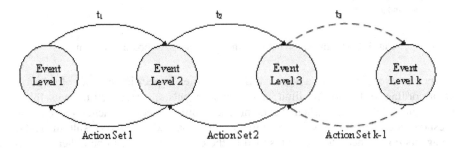

Fig. 2. The relationship between event evolution, passing *time* (*t*) and performed sets of *actions*

4 Primed Agents

The psychology literature clearly documents that people can be "primed" to activate one self-concept over others, and this priming can affect their resultant behavior. The dynamic constructivist view of culture [20] claims that this *frame switching* occurs when discrete constructs (categories, theories, stereotypes, schemas, etc.) of cultural self-concepts are brought to the forefront of an individual's mind in response to cues such as language and context. Individuals may have multiple networks of constructs and even contain conflicting constructs, as long as only one is activated or primed at a time.

One important way these constructs are formed as part of the self-concept is based on inclusion in a social group. Deaux et al. [21] performed a cluster analysis on trait property ratings to identify six distinct categories of social identity: relationships, vocation/avocation, political affiliation, stigma and ethnicity/religion. We base our trait model on these 6 groups, but make slight modifications. Based on the numerous studies of priming on gender and ethnicity we believed those two traits deserved their own group – thus we pulled gender out of the relationship group and split ethnicity/religion into ethnicity and religion. In addition, we felt age was an important category to include in a simulation that may require strenuous movement – thus we pulled it out into its own group also. We extend the theory of dynamic constructivism to simulating realistic individual *actions* based on the priming of one of these traits at a time. These factors are demonstrated with representative values in Table 1.

Table 1. Traits and their assigned values

Trait	Possible Values
Age	Child, adult, elder
Gender	Male, female
Ethnicity	American, European, Asian, African, Australian, Hispanic
Religion	Christian, Jewish, Muslim, Hindu, Buddhist
Vocation	Firefighter, policeman, teacher, student
Relational	Mother/father, daughter/son, husband/wife, friend/stranger
Stigma	Smoker, homeless, deaf
Political Affiliation	Democrat, Republican

Every agent may be assigned values for any set of the *traits* in the table. Agents may also possess multiples of any *trait*, such as having *relational$_1$* = *mother* and *relational$_2$* = *wife*. In addition, some of the *traits* contain secondary tags with additional information. For *relational$_1$* = *mother* there may be two secondary tags that specifically identify the agent's daughter and son.

Any of the *traits* can be brought to the forefront (i.e., primed). For simplicity in the examples that follow, priming is restricted to occurring only upon entering a location or interacting with another agent. It can, of course, be extended to any sort of interaction that a system may allow: reading, viewing, hearing – anything that may cause a trait to come to the forefront of the agent's self-concept. Additionally, priming is restricted to activating only one self concept at a time, paralleling the way it is activated according to the psychology literature. Determining a priority algorithm for priming of two or more traits is left for future work.

We give an example of priming in pseudocode below. This example is restricted to defining priming situations that are used in the Fire Event example in the next section:

```
function enter( location )
  if( location==myWorkplace )
        prime( myVocation )
  else if( location==myHome )
        prime( myMainRelationalStatus )

function interact( otherAgent )
  if( otherAgent==myParent )
        prime( myChildRelationalStatus )
  else if( otherAgent==myChild )
        prime( myParentalRelationalStatus )
  else if( otherAgent==myCoworker )
        prime( myVocation )
  else if( otherAgent.prime==age )
        prime( myAge )
```

Thus, if an agent has an *age trait=child* and they begin talking to someone who is primed as an *adult*, their childishness will come forward. Or, if an agent's *vocation trait* is firefighter, with a secondary tag *myWorkplace = firehouse*, he will be primed as a firefighter when he enters a firehouse. If his *vocation* is not firefighter, there is simply no priming when walking into the firehouse.

After an agent has been notified of a new event, or has run out of "interesting" actions to perform (based on becoming idle or bored as explained in 3.2), he will query the Message Board(s) to obtain possible actions to execute. Action choices over the set of possibilities are made based on the trait with which he is currently primed. We will demonstrate this further in the Fire Event example.

5 Fire Event Example

To illustrate the architecture we will construct a scenario of a Fire Event (FE) occurring inside a school. We represent the FE using a subset of possible agent *traits* because not all *traits* make sense as influences on behavior during every event. The *traits* we utilize are *age*, *vocation* and *relational*. The instantiated values for these traits are: child, adult, elder; firefighter, policeman, teacher, student; mother, father, daughter and son, respectively. Table 2 shows all functions of priming as well as specified *actions* during the evolving FE. Fig. 3 shows the FE as a finite state machine.

Recall that priming can occur when agents interact with each other and is based on either a secondary *relational* tag (e.g. myChild) or a primed *trait* in the other agent (e.g. age). It can also occur when agents enter a location or event radius that matches a secondary location tag (e.g. myWorkplace).

The beginning state of the world is:

- Agent 1 - walked into classroom, primed as teacher
- Agent 2 - walked into classroom, primed as student
- Agent 3 - bringing son to school, primed as mother
- Agent 4 - coming to school with his parent, primed as son
- Agent 5 - at firehouse, primed as firefighter
- Agent 6 - at police station, primed as policeman

Table 2. Priming and *actions* chosen during the evolving Fire Event (FE) example. *Note, neither firefighters nor policemen would have been called during the small and medium states of this event, but if they are within the *location* radius, they should still respond appropriately.

Trait	Value	Priming	Action selected during Fire Event:		
			Small	Medium	Large
Age	Child	interact(age)	stare	calmFollow	panickedFollow
	Adult	interact(age)	pourWater smother	extinguisher	leadAway
	Elder	interact(age)	pourWater smother	callPolice leadAway	calmFollow
Vocation	Firefighter	enter(firehouse) enter(emergency)	smother*	extinguisher*	fightFire
	Policeman	enter(station) enter(emergency)	smother*	extinguisher*	manageCrowd
	Teacher	enter(classroom) interact(student)	pourWater smother	extinguisher	leadAway
	Student	enter(classroom) interact(teacher)	stare	calmFollow	calmFollow
Relational	Mother/ Father	enter(home) interact(myChild)	pourWater smother	leadAway	leadAway
	Daughter/ Son	enter(home) interact(myParent)	stare	calmFollow	panickedFollow
Default			pourWater smother	extinguish	leadAway

The fire starts on the floor of the building where Agents 1-4 are located (note, we only use six agents here for simplicity, but any or all of these agents could be thought of as a set of agents primed with the specified trait). Because they are within the *influence region*, they are all notified of the FE by the school building Message Board. All acknowledge the FE because the *eEL* is higher than the *action* they were performing, and all query the Message Board to obtain appropriate behaviors. Agents 1 and 3 are assigned an *action* that is an aleatoric choice between pouring water on the fire and smothering the fire (with a .5 probability for each). Agent 1's choice is to pour water, and the action specifies the preparatory *action* of going to the nearest bathroom to obtain water (note that a feature of CAROSA and PARs are that actions can be composed of sub-actions, including preparatory actions; *thus these actions need not be explicitly requested by the event*). Agent 3's choice is to smother the fire, which has a preparatory *action* of obtaining a towel or blanket. Agent 2 and 4, primed as a student and son respectively, are transfixed by the small fire as they are assigned the *action* of staring. Agents 5 and 6 are not within the physical or communication *influence region* at this stage of the event because the fire is small, and thus are not notified.

If Agents 1 or 3 were able to complete either of their *actions* in time, the fire will change its state to *out*, but let's assume they took longer than the specified *time* to do this because the preparatory actions took a long time to complete. The state is updated to *medium* on the Message Board after 1 minute. This is reflected in the Message Board by increasing the *eEL*, altering the specified *actions* of agents and, because an alarm is set off, now includes firefighters and police as part of the communication *influence region*. Agent 1 is notified by the Message Board of a change and because the *eEL* has risen, aborts the *action* of obtaining water in order to perform the newly specified *action* for a primed teacher: obtain a fire extinguisher. Agent 3, for the same reasons and primed as a parent, is assigned the *action* of leading people away. Agents 2 and 4 modify their *actions* to perform a calm following of the nearest leader, in this case, Agent 3.

If Agent 1 was able to complete the action in time, the FE would evolve back to a *small* fire that could be smothered, but let's assume he took longer and it has grown to a *large* fire. Let's also assume Agents 2-4 have not yet moved out of the *influence region* and that Agents 5 and 6 have just arrived. Agent 1 and 3 now share responsibility for leading people away. Agent 2, primed as an obedient student, continues to follow calmly, but Agent 3, primed as a child, panics and begins to perform panicked following *actions* such as crying and pushing. Agent 5, primed as a firefighter, begins to fight the fire with a fire hose, while the primed policeman, Agent 6, manages the crowd by helping agents find the exit and then blocking anyone from entering. The fire will eventually end, either because the actions are performed repeatedly, or because the FE has lasted too long and will destroy the building.

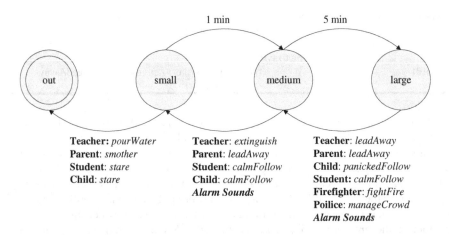

Fig. 3. The evolution of the Fire Event (FE)

6   Discussion and Conclusions

We have proposed a "Smart Event - Primed Agents" model. The Smart Event model embeds agent behaviors into the event in order to simplify the process of action selection. It does this by avoiding deep reasoning, while allowing for realistic and diverse agent behavior that is modified by differences in agent traits. To avoid the use of large "heavy" decision methods to simulate a variation in individual differences, we introduce a Primed Agent model that selects appropriate *actions* based solely on the most recently activated *trait*, analogous to human priming. The limited reasoning performed by each agent at run-time makes our method scalable and suitable for the simulation of large groups of differentiated agents with context-dependent behaviors.

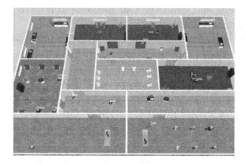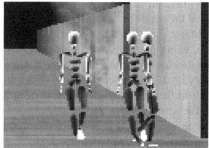

Fig. 4. A school building environment in the CAROSA framework (left) and agents responding to the fire event scenario (right)

To evaluate the complexity of our system, we compare it first to a needs-based model [15] that must make nm evaluations every t timesteps, where m is the number of agents, n is the number of needs each has, and t is the number of timesteps agents wait between re-evaluating their needs. Although, based on the CAROSA architecture, our agents also make a small, constant number of biological need evaluations regularly (hunger, thirst, tiredness, i.e., $3m$), for external events we believe it is more natural and less computationally intensive for the incoming event to trigger most state updates. Thus, our agents perform very few monitoring actions regularly. They must only make internal state evaluations when they update their primed trait, are notified of an event, or decide to act on an event.

In addition, the state evaluation that occurs during priming is not dependent on the number of events that occur in the world, but instead on a constant number of psychologically-based human traits and meaningful associations (i.e., myWorkplace, myChild, etc.) and should thus remain relatively small in the face of a large number of events, unlike a needs-based approach which has a need assigned for every type of event (i.e., need to buy a ticket, watch a performance, etc.). Thus a large number of evaluations are moved to occurring only every $t_l \gg t$, where t_l is the average time between priming and is much larger than t.

When notified of an event, we represent attention as a function with one simple evaluation: a comparison of the agent's current eEL to the event's eEL. Thus an agent must only make one comparison to decide whether or not to switch his *action*. In addition, because of the Message Board system and *influence region* specifications, we anticipate event notifications in a realistic simulation occurring no more frequently than every t timesteps, thus we believe that each agent may have to make 4 evaluations (3 biological and 1 eEL comparison) at most every t timesteps, which should be an improvement over n. Finally, upon becoming involved in an event, agents must only make another small evaluation because we have explicitly constrained the decision process to a simple evaluation of a few important, psychologically-based traits.

In decision network systems [16] a cognitive model aims to make deliberative agents that can exploit knowledge, reason about the world, and conceive and execute plans based on uncertainty. Decision networks require crafting the prior probabilities of each action in context and thus authoring behaviors has the potential to become very difficult in scenarios with a lot of actions and contexts. Our methods aim to re-move the need for agents to deliberate over uncertainty.

Many agent-based systems [6] focus on reasoning, planning and goal decomposi-tion, using preferences to make decisions between actions. Our system hypothesizes that this level of reasoning is much deeper than is necessary or realistic for an agent in everyday life situations. We use direct matching of event parameters with primed agent traits to facilitate a quick selection of individualistic behaviors from a plausible set.

The contributions of our framework are: a Smart Event model that acts as a re-source manager, assigning agent interactions and monitoring agent participation; a Primed Agents model based on human cognition that quickly selects the behaviors provided by the Smart Event without intensive reasoning; and a virtual human simula-tion model that strikes a balance between individualism and scalability while simpli-fying scenario authoring by allowing actions to be authored for sets of agents depend-ent on their traits, rather than individually coded for each agent.

In the future we intend to extend our scenarios to include additional events. These events could be completely new, non-emergency events such a coffee machine that needs to be cleaned or they could be sub-events of the FE such as a person getting injured or a fire extinguisher becoming empty. We also intend to expand the system of agent priming. There are many psychological theories on priming and cultural frame switching that could be used to refine our models, and explicit data resources that can be used to create a specific population and load appropriate action sets for specific events. Finally, we hope to test our theory that our simple Smart Event and Primed Agent model produces agent behaviors that are no less reasonable than those generated by more computationally intensive decision-theoretic and planning ap-proaches. To this end we take advantage of the extensive action representation framework extant in PAR and CAROSA to offload deliberative, aleatoric and pre-paratory actions. Animated scenarios are in development; agent graphics models will require robust action animations but this architecture will tell them what they should be doing when, where and how.

Acknowledgments. Partial support for this effort is gratefully acknowledged from the U.S. Army "SUBTLE" MURI W911NF-07-1-0216 and the Lockheed-Martin Corpo-ration through a Strategic Technology Thread Grant. We also appreciate technology support from Autodesk, nVidia, and the Susquehanna International Group.

References

[1] Pelechano, N., Allbeck, J., Badler, N.: Virtual Crowds: Methods, Simulation, and Con-trol. Morgan Claypool Publishers, San Rafael (2008)
[2] Helbing, D., Farkas, I., Vicsek, T.: Simulating Dynamical Features of Escape Panic. Let-ters to Nature, 487–490 (2000)
[3] Chenney, S.: Flow Tiles. In: ACM SIGGRAPH/ Eurographics Proceedings of Sympo-sium on Computer Animation, pp. 233–242 (2004)
[4] Reynolds, C.W.: Flocks, Herds and Schools: A Distributed Behavioral Model. ACM Computer Graphics 21(4), 25–34 (1987)

[5] Narain, R., Golas, A., Curtis, S., Lin, M.C.: Aggregate Dynamics for Dense Crowd Simulation. In: ACM SIGGRAPH Asia 2009 Papers, pp. 1–8 (2009)

[6] Laird, J.E., Newell, A., Rosenbloom, P.: SOAR: An Architecture for General Intelligence. Artificial Intelligence 33, 1–64 (1987)

[7] Funge, J., Tu, X., Terzopoulos, D.: Cognitive Modeling: Knowledge, Reasoning and Planning for Intelligent Characters. In: Proceedings of the 26th Annual Conference on Computer Graphics and Interactive Techniques, pp. 29–38 (1999)

[8] Silverman, B.G., Johns, M., Cornwell, J., O'Brien, K.: Human Behavior Models for Agents in Simulators and Games. Presence: Teleoperators and Virtual Environments 15(2), 139–162 (2006)

[9] Langer, E.J.: Rethinking the Role of Thought in Social Interaction. In: Harvey, J.H., Ickes, W., Kidd, R.F. (eds.) New Directions in Attribution Research, vol. 2, pp. 35–58. Erlbaum, Hillsdale (1978)

[10] Simon, H.: Models of Bounded Rationality. MIT Press, Cambridge (1982)

[11] Bargh, J.A., Chartrand, T.L.: The Unbearable Automaticity of Being. American Psychologist 54(7), 462–479 (1999)

[12] Bargh, J.A., Chen, M., Burrows, L.: Automaticity of Social Behavior: Direct Effects of Trait Construct and Stereotype Activation on Action. Journal of Personality and Social Psychology 71(2), 230–244 (1996)

[13] Carver, C.S., Ganellen, R.J., Froming, W.J., Chambers, W.: Modeling: An Analysis in Terms of Category Accessibility. Journal of Experimental Social Psychology 19, 403–421 (1983)

[14] Shih, M., Pittinsky, T.L., Ambady, N.: Stereotype Susceptibility: Identity Salience and Shifts in Quantitative Performance. Psychological Science 10, 80–83 (1999)

[15] Shao, W., Terzopoulos, D.: Autonomous pedestrians. In: Proceedings of the 2005 ACM SIGGRAPH/Eurographics Symposium on Computer Animation (SCA 2005), pp. 19–28 (2005)

[16] Yu, Q., Terzopoulos, D.: A Decision Network Framework for the Behavioral Animation of Virtual Humans. In: Proceedings of the 2007 ACM SIGGRAPH/Eurographics Symposium on Computer Animation, pp. 119–128 (2007)

[17] Kallmann, M., Thalmann, D.: Direct 3D interaction with smart objects. In: Proceedings of the ACM Symposium on Virtual Reality Software and Technology, pp. 124–130 (1999)

[18] Maïm, J., Haegler, S., Yersin, B., Mueller, P., Thalmann, D., Van Gool, L.: Populating Ancient Pompeii with Crowds of Virtual Romans. In: Proceedings of the 8th International Symposium on Virtual Reality, Archaeology and Cultural Heritage (VAST 2007), pp. 26–30 (2007)

[19] Badler, N.I., Allbeck, J.M., Zhao, L., Byun, M.: Representing and Parameterizing Agent Behaviors. In: Computer Animation, pp. 133–143 (2002)

[20] Hong, Y.-Y., Morris, M.W., Chiu, C.-Y., Benet-Martinez, V.: Multicultural Minds: A Dynamic Constructivist Approach to Culture and Cognition. American Psychologist 55(7), 709–720 (2000)

[21] Deaux, K., Reid, A., Mizrahi, K., Ethier, K.A.: Parameters of Social Identity. Journal of Personality and Social Psychology 68, 280–291 (1995)

Using Artificial Team Members for
Team Training in Virtual Environments

Jurriaan van Diggelen, Tijmen Muller, and Karel van den Bosch

TNO Defense, Safety and Security
Soesterberg, The Netherlands
{jurriaan.vandiggelen,tijmen.muller,karel.vandenbosch}@tno.nl

Abstract. In a good team, members do not only perform their individual task, they also coordinate their actions with other members of the team. Developing such team skills usually involves exercises with all members playing their role. This approach is costly and has organizational and educational drawbacks. We developed a more efficient and flexible approach by setting training in virtual environments, and using intelligent software agents to play the role of team members. We developed a general framework for developing agents that, in a controlled fashion, execute the behavior that enables the human player (i.e., trainee) to effectively learn team skills. The framework is tested by developing and implementing various types of team agents in a game-based virtual environment.

Keywords: human-agent teams, virtual environments, team training.

1 Introduction

A team of experts does not necessarily constitute an expert team. A team's performance is not only determined by how well the individual team members perform their tasks, but also by how well they practice their *team skills*. Not surprisingly, training team skills is an essential part of the education of many professions demanding a tight collaboration [10]. For example, fire fighters not only learn how to operate a fire hose (task behavior), but also how they must communicate relevant information about the fire's progress to their colleagues (team behavior).

Usually, team skills are trained by exercises with a (potentially large) number of participants, each playing a dedicated role in a given scenario. Such large scale team exercises have a number of drawbacks. First, this type of team training requires ample resources (both human and financial) and is difficult to organize. Furthermore, it occurs frequently that not all members of a team are available for training at the same time and location, and that role players (e.g. staff personnel) need to take their place. It can also be that the team members vary in competence, thus having different training needs (e.g. a team consisting of novice and advanced trainees). For example, an urban patrol scenario contains many roles which are either not relevant for soldiers practicing their team skills (e.g. *local inhabitant)*, or for which some soldiers holding that rank have already completed their training.

We propose to approach this problem by combining recent developments in virtual environments (VEs) and intelligent software agents. We aim at developing a

J. Allbeck et al. (Eds.): IVA 2010, LNAI 6356, pp. 28–34, 2010.

game-based platform for team training in which some team members are played by humans, and some are played by software agents. In this way, team training can be made less costly, as not all roles have to be fulfilled by humans anymore. Furthermore, training can be better tailored to the specific learning objectives of a specific individual, as we can control more precisely the team behavior of artificial team members than that of human team members (which may be trainees themselves).

Whereas computer-controlled characters in VEs are common in computer games, these characters are usually programmed with scripts which list a number of trigger/event rules. The type of behavior required for teamwork is too complex to be programmed in these scripting languages. Therefore, we have developed a framework for developing software agents whose behavior in a VE is based on concepts as goals, plans, and beliefs, and which is "aware" of its team.

The behavior of the software agent is directed by a teamwork model. Teamwork models have been studied for several decades by the AI community, e.g. [12]. Typical applications of these models are mixed human-agent teams [11], where computers assist humans in a flexible way, i.e. as a teammate. Our application to team training is novel, as our prime interest is not to develop a "perfect" team member which is always subjected to humans. Rather, we aim at developing a realistic team member which exhibits natural behavior and from which humans can *learn*. This makes human trainees better team players "in the real world" after they have completed their training. For example, a real team member sometimes forgets to communicate an important piece of information, for instance if he is too busy with other tasks. Implementing this property into an artificial team members allow us to design realistic experiences, from which the trainee can learn how to deal with such team task problems.

Our research objectives can thus be formulated as follows. Firstly, we aim at developing generic teamwork models tailored to training fundamental team skills. Secondly, we aim to implement these models to develop an agent-based artificial team member, situated in a virtual environment. This paper describes the concepts and design of our agent-based team training approach, followed by a proof-of-concept study, showing that it is a feasible alternative to human-based team training. We demonstrate our approach by presenting *Samurai*, a software agent that in a virtual environment performs a team task in a coordinated fashion with a human player (trainee).

The paper is organized as follows. The following section describes how teamwork is implemented in our system. Section 3 describes the implementation of Samurai and the integration of Samurai with the virtual environment. Section 4 gives the training case and event traces. A conclusion is given in Section 5.

2 Training of Teamwork

Teamwork is a topic of great complexity and breadth and no consensus has yet been reached on an exact definition. Most simply, a team is a group of people working together to achieve a common goal. This requires team members to maintain *common ground*, to be *mutually predictable*, and to be *mutually directable* [6]. Related literature reports different ways in which these properties can be implemented in artificial team members, with different levels of sophistication. We have implemented Samurai as follows. Samurai maintains common ground with the other team members by actively sharing relevant pieces of information with its team mates. Mutual predict-ability is achieved by applying an organizational structure to the team, which is com-monly known by all participants, and describes how the different team members (both human and agent) fulfill their tasks. Mutual directability is implemented by a *request* protocol, which allows one agent to ask another agent to perform an action.

Whereas we believe these properties to be essential for team membership, *how* these properties reveal themselves in behavior may vary. By explicitly modeling such differences in artificial team members we can expose trainees to different types of team behavior. In this paper, we will focus on two characteristics of the team mem-ber's behavior: unprovocative and provocative. Unprovocative indicates that the team member behaves in accordance with the procedures and goals of the team as a whole. This behavior imposes no challenges to fellow team members recognizing and cor-recting any omissions. In contrast, provocative behavior of a team member conflicts with good team behavior, thus requiring other team members to stay alert and to bring about corrections. These characteristics are shown in the rows of Table 1, , for each of the three teamwork properties discussed above. This leads to eight different possible configurations for team training.

Table 1. Different team member characteristics

		Team property		
		Mutual predictability	Common ground	Mutual directability
Training mode	Unprovocative	Organization aware	Always shares relevant information	Always obeys a request
	Provocative	Not organization aware	Sometimes fails to share relevant information	Sometimes refuses a request

In the upper cell of the first column, unprovocative mutual predictability is de-scribed as (fully) organization aware. The team members have complete knowledge of their organization, which team member fulfills which roles in the team, and how they perform their work. In provocative training, the team members are not com-pletely aware of the organization they are part of. This makes it more difficult for Samurai to predict the behavior of the trainee and the other way around. To overcome this issue, the trainee should learn to communicate with Samurai about his own role in the organization and also to find out about the role of Samurai himself.

In the second column, the different possibilities for common ground are shown. In unprovocative training, the team members always communicate relevant information with each other. In provocative training, they might sometimes fail to do this, because they forget it, or are too busy with other things. This requires the trainee to learn to actively collect relevant information.

In the third column, two possibilities for mutual directability are shown. On one extreme, the team members act as obedient servants, who blindly follow a request, regardless of what they are currently doing or what their own individual goals are. Whereas such behavior may appear convenient to the trainee, it is not necessarily in the team's interest, nor is it very realistic team behavior. A natural team member should be allowed to refuse a request, typically based on information that the requester does not have. This type of team member is willing to fulfill a request, when it believes this to be in the interests of the team. When it believes that its own plans are currently more important for the team, then the team member refuses the request.

3 Artificial Team Members

In this section, we will explain how we implemented the different types of team behavior outlined in the previous section. We will first explain the task behavior of an agent. Then, we will focus on team aspects.

The Cognitive Architecture

For the implementation of Samurai a cognitive architecture was developed in C++. The architecture consists of a framework for specifying practical reasoning rules, goals, beliefs, plans, together with an organization module including roles and role enactment, a dialogue module for processing natural language and a deliberation cycle.

Following Bratman's theory of practical reasoning [2], we model an agent's behavior by specifying *beliefs*, *goals* and *plans*. As is common for BDI-agent platforms (e.g. 3APL [6]), we use practical reasoning rules (or *PR-rules*) to determine how actions result from beliefs, goals and plans.

A PR-rule has the form *Head ← Guard | Body*. The head describes goals which form the activation event of the rule; the guard contains beliefs (using a predicate formula) that may or may not match with the agent's belief base; and the body describes the plan that is adopted when the rule fires. The activation and firing of rules is performed by the *deliberation cycle* (explained in Section 3.2).

As explained in Section 2, team members can know about each other's actions by using a shared organization model. Following well-known agent organization models, such as Moise [6], we define an organization as a number of *roles* (e.g. leader, scout) together with an *enactment model*, specifying which agents enact which roles. A role is specified as a set of goals and PR-rules. By enacting a role in the organization, the agent assumes the goals of the role (telling it *what* it should achieve), and it assumes the PR-rules (telling it *how* it should achieve the goals). Note that the agent may also have *individual* goals and PR-rules. These goals and PR-rules, contrary to the ones specified for its role, are not accessible to other agents.

A key factor in this approach is that the organization model is commonly known by all agents and is used by all to determine *information relevance*. As argued by Castelfranchi [4], information relevance for BDI agents should be examined in relation to their goals. Because the shared organization model allows agents to know some goals and PR-rules of other agents, they can proactively share information with other agents when they believe this helps them to achieve their goals.

This use of organization models not only serves the purpose of implementing behavior of individual agents in a team, but it also establishes the team properties 'mutual predictability' and 'common ground' among the team members. If a team consists of both virtual members (agents) and human members, then agents should be able to determine the role and tasks of the human players. As a consequence, the behavior of humans also needs to be captured in terms of goals and PR-rules. This allows a software agent to assess and reason about the goals and plans of humans too.

Deliberation Cycle

The deliberation cycle tells the agent what it should do next. This cycle is illustrated at the left hand side of the following figure:

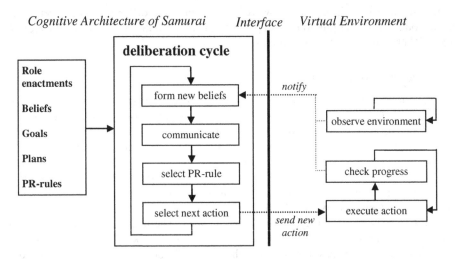

Fig. 1. Cognitive architecture and interaction with Virtual Environment

Given this process, unprovocative behavior is achieved if Samurai starts fully aware of the team organization (i.e. appreciating the roles of all team members), immediately shares all relevant information and always follows requests. The provocative training modes described in Table 1 are implemented by restricting access to the organization model (*Provocative mutual predictability*), applying a random 'forget' function to the sharing of relevant information (*Provocative common ground*), or by making Samurai attribute low priority to unmotivated incoming requests (*Provocative mutual directability*).

Interaction with Virtual Environment

Samurai, as well as the other members of the team, move around in a virtual environment. SABRE [8] was chosen as virtual environment for our experiment, as it was used before by NATO to study military team behavior. Furthermore, Neverwinter Nights, the commercial game SABRE is based on, offers a low-level scripting language with such functionality as locating specific objects and retrieving their attributes, and communicating with the (human) player through text messages.

For Samurai to be able to interact (i.e. sense and act) with this virtual environment an interface is needed. The outline of this interface is shown in Figure 1: the left hand side shows Samurai's architecture, while the right hand side shows the observation and execution model that is executed in parallel. The action execution mechanism is implemented in the virtual environment, because this environment defines which actions Samurai can take. Consequently, the deliberation cycle runs in parallel with the action execution mechanism, so the process of deciding what to do next does not halt action execution and Samurai can choose to interrupt an action at any time.

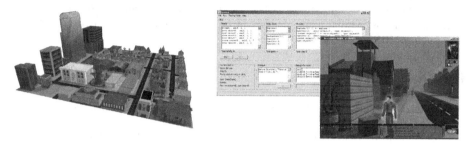

Fig. 2. The environment (left), the Samurai/SABRE interface (right)

4 Team Training Case

Using the Samurai/SABRE software framework described above, we implemented a cognitive model for a team training scenario. The scenario takes place in a small city with residential and commercial areas. The task of the team is to find, identify and neutralize weapon crates while maintaining the goodwill of the local population. To accomplish this, the team has various resources at its disposal, such as weapon scanners to scan the contents of a crate and lock-picking sets to open locked crates and doors. Results are measured in terms of goodwill of the population – for example, goodwill increases when weapon crates are neutralized by collecting its weapons, but decreases when private crates (i.e. not containing weapons) are opened.

We defined the team, using several roles: an *explorer* explores the environment to find and locate crates; *weapon scanner* has a tool to check if a crate contains weapons; a *lock picker* has a tool to break the lock of a crate; a *weapon collector* can remove any found weapons from the crates.

SABRE is representative for a team task, as its team members require each other's help to achieve the team goaland tools are distributed among the team members. Additionally, team coordination and cooperation is necessary for high performance, because there is limited time to execute the mission.

Depending on the objective of the training, Samurai can be set to provocative or unprovocative for each of the team properties listed in Table 1. These settings will affect the processes during training and consequently the team performance. We have tested our prototype by performing a pilot experiment in which trainees interacted with Samurai in provocative and unprovocative mode. Demonstration videos can be found online [13].

5 Conclusion

In this paper, we have proposed a generic architecture for modeling virtual team members for team training. The architecture was used to implement a virtual team member called Samurai for a search task in the virtual environment SABRE. The team behavior of Samurai can be controlled on different dimensions, making him provocative or unprovocative on multiple team properties. Consequently, the difficulty of cooperating with Samurai can be adapted to the ability of the human trainee, causing different learning experiences.

In the future, we plan to investigate empirically the effects of different levels of provocativeness on the learning of the trainee. Also, we plan to extend the software framework, allowing our virtual team member to be used in other virtual environments as well, such as VBS2.

References

[1] Baker, D.P., Salas, E.: Principles for measuring teamwork skills. Human Factors 34, 469–475 (1992)

[2] Bratman, M.E., Israel, D.J., Pollack, M.E.: Plans and resource-bounded practical reasoning. Computational Intelligence 4, 349–355 (1988)

[3] Burton, R.M., DeSanctis, G., Obel, B.: Organizational Design. Cambridge University Press, Cambridge (2006)

[4] Castelfranchi, C.: Guarantees for autonomy in cognitive agent architecture. In: Wooldridge, M.J., Jennings, N.R. (eds.) ECAI 1994 and ATAL 1994. LNCS (LNAI), vol. 890, pp. 56–70. Springer, Heidelberg (1995)

[5] Doswell, J.T.: Pedagogical Embodied Conversational Agent. In: Fourth IEEE International Conference on Advanced Learning Technologies, ICALT 2004, pp. 774–776 (2004)

[6] Hübner, J.F., Sichman, J.S., Boissier, O.: A Model for the Structural, Functional, and Deontic Specification of Organizations in Multiagent Systems. In: Bittencourt, G., Ramalho, G.L. (eds.) SBIA 2002. LNCS (LNAI), vol. 2507, Springer, Heidelberg (2002)

[7] Klein, G., Woods, D., Bradshaw, J.M., Hoffman, R.R., Feltovich, P.J.: Ten Challenges for Making Automation a Team Player. Joint Human-Agent Activity, IEEE Intelligent Systems 19(6) (2004)

[8] Leung, A., Diller, D., Ferguson, W.: SABRE: A game-based testbed for studying team behavior. In: Proceedings of the Fall Simulation Interoperability Workshop (SISO), Orlando, FL, September 18-23 (2005)

[9] Rickel, J., Johnson, W.L.: Extending Virtual Humans to Support Team Training in Virtual Reality. In: Exploring Artificial Intelligence in the New Millenium. Morgan Kaufmann Publishers, San Francisco (2002)

[10] Riedl, M.O., Stern, A.: Believable Agents and Intelligent Scenario Direction for Social and Cultural Leadership Training. In: Proceedings of the 15th Conference on Behavior Representation in Modeling and Simulation, Baltimore (2006)

[11] Sycara, K., Lewis, M.: Integrating intelligent agents into human teams. In: Team Cognition: Understanding the Factors that Drive Process and Performance, pp. 203–232. American Psychological Association, Washington (2004)

[12] Tambe, M.: Towards Flexible Teamwork. Journal of Artificial Intelligence Research, 83–124 (1997)

[13] Traum, D., Rickel, J., Gratch, J., Marsella, S.: Negotiation over Tasks in Hybrid Human-Agent Teams for Simulation-Based Training. In: Proceedings of the Second International Joint Conference on Autonomous Agents and Multiagent (2003)

[14] Cognitive Models Group, TNO,
http://cm.tm.tno.nl/index.php/en/virtual-team-member

A Comprehensive Taxonomy of Human Motives: A Principled Basis for the Motives of Intelligent Agents

Stephen J. Read, Jennifer Talevich, David A. Walsh, Gurveen Chopra, and Ravi Iyer

Department of Psychology, University of Southern California, Los Angeles, CA 90089
{read,talevich,dwalsh,gchopra,raviiyer}@usc.edu

Abstract. We present a hierarchical taxonomy of human motives, based on similarity judgments of 161 motives gleaned from an extensive review of the motivation literature from McDougall to the present. This taxonomy provides a theoretically and empirically principled basis for the motive structures of Intelligent Agents. 220 participants sorted the motives into groups, using a Flash interface in a standard web browser. The co-occurrence matrix was cluster analyzed. At the broadest level were five large clusters concerned with Relatedness, Competence, Morality and Religion, Self-enhancement / Self-knowledge, and Avoidance. Each of the broad clusters divided into more specific motives. We discuss using this taxonomy as the basis for motives in Intelligent Agents, as well as its relationship to other motive organizations.

Keywords: Human goals, human motives, motive taxonomy, motivation.

1 Introduction

Despite the fundamental role of goals and motives in human behavior, we have only the sketchiest idea of how they are structured and organized [1]; no consensually accepted, comprehensive, empirically based taxonomy of human motives exists. This lack of an accepted structure of human motivation undermines our ability to construct Intelligent Agents driven by psychologically valid models of motivation. Given the lack of a comprehensive taxonomy, our agents' models of human motivation must, of necessity, be somewhat ad hoc. Moreover, absence of an accepted structure obstructs communication among researchers, inhibits research, and slows theory development.

Although there has been considerable empirical work on the structure of human personality, as represented by the Big Five and related research, far less has been done on human motives and no agreed upon structure exists. The current project is focused on developing a comprehensive taxonomy of human motives.

A comprehensive taxonomy would greatly facilitate work on Intelligent Agents. It would provide a common framework for the construction of motivational systems in Intelligent Agents and would aid in the comparison of different models. Currently, researchers' choice of goals and motives tends to be relatively opportunistic or ad hoc, with different researchers choosing from different motivational accounts. This makes comparison and integration across models difficult and reduces our ability to

J. Allbeck et al. (Eds.): IVA 2010, LNAI 6356, pp. 35–41, 2010.

generalize. A further benefit is that because the motives are hierarchically structured, from more specific to more abstract and general, it allows the researcher to choose the level at which they want to operate, while still providing a structure for comparing across models. Finally, the current taxonomy also helps to address the perennial question of where the goals of an agent come from.

Although several researchers have attempted such a taxonomy (e.g., [2] [3] [4]), all have serious limitations. In previous work we [5] took initial steps toward addressing these limitations. We developed a much more comprehensive list of human motives than had been previously examined and from that generated a taxonomy of human motives that was based on a wide search of the constructs used in the motivational literature and that was empirically, rather than theoretically, generated. This resulted in a hierarchical taxonomy of 135 human motives consisting of 30 lower level clusters organized into progressively broader and more abstract categories.

However, our taxonomy still had several limitations. First, some of the clusters only had 2 motives, which did not provide for a stable cluster. Second, our taxonomy contained few Avoidance motives, things that people are motivated to avoid, such as social rejection or anxiety. However, a growing body of work clearly distinguishes between an Approach system that governs approach to rewarding stimuli and an Avoidance system that governs avoidance of aversive stimuli (e.g., [6] [7]). Thus, we needed a broader sample of motives. Third, our original sample of participants was small and limited, reducing the stability and generalizability of our results. The present study aims to address these limitations and further develop our taxonomy so as to provide a stronger foundation for work on motivated human behavior.

We used similarity judgments by naïve subjects as our guide to the motivational structures underlying people's behavior. We first generated an extensive set of motives based on a thorough review of the human motivation literature. We then had a large number of subjects sort 161 motives into categories on the basis of their semantic similarity, and then applied hierarchical cluster analysis to these judgments. This study was aimed at generating a comprehensive taxonomy of human motives that would: (1) include a comprehensive set of motives sampled from human motivational domains, and (2) tap into laypeople's conceptual organization.

2 Method

Motive selection. We started with the 135 motives from our earlier work [5]. We then identified additional motives that had not been in our earlier set, by drawing from a web study that asked respondents to list motives that characterized individuals described by each of 43 trait adjectives taken from the Big 5 dimensions. Finally, we added motives deemed central to recent theoretical accounts of motivation. One example is Avoid Impure Acts, related to Disgust and aspects of religion. We ended up with 161 motives.

Motive sorting. The categorization task was implemented as a Flash program inside a standard Web browser. The interface consisted of a scrolling list of the motives on the left side of the screen and a sorting area, which took up the remainder of the screen. Participants were asked to sort the motive into groups on the basis of their similarity. They sorted the motives by dragging them from the list, one at a time, onto the sorting area. If a motive was dragged onto an empty spot in the sorting area, the motive box changed into a category box. Additional motives could be dragged into this category box or dragged to empty parts of the sorting area to form new category boxes. Motives dragged to the sorting area were removed from the list. The "I'm done" button became active once participants had sorted at least 90 of the motives, but participants could continue to sort until they had sorted all 161 motives. The program continuously recorded participants' sorting throughout the entire sorting task.

Sample recruitment and demographics. Participants were recruited from the USC Psychology Department Subject pool, from regular visitors to the yourmorals.org website, which recruits participants to fill out a wide range of psychological measures, and through the use of online ads through Google, Yahoo, and ASK.com. 612 individuals sorted at least one motive, 438 individuals sorted at least 90 motives, which is the point at which the "I'm done" button became active, and 220 individuals sorted all 161 motives. Ages ranged from 18 to 70, about 60% of the sample was women, and about 70% were White.

3   Results

The sorting data was analyzed using hierarchical cluster analysis, with the number of times each pair of items was sorted into the same category treated as a measure of similarity. Higher numbers mean that the pair of items was viewed as more similar. The matrix of proximities or similarities was then analyzed using a cluster analysis technique called Ward's [8] method or Increasing Sums of Squares. This method is also known as the "within-groups sum of squares or the error sum of squares (ESS)" method and is designed to optimize the minimum variance within clusters. It outperforms other clustering methods in many cases. We analyzed the data from the 220 individuals who sorted all 161 motives. This is a large sample for this kind of motive analysis and should provide a fairly stable estimate.

The results seem clear. We separately examine five broad clusters and the lower level clusters that constitute them. A condensed version of the cluster diagram that combines some of the lowest level clusters is in Figures 1a and 1b. The original diagram and a complete list of the 161 motives are available from the first author.

3.1   Hierarchical Structure

At the broad level there is a strong correspondence between our results and other accounts of the structure of human motives. For example, Self-determination theory [9] argues that there are three basic psychological needs that people try to satisfy: Competence, Relatedness, and Autonomy. Relatedness and Competence are particularly clear in the current structure (see Figures 1a and 1b) and there is also evidence for clusters concerned with Autonomy although the structure is not as clear.

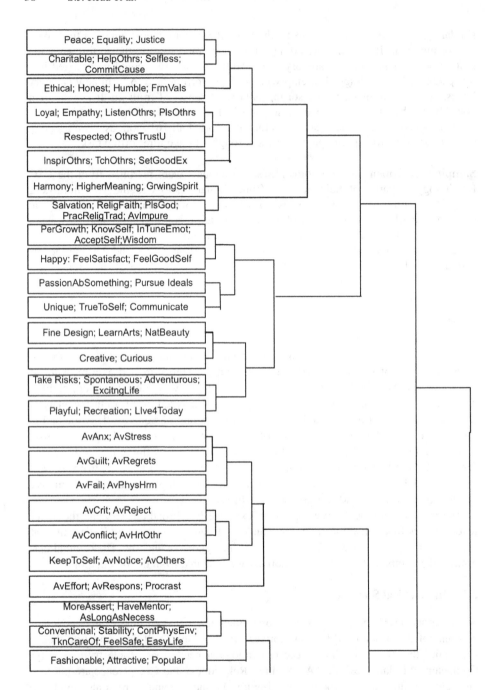

Fig. 1a. Condensed taxonomy, top half

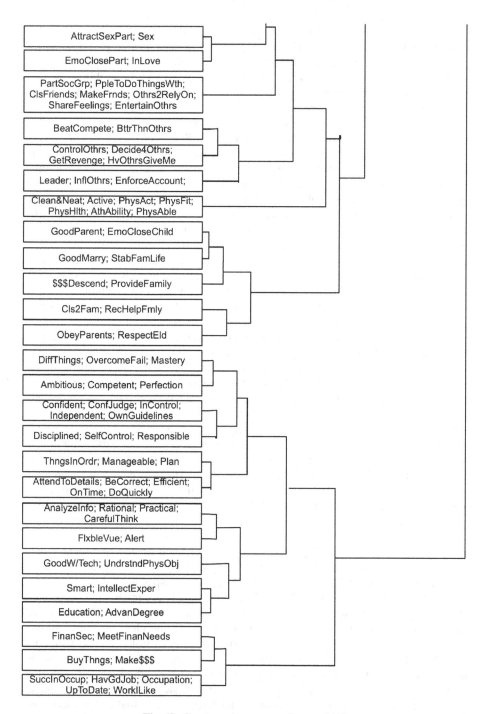

Fig. 1b. Condensed taxonomy, bottom half

A distinction similar to that between Competence and Relatedness is the frequently made distinction between Agentic and Communal orientations (e.g., [10]), which maps roughly onto Competence and Relatedness in Self-determination Theory. An Agentic orientation is focused on the individual achieving and doing things. In contrast, a Communal orientation is more group or community focused and is focused more on interactions with others and such things as caring for others.

The first high level cluster, at the top of the diagram (Figure 1a), is composed of two major clusters. One is a Morality, Religion, and Spirituality cluster. This cluster divides into one clear cluster concerned with religious faith and expression, a closely related, but separate cluster dealing with spirituality more generally, and a clear cluster dealing with two aspects of morality and ethics (e.g., peace and justice, helping others, ethical and honest; loyalty and listening to others, being respected and trusted, teaching and inspiring others). The other cluster seems to be something like Self-determination theory's Autonomy or something like a need for Self-Knowledge, with one cluster being concerned with personal growth, self-knowledge, and being happy and satisfied with the self, a second cluster concerned with being unique and passionate about something, a third cluster focused on aesthetics, natural beauty, and creativity/curiosity, and a final cluster consisting of adventurousness and playfulness.

The middle large cluster (spanning Figures 1a and 1b) is composed almost entirely of two sub clusters, one concerning Avoidance motives, which breaks down into a cluster concerning such things as avoiding stress, guilt, failure, or physical harm, a second cluster dealing with social avoidance, such as avoiding rejection/criticism, and conflict with others, and a third cluster concerned with avoiding effort or work.

The second subcluster of Relatedness or Communal motives has to do with various aspects of social interaction/relatedness with others. Within this, the top cluster seems to deal with desire for stability and safety and being popular or attractive. The next cluster (Sex/Love) consists of two closely related clusters, one having to do with attracting a sex partner and having sexual experiences and the other with being in love and emotionally close to a partner. The next cluster consists of a large number of motives having to do with affiliation and friendship. The next cluster seems to deal with issues of dominance and leadership. There is then a coherent cluster of items concerned with physical health, physical ability and physical activity.

The final set of clusters in the Relatedness cluster deal with various aspects of family. One cluster deals with parent-child relationships, another with marriage itself, and a third with providing for family. Then there are two related clusters that seem to deal more with one's relationship to one's own parents and siblings: being close to family and receiving help from family, and obeying parents and respecting elders.

The motives on the last large cluster (Figure 1b) clearly are related to Competence and Agency. Within this cluster we first see a cluster concerned with mastery and competence, followed by a cluster concerned with being confident, in control of self and environment, and being disciplined. Second, there is a cluster dealing with conscientiousness, a desire for things in order and a desire to be correct, efficient and on time. Third, there is a cluster that consists of items related to thinking and analyzing information, and being rational. Fourth, we see a cluster related to understanding physical objects and systems, being smart and having intellectual experiences, and being highly educated. The final cluster concerns financial security and making money, as well as having a good job and being successful in it.

4 Conclusion

This provides a remarkably coherent view of the structure of human motivation. The broad level of the taxonomy has strong parallels with broad distinctions made by other theorists, and the more specific levels of the hierarchy exhibit coherent clusters of motives that systematically join together into higher-level structures.

The current taxonomy has a number of advantages over previous attempts, including our own. It is based on a wider sample of motives, sampling more extensively from domains that have previously been under sampled. Moreover, it provides a consistent, replicable structure over a broader sample of participants. The taxonomy provides those interested in human motivation with a broad framework for the study and assessment of human motives, and their role in social behavior.

This taxonomy provides a firmer foundation for the construction of Intelligent Agents. Rather than making relatively ad hoc or intuitive choices of motives for an agent, the current comprehensive taxonomy of human motives can serve as the basis for the planning and decision making mechanisms of Intelligent Agents. This taxonomy provides a comprehensive structure of human motivation that helps identify which motives and goals an agent should have and why.

Acknowledgments. This research was funded by Contract No. W911NF-07-D-001 "Measuring Teamwork Skills and Predicting Reactions to Policies Using Computer Agents" from the Navy Personnel Research, Studies, and Technology Department.

References

1. Austin, J.T., Vancouver, J.B.: Goal constructs in psychology: Structure, process, and content. Psych. Bull. 120, 338–375 (1996)
2. Ford, M.E., Nichols, C.W.: A taxonomy of human goals and some possible applications. In: Ford, M.E., Ford, D.H. (eds.) Humans as self-constructing systems: Putting the framework to work. Erlbaum, Hillsdale (1987)
3. Murray, H.A.: Explorations in personality. Oxford University Press, New York (1938)
4. Wicker, F.W., Lambert, F.B., Richardson, F.C., Kahler, J.: Categorical goal hierarchies and classification of human motives. J. of Pers. 52, 285–305 (1984)
5. Chulef, A., Read, S.J., Walsh, D.A.: A Hierarchical Taxonomy of Human Goals. Motivation and Emotion 25, 191–232 (2001)
6. Clark, L.A., Watson, D.: Temperament: An organizing paradigm for trait psychology. In: John, O.P., Robins, R.W., Pervin, L.A. (eds.) Handbook of Personality: Theory and Research, 3rd edn., pp. 265–286. Guilford Press, New York (2008)
7. Gray, J.A., McNaughton, N.: The neuropsychology of anxiety: An enquiry into the functions of the septo-hippocampal system, 2nd edn. Oxford University Press, New York (2000)
8. Ward Jr., J.H.: Hierarchical grouping to optimize an objective function. American Statistical Association Journal 58, 236–244 (1963)
9. Deci, E.L., Ryan, R.M.: The "What" and "Why" of goal pursuits: Human needs and the Self-Determination Theory of behavior. Psych. Inquiry 11, 227–268 (2000)
10. Bakan, D.: The duality of human existence. Rand McNally, Chicago (1966)

The Impact of a Mixed Reality Display Configuration on User Behavior with a Virtual Human

Kyle Johnsen[1], Diane Beck[2], and Benjamin Lok[3]

[1] Faculty of Engineering, University of Georgia
[2] College of Pharmacy, University of Florida
[3] Department of Computer Information Science and Engineering, University of Florida
kjohnsen@uga.edu, beck@cop.ufl.edu, lok@cise.ufl.edu

Abstract. Understanding the human-computer interface factors that influence users' behavior with virtual humans will enable more effective human-virtual human encounters. This paper presents experimental evidence that using a mixed reality display configuration can result in significantly different behavior with a virtual human along important social dimensions. The social dimensions we focused on were engagement, empathy, pleasantness, and naturalness. To understand how these social constructs could be influenced by display configuration, we video recorded the verbal and non-verbal response behavior to stimuli from a virtual human under two fundamentally different display configurations. One configuration presented the virtual human at life-size and was embedded into the environment, and the other presented the virtual human using a typical desktop configuration. We took multiple independent measures of participant response behavior using a video coding instrument. Analysis of these measures demonstrates that display configuration was a statistically significant multivariate factor along all dimensions.

Keywords: virtual humans, embodied agents, human-centered computing, medicine, displays.

1 Introduction

A primary aspect of a mixed reality environment is the integration of the real and virtual worlds, i.e. the virtual portion of the world appears as an extension of the real world. This means that the virtual environment appears at life-size (correct proportions given the content and surrounding real environment), and is embedded (the display placed such that it makes sense in the real environment). Mixed reality may be powerful for embedding a virtual human (VH) agent into the real world (e.g. as a virtual patient, soldier, or tutor); however, there is little empirical evidence comparing alternatives (e.g. using a standard desktop PC environment). In this paper, we discuss our experiment and results in evaluating if a mixed reality environment is justified for a VH application: provider-patient communication skills training with VH agents.

For the evaluation, we focused on an important aspect of provider-patient communication training: training providers to react appropriately to challenges from lpatients (e.g. difficult questions). The hypothesis was that a mixed reality training environment

J. Allbeck et al. (Eds.): IVA 2010, LNAI 6356, pp. 42–48, 2010.

would elicit different behavior along critical social dimensions from trainees than would a typical desktop-based training environment.Totest this hypothesis, we compared two configurations (Described in more depth in Section 4.2).

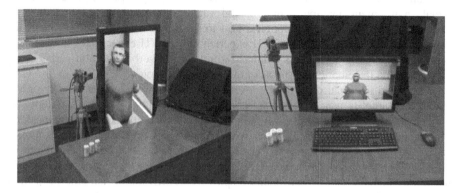

Fig. 1. The same VH displayed on a plasma television (Left) and a monitor (Right). A video camera records the experience for behavioral coding.

- Configuration PTV- A plasma TV (42" diagonal, oriented vertically) displayed the VH at life-size scale relative to the user. The display was placed in a chair across a desk from the user without a keyboard or mouse.
- Configuration MON- A typical LCD monitor (22" diagonal) displayed the VH at a smaller than life-size scale relative to the user. The display was placed on a desk in front of the user with a keyboard and mouse in a typical configuration.

2 Related and Previous Work

To generate a life-size VH relative to the user, mixed reality experiences may incoporate large-screen displays (projectors or large-screen televisions) [1, 2]. These large-screen displays show full-body life-size scale VHs. The use of a large-screen display may be justified from a cognitive perspective; researchers in media psychology have shown that, for *passive* media (e.g. television, movies), there is a strong positive correlation between imagery size and emotional response. People have a more powerful reaction to imagery on large screen displays [3]. Large screens also create a higher level of arousal and can amplify the effect of arousing imagery [4]. Furthermore, large screen displays motivate people to evaluate images of other people more favorably [5]. It seems reasonable then, that larger VHs would be more engaging to the user.

However, the reaction of a user to a VH is complex. There is the phenomenon of the uncanny valley [6], where, as an artificial entity approaches human form, there is a dramatic drop in acceptance. Also, some have found evidence that a mismatch between aesthetic realism and behavioural realism reduces copresence [7]. These theories motivate the current work, towards understanding how user behavior with a

VH is influenced by changing how the VH is displayed while controlling VH appearance and behavior.

Evaluating the effectiveness of visual display alternatives is a common task for new training applications. For applications involving spatial tasks (e.g. navigating a virtual environment, manipulating a spatial dataset), there exists an abundance of literature [8-11]. However, it is not clear how to generalize evaluations of displays for spatial tasks to the social tasks of VH experiences. In VH experiences, locomotion and object manipulation are less emphasized relative to verbal and non-verbal communication and the emotional aspects of that communication.

Closely tied to visual display, the level of physical immersion afforded by a VE system may amplify aspects of social communication with VHs. In one study, an immersive head-mounted display amplified the effect of user anxiety when speaking to an audience of VHs [12]. In other work, immersed CAVE display users took a leadership role over non-immersed small monitor display users in a collaborative virtual environment task [13]. Finally, a previous study on the system discussed in this work compared two virtual reality displays, an HMD and a fish-tank projection display [14]. Participants who interacted with a VH through an HMD were significantly more likely to self-rate their use of empathy higher. However, significant behavioral differences were not found between the two groups. This result directly led to the current work, comparing mixed reality configurations to easier-to-implement desktop configurations, that we hypothesize is a larger factor in user behavior.

3   Communication Skills Training Platform

The InterPersonal Simulator is a software and hardware platform designed to support interpersonal scenario training [1]. The InterPersonal Simulator shares many similarities to modern video game engines such as sound, rendering and animation support, scripting, and built in simulations (e.g. gazing and breathing). In addition, the InterPersonal Simulator supports user-VH conversations through speech and gesture recognition and a natural language script building system.

The open source, object-oriented rendering engine (OGRE) was used for rendering and animation and the FMOD sound system supported audio mixing and playback. The VH models were animated through a combination of vertex and skeletal animation. Recorded audio was used for the VH's voice.

A marker-based optical tracking system (2-Camera NaturalPoint Optitrack) was employed to track user head motion. Tracking head-motion enables a more immersive presentation of a virtual environment on a single-screen display by changing the viewing perspective to coincide with the user's head location, called fish-tank VR [15]. Both displays used in the study employed fish-tank head tracking for a immersion.

While normally the VH in the InterPersonal Simulator is driven solely by an autonomous agent, for the study VH responses were selected by a Wizard-of-Oz (WOz) operator controlling the VH via a hidden terminal and assisted by an autonomous agent system. The WOz could only initiate scripted responses and animations, and as such was not a true WOz (i.e. the wizard could not generate an arbitrary response from the VH). *Participants were told they were interacting with an autonomous agent through speech recognition.* Additionally, they were shown a tutorial video that taught them how to recognize when the patient did not recognize their speech accurately.

4 User Study

For the study, a VH experience was developed using the model of the peptic ulcer disease case [16]. The VH simulates a 35-year-old Caucasian male patient, Vic, who has come into an ambulatory clinic complaining about increasing pain in his abdominal region for the past month. A nurse and dietician had already seen Vic. Vic is anxiously waiting to be seen by the physician. Before the physician sees Vic, the student-pharmacist is asked to interview Vic.

Population. The VH patient was integrated as part of a clinical assessment exercise at the University of Florida's College of Pharmacy's doctorate program for working professionals. As part of a clinical assessment exercise the student the student is given a task to complete with a patient, typically a medical and medication history interview. For the experiment, thirty-nine students (12 men, 27 women) from the pharmacy program were recruited. The average age of the participants was 41.2 years old (min=26, max=65, σ=8.65). Also, the population was culturally diverse (11 Asian/Pacific Islander, 11 African-American, 2 Hispanic, and 15 Caucasian).

Procedure. Participants first filled out a background survey, conducted speech recognition training, and watched tutorial video. Then, the participant performed the interview. Participants were instructed to take less than fifteen minutes (the time given for standard clinical practice assessments) for the interview. The experimenter acting as the WOz was hidden in a far corner of the room behind a large desk, and was only able to hear the participant, simulating a human-quality speech recognition system.

Independent Variable. Participants were divided into two groups, PTV (using the plasma TV configuration), and MON (using the monitor configuration). The PTV condition (See Figure 1 left) was designed to create the mixed reality illusion of a person seated across a desk from the user, deemphasizing the display. By orienting the plasma TV vertically, the upper body of the VH (torso, arms, and head) was closely framed. The plasma TV was then placed in a standard desk-chair and placed behind a desk. A picture was taken of the area directly behind the plasma TV, and used as a texture for the background of the VE. This configuration is mixed reality in that it leveraged and extended the real environment (chair, desk, background).

The MON condition (See Figure 1 right) was designed to appear similar to a typical computer interface. The monitor was placed on the desk, with the VH displayed as sitting behind a virtual desk. Further, a keyboard and mouse were placed in front of the monitor (although these were non-functional). The same picture was used for the VE background texture. This configuration is not mixed reality because it was not designed to leverage the real environment.

The plasma TV (native 720x480) and monitor (native 1280x1024) had different native resolutions (although both were driven at 1024 x 768). The difference was not expected to influence user behavior, as the features of the virtual human were clearly visible in both displays. In addition, no participants commented on the resolution of the displays.

Measures. The dependent variable in this study was the behavior of students in response to two important moments during the interaction:

- **Moment 1 (M1):** The first moment occurred when the pharmacist entered the room, and introduced herself as the pharmacist. The patient (rudely) demanded, "Why aren't I speaking to the doctor?" This type of moment is a common occurrence for a pharmacist working in a clinical setting. Pharmacists are trained to respond pleasantly, to explain the purpose of the interview, and to comfort the patient.

- **Moment 2 (M2):** Around seven minutes into the interview, the patient said to the participant: "my dad died of cancer" and asked, "could this be cancer?" This moment was designed to evoke an empathetic response from the participant.

Participants' interactions with the VH were recorded using a video camera. The video camera was positioned next to the display and recorded the participant's face. The participant's face was recorded because facial expressions encode up to 60% of nonverbal information [17].

Five video evaluators independently rated all videos. Evaluators were blind to the condition of each participant (video was from the front and did not record the display condition) A video evaluation form was designed to rate the response of the participant to each critical moment. The instrument assessed four interrelated constructs, determined by the authors as likely to be influenced by display configuration and important to patient interactions:

- Engagement – how much the response indicated interest and involvement in the patient's problems, i.e. not disinterested

- Empathy – how much the response indicated that the participant attempted to understand the feelings of the patient, i.e. not inconsiderate

- Pleasantness – how friendly the participants' behavior was, i.e. not rude

- Naturalness – how much the participant's behavior was realistic, i.e. not robotic

5   Results and Discussion

The average correlation among video evaluators was medium (0.614), and a factor analysis of the average data showed a single significant (Eigen value > 1.0) factor for each moment. This means that each item in the rating scale was highly interrelated. The behavioral data was analyzed using a multivariate ANOVA for each critical moment survey. There was a significant multivariate effect of display type for both critical moments (Critical Moment 1 Wilks' $\lambda=.59$ $p=.02$, Critical Moment 2 $\lambda=.612$ $p=.01$). As seen in Figure 2, participants in the PTV condition were more engaged, empathetic, pleasant, and natural.

The video evaluation results suggest that the participants in the mixed-reality condition demonstrated more appropriate responses towards the VH patient than participants in the desktop condition. Participants in the mixed reality condition were rated

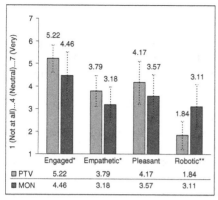
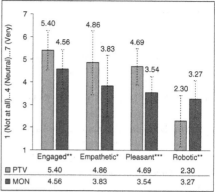

Fig. 2. Results for (Left) Moment 1 ("Why aren't I speaking to the doctor?") and (Right) Moment 2 (Could this be cancer?"). The dashed lines are +/- one standard deviation * (p<.05) ** (p<.01) *** (p<.001).

as significantly more engaged, empathetic, pleasant, and natural. In the desktop condition, participants appeared disconnected from the social interaction, and focused more on the general task (taking a medication history) than on the VH. A single dominant factor in the 4-item rating scale for each moment, suggesting that what observers were measuring was a single higher-level construct, such as appropriateness.

The raw magnitude of engagement is also worth noting. Participants in both the MON and PTV conditions were found to be engaged, but there was a main effect of display type in both M1 ($p=.03$) and M2 ($p=.03$), showing participants in the PTV condition were significantly more engaged. The reason for the high level of engagement in both conditions may have been the use of the WOz, and the isolation of the participant and the VH. During the interview, the participant was left alone in an office environment. With minimal interruptions occurring from technology, such as errors in speech recognition and outside influences, participants were engaged throughout the experience.

Overall, the results show that the visual display configuration is an important component to human-VH interactions, particularly those that may rely on or assess how the user responds to the VH. This work demonstrated that display configuration can have a strong influence on both cognition and behavior, and this result has important implications for designers of VH experiences. Designers should be aware of the limitations of small desktop display configuration. These types of display configurations are easily accessible and low-cost; however, interpersonal communication skills go beyond simple procedures. Interpersonal communication involves complex social and emotional behavior. Users may not treat VHs on a small monitor as they would a life-size VH. As a result, small monitor based VH experiences may be limited for the evaluation and training of interpersonal communication skills.

References

1. Johnsen, K., Dickerson, R., Raij, A., et al.: Experiences in using immersive virtual characters to education medical communication skills. IEEE Virtual Reality (2005)
2. Hill, R., Gratch, J., Marsella, S., Rickel, J., Swartout, W., Traum, D.: Virtual Humans in the Mission Rehearsal Exercise System. Künstliche Intelligenz 17, 5–10 (2003)
3. Lombard, M., Ditton, T.B.: The Role of Screen Size in Viewer Responses to Television Fare. Communication Reports 10, 95–106 (1997)
4. Reeves, B., Lang, A., Kim, E.Y., Tatar, D.: The Effects of Screen Size and Message Content on Attention and Arousal. Media Psychology 1, 49 (1999)
5. Lombard, M.: Direct Responses to People on the Screen: Television and Personal Space. Communication Research 22, 288–324 (1995)
6. Mori, M.: The Uncanny Valley. Energy 7, 33–35 (1970)
7. Bailenson, J.N., Swinth, K., Hoyt, C., Persky, S., Dimov, A., Blascovich, J.: The Independent and Interactive Effects of Embodied-Agent Appearance and Behavior on Self-report, Cognitive, and Behavioral Markers of Copresence in Immersive Virtual Environments. Presence: Teleoperators & Virtual Environments 14, 379–393 (2005)
8. Pausch, R., Proffitt, D., Williams, G.: Quantifying immersion in virtual reality. ACM SIGGRAPH, 13–18 (1997)
9. Bowman, D., Datey, A., Ryu, Y., Farooq, U., Vasnaik, O.: Empirical Comparison of Human Behavior and Performance with Different Display Devices for Virtual Environments. Human Factors and Ergonomics Society, 2134–2138 (2002)
10. Swan, J.E., Gabbard, I.I., Hix, J.L., Schulman, D., Kim, R.: A comparative study of user performance in a map-based virtual environment. In: IEEE Virtual Reality, pp. 259–266 (2003)
11. Tan, D.S., Gergle, D., Scupelli, P.G., Pausch, R.: With Similar Visual Angles, Larger Displays Improve Spatial Performance. In: ACM SIGCHI (2003)
12. Slater, M., Pertaub, D., Steed, A.: Public Speaking in Virtual Reality: Facing an Audience of Avatars. IEEE Computer Graphics and Applications 19, 6–9 (1999)
13. Slater, M., Sadagic, A., Usoh, M., Schroeder, R.: Small-Group Behavior in a Virtual and Real Environment: A Comparative Study. Presence: Teleoperators & Virtual Environments 9, 37–51 (2000)
14. Johnsen, K., Lok, B.: An Evaluation of Immersive Displays for Virtual Human Experiences. In: IEEE Virtual Reality (2008)
15. Ware, C., Arthur, K., Booth, K.S.: Fish tank virtual reality. In: ACM SIGCHI, pp. 37–42 (1993)
16. Schwinghammer, T.L.: Pharmacotherapy Casebook: A Patient-Focused Approach. McGraw-Hill Medical (2005)
17. Mehrabian, E.W.: Silent Messages. Wadsworth, Belmont (1971)

A Multimodal Real-Time Platform for Studying Human-Avatar Interactions

Hui Zhang, Damian Fricker, and Chen Yu

Indiana University, Bloomington, USA
{chenyu, huizhang, dfricker}@indiana.edu

Abstract. A better understanding of the human user's expectations and sensitivities to the real-time behavior generated by virtual agents can provide insightful empirical data and infer useful principles to guide the design of intelligent virtual agents. In light of this, we propose and implement a research framework to systematically study and evaluate different important aspects of multimodal real-time interactions between humans and virtual agents. Our platform allows the virtual agent to keep track of the user's gaze and hand movements in real time, and adjust his own behaviors accordingly. Multimodal data streams are collected in human-avatar interactions including speech, eye gaze, hand and head movements from both the human user and the virtual agent, which are then used to discover fine-grained behavioral patterns in human-agent interactions. We present a pilot study based on the proposed framework as an example of the kinds of research questions that can be rigorously addressed and answered. This first study investigating human-agent joint attention reveals promising results about the role and functioning of joint attention in human-avatar interactions.

Keywords: embodied agent, multimodal interaction, visualization.

1 Introduction

Interacting embodied agents, be they groups of people engaged in a coordinated task, autonomous robots acting in an environment, or an avatar on a computer screen interacting with a human user, must seamlessly coordinate their actions to achieve a collaborative goal. The pursuit of a shared goal requires mutual recognition of the goal, appropriate sequencing and coordination of each agent's behavior with others, and making predictions from and about the likely behavior of others. Such interaction is multimodal as we interact with each other and with intelligent artificial agents through multiple communication channels, including looking, speaking, touching, feeling, and pointing. In the case of human-human communication, moment-by-moment bodily actions are most of the time controlled by subconscious processes that are indicative of the internal state of cognitive processing in the brain (e.g., how much of an utterance they have processed, or how much of a situation they have comprehended)[1]. Indeed, both social partners in the interaction rely on those external observable behaviors to read the other person's intention and to initiate and carry on effective and

J. Allbeck et al. (Eds.): IVA 2010, LNAI 6356, pp. 49–56, 2010.

productive interactions [2]. In the case of human-agent interaction, human users interacting with virtual agents perceive them as "intentional" agents, and thus are automatically tempted to evaluate the virtual agent's behaviors based on their knowledge (and experience) of the real-time behavior of human agents. Hence, to build virtual agents that can emulate smooth human-human communication, intelligent agents need to meet with the human user's expectations and sensitivities to the real-time behaviors generated by virtual agents and perceive them in the similar way just as the user interacts with other humans.

2   Related Work

The above requirement poses a particular challenge in the design of intelligent virtual agents as we need those agents to not only generate appropriate behaviors but also execute those actions at the right moment and with the right timing. For example, head nodding at the right moment may reflect a listener's understanding as a back-channel feedback signal. In contrast, nodding at the unexpected moment may cause the speaker's confusion in reading/accessing the listener's attentional state. Similarly, a nodding action with abnormal timing may cause interruptions in communication. Indeed there is a growing research interest in studying real-time behaviors in human-computer interaction. In [3], an avatar generated reactive gaze behavior that is based on the user's current state in an interview scenario. In [4], sequential probabilistic models were used to select multimodal features from a speaker (e.g. prosody, gaze and spoken words) to predict visual back-channel cues (e.g. head nods). [5] built an engagement estimation algorithm based on analyzing gaze transition patterns from users. [6] developed a real-time gaze model for embodied conversational agents that generated spontaneous gaze movements based on the agent's internal state of cognitive processing.

3   A Real-Time Human-Agent Interaction Platform

The present work is specifically concerned with systematically studying the *exact timing* of *real-time interactions* between humans and virtual agents. To achieve this goal, we propose and implement a research framework for studying and evaluating different important aspects of multi-modal real-time interactions between humans and virtual agents, including establishment of joint attention via eye gaze coordination (an example application we will demonstrate by a pilot study described below), coupling of eye gaze, gestures, and utterances between virtual speaker and human listener in natural dialogues, and mechanisms for coordinating joint activities via verbal and nonverbal cues.

Specifically, there are three primary goals of building and using such a framework: 1) to test and evaluate moment-by-moment interactive behavioral patterns in human-agent interaction; 2) to develop, test and evaluate cognitive models that can emulate those patterns; 3) to develop, test and design new human-agent interfaces which include the appearance of the virtual agent, the control

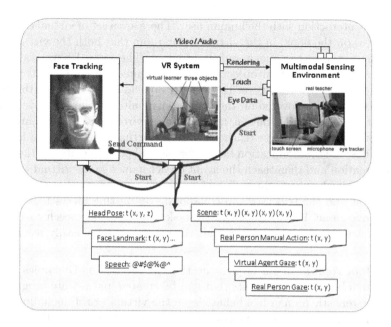

Fig. 1. An overview of system architecture. Top: A real person and a virtual human are engaged in a joint task with a set of virtual objects in a virtual environment. The platform tracks the user's gaze and hand movements in real time and feeds the information to the virtual agent's action control system to establish real-time perception-action loops with real and virtual agents. Bottom: multiple data streams are recorded from human-avatar interactions which are used to discover fine-grained behavioral patterns and infer more general principles.

strategy as well as real-time adaptive human-like behaviors. More importantly, we expect to use this platform to discover fundamental principles in human-agent interaction which can be easily extended to various scenarios in human-computer interactions. Two critical requirements for our framework are that it be able to collect, in an unprecedented way, fine-grained multi-modal sensorimotor data that can be used for discovering coupled behavioral patterns embedded in multiple data streams from both the virtual agent and the human user, and that the virtual agent can monitor the user's behaviors moment by moment, allowing the agent to infer the user's cognitive state (e.g. engagement and intention) and react to it in *real time*. To meet these requirements, we propose a framework consisting of four components (as shown in Figure 1): 1) an virtual experimental environment; 2) a virtual agent control system; 3) multi-modal sensory equipment; and 4) data recording, processing and mining. In the following, we will provide some details for each of the 4 components.

The Virtual Experimental Environment. This virtual environment consists of a virtual living room with everyday furniture, e.g. chairs and tables. This virtual scene is rendered on a computer screen with a virtual agent sitting on the sofa and partially facing toward the computer screen so that she can have a face-to-face interaction with the human user. There are a set of virtual objects on the table (or on the floor) in the virtual living room that both the virtual agent and the human user can move and manipulate. The virtual human's manual actions toward those virtual objects are implemented through VR techniques and the real person's actions on the virtual objects are performed through a touch-screen which is covered on the computer monitor. There are several joint tasks that can be carried out in this virtual environment. For example, the real person can be a language teacher while the virtual agent can be a language learner. Thus, the communication task is for the real person to attract the virtual agent's attention and then teach the agent object names so the virtual agent can learn the human language through social interaction. For another example, the virtual agent and the real user can collaborate on putting pieces together in a jigsaw puzzle game. In this collaborative task, they can use speech and gesture to communicate and refer to pieces that the other agent can easily reach.

The Virtual Agent. In our implementation, we use Boston Dynamics DI-Guy libraries to animate virtual agents that can be created and readily programmed to generate realistic human-like behaviors in the virtual world, including gazing and pointing at an object or a person in a specific 3D location, walking to a 3D location, and moving lips to synchronize with speech while speaking. In addition, the virtual human can generate 7 different kinds of facial expressions, such as smile, trust, sad, mad and distrust. All these combine to result in smooth behaviors being generated automatically. A critical component in the virtual human is to perceive the human user's behavior in real time and react appropriately within the right time span. As shown in Figure 1, this human-like skill is implemented by a combined mechanism including real-time eye tracking and motion tracking on the human side, real-time data transfer in the platform and real-time action control on the virtual human's side.

Multi-modal Sensory Equipment. As shown in Figure 1, our platform collects fine-grained behavioral data from both the virtual agent and the human user. On the human side, a Tobii 1750 eye tracker is used to monitor the user's eye movements at the frequency of 50Hz. The user's manual actions on virtual objects through the touch-screen is also recorded with timing information on a dedicated computer. Meanwhile, the system also records the user's speech in the interaction. More recently, we added a video camera pointing to the face of the user and a faceAPI package from seeingmachine (www.seeingmachine.com) is deployed and integrated into the whole system to record 38 3D face landmarks plus head rotation and orientation. On the virtual human side, our VR program not only renders a virtual scene with a virtual agent but also records gaze and manual actions generated by the virtual agent and his facial expressions. In addition, we also keep track of the locations of objects on the computer screen. As a result, we gather multimodal multi-stream temporal data streams from human-avatar interactions. All data streams are synchronized via system-wide timestamps.

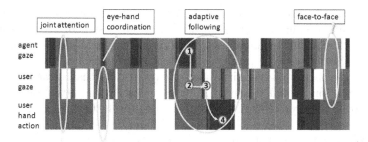

Fig. 2. Examples of multimodal data streams and data analysis. The three streams are derived from raw action data from both the user and the agent. The first one is the Region-Of-Interest(ROI) stream from the virtual agent's eye gaze, indicating which object the virtual agent attends to (e.g. gazing at one of the three virtual objects or looking straight toward the human user). The second stream is the ROI stream (three objects and the virtual agent's face) from the human user's gaze and the third one encodes which object the real person is manipulating and moving. We highlight 4 momentary interactive behaviors from those data streams (labeled from left to right on the top) to illustrate the kinds of patterns we investigate using our multimodal real-time platform: 1) joint attention: both agents visually attend to the same object (colored in red); 2) eye-hand coordination: the human user gazes at an object while moving it through the touch-screen; 3) adaptive following: this sequential pattern starts with the situation that the virtual agent and the human user attend to different objects (step 1), and then the human user checks the virtual agent's gaze (step 2) and follows the virtual agent attention to the same object (step 3) and finally reach to that object (step 4); 4) face-to-face: the virtual agent and the human user look towards each other's face. The goal of building the present framework is to study those moment-by-moment micro-level multimodal behaviors in human-avatar interactions.

Multimodal Data Processing and Mining. We have developed a visual data mining system that allows us to analyze rich multimodal datasets to search for detailed time-course patterns exchanged between the human user and the virtual agent [7]. This system has played a critical role in our previous studies on human-human interaction and human-robot interaction [8,9]. Our interactive visualization system provides an integrated solution with automatic and supervised data mining techniques that allow researchers to control (based on the visualization results) the focus of the automatic search for interesting patterns in multiple data streams. In particular, we use this system to not only detect the changes in each information channel (from either the human and the virtual agent data) but also consequential interactive patterns across two agents in real-time interaction. The insights from such active data exploration can subsequently be used for quantifying those interactive patterns as well as developing computational models of better human-agent interactions.

4   Preliminary Experiment

The overall goal of this research platform is to build a better human-agent communication system and understand multimodal agent-agent interaction. Joint visual attention has been well documented as an important indicator in smooth human-human communication. In light of this, our first pilot study focuses on joint attention between a human user and a virtual agent. More specifically, given the real-time control mechanism implemented in our platform, we ask how a human agent reacts to different situations wherein the virtual agent may or may not pay attention to and follow the human agent's visual attention. The joint task employed requires the human participant to teach the virtual agent a set of the (fictitious) names of various objects. We manipulated the engagement levels of the virtual agent to create three interaction conditions – engaged 10%, 50%, or 90% of total interaction time. When the virtual agent is engaged, she would follow the human teacher's attention inferred from the teacher's manual action and gaze, and then look toward the object that the real person is attending and meanwhile show interests by generating positive facial expressions. When she is not engaged, she would look at one of the other objects that the real teacher is not attending to with negative facial expressions. In this pilot study, there are in total 18 learning trials, each of which consists of 3 to-be-taught objects. The human teachers can manually move any of the three objects through the touch-screen to attract the virtual learner's attention first and then name it. Multimodal data from both interacting partners were recorded and analyzed to examine how real people adapted their behavior to interact with virtual agents possessing different level of social skills. For instance, we are interested in how frequently the real teacher checks the virtual agent's visual attention in three engagement conditions, how the virtual agent's engagement may influence what the real teacher says and what actions s/he generates toward the to-be-learned objects, what are sequential multimodal behavioral patterns within an agent, and how the real agent may generate coupled adaptive actions based on the virtual agent's state. More importantly, this new platform allows us to answer those questions based on moment-by-moment micro-level behavioral patterns as an objective way to access the smoothness of human-avatar interaction. Figure 2 shows an example to illustrate what kinds of multimodal behavioral patterns can be extracted from human-agent interaction and what kinds of research questions can be investigated using our platform. With this temporal window of only 30 seconds, the behaviors of both agents dynamically change moment by moment, creating various interactive patterns. Four joint activities are highlighted in Figure 2 (from left to right, see details in the caption): 1) joint attention; 2) eye-hand coordination; 3) adaptive following; and 4) face-to-face. We argue that multimodal human-avatar integration is made of those interactive patterns dynamically mixed with other joint activities between two interacting agents. Our ongoing research focuses on analyzing and comparing various joint action patterns across three engagement conditions to measure how the virtual agent's attentional state influences human users' moment-by-moment actions, and how human users adaptively adjust their reactive behavior based on their perception of the virtual agent's actions.

5   Conclusion and On-Going Work

In multimodal human-avatar interaction, dependencies and interaction patterns between two interacting agents are bi-directional, i.e., the human user shapes the experiences and behaviors of the virtual agent through his own bodily actions and sensory-motor experiences, and the virtual agent likewise directly influences the sensorimotor experiences and actions of the human user. The present paper describes a multimodal real-time human-avatar platform and demonstrates the potential of this platform for discovering novel and interesting results that can significantly advance the field of human-agent collaborative research. The learning task example is only one of many possible studies that could be conducted using the proposed framework. For example, another application of this framework is to determine the timing of back-channel feedback (from eye gaze, to gestures, to body postures, to verbal acknowledgments), which is critical for establishing common ground in conversations. This could include questions about how head movements, gestures and bodily postures are related to natural language comprehension, as well as general questions about the functional role of non-linguistic aspects of communication contributing to natural language understanding. Thus, with this real-time interactive system, we can collect multimodal behavioral data in different contexts, allowing us to systematically study the time-course of multimodal behaviors. The results from such research will provide insightful principles to guide the design of human-computer interaction. Moreover, those fine-grained patterns and behaviors can also be directly implemented in an intelligent virtual agent who will demonstrate human-like sensitivities to various non-verbal bodily cues in natural interactions.

References

1. Tanenhaus, M.K., Spivey-Knowlton, M.J., Eberhard, K.M., Sedivy, J.C.: Integration of visual and linguistic information in spoken language comprehension. Science 268, 1632–1634 (1995)
2. Shockley, K., Santana, M.V., Fowler, C.: Mutual interpersonal postural constraints are involved in cooperative conversation. Journal of Experimental Psychology: Human Perception and Performance 29, 326–333 (2003)
3. Kipp, M., Gebhard, P.: Igaze: Studying reactive gaze behavior in semi-immersive human-avatar interactions. In: Prendinger, H., Lester, J.C., Ishizuka, M. (eds.) IVA 2008. LNCS (LNAI), vol. 5208, pp. 191–199. Springer, Heidelberg (2008)
4. Morency, L.P., Kok, I., Gratch, J.: Predicting listener backchannels: A probabilistic multimodal approach. In: Prendinger, H., Lester, J.C., Ishizuka, M. (eds.) IVA 2008. LNCS (LNAI), vol. 5208, pp. 176–190. Springer, Heidelberg (2008)
5. Ishii, R., Nakano, Y.I.: Estimating user's conversational engagement based on gaze behaviors. In: Prendinger, H., Lester, J.C., Ishizuka, M. (eds.) IVA 2008. LNCS (LNAI), vol. 5208, pp. 200–207. Springer, Heidelberg (2008)
6. Lee, J., Marsella, S., Traum, D., Gratch, J., Lance, B.: The rickel gaze model: A window on the mind of a virtual human. In: Pelachaud, C., Martin, J.-C., André, E., Chollet, G., Karpouzis, K., Pelé, D. (eds.) IVA 2007. LNCS (LNAI), vol. 4722, pp. 296–303. Springer, Heidelberg (2007)

7. Yu, C., Zhong, Y., Smith, T., Park, I., Huang, W.: Visual data mining of multimedia data for social and behavioral studies. Information Visualization 8, 56–70 (2009)

8. Yu, C., Smith, L., Shen, H., Pereira, A.F., Smith, T.: Active information selection: Visual attention through the hands. IEEE Transactions on Autonomous Mental Development 2, 141–151 (2009)

9. Yu, C., Scheutz, M., Schermerhorn, P.: Investigating multimodal real-time patterns of joint attention in an hri word learning task. In: HRI 2010: Proceeding of the 5th ACM/IEEE international conference on Human-robot interaction, pp. 309–316. ACM, New York (2010)

Realizing Multimodal Behavior

Closing the Gap between Behavior Planning and Embodied Agent Presentation

Michael Kipp, Alexis Heloir, Marc Schröder, and Patrick Gebhard

DFKI, Saarbrücken, Germany
`firstname.surname@dfki.de`

Abstract. Generating coordinated multimodal behavior for an embodied agent (speech, gesture, facial expression...) is challenging. It requires a high degree of animation control, in particular when reactive behaviors are required. We suggest to distinguish *realization planning*, where gesture and speech are processed symbolically using the behavior markup language (BML), and *presentation* which is controlled by a lower level animation language (EMBRScript). Reactive behaviors can bypass planning and directly control presentation. In this paper, we show how to define a behavior lexicon, how this lexicon relates to BML and how to resolve timing using formal constraint solvers. We conclude by demonstrating how to integrate reactive emotional behaviors.

1 Introduction

Embodied agents have the potential to make human-computer interaction more intuitive, engaging and accessible. To take full effect, they have to use all modalities of the body (speech, gesture, facial expression, posture etc.) in meaningful coordination. The SAIBA framework aims suggests three principal modules for the behavior production process [1]: *intent planning* for determining the overall content of the message in terms of abstract communicative goals, *behavior planning* for deciding on the choice of words, gestures, facial expressions etc. in terms of modalities but not body part and *realization* for rendering these behaviors with a concrete agent body and voice. BML (behavior markup language) was suggested as a standard language to formulate sequences of abstract behaviors (speech, gesture, gaze ...), independent of concrete animation or speech synthesis platforms. For instance, a gaze behavior toward a person X could be defined, independent of whether this is realized just with the eyes only, a turn of the head, the upper body or by repositioning the whole body. BML also allows to define complex temporal synchronization constraints between behaviors. However, there has been no general solution how to actually solve these in a principled way. We have argued that SAIBA leaves a significant gap between behavior planning and realization [2]. Many choices of actual animation must be either made in the realizer or specified using custom BML extensions, which compromises its conceptual clarity. Therefore, we suggest to separate these processes into *realization*

J. Allbeck et al. (Eds.): IVA 2010, LNAI 6356, pp. 57–63, 2010.

planning and *presentation* (Fig. 1). The realization planner converts abstract, underspecified and cross-referenced behavior specifications (BML) into linear, executable presentation scripts (so this includes multimodal coordination). The presentation module contains a 3D character animation engine and possibly a separate audio player for the voice. Presentation calls for a new language for the animation part which we call EMBRScript [3] which we also use to define the behavior lexicon.

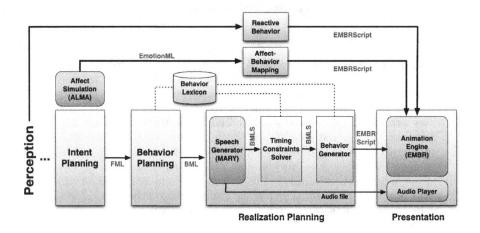

Fig. 1. Overview of our architecture. Reusable standard components depicted as light blue rounded boxes.

One of the earliest frameworks for virtual character control was Improv [4] which provided a scripting language for authoring both the animation and the behavior of real-time animated actors. This system was the first to make a distinction between abstract behavior specifications and executable animation scripts. However, the animation scripts were very low-level, an abstract framework on the level of behaviors was missing. In the BEAT [5] pipeline architecture a translation mechanism from behavior specifications to animation commands exists but the translation process is not explicitly described. SmartBody was the first system to implement BML for agent control [6] but required many custom extensions to BML. Greta [7] is also based on SAIBA and separates realization into behavior planning and realization in the sense that MPEG4 scripts for the player are produced. However, it is not clear how the translation process is done in terms of e.g. temporal constraints resolution. While most existing frameworks implicitly make the distinction between realization planning and presentation, they do not offer declarative languages to control animation and/or define behavior lexemes. The problem of time constraint resolution has not been dealt with in a principled way.

Our research makes the following contributions: (1) Separating realization planning from presentation, (2) clarifying the role of behavior lexicons, (3) a principled approach to resolving BML time constraints and (4) demonstrating reactive behavior integration.

2 Framework

The pipeline architecture of our framework is shown in Fig. 1. We focus on realization planning where processing starts with a BML[1] document that describes, e.g., the text to be spoken, gestures, head nods etc. – together with timing constraints regarding the behaviors' sync points. Realization planning consists of generating speech, resolving all behavior timings and retrieving lexeme data for the production of an executable animation script, together with an audio file of the speech. The presentation layer represents character animation and audio playback. We can now issue reactive behaviors like gaze following or continuous adjustments to the current emotion (face, posture) by sending it directly to the presentation module, by-passing intent and behavior planners.

Components. Our system is implemented on top of the SEMAINE API, an open-source distributed multi-platform component integration framework for real-time interactive systems [8]. Components communicate via standard representation formats, including BML, BMLS and EmotionML. For realtime 3D character animation we use our free EMBR software[2] (Embodied Agents Realizer) [3,2] which allows fine-grained animation control via a pose-based specification language called EMBRScript. EMBR allows gesturing, facial expressions, pose shifts, blushing and gaze control and autonomous behaviors like breathing and blinking. For the synthesis of speech we use the *text-to-speech* and *speech realizer* components MARY of the SEMAINE system.

Reactive Affect-Behavior Mapping. To demonstrate the modeling of reactive behavior, we implemented a direct coupling of emotional state with behaviors like facial expression, head orientation, breathing and blushing. We use ALMA [9] for affect simulation which continually produces EmotionML [10] to express the current *emotion* and *mood* of the agent. This is mapped to behaviors that are directly sent to the presentation component as EMBRScript documents. For instance, *mood* affects blushing and breathing with its *arousal* component. We defined mappings for emotion events (joy, anger, liking...) to trigger behaviors (facial expressions) and physiological changes (breathing, blushing), based on the literature. The emotion intensity determines the duration and the visible intensity (e.g. blushing level, extent of smile, raised eye brow level) of an emotional cue.

3 Realization Planning

Realization planning input is a behavior specification (BML) to be translated into an executable animation script (EMBRScript). We propose a pipeline where

---

[1] http://wiki.mindmakers.org/projects:bml:draft1.0
[2] http://embots.dfki.de/EMBR

the input BML is successively enriched. We call "solved BML", short BMLS, a subset of BML where all time references are resolved.

Behavior Lexicon. Behaviors specified in BML have to be translated to animation plans. Synchronization points must be resolved for each behavior. Both tasks require a central database of behaviors, the *behavior lexicon L*, which effectively restricts the language BML to a subset BML(L).

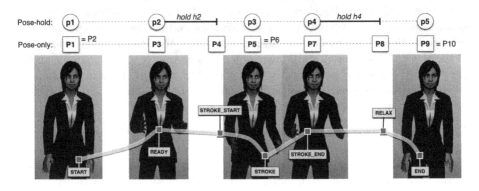

Fig. 2. EMBRScript template for lexeme "beats" with parameter handedness=both. Only the poses P3 ("ready"), P5 ("stroke") and P7 ("stroke_end") need markup, the rest is implicit. The top line shows the pose-hold representation of EMBRScript the line below the pose-only representation.

The behavior lexicon L consists of a collection of *lexemes* $\{l_1, \ldots, l_n\}$. Lexemes are *parametrizable* with regard to BML attributes (e.g. handedness, number of repetitions), i.e. every lexeme represents a *set of variants*. Each lexeme must declare which of the BML *sync points* (start, ready, stroke_start, stroke, stroke_end, relax, end) can be used in conjunction with this lexeme. In our framework, we use EMBRScript to define the variants of a lexeme which are based on key poses, some of which can be equated with BML sync points (see Fig. 2). The key pose representation allows to easily modify the motion by shifting poses in time or adjusting hold durations. For every lexeme we define several EMBRScript templates that correspond to a concrete parametrization, e.g. three templates for handedness variants: left, right or both. We mark up those poses that correspond to sync points. Because of the pose-hold representation, we only need to mark up three sync points at most (namely ready, stroke and stroke_end). We can quickly create lexeme templates using a graphical tool for pose creation, sync point markup and interactive animation viewing. We currently have 51 gesture lexemes in our lexicon, instantiated by 121 EMBRScript templates.

Speech Generator. The text-to-speech (TTS) component reads BML markup and sends audio data to the presentation module (Fig. 1). For temporal synchronization with the face and gestures, the TTS needs to output (a) the phonetic symbols and their timings and (b) the absolute time of BML sync points. We

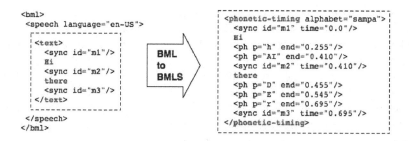

Fig. 3. BML transformed to BMLS$_{speech}$: phoneme timings and sync points resolved

transport this information under the new `phonetic-timing` tag. Note that this tag can also be used in the case that an application uses pre-recorded audio files instead of synthesized speech. BML is transformed to BMLS$_{speech}$ as depicted in Fig. 3, where the `text` tag is replaced by the more informative `phonetic-timing` tag, effectively decoupling the steps of audio generation and synchronized visual realization planning.

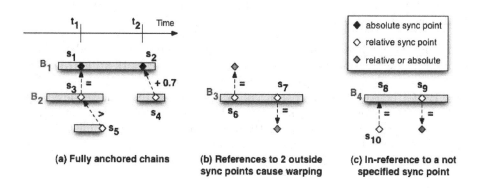

Fig. 4. Cases of sync point linkages

Timing Constraints Solver. The timing constraints solver receives BMLS$_{speech}$ where speech sync points contain absolute time. The task is to resolve relative sync points also for nonverbal behaviors like in `<gesture start="h1:end"/>`. We translate this problem to a formal constraint problem and explain this by example. Fig. 4 shows behaviors and how their sync points can relate to each other. Case (a) is probably most frequent: sync points refer to other sync points, and every "chain" of references is grounded in an absolute sync point. For the constraint problem formulation we introduce V^s for every sync point s. Absolute times can be directly assigned: $V^{s1} = t_1$ and $V^{s2} = t_2$. Relative sync point relationships are expressed via their respective constraint variables. For the example in Fig. 4 this translates to $V^{s3} = V^{s1}$ and $V^{s4} = V^{s2} + 0.7$ and $V^{s5} > V^{s3}$.

Fig. 4, case (b), a behavior B_3 has two (or more) sync points s_6 and s_7 which means B_3 has to be stretched or compressed. In case (c), behavior B_4 *is referenced* by another behavior with respect to sync point s_8, although s_8 is *not* specified at all in B_4. This makes sense only if there is another sync point s_9 that "anchors" behavior B_4. However, how do we formulate a constraint for resolving s_{10}? For this, we have to consult our lexicon and introduce s_8 as a virtual sync point, deriving its relation to s_9 from the lexeme template. In the lexicon, each behavior has a pre-specified timing of sync points. We formulate constraints thus that the changes to the original lexeme are kept minimal. So let us assume that of behavior B_4, one sync point s_9 is specified and another one, s_8, is "virtual", i.e. it is referred to but not specified itself. Then, we introduce intra-behavior constraints to express the relationship between s_8 and s_9: $V^{s8} + V^\Delta = V^{s9}$ and $V^\epsilon = |lexeme_\Delta(s_8, s_9) - V^\Delta|$. Here, $lexeme_\Delta$ is a constant that is equal to the distance of the two sync points in the original lexeme template. V^Δ is the actual distance when realized and V^ϵ is the deviation from the original distance. In our constraint solver, we ask for minimization of all V^ϵ variables. We implemented the described system with the Java constraint solver JaCoP [3].

Note that we can now define the *realizability* of an BML(L) input document in terms of three conditions: (1) every sync point of behavior b must be marked-up in the lexeme of b in lexicon L, (2) every chain of relative sync points must be grounded, i.e. end in an absolute sync point[4] and (3) every lexeme reference in BML must have a counterpart in L.

Behavior Generator. The behavior generator receives BMLS and produces final EMBRScript. For viseme generation, the phonetic mark-up is translated to a sequence of morph targets (currently 16 visemes). For gesture generation, each BMLS behavior tag B that refers to a lexeme in the behavior lexicon is looked up based on the parameters (e.g. handedness) to retrieve the correct lexeme variant in the form of an EMBRScript template e. This template is then modified according the the resolved sync points in B.

4   Conclusion

We presented a framework for realizing multimodal behaviors for an embodied agent. Our framework is based on the modified SAIBA framework where realization and presentation are separated, and utilizes existing and coming standards for data exchange (BML and EmotionML). We showed how to resolve timing constraints in BML and how to expand gesture lexemes to executable scripts. We demonstrated the potential for reactive behaviors by implementing a direct affect-behavior mapping. Our work clarifies that BML is tightly linked to the behavior lexicon. The *realizability* of a BML document depends internally on the linking of relative constraints and externally on the lexicon entries (lexemes)

---

[3] http://jacop.osolpro.com

[4] Here, we need an extended definition of a "chain" where, if sync point s refers to behavior b, the only condition is that b has at least one other sync point.

and the semantic meta-data of each lexeme. We advocate to use standardized XML languages for data exchange, even within modules, in the form of "solved BML" (BMLS), to facilitate the exchange of components in the community.

In future research we plan to integrate a dialogue manager and rich sensor input, e.g. tracking gaze, facial expressions and biosignals. These signals can directly be mapped to presentation for reactive behaviors like gaze following.

Acknowledgments. This research has been carried out within the framework of the Excellence Cluster Multimodal Computing and Interaction (MMCI), sponsored by the German Research Foundation (DFG).

References

1. Vilhjalmsson, H., Cantelmo, N., Cassell, J., Chafai, N.E., Kipp, M., Kopp, S., Mancini, M., Marsella, S., Marshall, A.N., Pelachaud, C., Ruttkay, Z., Thórisson, K.R., van Welbergen, H., van der Werf, R.J.: The behavior markup language: Recent developments and challenges. In: Pelachaud, C., Martin, J.-C., André, E., Chollet, G., Karpouzis, K., Pelé, D. (eds.) IVA 2007. LNCS (LNAI), vol. 4722, pp. 99–111. Springer, Heidelberg (2007)
2. Heloir, A., Kipp, M.: EMBR - a realtime animation engine for interactive embodied agents. In: Proc. of the Intl. Conf. on Intelligent Virtual Agents (2009)
3. Heloir, A., Kipp, M.: Realtime animation of interactive agents: Specification and realization. Applied Artificial Intelligence (2010)
4. Perlin, K., Goldberg, A.: Improv: A System for Scripting Interactive Actors in Virtual Worlds. In: Proc. of SIGGRAPH 1996, vol. 29(3) (1996)
5. Cassell, J., Vilhjálmsson, H., Bickmore, T.: BEAT: the Behavior Expression Animation Toolkit. In: Proceedings of SIGGRAPH 2001, pp. 477–486 (2001)
6. Thiebaux, M., Marshall, A., Marsella, S., Kallman, M.: Smartbody: Behavior realization for embodied conversational agents. In: Proc. of the Intl. Conf. on Autonomous Agents and Multiagent Systems (2008)
7. Niewiadomski, R., Bevacqua, E., Mancini, M., Pelachaud, C.: Greta: an interactive expressive ECA system. In: AAMAS 2009: Proc. of The 8th International Conference on Autonomous Agents and Multiagent Systems, Budapest, Hungary, pp. 1399–1400 (2009)
8. Schröder, M.: The SEMAINE API: towards a standards-based framework for building emotion-oriented systems. In: Advances in Human-Computer Interaction (2010)
9. Gebhard, P.: ALMA - a layered model of affect. In: Proceedings of the Fourth International Joint Conference on Autonomous Agents and Multiagent Systems, pp. 29–36. ACM Press, New York (June 2005)
10. Schröder, M., Baggia, P., Burkhardt, F., Pelachaud, C., Peter, C., Zovato, E.: Emotion markup language (EmotionML) 1.0. W3C first public working draft, World Wide Web Consortium (October 2009)

Designing an Expressive Avatar of a Real Person

Sangyoon Lee, Gordon Carlson, Steve Jones, Andrew Johnson,
Jason Leigh, and Luc Renambot

Electronic Visualization Laboratory, University of Illinois at Chicago,
851 S. Morgan St. Chicago, IL 60607, USA
{slee14,gcarls4,sjones,ajohnson,spiff,renambot}@uic.edu

Abstract. The human ability to express and recognize emotions plays an important role in face-to-face communication, and as technology advances it will be increasingly important for computer-generated avatars to be similarly expressive. In this paper, we present the detailed development process for the Lifelike Responsive Avatar Framework (LRAF) and a prototype application for modeling a specific individual to analyze the effectiveness of expressive avatars. In particular, the goals of our pilot study ($n = 1,744$) are to determine whether the specific avatar being developed is capable of conveying emotional states (Ekmans six classic emotions) via facial features and whether a realistic avatar is an appropriate vehicle for conveying the emotional states accompanying spoken information. The results of this study show that happiness and sadness are correctly identified with a high degree of accuracy while the other four emotional states show mixed results.

Fig. 1. Dr. Alex Schwarzkopf and His Virtual Representation

1 Introduction

An avatar, a human-like computer interface, has been actively developed in various forms and is becoming more and more prevalent in diverse target applications [1]. With widespread adoption of advanced computer graphics, artificial intelligence and various

J. Allbeck et al. (Eds.): IVA 2010, LNAI 6356, pp. 64–76, 2010.

sensing technologies, a lifelike avatar becomes capable of increasingly natural interaction. The human ability to express and to recognize emotions plays an important role in face-to-face communication. As an avatar interface relies on the naturalness of peoples everyday communication with others, understanding its nature is a fundamental key to success. We understand people better as well as convey our ideas more appropriately given with such a capability in everyday life [2] . Our work makes three different contributions. First, it presents our experiences in creating the avatar framework. Second, we demonstrate an avatar creation process in detail. Finally, we conduct a user study with a prototype application to analyze the effectiveness of avatar emotion compared to that of a human. The rest of the paper is organized as follows. Section 2 reviews studies related to our work. In section 3, we describe an implemented Lifelike Responsive Avatar Framework (LRAF) system including a framework and avatar creation method. User study results are presented in section 4 and the conclusion is in section 5.

2   Related Work

Research on avatars or virtual humans has been ongoing for decades. Yee et al. conducted a meta-analysis of the effectiveness of avatar usage across 40 research projects. They found that visual human-like embodied agent interfaces and their realistic behavior showed significant effects in subjective responses but not in task performance [1]. In contrast to this, a more natural behavior model such as a relational agent provided users with a better experience not only in subjective but also in behavioral measures with a virtual nurse application [3] and a long-term daily exercise application [4]. This implies that the application domain can affect the effectiveness of an avatar. One counterexample in the early study is a poker game with emotional avatars by Koda et al. Some subjects believed that a poker player should not show any emotion during game play [5]. Our research focuses on an avatar's expressive capability. To this end, Ekmans classic study [6] has been widely adopted to model human emotion in avatar interfaces. Diana et al. proposed an affective model for the generation of emotional states using MPEG-4 Facial Animation Parameters and evaluated its recognition rate [7]. A series of studies by Wallraven et al. used a 4D-scanner to capture human expressions and create a computer-animated head. They compared perception accuracy with various rendering techniques such as texture and shape blurring [8] and stylizations of rendering [9]. They found that more realistic rendering was better at providing subjective certainty and quality of the conveyed expression. More recent studies of expressive virtual humans with various graphical features such as dynamic wrinkles, blushing, and tears also confirmed these results [10,11]. However, creation of realistic graphics to resemble a human subject requires either high fidelity hardware or a fair amount of a designers effort. In this study, we present our robust method to create an avatar of a person without unique hardware or a high degree of human intervention.

3   Design and Implementation

Creating a compelling avatar requires many complex steps involving programming, observation, design, and evaluation. In this section, we present our implementation of a framework, and the method of developing an avatar based on a specific target person. Our first prototype application is designed to allow the user to interact with a senior National Science Foundation program director to retrieve domain specific knowledge about the program which he led (Figure 2).

Fig. 2. LRAF prototype application. A user interacts with a life-size avatar on a 50" display. Our first prototype application is a life-like embodiment of a particular person, retiring National Science Foundation program director Dr. Alex Schwarzkopf. The import aspect of our design goal is to ensure a user's experience as natural and realistic as possible. To this end, a deployed large display matches a target persons physical measures in the realized representation and an ambient microphone enables a user to interact with an avatar more naturally. It is designed to be a life-size avatar simulating face-to-face communication with a real person.

3.1   LifeLike Responsive Avatar Framework (LRAF)

The LifeLike Responsive Avatar Framework is composed of multiple modules to accommodate the various features of a lifelike avatar. Figure 3 shows the high-level framework architecture. In the following subsections, we will give more details of the framework.

Graphics Library and Animation. LRAF relies on the Object-Oriented Graphics Rendering Engine (OGRE) library for its low-level graphics modules [12]. OGRE is an open-source platform independent rendering engine that supports most modern graphics features such as skeletal / shape animation, shader languages, and flexible plug-in architecture. Custom rendering techniques are implemented in addition to the standard set of features.

LRAF avatar animation is a combination of a full body skeletal animation and shape-based facial animation. The Facial Expression Synthesizer controls verbal and nonverbal expressions together - verbal expressions for lip synchronization and nonverbal expression for emotion and other behavioral aspects. The synthesizer integrates

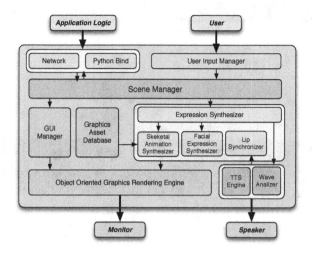

Fig. 3. LRAF architecture diagram

all the weight parameters to blend a facial expression. The Skeletal Animation Synthesizer manages full body animation. Avatars intended to mimic human behavior need to behave somewhat non-deterministically or else they will appear unnatural and mechanistic. To accomplish this we devised the concept of a Semi-Deterministic Hierarchical Finite State Machine (SDHFSM). An SDHFSM is a hierarchical finite state machine where a sub-state is chosen either based on a set of constraints or randomly given multiple possible options (Figure 4).

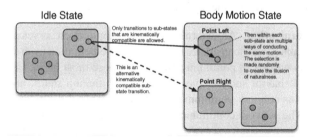

Fig. 4. Semi-Deterministic Hierarchical Finite State Machine

Voice and Lip Synchronization. There are two main approaches to generating an avatar voice, a Text-To-Speech (TTS) synthesizer, and a prerecorded human voice. LRAF supports both functionalities to synchronize lip animation. TTS can synthesize speech from unrestricted text. Since Microsofts SAPI TTS engine generates a discrete viseme event while synthesizing a voice in real time, we used a linear blending algorithm to fill the gaps between the distinct lip shapes. The TTS voice module constantly monitors and enqueues a viseme event to the lip synchronizer. The lip synchronizer computes the weight parameters for each viseme blendshape by multiplying the elapsed frame time, the current

Fig. 5. LRAF application using Python binding. A tour guide astronaut avatar describes features of the high-resolution Carina Nebula image on a tile display system.

amplitude of the audio mixer and a constant factor. This is not a precise mouth coarticulation model but it is a feasible solution. We are looking into a better algorithm to improve this in the future, such as King and Parents blendshape based coarticulation model [13]. A recorded voice can be more realistic than a synthesized voice as it uses a real persons voice. We have used a FFT waveform analyzer to monitor several frequency bands. Each band or group of bands can be used to drive a specific lip shape. As the recorded voice plays, the lip synchronizer continuously computes the weight parameters based on the power level of the assigned frequency bands.

External Communication. An external module or application serves as the brain for the avatar. This separation encapsulates the LRAF implementation from the application. LRAF supports two types of communication that expose most of the LRAF interfaces to control avatar behavior such as speech content, animation states, and expressions. One is synchronous network communication and the other is a binding to the Python script language. The network communication model is used in our first prototype application [14].

The Python binding extends the LRAF C++ abstract class Activity to Python. Application developers can inherit this class and implement it in a script based on application requirements. The Activity class defines a hierarchical task model with an internal FSM template. The script can then connect LRAF to an external application that benefits from an avatar-mediated interface (Figure 5).

3.2   Avatar Design

Developing a fully expressive conversational agent takes multiple steps to incorporate various aspects of human characteristics. We mainly used commodity software packages to reproduce a real person as the target model of our prototype agent.

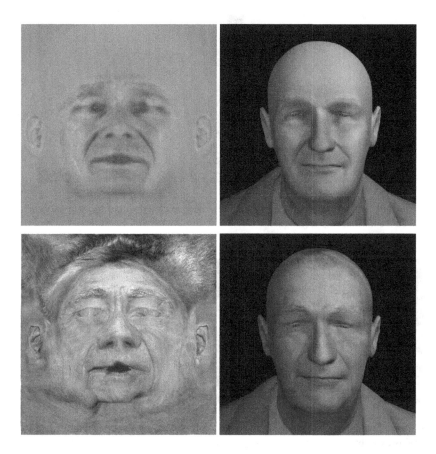

Fig. 6. Skin Texture Enhancement. Top row: default texture (512x512 resolution) from Face-Gen and its rendering result. Bottom row: high-resolution skin texture (4096x4096 resolution) acquired by projecting high quality photos of a target person onto 3D mesh model.

Head Generation. An avatar head is the most complicated piece of the avatar. Primarily, it should support fundamental facial expressions and look reasonably like our target person, Dr. Schwarzkopf. We used Singular FaceGen Modeler to create a base mesh model of the avatar head. It provided an easy way to generate a head model with two photos of the real person, front and side. This model features 39 blendshapes including 7 emotions, 16 modifiers and 16 phonemes. A modifier is similar to a FACS Action Unit that controls small parts of the face such as a blink and eyebrow up / down.

While this is an efficient way to begin, a generated base mesh model and its texture is often not detailed enough or not similar enough to the target model. In particular we noticed that the accuracy of resemblance is lower if the target person is elderly and has many skin wrinkles in the photos. The default texture resolution is also not enough to fully realize the detailed facial features in a high-resolution display. Fine tuned adjustment of facial proportion and texture reconstruction are necessary to achieve the best resemblance. Figure 6 illustrates this realism enhancement by applying photo-based

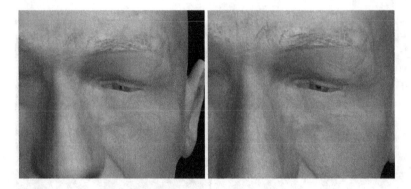

Fig. 7. Effedt of Normal Map for Skin Details. Left image rendered with color map only and right image used the normal map technique.

Fig. 8. Dynamic texturing on glasses. Live webcam image (left) is blended on the reflective surface of glasses(right).

texture projection. In our current pipeline, a designer manually applies texture projection and blends multiple resulting images into one high-resolution texture. Even with a higher resolution color texture map, the resulting rendering of the skin is rather plain and too smooth. To realize human skin characteristics further, it is necessary to add more subtle features such as wrinkles and pores. The most widely adopted method to implement those details in graphics is to use a tangent space normal map. This technique utilizes the vast computation power of graphics hardware in pixel space without losing frame rate compared to a high-density polygonal mesh model approach. A normal map texture is generated by the color texture based normal extraction method [11]. The final rendering result of a normal map is presented in Figure 7.

A small graphical gadget can improve the user experience and embodiment in interacting with the avatar. One example to fill the gap between the virtual and real worlds is the use of a live video feed on a reflective material in the virtual scene (Figure 8). During our preliminary internal review, most users noted higher engagement with this feature. It will be useful to evaluate this effect in a future study.

Full body Modeling and Motion Acquisition. An avatar full body model was designed in Autodesk Maya software. All physical dimensions of the model matched the target person. Since we use a skinned mesh to animate an avatar body, we built the body skeleton with roughly 70 bones including all of the finger bones and rigged it to the body mesh. Finally, the head model was combined with the body. As we digitized the person, all behaviors and gestures were based on the target person. We utilized an optical motion capture system, Vicon MX-F40, to acquire full body motion and mannerisms. Then a segmentation of each individual motion clip was processed to construct an internal motion database. Each motion clip corresponds to a unit action such as look left / right, various pointing, idle, and other actions. The animation module in LRAF selects proper motion clips and blends them in real time.

Personification and Review. As we develop a specific person's virtual representation, the realism of the agent relies not only on visual realism but also on behavioral characteristics. So far we have discussed how we create a visually compelling agent with the help of advanced graphics. The use of a motion capture system partially solves the problem of simulating the gestural aspects of the agent as it precisely replicates a target persons kinematic movement. For instance, an 82 year old man's keyboard typing may just be pressing keys with one or two index fingers and his natural posture of sitting on a chair is slightly leaning toward one side rather than straight-up. However, developing a more fine-grained mannerism model is still a very active research area and requires a significant amount of effort in observation, modeling, and evaluation. In our first prototype application, we started with several obvious and most distinct mannerisms. For instance, the subject's blink rate is more frequent than the rate of an average male adult. His often used expressions in conversation such as "Hello, friend." and "Keep the peace." are included in the speech corpus. After establishing the design process of this avatar, we applied the same method to produce several virtual representations for other target persons (i.e., the space astronaut in Figure 5). Our method successfully managed to produce a realistic avatar with a few days work. This work involved taking photographs of a person, head generation, texture re-touching, and fitting to a full body model. We either purchased a commercial body models or exported a similar one from a popular modeling package such as Poser. Assuming each individual has unique gestures and full body expression, motion acquisition process remains as labor-intensive effort without much automation.

4   Pilot Study

The goals of the pilot study were twofold: First, determine whether the specific avatar being developed was capable of conveying emotional states; and second, determine, more generally, whether realistic avatars are good vehicles for conveying emotional states accompanying spoken information. In this study we used still renderings of an avatar and photos of the human the avatar was based on to determine whether users identified the emotional states comparably between the avatar and the human upon which it was based. The rendering images used in this study are the intermediate result of graphical enhancement as the survey was conducted while we continuously improved our visual representation techniques.

4.1   Design and Procedure

The human model of the avatar, Dr. Alex Schwarzkopf, was chosen for our study. Our work here is based on Ekmans [6,15,16] approach to expressing emotions which have shown positive results in using comparative images to study human emotion recognition. The study draws on methods from two studies [17,18] and merges them together to focus specifically on the avatar, and to incorporate a larger pool of research subjects available online. Images were used for two reasons: 1) videos create significant issues of reliability in large online studies and 2) previous studies using this approach have yielded useful results. To extend this work into the avatar world, photographs were taken of Alex exhibiting six classic emotional states: anger, fear, disgust, happiness, sadness, and surprise. Three photos of each emotional state were selected based on how well they corresponded to the elements of Ekmans emotional characteristics (18 total human images). Images of the avatar were rendered to mimic the photos of Alex as closely as possible by manipulating key facial variables (18 total avatar images) in a process to similar studies listed previously. Eyeglasses were removed to avoid interfering with facial features. The avatar renderings used were not photorealistic but had the prominent facial features necessary. In some cases, we appended phoneme shape, head orientation, and eye gaze in addition to the modifier shape to obtain the best match (Figure 9).

Subjects were directed to an online survey tool where they were shown the 36 images, randomly ordered, and asked to identify which of the six emotional states the face was displaying. Subjects were only allowed to pick from the six emotional states and there was no other or none option. Subjects were recruited from across the student population of a major research university with approximately 25,000 students. Mass emails, posters, and word of mouth in classrooms were used in conjunction with recruiting incentives. After removing erroneous or invalid data 1,744 subjects participated (n=1744). Gender was split almost evenly: 864 males and 867 females, and ages ranged from 18 to 64 (*mean*=23.5, *median*=22, *mode*=20).

Fig. 9. A Sample Happiness Emotion. Avatar emotion is rendered with weight parameters as follows: Smile(1.0), BlinkLeft(0.2), BlinkRight(0,1), BrowUpLeft(0.2), BrowUpRight(0.1), and Phoneme B(0.65).

4.2   Result and Discussion

We sought two measures: (1) did the subjects correctly identify the emotion displayed and (2) did the subjects match the emotion for each human/avatar pair? Subjects did not identify anger in either the human or avatar to a useful degree. In four of the six anger

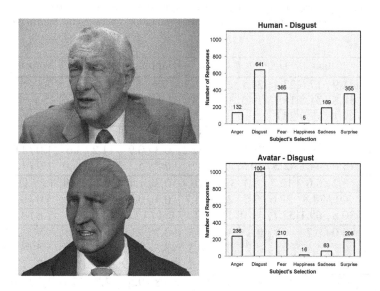

Fig. 10. Disgust emotion pair of images and results

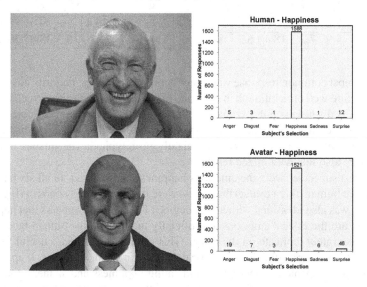

Fig. 11. Happiness emotion pair of images and results

Table 1. Percentage of valid responses identifying the emotion displayed. Three pairs of images (each pair made up of one avatar rendering and one photo of the real human) for each emotion tested. Left column indicates what emotion was intended to be depicted. Columns represent what percentage of subjects identified each emotion in the image. Percentages in bold represent the most popular selection made by subjects regarding that pair. The far right column represents the number of valid responses from subjects (n). Highlighted pairings are the most successful based on Paired Samples T Test for each human/avatar pairing (threshold is $p < 0.05$). Thus, the table illustrates that subjects seem to recognize happiness and sadness between the human picture and avatar rendering.

Emotions	Anger	Disgust	Fear	Happiness	Sadness	Surprise	n
Anger	**41.9** / 17.6	27.4 / **34.1**	2.4 / 12.3	17.6 / 8.5	3.3 / 22.5	7.5 / 5.1	1597
	30.5 / **31.8**	18.3 / 19.3	10.2 / 3.1	2.9 / 27.7	13.1 / 10.6	25.1 / 7.4	1624
	49.1 / 17.0	28.0 / 21.4	3.5 / 12.1	0.4 / 10.0	14.0 / **32.5**	4.9 / 6.9	1587
Disgust	6.4 / 17.1	35.3 / **27.3**	0.6 / 3.4	**49.5** / 26.5	2.8 / 19.4	5.4 / 6.3	1587
	7.8 / 13.6	**38.0** / **57.9**	21.6 / 12.1	0.3 / 0.9	11.2 / 3.6	21.0 / 11.9	1684
	13.6 / **44.1**	**42.3** / 30.5	7.4 / 3.9	0.2 / 5.3	34.7 / 15.0	1.9 / 1.3	1593
Fear	3.2 / 3.0	12.5 / 8.3	39.6 / 16.4	0.3 / 1.1	**40.2** / **59.9**	4.2 / 11.3	1592
	3.9 / **78.8**	22.6 / 9.5	25.6 / 4.7	0.4 / 0.7	**42.4** / 5.4	5.0 / 0.9	1612
	30.8 / **69.1**	**32.7** / 11.0	14.8 / 2.1	0.4 / 12.0	13.6 / 1.6	7.6 / 4.3	1601
Happiness	0.0 / 0.7	0.1 / 0.8	0.1 / 0.3	**98.7** / **93.9**	0.2 / 0.9	0.9 / 3.3	1599
	0.2 / 1.1	0.2 / 0.5	0.4 / 0.5	**93.5** / **89.1**	0.2 / 0.5	5.5 / 8.2	1685
	0.3 / 1.2	0.2 / 0.4	0.1 / 0.2	**98.6** / **94.9**	0.1 / 0.4	0.7 / 2.9	1600
Sadness	0.7 / 20.9	20.2 / 13.5	1.8 / 5.8	0.8 / 9.5	**74.7** / **46.7**	1.7 / 3.6	1595
	0.9 / 1.9	2.7 / 4.7	2.2 / 6.3	0.2 / 0.6	**93.6** / **85.5**	0.4 / 1.1	1610
	1.1 / 1.6	7.7 / 4.1	3.2 / 3.7	0.2 / 1.8	**85.6** / **87.6**	2.2 / 1.2	1586
Surprise	5.3 / 4.1	13.2 / 10.5	23.3 / 27.7	0.9 / 1.9	8.6 / 27.6	**48.5** / **28.2**	1666
	5.6 / 8.8	7.3 / 6.3	18.4 / 2.7	2.7 / 21.1	**36.4** / 2.6	29.6 / **58.5**	1604
	5.9 / 7.2	18.4 / 6.2	8.8 / 5.2	1.9 / 31.5	29.2 / 10.3	**35.8** / **39.6**	1594

images the most common response was anger but it was never the majority answer. Disgust did not fare well either though in one pair (Figure 10) subjects did correctly identify the emotion as disgust even if less overwhelmingly in the avatar image. Subjects could not correctly identify the human or avatar images with regard to fear, indicating that perhaps the human images were not sufficiently prototypical. The images indicating surprise were also met with mixed results.

The largest successes were the emotions happiness and sadness. In all six happiness images (three human, three avatar) the results were overwhelmingly correct (Figure 11) and sadness was also identified with a high degree of accuracy. It appears that happiness and sadness are the easiest emotions to artificially indicate on the human face and the easiest to accurately replicate on the avatar. This pilot study provides useful feedback for our work and informs the decisions we will make in the next phases. It appears the current avatar is capable of successfully indicating happiness and sadness. Our avatar indicates happiness to roughly the same degree as the human upon which it was based;

the same is true of sadness (Table 1). The other four emotions anger, fear, surprise, and disgust are not currently indicated by our avatar to any useful degree.

While the avatar did not successfully display the other four emotions, the human photos did not achieve reliable levels of emotional indication either. In fact, there were several pairs where the avatar and human photos were identified in the same incorrect way (e.g. confusing sadness and disgust). One interpretation is that the avatar was sometimes being interpreted the same way as the human, but the human image was not a good prototypical indication of the given emotion. It is possible that the avatar was fundamentally recreating the human expression but that we chose the wrong human face on which to base the avatar. Further research needs to be done to determine whether the remaining four emotions can be better indicated by the human model and, if not, whether we may want to choose a new human to serve as the basis for the avatar.

5   Conclusion and Future Work

In this research, we have developed the Lifelike Responsive Avatar Framework and presented how we created a prototype application for modeling a specific person. With this method we were able to reproduce another avatar in several days without extensive manual intervention. Pilot study results showed that the current avatar is capable of successfully indicating two emotions, happ iness and sadness, but not necessarily the other four. Similarly the human photos in our pilot study showed mixed results for these four emotions.

One aspect we did not consider in the pilot study is that a human recognizes emotions within a context accompanying temporal changes over time and/or spoken information. Further investigation of how those factors affect on avatar emotion is necessary in the future. One good example of a context sensitive task oriented study is[19]. Stern et al performed a user study to examine persuasiveness and social perception of synthetic versus human voice in the context of the persuasive speech. Given all visual realism and higher modality an avatar model studied in small scale should also be evaluated with respect to application quality and performance as a whole in the future. Further dynamic face features such as wrinkle generation [10,11,20] will also be considered in later study.

Considering the results discussed in this work, we conclude that our framework and avatar design method is at least partially capable of successfully conveying human emotions and its accuracy is close to that of the target person.

Acknowledgments. This publication is based in part on work supported by the National Science Foundation (NSF), awards CNS-0420477, CNS-0703916.

References

1. Yee, N., Bailenson, J., Rickertsen, K.: A meta-analysis of the impact of the inclusion and realism of human-like faces on user experiences in interfaces. In: Proceedings of the SIGCHI conference on Human factors in computing systems (2007)

2. Ekman, P.: Emotions revealed. Henry Holt, New York (2003)
3. Bickmore, T., Pfeifer, L., Jack, B.: Taking the time to care: empowering low health literacy hospital patients with virtual nurse agents. In: Proceedings of the 27th international conference on Human factors in computing systems (2009)
4. Bickmore, T., Picard, R.: Establishing and maintaining long-term human-computer relationships. ACM Trans. Comput. Hum. Interact. 12(2), 293–327 (2005)
5. Koda, T., Maes, P.: Agents with faces: the effect of personification. In: 5th IEEE International Workshop on Robot and Human Communication, pp. 189–194 (November 1996)
6. Ekman, P.: Emotion in the Human Face. Pergamon Press, New York (1972)
7. Diana, A., Javier, V., Francisco, J.: Generation and visualization of emotional states in virtual characters. Comput. Animat. Virtual Worlds 19(3-4), 259–270 (2008), 1410372
8. Wallraven, C., Breidt, M., Cunningham, D., Bülthoff, H.: Psychophysical evaluation of animated facial expressions. In: APGV 2005: Proceedings of the 2nd symposium on Applied perception in graphics and visualization (August 2005)
9. Wallraven, C., Fischer, J., Cunningham, D., Bartz, D., Bülthoff, H.: The evaluation of stylized facial expressions. In: APGV 2006: Proceedings of the 3rd symposium on Applied perception in graphics and visualization (July 2006)
10. Courgeon, M., Buisine, S., Martin, J.C.: Impact of expressive wrinkles on perception of a virtual character's facial expressions of emotions. In: Ruttkay, Z., Kipp, M., Nijholt, A., Vilhjálmsson, H.H. (eds.) IVA 2009. LNCS, vol. 5773, pp. 201–214. Springer, Heidelberg (2009)
11. de Melo, C.M., Gratch, J.: Expression of emotions using wrinkles, blushing, sweating and tears. In: Ruttkay, Z., Kipp, M., Nijholt, A., Vilhjálmsson, H.H. (eds.) IVA 2009. LNCS, vol. 5773, pp. 188–200. Springer, Heidelberg (2009)
12. The OGRE Team: Ogre - open source 3d graphics engine, http://www.ogre3d.org
13. King, S.A., Parent, R.: Creating speech-synchronized animation. IEEE Transactions on Visualization and Computer Graphics 11(3), 341–352 (2005)
14. DeMara, R.F., Gonzalez, A.J., Hung, V., Leon-Barth, C., Dookhoo, R.A., Jones, S., Johnson, A., Leigh, J., Renambot, L., Lee, S., Carlson, G.: Towards interactive training with an avatar-based human-computer interface. In: The Interservice/Industry Training, Simulation & Education Conference, I/ITSEC (December 2008)
15. Ekman, P., Davidson, R.J.: The nature of emotion. Oxford Press, New York (1994)
16. Scherer, K.R., Ekman, P.: Handbook of methods in nonverbal behavior research, p. 593. Cambridge University Press, Cambridge (1982)
17. Mendolia, M.: Explicit use of categorical and dimensional strategies to decode facial expressions of emotion. Journal of Nonverbal Behavior (January 2007)
18. Ellison, J., Massaro, D.: Featural evaluation, integration, and judgment of facial affect. Journal of Experimental Psychology: Human Perception and Performance (January 1997)
19. Stern, S.E., Mullennix, J.W., Yaroslavsky, I.: Persuasion and social perception of human vs. synthetic voice across person as source and computer as source conditions. Int. J. Hum. Comput. Stud. 64(1), 43–52 (2006)
20. Maddock, S., Edge, J., Sanchez, M.: Movement realism in computer facial animation. In: 19th British HCI Group Annual Conference, Workshop on Human-animated Characters Interaction (January 2005)

Interactive Motion Modeling and Parameterization by Direct Demonstration

Carlo Camporesi, Yazhou Huang, and Marcelo Kallmann

University of California, Merced

Abstract. While interactive virtual humans are becoming widely used in education, training and therapeutic applications, building animations which are both realistic and parameterized in respect to a given scenario remains a complex and time–consuming task. In order to improve this situation, we propose a framework based on the direct demonstration and parameterization of motions. The presented approach addresses three important aspects of the problem in an integrated fashion: (1) our framework relies on an interactive real-time motion capture interface that empowers non–skilled animators with the ability to model realistic upper-body actions and gestures by direct demonstration; (2) our interface also accounts for the interactive definition of clustered example motions, in order to well represent the variations of interest for a given motion being modeled; and (3) we also present an *inverse blending* optimization technique which solves the problem of precisely parameterizing a cluster of example motions in respect to arbitrary spatial constraints. The optimization is efficiently solved online, allowing autonomous virtual humans to precisely perform learned actions and gestures in respect to arbitrarily given targets. Our proposed framework has been implemented in an immersive multi-tile stereo visualization system, achieving a powerful and intuitive interface for programming generic parameterized motions by demonstration.

Keywords: Learning by demonstration, motion blending, virtual humans, virtual reality.

1 Introduction

A central goal in the area of autonomous virtual humans is to achieve virtual assistants that can effectively interact, learn, train, and assist people in a variety of tasks. We focus on the particular problem of modeling motions for interactive training applications requiring complex gestures and actions to be reproduced realistically and with precise parameterizations in respect to spatial constraints in the environment.

Modeling and parameterization of realistic motions is clearly an important problem in a wide range of applications involving virtual humans. One approach for achieving precise parameterizations is to rely on algorithmically synthesized actions and gestures [19, 13], however it remains difficult to achieve realistic full-body results and a specific computational model is needed for every action to be simulated.

Another important limitation of algorithmic approaches in many training applications is that the motions to be reproduced may only be known by experts in the subject

J. Allbeck et al. (Eds.): IVA 2010, LNAI 6356, pp. 77–90, 2010.

area of the training. Such cases are clearly better handled by motion modeling solutions based on motion capture.

Several systems based on motion captured (or hand-crafted) animations have been developed and are able to achieve highly realistic results [8, 28]. However the process of building the set of needed motions for each given scenario is often time–consuming, and it remains difficult to precisely parameterize pre-defined animations in respect to spatial constraints.

We propose in this paper an interactive motion modeling framework for addressing these many difficulties in an integrated fashion. Our framework is designed to be used in two distinct phases: in the **modeling phase** the user demonstrates to the virtual human how to perform parameterized motions, such that in the **training phase** the virtual human is then able to reproduce the motions in interactive training sessions with apprentice users learning the training subject.

Our system targets the situation where, in the modeling phase, experts in the training subject are able to model the needed actions and gestures by direct demonstration, without the need of having previous experience with the system. In the training phase, the stored example motions are then re-used by the virtual human to train apprentice users. Our framework in particular enables the virtual human to reproduce motions in respect to arbitrary target locations in the environment. Figure 1 presents one typical scenario modeled by our system.

(a)   (b)

Fig. 1. (a) In this scenario, during the modeling phase, the user demonstrates several examples of pointing motions in order to demonstrate operations with a stereo system and a telephone. (b) During the training phase, the user requests the virtual human to precisely perform the same pointing motions for arbitrary targets, here specified by the apex of the yellow cone which is controlled via a WiiMote controller. The training phase is used here to test if the example motions are sufficiently covering the volume of interest in the scenario. The user can interactively switch between the two phases until all required motions are correctly defined. Note that the simulated images in this figure appear fuzzy since they are being projected for stereo visualization.

Our motion-based interactive framework allows the design of new types of interaction techniques, which can be developed according to the training scenario at hand. For example, the apprentice may request the virtual human to perform actions at different locations and under different conditions, feedback can be provided based on on-line comparisons between the motions from the expert and the apprentice, etc. Such scenarios are clearly applicable to a variety of training applications, for example, sports training, rehabilitation of motor-impaired patients, training of medical procedures, demonstration of generic procedures, delivery of instructions, etc.

The work presented in this paper addresses the main computational challenges involved in building such interactive systems. Our proposed framework is based on three main computational modules:

- First, a real-time motion capture interface is developed for allowing users to interactively model motions by direct demonstration. In order to be effective for a variety of situations, our solution includes calibration and mapping from a reduced set of tracking sensors.
- During the motion modeling phase, motions can be recorded and re-played on-line, allowing users to effectively model generic actions and gestures in an intuitive way. The modeling interface also allows the definition of clusters of example motions, in order to represent spatial variations of a same motion. These variations are used during the training phase in order to precisely parameterize the motions in respect to arbitrarily given spatial targets.
- Finally, given a cluster of example motions built by the user during the modeling phase, we present an optimization technique for computing motions on-line precisely respecting arbitrarily given spatial constraints. Our technique is called *inverse blending* and the solution motions are obtained by blending operations with the example motions in a given cluster, therefore the solutions remain humanlike and similar to the example motions. This technique is critical for achieving precise parameterizations of realistic actions and gestures, without the need of any pre–computation. Examples are presented with the modeling of pointing and pouring motions, which are precisely parameterized in respect to arbitrarily given target locations.

Our interactive motion modeling framework has been implemented in an immersive multi-tile *power wall* stereo visualization system (shown in Figure 1). The ability to perform simulations in a large visualization system is important for achieving immersive full-scale interactions, in analogy to the way humans naturally interact with each other. As a result our obtained system represents a powerful and intuitive approach for programming generic parameterized motions by demonstration.

The reminder of this paper is organized as follows: after discussing related work in the next section, we present our motion capture interface in Section 3 and our modeling interface in Section 4. We then present our inverse blending optimization technique in Section 5. Finally, Section 6 discusses our results and Section 7 concludes this paper.

2 Related Work

Our approach of direct demonstration of motions is strongly related to several imitation-based learning methods previously proposed for different applications in robotics [26,2] and computer graphics [5,6]. The work of Cooper et al. [5] in particular also employs a full-body motion capture interface for building a database of motions, however with the focus on building motion databases with good coverage for motion controllers, and not on achieving an immersive and interactive system to teach motions to virtual humans.

Although several existing systems address different aspects related to our work, we are actually not aware of other systems with all the same characteristics as ours. We therefore proceed with our related work analysis in respect to the different computational solutions employed in our overall system.

Several methods have been proposed in the literature for addressing the problem of motion reconstruction from a reduced marker set. A popular approach is to employ statistical models [31] and machine learning [4] for extracting from a motion database the motion closest to the input signal. The performance of these methods however greatly depends on the used databases and they are usually not suitable for real-time applications. Algorithmic approaches based on simulation or optimization have also been proposed [11, 24] but are computationally expensive and are not suitable for achieving humanlike motions.

Algorithmic approaches based on Inverse Kinematics (IK) can run in real-time and may be suitable for motion reconstruction if enough markers are provided to well limit the overall posture space of possible solutions. Inverse Kinematics has also been employed to optimize full–body postures for tracking the input stream from a reduced marker set [20, 7]. However the convergence time for iterative Jacobian-based solvers over the full–body of a character may require several iterations and can introduce lag in a real-time interface.

Our interactive interface focuses on achieving a fast solution for reconstructing humanlike motions by employing an analytical IK solver [12] applied only to the arms of the character. We then rely on simple mappings from additional markers in order to fully reconstruct upper-body motions very efficiently in real-time. As our present work focuses on modeling upper-body actions, we do not address in this work tracking of legs or reconstruction of locomotion.

One of the main purposes of our system is to model actions and gestures to be used in training applications. Previous work on gesture synthesis has mainly focused on sequencing pre-defined animations [8, 27, 28], or by algorithmic synthesis, such as by employing IK solvers towards specified trajectories [19, 13]. By modeling gestures with our motion blending techniques we are able to achieve the benefits of both approaches, i. e., realistic animations which can be also parameterized with spatial targets.

The topic of character animation based on motion capture has been extensively studied in the literature for several applications [1, 14, 25, 15, 16]. Although the majority of works focus on the locomotion problem, motion blending (or motion interpolation) has also been well addressed in previous works for modeling gestures and actions.

Different methods have been proposed related to motion blending, for example, hierarchical filtering [3], parameterization using Fourier coefficients [29], stochastic sampling [30], and interpolation based on radial basis functions (RBFs) [22]. The problem of end-effector control with motion blending has also been addressed before [23, 32], and more generically, spatial properties are also addressed by the geostatistical interpolation scheme [18].

Another approach used for addressing spatial constraints is to generate and add pseudo motion examples [23, 14], which however increases the needed computation and storage. The scaled Gaussian process latent variable model [9] optimizes interpolation kernels specifically for maintaining constraints described by latent spaces.

The main limitation of these methods is that alone they are not able to precisely meet given spatial constraints. For instance, the active learning methodology [5] relies on Inverse Kinematics solvers in addition to blending, however risking to penalize the obtained realism.

Our proposed method for motion parameterization is based on the optimization of blending weights until best meeting generic spatial constraints defining the target parameterization. Our approach is simple and intuitive, and yet has not been addressed in previous work. Our method can be seen as a post-processing step for optimizing a given set of blending weights, which can be initially computed by any motion blending technique. Only error metrics for the spatial constraints to enforce are necessary in order to optimize the blending weights using a given motion interpolation scheme. We show in this paper that our optimization framework is able to well parameterize pointing and pouring actions on-line and without the need of any pre–computation.

3   Motion Capture Interface

A variety of commercially available solutions are able to map full–body motions to a virtual character in real-time, however the available options are usually expensive and often require the user to wear cumbersome tracking devices.

For instance, retro-reflective motion capture systems require the user to wear a full–body suit with a number of markers carefully placed; systems based on magnetic sensors rely on 15 to 20 magnetic sensors connected with cables; and exo-skeleton systems are heavy and often restrictive.

As shown in Figure 2 (a), our real-time upper-body motion capture solution is based on tracking four key limbs of the user: the two hands, the head, and the lower or mid joint of the spine. We track both the position and orientation of each of these parts in global coordinates. The user wears simple straps with markers on each of the considered body parts and we rely on a 10-camera Vicon system for performing the real-time tracking. Although we rely on an instrumented room with cameras, our solution can be ported to any other system able to track these four parts. We also rely on a data glove for capturing finger motions in real-time.

Before starting an interactive session, a calibration process is necessary in order to map the user's body to the skeleton of the virtual human in the scene. We choose not to adapt the dimensions of the virtual human in order to maintain a consistent database of motions which can be shared by different users.

The calibration consists of measuring scaling factors, and requires the user and the virtual agent to stand in a T–pose posture. Let e_i denote the positions of the hands and the head of the user in global coordinates, $i = \{1, 2, 3\}$. Let p be the global position of a point on the user spine at the same height as the shoulder. This point is computed from the spine and hand markers at T–pose. Similarly, let e_i^v and p^v be the same points but computed in respect to the virtual human skeleton. Scaling factors s_i are then computed with:

$$s_i = \frac{\|e_i^v - p^v\|}{\|e_i - p\|}. \tag{1}$$

The scaling factors are obtained during the T-pose calibration and then applied during the modeling phase of the system in order to have the end-effector positions of the

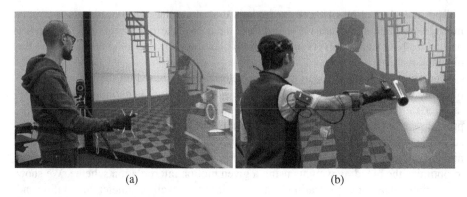

(a)   (b)

Fig. 2. The figure shows (a) the camera-based motion interface and (b) our *gesture vest* interface based on inertial sensors [10]

user and the virtual human matching. Each time new readings are processed, each scaling factor s_i multiplies the translation component of its corresponding body part being tracked, after transforming it to local coordinates in respect to the root joint.

The following additional operations are then performed on-line in order to complete the motion mapping:

- First, the global position of the virtual human is updated according to the tracked spine location of the user. In our current version, we focus only on capturing upper–body actions and gestures without any locomotion, and so no attention is given for tracking or solving leg motions.
- The spine of the virtual human is bent considering the amount of rotation between the tracked spine orientation and the head orientation. This rotation is subdivided by the number of joints being used to represent the spine of the virtual human, and distributed among these joints, similarly to the approach described by Monheit et al. [17]. The rotation of the head joint is directly mapped from the head markers, which are actually placed attached to the polarized glasses used for stereo visualization (see Figure 2 (a)).
- The arm posture reconstruction is performed using a fast analytical IK solver considering arm-body collision avoidance by automatic variation of the arm swivel angle [12]. The swivel angle is set to start at a low default value such that the elbows remain low, as is the case in usual arm motions. In some cases when the arm is extended, due tracking and calibration imprecisions, the IK may report that an end-effector cannot reach its target position, in which case we take the closest possible solution. The motion of the fingers is directly mapped from a data-glove. As shown in Figure 2 (a), four markers attached at the extremities of two crossed sticks (fixed on the data-glove) are used for tracking the 6 degrees of freedom hand targets.

Although a precise reconstruction cannot be guaranteed, the mapping is extremely fast and results in very fluid interactions always running well above 30 frames per second. Achieving a fluid and lag-free interface has showed to be extremely important for the effective use of the system. The proposed use of a reduced marker set allows the accommodation of systems with fewer (or lower–cost) cameras and also allows the system to be ported to other tracking solutions.

We have in particular also experimented with an alternate motion capture solution based on our portable and easy–to–wear *gesture vest* prototype system [10]. This device is composed of 5 inertial sensors placed on the arms, head and spine of the user. The device produces very accurate motions, is portable and wireless, and is in particular well suited for capturing one-arm gestures. Figure 2 (b) illustrates one interactive modeling section using this equipment. This system is also integrated with a data glove in order to capture hand shapes.

The main drawback of this solution is that alone it cannot track information in global coordinates in respect to our visualization system, making it difficult to be used in our applications related to specification of spatial constraints. When the system is integrated with a global tracking device then it becomes perfectly suitable for our applications. Note that in Figure 2 (b) the user is wearing a hat being tracked by the camera system in order to provide global positioning information.

Depending on the application, and on the availability of additional trackers, our gesture vest solution represents a suitable alternative for achieving a small, portable and low–cost solution. The system can be in particular effective for large-scale training scenarios with many users, since the sensors scale well and do not suffer from occlusion limitations.

4   Interactive Motion Modeling Interface

The ability to run our system in integration with a large immersive display is of main importance in our interactive interface. It allows the user to interact with full-scale virtual environments with immersive stereo vision perception, achieving realistic and accurate reproduction of conditions during both the modeling and training phases.

In order to allow full operation of the system by a single user, our current solution for the motion modeling phase focuses on tracking single-arm actions and gestures performed by the right arm. In this way the user only wears a data glove on the right hand, and the left hand holds a WiiMote controller which provides control over all the system functionality, achieving a simple and effective interactive user interface.

By clicking buttons on the WiiMote controller, the user can change the camera view between several modes, can control the recording and replay of motions, initiate the definition of clustered example motions, add or delete motions from each cluster, etc.

The definition of clusters of example motions is an important concept of our system. The definition of a cluster is necessary for specifying each parameterized action or gesture. When the user selects to start a new cluster, every recorded motion becomes associated with the cluster. Motions in a cluster will be blended during the training phase and therefore they have to consistently represent variations of a same type of motion. For instance, a pointing cluster will contain several pointings of the same type but each pointing to a different location in the environment.

One important information to be associated to each motion in a cluster is its parameterization frame. For example, this frame will be the stroke frame of a gesture or the final frame of a one-way pointing motion. The parameterization frame identifies which frame of the motion is to be parameterized in respect to new target locations during the training phase. We currently let the user specify this frame by pressing a button of the WiiMote controller at the right moment with the left hand, while the motion is being demonstrated with the right arm. The frame location can be then adjusted forward and backwards interactively if needed. This solution is acceptable in several cases but we recognize it may divert the attention of the user from well performing the motion being demonstrated. We therefore also let the user to interactively select this frame after the motion is performed. We also allow the user to trim the initial and final frames of each recorded example motion.

Clusters of motions can be edited, stored and reloaded as needed. Whenever the user wishes to test a modeled cluster, the system can be switched to training phase and the WiiMote controller is then used to specify targets to be solved by inverse blending. In this way the virtual human is able to perform a new motion precisely reaching given targets and well preserving the quality of the original demonstrated motions. The WiiMote controller also has a haptic feedback which is used during the training phase to tell the user when asked targets are colliding with the environment.

The interconnection of the several modules of our system is further illustrated in Figure 3. In the next section we describe our inverse blending optimization technique used during the training phase.

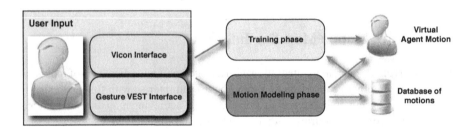

Fig. 3. Overview of the main parts of the system. The arrows illustrate the data flow during the modeling and training phases.

5   Inverse Blending

The first step for applying the inverse blending optimization is to model each spatial constraint of interest with an error metric function f, which measures how well each constraint is being satisfied at the given parameterization frame. Although the examples presented in this work only use positional constraints for end-effectors, generic types of spatial constraints C can also be taken into account.

Constraints can also have an arbitrary number of degrees-of-freedom (DOF), for example, pointing to a distant location imposes a 2–DOF positional constraint enforcing that the pointing line through the finger reaches a desired target, while precisely pin-pointing a button on a dial pad needs a 3–DOF positional constraint (the target for pointing), and an optional rotational constraint for determining a preferred pointing orientation style (see Figure 4).

The optimization starts by selecting k example motions M_j from the example motion cluster that best satisfy the constraint function f, $j = \{1, \ldots, k\}$. For example, in a typical reaching task, the k motion examples having the hand joint closest to the target will be selected. For the case of reaching motions, the hand location at the final pose of the motion is typically used as the parameterization frame. For gestures, the frame of the gesture stroke point is used.

Our optimization procedure is based on a traditional but efficient motion blending scheme, where an initial blended motion M is obtained with $M(w) = \sum_{j=1}^{k} w_j M_j$, where $w = \{w_1, \ldots, w_k\}$ are blending weights initialized from a traditional RBF interpolation scheme. Any suitable kernel function can be used and we employ the popular $exp^{-\|e\|^2/\sigma^2}$ kernel. Since our optimization runs on-line during interaction with the user, we do not attempt to optimize kernel functions in respect to the constraints [22, 18]. Instead, our blending weights will be optimized independently of the interpolation kernel.

In order to enforce a given constraint C, our goal is to find the optimal set of blending weights w, which produces the minimum error e^*, measured by the constraint error function f:

$$e^* = min_{w_j \in [0,1]} \ f\left(\sum_{j=1}^{k} w_j M_j\right). \tag{2}$$

This formulation can also account for multiple constraints by combining the error metric of each constraint in a single weighted summation. Two coefficients are then introduced for each constraint C_i, $i = \{1, \ldots, n\}$: a normalization coefficient n_i and a prioritization coefficient c_i. The purpose of coefficient n_i is to balance the magnitude of the different error metrics associated to each constraint. Coefficient c_i allows the specification of relative priorities between the constraints.

The result is essentially a multi-objective optimization problem, with the goal being to minimize an error metric composed of the weighted summation of the individual error metrics:

$$e = \ min_{w_j \in [0,1]} \sum_{i=1}^{n} (c_i \ n_i \ f_i \left(M(w)\right)). \tag{3}$$

Independent of the number of constraints being addressed, when constraints are fully satisfied, $e \rightarrow 0$. Figure 4 shows several results obtained by our optimization scheme.

Several optimization routines were implemented for solving our inverse blending problems, including: steepest ascent hill-climbing, the Nelder-Mead method and the gradient decent method [21]. Performance evaluations were conducted by solving 5000 inverse blending problems for different scenarios: pointing, pouring and grasping. The Nelder-Mead method [21] has been proved to be the method of choice for our case where k remains below 15. The method requires a simple implementation and can typically achieve optimal blending weights within 2 milliseconds of computation time.

With suitable example motions in a given cluster, inverse blending can produce motions exactly satisfying given spatial constraints and fast enough for real-time applications. The several examples presented by this paper demonstrate its successful execution

Fig. 4. The image shows results obtained with three different motion clusters. (a) Pointing motions parameterized by a 2–DOF directional constraint results in precise pointing to distant targets. (b) Pouring motions can be parameterized by a 2–DOF planar constraint specifying the precise location above the pouring target, and an additional constraint specifying an acceptable height range, so that liquids can correctly flow down into containers. (c) Precise pinpointing to given targets requires a 3–DOF positional constraint, with optional rotational constraints for further controlling the final poses obtained. The shown pinpointing examples show different orientations obtained, which match the x-axis of the tri-axes manipulator.

in different scenarios. To evaluate the performance of our method, a reaching task was designed to measure the errors produced by our method against a single RBF interpolation, with the 16 reaching motions in the database from Mukai and Kuriyama [18]. A total of 114 reaching goals (each specifying a 3–DOF positional constraint) were placed evenly on a spherical surface within reach of the character. These goals are highlighted with small yellow dots in Figure 5. The end locations of the hand trajectory in each example motion are shown as gray dots.

For each reaching target on the surfaces shown in Figure 5, we first used the RBF interpolation alone to generate a reaching motion and recorded the final hand position where the character actually reaches. These final positions are used to construct a mesh grid, which is shown on the upper row of Figure 5. Each triangle on the mesh is colored in respect to the average errors from its vertices, representing the distance error between the final hand positions and their corresponding reaching targets. We then use inverse blending optimization to perform the same tasks, and the mesh constructed is shown on the lower row of Figure 5. The reaching motions generated by inverse blending can precisely reach most of the targets, and the measured errors were practically zero across most of the mesh. Only at the boundary of the surface that errors start to appear. In this specific task, the radius of the spherical surface was set to $80cm$, and both methods used eight example motions from the database ($k = 8$) for computing each reaching task.

It is important to note that the ability of enforcing constraints greatly depends on the existing variations among the used motion examples being blended. The number of needed example motions also depend on the size of the target volume space. The

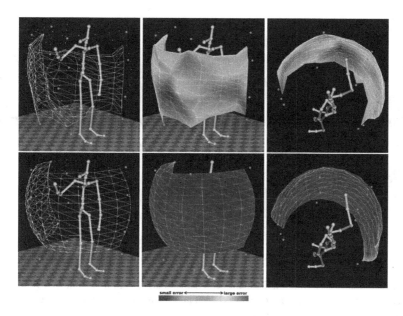

Fig. 5. Visualization of errors obtained by RBF interpolation and inverse blending. The upper row shows the results obtained with RBF interpolation. The blue smooth meshes on the lower row show the inverse blending results, which can well satisfy the given 3–DOF positional constraints.

computational time required for finding solutions will also depend on the quality and number of considered motion examples (the k value). However, as showed in our several examples, these limitations can be well addressed by appropriately modeling example motions, and balancing the coverage vs. efficiency trade-off specifically for each action being modeled.

6   Results and Discussion

Examples demonstrating several aspects of our interactive system are presented in the video accompanying this paper (available at http://graphics.ucmerced.edu/).

We believe that our system achieves an effective overall design for modeling parameterized motions, which are extremely important for several types of applications (see Figure 6). Our framework well addresses the modeling of generic gestures and actions to be executed by interactive virtual humans, and furthermore allows non–skilled animators to intuitively obtain realistic results. Our proposed motion interface has therefore the potential to impact many applications.

Our first results open several new opportunities for further development of our interface design. For instance, we intend to quantify the advantages and limitations of employing an immersive stereo visualization display, and further explore the benefits of displaying the user's avatar during the modeling phase, as opposed to simply rely on an immersive direct motion performance. Direct performance offers better precision when interacting with the virtual environment, however note that the user is not required

Fig. 6. In this example pouring motions are demonstrated and added to a parameterized pouring action cluster (top sequence). Once completed, the cluster is used to generate new pouring actions to arbitrary locations (bottom sequence).

to demonstrate motions exactly meeting constraints, since the inverse blending will be responsible for that during the training phase.

Several improvements to our current motion capture interface can also be performed. For instance, a two-arm tracking interface can be easily integrated by including a few voice commands and/or finger gestures for operating the system, in order to free the left hand from holding the WiiMote controller. The integration of locomotion is also important, and in the scope of our target applications, we plan to include automatic locomotion and body positioning algorithms for controlling the virtual human instead of learning lower-body locomotion animations from the user. An independent gaze model also appears to be necessary.

We also intend to apply our system to concrete training scenarios. Additional constraints and parameterizations will be included, for instance related to parameterizing motion variations according to emotional levels, importance, etc. Our inverse blending technique can handle any generic parameterizations as long as suitable motion clusters can be provided.

7   Conclusions

We have presented in this paper a novel motion modeling framework based on the direct demonstration and parameterization of motions. We have in particular presented the several algorithmic solutions required for enabling the development of the proposed design: a fast procedure for motion mapping from a reduced marker set, an intuitive motion interface for enabling the direct demonstration of parameterized actions and gestures, and an inverse blending optimization technique able to efficiently achieve realistic and parameterized motions in respect to arbitrarily given targets.

Our proposed framework has been implemented in an immersive multi-tile stereo visualization system, achieving a powerful and intuitive interface for programming generic parameterized motions by demonstration. We believe that the overall concept of our system has the potential to impact many applications.

Acknowledgements. This work was partially supported by NSF Awards IIS-0915665 and CNS-0723281, and by a CITRIS seed funding grant.

References

1. Arikan, O., Forsyth, D.A., O'Brien, J.F.: Motion synthesis from annotations. ACM Transaction on Graphics (Proceedings of SIGGRAPH) 22(3), 402–408 (2003)
2. Billard, A., Matarić, M.J.: Learning human arm movements by imitation: Evaluation of a biologically inspired connectionist architecture. Robotics and Autonomous Systems 37(2-3), 145–160 (2001)
3. Bruderlin, A., Williams, L.: Motion signal processing. In: SIGGRAPH 1995, pp. 97–104. ACM, New York (1995)
4. Chai, J., Hodgins, J.K.: Performance animation from low-dimensional control signals. In: SIGGRAPH 2005: ACM SIGGRAPH 2005 Papers, pp. 686–696. ACM, New York (2005)
5. Cooper, S., Hertzmann, A., Popović, Z.: Active learning for real-time motion controllers. ACM Transactions on Graphics (SIGGRAPH 2007) 26(3) (August 2007)
6. Dontcheva, M., Yngve, G., Popović, Z.: Layered acting for character animation. ACM Transactions on Graphics 22(3), 409–416 (2003)
7. Raunhardt, R.D.: Motion constraint. Visual Computer, 509–518 (2009)
8. Gebhard, P., Kipp, M., Klesen, M., Rist, T.: What are they going to talk about? towards life-like characters that reflect on interactions with users. In: Proc. of the 1st International Conference on Technologies for Interactive Digital Storytelling and Entertainment (TIDSE 2003) (2003)
9. Grochow, K., Martin, S., Hertzmann, A., Popović, Z.: Style-based inverse kinematics. ACM Transactions on Graphics (Proceedings of SIGGRAPH) 23(3), 522–531 (2004)
10. Huang, Y., Kallmann, M.: Interactive demonstration of pointing gestures for virtual trainers. In: Proceedings of 13th International Conference on Human-Computer Interaction, San Diego, CA (2009)
11. Yamaguchi, J., Takanishi, A., Kato, I.: Development of a biped walking robot compensating for three-axis moment by trunk motion. In: Proc. IEEE/RSJ Int. Conf. Intelligent Robots and Systems, pp. 561–566 (1993)
12. Kallmann, M.: Analytical inverse kinematics with body posture control. Computer Animation and Virtual Worlds 19(2), 79–91 (2008)
13. Kopp, S., Wachsmuth, I.: Model-based animation of co-verbal gesture. In: Proceedings of Computer Animation, pp. 252–257 (2002)
14. Kovar, L., Gleicher, M.: Automated extraction and parameterization of motions in large data sets. ACM Transaction on Graphics (Proceedings of SIGGRAPH) 23(3), 559–568 (2004)
15. Kovar, L., Gleicher, M., Pighin, F.: Motion graphs. ACM Trans. Graph. 21(3), 473–482 (2002)
16. Lee, J., Chai, J., Reitsma, P.S.A., Hodgins, J.K., Pollard, N.S.: Interactive control of avatars animated with human motion data. ACM Transactions on Graphics 21(3), 491–500 (2002)
17. Monheit, G., Badler, N.I.: A kinematic model of the human spine and torso. IEEE Comput. Graph. Appl. 11(2), 29–38 (1991)
18. Mukai, T., Kuriyama, S.: Geostatistical motion interpolation. In: ACM SIGGRAPH, pp. 1062–1070. ACM, New York (2005)

19. Noma, T., Zhao, L., Badler, N.I.: Design of a virtual human presenter. IEEE Computer Graphics and Applications 20(4), 79–85 (2000)
20. Peinado, M., Meziat, D., Maupu, D., Raunhardt, D., Thalmann, D., Boulic, R.: Full-Body Avatar Control with Environment Awareness. IEEE Computer Graphics And Applications 29, 62–75 (2009)
21. Press, W.H., Teukolsky, S.A., Vetterling, W.T., Flannery, B.P.: Numerical Recipes 3rd Edition: The Art of Scientific Computing. Cambridge University Press, New York (2007)
22. Rose, C., Bodenheimer, B., Cohen, M.F.: Verbs and adverbs: Multidimensional motion interpolation. IEEE Computer Graphics and Applications 18, 32–40 (1998)
23. Rose, C.F., Sloan, P.P.J., Cohen, M.F.: Artist-directed inverse-kinematics using radial basis function interpolation. Computer Graphics Forum (Proceedings of Eurographics) 20(3), 239–250 (2001)
24. Kagami, S., et al.: Autobalancer: An online dynamic balance compensation scheme for humanoid robots. In: Int. Workshop Alg. Found. Robot (2000)
25. Safonova, A., Hodgins, J.K.: Construction and optimal search of interpolated motion graphs. In: SIGGRAPH 2007: ACM SIGGRAPH 2007 papers, p. 106. ACM, New York (2007)
26. Schaal, S., Ijspeert, A., Billard, A.: Computational approaches to motor learning by imitation. The Neuroscience of Social Interaction 1431, 199–218 (2003)
27. Stone, M., DeCarlo, D., Oh, I., Rodriguez, C., Stere, A., Lees, A., Bregler, C.: Speaking with hands: creating animated conversational characters from recordings of human performance. ACM Transactions on Graphics 23(3), 506–513 (2004)
28. Thiebaux, M., Marshall, A., Marsella, S., Kallmann, M.: Smartbody: Behavior realization for embodied conversational agents. In: Seventh International Joint Conference on Autonomous Agents and Multi-Agent Systems, AAMAS (2008)
29. Unuma, M., Anjyo, K., Takeuchi, R.: Fourier principles for emotion-based human figure animation. In: SIGGRAPH '95, pp. 91–96. ACM, New York (1995)
30. Wiley, D.J., Hahn, J.K.: Interpolation synthesis of articulated figure motion. IEEE Computer Graphics and Applications 17(6), 39–45 (1997)
31. Zheng, Y., et al.: Generating human interactive behaviours using the windowed viterbi algorithm. Computer Vision and Computer Graphics. Theory and Applications, 70–82 (2009)
32. Yamane, K., Kuffner, J.J., Hodgins, J.K.: Synthesizing animations of human manipulation tasks. In: SIGGRAPH '04: ACM SIGGRAPH 2004 Papers, pp. 532–539. ACM, New York (2004)

Speed Dating with an Affective Virtual Agent - Developing a Testbed for Emotion Models

Matthijs Pontier[1,2], Ghazanfar Siddiqui[1,2,3], and Johan F. Hoorn[1]

[1] VU University Amsterdam, Center for Advanced Media Research Amsterdam,
De Boelelaan 1081, 1081HV Amsterdam, The Netherlands
[2] VU University Amsterdam, Department of Artificial Intelligence, De Boelelaan 1083,
1081HV Amsterdam, The Netherlands
[3] Quaid-i-Azam University Islamabad, 45320, Pakistan
{mpr210,ghazanfa}@few.vu.nl
http://www.few.vu.nl/~{mpr210,ghazanfa}

Abstract. In earlier studies, user involvement with an embodied software agent and willingness to use that agent were partially determined by the aesthetics of the design and the moral fiber of the character. We used these empirical results to model agents that in their turn would build up affect for their users much the same way as humans do for agents. Through simulations, we tested these models for internal consistency and were successful in establishing the relationships among the factors as suggested by the earlier user studies. This paper reports on the first confrontation of our agent system with real users to check whether users recognize that our agents function in similar ways as humans do. Through a structured questionnaire, users informed us whether our agents evaluated the user's aesthetics and moral stance while building up a level of involvement with the user and a degree of willingness to interact with the user again.

Keywords: Cognitive Modeling, Emotion Modeling, Speed Dating, Virtual Humans, Empirical Testing.

1 Introduction

In prior work, we described how certain dimensions of synthetic character design were perceived by users and how they responded to them [20]. A series of user studies resulted into an empirically validated framework for the study of user-agent interaction with a special focus on the explanation of user engagement and use intentions. We put together results of various studies so as to clarify the individual contributions of agent's affordances, ethics, aesthetics, facial similarity, and realism to the use intentions and engagement of the human user. The interactions between these agent features and their contribution to human user's perception of agents were summarized in a schema called Interactively Perceiving and Experiencing Fictional Characters (I-PEFiC). To date, this framework has a heuristic value because the extracted guidelines are important for anyone who designs virtual characters.

The evidence-based guidelines of I-PEFiC strengthen (e.g., 'beauty leads to involvement') and demystify ('ethics is more important than realism') certain views

J. Allbeck et al. (Eds.): IVA 2010, LNAI 6356, pp. 91–103, 2010.
© Springer-Verlag Berlin Heidelberg 2010

regarding synthetic character design, giving them experimental support. For example, not only a system's interaction possibilities have a direct effect on the willingness to use an agent but the ethical behavior of the agent as a personality does so too. Moreover, moral behaviors of the agent will be checked for relevance to user's goals and concerns and through that side-track, exert indirect effects on use intentions as well.

In a simulation study [12], we were capable of formalizing the I-PEFiC framework and make it the basic mechanism of how agents and robots build up affect for their human users. In addition, we designed a special module for affective decision making (ADM) which made it possible for the agent to select actions for or against its user.

When we compared I-PEFiC^{ADM} to EMA [8], [15] and CoMERG [4], we found out that the models are complementary to each other. For instance, CoMERG covers a wide variety of emotion regulation strategies. EMA, on the other hand, contains very sophisticated mechanisms for both appraisal and coping, and generating specific emotions based on this appraisal. Therefore, we concluded it would make sense to integrate them [3].

We integrated the three models into Silicon Coppélia [17], and performed simulation experiments to test the behavior of the model. The robotic behavior based on Silicon Coppélia was consistent with the theories the model is based on, and seemed compelling intuitively. However, we tested our models using agent's interacting with each other, not with a real user.

In order to be able to do so, we developed a speed dating application as a testbed for emotion models. In this application, the user interacts with a virtual human on a website. We chose the emotionally laden setting of the speed date because that would make it easy to ask the user what the invisible counterpart would think of them, ethically, aesthetically, and whether they believed the other would want to make an appointment with them, etc.

This testbed served for the first confrontation of Silicon Coppélia with actual users. To make it fit the speed dating domain, we made some changes to Silicon Coppélia, which are described in section 3. We implemented this changed model in the virtual human, thereby enabling it to behave emotionally human-like.

We focused on five factors of Silicon Coppélia that are particularly of interest to a speed-date situation: Good looks (factor Aesthetics), moral behavior (factor Ethics), relevance to personal concerns (Relevance) [8], feeling involved (Involvement), and willingness to meet again (Use Intentions). We wondered whether users would recognize that agents were making ethical and aesthetic assessments and that these assessments were affecting the agent's level of involvement with them as a dating partner as well as the agent's intentions to use (i.e., meet) them again either in another dating session or in real life. Therefore, with our speed-dating application in which the agent was represented by an embodied avatar, we wished to test the following hypotheses.

H1:   Users recognize a direct positive effect of agent-assessed Aesthetics on the agent's Involvement with the user

H2:   Agent-assessed Ethics of the user has a positive direct effect on Use Intentions of the agent to meet the user again

H3:   Relevance of user behavior to agent concerns has a mediating effect on the relation between agent-assessed Ethics and Use Intentions (see H2)

2   Models Incorporated in the Agent

As suggested in [3], three models were integrated into Silicon Coppélia: EMA [8], [15], CoMERG [4], and I-PEFiC[ADM] [12]. For this study, we implemented Silicon Coppélia into a speed dating agent. Some changes were made to the model to make it fit the speed dating domain. This section will shortly describe Silicon Coppélia, thereby focusing on the parts where changes were made. More detailed descriptions of Silicon Coppélia and the models it is based on can be found in [3], [4], [8], [12], [15], [17]. Figure 1 shows Silicon Coppélia in a graphical format.

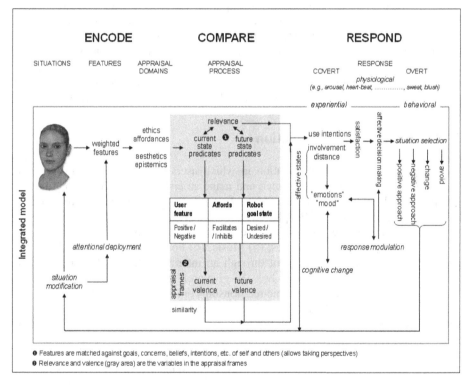

Fig. 1. Integration of CoMERG, EMA and I-PEFiC[ADM] in "Silicon Coppélia"

Silicon Coppélia consists of a loop with a situation as input, and actions as output, leading to a new situation. In this loop there are three phases: the encoding, the comparison and the response phase.

In the *encoding* phase, the agent receives others in terms of ethics (good vs. bad), affordances (aid vs. obstacle), aesthetics (beautiful vs. ugly), and epistemics (realistic vs. unrealistic). The agent can be biased in this perception process. The agent has desires with a certain strength for reaching or preventing goal-states that are defined in the system.

In the *comparison* phase, the agent uses beliefs that actions facilitate or inhibit these desired or undesired goal-states to calculate a general expected utility of each action. Further, the perceived features in others, and certain appraisal variables, such as the belief that someone is responsible for reaching or not reaching a goal-state, are appraised for relevance (relevant or irrelevant) and valence to the agent's goals (positive or negative outcome expectancies).

In the *response* phase of the model, this leads to feelings of involvement and distance towards the other, and to use intentions: the agent's willingness to employ the other as a tool to achieve its own goals. Note that with response both overt (behavioral) and covert (experiential) responses are meant in this phase. Emotions such as hope, joy and distress are generated using appraisal variables like the perceived likelihood of goal-states. The agent uses an affective decision making module to calculate the expected satisfaction of possible actions. In this module, affective influences and rational influences are combined in the decision making process. Involvement and distance represent the affective influences, while use intentions and general expected utility represent the more rational influences. When the agent picks and performs an action, a new situation emerges, and the model starts at the first phase again.

3 The Speed-Date Application

We designed a speed date application in which users could interact with a virtual human, named Tom, to get acquainted and make an appointment. The dating partner was performed by our software agent based on Silicon Coppélia, and represented by an avatar created in Haptek's PeoplePutty software [11].

During the speed date, partners could converse about seven topics: (1) Family, (2) Sports, (3) Appearance, (4) Hobbies, (5) Music, (6) Food, and (7) Relationships. For each topic, the dating partners went through an interaction tree with responses that they could select from a dropdown box. To give an idea of what the interaction trees look like, we put the tree for the topic relationships online as an appendix [21].

The agent is capable of simulating five emotions: hope, fear, joy, distress, and anger, which were expressed through the face of the avatar with either a low or a high intensity (depending on little or much relevance of user choices to agent's goals and concerns). Like this, we created 32 (2^5) different emotional states in PeoplePutty; one for each possible combination of two levels of intensity of the five simulated emotions.

We created a Web page for the application (Figure 2), in which the virtual agent was embedded as a Haptek player. We used JavaScript [1], a scripting language, in combination with scripting commands provided by the Haptek software [11], to control the Haptek player within the Web browser. In the middle of the Web site, the affective conversational agent was shown, communicating messages through a voice synthesizer and additionally shown in a text area right above the avatar. Figure 2 shows that the avatar looks mildly angry in response to the user's reply "Well, that's none of your business". When the 'start speed date' button above the text area was pressed, the agent introduced itself and started by asking the user a question. The user selected an answer from the dropdown box below the agent. Then the agent responded and so on until the interaction-tree was traversed. When a topic was done,

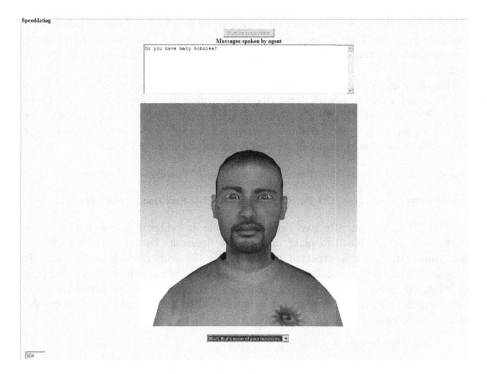

Fig. 2. The speed-dating application

the user could select a new topic or let the agent pick one. When all topics were completed, the message "the speed dating session is over" was displayed and the user was asked to fill out the questionnaire.

3.1 Determining Which Responses to Select

In the speed dating application, the agent perceives the user according to I-PEFiC^{ADM} [12]. It had beliefs that features of the user influenced certain goal-states in the world. For our speed-date setting, the possible goal-states are 'get a date', 'be honest', and 'connecting well' on each of the conversation topics. The agent has beliefs in the range [-1, 1] about the facilitation of these goal-states by each possible response. Further, the agent attaches a general level of positivity and negativity to each response.

During the speed date, the agent updates the assessed goodness of the human user according to the positivity it perceives in the user's responses. It updates the agent-assessed badness on the basis of the negativity it perceives in the user's responses. The ethical values are updated according to the following formulae:

New_Perc(Good) $= \beta_{eth} *$ Old_Perc(Good) $+ (1\text{-}\beta_{eth}) *$ Perc(Positivity_Response)

New_Perc(Bad) $= \beta_{eth} *$ Old_Perc(Bad) $+ (1\text{-}\beta_{eth}) *$ Perc(Negativity_Response)

In these formulae, the persistency factor β_{eth} is the proportion of the old perceptions that is taken into account to determine the new perceptions. The remaining part of the perceptions is determined by the positivity and negativity in the response of the human user.

The agent establishes beliefs about the beauty of the human user in the domain [0, 1], based on user responses during the conversation topic 'appearance'. The agent updates the assessed beauty and ugliness of the user, using the following formulae. In these formulae, β_{aesth} serves as the persistency factor, and Perc(Beauty_Response) represents the perceived beauty of the user based on the user's response.

New_Perc(Beauty) = β_{aesth} * Old_Perc(Beauty) + (1-β_{aesth}) * Perc(Beauty_Response)

New_Perc(Ugly)　　= β_{aesth} * Old_Perc(Ugly) + (1-β_{aesth}) * (1-Perc(Beauty_Response))

I-PEFiC^{ADM} has an affective decision module in which rational and affective dimensions are combined to make an affective decision. To determine the rational dimensions, the general expected utility (GEU) [8] with respect to the goals is calculated. The agent also calculates the GEU of the actions of the human participant regarding the agent's own goals. The agent uses this to determine the perceived affordances of the participant in terms of being an aid or an obstacle in achieving the agent's goals, using the following formulae:

IF　　　　GEU_action(Human_Action) > 0

THEN　　New_Perc(Aid)　　= Old_Perc(Aid) + α_{aff} * GEU(Human_Action) * (1-Old_Perc(Aid))

　　　　　New_Perc(Obst)　　= Old_Perc(Obst) - α_{aff} * GEU(Human_Action) * Old_Perc(Obst)

IF　　　　GEU_action(Human_Action) < 0

THEN　　New_Perc(Aid)　= Old_Perc(Aid) + α_{aff} * GEU(Human_Action) * Old_Perc(Aid)

　　　　　New_Perc(Obst) = Old_Perc(Obst) - α_{aff} * GEU(Human_Action) * (1-Old_Perc(Obst))

In these formulae, α_{aff} is a *modification factor* that determines how quickly the variable was updated. This modification factor is multiplied with the *impact value* GEU(Human_Action). Multiplying with a *limiter* (in the case of the first formula this is (1-Old_Perception(Aid))) avoids that the formula goes out of range. It also manages that if an agent's assessments approach an extreme value, it will be harder to push it further to the extreme and easier to move it back to a less extreme value.

Our speed-dating agent is capable of developing a bias [0, 2] in the assessment of the moral fiber of the user. This bias is initiated at a neutral value of 1. In [17], the believed responsibility of oneself and others for reaching certain goal states is calculated. This believed responsibility is used to calculate a bias in perceiving the ethics of the human user, using the formulae presented next. Note that these formulae have the same form (with a modification factor, an impact value, and a limiter) as those for calculating the perceived aid and obstacle described earlier:

IF　　　　-Belief(Human_Responsible, Goal) * Ambition(Goal) > 0

THEN　　New_Bias(Good) = Old_Bias(Good) - $\alpha_{b\text{-}eth}$ * Ambition(Goal) * Old_Bias(Good)

　　　　　New_Bias(Bad) = Old_Bias(Bad) + $\alpha_{b\text{-}eth}$ * Ambition(Goal) * (2 - Old_Bias(Bad))

IF   -Belief(Human_Responsible, Goal) * Ambition(Goal) < 0

THEN   New_Bias(Good) = Old_Bias(Good) + $\alpha_{b\text{-}eth}$ * -Ambition(Goal) * Old_Bias(Good)

          New_Bias(Bad) = Old_Bias(Bad) - $\alpha_{b\text{-}eth}$ * -Ambition(Goal) * (2 - Old_Bias(Bad))

Using these variables, the agent determines its response. The agent-assessed ethics, aesthetics, realism, and affordances of the user lead, while matching these aspects with the goals of the agent, to 'feelings' of Involvement and Distance towards the human user and a general expected utility of each action, as described in [17]. Each time, the agent can select its response from a number of options. The expected satisfaction of each possible response is calculated based on the Involvement and Distance towards the user and the general expected utility of the response, using the following formula:

$$ExpectedSatisfaction_{(Action)} = w_{eu} * GEU_{(Action)} +$$
$$w_{pos} * (1 - abs(positivity - bias_I * Involvement)) +$$

$$w_{neg} * (1 - abs(negativity - bias_D * Distance))$$

The agent searches for an action with the level of positivity that comes closest to the level of (biased) involvement, with the level of negativity closest to the level of (biased) distance, and with the strongest action tendency.

3.2 Determining Which Emotions to Express

During the speed date, the agent simulates a series of emotions, based on the responses given by the user. Hope and fear are calculated each time the user gives an answer. Hope and fear of the agent are based on the perceived likelihood that the agent will get a follow-up date. The likelihoods are used in the following function to calculate the hope for achieving a goal. This function is similar to the function described in [5].

IF   f >= likelihood
THEN   hope_for_goal = -0,25 * (cos(1 / f * π * likelihood(goal)) -1,5) * ambition(goal)

IF   f < likelihood
THEN   hope_for_goal = -0.25 * (cos(1 / (1-f) * π * (1-likelihood(goal))) -1.5) * ambition(goal)

In these functions, f is a shaping parameter (in the domain [0, 1]) that can be used to manipulate the location of the top of the hope curve. The value of this parameter may differ per individual, and represents 'fatalism' (or 'pessimism'): The top of the likelihood/hope-curve is always situated at the point where likelihood = f. Thus, for an f close to 1, the top of the curve is situated to the extreme right (representing persons that only 'dare' to hope for events that are likely to happen). Similarly, for an f close to 0, the top of the curve is situated to the extreme left (representing persons that already start hoping for very unlikely events). In our current study, f was set at 0.5.

We created a smooth function instead of a linear function, because this matches the emotion curves found for humans the best. Further, a higher ambition level leads to higher hopes. If the ambition level is negative (i.e., the goal is undesired), the outcome of hope_for_goal will be a negative value.

The following algorithm is executed on the found values for hope_for_goal:

1. Sort the values in two lists: [0→1] and [0→-1]
2. Start with 0 and take the mean of the value you have and the next value in the list. Continue until the list is finished. Do this for both the negative and the positive list.
3. Hope = Outcome positive list. Fear = abs(Outcome negative list).

The values are sorted in a list with positive hope_for_goal's (i.e., hope for desired goals), and negative hope_for_goal's (i.e., fear for undesired goals). For both the lists, 0 is the starting point and the mean of the value you have and the next value in the list (where the next value is the value closest to 0 that is left in the list) is picked until the end of the list is reached. The new level of hope for the agent is the outcome of the positive list and the new level of fear for the agent is the absolute value of the outcome of the negative list.

The joy and distress of the agent are based on reaching or not reaching desired or undesired goal-states. If a goal-state becomes true (i.e., the agent matches well with the user on a certain conversation topic), the levels of joy and distress are calculated by performing the following formulae:

IF   (ambition (goal) * belief(goal)) > 0
THEN   new_joy   = old_joy + mf_joy * ambition(goal) * belief(goal) * (1-old_joy)
        new_distress   = old_distress + mf_distress * -ambition(goal) * belief (goal) * old_distress

IF   (ambition (goal) * belief (goal)) < 0
THEN   new_joy   = old_joy + mf_joy * ambition(goal) * belief(goal)* old_joy
        new_distress   = old_distress + mf_distress * -ambition(goal) * belief (goal) * (1-old_distress)

In these formulae, mf_joy and mf_distress are modification factors that determine how quickly joy and distress are changed if the agent reaches a certain goal-state. In this paper, the values were both set to 1. These modification factors are multiplied with the impact value, which is ambition(goal) for joy and -ambition(goal) for distress. This way, if a desired goal is achieved, joy is increased and distress is decreased. Conversely, achieving an undesired goal decreases joy and increases distress. Multiplying with limiter (1-old_joy) for joy and old_distress for distress if the goal is desired, keeps the formula from going out of range and drives possible extreme values of joy and distress back to a milder level. If the achieved goal-state is undesired, old_joy is used as limiter for joy and (1-old_distress) as a limiter for distress, because the values of joy and distress will move into the opposite direction of when the goal is desired.

The anger of the agent is calculated using the believed responsibility of the human user for the success of the speed date:

IF   Belief(Human_Responsible, Goal)) * Ambition(Goal) > 0
THEN   Anger(Agent)   = old_anger + mf$_{anger}$ * (-Belief(Human_Responsible, Goal)) *
                Ambition(Goal) *   (1 - old_anger)

IF   Belief(Human_Responsible, Goal)) * Ambition(Goal) < 0
THEN   Anger(Agent)   = old_anger + mf$_{anger}$ * (-Belief(Human_Responsible, Goal)) *
                Ambition(Goal) *   old_anger

To calculate the level of the agent's anger with the user in the range [0, 1], the above formula is used, with Belief(Human_Responsible, Goal) * Ambition(Goal) as *impact value*. This way, if an agent believes a desired goal state should have been reached, but it has not, the agent will become angrier with the user who the agent holds responsible for not achieving the desired goal state. The agent will become less angry with the user who is believed to have tried helping to reach the desired goal state. The reverse happens, when the goal state is undesired. Because people do not stay angry forever, anger is multiplied with a decay factor at each time step.

All five emotions implemented into the system (i.e., hope, fear, joy, distress, and anger) are simulated in parallel (see [20]). If the level of joy, distress, or anger is below 0.5, a low intensity of the emotion was facially expressed by the agent. If the level of joy, distress, or surprise was greater or equal than 0.5, a high intensity of the emotion was expressed by the agent. Because within the given parameter settings, hope and fear rarely reached extreme values, this boundary was set to 0.25 for hope and fear.

4   Experiment

To examine the hypotheses H1-3, a user study was performed in which users diagnosed the cognitive mechanisms by which their robotic dating partner came to an assessment of and affective attitude towards its user.

4.1 Participants

A total of 18 participants ranging in age from 18 to 24 years (M = 19.17, SD = 1.86) volunteered for course credits. All participants were Dutch female students of VU University Amsterdam (Communication Science Program). We confronted female participants with male agents, because the ability to describe emotional feelings as clearly as possible was considered a prerequisite to assess the agent's affective performance. Previous research suggests that women are better equipped to do an emotional assessment of others [2]. Participants were asked to rate their experience in dating and computer-mediated communication on a scale from 1 to 7 and appeared to be reasonably experienced in dating (M = 4.00, SD = 1.72) and communicated frequently via a computer (M = 5.50, SD = 1.04).

4.2 Procedure

Preceding the experiment, the participants were told a cover story that they were participating in a speed-dating session with a male participant, named Tom, who was at another location. After a session of about 10 minutes, the participants filled out a questionnaire of 94 items. At the end of the experiment, the participants were thanked for their participation and were debriefed that the avatar they communicated with represented not a real human but a computer-generated agent used to test our affect generation and regulation software.

4.3 Measurements

We developed a 94-item questionnaire in Dutch in which the dependent variables of H1-3 were incorporated. All items were in the form of statements of the type "I think that Tom finds me attractive" measured on a 7-point Likert-type rating scale, which ranged from 'totally disagree' (1) to 'totally agree' (7). Negatively phrased items were reverse-coded before entering the analysis.

Ethics measured in how far the participants perceived the agent as good or bad, using the four items 'trustworthy', 'credible', 'malicious' and 'mean'. The scale appeared to be reliable (Cronbach's $\alpha = .83$). *Aesthetics* measured in how far the participant perceived the agent as beautiful or ugly, using the four items 'attractive', 'good-looking', 'ugly' and 'bad-looking'. The scale appeared to be very reliable (Cronbach's $\alpha = .94$). *Relevance* was measured by three items indicating how important or useless the user was in 'creating a good atmosphere' and in 'completing each other during conversation'. This scale appeared to be very reliable (Cronbach's $\alpha = .88$). *Use Intentions* were measured with four items. These were 'happy to have met', 'wanting to meet in another context', 'sad to have met' and 'wanting to get rid of'. The scale appeared to be very reliable (Cronbach's $\alpha = .90$). *Involvement* was measured with four items, which were 'appeal', 'good feeling', 'feeling connected' and 'feeling engaged'. Also this scale appeared to be very reliable (Cronbach's $\alpha = .93$).

The remaining items referred to sociodemographic variables or were derived from questionnaires dedicated to other emotion regulation models [10], [19], [20] so to assess the psychometric quality of the items, which was on the whole quite disappointing. The results of the pre-test of these additional items fall beyond the scope of the present paper and will be reported elsewhere.

5 Analysis and Results

The items on each scale were averaged for each participant and the grand mean scale values across participants were used in a series of linear regressions to explore the hypotheses H1-3.

H1 predicted that users would see that the agent assessed their looks (factor Aesthetics), which was then used by the agent to determine a level of Involvement with the user. The direct relation between agent-assessed Aesthetics (M = 4.10, SD = 1.32) and Involvement (M = 2.46, SD = 1.24) was analyzed using linear regression. H1 was confirmed in that Aesthetics predicted Involvement ($R^2 = .708$, r(16) = .85, p < .01) indicating a significant positive relation between the two variables. Therefore, H1 could be confirmed.

H2 and H3 were tested in unison, stating that there should be direct effects of agent-assessed Ethics of the user on Use Intentions (H2) complemented by indirect effects of Ethics through the Relevance of the user to agent's goals and concerns (H3). We performed a Sobel-test [18] to investigate the effects of Ethics (M = 4.10, SD = .92) on Use Intentions (M = 3.65, SD = 1.24) and the predicted mediating role of Relevance (M = 4.08, SD =.92). Ethics served as the independent variable, Relevance as the mediator, and Use Intentions as the dependent variable. The results showed a significant direct effect of Ethics on Use Intentions (Sobel z = .88, t(16) = 2.51, p < .05), supporting H2. However, no significant direct effects were found between Ethics and Relevance or Relevance and Use Intentions. The predicted indirect effect of Ethics through Relevance was not significant either (Sobel z = 28, p = .24), so that H3 was rejected.

6 Discussion

We developed a speed-dating application, in which a human user could communicate with an affective agent via multiple-choice questions on a website. Because of the emotionally laden setting of a speed date, this application serves well as a testbed for emotion models. Many emotion models work with (interrelated) goals. In this application, already some goals and their relation has been pre-defined. Further, using the Haptek software [11], the agent can easily be modified, for example by changing the appearance, the voice, and the types and intensities of facial expressions shown by the agent.

In a previous study, various emotion models, such as [6], [16], were validated by comparing human self-reported emotion intensities while playing a game with predictions of the emotion models [9]. However, this did not involve letting humans judge the behavior generated by the models as a validation method.

In the current study, we used the application to test Silicon Coppélia [17], an affect generation and regulation system that builds up an affective attitude of the agent towards its user, and makes decisions based on rational as well affective influences. In a user study with young females, we assessed in how far users recognized that a male agent, named Tom, was responding according to the predictions by Silicon Coppélia, described in the introduction.

H1 was confirmed in that female users recognized a direct positive effect of Tom's assessed aesthetics of the female user on Tom's involvement with her. Put differently, females recognized that when Tom found them attractive, he became more involved in terms of having 'good feelings' about them and 'feeling connected'. Note that Tom did not explicitly express these affective states but that the female users were under the impression that this is how Tom felt about them. By confirming H1, we found the mirror-image of a well-established empirical finding [20] that users become more involved with an embodied agent when they find it aesthetically more pleasing. We now have confirmation that on this aspect, our software behaves in a human-like fashion.

H2 was confirmed in that the female users recognized that Tom assessed their moral fiber and that this had a direct and positive effect on Tom's intentions to use (or better meet) the user again, either in another dating session or offline. In other words, female users saw that Tom was more inclined to meet them again when he thought they were more 'credible' and 'trustworthy'. Again, the confirmation of H2 is the mirror image of earlier findings [20], indicating that our software assesses humans like humans assess embodied software agents.

H3 was refuted in the sense that ethical aspects of the female user were not played through relevance to Tom's goals in order to evoke effects on Tom's use intentions. Female users only saw the direct effects of Tom's ethical assessment on how he felt about them (H2). The absence of the mediating effect of relevance shows the limitations of our software in authentically simulating human-like affective behavior. Mimicking indirect affective mechanisms seem to be a bridge too far. For now.

There are two problems to crack if we want to explain the absence of the effect of relevance as a mediating variable. First, it might be that the items were not indicating relevance as a concept well enough, although they were psychometrically congruent. However, this might mean that although the items measured the same, it was not relevance to the agent's goals and concerns that they measured. Thus, better concept analysis and pre-testing of items should improve the contents of the relevance scale. Second, it might be that the behavioral representation of relevance in the interaction options was not expressed well enough. This would take a round of redesign and user testing to see whether there is a way to surpass a certain threshold of recognition.

Future research with human users, however, should not only focus on ethics, aesthetics, involvement and use intentions. Although important, they are flanked by other factors such as realism and affordances [20]. Further, it is not yet assessed whether models such as EMA [8], [14], [15] or Gross [4] have added value for producing affective behavior that is recognizable for humans.

The application is generic in the sense that (emotion) models can easily be connected to the agent. After connecting, the agent bases its behavior (i.e., speech acts, facial expressions, etc.) on these models. Thereby, if the models are correct, it should be able to simulate behavior that is perceived as emotionally human-like by humans. By implementing several (versions of) models into the agent, multiple test-conditions can be created to compare the different models.

Also, the application can easily be adjusted to let a human control the speed dating agent, which enables doing Wizard of Oz studies [13]. In future research, we plan to compare the performance of models such as I-PEFiC^{ADM}, EMA, and Gross with a Wizard of Oz condition of human-human interaction, which allows for making stronger claims to the behavioral fidelity of an agent's affective response mechanisms.

Acknowledgements

We would like to thank Tibor Bosse for commenting on earlier drafts of this paper. We are also grateful to the master students H. Blok, J. Jobse, S. Bor, Y. Kobayashi, R. Changoer, D. Langeveld, P. Dirks, B. Rond, K. van Gool, and E. Stam for their help in designing the interactions between the agent and its user, for their help in developing and testing the questionnaire, and for performing statistical analyses.

References

1. About JavaScript – MDC,
   http://developer.mozilla.org/en/docs/About_JavaScript
2. Barrett, L.F., Robin, L., Pietromonaco, P.R., Eyssell, K.M.: Are Women The "More Emotional Sex?" Evidence from Emotional Experiences in Social Context. Cognition and Emotion 12, 555–578 (1998)

3. Bosse, T., Gratch, J., Hoorn, J.F., Pontier, M.A., Siddiqui, G.F.: Comparing Three Computational Models of Affect. In: Proceedings of the 8th International Conference on Practical Applications of Agents and Multi-Agent Systems, PAAMS, pp. 175–184 (2010)

4. Bosse, T., Pontier, M.A., Treur, J.: A Dynamical System Modelling Approach to Gross´ Model of Emotion Regulation. In: Lewis, R.L., Polk, T.A., Laird, J.E. (eds.) Proceedings of the 8th International Conference on Cognitive Modeling, ICCM 2007, pp. 187–192. Taylor & Francis, Abington (2007)

5. Bosse, T., Zwanenburg, E.: There's Always Hope: Enhancing Agent Believability through Expectation-Based Emotions. In: Pantic, M., Nijholt, A., Cohn, J. (eds.) Proceedings of the 2009 International Conference on Affective Computing and Intelligent Interaction, ACII 2009, pp. 111–118. IEEE Computer Society Press, Los Alamitos (2009)

6. Dias, J., Paiva, A.: Feeling and Reasoning: a Computational Model for Emotional Agents. In: Bento, C., Cardoso, A., Dias, G. (eds.) EPIA 2005. LNCS (LNAI), vol. 3808, pp. 127–140. Springer, Heidelberg (2005)

7. Frijda, N.H., Swagerman, J.: Can Computers Feel? Theory and Design of an Emotional System. Cognition and Emotion 1, 235–258 (1987)

8. Gratch, J., Marsella, S.: Evaluating a computational model of emotion. Journal of Autonomous Agents and Multiagent Systems (Special issue on the best of AAMAS 2004) 11(1), 23–43 (2006)

9. Gratch, J., Marsella, S., Wang, N., Stankovic, B.: Assessing the validity of appraisal-based models of emotion. In: Pantic, M., Nijholt, A., Cohn, J. (eds.) Proceedings of the International Conference on Affective Computing and Intelligent Interaction, ACII 2009. IEEE Computer Society Press, Los Alamitos (2009)

10. Gross, J.J.: Emotion Regulation in Adulthood: Timing is Everything. Current Directions in Psychological Science 10(6), 214–219 (2001)

11. Haptek, Inc., http://www.haptek.com

12. Hoorn, J.F., Pontier, M.A., Siddiqui, G.F.: When the user is instrumental to robot goals. First try: Agent uses agent. In: Proceedings of IEEE/WIC/ACM Web Intelligence and Intelligent Agent Technology 2008, WI-IAT 2008, IEEE/WIC/ACM, Sydney AU, pp. 296–301 (2008)

13. Landauer, T.K.: Psychology as a mother of invention. In: Proceedings of the SIGCHI/GI conference on Human factors in computing systems and graphics interface, pp. 333–335 (1987)

14. Marsella, M., Gratch, J.: EMA: A Process Model of Appraisal Dynamics. Journal of Cognitive Systems Research 10(1), 70–90 (2009)

15. Marsella, S., Gratch, J.: EMA: A Model of Emotional Dynamics. Cognitive Systems Research 10(1), 70–90 (2009)

16. Neal Reilly, W.S.: Believable Social and Emotional Agents. CMU, Pittsburgh (1996)

17. Pontier, M.A., Siddiqui, G.F.: Silicon Coppélia: Integrating Three Affect-Related Models for Establishing Richer Agent Interaction. In: IEEE/WIC/ACM International Conference on Web Intelligence and Intelligent Agent Technology. WI-IAT, vol. 2, pp. 279–284 (2009)

18. Preacher, K.J., Hayes, A.F.: SPSS and SAS procedures for estimating indirect effects in simple mediation models. Behavior Research Methods, Instruments, & Computers 36(4), 717–731 (2004)

19. Smith, C.A., Lazarus, R.S.: Emotion and Adaptation. In: Pervin, L.A. (ed.) Handbook of Personality: Theory & Research, pp. 609–637. Guilford Press, New York (1990)

20. Van Vugt, H.C., Hoorn, J.F., Konijn, E.A.: Interactive engagement with embodied agents: An empirically validated framework. Computer Animation and Virtual Worlds 20, 195–204 (2009)

21. http://www.few.vu.nl/~ghazanfa/IVA2010/

Individualized Gesturing Outperforms Average Gesturing – Evaluating Gesture Production in Virtual Humans

Kirsten Bergmann[1,2], Stefan Kopp[1,2], and Friederike Eyssel[1]

[1] Center of Excellence in "Cognitive Interaction Technology" (CITEC), Bielefeld University
[2] Collaborative Research Center 673 "Alignment in Communication", Bielefeld University
P.O. Box 100 131, D-33501 Bielefeld, Germany
{kbergmann, skopp}@techfak.uni-bielefeld.de,
friederike.eyssel@uni-bielefeld.de

Abstract. How does a virtual agent's gesturing behavior influence the user's perception of communication quality and the agent's personality? This question was investigated in an evaluation study of co-verbal iconic gestures produced with the Bayesian network-based production model GNetIc. A network learned from a corpus of several speakers was compared with networks learned from individual speaker data, as well as two control conditions. Results showed that automatically GNetIc-generated gestures increased the perceived quality of an object description given by a virtual human. Moreover, gesturing behavior generated with individual speaker networks was rated more positively in terms of likeability, competence and human-likeness.

Keywords: Evaluation, Gesture Generation, Inter-subjective Differences.

1   Introduction

A major goal in developing intelligent virtual agents (IVAs) is to advance the interaction between humans and machines towards natural and intuitive conversation. Human-human conversation is characterized by a high degree of multi-modality combining speech and other non-verbal behavior such as gestures, facial expressions, gaze, body posture, and intonation. Thus, IVA researchers are faced with two major problems: first, how to master the technical challenge to generate flexible conversational behavior automatically in IVAs and, second, how to ensure that the produced synthetic behavior improves the human-agent conversation valued by human users. The first issue has sparked the interest of many researchers in the field of IVA. For instance, with regard to iconic gestures, different modeling approaches are tested, with the goal to identify systematic characteristics of co-verbal gestures, shared among speakers, and have tried to cast these commonalities into generative models [6,16,19]. Others have emphasized individual differences in communicative behavior, e.g. [27,8], or tried to model individual gesture style for IVAs [29,12,26]. It is obvious that for the generation of multimodal behavior the consideration of both, commonalities that account for an agreed (or even conventionalized) sign system, and idiosyncrasies that make for a coherent individual style is an important issue. In previous work [1] we have proposed the GNetIc (*Gesture*

J. Allbeck et al. (Eds.): IVA 2010, LNAI 6356, pp. 104–117, 2010.

Net for Iconic Gestures) approach to automatically derive novel gestures from contextual demands, for instance, the given communicative goal, discourse status, or referent features. Importantly, by combining rule-based and data-based models, GNetIc can simulate both systematic patterns shared among several speakers, as well as idiosyncratic patterns specific to an individual. That is, GNetIc can produce novel gestures as if being a certain speaker.

The second major problem to be addressed concerns the question of how to ensure positive effect and user acceptance. There is increasing evidence that endowing virtual agents with human-like, non-verbal behavior may lead to enhancements of the likeability of the agent, trust in the agent, satisfaction with the interaction, naturalness of interaction, ease of use, and efficiency of task completion [4,13]. Concerning the particular question how humans perceive a virtual agent showing co-speech gestures, Krämer et al. [21] found no effect on agent perception when comparing a gesturing agent with a non-gesturing one. The agent displaying gestures was perceived just as likable, competent, and relaxed as the agent that did not produce gestures. In contrast, Cassell and Thórisson reported that non-verbal behavior (including beat gestures) caused users to give higher scores on language ability and life-likeness of the agent, as well as smoothness of interaction [7]. A study by Rehm and André revealed that the perception of an agent's politeness depended on the graphical quality of the employed gestures [28]. Moreover, Buisine and Martin [5] found effects of different types of speech-gesture cooperation in agent's behavior. They found that redundant gestures increased ratings of explanation quality, expressiveness of the agent, likeability and a more positive perception of the agent's personality. In an evaluation of speaker-specific gesture style simulation, Neff et al. [26] reported that the proportion of subjects who correctly recognized a speaker from generated gestures was significantly above chance.

The goal of this paper is to evaluate the GNetIc production model to explore if and how automatically generated gestures can be beneficial for human-agent interaction. In particular, we were interested in (1) the quality of the produced iconic gestures as rated by human users; (2) whether an agent's gesturing behavior can systematically alter a user's perception of the agent's likeability, competence, and human-likeness; and (3) whether producing gestures like a particular individual or like the average speaker is preferable. To investigate these questions, we exploit the flexibility afforded by GNetIc to generate speech-accompanying gestures in different conditions: individual speaker networks (representing an individualized gesturing style), networks learned from corpus data of several speakers, random gestures, or no gestures at all. The following section briefly describes the GNetIc production model. Section 3 describes the setting and procedure of the evaluation study. Results are presented in Section 4. Finally, we discuss the results and draw conclusions in Section 5.

2   Gesture Generation with GNetIc

Iconic gestures, in contrast to language or other gesture types such as emblems, have no conventional form-meaning mapping. Apparently, iconic gestures communicate by virtue of iconicity, i.e., their physical form corresponds to object features such as shape or spatial properties. Empirical studies have revealed, however, that similarity with the referent cannot fully account for all occurrences of iconic gesture use [31]. Recent findings actually indicate that a gesture's form can be influenced by a variety of contextual constraints, and that distinctive differences in personal and cultural backgrounds can lead to obvious inter-subjective differences in gesturing (cf. [15]). Consider, for instance, gesture frequency: while some people rarely make use of their hands while speaking, others do so almost without interruption. Similarly, individual variation becomes apparent in preferences for general gestural representation techniques [24,17,31] or the choices of morphological features, such as handshape or handedness [2].

Taken together, iconic gesture generation on the one hand generalizes across individuals to a certain degree, while on the other hand, inter-subjective differences must be taken into consideration by an account of why people use gestures the way they actually do. To tackle the challenge of considering both general and individual patterns in gesture formulation, we have proposed GNetIc [1]. In this approach, we employ Bayesian Decision networks which provide a representation of a finite sequential decision problem, combining probabilistic and rule-based decision-making. Gesture features empirically found to be highly idiosyncratic, *Idiosyncratic Gesture Features* (IGFs) henceforth, are represented as nodes conditioned by probability distributions. These distributions can be learned from corpus data–either from data of several speakers or for an individual speaker's data separately [3]. Resulting networks differ in their global network structure as well as in their local conditional probability distributions, revealing that individual differences are not only present in the overt gestures but can be traced back to the production process they originate from.

Table 1. Gesture features, their types and the values as determined with GNetIc

Feature Type	Gesture Features	Values
Idiosyncratic Gesture Features (IGFs)	Gesture (G)	*yes, no*
	Representation Technique (RT)	*indexing, placing, shaping, drawing, posturing*
	Handedness (H)	*rh, lh, 2h*
	Handshape (HS)	*ASL handshapes, e.g. ASL-B, ASL-C*
Common Gesture Features (CGFs)	Palm Orientation (PO)	*up, down, left, right, towards, away*
	Finger Orientation (FO)	*up, down, left, right, towards, away*
	Movement Type (MT)	*up, down, left, right, towards, away*
	Movement Direction (MD)	*up, down, left, right, towards, away*

Other gesture features, in contrast, are more universal. These features basically realize the form-meaning mapping between referent shape and gesture form, thus, accounting for most of the iconicity in the resulting gestures. In the following, we will refer to these features as *Common Gesture Features* (CGFs). In GNetIc networks, the use of these features is modeled in a rule-based way, that is, by nodes containing a set of if-then rules. Table 1 summarizes GNetIc gesture features and their properties.

Figure 1 illustrates the overall decision network. It contains four nodes representing the IGFs (see Table 1; drawn as ovals) which are connected to their predecessors by the network structure learned from speaker-specific data. The dependencies (edges) of nodes representing the CGFs (drawn as rectangles) are defined universally and do not vary across individual networks. Nevertheless, since each CGF-node has IGF-nodes as predecessors, the rule-based CGF decisions depend on IDFs whose (individual) values have been determined previously. Furthermore, each CGF-node is determined from the visuo-spatial features of the referent accounting for iconicity in the resulting gesture.

Whether the non-verbal behavior produced by GNetIc is a reasonable simulation of real speaker behavior, has been investigated in [1,3]. To do so, we conducted a corpus-based cross-validation study in which we compared the model's predictions with the actual gestures we had observed empirically. Results for both, IGF- and CGF-nodes, were quite satisfying with deviations lying well within what can be considered the natural fuzziness of human gesturing behavior. However, to find out whether the automatically generated gestures are actually comprehensible as intended and thus helpful in human-agent interaction, we still needed to conduct a study to evaluate GNetIc with real human users. This study is described in the following.

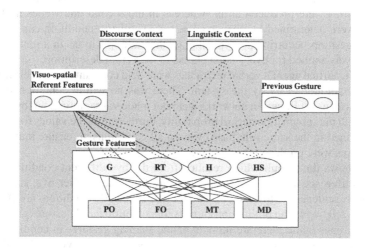

Fig. 1. General structure of a GNetIc decision network. Gesture production choices are taken either probabilistically (IGF-nodes drawn as ovals) or rule-based (CGF-nodes drawn as rectangles), solely depending on the values of connected contextual variables. Links are either learned from corpus data (dotted lines) or defined by a set of if-then rules (solid lines).

3   Evaluation Study

The present study was designed to investigate three questions. First, can we achieve a reasonable quality in the iconic gestures automatically derived with GNetIc as perceived by users? Second, is the user's perception of an agent in terms of likeability, competence, and human-likeness altered by the agent's gesturing behavior? And third, is it preferable to produce gestures like a particular individual or like the average speaker?

3.1   Independent Variables

In a between-subject design, participants were presented with a description of a church building given by the virtual human Max [20]. All descriptions were produced fully autonomously at runtime using a speech and gesture production architecture into which GNetIc is integrated [1]. We manipulated the gesturing behavior of the agent resulting in five different conditions in which Max, notably, received the identical communicative goals and produced identical verbal utterances throughout. Furthermore, all gestures were generated from the same knowledge base, a visuo-spatial representation of referent features (IDT, [30]). In two individual conditions, *ind-1* and *ind-2*, the GNetIc networks were learned from data of individual speakers from our SaGA corpus [22] (subject P5 in *ind-1*, subject P7 in *ind-2*). We have chosen these two speakers because both speakers gestured quite frequently and approximately at the same rate. In a *combined* condition, the GNetIc network was generated from data of five different speakers (including P5 and P7). These speakers' gesture styles are thus amalgamated in one network. As a consequence, Max' gesturing behavior is not as consistent as with individual networks with regard to the IDF choices. Finally, we added two control conditions. In the first one, *no gestures* were produced at all, whereas in the second one values in the four IGF-nodes were determined by chance (*random*). The latter condition can result, for instance, in gestures occurring at atypical (e.g., thematic) positions in a sentence since the network was applied for every noun phrase in the verbal description.

Overall, the virtual agent's verbal utterances were held constant and all gestures were created fully autonomously by the system. There was no within-condition variation, because choices in the Bayesian networks were not made via sampling, but by choosing the values with maximum a-posteriori probability. Furthermore, the values for the CGFs were determined in the same rule-based way in all conditions, to ensure that no "non-sense" gestures were produced throughout.

Table 2 shows the stimuli which resulted from the five different conditions. There is no wide difference across conditions in gesture frequency (either five, six or seven gestures in six sentences). However, the two individual GNetIc conditions are character-ized by less variation in the production choices. In condition *ind-1* gestures are predom-inantly static ones while there are more dynamic shaping gestures in condition *ind-2*. Moreover, the gestures in condition *ind-1* are mostly performed with c-shaped hands, whereas in *ind-2* some gestures are performed with a flat handshape. In the *combined* GNetIc condition, a combination of different techniques is obvious. A similar mixture of techniques is observable in the *random* condition which is further characterized by inconsistency in handedness and handshapes. Moreover, gestures in this condition can occur at atypical positions in a sentence.

3.2   Dependent Variables

Immediately upon receiving the descriptions by Max, participants filled out a ques-tionnaire in which two types of dependent variables had to be assessed on seven-point Likert-scales. First, participants were asked to evaluate the presentation quality with re-spect to Max's language capability (eloquence) as well as gesture quantity and quality. With regard to gesture quality we used the attributes spatial extent, temporal extent, fluidity, and power as proposed in [12]. Further, subjective measures were taken as to how comprehensible Max's explanations were, as well as how vivid the agent's mental concept (or mental image) of the church was. Second, participants were asked to state their person perception of the virtual agent. To this end, we chose 18 items [9,14], e.g., 'pleasant', 'friendly', 'helpful' (translated from German) which had to be assessed on a scale from one to seven how well they apply to Max.

Table 2. Stimuli presented in the five different conditions: verbal description given in each condition (left column; translated to English; gesture positions labelled with squared brackets); GNetIc networks from which the gesturing behavior were produced (top row); gestures produced (right columns).

	no gesture	random	combined	ind-1	ind-2
[The church is squared]...					
...and in the middle there is [a small spire.]					
[The spire]...					
...has [a tapered roof].					
And [the spire]...					
has [a clock].					
There is [a door] in front.					
And in front of the church there is [a low, green hedge].					
There is [a large deciduous tree] to the right of the church.					

3.3 Participants

At total of 110 participants (22 in each condition), aged from 16 to 60 years (M = 23.85, SD = 6.62), took part in the study. 44 participants were female and 66 were male. All of them were recruited at Bielefeld University and received 3 Euros for participating.

3.4 Procedure

Participants were instructed to carefully watch the presentation given by the virtual agent Max in order to be able to answer questions regarding content and subjective evaluation of the presentation afterwards. Figure 2 shows the setup used for stimulus presentation: Max was displayed on a 80 x 143 cm screen and thus appeared in life-size of 1.25 m. Life-sized projections have been shown to yield visual attention and fixation behavior towards gestures that is similar to behavior in face-to-face interactions [11]. Participants were seated 170 cm away from the screen and their heads were approximately leveled with Max's head.

Fig. 2. Set-up of the stimulus presentation phase

They were randomly assigned to one of the five conditions. The object description given by Max was preceded by a short introduction: Max introduced himself and repeated the instruction already given by the experimenter to get participants used to the speech synthesis. The following object description was always six sentences long and took 45 seconds. Each sentence was followed by a pause of three seconds. Participants have been left alone for the stimulus presentation, and after receiving the questionnaire to complete it (neither experimenter nor Max present).

4   Results

In the following we report results regarding the effect of experimental conditions on perceptions of presentation quality and agent perception. The third, more methodologically oriented question of preference for individual vs. average models will be discussed based on these results in the next section.

4.1   Quality of Presentation

We investigated the perceived quality of presentation with regard to gestures, speech, and content. Participants were asked to evaluate each variable on a seven-point Likert-scale with '1' standing for the most negative evaluation and '7' standing for the most positive one. To test the effect of experimental conditions on the dependent variables, we conducted analyses of variance (univariate ANOVA) and paired-sample t-tests. Mean values and standard deviations for all variables in the different conditions are summarized in Table 3 and visualized in Figure 3 for dependent variables with significant main effects.

Gesture Quantity. With regard to gesture quantity, the overall mean value for the four gesture conditions is M=3.75 (SD=1.06) on a seven-point Likert-scale (too few–too many). There is no significant main effect for experimental conditions. That is, participants were quite satisfied with the gesture rate. For the *no gesture* condition participants rated gesture quantity as rather too low (M=2.48, SD=1.21).

Gesture Quality. No main effect for experimental conditions was obtained for the four attributes characterizing gesture quality: spatial extent (too small–too large, M=3.77, SD=0.97), temporal extent (too slow–too fast, M=3.53, SD=0.85), fluidity (not fluid–very fluid, M=3.70, SD=1.51), and power (weak–powerful, M=3.87, SD=1.30). In all four gesture conditions the four quality attributes were rated with mean values between 3.0 and 4.0 on a seven-point Likert-scale, i.e., all attributes of gesture quality have been perceived as relatively good.

Eloquence. For the dependent variable eloquence, there was a significant mean effect ($F(4,79)=3.12$, p=.02). This is due to the fact that the mean of condition for *ind-2* differed from all other conditions (*ind-2/no gesture*: $t(21)=2.64$, p=.02; *ind-2/random*: $t(25)=2.94$, p=.01; *ind-2/combined*: $t(25)=4.02$, p=.001; *ind-2/ind-1*: $t(31)=2.43$, p=.02). That is, gestures produced with a suitable individual gesture network have the potential increase the perceived eloquence (recall that the verbal explanations were identical in all conditions).

Table 3. Mean values for the dependent variables of presentation quality in the five conditions (standard deviations in parentheses)

	ind-1	*ind-2*	*combined*	*no gestures*	*random*
Gesture Quantity	3.91 (1.15)	3.95 (0.95)	3.59 (0.91)	2.48 (1.21)	3.55 (1.22)
Spatial Extent	3.77 (0.87)	4.14 (0.83)	3.59 (1.05)	–	3.55 (1.05)
Temporal Extent	3.68 (0.83)	3.64 (0.66)	3.50 (1.01)	–	3.30 (0.87)
Fluidity	4.09 (1.48)	4.00 (1.57)	3.05 (1.32)	–	3.65 (1.53)
Power	3.59 (1.10)	4.09 (1.27)	3.91 (1.38)	–	3.90 (1.48)
Eloquence	3.50 (1.74)	4.91 (1.14)	3.05 (1.46)	3.69 (1.11)	3.25 (1.61)
Comprehension	5.18 (1.33)	5.27 (1.16)	4.68 (1.49)	4.95 (1.32)	4.18 (1.37)
Gestures helpful	5.68 (1.56)	5.82 (0.85)	4.70 (1.62)	1.82 (1.14)	4.10 (2.05)
Vividness	5.32 (1.62)	5.45 (1.13)	4.18 (1.81)	4.08 (1.32)	3.81 (1.80)

Overall Comprehension. Another variable we were interested in was the comprehensibility of the overall description (not comprehensible–easily comprehensible). Although the ANOVA marginally failed to reach significance (F(4,105)=2.37, p=.057), we analyzed simple effects for experimental conditions. The means for both individual GNetIc conditions significantly outperformed the mean of the *random* gesture condition (*ind-1/random*: t(42)=2.46, p=.018; *ind-2/random*: t(41)=2.85, p=.007). In tendency, the *no gesture* mean differed from the *random* mean. That is, participants reported greater comprehension of the presentation when the agent produced no, rather than random gestures.

Gesture's Helpfulness for Comprehension. With regard to perceived helpfulness of gesturing we obtained a significant main effect (F(4,104)=25.86, p<.001). Not surprisingly, participants in the *no gesture* condition rated gesturing as less helpful than participants in the other conditions (*t*-test, p<.001 in each case). In addition, gestures in both individual conditions (*ind-1, ind-2*) were rated more helpful than in the *random* condition (*ind-1*: t(41)=2.87, p=.006; *ind-2*: t(41)=3.63, p=.001).

Vividness. Furthermore, we asked participants to rate the vividness of the agent's conception of the presented content. Random gesturing tended to hamper this impression even more than no gesturing and combined gesturing. Furthermore, the ANOVA revealed a significant main effect (F(4,79)=3.50, p=.01). Results of *t*-tests showed significant mean differences between both individual GNetIc conditions and the other three conditions (*ind-1/no gesture*: t(29)=2.47, p=.02; *ind-1/random gestures*: t(30)=2.66; p=.01; *ind-1/combined*: t(41)=2.19, p=.03; *ind-2/no gesture*: t(22)=2.76, p=.01; *ind-2/random gestures*: t(25)=2.91, p=.01; *ind-2/combined*: t(31)=2.12, p=.04). That is, producing gestures with an individualized network helps a virtual agent to create the impression of having a better idea of what is being described in human recipients.

4.2 Agent Perception

We assessed how Max is perceived using several items, e.g. 'pleasant', 'friendly', 'helpful', on seven-point Likert scales. To measure the reliability of these items we grouped them into three scales 'likeability', 'competence", and 'human-likeness' (see Table 4) and calculated Cronbach's alpha for the indeces. The alpha values for all three scales were above 0.7, which justifies combining these items into one mean value as a single index for this scale. We analyzed the main effect for experimental conditions by applying ANOVAs and further investigated the pattern of means by computing paired-samples *t*-tests. Mean values and standard deviations for all variables under the different conditions are summarized in Table 5 and visualized in Figure 3.

Likeability. Regarding likeability, we found a significant main effect for experimental conditions (F(4,104)=3.88, p=.01). Mean ratings for the two individual GNetIc conditions were higher than in the other conditions. In particular, this relationship was significant when comparing the *ind-2* condition with *no gesture* (t(36)=2.68, p=.01) and *random* conditions (t(38)=3.58, p=.001). The mean difference between *ind-2* and the *combined* condition marginally failed to reach significance (t(40)=1.99, p=.054). For individual condition *ind-1*, the difference of mean evaluation of likeability in comparison with *random* gestures is significant (t(42)=2.06, p=.05). In addition, means for the *combined* GNetIc condition were higher than in both control conditions. In other

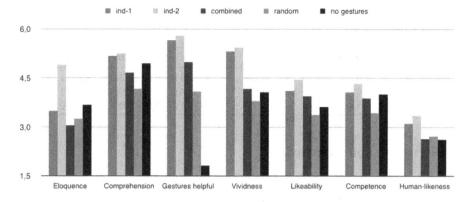

Fig. 3. Mean values of the dependent variables in the five conditions (see Tables 3 and 5 for SDs)

words, all three GNetIc conditions outperformed the control conditions (*random* and *no gestures*), whereby best evaluations for likeability were obtained by participants in the individual GNetIc conditions.

Competence. With regard to the evaluation of the agent's competence we also found a significant main effect (F(4,101)=2.65, p=.04). The GNetIc conditions received higher mean evaluations than the *random* condition. This relationship was strongly significant when comparing *ind-2* with *random* (t(42)=3.94, p=.001). Comparing *ind-1* and *random* we also found a significant main effect (t(41)=2.08, p=.04). The *combined* GNetIc condition also received a higher mean evaluation than the *random* condition which is, however, not significant. Notably, there is no significant difference between the GNetIc conditions and the *no gesture* condition.

Human-likeness. Finally, the analysis of ratings for human-likeness revealed a main effect (F(4,104)=2.08, p=.09). Both individual GNetIc conditions outperformed the other conditions. Again, this relationship is stronger for the condition *ind-2* (*ind-2/no gesture*: t(42)=2.40, p=.02; *ind-2/random gestures*: t(42)= 2.09, p=.04; *ind-2*/combined: t(41)= 2.30, p=.03). For the other individual GNetIc condition *ind-1*, the mean rating of human-likeness is also higher than in the *combined* GNetIc condition and the two control conditions, but these differences are not significant. No difference at all is present between the *combined* GNetIc condition and the two control conditions (*random* and *no gesturing*).

Table 4. Reliability analysis for the three scales 'likeability', 'competence'', and 'human-likeness'

Scale	Items	Cronbach's Alpha
likeability	pleasant, sensitive, friendly, likeable, affable, approachable, sociable	.86
Competence	dedicated, trustworthy, thorough, helpful, intelligent, organized, expert	.84
Human-likeness	active, humanlike, fun-loving, lively	.79

Table 5. Mean values for the agent perception scales in the five different conditions (standard deviations in parentheses)

	ind-1	ind-2	combined	no gestures	random
Likeability	4.12 (1.18)	4.47 (0.81)	3.95 (0.87)	3.62 (1.24)	3.39 (1.14)
Competence	4.07 (1.11)	4.34 (0.55)	3.89 (0.84)	4.01 (1.09)	3.44 (1.07)
Humanlikeness	3.11 (1.29)	3.37 (1.07)	2.64 (1.01)	2.62 (1.00)	2.73 (0.99)

5   Discussion and Conclusion

The goal of this paper was to evaluate the GNetIc production model and to explore the impact of automatically generated gestures on human-agent interaction. A network learned from a corpus of several speakers was compared with networks learned from individual speaker data, as well as two control conditions (no and random gestures). Results can be summarized in four points: First, Max's gesturing behavior was rated positively regarding gesture quantity and quality, and we found no difference across gesture conditions concerning these issues. Second, both individual GNetIc conditions outperformed the other conditions in that gestures were perceived as more helpful, overall comprehension of the presentation was rated higher, and the agent's mental image was judged as being more vivid. Similarly, the two individual GNetIc conditions outperformed the control conditions regarding agent perception in terms of likeability, competence, and human-likeness. Third, the *combined* GNetIc condition was rated worse than the individual GNetIc conditions throughout. Fourth, the *no gesture* condition was rated more positively than the *random* condition, in particular for the subjective measures of overall comprehension, the gesture's role for comprehension, and vividness of the agent's mental image. That is, with regard to these aspects it seems even better to make no gestures than to randomly generate gestural behavior even though it is still considerably iconic (cf. gestures in Table 2). It is remarkable that the significant effects reported in this paper already occur after the presentation of 45 seconds lasting stimuli each of them containing up to seven gestures. Future research should, however, also investigate how users perceive longer presentations or interactions between agent and user who was just a passive recipient in the present study.

The results reported here bear important and exciting consequences for IVA research. First, from the methodological point of view of building IVAs, we now have evidence that building generative models of co-verbal iconic gesture use, going beyond gesture lexicons is possible and can yield good results with actual users. Notably, we did not reproduce individual speaker's behavior "literally". Rather, we trained the model from their data so as to extract their preferences and strategies in composing gestures. In result, we can say that we obtained models that create novel gestures as if being the respective speaker and users rated the produced gestures positively.

Second, from the point of view of human communication research our results show that computational modeling with IVAs is a highly valuable tool to discover mechanisms and principles of communicative behavior. Here we explicated process models of how speakers form gestures and we showed that these models actually produce reasonable behavior. Furthermore, different models result in perceivably different behavior, with consistently differing perception and evaluation by human recipients.

Third, and probably most surprising, we found that the common approach to inform behavior models from empirical data by averaging over a population of subjects is not necessarily the best choice. Our findings suggest that modeling individual speakers with proper abilities for the target behavior (in our case good iconic gesturing) results in even better behavior judged from the perspective of human interaction partners. This may be due to the fact that individual networks ensure a greater coherence of the produced behavior. As a consequence, the agent may appear more coherent and self-consistent which, in turn, may make its behavior more predictable and easier to interpret for the user. This is in line with Nass et al. who found that people like ECAs more when they show consistent personality characteristics across modalities [25]. On the contrary, however, Foster & Oberlander recently argued for more variation in the generation of non-verbal behavior based on evidence from the evaluation of automatically produced head and eyebrow motion [10]. In any case, as a consequence for future IVA research, it seems reasonable according to our results to detect particularly appropriate speakers and to individualize agents in their way (e.g., in our data *ind-2* outperforms *ind-1*). This may also help to point up a solution to the task of producing iconic gestures, which is daunting because of the seemingly under-constrained problem of having to pick from a myriad of possible options, which appear to be more or less equivalent and whose contingencies are hardly known. Adhering to an individual style of gesturing can provide additional constraints to resolve this problem of behavior formulation, and it can actually help to produce good behavior and increase the acceptance of the agent.

Such an individualization, however, bears the danger of narrowing acceptance down to a certain population of users, since gesture perception as well as production may be subject to inter-individual differences. For instance, Martin et al. found the rating of gestural expressivity parameters to be influenced by human addressee's personality traits [23]. Although our data does not suggest such a risk immediately, since individual conditions did not received higher standard deviations, an elaborated study should also take the addressee into account. Further, a quest for individualization should, in our view, be accompanied by efforts to also make agents able to deviate from this individualized behavior in reciprocal interaction, in order to achieve inter-personal coordination and to induce social resonance [18].

Acknowledgements. This research is partially supported by the Deutsche Forschungsgemeinschaft (DFG) in the Collaborative Research Center 673 "Alignment in Communication" and the Center of Excellence in "Cognitive Interaction Technology" (CITEC).

References

1. Bergmann, K., Kopp, S.: GNetIc–Using Bayesian decision networks for iconic gesture generation. In: Ruttkay, Z., Kipp, M., Nijholt, A., Vilhjálmsson, H.H. (eds.) IVA 2009. LNCS, vol. 5773, pp. 76–89. Springer, Heidelberg (2009)
2. Bergmann, K., Kopp, S.: Increasing expressiveness for virtual agents–Autonomous generation of speech and gesture in spatial description tasks. In: Decker, K., Sichman, J., Sierra, C., Castelfranchi, C. (eds.) Proceedings of the 8th International Conference on Autonomous Agents and Multiagent Systems, Budapest, Hungary, pp. 361–368 (2009)
3. Bergmann, K., Kopp, S.: Modeling the production of co-verbal iconic gestures by learning bayesian decision networks. Applied Artificial Intelligence (to appear)

4. Bickmore, T., Cassell, J.: Social dialogue with embodied conversational agents. In: van Kuppevelt, J., Dybkjaer, L., Bernsen, N. (eds.) Advances in Natural, Multimodal Dialogue Systems, New York, Kluwer Academic Publishers, Dordrecht (2005)
5. Buisine, S., Martin, J.-C.: The effects of speech-gesture cooperation in animated agents' behavior in multimedia presentations. Interacting with Computers 19, 484–493 (2007)
6. Cassell, J., Stone, M., Yan, H.: Coordination and context-dependence in the generation of embodied conversation. In: Proceedings of the First Intern. Conf. on NLG (2000)
7. Cassell, J., Thórisson, K.: The power of a nod and a glance: Envelope vs. emotional feedback in animated conversational agents. Applied Artificial Intelligence 13, 519–538 (1999)
8. Dale, R., Viethen, J.: Referring expression generation through attribute-based heuristics. In: Krahmer, E., Theune, M. (eds.) Proceedings of the 12th European Workshop on Natural Language Generation, Athens, Greece, pp. 58–65 (2009)
9. Fiske, S.T., Cuddy, A.J., Glick, P.: Universal dimensions of social cognition: Warmth and competence. Trends in Cognitive Science 11(2), 77–83 (2006)
10. Foster, M., Oberlander, J.: Corpus-based generation of head and eyebrow motion for an embodied conversational agent. Language Resources and Evaluation 41, 305–323 (2007)
11. Gullberg, M., Holmqvist, K.: What speakers do and what listeners look at. Visual attention to gestures in human interaction live and on video. Pragmatics & Cognition 14, 53–82 (2006)
12. Hartmann, B., Mancini, M., Pelachaud, C.: Implementing expressive gesture synthesis for embodied conversational agents. In: Gibet, S., Courty, N., Kamp, J.-F. (eds.) GW 2005. LNCS (LNAI), vol. 3881, pp. 188–199. Springer, Heidelberg (2006)
13. Heylen, D., van Es, I., Nijholt, A., van Dijk, B.: Experimenting with the gaze of a conversational agent. In: van Kuppevelt, J., Dybkjær, L., Bernsen, N. (eds.) Proceedings International CLASS Workshop on Natural, Intelligent and Effective Interaction in Multimodal Dialogue Systems, pp. 93–100 (2002)
14. Hoffmann, A., Krämer, N., Lam-Chi, A., Kopp, S.: Media equation revisited. Do users show polite reactions towards an embodied agent? In: Ruttkay, Z., Kipp, M., Nijholt, A., Vilhjálmsson, H.H. (eds.) IVA 2009. LNCS, vol. 5773, pp. 159–165. Springer, Heidelberg (2009)
15. Hostetter, A., Alibali, M.: Raise your hand if you're spatial–Relations between verbal and spatial skills and gesture production. Gesture 7(1), 73–95 (2007)
16. Huenerfauth, M.: Spatial, temporal and semantic models for American Sign Language generation: Implications for gesture generation. Semantic Computing 2(1), 21–45 (2008)
17. Kendon, A.: Gesture–Visible Action as Utterance. Cambridge University Press, Cambridge (2004)
18. Kopp, S.: Social resonance and embodied coordination in face-to-face conversation with artificial interlocutors. Speech Communication 52, 587–597 (2010)
19. Kopp, S., Tepper, P., Ferriman, K., Striegnitz, K., Cassell, J.: Trading spaces: How humans and humanoids use speech and gesture to give directions. In: Nishida, T. (ed.) Engineering Approaches to Conversational Informatics, pp. 133–160. John Wiley, New York (2007)
20. Kopp, S., Wachsmuth, I.: Synthesizing multimodal utterances for conversational agents. Computer Animation and Virtual Worlds 15(1), 39–52 (2004)
21. Krämer, N., Tietz, B., Bente, G.: Effects of embodied interface agents and their gestural activity. In: Rist, T., Aylett, R.S., Ballin, D., Rickel, J. (eds.) IVA 2003. LNCS (LNAI), vol. 2792, pp. 292–300. Springer, Heidelberg (2003)
22. Lücking, A., Bergmann, K., Hahn, F., Kopp, S., Rieser, H.: The Bielefeld speech and gesture alignment corpus (SaGA). In: Kipp, M., Martin, J.-C., Paggio, P., Heylen, D. (eds.) Proceedings of the LREC 2010 Workshop on Multimodal Corpora (2010)
23. Martin, J.-C., Abrilian, S., Devillers, L.: Individual differences in the perception of spontaneous gesture expressivity. In: Integrating Gestures, p. 71 (2007)
24. Müller, C.: Redebegleitende Gesten: Kulturgeschichte–Theorie–Sprachvergleich. Berlin Verlag, Berlin (1998)

25. Nass, C., Isbister, K., Lee, E.-J.: Truth is beauty: Researching embodied conversational agents. In: Cassell, J., et al. (eds.) Embodied Conversational Agents, pp. 374–402. MIT Press, Cambridge (2000)
26. Neff, M., Kipp, M., Albrecht, I., Seidel, H.-P.: Gesture modeling and animation based on a probabilistic re-creation of speaker style. ACM Transactions on Graphics 27(1), 1–24 (2008)
27. Oberlander, J., Gill, A.: Individual differences and implicit language: personality, parts-of-speech and pervasiveness. In: Proceedings of the 26th Annual Conference of the Cognitive Science Society, Chicago, IL, pp. 1035–1040 (2004)
28. Rehm, M., André, E.: Informing the design of agents by corpus analysis. In: Nishida, T., Nakano, Y. (eds.) Conversational Informatics. John Wiley & Sons, Chichester (2007)
29. Ruttkay, Z.: Presenting in style by virtual humans. In: Esposito, A., Faundez-Zanuy, M., Keller, E., Marinaro, M. (eds.) COST Action 2102. LNCS (LNAI), vol. 4775, pp. 23–36. Springer, Heidelberg (2007)
30. Sowa, T., Wachsmuth, I.: A computational model for the representation an processing of shape in coverbal iconic gestures. In: Coventry, K.R., Tenbrink, T., Bateman, J.A. (eds.) Spatial Language and Dialogue, pp. 132–146. Oxford University Press, Oxford (2009)
31. Streeck, J.: Depicting by gesture. Gesture 8(3), 285–301 (2008)

Level of Detail Based Behavior Control for Virtual Characters

Felix Kistler, Michael Wißner, and Elisabeth André

Augsburg University, Multimedia Concepts and their Applications,
D-86159 Augsburg, Germany
{kistler,wissner,andre}@informatik.uni-augsburg.de
http://mm-werkstatt.informatik.uni-augsburg.de/

Abstract. We take the idea of Level of Detail (LOD) from its traditional use in computer graphics and apply it to the behavior of virtual
characters. We describe how our approach handles LOD determination
and how we used it to reduce the simulation quality of multiple aspects
of the characters' behavior in an existing application.

1 Introduction

Traditionally, Level of Detail (LOD) is a concept found in 3D graphics programming aiming at reducing the total amount of polygons in a scene and thus
increasing the overall performance. To this end, for each 3D-Object in the scene,
the distance from the camera to this object is taken into account. The further
away an object is from the camera, the less important it becomes for the user
and the fewer polygons are drawn for it, following the rationale that the human
eye will not be able to tell the difference. Different LODs can be discrete and
are switched at certain distance thresholds or they can be continuous and the
number of polygons is updated dynamically. Recent research extends the idea
of LOD to the simulation of the behavior of virtual characters, using the terms
"Simulation LOD" or "LOD AI". The general idea is to find uninteresting or
unimportant characters in the scene and reduce the simulation quality of their
behavior accordingly. When applying LOD to the behavior of characters in this
manner, new questions arise regarding the definition and usage of the different
LODs: Is distance from the camera still a viable method to determine LOD for
a certain character? Or are there situations in which a character might be interesting enough to exhibit its complete behavior, regardless of the distance to the
camera? Which aspects of the behavior simulation can be reduced and how?

In this work we address the above questions and present our approach of an
LOD-based behavior control system. We also report how we integrated and tested
our system in an existing application, the Virtual Beer Garden. The Virtual Beer
Garden is a Sims-like virtual environment where characters try to satisfy certain
needs by interacting with each other or smart objects in the environment.

The novelty of our approach lies in the wide range of reducible aspects of
behavior and the fact that the behavior reduction is applied at execution time
and not beforehand during behavior selection.

J. Allbeck et al. (Eds.): IVA 2010, LNAI 6356, pp. 118–124, 2010.

2   Related Work

Table 1 shows an overview of previous work on "Simulation LOD" or "LOD AI", as well as our approach.

As can be seen from the table, with a wide range of reducible aspects of behavior, LOD determination based on distance and visibility and a rather large number of different LODs, our work focuses on a more flexible approach which is applicable to many different applications and scenarios.

Table 1. Comparison of different LOD approaches

Authors	LOD based on	Number of LODs	LOD applied to	AI behaviors
Chenney et al. [1]	potential visibility	2	updating movement	navigation, collision avoidance
O'Sullivan et al. [2]	distance	not specified	geometry, animations, collision avoidance, gestures and facial expressions, action selection	navigation, collision avoidance, complex dialogs with other agents
Brockington [3]	distance	5	scheduling, navigation, action selection in combat	navigation, collision avoidance, complex combat interactions
Niederberger and Gross [4]	distance and visibility	21	scheduling, collision avoidance, path planning, group decisions	navigation, collision avoidance
Brom et al. [5]	simplified distance	4	action selection (with AND-OR trees), environment simplification	navigation, complex interactions with objects and other agents
Paris et al. [6]	distance	3	navigation, collision avoidance	path planning, navigation, collision avoidance
Lin and Pan [7]	distance	not specified	geometry, animations	locomotion
Osborne and Dickinson [8]	distance	not specified	navigation, flocking, group decisions	navigation
Our work	distance and visibility	10	updating movement, collision avoidance, navigation, action execution	navigation, collision avoidance, desire-based interactions with agents and smart objects, dialogs

3   LOD Based Behavior Control System

Our LOD based Behavior Control System is based on the Horde3D GameEngine [9]. The engine is component-based and due to this modular design it can be simply enhanced by new components as done in our implementation described in this section.

3.1   LOD Determination

The most important goal in determining the different levels of detail is to keep the later usage as generic as possible. Because of that the LOD should offer enough different nuances in its classification. The current implementation calculates the LOD in up to ten configurable levels according to the distance from the camera, and further adds an again configurable value, if the object is not visible from the current camera (as suggested by Niederberger and Gross).

The different LODs for an entity in the game world can be configured within the XML-based scene graph. Figure 1 shows an example XML configuration. d0-d5 configure the discrete distances for the LOD levels in the game environment. "invisibleAdd" is the value added to the LOD in case of invisibility of the object.

In the LOD calculation, all objects whose distance to the camera is lower than d0 are assigned a LOD value of 0. For all others the following applies:

$$LOD(x) = d(x) + add(x)$$
$$\text{where } d(x) = i \text{ for } d_i(x) \leq r(x) < d_{i+1}(x)$$
$$\text{with } r(x) = \text{ "distance of x to the camera"}$$
$$\text{with } d_i(x) = \text{ "discrete distance } d_i \text{ as configured for x"}$$
$$\text{and } add(x) = \begin{cases} invisibleAdd(x) & \text{if } x \text{ is invisible} \\ 0 & \text{otherwise} \end{cases}$$

Let us assume the "invisibleAdd" of an object x is set to 2 and its distance to the camera is 100, which is between d3(x) and d4(x). Then it's first assigned an LOD value of 3. If x is also invisible for the current camera, the "invisibleAdd" is added. Thus the LOD of x becomes 5 in total.

The visibility determination takes place by testing the bounding box of an object against the camera frustum. In that way nearly visible agents are also counted as visible, in opposite to Niederberger and Gross. As most of the time only few agents fall into this category, this additional classification is of little consequence, though.

If occlusion culling is activated in the application, this extra information is also taken into account for the LOD determination. As a result objects or agents occluded by others get the "invisibleAdd" as well.

```
<AILOD d0="25" d1="40" d2="60" d3="90" d4="130" d5="200" invisibleAdd="2" />
```

Fig. 1. XML configuration for the LOD determination

Fig. 2. LOD classification
Left: Small section of the Virtual Beer Garden environment, showing both visible and invisible agents at the same distance.
Right: Complete scene, showing many agents with LOD 7

Figure 2 shows two examples of the LOD classification. Note that the transparent, white pyramid represents the camera frustum for the LOD calculation. Also, all objects and characters for which the LOD is calculated are marked with colored circles according to their LOD value. LOD 0 is white and LODs 1-6 are incrementally darkening until black at LOD 7.

3.2 LOD Usage and Sample Application

As the Horde3D GameEngine is organized in (preferably independent) components, it seems logical to apply the Level Of Detail in each of these components separately to gain the most benefit. Moreover, each component's LOD usage can be configured individually to suit the current application's needs. However, the current LOD implementation only focuses on the AI relevant components. The following simplifications are caused by the LOD implementation so far:

- The path planning is reduced at a higher LOD level.
- The movement of the characters is simulated differently. It varies from the complete continuous movement with full animation, over continuous movement without animation, to a more and more infrequent update of the movement (so the agents move with a jerk), and ends with the direct jump to the designated destination.
- Update rates are reduced at a higher LOD.
- Repulsive forces in the governing crowd simulation are ignored from a specific LOD on. As a result, agents walk through each other and through small objects.
- Speech is only output up to a certain LOD.
- Animations are omitted at higher LODs.
- Some behavior is dropped at higher LODs.

Virtual Beer Garden. The application we applied our LOD system to is the Virtual Beer Garden [10], a typical Bavarian beer garden, with trees, benches and tables, toilets, and a booth in which two characters sell beer and salads. Further there are waitresses which bring away empty beer steins and salad bowls. But the main characters are the patrons. They enjoy themselves by drinking beer, eating salad and chatting. They further go to the toilet, if they need. To have a more profound LOD application, we changed the environment so that it now contains for different beer gardens with a free open space in between (see figure 2 right).

The characters' movement in the application is governed by a crowd simulation which is also controlled by our LOD based system [11]. Before we describe how we applied our LOD system to the characters' AI, we will first explain it. It is based on a desire system and the use of smart objects, similar to The Sims (cf. [12], [13]).

All actions are driven by the agents' desires, which are defined by: a unique name, the current level in the range of 0 (no desire) to 100 (soon to be satisfied), an initial value (if unconfigured, initialized by a random number), an increment which continuously increases or decreases the desire, and finally a weight to prioritize desires.

To satisfy these desires, a character has to interact with the so-called smart objects, which provide information about the interaction procedure. This information normally includes exact action instructions, pre- and postconditions and additional pieces of information for the interaction, similar to the approach described by Abaci et al. [14]. The action instructions of our smart objects are divided into a sequence of preparations and a sequence of actions for the actual interaction. Both sequences are added to the characters' action queue, which they processes step by step. Possible actions include: Going to a certain position, speaking a sentence, playing an animation, picking up or setting down an object and adding a certain value to a desire. The information flow between a character and a smart object is also shown in figure 3.

In addition to the smart objects interactions, the agents can interact with each other. For example, if a character has emptied its beer stein, it can ask a waiter to refill it. If a character wants to fulfill such a desire, it first has to find

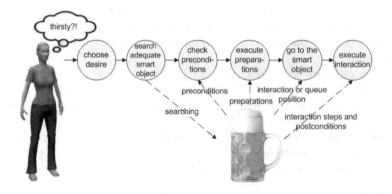

Fig. 3. Information flow between character and smart object

a partner in its search radius that feels this need, too - at least with a value of 40. If the agent has found such a partner, it will walk toward the other and waits if there is still another interaction to finish. Now, each interaction partner gets an action sequence, and they both take turns at working it off. The agent interactions in the Virtual Beer Garden mainly consist of smalltalk, but also of goal-oriented dialog, such as sales conversations between the waiter or the cook and the customer at the booth.

The characters' interaction with the smart objects is reduced by the LOD system in the following way: Based on whether a step in the interaction sequence is critical for the outcome of the interaction, the agents can skip it. To this end, the smart objects offer a maximum LOD and an alternative waiting time for each step of the interaction. At each step, the agent checks its LOD against this maximum and if it's above, the agent waits for the indicated amount of time instead of actually performing the action.

As the action selection is predetermined by the smart objects interactions, there is a high guarantee for a consistent behavior in the game progress, even if the LOD applications skips the partial steps of the interactions. This reveals an advantage over other AI techniques.

4 Conclusion and Future Work

In this work we presented our idea of an LOD based behavior control system for virtual characters based on discrete distances from an application's camera and also reported how we applied it to an existing application. We showed that many aspects of the characters' behavior can be reduced with our implementation due to its general approach. Applying the behavior reduction at the action execution level also provides us with high consistency during LOD changes.

Ideas for future work include three different kinds of improvement: First, the approach could be extended to additional behaviors, such as the gaze behavior system we described in [15] or other sensory input. Second, the approach could be made more dynamic, especially regarding the animations. As of now, they are either played or not. Here, it would be interesting to created simplified animations that could be used in between, as described by [16]. Finally, the LOD approach could also be adapted to other behavior control techniques for virtual characters, such as HTN Planners, Hierarchical Finite State Machines or Behavior Trees.

References

1. Chenney, S., Arikan, O., Forsyth, D.A.: Proxy Simulations For Efficient Dynamics. In: Proceedings of Eurographics (2001)
2. O'Sullivan, C., Cassell, J., Vilhjalmsson, H., Dingliana, J., Dobbyn, S., McNamee, B., Peters, C., Giang, T.: Levels of detail for crowds and groups. Computer Graphics Forum 21(4), 733–742 (2002)
3. Brockington, M.: Level-Of-Detail AI for a Large Role-Playing Game. In: AI Game Programming Wisdom, pp. 419–425. Charles River Media (2002)

4. Niederberger, C., Gross, M.: Level-of-detail for cognitive real-time characters. The Visual Computer: Int. Journal of Computer Graphics 21(3), 188–202 (2005)
5. Brom, C., Šerý, O., Poch, T.: Simulation Level of Detail for Virtual Humans. In: Pelachaud, C., Martin, J.-C., André, E., Chollet, G., Karpouzis, K., Pelé, D. (eds.) IVA 2007. LNCS (LNAI), vol. 4722, pp. 1–14. Springer, Heidelberg (2007)
6. Paris, S., Gerdelan, A., O'Sullivan, C.: CA-LOD: Collision Avoidance Level of Detail for Scalable, Controllable Crowds. In: Proc. of the 2nd Int. Workshop on Motion in Games, pp. 13–28. Springer, Heidelberg (2009)
7. Lin, Z., Pan, Z.: LoD-Based Locomotion Engine for Game Characters. In: Hui, K.-c., Pan, Z., Chung, R.C.-k., Wang, C.C.L., Jin, X., Göbel, S., Li, E.C.-L. (eds.) EDUTAINMENT 2007. LNCS, vol. 4469, pp. 214–224. Springer, Heidelberg (2007)
8. Osborne, D., Dickinson, P.: Improving Games AI Performance using Grouped Hierarchical Level of Detail. In: Proc. of the 36th Annual Convention of the Society for the Study of Artificial Intelligence and Simulation of Behaviour (2010)
9. Horde3D GameEngine: University of Augsburg (2010), http://mm-werkstatt.informatik.uni-augsburg.de/projects/GameEngine/
10. Rehm, M., Endrass, B., Wißner, M.: Integrating the User in the Social Group Dynamics of Agents. In: Workshop on Social Intelligence Design, SID (2007)
11. Wißner, M., Kistler, F., André, E.: Level of Detail based Behavior Control for Virtual Characters in a Crowd Simulation. In: CASA 2010 Workshop on Crowd Simulation (2010)
12. Champandard, A.J.: Living with The Sims' AI: 21 Tricks to Adopt for your Game (2010), http://aigamedev.com/open/highlights/the-sims-ai/
13. Tirrell, J.W.: Dumb People, Smart Objects: The Sims and the Distributed Self (2010), http://www.jtirrell.com/jtirrell/dumb_people
14. Abaci, T., Cíger, J., Thalmann, D.: Planning with smart objects. In: The 13th Int. Conf. in Central Europe on Computer Graphics, Visualization and Computer Vision, pp. 25–28 (2005)
15. Wißner, M., Bee, N., Kienberger, J., André, E.: To See and to Be Seen in the Virtual Beer Garden - A Gaze Behavior System for Intelligent Virtual Agents in a 3D Environment. In: Mertsching, B., Hund, M., Aziz, Z. (eds.) KI 2009. LNCS, vol. 5803, pp. 500–507. Springer, Heidelberg (2009)
16. Giang, T., Mooney, R., Peters, C., O'Sullivan, C.: ALOHA: Adaptive Level of Detail for Human Animation: Towards a new Framework. In: EUROGRAPHICS, Short Paper Proceedings, pp. 71–77 (2000)

Virtual Agents Based Simulation for Training Healthcare Workers in Hand Hygiene Procedures.

Jeffrey Bertrand[1], Sabarish V. Babu[2], Philip Polgreen[3], and Alberto Segre[1]

[1] Department of Computer Science, University of Iowa,
14 MacLean Hall, Iowa City, Iowa – 52242-1419
[2] Human-Centered Computing Division, School of Computing, Clemson University,
100 McAdams Hall, Clemson, South Carolina – 29634-0974
[3] Department of Internal Medicine, University of Iowa,
200 Hawking Drive, Iowa City, Iowa - 52242
{jeffrey-bertrand,philip-polgreen,alberto-segre}@uiowa.edu,
sbabu@clemson.edu

Abstract. The goal of our work is the design and implementation of a virtual agents based interactive simulation for teaching and training healthcare workers in hand hygiene protocols. The interactive training simulation features a virtual instructor who teaches the trainee the Five Moments of hand hygiene, recommended by the Centers of Disease Control and the World Health Organization, via instructions and demonstrations in a tutorial phase. In an interactive training phase, a virtual health care worker demonstrates by interacting with a virtual patient and the patient's environment in ten randomly generated virtual scenarios. After watching each scenario the trainee evaluates if the virtual healthcare worker's actions are in accordance with the Five Moments of Hand Hygiene procedure. In a feedback phase, the trainee receives feedback on their performance in the training phase after which the trainee can either exit or return to any phase of the interactive simulation. We describe the design and development of the hospital environment, simulated virtual instructor, health care worker and patient, and the interactive simulation components towards teaching and training in healthcare best practices associated with hand hygiene.

Keywords: Virtual Humans, Medical Virtual Reality, 3D Human-Computer Interaction.

1 Introduction

According to the Centers for Disease Control (CDC), healthcare-associated infections affect about two million patients in US hospitals each year [1]. Tragically, many of these hospital-acquired infections are preventable. Despite the fact that hand hygiene is one of the most important measures for preventing healthcare-associated infections [2, 3], hand hygiene rates among healthcare workers remain unacceptably low [4]. Interventions which include feeding hand hygiene rates back to healthcare workers can lead to improvements in hand hygiene practices [2], and improved rates can

J. Allbeck et al. (Eds.): IVA 2010, LNAI 6356, pp. 125–131, 2010.

decrease healthcare-associated infections [2, 5, 3]. Thus, measuring hand hygiene is an important component of infection control programs, and one that is recommended by both the Centers for Disease Control and Prevention (CDC) and the World Health Organization (WHO) [2, 6]. Furthermore, the Joint Commission, the largest organization that inspects hospitals in the US, currently mandates that all hospitals monitor hand-hygiene compliance and during inspections asks hospitals not only what their rates are but also what they are doing to improve compliance. Currently, most observations are performed and recorded by human observers, and to date, this method is considered the "gold standard" for hand-hygiene measurement [7]. In short, the five moments or situations when health care workers should follow proper procedures of hand hygiene are defined as: before touching a patient, before clean/aseptic procedures, after body fluid exposure/risk, after touching a patient, and after touching the patient's surroundings.

To help educate healthcare workers about when to practice hand hygiene the WHO have defined a set of circumstances when hand-hygiene should be practiced using an alcohol rub or soap and water. These are referred to as the Five Moments. In prior research, interactive virtual humans have been used to teach and train verbal and non-verbal social behaviors in a variety of tasks in face-to-face conversation [8, 9]. While there are short videos and posters to describe the Five Moments, to our knowledge there are no interactive virtual environments simulations with virtual humans for healthcare worker education that stress the importance of how observations should be done. We believe that training infection control professionals to appropriately observe and record hand hygiene is critical. We propose that these observation skills would more effectively be learned in an immersive, active, engaging environment. Indeed, most of the studies reviewed in the recent Agency for Healthcare Research and Quality report on the effectiveness of continuing medical education suggest that interactive techniques are more effective than non-interactive ones [10].

1.1 Related Work

Johnson et. al. have developed an immersive virtual patient framework for training medical students in patient interview training skills in simulated inter-personal conversation with virtual patients [8]. Parsons et. al. are using virtual human patients towards training of novice mental health clinicians in conducting patient interviews using virtual patients that exhibit psychological disorders such as conduct disorder [9]. ELECT BiLAT, developed at the ICT at USC, is a simulated virtual environment with virtual humans towards training army officers' culture-specific verbal and non-verbal behaviours in Middle Eastern culture [11]. Babu et. al. showed that immersive virtual humans in natural multimodal interaction can teach and train users social conversational nonverbal behaviours associated with south Indian culture [12]. Fear Not! Is an Interactive Virtual Environment (IVE) developed for education against bullying behaviours in schools [13].

Our novel contribution is the design and development of an interactive virtual environment simulation with virtual humans towards teaching and training health care workers in clinical best practices associated with hand hygiene.

Table 1. Description and screenshots of the tutorial, interactive training, and feedback phases of the hand hygiene training simulation

Description	*Screenshots*
1. Tutorial Phase: Dr. Evan welcomes the trainee to the hand hygiene training simulation.	
Dr. Evan informs the trainee that he will be tested in the next session after the tutorial on Five Moments of hand hygiene, and must pay attention to his instructions and demonstrations in the tutorial session.	
Dr. Evan then teaches each condition of the Five Moments of hand hygiene by providing verbal and non-verbal instruction and demonstration. In this example, Dr. Evan teaches the first moment of hand hygiene, which is to wash your hands before contact with a patient. Clockwise the screen shots on the right show the instruction of the first moment of hand hygiene as provided by Dr. Evan, followed by a demonstration where Simon (the virtual healthcare worker) washes his hands using an alcohol based sanitizer, and then proceeds to appropriately meet the patient.	
2. Training Phase: Dr. Evan presents ten randomly generated scenarios for the trainee to evaluate whether Simon is interacting with the patient in accordance with the proper protocols of hand hygiene or not. Screen shots of Simon interacting with the virtual patient and the evaluation interface where the trainee records his observations are shown on the right respectively.	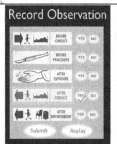

3. Feedback Phase:
Dr. Evan then provides feedback on how well the trainee performed in the interactive training session and presents the trainee with a score. The simulation then allows the trainee to revisit the tutorial, interactive training, and feedback sessions via the simulation interface.

2 Interactive Training Scenario

The interactive training scenarios are based on the notion of the trainee learning the hand hygiene protocols by playing the part of a health inspector that hospitals now employ in order to monitor compliance with the WHO/CDC recommended Five Moments of hand hygiene procedure. The trainee experiences three main phases in the training simulation. An initial title interface is used to guide the trainee through the simulation; the trainee also has the ability to revisit some of the modules if she wishes to do so. A simulation flow is shown in Figure 1 to highlight the programmatic sequence of events as part of the training simulation. In Table 1, we provide a description and screenshots of sample interactions of the trainee in the tutorial, interactive training, and feedback phases of the virtual agents based hand hygiene protocol training simulation.

Here are the three main phases of the training simulation:

1. A *tutorial phase* in which the trainee learns the Five Moments of hand hygiene one after another in succession from the virtual instructor "Dr. Evan". The virtual doctor informs the trainee that she will be tested in the Five Moments of hand hygiene procedure after the tutorial session. Dr. Evan then teaches the trainee the situations pertaining to each moment of hand hygiene with demonstrations, using speech, gestures and expressions.

2. An *interactive training phase* in which the trainee experiences ten randomly generated scenarios consisting of a virtual nurse "Simon" interacting with virtual patients in a hospital environment. The trainee has to evaluate if Simon follows the proper hand hygiene procedure after observing each scenario in which Simon interacts with virtual patients and/or their surroundings. The trainee records her observations via an evaluation interface.

3. A *feedback phase* in which the trainee receives a score of her performance in accurately identifying the cases when Simon in each of the randomly generated training scenario acted in accordance with the Five Moments of hand hygiene.

In the interactive training phase, the user is presented with ten scenarios in which the virtual nurse Simon interacts with the patient correctly or incorrectly according to the Five Moments of hand hygiene. These random scenarios are defined as follows. For moment one (before touching a patient), Simon either washes his hands or does not before shaking hands with the patient. In moments two (before clean/aseptic procedure) and three (after body fluid exposure), Simon gives the patient an injection and may or may not wash his hands before or afterwards. Simon checks the patient's pulse in the fourth moment (after touching a patient) and may or may not wash his hands afterwards. And, in the fifth moment (after touching the patient's surroundings) Simon types on the computer next to the patient to demonstrate touching the patient's surroundings and then may or may not wash his hands. The animations are exhibited in random order every time the simulation scenarios are initiated.

3   Components of the Simulation Framework

All assets of the simulation were created in the Blender Open Source Framework [14], with the exception of the virtual humans which were modeled using Poser 8. The Blender game engine was chosen due to its integrated development environment for modeling, texturing, animation, simulation logic, and real-time animation engine characteristics. The built-in Python script engine was used to script behaviors for the virtual humans, simulation events, as well as the 2D evaluation interface.

Blender also provided the support for many advanced areas of virtual human modeling and animation such as armature-based and mesh-based animations, and integrating motion capture data for virtual humans. On the graphical rendering side Blender provided features such as occlusion and view frustum culling, networking, and collision detection. Poser 8 was used to render lip-synched animations with respect to the interactive speech behaviors of Dr. Evan.

In order to create training simulations that can be evaluated in a future usability study by health care workers in the University of Iowa Hospital, we decided to graphically recreate the virtual training environment as close as possible to the real UI hospital. This will enable the training experience to be as meaningful as possible for the trainees at the UI hospital. CAD files of the UI hospital were used in modeling the environment, and objects such as doors, beds, medical equipment were used to populate the scene according to the locations of objects provided in the CAD files.

a.   Design of Dr. Evan, Simon and the Virtual Patient:
In order to make our virtual humans believable we endeavored to model and animate realistic virtual characters in our training simulation. Poser 8 was used to create character geometry as well as the clothing and accessories such as hair. The resulting high polygon model was imported into Blender and was decimated in order to enable real time rendering of the characters. We employed techniques such as normal mapping and retopology that mimics the high polygon model very closely to generate highly realistic appearance, which can be animated in real time. The final virtual humans used in the simulation were around 7,000 polygons each. Once the models were complete, an armature and facial rig was created.

b.   Armature and Facial Rigging:
In order to animate the virtual humans, an advanced armature rig was created in the Blender environment. The armature was developed to support inverse kinematics on the spine, arms, fingers, and legs. An advanced facial rig was also created to control facial expressions, and create speech behaviors. A combination of armature bone motion and shape morphing enabled us to create a wide variety of facial and body gestures. Gaze bones were used to animate pre-canned gaze behaviors. The next step was skinning, where using the Blender "painting" feature we mapped the mesh to the armature. A weighted mapping procedure was used to account for the influence of a group of adjacent bones on the underlying mesh.

c.   Animation and Scenario Modeling:
Verbal and non-verbal actions of the agents were created using a series of keyframes in the Blender Action Editor. Keyframes were used to define every movement for

each bone in the armature. The Blender Interpolation Graph Editor interpolates the animation between keyframes. Every keyframe is composed of seven parameters pertaining to location, quaternion rotation, and scale of a single bone. The action editor is a collection of keyframes that defines an action i.e. administering an injection or washing hands. Our initial efforts to keyframe all the animations turned out to be tedious and time consuming. Therefore, we imported motion capture files from the Carnegie-Mellon Motion Database [15] pertaining to walking, hand washing, and patient intervention.

The Blender non-linear editor was used to encapsulate the actions into strips that are stacked and blended to create smooth animations. The non-linear editor facilitated the compositing, blending, and interpolating multiple strips of animation. Facial expressions were controlled using a set of keyframed shape keys. A shape action contains an interpolation graph that controls the influence of the shape key. A combination of shape-key animations creates a wide variety of expressions, such as blinking, smiling and frowning. These animations were evoked at appropriate times via simple Python scripts towards simulation logic in the Blender non-linear editor.

The agent's armature was parented to a path, and the path had a speed control interpolation graph associated with it, making it easy to control the speed of walking. The non-linear editor also enabled stride bone calculation. A stride bone was used to sync an agent's footsteps to the ground plane. The virtual agent was then parented to a Bezier curve to define the path in the demonstration scenario, and stride bone parameters were set to affix their footsteps on to the floor plane as they proceed along the path.

4 Summary and Future Work

Our novel contribution is a virtual agents based simulation for the teaching and training of health care best practices associated with hand hygiene. The simulation is designed to interactively teach and train hospital workers in the Five Moments of hand hygiene procedure recommended by the CDC and WHO organizations. Our simulation features an interactive virtual doctor "Dr. Evan", a virtual nurse "Simon", and a virtual patient in training scenarios geared towards memorizing, observing, and utilizing the Five Moments of hand hygiene procedure.

Future work will focus on the evaluation of our hand hygiene simulation by health care workers at the University of Iowa Hospital in teaching and promoting awareness of the Five Moments of hand hygiene. The usability study will also include comparison of our current instruction, interactive training, and feedback system, vs. video based instruction, vs. traditional textual instruction on the effectiveness of learning health care best practices associated with sanitation and hand hygiene.

Acknowledgments. The authors thank Monika Ahuja, Evan Wilcek, Michelle Everett, and Ryan Garman for their assistance. The authors also gratefully acknowledge the US National Institutes of Health, National Institutes of Science, and the University of Iowa Internal Funding Initiative Social and Behavioral Sciences Funding program for their support of our research.

References

1. Jarvis, W.R.: Selected Aspects of the Socioeconomic Impact of Nosocomial Infections: Morbidity, Mortality, Cost, and Prevention. Infection Control and Hospital Epidemiology 7, 552–557 (1996)
2. Boyce, J.M., Pittet, D.: Guidelines for Hand Hygiene in Health-Care Settings: Recommendations of the Healthcare Infection Control Practices Advisory Committee and the HIC-PAC/SHEA/APIC/IDSA Hand Hygiene Task Force. Infection Control and Hospital Epidemiologyl 23, S3–S41 (2002)
3. Pittet, D., Hugonnet, S., Harbarth, S., Mourouga, P., Sauvan, V., Touveneau, S., Perneger, T.V.: Effectiveness of a Hospital-Wide Programme to Improve Compliance with Hand Hy-giene Infection Control Programme. Lancet 9238, 1307–1312 (2000)
4. Erasmus, V., Daha, T.J., Brug, H., Richardus, H.H., Behrendt, M.D., Vos, M.C., Van Beeck, E.F.: Systematic Review of Studies on Compliance with Hand Hygiene Guidelines in Hospital Care. Infection Control and Hospital Epidemiology 31, 283–294 (2010)
5. Pessoa-Silva, C.L., Hugonnet, S., Pfister, R., Touveneau, D.S., Posfay-Barbe, K., Pittet, D.: Reduction of Health Care Associated Infection Risk in Neonates by Successful Hand Hygiene Promotion. Pediatrics 120(2), e382–e390 (2007)
6. Pittet, D., Allegranzi, B., Boyce, J.M.: The World Health Organization Guidelines on Hand Hygiene in Health Care and Their Consensus Recommendations. Infection Control and Hospital Epidemiology. World Health Organization World Alliance for Patient Safety First Global Patient Safety Challenge Core Group of Experts 30, 611–622 (2009)
7. Boyce, J.M.: Hand Hygiene Compliance Monitoring: Current Perspectives From the USA. Journal of Hospital Infections 70(S1), 2-7 (2007)
8. Johnson, K., Dickerson, R., Raij, A., Lok, B., Jackson, J., Shin, M.C., Hernandez, J., Stevens, A., Lind, D.S.: Experiences in Using Immersive Virtual Characters to Educate Medical Communication Skills. In: Proceedings of the IEEE Virtual Reality Conference, pp. 179–186 (2005)
9. Parsons, T., Kenny, P., Rizzo, A.: Virtual Human Patients for Training of Clinical Interview and Communication Skills. In: Proceedings of the Virtual Reality and Associated Technology Conference (2008)
10. Marinopoulos, S.S., Dorman, T., Ratanawongsa, W.L.M., Ashar, B.H., Magaziner, J.L., Miller, R.G., Thomas, P.A., Prokopowicz, G.P., Qayyum, R., Bass, E.B.: Effectiveness of Continuing Medical Education. Evidence Report/Technology Assessment No. 149, Publication 07-E006, Agency for Healthcare Research and Quality, Rockville, MD (January 2007)
11. Hill, R.W., Belanich, J., Lane, H.C., Core, M., Dixon, M., Forbell, E., Kim, J., Hart, J.: Pedagogically Structured Game-Based Training: Development of the Elect Bilat Simulation. In: Proceedings of the 25th Army Science Conference (2006)
12. Babu, S., Suma, E., Barnes, T., Hodges, L.F.: Can Immersive Virtual Humans Teach Social Conversational Protocols? In: Proceeding of the IEEE Int'l Conf. Virtual Reality, pp. 215–218 (2007)
13. Aylett, R., Figueiredo, R., Louchart, S., Dias, J., Paiva, A.: Making It Up as You Go Along – Improvising Stories for Pedagogical Purposes. In: Gratch, J., Young, M., Aylett, R.S., Ballin, D., Olivier, P. (eds.) IVA 2006. LNCS (LNAI), vol. 4133, pp. 304–315. Springer, Heidelberg (2006)
14. Mullen, T.: Mastering Blender. Wiley Publishing, Indianapolis (2009)
15. Carnegie Mellon Motion Capture Database, http://mocap.cs.cmu.edu/

Modeling Behavioral Manifestations of Coordination and Rapport over Multiple Conversations

Speaking Rate as a Relational Indicator for a Virtual Agent

Daniel Schulman and Timothy Bickmore

College of Computer and Information Science, Northeastern University
360 Huntington Ave – WVH 202, Boston MA 02115
{schulman,bickmore}@ccs.neu.edu

Abstract. Many potential applications of virtual agents require an agent to conduct multiple conversations with users. An effective and engaging agent should modify its behavior in realistic ways over these conversations. To model these changes, we gathered a longitudinal video corpus of human-human counseling conversations, and constructed a model of changes in articulation rates over multiple conversations. Articulation rates are observed to increase over time, both within a single conversation and across conversations. However, articulation rates increased mainly for words spoken separately from larger phrases. We also present a preliminary evaluation study, showing that implementing such changes in a virtual agent has a measurable effect on user attitudes toward the agent.

Keywords: Speaking Rate, Embodied Conversational Agent, Relational Agent, Rapport.

1 Introduction

Embodied Conversational Agents (ECAs) simulate face-to-face conversation with users by reproducing human verbal and nonverbal conversational behavior as much as possible [1]. ECAs have been employed in a variety of applications domains, including education, counseling, and social engagement. Many of these application domains require that an ECA have multiple conversations with each user, possibly over a long period of time. Since the conversational behavior of human dyads is known to change over time as their relationship evolves [2,3], it is important that ECAs be able to simulate this behavior as well.

Toward that goal, we discuss a preliminary investigation of one aspect of verbal behavior: changes in the articulation rate of speech, defined here in terms of the duration of words spoken, excluding any silences or pauses. Our methodology is based on the collection and analysis of a longitudinal corpus of human-human interaction, in which we examine multiple conversations over time between the

J. Allbeck et al. (Eds.): IVA 2010, LNAI 6356, pp. 132–138, 2010.
© Springer-Verlag Berlin Heidelberg 2010

same participants, in the context of developing interpersonal relationships. In our initial analysis, we construct a model of changes in articulation rates, both within and across conversations. We then present a preliminary evaluation in which some of the changes predicted by this model are incorporated in an ECA.

2   Related Work

A number of studies have examined the effects of speaking rates on listeners, focusing particularly on how changes in speaking rate affect the listener's perceptions of the speaker's personality. Smith et. al. found that increased speaking rate was perceived as increased competence, while perceived benevolence was highest at normal speech rates, and lower otherwise [4]. Nass and Lee showed that users perceived synthesized computer speech as more extroverted when it was generated with greater speech rate, volume, pitch, and pitch variation. Users tended to prefer speech perceived as matching their own introversion/extroversion [5].

Several researchers have examined differences in speaking rates, and other features of verbal behavior, usually with a cross-sectional design (comparing friends to strangers or acquaintances). Planalp and Benson showed that observers could judge with 80% accuracy whether audiotaped conversations were between strangers or friends. Several cues that observers commonly cited (although a small percentage of all cited) were related to articulation rates, such as "pace", "tone of voice", and "smoothness" [6]. Yuan et. al. compared several large corpora of conversational telephone speech in English and Chinese. Corpora consisting primarily of conversations between friends or family members had a higher average speaking rate than those consisting primarily of conversations between strangers [7].

Cassell et. al. compared dialogue between dyads who were either friends or strangers, using a direction-giving task. Friends used significantly more turns per minute than strangers, although it is not known whether this was due to changes in speaking rate. Friends also used significantly fewer acknowledgments when receiving directions [3].

3   A Longitudinal Corpus of Counseling Conversations

We gathered a video corpus intended to allow exploratory analysis that could identify possible changes in verbal and nonverbal behavior over multiple conversations. The corpus contains multiple conversations over time between the same people, and thus can be used for longitudinal analysis. This allows us to examine changes over time and separate them from differences between individuals.

We also wished to focus on a real-world task that naturally would involve multiple conversations over time, and in which changes in verbal and nonverbal behavior might plausibly have an effect on task outcomes. Therefore, we chose to study health behavior change counseling for exercise promotion, an area to which conversational agents have been applied (e.g., [8]). The rapport and relationship between counselor and client is known to affect outcomes [9], and there has been research interest in verbal and nonverbal behavior that may be related to the development of this relationship (e.g., [2]).

3.1   Procedure

Participants were asked to complete six sessions, at approximately one week intervals. The counselor was instructed to conduct a short conversation with each participant at each session, and that the conversation should encourage the participant to increase his or her daily physical activity. The conversations were video recorded.

Six participants were recruited via ads placed on craigslist.org. Participants were required to be not currently exercising regularly. Participants ranged in age from 22 to 65, although all but two were 25 or younger (median age 24). Five of the six participants were female. A single counselor (also female) interacted with all participants.

A total of 32 conversations were recorded; five of the six participants completed all six sessions. The resulting corpus comprises approximately 8.3 hours of recorded video, with approximately 100,000 words of spoken dialogue.

4   A Model of Changes in Articulation Rate

We performed a full word-aligned orthographic transcription of the corpus, producing an estimate of the duration of every spoken word. The corpus was also divided into "segments", with a segment consisting of a sequence of words by a speaker uninterrupted by silence. Note that a single turn or utterance by a speaker may contain multiple segments, if it included any intra-turn pauses. To account for differences in word lengths, the duration of each word was normalized by the number of phonemes, determined using the CMU pronouncing dictionary (version 0.7a; http://www.speech.cs.cmu.edu/cgi-bin/cmudict), with manual correction for words that did not appear in the dictionary.

We used a linear mixed-effect model to account for the longitudinal nature of the data [10], analyzed with Bayesian methods using R 2.10 and the MCMCglmm package [11]. Uninformative or very weakly-informative prior distributions were used for all effects.

To model change across conversation, we included a fixed effect of the number of previous sessions, while random effects allow for variability across subjects. Two covariates were motivated by prior work: (a) the position of a segment within a conversation [12], and (b) the length of a segment [13]. Inspection of preliminary models showed that predictions were poor for single-word segments (words bounded by silence); these had longer duration than predicted, even including segment length as a covariate. Therefore, we included, as an additional predictor ("Multiword"), whether a word was in a multi-word segment.

4.1   Results

Table 1 shows the full regression model. Word durations in later conversations tended to be shorter than word durations in earlier conversations. However, this change was observed *only* for single-word segments (shown by the fixed effects

Table 1. A Mixed-effect Regression Model Predicting Articulation Rate (average seconds per phoneme, log-transformed)

Parameter	Fixed Effect[b]		Random Effect[b]	
Intercept	-2.070***	[-2.120,-2.021]	0.031	[0.017,0.087]
Session[c]	-0.015**	[-0.024,-0.005]	0.003	[0.001,0.011]
Who[d]	0.100*	[-0.002,0.176]	0.066	[0.034,0.208]
Multiword[e]	-0.592***	[-0.616,-0.564]		
Pos[f]	-0.045***	[-0.057,-0.035]		
Session × Who	0.002	[-0.001,0.005]		
Who × Multiword	-0.065***	[-0.091,-0.037]		
Session × Multiword	0.012**	[0.005,0.019]		
Multiword × Len[g]	-0.105***	[-0.108,-0.100]		
Multiword × Pos	0.038***	[0.025,0.049]		
Multiword × Len × Pos	-0.004*	[-0.008,-0.001]		

[a] *p<.05, **p<.01, ***p<.001
[b] Posterior mode and 95% credible interval.
[c] Previously completed sessions (starts at zero).
[d] 0=counselor, 1=client
[e] 1 if the word is part of a longer segment, 0 otherwise.
[f] Number of segment within a conversation, centered and standardized.
[g] Length of segment in words, log-transformed, centered, and standardized.

"Session" and "Session × Multiword"). Similarly, within conversations, words near the end of a conversation tended to be shorter, again largely for single word segments (shown by "Pos" and "Multiword × Pos").

Given these results, we next examined the occurrences of single-word segments within the corpus. The most common such words ("okay", "yeah", "mm-hmm", "um", "so", "yknow", "and", "right", "but", "great"; approximately 70% of all instances), appear to consist mainly of backchannels and acknowledgements (e.g., "okay", "yeah"), and discourse markers (e.g., "so", "and").

In sum, we observed that the durations of single-word acknowledgements and discourse markers decreased over time, both within a single conversation and across multiple conversations.

5 A Preliminary Study of the Effects of Articulation Rate Changes in Conversational Agents

The changes predicated by the model are quite subtle: after five conversations, the average speaker increased their articulation rate approximately 8% (and only on specific words). We conducted a preliminary evaluation in order to test whether the model-predicted differences, when incorporated in a conversational agent's speech, were perceptible to users, and whether they had any measurable effect on attitudes toward the agent. Participants had two similar conversations, with two similar agents, which differed in articulation rates: In the SLOW condition, the articulation rate of the agent's speech was left unchanged, while in FAST, the articulation rate of acknowledgments and discourse markers was increased by the amount our model predicted would occur after five conversations (8%), and also increased at the predicated rate within a conversation (to a total of approximately 13%).

5.1 Apparatus and Measures

The two agents were chosen to have a similar appearance, and both used synthesized speech with synchronized nonverbal behavior. Participants used multiple-choice spoken input, with up to 6 utterance choices displayed by the agent at each turn. However, the agents were controlled via a Wizard-of-Oz setup [14], in order to eliminate any possible effects of speech recognition errors.

Both dialogues consisted of social dialogue only. The dialogues were designed to be approximately the same length (about 40 turns , varying slightly based on participant choices), and contained similar (but not identical) topics. Topics with a low intimacy level were used, such as weather, local sports, and features of the experiment location. Dialogues were manually tagged to identify acknowledgments and discourse markers that should increase in articulation rate when in the FAST condition.

Perceived rapport was assessed with the bond subscale of the Working Alliance Inventory [15] following each conversation. Participant introversion/extroversion was assessed using a 16-item subset of the Interpersonal Adjective Scales [16].

5.2 Procedure

The order of conditions, agents, and dialogues were randomly assigned. Following a demographics questionnaire, participants received brief instruction in how to interact with the agent. Participants were told they would be interacting with two different agents, but were not informed of differences in articulation rates, or any other specific differences. The experimenter left the room during the conversations, and returned to administer questionnaires afterward.

5.3 Results

8 participants (5 female, mean age 34.6, age range 23–63) were recruited via a contact list of potential participants who had expressed interest in previous studies but had not participated. All reported high levels of computer proficiency, and all but one were college graduates.

No significant difference was observed in perceived rapport (Working Alliance Inventory) between the SLOW and FAST speech (paired $t(7)=-0.296$, $p=0.78$). However, given results by Nass and Lee [5], we also analyzed the effect of the participant's extroversion. A linear regression showed that extroversion predicted the difference in perceived rapport between SLOW and FAST ($R^2=0.55$,

$F(1,6)=7.39, p=0.035$). Participants who were more extroverted were more likely to report a higher perceived rapport in the FAST condition.

Only one participant reported noticing a difference in speaking rate. When participants were asked to "guess" which agent spoke faster, 5 of 8 identified the correct agent; this is not significantly different from chance ($\chi^2(1)=0.5$, $p=0.48$). Therefore, we cannot conclude that participants consciously distinguish this difference in speaking rates in conversation.

6 Discussion

Our corpus shows evidence of changes in articulation rates over time, both within conversations and across multiple conversations. This complements results from earlier, cross-sectional studies, providing evidence that these changes in verbal behavior are in fact changes over time rather than pre-existing differences.

We also show a previously unreported nuance: increases in articulation rates were observed mainly in words bordered by silence, and these words were often acknowledgments or discourse markers. One possible explanation is that these words are the ones most easily spoken faster; longer segments of speech already tend to have faster articulation rates [13]. Alternatively, markers such as "so" may be used by speakers to coordinate their interaction. Faster articulation rates may indicate a decrease in explicit coordination as speakers increase in familiarity.

We show some preliminary evidence that changes in articulation rates of a speaker may have a measurable effect, even though listeners may not necessarily be able to consciously perceive the changes. However, the characteristics of the listener may be equally important: Extroverted listeners may prefer a speaker that "jumps right in" with a speaking style that indicates greater familiarity.

Both studies are limited by a small number of participants, and the corpus includes only a single counselor. Additional research is needed to determine whether these results will generalize across people, languages or dialects, or cultural backgrounds. To address some of these limitations, we plan a longitudinal evaluation study, in which participants have multiple conversations with an ECA designed according to the model developed here.

This work discusses how only a single aspect of verbal behavior changes over time. However, the observation that there are changes in verbal and/or nonverbal behavior both across and within conversations has implications for researchers working with virtual agents. We believe that the ability of virtual agents to change their behavior in realistic ways over time is important for making them more lifelike, engaging, and effective, especially as people work with them for longer periods of time.

Acknowledgments. Thanks to Jenna Zaffini for her work in collecting the video corpus, Connor Westfall for assistance with the evaluation study, and to the other members of the Relational Agents Group for their help and many useful discussions.

References

1. Cassell, J.: Embodied conversational agents. MIT Press, Cambridge (2000)
2. Tickle-Degnen, L., Gavett, E.: Changes in nonverbal behavior during the development of therapeutic relationships. In: Philippot, P., Feldman, R.S., Coats, E.J. (eds.) Nonverbal behavior in clinical settings, pp. 75–110. Oxford University Press, New York (2003)
3. Cassell, J., Gill, A.J., Tepper, P.A.: Coordination in conversation and rapport. In: Workshop on Embodied Language Processing, Association for Computational Linguistics, pp. 41–50 (2007)
4. Smith, B.L., Brown, B.L., Strong, W.J., Rencher, A.C.: Effects of speech rate on personality perception. Language and Speech 18(2), 145–152 (1975)
5. Nass, C., Lee, K.M.: Does computer-generated speech manifest personality? an experimental test of similarity-attraction. In: CHI 2000: Proceedings of the SIGCHI conference on Human factors in computing systems, pp. 329–336. ACM, New York (2000)
6. Planalp, S., Benson, A.: Friends' and acquaintances' conversations I: Perceived differences. Journal of Social and Personal Relationships 9(4), 483–506 (1992)
7. Yuan, J., Liberman, M., Cieri, C.: Towards an integrated understanding of speaking rate in conversation. In: International Conference on Spoken Language Processing, INTERSPEECH-2006 (2006)
8. Bickmore, T.: Relational agents: Effecting change through human-computer relationships (2003)
9. Horvath, A.O., Symonds, D.B.: Relation between working alliance and outcome in psychotherapy: A meta-analysis. Journal of Counseling Psychology 38(2), 139–149 (1991)
10. Verbeke, G., Molenberghs, G.: Linear Mixed Models for Longitudinal Data. Springer, Heidelberg (2001)
11. Hadfield, J.: MCMC methods for multi-response generalized linear mixed models: The MCMCglmm R package. Journal of Statistical Software 33(2), 1–22 (2009)
12. Quené, H.: Multilevel modeling of between-speaker and within-speaker variation in spontaneous speech tempo. The Journal of the Acoustical Society of America 123(2), 1104–1113 (2008)
13. Nakatani, L.H., O'Connor, K.D., Aston, C.H.: Prosodic aspects of american english speech rhythm. The Journal of the Acoustical Society of America 69(S1), 82 (1981)
14. Dahlbäck, N., Jönsson, A., Ahrenberg, L.: Wizard of oz studies: why and how. In: IUI 1993: Proceedings of the 1st international conference on Intelligent user interfaces, pp. 193–200. ACM, New York (1993)
15. Horvath, A.O., Greenberg, L.S.: Development and validation of the working alliance inventory. Journal of Counseling Psychology 36(2), 223–233 (1989)
16. Wiggins, J.S.: A psychological taxonomy of trait-descriptive terms: The interpersonal domain. Journal of Personality and Social Psychology 37(3), 395–412 (1979)

DelsArtMap: Applying Delsarte's Aesthetic System to Virtual Agents

Michael Nixon, Philippe Pasquier, and Magy Seif El-Nasr

School of Interactive Arts and Technology, Simon Fraser University

Abstract. Procedural animation presents significant advantages for generating content, especially character animation, in virtual worlds. Artistic, aesthetic models have much to offer procedural character animation to help address the loss of expressivity that sometimes results. In particular, we examine the contribution of François Delsarte's system and formalize it into a mapping between emotional states and static character poses. We then show an implementation of this model in UNITY.

1 Introduction

Artificial agents have been defined as computer systems capable of flexible autonomous action in some environment in order to meet their design objectives [18]. Intelligent virtual agents (IVAs) are a particular type of artificial agents embodied with a graphical front-end or a physical robotic body. Conversational agents are IVAs capable of engaging in interactions with humans employing verbal or non verbal means. These have been proven useful as a way to progress towards more natural human-computer interactions [14]. This often involves the portrayal of a believable human character, which goes beyond realism to incorporate an aesthetic agenda.

Believability is the term that has arisen to describe how natural an agent seems, and it relies on the coordinated and consistent expression of meaningful body movements. In particular, Bates took his cue from animators and argues that the realism of the work is dependant largely on the agents' ability to demonstrate true-to-life emotional responses [4]. He provides three requirements for this: defining the emotions clearly though a system of emotional classification, demonstrating a thought process behind setting the emotional state, and determining the appropriate timing and volume of the emotion to duplicate recognizable and realistic emotional responses. The result is characters that are better quality and provide a broader appeal to audiences who want socially and emotionally engaging experiences [8].

Our work addresses the gap between psychology and animation that affects those intelligent virtual agents using a graphical body. The value of basing such characters on sound models has already been shown [8]; however, reliably communicating these psychological and emotional states is an unsolved problem. Ideally, these characters would be capable of a full range of meaningful expressions, as this would meaningfully contribute to their ability to convey emotions and personality traits.

J. Allbeck et al. (Eds.): IVA 2010, LNAI 6356, pp. 139–145, 2010.

Given the need for a system that makes connections between emotion and personality models and resulting animation, we investigate the work of the artist François Delsarte. It provides interesting insights into the meanings behind movement and provides a foundation that is trusted by artists for aesthetically pleasing and meaningful movement. Our contribution is to formalize Delsarte's observations into a mapping between emotional states and poses. We also show an implementation in the UNITY Game Development Tool [1]. This provides a platform for future user studies.

2 Background

The trend towards lifelike computer characters started in the late 1990's, and the research agenda of the Oz Project at Carnegie Mellon University both exemplified and helped to define it. Their 'broad agents' [5] incorporated an emotional component (Em, based on the OCC model of appraisal) and a behavioural component (Hap, a goal-based tree structure) and demonstrated how sound representations of personality and emotion could lead to believable virtual characters. However, for all its foundational contribution to believable characters, the work generally leaves animation techniques unaddressed. The Edge of Intention, the animated world they produced, did not use human characters. As such, there remains work to be done in the development of an aesthetic model for human movement to fit between the emotional and behavioural components.

Depicting believable characters faces two major challenges: on the one hand, the deeply important emotions that motivate actions, and the personality traits that characterize them, must be portrayed. In fact, being able to "infer emotional or mental state by observing ... behavior [3]" is an accepted definition of believability. Lifelike behaviour also leverages a powerful property of virtual environments to create a positive feedback loop of engagement and active belief creation [11].

Delsarte (1811-1871) was a French artist who wanted to improve actors' training and so created a system of expression based on his systematic observations of the human body and its interactions. This artistic aesthetic system links meaning and motion and has influenced both acting and modern dance [15]. Though "couched in a language and terminology from the 1800s that strikes a 21st century reader as perhaps quaint and metaphysical", this technique structurally describes how attitude and personality are conveyed by body postures and gestures [10].

Delsarte's primary law is that of correspondence, because he believed that each gesture is expressive of an internal meaning. This forms the foundation for connecting emotions and traits to motion within his system. Delsarte also provides several principles of motion, including the meaning of certain zones of the body, and the meaning of different directions of movement. Motions away from the centre (e.g. the body) are termed "excentric" and have relation to the exterior world. Motions towards the centre are termed "concentric" and have relation to the interior. Balanced motion is "normal" and moderates between the two. Finally, these three provide nine possible combination poses per body zone for which Delsarte provides the meaning. These poses form the basis for the mapping we describe in Section 3.

Delsarte's system has been the basis and inspiration for artists, although it has not been thoroughly validated across the entire body. His work on hand positions has been studied [10] through the use of participant observation. Results showed that people interpret the animation of an un-textured hand according to Delsarte's mapping "remarkably consistently." This study's methodology also provides a model for future studies through the comparison of a pose from Delsarte and its perceived perception. The use of Delsarte's system by animators [12] has also been studied using a similar methodology and indicates that it can lead to emotions being conveyed more accurately. These results indicate that Delsarte's system is a promising starting point for creating believability in IVAs; however, the real test lies in formalizing these observations into a validated model that links psychological states and movement.

Laban Movement Analysis (LMA) is another system that has been used as the basis for the animation of intelligent virtual agents. LMA [9] grew out of the theories of Rudolf Laban (1879-1958) and provides a rich vocabulary for describing and analyzing movement. This focus on rich description as opposed to prescriptive instruction is what distinguishes LMA from Delsarte's movement system. One IVA system that uses LMA is the Jack system [2], which provides a polygonal human model with ranges of motion appropriate for ergonomic evaluations. Its use of movement synthesis is parameterized using Laban's Effort notation to indicate how a motion operates in terms of Laban's effort qualities: Space, Weight, Time, and Flow.

3   DelsArtMap: Emotion Mapping

In this section, we describe our mapping between emotion and character poses. This mapping is based on our reading of Delsarte's principles regarding the meaning of body positions and movement [15,16]. For each given pose, Delsarte states in his own words what is conveyed. The extant illustrations from Delsarte's pupils demonstrate our source material as to what each pose could look like. Our mapping formalizes Delsarte's principles and correspondences. The possible uses of this mapping include generating key frames for animation, modulating gestures, and posing communicative agents.

DelsArtMap provides a mapping between an emotion and stances for the legs, arms, head, and torso. In order to generate a stance, the character's motivating emotion must be specified, along with the strength of the emotion as a real number in the range $[0, 5]$. As well, the object of the character's emotion or intent can also be specified by providing its position $<x, y, z>$ in the three-dimensional environment. This object can also be unspecified ($<$null$>$). We chose to work with a set of emotions described by researchers [6,17] as universal and unique. They are {Happiness, Pride, Sadness, Fear, Anger, Contempt, Shame, Guilt, Neutral}. Neutral describes a base state without an overt emotion.

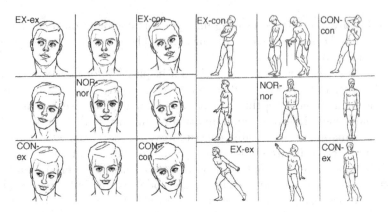

Fig. 1. Left: Delsarte's nine poses for the head; Right: Delsarte's nine poses for legs [15]

This mapping generates poses for the following regions of the body: the arms and hands, the torso, the legs and feet, and the head. However, although Delsarte describes the facial display of emotion – and in fact locates the ability to convey specific emotion there – we are not addressing it at this time, since it is being covered by other projects (e.g. iFace [19]) and rigorously explored through scientific research (e.g. Ekman [7]).

According to Delsarte, body parts move in three directions: excentric (ex), normal (nor), and concentric (con), as described in Section 2. Furthermore, besides the primary "grand division" that has the strongest influence, each action is also sub-divided further according to the same system depending on any moderating effect. Delsarte's system provides meanings for each set of nine-fold possibilities based on their affinity for the body (vital), soul (emotional), or mind (mental). These correspondences can be matched to contemporary models of emotions. For each region and emotion, a grand and sub-division mapping based on Delsarte's principles is provided. The chosen emotion determines which pose is referenced, as shown in Figure 1. The strength of the emotion determines to what degree the pose resembles the specified full-strength division. It is important to note that reducing the strength of the emotion leads the emotion to become more concentric, and to blend with the appropriate zero-strength mapping. We formalize this mapping as:

Definition 1. *DelsArtMap(emotion, strength, object)* $\rightarrow$
Pose[(region$_1$, granddivision$_1$, subdivision$_1$)...(region$_n$, granddivision$_n$, subdivision$_n$] where region $\in$ *{head, arms, legs, torso}, granddivision* $\in$
{excentric, normal, concentric}, subdivision $\in$*{excentric, normal, concentric}*

The poses of the head are well-defined and symmetrical. Their mapping is shown in Table 2. Specifying an object for the emotion is very relevant for the head, because turning away (excentric) or toward (concentric) is relative to an object. Without one, the pose will use the nor grand division with the specified sub-division instead. It is possible, as shown in Table 2, for two emotions to have the same value in a certain region. These emotions are typically recognizable by having separate values in another region.

Figure 1 depicts each of the nine pose combinations. In it, the excentric grand division is shown in the left column, demonstrating the head turned away from the object of its emotion. The right column shows the concentric grand division, with the head turned towards the object. The top row shows the excentric sub-division, with the head raised. The bottom row shows the concentric sub-division, with the head lowered. The middle column and row show the normal grand and sub-division, respectively.

Hand movements frequently serve as emblems with specific meaning, illustrators that accompany verbal messages, regulators that govern turn-taking in speech, and adaptors – fragmented patterns of behaviour that respond to buried triggers [6]. However, the arms and hands also communicate emotions. Delsarte's doctrine of special organs similarly indicates that the meaning of a gesture is coloured by the realm in which it starts and ends. In order to pose the arms and hands, this could be taken into consideration, however, it is much more relevant when movement are generated. Therefore, our mapping is based on Delsarte's observations about the "attitudes" (i.e. stances) of the arms. The chosen emotion again determines which pose is used, according to the mapping in Table 1. Due to the many ways the arms are used, they are the most complicated under Delsarte's system, lacking the symmetry of the head.

Table 1. Arms - emotion mapping

Emotion	0 strength mapping	full strength mapping	full strength Description
Happiness	Normal-Concentric	Excentric-Normal	Arms extended from shoulders
Pride	Normal-Normal	Normal-Excentric	Elbows bent, hands on hips
Sadness	Normal-Concentric	Normal-Concentric	Arms hanging at sides
Fear	Normal-Concentric	Concentric-Concentric	Arms hanging behind body
Anger	Normal-Excentric	Excentric-Excentric	Arms extended full in front
Contempt	Normal-Normal	Concentric-Normal	Arms crossed over chest
Shame	Normal-Concentric	Excentric-Concentric	Arms hang in front of body
Guilt	Normal-Concentric	Excentric-Concentric	Arms hang in front of body
Neutral	n/a	Normal-Concentric	Arms hang at sides

The chosen emotion determines which pose from Figure 1 is used, according to the mapping in Table 2. The legs start posed to face the object of their character's emotion, if one is specified. In Figure 1, the excentric grand division of the legs is demonstrated in the left column, showing the more outgoing poses. The right column shows the concentric grand division, with its 'shrinking' poses.

Table 2. Left: Head - emotion mapping; **Right:** Legs - emotion mapping

Emotion	0-strength	full strength	0-strength	full strength
Happiness	Normal-Normal	Normal-Excentric	Normal-Normal	Normal-Excentric
Pride	Excentric-Normal	Excentric-Excentric	Excentric-Normal	Excentric-Concentric
Sadness	Concentric-Normal	Concentric-Concentric	Normal-Normal	Normal-Concentric
Fear	Concentric-Normal	Concentric-Concentric	Normal-Normal	Excentric-Normal
Anger	Excentric-Normal	Excentric-Normal	Excentric-Normal	Excentric-Excentric
Contempt	Excentric-Normal	Excentric-Excentric	Excentric-Normal	Excentric-Concentric
Shame	Concentric-Normal	Concentric-Concentric	Concentric-Normal	Concentric-Excentric
Guilt	Concentric-Normal	Concentric-Concentric	Concentric-Normal	Concentric-Concentric
Neutral	n/a	Normal-Normal	n/a	Normal-Normal

According to Delsarte, the torso primarily provides meaning in relation to hand gestures. However, the torso also provides meaning through expansion, indicating excitement or vehemence, and contraction, indicating timidity or prostration. For the purposes of DelsArtMap, the following hold: the torso expands in proportion to the strength of the emotion for the following: happiness, pride, anger, and contempt. The torso contracts accordingly for the following: sadness, anger, shame, and guilt.

4   Implementation

The mapping described above in Section 3 is implemented within the UNITY Game Development Tool [1]. Within UNITY, a fully "rigged" humanoid character created by Chelsea Hash at the NYU Social Game Lab is controlled by the DelsArtMap mapping, which we implemented in the C# language. Since UNITY neatly exports to a web format viewable with a free plugin download, the system [13] and source code is available online at http://meinleapen.com/delsartmap/delsartmap.html.

5   Conclusion

As we observed in Section 1, the coordinated and consistent expression of meaningful body movements is an important component of believability. This is particularly important to consider when procedurally animating embodied IVAs. In search of a solution, this paper investigates Delsarte's movement system and describes DelsArtMap, a mapping between emotions and poses based on his system. It also demonstrates an implementation of this mapping on a generic humanoid model within the UNITY Game Development Tool where the character moves to take on an emotional pose and amplitude specified by the user. This implementation constitutes an interpretation of how Delsarte's nine-fold body part poses can be turned into joint angles within an animated environment. DelsArtMap shows how Delsarte's observations can be used for the animation of believable characters and provides a framework application for future evaluation and development. The next step is to validate DelsArtMap through a user study using this implementation as a testing framework.

Acknowledgements

We would like to thank the NYU Social Game Lab, led by Dr. Katherine Isbister, for the use of the character model and 3D environment they developed for the 'Emotion in Motion' project (see http://socialgamelab.bxmc.poly.edu/projects/emotionandmotion/).

References

1. UNITY: game development tool (2010), http://unity3d.com/
2. Badler, N.I.: Real-time virtual humans. In: Pacific Conference on Computer Graphics and Applications, pp. 4–13. IEEE Computer Society Press, Seoul (1997)
3. Badler, N.I., Allbeck, J., Zhao, L., Byun, M.: Representing and parameterizing agent behaviors. In: Proceedings of Computer Animation, 2002, pp. 133–143. IEEE Computer Society, Geneva (2002)
4. Bates, J.: The role of emotion in believable agents. Communications of the ACM, Special Issue on Agents 37(7), 122–125 (1994)
5. Bates, J., Loyall, A.B., Reilly, W.S.: An architecture for action, emotion, and social behavior. In: Castelfranchi, C., Werner, E. (eds.) MAAMAW 1992. LNCS, vol. 830, pp. 55–68. Springer, Heidelberg (1994)
6. Ekman, P., Friesen, W.V.: The repertoire of nonverbal behavior: Categories, origins, usage and coding. Semiotica 1, 49–98 (1969)
7. Ekman, P.: Facial expression and emotion. American Psychologist 48, 384–392 (1993)
8. Isbister, K.: Better Game Characters by Design: A Psychological Approach. Morgan Kaufmann, San Francisco (2006)
9. Laban, R.: The mastery of movement. Plays Inc., Boston (1971)
10. Marsella, S., Carnicke, S.M., Gratch, J., Okhmatovskaia, A., Rizzo, A.: An exploration of delsarte's structural acting system. In: Gratch, J., Young, M., Aylett, R.S., Ballin, D., Olivier, P. (eds.) IVA 2006. LNCS (LNAI), vol. 4133, pp. 80–92. Springer, Heidelberg (2006)
11. Murray, J.H.: Hamlet on the Holodeck: The Future of Narrative in Cyberspace. The MIT Press, Boston (1998)
12. Nixon, M.: Enhancing Believability: Evaluating the Application of Delsarte's Aesthetic System to the Design of Virtual Humans. Master's, Simon Fraser University (October 2009)
13. Nixon, M., Pasquier, P., Seif El-Nasr, M.: Delsarte pose system (2010), http://meinleapen.com/delsartmap/delsartmap.html
14. Preece, J., Rogers, Y., Sharp, H., Benyon, D., Holland, S., Carey, T.: Human-Computer Interaction: Concepts And Design. Addison-Wesley, Reading (1994)
15. Shawn, T.: Every Little Movement. Dance Horizons, Brooklyn (1954)
16. Stebbins, G.: Delsarte System of Expression. Dance Horizons, Brooklyn (1977)
17. Wallbott, H.: Bodily expression of emotion. European Journal of Social Psychology 28, 879–897 (1998)
18. Wooldridge, M.: An Introduction to MultiAgent Systems. John Wiley & Sons, Chichester (2009)
19. Zammitto, V., DiPaola, S., Arya, A.: A methodology for incorporating personality modeling in believable game characters. In: Proceedings of International Conference on Games Research and Development (CyberGames), Beijing, China (October 2008)

Backchannel Strategies for Artificial Listeners

Ronald Poppe, Khiet P. Truong, Dennis Reidsma, and Dirk Heylen*

Human Media Interaction Group, University of Twente
P.O. Box 217, 7500 AE, Enschede, The Netherlands
{poppe,truongkp,dennisr,heylen}@ewi.utwente.nl

Abstract. We evaluate multimodal rule-based strategies for backchannel (BC) generation in face-to-face conversations. Such strategies can be used by artificial listeners to determine when to produce a BC in dialogs with human speakers. In this research, we consider features from the speaker's speech and gaze. We used six rule-based strategies to determine the placement of BCs. The BCs were performed by an intelligent virtual agent using nods and vocalizations. In a user perception experiment, participants were shown video fragments of a human speaker together with an artificial listener who produced BC behavior according to one of the strategies. Participants were asked to rate how likely they thought the BC behavior had been performed by a human listener. We found that the number, timing and type of BC had a significant effect on how human-like the BC behavior was perceived.

1 Introduction

We introduce and evaluate strategies to automatically generate listener backchannels in face-to-face interactions between a human speaker and an artificial listener. In our case, the artificial listener is an intelligent virtual agent that aims at sustaining a conversation with a human interlocutor. Backchannels (BCs) are an important aspect of conversation management, specifically for this type of speaker-listener dialog. Their function is to signal attention and interest, without interrupting the speaker's discourse. The use of appropriately timed BCs has been found to improve the speaker's narrative, and increase the amount of time spent speaking [1]. In interactions between a human speaker and an artificial listener, BCs should be automatically generated for the artificial listener. While placement of BCs within the discourse structure is reasonably well understood (see e.g. [2,3]), it is difficult to determine and analyze this lexical structure in real-time. In practice, one has to resort to features that can be obtained with low processing requirements such as gaze direction, pitch slopes and pauses in the speaker's speech (e.g. [4,5]).

Several authors have addressed real-time prediction of BC timing in audio-only settings using machine learning [6,7] or rule-based algorithms [8]. Machine

* The research leading to these results has received funding from the European Community's Seventh Framework Programme (FP7/20072013) under Grant agreement no. 211486 (SEMAINE).

J. Allbeck et al. (Eds.): IVA 2010, LNAI 6356, pp. 146–158, 2010.

learning algorithms can automatically extract decision rules from labeled training samples. These samples must be representative of the target domain. In practice, it is often difficult to interpret the decision rules, which makes generalization to other contexts difficult. This would require retraining and labeled samples must be available for the new domain. To avoid these issues, Ward and Tsukahara [8] manually defined a rule-based algorithm that predicts BCs based on the speaker's pitch contours. They obtained reasonable results while the algorithms are easy to understand and verify.

The above works have considered an audio-only setting, which is different from the face-to-face setting with an artificial listener that we consider in this research. For example, Dittmann and Llewellyn [9] observed that the mere fact that conversational partners can see each other is a signal of attention and thus reduces the need for BCs. Also, the turn-taking process, including BC feedback, is arguably more complex. Duncan [2] identifies speech, gaze and gesture as relevant components of natural turn-taking, while turn-taking in audio-only settings only considers speech. Morency et al. [10] presented one of the few real-time multimodal BC prediction systems. They automatically select features from speech and gaze, and train conditional random fields to model sequential probabilities.

Systems that automatically predict BC timings are usually evaluated using the correlation between the predicted and actually performed BCs. This approach does not take into account individual differences. A given moment where an individual does not provide a BC is not necessary an inappropriate moment for BC feedback. However, in the evaluation of BC prediction algorithms, such a predicted BC would be regarded as a false positive. Individual differences also affect the training of machine learning models as samples without BCs are labeled as negatives which consequently decreases the quality of the model. This issue was addressed by Huang et al. [11], who had observers watch a video of a speaker and indicate where they would provide BCs as if they were actual listeners. They analyzed which BC opportunities were shared by several raters and used these samples as positives. The output of their approach was rated by human observers on believability, rapport, wrong head nods and missed opportunities. This evaluation based on human perception is in contrast with corpus-based evaluation. Even though one would expect that the actual listener would demonstrate human-like BC behavior, there is no guarantee that the behavior will be judged as most human-like. Indeed, Huang et al. found that a face-to-face setting was not best rated by human observers.

In this paper, we focus on face-to-face conversations with an artificial listener and introduce and evaluate several strategies that define BC timings using intuitive rules. We introduce strategies that use features from the speaker's speech and gaze. In addition to multimodal input, we also deliberately generate both visual and vocal BCs. The strategies are evaluated with a human perception experiment where participants judge the naturalness of the artificial listener's BC behavior, performed by a virtual agent. Our samples are short, which allows for a closer analysis of the relative strengths of the different strategies. We investigate the influence of the amount, timing and type of BCs.

We discuss related work on BCs and artificial listeners in the next section. The six BC strategies that we will evaluate are described in Section 3. We present our experiment in Section 4 and discuss the results in Section 5.

2   Related Work

Research into turn-taking behavior defines the person who holds the turn as the speaker and the person who is being addressed as the listener. The term BC feedback was first used by Yngve [3], who described it as messages sent by the listener without the intent to take the turn. Subsequent research focused on the role of BCs within the turn-taking process. Duncan [12] observed that BCs are often used as a response to a speaker's turn-yielding signal, implying that they might be cued by the speaker. BCs take many forms including short vocalizations (e.g. "hmm", "uhhuh"), sentence completions, requests for clarification, brief restatements and bodily manifestations such as head nods [2]. Bavelas et al. [1] identified specific and generic responses. The former are tightly connected to the speaker's narrative, the latter are mere signals of continued attention.

Apart from the role of BCs in conversation, researchers have focused on identifying the nonverbal context of BCs. Dittmann and Llewellyn [13], Duncan [2] and Yngve [3] noted that BCs are often produced after rhythmic units in the speaker's speech, and specifically at the end of grammatical clauses. Kendon [14] and Bavelas et al. [15] looked at the relation between gaze and BCs, and found that the listener is likely to produce a BC when there is a short period of mutual gaze between speaker and listener. These moments usually occur at the end of a speaker's turn.

Corpus-based research revealed that BCs are also often produced when the speaker's speech ends with a rising or falling pitch [5]. Bertrand et al. [4] additionally took into account gaze and lexical features and observed that BCs often appear after nouns, verbs and adverbs. Cathcart et al. [16] further found that BCs are often preceded by a short pause in the speaker's discourse.

These systematics have motivated researchers to train machine learning models to automatically and in real-time predict the timing of BCs given the speaker's discourse. For instance, such systems can be used to insert BC feedback in spoken telephone dialogs. Given the real-time requirements, these systems have to rely on audio features that are easy to extract. Noguchi [6] learned decision trees based on pitch and power features. Okato et al. [7] used Hidden Markov Models where state transitions corresponded to changes in prosodic context. Instead of using a learned model, Ward and Tsukahara [8] manually defined an algorithm for the prediction of BC timing using a small number of rules. It focuses on a sustained lowered pitch within the speaker's utterance.

In face-to-face conversations between a human speaker and an artificial listener, also visual cues from the speaker should be taken into account. Morency et al. [10] automatically selected audio and gaze features extracted from a corpus of training samples. For the prediction of BC timings, they trained conditional random fields, a sequential probabilistic model. Maatman et al. [17] aimed at creating rapport between an artificial listener and a human speaker. They observed several aspects of the speaker's nonverbal behavior, including speech pitch and loudness, gaze, head nods and shakes and posture shifts. A modification of Ward and Tsukahara's algorithm [8] was combined with a mimicking strategy to identify BC opportunities. The approach was evaluated in [18] and was found to improve the overall impression of the communication compared to a similar setting without the animation of BCs. However, they only used head nods as BC type. Huang *et al.* [11] also conducted a human perception experiment to evaluate the quality of their BC strategy, but they also only animated nods.

In natural face-to-face conversations, people use a range of different BC types including nods, vocalizations, smiles and frowns [2]. There is some research on how different BC types are perceived in terms of positivity, politeness and attentiveness. For example, Heylen *et al.* [19] investigated the perception of facial expressions as BCs. Granström *et al.* [20] also took into account systematic variations in the pitch contour of vocalizations. However, this research considered isolated BCs without context such as the speaker's discourse. Given differences in perceived meaning of BC types, it would make sense to explicitly take into account BC type in the generation of an artificial listener's BC behavior. In the research described in this paper, we evaluate several rule-based BC strategies using a human perception experiment. Participants rated fragments of a conversation between a human speaker and an artificial listener who displayed BC behavior according to one of the strategies. We used two different BC types (a nod and a vocalization). We investigate how the amount, timing and type of BC influences the perception of naturalness of the BC behavior.

3   Backchannel Strategies

We define six strategies to determine the placement of listener BCs in real-time based on the speaker's speech, gaze or both. We discuss the strategies below.

- **Copy.** This strategy contains all BCs that have been performed by the actual listener in interaction with the speaker.

- **Random.** An approximation of an Erlang distribution is used to generate BC timings without taking into account any signal from the speaker. We use one normal distribution to model the timing of the first BC, and one to model the time between two BCs. For the generation of BC onsets, we iteratively sample from the distributions until the end of the fragment is reached. We resample when the time between subsequent BCs is below 1s. One random distribution for each strategy-fragment combination is generated.

- **Ward & Tsukahara.** We use the rule by Ward and Tsukahara [8] that has been used for BC prediction in English audio-only settings, reprinted as Algorithm 1.

Algorithm 1. WARD&TSUKAHARA strategy for BC placement

Provide BC feedback upon detection of:
P1 a region of pitch less than the 26th-percentile pitch level and
P2 continuing for at least 110ms,
P3 coming after at least 700ms of speech,
P4 provided that no BC has been output within the preceding 800ms,
P5 after 700ms wait.

– **Gaze.** Several researchers have observed the relation between (mutual) gaze and BCs. In a setting similar to ours, Bavelas *et al.* [15] observed that listeners tend to look at the speaker for fairly long intervals, while speakers would look at the listener for frequent but much shorter periods. When the speaker looks at the listener, this starts a brief period of mutual gaze, in which a BC is likely to occur. Similar observations have been made by Duncan [12] and Kendon [14]. We use this mechanism to determine the timing of BCs based on the speaker's gaze at the listener only, formalized in Algorithm 2.

Algorithm 2. GAZE strategy for BC placement

Provide BC feedback upon detection of:
P1 gaze at the listener,
P2 coming after at least 1000ms of no gaze,
P3 after 500ms wait.

– **Pitch & Pause.** It has been observed that BCs frequently occur in a pause after a speaker's utterance [3,13]. We include this observation in our strategy for BC placement in Algorithm 3. We use a minimum pause duration of 400ms as a compromise between the 200ms as used in Maatman *et al.* [17] and the 700ms used by Ward and Tsukahara [8]. We further take into account the preceding speech. Instead of a region of low pitch, we focus on rising or falling pitches, as suggested by several researchers [9]. Gravano and Hirschberg [5] found in their audio-only corpus that over 80% of all BCs were preceded by either a rising or falling pitch contour.

Algorithm 3. PITCH&PAUSE strategy for BC placement

Provide BC feedback upon detection of:
P1 a pause of 400ms,
P2 preceded by at least 1000ms of speech,
P3 where the last 100ms,
P4 contain a rising or falling pitch of at least 30Hz.
P5 provided that no BC has been output within the preceding 1400ms.

– **Pitch, Pause & Gaze.** In this strategy, we combine the BCs of the GAZE and PITCH&PAUSE strategies, both described above. Our rationale is that both should identify relevant BC locations. To avoid overlapping BCs, we set the minimum time between two BCs to 1s. In a situation where both strategies identify the same locations, the combined strategy will result in similar placement of BCs.

4 Experiment Setup

We conducted a user experiment where human observers rated fragments from actual conversations. We replaced the listener by an artificial listener and generated BC behavior according to the strategies described in the previous section. In this section, we explain the construction of the stimuli and the setup of the experiment.

4.1 Stimuli

We used the Semaine Solid SAL data [21], which contains dialogs between a human listener and a human speaker. The task of the listener was to sustain the conversation with the user, while playing one of four predefined roles with the intention to evoke emotionally colored reactions. We only consider interactions with Prudence, the pragmatic character, played by two different operators.

We extracted speaker fragments bounded by 1.5s of non-speech. We discarded fragments that were shorter than 10s, did not contain BCs or that contained interjections (e.g. "that's good"). From the remaining fragments, we selected 8 samples for each of the two operators. We further removed the listener's vocalizations from the speaker's audio signal. The average sample length was 19.9s, with an average of 2.6 BC per fragment.

Speaking/pause and pitch information were obtained using Praat [22], speaker's gaze towards the listener was annotated manually. For the COPY strategy, we annotated the onset of all BCs. In the case of repeated nods, we took the most articulated nod. When two BCs overlapped in time (e.g. nod and vocal), we annotated a single instance. For the RANDOM strategy, the mean (SD) start of the first BC was at 6.97s (6.20s), and 5.00s (2.73s) between subsequent BCs.

In order to evaluate the BC strategies, we replaced the video of the listener by a virtual agent. We used Elckerlyc [23], a BML realizer that allows for easy control of verbal and nonverbal behavior of the artificial listener. Given that we do not focus on the content of the speaker's utterance, we choose two common generic (see [1]) BCs in face-to-face interaction: a nod and vocalization ("uh-huh"). There is surprisingly little known about potential semantic differences between visual and vocal BCs. Duncan [2] found no difference in the placement within the speaker's discourse. This was also observed by Dittmann and Llewellyn [9], who did note that a nod on average precedes a vocalization by 175ms. The large number of BCs in our sample sets did not allow for a controlled design and we introduced BC type as an uncontrolled variable in our experiment. At each defined BC onset, we randomly animated a nod, a vocalization or a combination of both. We used the same ratios as performed by the actual listeners, calculated over all fragments.

Fig. 1. Example stimulus with artificial listener (left) and actual speaker (right)

We also animated, for each fragment and strategy, the listener's blinks where they occurred in the actual recording. The rationale for this decision is that blinks can sometimes be regarded as BCs, but it is unclear to what extend they can be replaced by a different type of BC. In addition, the use of blinks prevents the artificial listener from looking too static. The final stimuli consisted of the animated listener and the video of the speaker, shown side-by-side (see Figure 1).

4.2   Procedure

The participants were explained they would be participating in an experiment to determine the quality of BC strategies. They were told they would be shown fragments of a conversation between a speaker and an animated listener who would only show nods and blinks, and say "uhhuh". Participants were asked to rate, for each fragment, "how likely do you think the listener's backchannel behavior has been performed by a human listener". They made their judgements by setting a slider that corresponded to a value between 0 and 100. For each fragment, the participants could type in optional remarks. After completing the experiment, they were asked to provide general comments on the study.

Given the large number of combinations (16 fragments and six strategies), we divided fragments into two distinct sets. Each set contained four fragments of each of the two operators, performed with all six BC strategies. Each participant therefore rated 48 samples. We defined a pseudo-random order, with the only constraint that a fragment would not appear twice in succession. Half of the participants viewed the clips in the specified order, the other half in the reverse order. Order and set were crossed to yield four groups.

Due to the different sets of fragments, we formally have two experiments, one for each set. Each experiment has strategy and fragment as within-subjects variable and order as between-subjects variable.

4.3   Participants

We recruited 20 colleagues and doctoral students (4 female, 16 male) with a mean age of 28.4 (min 24, max 55). Each of the participants was assigned randomly to a group with the lowest number of respondents.

5   Results and Discussion

The 20 participants rated in total 960 samples. Initially, we ignored the variable of fragment which allowed us to combine the results of both sets of fragments. We performed a repeated measures ANOVA with set and order as between-subjects variables, and strategy as within-subjects variable. The average score per strategy for each participant was used as the dependent variable. In the analysis, only the variable strategy proved significant ($F(5, 80) = 22.141$, $p < 0.01$). See Figure 2 and Table 1 for an overview and the scores per strategy. Post-hoc analysis revealed significant differences between all pairs of strategies ($p < 0.05$), except between the RANDOM, PITCH&PAUSE and PITCH,PAUSE&GAZE strategies. The high SDs for each strategy are partly explained by differences in rating scores of individual participants. While the average score over all samples was approximately 42, the range for individual participants was between 17 and 62. An analysis with (normalized) z-scores resulted in the same interaction effects.

When looking at the scores of the different strategies, our first observation is that the COPY strategy performed the best on average. This is not surprising as the timing of BCs was performed by the actual listener, although in many cases the animated BC type was different from the type that was actually performed. The relatively low score of the COPY condition might partly be attributed to the BC type. We used two generic BC types, which might not be the most suitable choice in all cases. Also, we expect that part of the lower score can be attributed to inter-personal differences in BC behavior. Several participants reported that they performed BCs based on the speaker's video as if they were the listener.

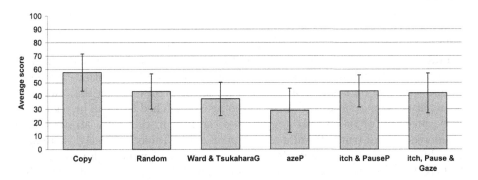

Fig. 2. Average scores (with SD) for all strategies, calculated over all responses

Table 1. Summary of results per strategy. A generated BC is matching if its onset appears within a margin of 200ms of the onset of a BC in the COPY strategy

	COPY	RANDOM	WARD& TSUKAHARA	GAZE	PITCH& PAUSE	PITCH,PAUSE & GAZE
Average score	57.67	43.39	37.69	29.04	43.56	42.03
Standard deviation	13.93	13.26	12.60	16.57	12.02	14.98
Number of BCs	51	47	54	25	25	49
Nods (%)	41.18	48.94	50.00	64.00	48.00	46.94
Nod + vocals (%)	58.82	48.94	50.00	36.00	52.00	53.06
Vocals (%)	0.00	2.13	0.00	0.00	0.00	0.00
Matching precision (%)		12.77	9.26	4.00	40.00	22.49
Matching recall (%)		11.76	9.80	1.96	19.60	21.57

Simultaneously, they monitored the animation of the listener to see how well the animated BCs corresponded with their own BCs.

We further observe that the RANDOM, PITCH&PAUSE and PITCH,PAUSE&GAZE strategies performed relatively well, while the WARD&TSUKAHARA and GAZE strategies received significantly lower scores.

Number of BCs. In a first attempt to explain these differences, we analyzed the effect of the number of BCs. We calculated the correlation between the number of BCs per minute and the average score, for each fragment and each strategy. The effect appeared to be significant ($r(94) = 0.400$, $p < 0.01$). The range of BCs per minute was between 0 and 23. Given this correlation, it is more likely that strategies with a lower number of generated BCs will have lower scores. This is true for the GAZE strategy, but the PITCH&PAUSE strategy scored similar to the RANDOM strategy while only half the number of BCs was generated (see Table 1). Also, the additional BCs of the GAZE strategy did not increase the score of the PITCH,PAUSE&GAZE strategy compared to the PITCH&PAUSE strategy. Clearly, the number of BCs is not the only important factor.

Timing of BCs. To quantitatively investigate the timing of the BCs, we calculated how well these matched the BCs in the COPY strategy. While an unmatched BC does not imply that the BC is inappropriate, a matched BC is likely to be more accurately timed as the COPY strategy was rated as the most natural strategy. We consider a generated BC matching if there is a BC in the corresponding fragment of the COPY strategy whose onset is within a 200ms margin. This margin is strict but realistic given the precise timing that humans use in natural conversations [2]. The percentage of matched BCs can be regarded as the precision of the BC strategy, where the BCs in the COPY strategy are considered ground truth. Results are summarized in Table 1. Clearly, there are large differences between strategies. We note in particular the high precision of the PITCH&PAUSE strategy. Despite the lower number of generated BCs, the absolute number of matching BCs is higher than in the RANDOM strategy (10 and 6, respectively). From these observations, we conclude that both the number and timing of BCs contribute to the level of perceived naturalness.

Of note is also the relatively high precision of the RANDOM strategy. In the RANDOM and COPY strategies there was a BC every 6.77s and 6.24s, respectively. The average matching precision and recall between two uniform random distributions with the probability of observing a BC every 6.5s and a window size of 400ms (200ms in both directions) are 6.15%. The actual precision and recall of the RANDOM strategy are a factor two higher. We are left to conclude that the Erlang distribution that we used to model BCs in the RANDOM strategy is a good approximation of natural BC timings and/or that the timing of the specific set of generated BCs in the RANDOM strategy is exceptionally accurate.

Despite the higher number of BCs in the WARD&TSUKAHARA strategy, the score is much lower compared to the PITCH&PAUSE strategy. We observed that the matching precision of the WARD&TSUKAHARA strategy was low, which leads us to believe that the timing was less accurate. A possible explanation could be that Ward and Tsukahara [8] developed their strategy for audio-only settings and these might be systematically different from face-to-face settings when looking at speech and pitch features. This issue requires further research.

In an attempt to explain the low score for the GAZE strategy, we checked whether BCs would be systematically earlier or later compared to the COPY strategy. We found three times more matching BCs when the final rule of the GAZE strategy (Algorithm 2) was left out (corresponding to an overlap precision of 12.00%). This would also affect the PITCH,PAUSE&GAZE strategy. Again, there is no guarantee that the timing of the modified strategy will result in higher perceived naturalness. For the WARD&TSUKAHARA strategy, we did not find such a systematic bias.

Type of BCs. An important variable that we did not control for in our experiment was the BC type (nod, vocalization or combination of both). We take a closer look at the influence of type on the score. From Table 1, we see that there are some differences in the ratios between strategies, caused by the random factor in the generation of the BCs. We calculated the correlation between score and the percentage of vocalizations per fragment and strategy. We found a significant correlation ($r(94) = 0.201$, $p < 0.05$) which indicates that a higher percentage of vocals was found to be more natural. A fragment with only vocalizations on average scored almost 10 points higher than a fragment without vocalizations. This is somewhat at variance with remarks made by the participants. These reported that vocalizations placed within the speaker's discourse were disruptive and consequently rated lower. However, they also mentioned that vocalizations produced at appropriate moments gave them the impression that the BC behavior was performed by a human listener.

Participants also remarked that they found it unlikely that human listeners would nod when the speaker was not looking at them. It would therefore make sense to use information about the speaker's gaze also in the decision which BC type to animate.

Apart from the difference between individual BC types, the ratios of BC types performed by the actual listener are different from those reported in Dittmann and Llewellyn [9]. In a similar setting with one speaker and one listener they found approximately 60% of the observed BCs were vocalizations alone and around 22% were combinations of a nod and a vocalization. In contrast, we observed around 4% vocalizations alone and 30% combined BCs. One reason for the lower number of vocalizations in our experiment is that we did not select fragments with interjections that overlapped with the speaker's speech. Differences in familiarity, topic and conversation length might also have contributed to the discrepancy. Overall, the participants might have judged the BC behavior less natural due to potential differences in the ratio of BC type that we used and the ratio that is common for the type of conversation we considered in this experiment. However, this was not reported by any of the participants.

Role of blinks. Another factor in our stimuli was the presence of blinks. For each fragment and strategy, we animated blinks at the exact same moments as where the actual listener blinked. Especially for the fragments where no BCs were generated, this made the participants feel that they were still looking at an attentive listener. Several participants explicitly mentioned that they considered some blinks as BCs. Further research is needed to determine in which contexts blinks can be regarded as BCs, and whether they can be exchanged with different BC types.

6   Conclusions and Future Work

We have evaluated rule-based backchannel (BC) strategies in face-to-face conversations with the goal of improving BC behavior for artificial listeners. To this end, we used six different strategies to determine BC timings using features of the speaker's speech and gaze. We animated the BC behavior of an artificial listener for each of the six strategies, for a set of 16 fragments of recorded conversations. Given the multimodal nature of face-to-face conversations, we animated either a visual (nod) or vocal ("uhhuh") BC. Our stimuli consisted of a video of a human speaker and an animation of the artificial listener, shown side by side. In a user experiment, we had participants rate the likeliness that the BC behavior performed by the artificial listener had been performed by a human listener.

It appeared that a higher number of generated BCs increases the naturalness of the BC behavior. In addition, timing proved important. In fact, the strategy where the BC timings were identical to those in the original listener's video was rated the best. A third important yet uncontrolled factor was the type of animated BC. A positive correlation was found between the percentage of vocalizations and the rating. However, several participants in the experiment indicated that they thought it was unlikely that a human listener would produce vocalizations during the speaker's discourse. In our experiment, the use of the speaker's gaze did not result in more human-like BC behavior.

We believe that successful BC strategies in face-to-face conversations should accurately place BCs at a number of key moments. This is exactly what the PITCH&PAUSE strategy does. In addition, there should be a sufficient number of BCs throughout the speaker's turn. The PITCH&PAUSE strategy could therefore be combined with an Erlang model as used in the RANDOM strategy, or the algorithm of Ward and Tsukahara [8]. Finally, we propose to use keyword spotting (e.g. as in [24]) to respond immediately to acknowledgement questions such as "you know?" and "right?".

Future work will be focused on three aspects. First, we are currently working on a corpus-based evaluation, which allows to validate much more data and consequently overcome a potential bias due to the selection of a limited number of fragments [25]. This comes at the cost of a less precise evaluation as a high correlation with the actually performed BCs does not guarantee a high level of naturalness. We are looking at ways to combine the corpus-based evaluation with the annotation approach introduced in [11].

Second, we intend to look closer at the perception of animated BC types in different contexts. Insights in this direction could be used to determine not only when but also how to animate a BC. For example, to produce a visual BC only when the speaker looks at the listener. Finally, we aim to apply our strategies online, to generate BCs for an artificial listener in conversation with a human speaker.

References

1. Bavelas, J.B., Coates, L., Johnson, T.: Listeners as co-narrators. Journal of Personality and Social Psychology 79(6), 941–952 (2000)
2. Duncan Jr., S.: On the structure of speaker-auditor interaction during speaking turns. Language in Society 3(2), 161–180 (1974)
3. Yngve, V.H.: On getting a word in edgewise. In: Papers from the Sixth Regional Meeting of Chicago Linguistic Society, pp. 567–577. Chicago Linguistic Society (1970)
4. Bertrand, R., Ferré, G., Blache, P., Espesser, R., Rauzy, S.: Backchannels revisited from a multimodal perspective. In: Proceedings of Auditory-visual Speech Processing, Hilvarenbeek, The Netherlands, pp. 1–5 (August 2007)
5. Gravano, A., Hirschberg, J.: Backchannel-inviting cues in task-oriented dialogue. In: Proceedings of Interspeech, Brighton, UK, pp. 1019–1022 (September 2009)
6. Noguchi, H., Den, Y.: Prosody-based detection of the context of backchannel responses. In: Proceedings of the International Conference on Spoken Language Processing (ICSLP), Sydney, Australia, pp. 487–490 (November 1998)
7. Okato, Y., Kato, K., Yamamoto, M., Itahashi, S.: Insertion of interjectory response based on prosodic information. In: Proceedings of the IEEE Workshop Interactive Voice Technology for Telecommunication Applications, Basking Ridge, NJ, pp. 85–88 (1996)
8. Ward, N., Tsukahara, W.: Prosodic features which cue back-channel responses in English and Japanese. Journal of Pragmatics 32(8), 1177–1207 (2000)
9. Dittmann, A.T., Llewellyn, L.G.: Relationship between vocalizations and head nods as listener responses. Journal of Personality and Social Psychology 9(1), 79–84 (1968)

10. Morency, L.P., de Kok, I., Gratch, J.: A probabilistic multimodal approach for predicting listener backchannels. Autonomous Agents and Multi-Agent Systems 20(1), 80–84 (2010)
11. Huang, L., Morency, L.-P., Gratch, J.: Parasocial consensus sampling: Combining multiple perspectives to learn virtual human behavior. In: Proceedings of the International Conference on Autonomous Agents and Multiagent Systems (AAMAS), Toronto, Canada (to appear, 2010)
12. Duncan Jr., S.: Some signals and rules for taking speaking turns in conversations. Journal of Personality and Social Psychology 23(2), 283–292 (1972)
13. Dittmann, A.T., Llewellyn, L.G.: The phonemic clause as a unit of speech decoding. Journal of Personality and Social Psychology 6(3), 341–349 (1967)
14. Kendon, A.: Some functions of gaze direction in social interaction. Acta Psychologica 26(1), 22–63 (1967)
15. Bavelas, J.B., Coates, L., Johnson, T.: Listener responses as a collaborative process: The role of gaze. Journal of Communication 52(3), 566–580 (2002)
16. Cathcart, N., Carletta, J., Klein, E.: A shallow model of backchannel continuers in spoken dialogue. In: Proceedings of the Conference of the European chapter of the Association for Computational Linguistics, Budapest, Hungary, vol. 1, pp. 51–58 (2003)
17. Maatman, M., Gratch, J., Marsella, S.: Natural behavior of a listening agent. In: Panayiotopoulos, T., Gratch, J., Aylett, R.S., Ballin, D., Olivier, P., Rist, T. (eds.) IVA 2005. LNCS (LNAI), vol. 3661, pp. 25–36. Springer, Heidelberg (2005)
18. Gratch, J., Okhmatovskaia, A., Lamothe, F., Marsella, S., Morales, M., van der Werf, R.J., Morency, L.P.: Virtual rapport. In: Gratch, J., Young, M., Aylett, R.S., Ballin, D., Olivier, P. (eds.) IVA 2006. LNCS (LNAI), vol. 4133, pp. 14–27. Springer, Heidelberg (2006)
19. Heylen, D., Bevacqua, E., Tellier, M., Pelachaud, C.: Searching for prototypical facial feedback signals. In: Pelachaud, C., Martin, J.-C., André, E., Chollet, G., Karpouzis, K., Pelé, D. (eds.) IVA 2007. LNCS (LNAI), vol. 4722, pp. 147–153. Springer, Heidelberg (2007)
20. Granström, B., House, D., Swerts, M.: Multimodal feedback cues in human-machine interactions. In: Proceedings of the International Conference on Speech Prosody, Aix-en-Provence, France, pp. 11–14 (2002)
21. Valstar, M.F., McKeown, G., Cowie, R., Pantic, M.: The Semaine corpus of emotionally coloured character interactions. In: Proceedings of the International Conference on Multimedia & Expo, Singapore, Singapore (to appear, 2010)
22. Boersma, P., Weenink, D.: Praat: doing phonetics by computer. Software (2009), http://www.praat.org
23. Van Welbergen, H., Reidsma, D., Ruttkay, Z., Zwiers, J.: Elckerlyc - A BML realizer for continuous, multimodal interaction with a virtual human. Journal of Multimodal User Interfaces (to appear, 2010)
24. Jonsdottir, G.R., Gratch, J., Fast, E., Thórisson, K.R.: Fluid semantic backchannel feedback in dialogue: Challenges and progress. In: Pelachaud, C., Martin, J.-C., André, E., Chollet, G., Karpouzis, K., Pelé, D. (eds.) IVA 2007. LNCS (LNAI), vol. 4722, pp. 154–160. Springer, Heidelberg (2007)
25. Truong, K.P., Poppe, R., Heylen, D.: A rule-based backchannel prediction model using pitch and pause information. In: Proceedings of Interspeech, Makuhari, Japan (to appear, 2010)

Learning Backchannel Prediction Model from Parasocial Consensus Sampling: A Subjective Evaluation

Lixing Huang, Louis-Philippe Morency, and Jonathan Gratch

Institute for Creative Technologies, University of Southern California,
13274 Fiji Way, Marina del Rey, CA 90292, USA
{lhuang,morency,gratch}@ict.usc.edu

Abstract. Backchannel feedback is an important kind of nonverbal feedback within face-to-face interaction that signals a person's interest, attention and willingness to keep listening. Learning to predict when to give such feedback is one of the keys to creating natural and realistic virtual humans. Prediction models are traditionally learned from large corpora of annotated face-to-face interactions, but this approach has several limitations. Previously, we proposed a novel data collection method, Parasocial Consensus Sampling, which addresses these limitations. In this paper, we show that data collected in this manner can produce effective learned models. A subjective evaluation shows that the virtual human driven by the resulting probabilistic model significantly outperforms a previously published rule-based agent in terms of rapport, perceived accuracy and naturalness, and it is even better than the virtual human driven by real listeners' behavior in some cases.

Keywords: Parasocial Interaction, Virtual Human, Backchannel Prediction.

1 Introduction

When people interact face-to-face, actions often speak louder than words. A speaker's facial expressions, gestures and postures can dictate the meaning of an utterance; whereas a listener's nonverbal reactions provide moment-to-moment feedback that can alter and serve to co-construct subsequent speech [21,22,23]. Beyond its impact on meaning, nonverbal signals communicate emotion and personality, enhance the persuasiveness of speech, express social status and regulate conversational flow. Not surprisingly, considerable effort has been directed at endowing virtual humans with the ability to recognize, understand and exploit the nonverbal channel [16,17,18].

Virtual humans that produce such nonverbal signals can induce desirable social changes in their human interaction partners. Synthetic nonverbal behaviors can enhance the persuasiveness of virtual human speech [7], encourage people to take their medicine [12], and promote more cooperation in economic games [11]. Our own studies with the Rapport Agent [3] suggest that nonverbal behavior plays a causal role in achieving these effects. As a result of its contingent nonverbal feedback, human speakers speak more fluently with the Rapport Agent [6], disclose more intimate information about themselves [13] and may better remember recent events [14]. Indeed,

J. Allbeck et al. (Eds.): IVA 2010, LNAI 6356, pp. 159–172, 2010.
© Springer-Verlag Berlin Heidelberg 2010

these and related studies suggest that a virtual human's behavior may be more important than its appearance in achieving social effects [8].

Although early research on virtual humans relied on hand-crafted algorithms to generate nonverbal behaviors, informed by psychological theories or personal observations of face-to-face interaction [4], recent scholarship has seen an explosion in interest in data-driven approaches that automatically learn virtual human behaviors from annotated corpora of human face-to-face interactions. Several systems now exist that automatically learn a range of nonverbal behaviors including backchannel feedback [2], conversational gestures [9,15] and turn-taking cues [10].

It is widely assumed that natural human-to-human interaction constitutes the ideal dataset from which to learn virtual human behaviors, however, there are drawbacks with such data. First, natural data can be expensive and time-consuming to collect. Second, human behaviors contain variability so that some of the behavior samples may conflict with the social effect that we want the virtual human to produce. Finally, each instance in face-to-face interaction only illustrates how one particular individual responds to another, yet such data fails to give us insight on how well such responses generalize across individuals. Rather than simply exploring more powerful learning algorithms that might overcome these drawbacks, we argue that attention should also be directed at innovative methods for collecting behavioral data.

Recently, we proposed a novel data collection approach called *Parasocial Consensus Sampling* (PCS) [1] to inform virtual human nonverbal behavior generation. Instead of interacting face-to-face, participants were guided through a "parasocial" interaction in which they attempted to produce natural nonverbal behaviors to pre-recorded videos of human interaction partners. Through this method we were able to quickly collect large amounts of behavioral data, but more importantly, we were able to assess how multiple individuals might respond to the identical social situation. These multiple perspectives afford the possibility of driving virtual humans with the consensus view on how one should respond, rather than simply concatenating many idiosyncratic responses. A test of this approach, applied to the problem of generating listener nonverbal feedback, showed that 1) participants felt comfortable producing behavior in this manner and 2) the resulting consensus perceived more accurate and more effective than natural feedback (i.e., feedback from the natural listener in face-to-face conversation). Although this was a promising first step, it remains to demonstrate that consensus data can be used to train an effective predictive model.

In this article, we take this next logical step in demonstrating the power of the PCS: using consensus data, we train a predictive model of listener backchannel feedback. We compare the performance of this model against our previous Rapport Agent that generated behaviors according to a hand-crafted mapping. Our subjective evaluation shows the virtual human driven by this probabilistic model performs significantly better than the Rapport Agent [6] in terms of rapport, perceived accuracy and naturalness, and it is even better than the virtual human driven by real listener's behavior in some cases.

2   Background: Parasocial Consensus Sampling

Horton and Wohl [19] first introduced the concept of parasocial interaction. This describes people's natural tendency to interact with media representations of people as if they were interacting face-to-face with the actual person. Many researchers [20,29,30] have documented that people readily produce such "parasocial" responses and these responses bear similarity to what is found in natural face-to-face interactions, even if the respondents are clearly aware they are interacting with pre-recorded media. By exploiting this characteristic of humans, we proposed the parasocial consensus sampling framework [1].

Parasocial Consensus Sampling is a new methodological framework that collects typical human responses in social interactions.

Unlike the traditional way to collect human behavioral data, where participants' behaviors are recorded during the social interaction, *parasocial* consensus sampling guides multiple independent individuals to vicariously experience the same media representation of social interaction in order to gain the typicality (i.e., consensus view) of human response.

The idea of parasocial *consensus* is to combine multiple parasocial responses to the same media clip in order to develop a composite view of how a typical individual would respond. For example, if a significant portion of participants smile at certain points in a videotaped speech, we might naturally conclude that smiling is a typical response to whatever is occurring in the media at these moments. More formally, a parasocial consensus is drawing agreement from the feedback of multiple independent participants when they experience the same media representation of an interaction. It does not reflect the behavior of any one individual but can be seen more as a proto-typical or summary trend over some population of individuals which, advantageously, allows us to derive both the strength and reliability of the responses.

Although we can never know how every person will respond to a given situation, *sampling* is a way to estimate the consensus by randomly selecting individuals from a given population. Thus, parasocial consensus sampling is a way to estimate the consensus behavioral response in face-to-face interactions by recording the parasocial responses of multiple individuals to the same media (i.e., by replacing one partner in a pre-recorded interaction with multiple vicarious observers). By repeating this process over a corpus of face-to-face interaction data, we can augment the traditional databases used in learning virtual human interactional behaviors with estimates of the strength and reliability of such responses and, hopefully, learn more reliable and effective behavioral mappings to drive the behavior of virtual humans.

2.1 Definition

We define parasocial consensus sampling as a composite of five elements:

(1) *Interactional Goal*: this is the intended goal of the virtual human interactional behaviors. Before participating in parasocial consensus sampling, participants should be explicitly or implicitly encouraged to behave in a manner which is consistent with this goal, for example, creating rapport.

(2) *Target behavioral response*: this is the particular response or set of responses that the virtual human is going to generate in order to create a specific interactional goal. Participants should be encouraged to produce such behaviors when they are participating in the parasocial interaction. Candidate behavioral responses include backchannel feedback, turn-taking, evaluative facial expressions and paraverbals such as "uh-huh".

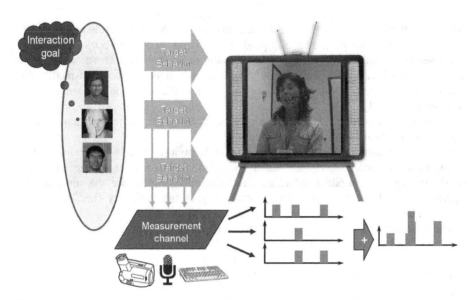

Fig. 1. Parasocial Consensus Sampling (PCS) works as follows: we first recruit participants from some *population*, and then encourage them to give *particular responses* (e.g. backchannels, facial expressions, and so on), measured via some *channel* (i.e. visual channel, audio channel, and mechanical channel), in order to create the *interactional goal* within the parasocial interaction with the *media* representation of social interaction.

(3) *Media*: this is the set of stimuli that will be presented to the participants in order to stimulate their parasocial responses. Ideally this would be a media clip derived from a natural face-to-face interaction where the participants can view the clip from a first-person perspective. For example, if the original interaction was a face-to-face conversation across a table, the camera position should approximate as close as possible the perspective of one of the conversation partners.

(4) *Target population*: this is the population of individuals we wish the virtual human to learn. This might consist of members selected from particular group (e.g., women, speakers of African-American vernacular, or patients with clinical depression). Participants should be recruited from this target population.

(5) *Measurement channel*: this is the mechanism by which we measure the parasocial response. The most natural way to measure the response would be to encourage participants to behave as if they were participating in face-to-face interaction and record their responses. However, to take advantage of the imaginary nature of parasocial interaction, participants might be encouraged to elicit responses in a more easily measured way. For example, if we are interested in the consensus of when to smile in an interaction, we can ask participants to exaggerate the behavior or even to press a button whenever they feel the response is appropriate. Candidate measurement channels include the visual channel (e.g. videotaping), audio channel (e.g. voice recording) or mechanical channel (e.g. press a button).

2.2   PCS in Action: Collect Listener Backchannel Feedback

Prior research [2,4] has suggested that backchannel feedback [31] plays an important role in establishing rapport between interactants and this paper is going to learn a probabilistic model to predict the backchannel feedback. First, we illustrate how to apply parasocial consensus sampling framework to collect listener backchannel feedback data.

Parasocial consensus sampling consists of five key elements: interactional goal, target behavioral response, media, target population and measurement channel. We customized the parasocial consensus sampling in our work as follows:

- *Interaction Goal*: Create rapport
- *Target Behavioral Response*: Backchannel feedback
- *Media*: Pre-recorded videos
- *Target Population*: General public
- *Measurement Channel*: Keyboard

We recruited 9 fluent English speakers (2 female, 7 males) from a local temporary employment agency to participate in the parasocial interactions with the human speaker videos from our previously collected corpus of face-to-face interactions [5]. The average age of the participants is 45.2 years old, and the standard deviation is 12.6. Participants were instructed to pretend they were in a video teleconference with the speaker in the video and to establish rapport by conveying they were actively listening and interested in what was being said. To convey this interest, participants were instructed to press the keyboard each time they felt like providing backchannel feedback such as head nods or paraverbals (e.g. "uh-huh" or "OK"). In a *one-day* experiment, each of the 9 participants interacted with a total of 45 videos, which is much more efficient than the original approach that collecting behavioral data from face-to-face interaction. They gave about 18000 backchannel feedback in total; on average, it is about 7 or 8 backchannels per minute. In next section, we are going to show how to learn a probabilistic model from the parasocial consensus sampling data.

3   Learning a Probabilistic Model from PCS

To learn probabilistic models from parasocial consensus sampling data, we must build a consensus model from the individual parasocial coders and then uses this consensus data to learn a probabilistic model. One advantage of learning from a consensus is it separates what is idiosyncratic from what is essential. Our goal is to learn a probabilistic model which will generalize the PCS data to new sequences (or live interactions) not seen in the training set. The probabilistic model is trained from the speaker's actions (e.g., pause, eye gaze, and specific lexicon words) to predict the listener backchannel feedback (i.e., head nods).

3.1   Building Consensus

The backchannel PCS dataset described in Section 2.2 consists of N sets of parasocial responses: T_1, T_2, ..., T_N , where N is the number of participant. For each parasocial interaction T_i, the PCS dataset contains the response timestamps $T = \{t_1, t_2, \ldots\}$ indicating when the participant gave a response. These response timestamps are combined to create the consensus following a three-step approach:

(a) *Convert timestamps*: Each response timestamp can be viewed as a window of opportunity where backchannel feedback is likely. Following the work of Ward and Tsukahara [4], we create a one second time window centered about each timestamp. The timeline is then sampled at a constant frame rate of 10Hz [4]. Figure 2 illustrates this approach.

Fig. 2. t1, t2, t3 are the time spots when a participant gives backchannel feedback in a parasocial interaction. A 1.0s window of opportunity is put around each timestamp so that the time spot is in the middle of the window. The samples within the window are set to 1 to indicate the presence of feedback, while others are set to 0.

(b) *Correct for individual differences* (optional): Our current data collection requires participants to press a button when they expect a response and it is well known that individuals can differ significantly in their reaction time on such tasks [27,28]. Therefore, the quality of consensus data can be improved if we first factor out these individual differences before combining response timestamps into a consensus. We can estimate this delay by comparing the parasocial interaction with the face-to-face interaction. We follow the approach in [2,4] to count how often PCS matches the real listener's behaviors and find the time offset that maximizes this score. This process was repeated independently on the nine participants of the PCS data. The reaction time values varied from 600ms to 1200ms, with average of 970ms. The 10 video sequences used for our subjective evaluation described in Section 4 were not part of the video sequences used to select the reaction times.

(c) *Build consensus view from multiple interactions*: a histogram is computed over time by looking at all the parasocial interactions. Whenever there is backchannel feedback occurring on a sample (sampled at 10Hz), the histogram of that sample is increased by 1. Thus, each sample is associated with a number indicating how many participants agree to give backchannel feedback at that point. Figure 3 shows an example of one parasocial consensus and compares it to the backchannel feedback from the real listener in the original face-to-face interaction.

By looking at the real listener's feedback, it seems that pause is a good elicitor of listener feedback, but the relative strength of this feature is unclear. In contrast, the parasocial consensus clearly shows that the pauses differ in their propensity to elicit feedback. Looking more carefully at the example we see the utterances before the first two pauses are statements, while the last one expresses an opinion, suggesting that pauses after opinions may be better predictors of listener feedback. Also, the speaker expressed emphasis on the third utterance. This result gives us a tool to better analyze and understand features that predict backchannel feedback.

By applying a threshold, the *consensus level*, to the parasocial consensus, feedback with less importance can be filtered out. Following the work in [1], we select a

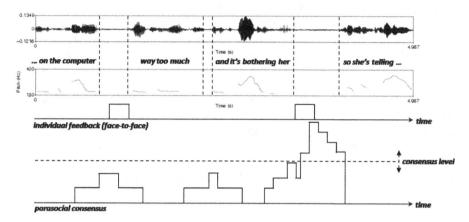

Fig. 3. Example segment showing a parasocial consensus of listener backchannel varies over time. While individual feedback (from the original face-to-face interaction) only gives discrete prediction, our parasocial consensus shows the relative importance of each feedback. By applying a consensus level to the parasocial consensus, we get only important feedback.

consensus level that makes the number of backchannels from parasocial consensus closest to that from the original face-to-face interaction data.

3.2 Learning Probabilistic Model

To build the predictive model for virtual humans, we find the relationship between speaker's features and the consensus. Recently, there has been seen an explosion in interest in data-driven approaches that automatically find such patterns using machine learning methods [2,9,10,15]. Given the time-series nature of human behavior, sequential model is a good one to learn the internal dynamic structure existing in human behavior. We apply a similar strategy as [2] to learn a *Conditional Random Field* (CRF) model from parasocial consensus sampling data. This method takes as input a sequence of human speaker's features and returns a sequence of probabilities to give backchannel feedback.

Although semantic information is an important feature in predicting backchannel feedback, it has been mentioned in other work [2,4] that non-verbal information itself also provides lots of clues in backchannel prediction. In this paper, we try to push the state of the art of non-verbal feature based models. Four speaker features are selected as suggested in [2]:

- *Pause* using binary encoding
- *Speaker looking at the listener* using ramp encoding with a width of 2 seconds and a 1 second delay
- *'and'* using step encoding with a width of 1 second and a delay of 0.5 seconds
- *Speaker looking at the listener* using binary encoding

All the features mentioned above were hand labeled by coders. While training, we split the data set (the videos used for evaluation in Section 4 are not included) into training set and validation set. This is done by N-fold cross validation. This means N-1 folders are used for training, and the remaining folder is used as validation data for testing the model. This process is repeated N times, and then the best model is selected based on the performance of our models. The performance is measured by F_1 score, which is the harmonic mean of precision and recall. Precision is the probability that predicted backchannels correspond to actual listener behavior; recall is the probability that a backchannel produced by an actual listener was predicted by the model.

Given new test sequence, CRF outputs probability over time to indicate the likelihood of giving backchannel feedback. The local maximum of the probability are selected as the candidates. In order to generate the final backchannel feedback, we have to pick up a feedback level as shown in Figure 4. In this paper, we set the feedback level so that the number of feedback from CRF model is closest to that from the training set.

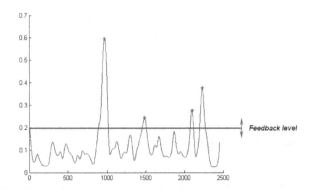

Fig. 4. Generate the final backchannel feedback by applying the feedback level to the output of CRF model. The stars (*) are the final backchannels.

4   Subjective Evaluation

In evaluating the performance of the probabilistic model, we conduct a subjective evaluation experiment to assess whether the virtual human driven by the CRF model can be used to achieve the interactional goal: creating rapport, when compared against the Rapport Agent and the original human listener. Specially, we compose videos illustrating a human speaker interacting with the virtual human (Figure 5) and contrast subjective impressions of different models for generating the virtual human's behavior.

We claim that a potential advantage PCS over traditional training methods is that the consensus data better reflects the intended interactional goal than typical face-to-face data. To better assess this claim we assess the approach against three classes of face-to-face interactions: high-rapport interactions where the original human listener exhibited high rapport; low-rapport interactions where the original human listener exhibited low rapport, and "typical" interactions that contain a mixture of both.

Fig. 5. Videos for subjective evaluation

4.1 Backchannel Prediction Models

We selected 10 speaker videos not used in training the CRF model. When these face-to-face interactions were originally conducted, speakers were asked to assess the rapport they felt with their conversation partner. Five videos were those from our corpus with the lowest rapport score and 5 were those with the highest rapport score. We created three variants of each of these videos, replacing the human listener with a virtual human whose behavior was driven by one of three different prediction models:

(1) *PCS-CRF*: the virtual human is driven by the CRF model trained on parasocial consensus. The training set doesn't include the 10 videos used for evaluation.

(2) *Natural*: the virtual human is driven by the real listener's backchannel feedback from the original face-to-face interaction.

(3) *Rapport Agent*: Gratch et al. [6] built the Rapport Agent by applying a rule-based model to predict when to give backchannel feedback. The backchannels were predicted from two rules: (a) If the speaker nods, the listener should nod back, (b) if there are backchannel opportunities in the speaker's speech, the listener should nod back. The Rapport Agent uses Watson [26] to detect head nods and LAUN [6] to detect backchannel opportunities using the approach of Ward and Tsukahara [4]. We replicate the Rapport Agent's behavior by using the same two tools to extract features from human speaker videos and applying the same rules for backchannel prediction.

4.2 User Study

We recruited 17 participants to evaluate the quality of the virtual human's behavior. Before watching videos, they were told "you are going to evaluate different versions of a virtual agent in the context of interacting with a human speaker. In each video, there is a speaker telling a story and the virtual agent giving nonverbal feedback to the speaker by nodding. We need you to evaluate the timing of the agent's head nods." After watching each video, participants evaluated the virtual human's behavior by answering 7 questions:

Rapport Scale:

1. *Close Connection*: Do you feel a close connection between the agent and the human speaker? (1(not at all) – 7(yes, definitely close connection))
2. *Engrossed*: Did the agent appear to be engrossed in listening to the story? (1(not engrossed at all) – 7(very much engrossed))
3. *Rapport*: Did there seem to be rapport between the agent and the speaker? (1(no rapport at all) – 7(yes, there's rapport))
4. *Listen Carefully*: Did the agent appear NOT to be listening carefully to the speaker? (1(No, he doesn't listen at all) – 7(Yes, he is listening very carefully))

Perceived accuracy:

5. *Precision*: How often do you think the agent nodded his head at an inappropriate time? (1(always inappropriate) – 7(always appropriate))
6. *Recall*: How often do you think the agent missed head nod opportunities? (1(missed a lot) – 7(never missed))

Naturalness:

7. Do you think the virtual agent's behavior is natural? (1(not natural at all) - 7(yes, absolutely natural))

4.3   Results

ANOVA test is applied to find whether there is significant difference among the three versions. The four items related to rapport are averaged into a single scale that showed good reliability (Cronbach's alpha = 0.98).

The results are summarized from Figure 6 to 9. In each figure, from left to right, they are mean values for all 10 videos (Overall), 5 high-rapport videos (High Rapport), and 5 low-rapport videos (Low Rapport) respectively. The start (*) means there is significant difference between the versions under the bracket.

4.3.1   Rapport Scale

Overall, the virtual human driven by the CRF model (PCS-CRF) is significantly better than the Rapport Agent [6]. It demonstrates a better prediction model can be learned from parasocial consensus sampling data. If applied to virtual human systems, it has the potential to create better social effects than the Rapport Agent did.

By looking at the virtual human driven by PCS-CRF and the one driven by real listener's behavior, we don't see significant difference overall, but there is significant

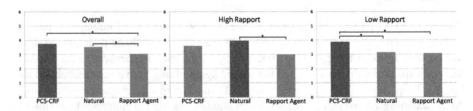

Fig. 6. *Rapport Scale.* Overall, the virtual human driven by CRF is significantly better than Rapport Agent. For low-rapport videos, the virtual human driven by CRF is significantly better than the one driven by real listener's behavior.

difference between the two in the low-rapport videos, which shows PCS-CRF can do as well as real human listeners who succeed in creating rapport and do better than those who fail to.

4.3.2 Perceived Accuracy

For the *Precision* question, PCS-CRF does significantly better than the Rapport Agent; while there is no difference between the two for the *Recall* question. The Rapport Agent gave responses whenever he saw the speaker nodded or the presence of backchannel opportunities. Such simple rules may lead to many unnecessary head nods so that the recall is high (Fig. 8), while the precision is low (Fig. 7). This explains the reason why PCS-CRF outperforms Rapport Agent.

By comparing the virtual human driven by CRF and the one driven by real listener's behavior, we don't see significant difference between them for the *Precision* question, which is expected, since real listeners are not likely to give wrong feedback in natural face-to-face interactions. However, there is significant difference between the two for the *Recall* question, and the difference mainly comes from the low-rapport videos. This explains why PCS-CRF does better than real listener's behavior in the low-rapport videos. Real listeners sometimes don't give enough appropriate backchannel responses within the interactions and thus fail to create rapport. On the other hand, PCS-CRF is learned from consensus data which is not likely to fail in this regard unless most of the parasocial interactions fail to create rapport at the same time.

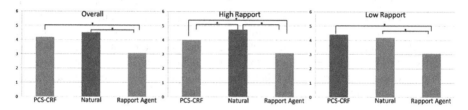

Fig. 7. *Precision.* The virtual human driven by CRF provides backchannel feedback more precisely than the Rapport Agent.

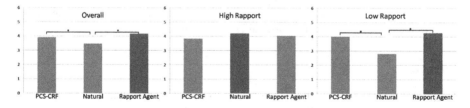

Fig. 8. *Recall.* The virtual human driven by real listener's behavior misses more opportunities to provide backchannel feedback than the other two versions do.

4.3.3 Naturalness

By comparing the Natural question (Fig. 9) with the Rapport Score question (Fig. 6), we find the virtual human is perceived more natural when it creates more rapport

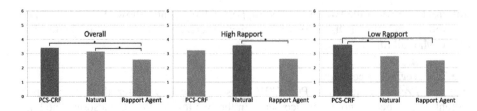

Fig. 9. *Natural.* Overall, The virtual human driven by CRF is more natural than Rapport Agent. For low-rapport videos, the virtual human driven by CRF is more natural than the one driven by real listener's behavior.

within the interaction, which confirms previous finding that creating rapport does lead to positive social effects.

5   Conclusion and Future Work

In this paper, we learned a probabilistic model for predicting listener backchannel feedback from parasocial consensus sampling data. By comparing the virtual humans driven by (1) CRF model trained on PCS data, (2) real listener's behavior and (3) Rapport Agent's behavior, we found that the virtual human driven by CRF model is significantly better than the one driven by Rapport Agent's behavior, and it has almost the same performance as the one driven by real listener's behavior. The result demonstrated we could learn a better prediction model from PCS data and proved the validity of this data collection framework in advance. As future work, we are planning to assess the power of the PCS framework with other conversation cues such as smiling, turn-taking and interruptions, other interactional goals besides rapport, and other measurement channels, such as vision-based methods.

Acknowledgement

This material is based upon work supported by the National Science Foundation under Grant No. 0729287. The content does not necessarily reflect the position or the policy of the Government, and no official endorsement should be inferred.

References

1. Huang, L., Morency, L.-P., Gratch, J.: Parasocial Consensus Sampling: Combining Multiple Perspectives to Learn Virtual Human Behavior. In: Proceedings of 9th International Conference on Autonomous Agents and Multiagent Systems (2010)
2. Morency, L.-P., de Kok, I., Gratch, J.: Predicting Listener Backchannels: A Probabilistic Multimodal Approach. In: Prendinger, H., Lester, J.C., Ishizuka, M. (eds.) IVA 2008. LNCS (LNAI), vol. 5208, pp. 176–190. Springer, Heidelberg (2008)
3. Gratch, J., Wang, N., Gerten, J., Fast, E., Duffy, R.: Creating Rapport with Virtual Agents. In: Pelachaud, C., Martin, J.-C., André, E., Chollet, G., Karpouzis, K., Pelé, D. (eds.) IVA 2007. LNCS (LNAI), vol. 4722, pp. 125–138. Springer, Heidelberg (2007)

4. Ward, N., Tsukahara, W.: Prosodic features which cue backchannel responses in English and Japanese. J. Pragmatics 23, 1177–1207 (2000)
5. Gratch, J., Okhmatovskaia, A., Lamothe, F., Marsella, S., Morales, M., Werf, R.J., Morency, L.-P.: Virtual Rapport. In: Gratch, J., Young, M., Aylett, R.S., Ballin, D., Olivier, P. (eds.) IVA 2006. LNCS (LNAI), vol. 4133, pp. 14–27. Springer, Heidelberg (2006)
6. Gratch, J., Wang, N., Okhmatovskaia, A., Lamothe, F., Morales, M., Morency, L.-P.: Can Virtual humans be more engaging than real ones? In: Jacko, J.A. (ed.) HCI 2007. LNCS, vol. 4552, pp. 286–297. Springer, Heidelberg (2007)
7. Bailenson, J.N., Yee, N.: Digital Chameleons: Automatic assimilation of nonverbal gestures in immersive virtual environments. Psychological Science 16, 814–819 (2005)
8. Bailenson, J.N., Yee, N., Merget, D., Schroeder, R.: The Effect of Behavioral Realism and Form Realism of Real-Time Avatar Faces on Verbal Disclosure, Nonverbal Disclosure, Emotion Recogition, and Copresence in Dyadic Interaction. PRESENCE: Teleoperators and Virtual Environments 15(4), 359–372 (2006)
9. Lee, J., Marsella, S.: Learning a Model of Speaker Head Nods using Gesture Corpora. In: 8th International Conference on Autonomous Agents and Multiagent Systems (2009)
10. Jonsdottir, G.R., Thorisson, K.R., Nivel, E.: Learning Smooth, Human-Like Turntaking in Realtime Dialogue. In: Prendinger, H., Lester, J.C., Ishizuka, M. (eds.) IVA 2008. LNCS (LNAI), vol. 5208, pp. 162–175. Springer, Heidelberg (2008)
11. de Melo, C., Gratch, J.: Expression of Moral Emotions in Cooperating Agents. In: Ruttkay, Z., Kipp, M., Nijholt, A., Vilhjálmsson, H.H. (eds.) IVA 2009. LNCS, vol. 5773, pp. 301–307. Springer, Heidelberg (2009)
12. Bickmore, T., Puskar, K., Schlenk, E., Pfeifer, L., Sereika, S.: Maintaining Reality: Relational Agents for Antipsychotic Medication Adherence. J. Interacting with Computers special issue on Mental Health (2010)
13. Kang, S.-H., Gratch, J., and Watts, J. The Effect of Affective Iconic Realism on Anonymous Interactants' Self-Disclosure. In: Proceedings of Interaction Conference for Human-Computer Interaction (2009)
14. Wang, N., Gratch, J.: Can a Virtual Human Build Rapport and Promote Learning? In: Proceedings of 14 International Conference on Artificial Intelligence in Education (2009)
15. Kipp, M., Neff, M., Kipp, K.H., Albrecht, I.: Towards natural gesture synthesis: Evaluating gesture units in a data-driven approach to gesture synthesis. In: Pelachaud, C., Martin, J.-C., André, E., Chollet, G., Karpouzis, K., Pelé, D. (eds.) IVA 2007. LNCS (LNAI), vol. 4722, pp. 15–28. Springer, Heidelberg (2007)
16. Cassell, J., Sullivan, J., Prevost, S., Churchill, E.F.: Embodied Conversational Agents. MIT Press, Cambridge (2000)
17. Gratch, J., Rickel, J., Andre, E., Badler, N., Cassell, J., Petajan, E.: Creating Interactive Virtual Humans: Some Assembly Required. IEEE Intelligent Systems, 54–63 (July/August 2000)
18. Vinayagamoorthy, V., Gillies, M., Steed, A., Tanguy, E., Pan, X., Loscos, C., Slater, M.: Building Expression into Virtual Characters. In: Eurographics 2006 (2006)
19. Horton, D., Wohl, R.R.: Mass communication and parasocial interaction: Observation on intimacy at a distance. Psychiatry 19, 215–229 (1954)
20. Levy, M.R., Watching, T.V.: News as parasocial interaction. J. Broadcasting 23, 60–80 (1979)
21. Heylen, D.: Understanding Speaker-Listener Interactions. In: Proceedings of 10th Annual Conference of the International Speech Communication Association (2009)
22. Bavelas, J.B., Coates, L., Johnson, T.: Listener Responses as a Collaborative Process: The Role of Gaze. J. Communication 52(3), 566–580 (2006)

23. Bavelas, J.B., Coates, L., Johnson, T.: Listeners as co-narrators. J. Personality and Social Psychology 79(6), 941–952 (2000)
24. Bernieri, F.J., Gillis, J.S., Davis, J.M., Grahe, J.E.: Dyad Rapport and the Accuracy of Its Judgment Across Situations: A Lens Model Analysis. J. Personality and Social Psychology 71(1), 110–129 (1996)
25. Gifford, R.: A Lens-Mapping Framework for Understanding the Encoding and Decoding of Interpersonal Dispositions in Nonverbal Behavior. J. Personality and Social Psychology 66(2), 398–412 (1994)
26. Morency, L.-P., et al.: Contextual Recognition of Head Gestures. In: Proceedings of 7th International Conference on Multimodal Interactions (2005)
27. Montare, A.: The simplest chronoscope: group and interindividual differences in visual reaction time. J. Perceptual and motor skills 108(1), 161–172 (2009)
28. Reaction time, http://en.wikipedia.org/wiki/Reaction_time
29. Houlberg, R.: Local television news audience and the para-social interaction. J. Broadcasting 28, 423–429 (1984)
30. Rubin, A.M., Perse, E.M., Powell, R.A.: Loneliness, para-social interaction, and local television news viewing. Human Communication Research 12, 155–180 (1985)
31. Yngve, V.: On Getting a Word in Edgewise. In: 6th Regional Meeting of the Chicago Linguistic Society, pp. 567–577.

RIDE: A Simulator for Robotic Intelligence Development

HyunRyong Jung[1] and Meongchul Song[2]

[1] College of Computing, Georgia Institute of Technology, Atlanta, GA, USA
hjung46@gatech.edu, jhr1021@gmail.com
[2] The Advanced Software Research Center, SAIT, Samsung Electronics,
Yongin-si, Gyeonggi-do, 446-712 South Korea
meong.song@samsung.com

Abstract. Recently, robot hardware platforms have improved significantly and many researchers are working on applying artificial intelligence to robots. However, developing robots is challenging and takes exorbitant costs. Also, even if you primarily focus on robot intelligence, you may not be able to evaluate intelligence algorithms without recognition, manipulation among others. In this paper, we present Robot Intelligence Development Environment (RIDE), a simulator for robotic intelligence development. RIDE makes it possible to test robot intelligence easily with its RIDE editor and built-in synthetic vision mechanism. Also we show the feasibility of RIDE with case studies.

Keywords: Simulator, Robot, Intelligence, Synthetic Vision.

1 Introduction

For robotic researchers and developers, especially in the area of intelligence and navigation, during the development of algorithms, robot configurations and experiment environments are subject to frequent changes since interactive test of algorithms under various scenarios are essential. Robotic simulators are alternatives to overcome these problems and requirements. Today, there are a lot of robotic simulators. However, with the exception of some commercial products, few offer their own editing tools in order to build virtual robots easy and add additional information for simulation.

Another thread of consideration for robotic intelligence development is to reduce the burden of implementing recognition functionalities. Synthetic vision is such an approach. Basically, synthetic vision can be regarded as simulated vision for robots [2]. It renders test environments in camera images from the robot's point of view and provides recognition results such as object recognition and disparity map.

However, there are almost no robot simulator that supports synthetic vision and editor to reduce effort in testing robot intelligence. This motivated us the development of a simulator, Robot Intelligence Development Environment (RIDE), which is capable of convenient configuration of robot and test environments, and supports synthetic vision.

This paper is organized as follows. Section 2 presents a brief survey of existing open source and commercial robotic simulators. The architecture and characteristics of RIDE are described in Section 3 Next, in Section 4 we present case studies

J. Allbeck et al. (Eds.): IVA 2010, LNAI 6356, pp. 173–179, 2010.

conducted to demonstrate the capabilities of RIDE. Finally, the paper provides conclusions and future work in Section 5.

2 Related Work

There are a variety of robotic simulators for their own purposes. Table 1 compares various existing open source and commercial robotic simulators that offer 3D simulation environments.

Table 1. Comparison of Existing Open Source and Commercial Simulators

	License	Editor	Operating Systems	Physics Library	Graphics Library	Plug-in / Support	Sensors
USARSim	GPL[a]	Yes	Windows, Linux, MacOS	Karma	Unreal Engine 2.0	Player	touch, camera, odometer, range, IMU, encoder, RFID, sound, HumanMotion
OpenRave	LGPL[b]	No	Windows, Linux, MacOS	ODE	OpenGL (GLEW)	Controllers, IK[e], Solvers, Planners	laser, camera
Gazebo	GPL	No	Linux, MacOS	ODE	OpenGL (GLUT)	Player	laser, sonar, GPS, IMU, monocular and stereo camera
OpenSim	GPL/OSS[c]	No	Linux	ODE	Open Scene Graph	IKOR[f]	link proximity
Simbad	GPL	No	Windows, Linux, MacOS	—	Java3D	PicoNode, PicoEvo	camera, distance, bumper
Webots	Commercial	Yes[d]	Windows, Linux	ODE	OpenGL	—	range, light, touch, GPS, camera, encoder, distance, force
Marilou	Commercial	Yes	Windows	ODE	DirectX	—	GPS, odometer, distance, bumper, force, accelerometer, camera

[a]The GNU Public License; [b]The GNU Lesser General Public License; [c]Open Source Software; [d]Editor for scene tree; [e]Inverse kinematics; [f]Inverse kinematics for redundant manipulators

Most simulators primarily focus on experimenting robotic navigation and motion algorithms. There are in fact simulators which already support some aspects discussed in Section 1. Gazebo [8] and Webots [9] are the most convenient simulators for intelligence experiments in the categories of open source projects and commercial products, respectively. However, to our knowledge, there is currently no simulator that offers capabilities of distance detection and vision recognition based on synthetic vision, and configuring recognition information in editor altogether.

3 Robot Intelligence Development Environment

RIDE is able to test robots as other robotic simulators do. In addition, it supports synthetic vision, which makes it possible to convenient experiment of robot intelligence algorithms and scenarios. In this section, we describe the architecture and main components of RIDE and our approach to synthetic vision.

3.1 Architecture

Since convenient configuration of robots and test environments is one of our major design goals, RIDE offers an editor tool, RIDE-Editor. It runs on Microsoft Windows and mainly consists of RIDE-Editor and RIDE-Sim, an application to simulate the robot under the given experiment environment.

A user configures a virtual robot using the RIDE-Editor. More specifically, a user provides the robot's part, input device, and output device information and configures relationships between the devices, which are represented as Virtual Robot Information. Also, the user provides test environments and recognition information using the RIDE-Editor represented as Virtual Environment Information. The stored information is used to experiment the robot in RIDE-Sim. RIDE-Sim communicates with robot control programs via the communication middleware and controls the robot by executing the robot control programs.

3.2 RIDE-Editor

Other than commercial robot simulators, none of the open source simulators provides an editor tool to configure the robot and test environment (see TABLE I). This makes it difficult to test robots or environments that are not provided by specific simulators. RIDE system has RIDE-Editor tool to support a user to configure robots and simulation environments.

RIDE-Editor provides viewports to configure robots and environments with ease. Using the RIDE-Editor GUI, a user examines robot parts, input devices and output devices; changes the size, location, mass and textures of a part; setup relationships between parts, input devices and output devices. For example, a user specifies an IR sensor should be connected to a specific part or a motor. In addition, object recognition information can be added in RIDE-Editor and used in synthetic vision. For instance, if you create a box and categorize it as a refrigerator, you can get recognition result from synthetic vision without using object recognition algorithm.

RIDE-Editor provides part, input device, output device, obstacles, and categories for robot and environment construction. Specifically, RIDE-Editor provides box and sphere for primitive parts, and tri-meshes (triangle meshes) for user-defined parts; camera, IR sensor, torque sensor, force sensor, and microphone for input devices; velocity- and position- control motors, and speaker for output devices.

Aforementioned devices are used to configure robots. Test environments consist of obstacles which could be boxes, spheres, or tri-meshes. Category items represent synthetic vision-based recognition results.

3.3 RIDE-Sim

RIDE-Sim is a robotic simulator tool and utilizes ODE for physics library and RIDE-Engine, our own 3D graphics engine. RIDE-Engine supports light, camera, and texture, and used by both RIDE-Editor and RIDE-Sim. Most open source 3D graphics engines are lack of functionalities that are required by our robot simulator such as multi-viewport, and accessing depth buffer, and etc. So, we developed optimized and light-weight RIDE-Engine that suits to RIDE system.

Multiple robots can be configured in test environments under RIDE-Sim. RIDE-Sim refers parts, input and output devices information configured in RIDE-Editor. A robot control program controls output devices or retrieve input devices' information, i.e., sensor information, by accessing robot, input or output device IDs specified in RIDE-Sim. Robot and obstacle information is maintained in robot information file (RIF) and obstacle information file (OIF), respectively. During the simulation process, part and input/output device information is verified using RIDE-Sim GUI and robot's camera images are also available to examine. The user is also able to control simulation environment, edit scene textures, light and ODE parameters.

3.4 Synthetic Vision

Artificial vision, which utilizes sensors such as cameras and scanners, is a very important topic in the field of robotics and artificial intelligence. However, 3D recognition and interpretation do not support distance detection, pattern recognition, or noisy image processing very well [1]. With the synthetic vision [2] [3] [4] [7], it is possible to solve aforementioned problems during the simulation and as a result robotic researchers are able to focus on verifying intelligence scenarios.

Synthetic vision solves distance detection by utilizing output images from the robot's vision sensors and computes camera space coordinates based on screen coordinates (see Equation 1). M and P represent modeling and projection matrices, respectively, and q_{real} and q_{norm} represent points on real screen and normalized points, respectively.

$$q_{real} = q_{norm}(M \cdot P)^{-1} \qquad (1)$$

Fig. 1 (a), (b), and (c) show example distance detection results. A bright object indicates that it is far from the camera. Combined with the distance information obtained by synthetic vision, navigation, robotic intelligence, and scenario simulations can be conducted without employing separate distance detection algorithms.

A virtual robot performs object recognition first by rendering, using flat shading technique, objects found in the synthetic vision's viewing frustum. Next, it analyzes color values from the image and determines the detected objects. Finally, it compares the color values of the detected objects with those of pre-defined category objects [3] [4], and returns the recognition results. Fig. 1 (d), (e), and (f) show the results of rendered objects under various situations, where category information of objects is provided in advance by RIDE-Editor. If verifying recognition *per se* is not a goal,

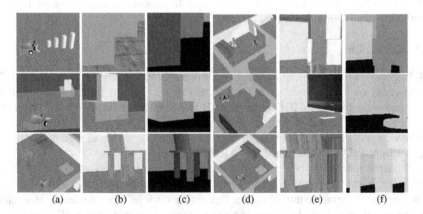

(a)	(b)	(c)	(d)	(e)	(f)

Fig. 1. Distance detection using synthetic vision (a) test environment (b) camera images (c) distance detection results, Perception results (d) location of a virtual robot (e) images from robot's camera (f) rendered images using flat shading

then a robot control program uses the recognition results obtained by synthetic vision. Upon the request from a robot control program, RIDE-Sim performs recognition using flat shading and synthetic vision, and returns the recognition results to the robot control program.

4 Case Studies

In this section, we present various robotic simulation test cases to exhibit the advantages and capabilities of RIDE. RIDE is able to perform tele-operation, and facial expression simulations like other robotic simulators. In addition, we show that we can conveniently simulate robotic intelligence using RIDE.

4.1 Tele-presentation and Map-Building

Test environment for the simulation and a mobile robot were constructed by the RIDE-Editor as in Fig. 2 (a) and (b), respectively. The robot consists of three infra-red sensors, two cameras and two motors, and has tele-presentation and map-building capabilities. Next, we implemented a robot control program for tele-operation (see Fig. 2 (c)). Using the robot control program, we control the robot's movement and verify infra-red sensor values and camera images. The result map, Fig. 2 (d), was constructed based on synthetic vision. Aforementioned, many existing robotic simulators do not support camera-based distance detection. Therefore, robotics researchers have to utilize stereo vision algorithms directly or indirectly. One of the advantages of using RIDE is provision of built-in synthetic vision mechanism, which makes it possible for navigation algorithm developers to use the camera image based distance detection without their own stereo vision implementations.

4.2 Facial Expression

The purpose of the case study is to test facial expressions. We constructed a face with eyes, eyebrows, and eyelids that features 8 DOF. RIDE offers an editor tool, RIDE-Editor, which supports convenient construction of robot configuration so that robotic researchers test robots with ease. The simple robot, i.e., the face, used in the case study was capable of expressing two emotions, happiness and anger. The behaviors of actuators were mapped to each emotion and the robot shows its emotions using facial expression. The expressions for emotions were configured using the robot control program. If combined with the synthetic vision, it is possible to conduct simulations that express robot's emotions with respect to recognized faces and objects.

4.3 Goal-Based Cognitive System and Navigation

The last and the most important case study to present is the simulation of goal-based cognition. The robot control program architecture shown in Fig. 3 (a) describes architecture of a mobile robot. The architecture is based on the cognitive architecture in [5]. The robot is capable of goal-based cognition [6] and navigation. The cognitive architecture mainly consists of five systems: they are sensory system, perception system, navigation system, action system and motor system.

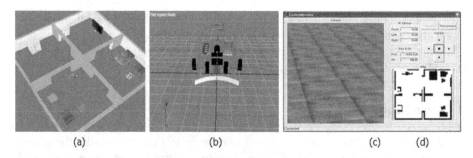

(a)   (b)   (c)   (d)

Fig. 2. Tele-operation and map-building experiment (a) test environment (b) mobile robot (c) robot control program for tele-operation (d) map building result

Goal selection is done according to the policies specified in the working memory. For the case study, a main goal is defined as moving the robot from a starting location to a destination and is a combination of one or more goals. If a goal needs to be divided into one or more sub-goals, new sub-goals are generated. A sub-goal is either a path planning goal or a path following goal. A path planning sub-goal is one to plan paths to achieve its parent goal and a path following sub-goal to move the robot according to the planned paths. Goals are executed until the main goal is achieved.

The robot consists of two motors and a camera. Map-building process is accomplished based on the distance detection results obtained from synthetic vision; Path planning uses the A* algorithm. The experiment result is shown in Fig. 3 (b) and (c). The robot updates the map during the experiment which, in turn, modifies initially planned path. Different from many other existing robotic simulators, where researchers need to adapt or implement their own algorithms to detect distances from the camera input images, RIDE offers convenient testing of navigation algorithms without the implementation of distance detection.

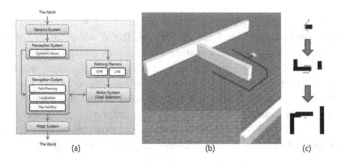

(a)   (b)   (c)

Fig. 3. Navigation based on goal-based cognition (a) architecture for goal-based cognitive system (b) navigation trace (c) constructed map

5 Conclusion

We presented RIDE, a robotic simulator, and case studies demonstrating its capabilities. The philosophy behind RIDE is the development of a convenient research tool for artificial intelligence development more than just a robotic simulator. RIDE-Editor provides convenient construction of robots and simulation environments and built-in synthetic vision makes it possible for robotic researchers to focus on intelligence algorithm development.

References

1. Gagalowicz, A.: Collaboration between computer graphics and computer vision. In: Thalmann, D. (ed.) Scientific Visualization and Graphics Simulation, pp. 233–248. John Wiley & Sons, New York (1990)
2. Noser, H., Renault, O., Thalmann, D., Thalmann, N.M.: Navigation for digital actors based on synthetic vision, memory and learning. Computer Graphics 19, 7–19 (1995)
3. Enrique, S., Watt, A., Maddock, S., Policarpo, F.: Using synthetic vision for autonomous non-player characters in computer games. In: Proc. 4th Argentine Symposium on Artificial Intelligence, Santa Fe, Argentina (2002)
4. Kuffner, J., Latombe, J.-C.: Fast synthetic vision, memory, and learning models for virtual humans. In: Proc. Computer Animation (1999)
5. Burke, R., Isla, D., Downie, M., Ivanov, Y., Blumberg, B.: Creature smarts: the art and architecture of a brain. presented at The Game Developers Conference, San Jose, CA (2001)
6. Buckland, M.: Programming Game AI by Example. Wordware Publishing, Inc.
7. Peters, C., Carol O'Sullivan, C., Peters, C., Sullivan, O.: Synthetic Vision And Memory for Autonomous Virtual Humans. Computer Graphics Forum (2002)
8. http://playerstage.sourceforge.net/gazebo/gazebo.html
9. http://www.cyberbotics.com/

A Velocity-Based Approach for Simulating Human Collision Avoidance

Ioannis Karamouzas and Mark Overmars

Games and Virtual Worlds, Utrecht University, The Netherlands
{ioannis,markov}@cs.uu.nl

Abstract. We present a velocity-based model for realistic collision avoidance among virtual characters. Our approach is elaborated from experimental data and is based on the simple hypothesis that an individual tries to resolve collisions long in advance by slightly adapting its motion.

1 Introduction

In this paper, we address the problem of visually compelling and natural looking avoidance behaviour between interacting virtual characters. We first exploit publicly available motion capture data to gain more understanding into how humans solve interactions in real-life. Based on our analysis and some known facts about human locomotion, we propose a model for realistic collision avoidance.

In our approach, each character anticipates future collisions and tries to resolve them in advance by slightly adapting its orientation and/or speed. Consequently, the characters avoid all collisions as early as possible and with minimal effort which results in a smooth and optimal flow.

Experiments show that our model exhibits emergent phenomena, like lane formation, that have been observed in real crowds. The technique is relatively easy to implement and can be used to simulate crowds of thousands of characters at real-time frame rates.

Since we use the velocity space to plan the avoidance maneuvers of each virtual character, our approach is similar in nature to the methods that are based on the *Velocity Obstacle* formulation [1,2]. However, we significantly reduce the set of admissible velocities by taking into account how imminent potential collisions are. Our method bears also some resemblance to the model proposed by Pettré *et al.* [3], as we use their experimental study to elaborate our collision avoidance algorithm. Our analysis, though, focuses on the *predicted time to collision* between interacting participants and the deviation from their desired velocities, whereas they studied the effect that the *minimum predicted distance* has on the participants' accelerations.

2 Experimental Analysis

30 subjects participated in the experiment and in total 429 trials were recorded. Each trial consists of two participants crossing paths orthogonally while walking

J. Allbeck et al. (Eds.): IVA 2010, LNAI 6356, pp. 180–186, 2010.

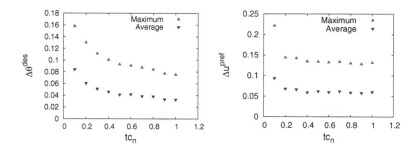

Fig. 1. left : maximum and average deviation from the desired orientation as a function of the normalized time to collision, **right** : maximum and average deviation from the preferred speed as a function of the normalized time to collision.

toward the opposite corners of a square area. We refer the reader to [3] for a detailed explanation of the experimental protocol.

In each trial, similar to [3], the *interaction* starts at time t_s when the two participants can see each other and ends at time t_f when the distance between the participants is minimal. During the interaction period, $t_s < t < t_f$, we estimate the future motions of the two participants by linearly extrapolating their current trajectories. Then, we can determine whether and when the participant P_1 will collide with P_2 as follows:

$$\|(\mathbf{x}_2 + t\mathbf{v}_2) - (\mathbf{x}_1 + t\mathbf{v}_1)\| = r_1 + r_2, \tag{1}$$

where $\mathbf{x}$ defines the position of the participant's trunk, approximated by interpolating the two shoulder markers of the participant and r denotes the radius of a participant derived from the distance between the two markers. The participant's velocity $\mathbf{v}$ is calculated using forward finite difference, i.e. $\mathbf{v} = d\mathbf{x}/dt$. Solving the above equation, we can predict the time to collision $tc(t)$ between P_1 and P_2 at time t. To be able to run comparisons over all trials, the predicted time to collision for any time $t_s < t < t_f$ is normalized as follows:

$$tc_n(t) = \frac{tc(t)}{\max_{t \in [t_s, t_f]} \{tc(t)\}} \tag{2}$$

$tc_n(t)$ ranges from 0 to 1, where 0 indicates that the two participants are already colliding and 1 corresponds to the maximum time to collision between the two participants for the current trial.

Time to collision and desired orientation. Fig. 1 (left) plots the participants' deviations from their desired orientations as a function of the normalized time to collision. We grouped the tc_n into 10 clusters of equal length and then, we determined the maximum and average deviation angle per cluster. As can be inferred from the figure, the maximum deviation angle is quite small for predicted collisions that will take place in the far future, $tc_n \geq 0.9$. After a small

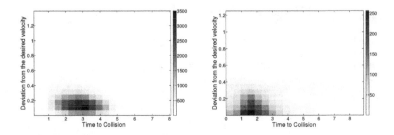

Fig. 2. Density of the deviation from the desired velocity as a function of the predicted time to collision. **left** : participants that cross paths orthogonally, **right** : participants that have to avoid head-on collisions.

increase, the max deviation angle remains more or less constant for a long period, $0.5 \leq tc_n \leq 0.8$. As soon as potential collisions starts to become imminent ($tc_n < 0.4$), the deviation angle increases reaching to a peak when the tc_n tends to 0. Similar trend is also observed when looking at the evolution of the average deviation angle with respect to tc_n.

Time to collision and preferred speed. During the interaction period, we define the preferred speed of a participant by taking the average speed over this period. Compared to the orientation deviation, the deviation from the preferred speed remains constant for a longer period of time, $tc_n \geq 0.2$, as shown in Fig. 1 (right). Note also the abrupt increase of the maximum deviation at $tc_n < 0.2$, which allows the participants to successfully resolve threatening collisions by refining their speed.

Discussion. To obtain a clear overview of how participants solve interactions, we also cumulated all pairs of predicted collision times and corresponding deviation velocities $\Delta \mathbf{v}^{des}$ for all trials, where $\Delta \mathbf{v}_i^{des}(t) = \|\mathbf{v}_i(t) - \mathbf{v}_i^{des}\|$ and the desired velocity $\mathbf{v}_i^{des}$ is determined by the participant's preferred speed and orientation. Fig. 2 (left) shows the density plot of the corresponding bivariate data. As can be seen, in most of the trials the majority of the participants prefer to solve interactions in advance, that is when $2.0 \leq tc \leq 4.0$, favouring small changes in their velocities. Note also that very rarely participants have to adapt their motions at imminent collision times which shows the ability of people to efficiently predict and avoid collisions.

In conclusion, our analysis have shown that individuals resolve collisions long in advance by slightly adjusting their motions. Note that the current study focuses on participants that have perpendicular trajectories. Another challenging case is when interacting participants have to avoid head-on collisions. For that reason, we have recently conducted an experimental study [4] similar to the one proposed by Pettré *et al.* Preliminary analysis of the corresponding interactions data seems to support our current observations (see Fig. 2, right). Note, though, that due to the fact that the participants have exactly opposite desired directions, some miscommunication on how they pass each other might be detected. Thus, as can be seen in the figure, there are cases that collisions are resolved at the last moment.

3   Collision Avoidance

In our problem setting, we are given a virtual environment in which n heterogeneous agents $A_1, ... A_n$ have to navigate without colliding with the environment and with each other. For simplicity we assume that each agent moves on the 2D plane and is modeled as a disc with radius r_i. At a fixed time t, the agent A_i is at position $\mathbf{x}_i$, defined by the center of the disc, and moves with velocity $\mathbf{v}_i$. The motion of the agent is limited by a maximum speed $u_i^{\max}$. Furthermore, at every time step of the simulation, the agent has a desired velocity $\mathbf{v}_i^{des}$ that is directed towards the agent's goal position g_i and has magnitude equal to the agent's preferred speed u_i^{pref}.

Then, the agent A_i solves interaction with the other agents in three steps:

Step 1 - Retrieve the set of colliding agents. In the first step of our algorithm, we compute the set CA_i of first N agents that are on collision course with the agent A_i. We first extrapolate the future position of A_i based on its desired velocity $\mathbf{v}_i^{des}$. Similarly, we predict the future motions of all the nearest agents that A_i can see by linearly extrapolating their current velocities (A_i can only estimate the actual velocities of the other agents and not their desired ones).

Based on the predicted trajectories, we can now determine whether the agent A_i will collide with another agent A_j. We assume that a collision occurs when A_j lies inside or touches the personal space of A_i, resulting in the following equation:

$$\|(\mathbf{x}_j + \mathbf{v}_j t) - (\mathbf{x}_i + \mathbf{v}_i^{des}t)\| \leq r_j + (r_i + \mu_i), \qquad (3)$$

where $r_i + \mu_i$ denotes the size of A_i's personal space (default value of the minimum security distance μ is set to $\mu = 0.8m$). Solving the above equation for t, we can deduct the possible collision time tc_{ij} between A_i and A_j. If $tc_{ij} \geq 0$, the agent A_j is inserted into the set of the agents that are on collision course with A_i.

We sort this set in order of increasing collision time and keep the first N agents. Experiments have indicated that this number can be kept small (default value is $N = 5$). This not only reduces the running time of our algorithm, but also reflects natural human behaviour. In real-life, an individual takes into account a limited number of other walkers, usually those that are on collision course with him/her in the coming short time.

Step 2 - Determine the set of admissible orientations and speeds. In the second step of the algorithm, we retrieve the set of candidate orientations $O_i \in \mathbb{R}^2$ and speeds $U_i \in \mathbb{R}$ that the agent A_i can select in order to resolve the collisions with the agents that belong to the set CA_i. First, we determine the collision time tc with the most threatening agent, that is the agent in the set CA_i with which A_i will collide first. Then, based on our analysis in Section 2, we compute the

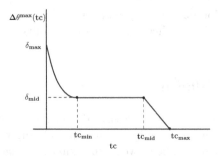

Fig. 3. Maximum orientation deviation for an agent, as a function of the predicted time to collision

maximum angle that the agent A_i can deviate from its desired velocity. The maximum deviation angle $\Delta\theta_i^{\max}$ is approximated by a piecewise function (see Fig. 3) as depicted in Fig. 3.

In the figure, the $tc_{\max}$ defines the maximum time that A_i anticipates a collision. Note that, in the experimental analysis, the maximum collision time averaged over all experiments is $4.2s$. However, in our simulations, each agent has to simultaneously solve interactions with multiple agents. Thus, a higher anticipation time is used ensuring smooth avoidance behaviour (default value is $tc_{\max} = 8s$). The threshold tc_{mid} regulates the start of the constant part of the function, whereas the $tc_{\min}$ defines collisions that are imminent to A_i leading to higher deviation angles (default values are $tc_{\mathrm{mid}} = 6s, tc_{\min} = 2.5s$). The parameter $\delta_{\max}$ determines the maximum admissible angle the A_i can deviate from its desired direction of motion. In our simulations, we assume that virtual characters cannot backtrack and thus, $\delta_{\max} = \pi/2$. Finally, the parameter δ_{mid} defines the deviation angle during the constant interval of the function (default value is $\delta_{mid} = \pi/6$).

Having retrieved the maximum deviation angle $\Delta\theta_i^{\max}$, we determine the agent's admissible orientation domain O_i as follows:

$$O_i = \{\, \mathbf{n}_\theta \mid \theta \in [\theta^{des} - \Delta\theta_i^{\max}, \theta^{des} + \Delta\theta_i^{\max}] \,\}, \qquad (4)$$

where $\mathbf{n}_\theta = [\cos\theta, \sin\theta]^T$ is the unit vector pointing in direction θ and θ^{des} is the orientation derived from A_i's desired velocity.

A similar approach is also used to determine the admissible speed domain U_i of the agent A_i. Based on the speed deviation plot, shown in Fig. 1, the U_i is approximated as follows:

$$U_i = \begin{cases} u \mid u \in [0, u^{\max}], & \text{if } 0 \le tc \le tc_{\min} \\ u \mid u \in [u^{pref}, u^{pref} \pm \Delta u_i^{\max}], & \text{if } tc_{\min} < tc \le tc_{\max} \\ u^{pref}, & \text{if } tc_{\max} < tc \end{cases} \qquad (5)$$

where for the maximum speed deviation $\Delta u_i^{\max}$ holds that $\Delta u_i^{\max} \le \min(u^{\max} - u^{pref}, u^{pref})$. In our simulations, we set the default value of $\Delta u_i^{\max}$ to $\Delta u_i^{\max} = 0.4m/s$, whereas the default value for $u^{\max}$ is set to $u^{\max} = 2.4m/s$.

Step 3 - Select an optimal solution velocity. In the final step of the algorithm, we compute an optimal solution velocity for the agent A_i. First, we deduce the set of feasible avoidance velocities FAV_i from the agent's admissible orientation and speed domains as follows:

$$FAV_i = \{u \, \mathbf{n}_\theta \mid u \in U_i \wedge \mathbf{n}_\theta \in O_i\} \tag{6}$$

In practice, an infinite number of feasible velocities exist. Thus, we restrict the O_i domain into a discrete set of orientation samples (default size of the discretization step is set to 0.13 radians). Similarly, we discretize the U_i domain into a set of adjacent speed samples (default distance between adjacent samples is set to 0.1).

Next, we select the agent's a new velocity $\mathbf{v}_i^{new}$ from the set of feasible velocities. Among the candidate velocities $\mathbf{v}^{cand}$, we retain the solution minimizing the kinetic energy of the agent, the risk of collisions with the other agents and the deviation from the agent's desired velocity:

$$\mathbf{v}_i^{new} = \underset{\mathbf{v}^{cand} \in FAV_i}{\arg\min} \Big\{ \overbrace{\alpha(1 - \frac{cos(\Delta\phi)}{2}) + \beta\frac{\big| \|\mathbf{v}^{cand}\| - \|\mathbf{v}\| \big|}{u^{max}}}^{\text{Energy}} + \underbrace{\gamma\frac{\|\mathbf{v}^{cand} - \mathbf{v}_i^{des}\|}{2u^{max}}}_{\text{Deviation}} + \underbrace{\delta\frac{tc_{max} - tc}{tc_{max}}}_{\text{Collisions}} \Big\}$$

where $\Delta\phi$ defines the angle between the agent's current velocity vector and $\mathbf{v}^{cand}$. Consequently, the energy expenditure in our cost function is approximated by taking into account changes both in the speed and the direction of the agent. Regarding the collision cost, tc denotes the minimum predicted collision time between the agent A_i and the agents in the set CA_i, assuming that A_i selects a velocity $\mathbf{v}^{cand}$; note that tc is upper bounded by tc_{max}. The constants $\alpha, \beta, \gamma, \delta$ define the weights of the specific cost terms and can vary among the agents to simulate a wide variety of avoidance behaviours (default values are $\alpha = 5$, $\beta = 0.5$, $\gamma = \delta = 1$).

Having retrieved the new velocity $\mathbf{v}_i^{new}$, the agent advances to its new position $\mathbf{x}^{new}$ as follows:

$$\mathbf{x}_i^{new} = \mathbf{x}_i + \mathbf{v}_i^{new} \Delta t, \tag{7}$$

where Δt is the time step of the simulation. During each simulation cycle, we also update the orientation of the agent. The energy term in our cost function does not allow the agent to abruptly change its direction, ensuring smooth avoidance motions. Thus, the new orientation θ_i^{new} of the agent is directly inferred from the solution velocity, that is $\theta_i^{new} = \arctan(\mathbf{v}_i^{new})$.

4   Experimetal Results

We evaluated the quality of our approach against a wide range of test-case scenarios. These scenarios range from simple interactions between pairs of agents to more challenging and large test cases.

We refer the reader to http://people.cs.uu.nl/ioannis/interactions for the resulting simulations. In all of our simulations, the agents smoothly evade collisions with other agents and static obstacles. In addition, our approach exhibits emergent phenomena that have been observed in real crowds, such as the dynamic formation of lanes, queuing behaviour, as well as the emergence of slowing down and stopping behaviour to efficiently resolve imminent collisions.

We have also run comparisons with the Reciprocal Velocity Obstacle method [2]. We choose the RVO because of its increased popularity among the methods that are based on the VO formulation, and its many existing variants. The main difference between our approach and VO methods is that in the latter, at every simulation step, each agent tries to find an optimal collision-free velocity. Consequently, in rather confined and crowded environments, the agent may not be able to find such a velocity and thus, the only solution would be to abruptly adjust its direction or change its speed and stop. In contrast, our approach favours small changes in the velocity of each agent, even though such changes may lead to a collision in the (far) future. Assuming that the other agents will also slightly adapt their motions, collisions are resolved in advance with minimal effort.

Besides the quality, we are also interested in the performance of our proposed approach. To test its usability in real-time applications, we selected a varying number of agents and placed them randomly across an environment filled with small-sized obstacles. Each agent had to advance toward a random goal position avoiding collisions with the obstacles and the other moving agents; when it had reached its destination, a new goal was chosen. The running time of our method on a 2.4 GHz Core 2 Duo CPU (on a single thread) scaled almost linearly with the number of agents. Even for 3000 agents, it took 129 ms per simulation step to compute the three steps of our collision avoidance algorithm. Since, in our system, the velocities of the agents were updated at 5 fps, it is clear that our approach can simulate thousands of virtual characters at interactive rates.

Acknowledgments

This research has been supported by the GATE project, funded by the Netherlands Organization for Scientific Research (NWO) and the Netherlands ICT Research and Innovation Authority (ICT Regie).

References

1. Fiorini, P., Shiller, Z.: Motion planning in dynamic environments using velocity obstacles. International Journal of Robotics Research 17, 760–772 (1998)
2. van den Berg, J.P., Lin, M., Manocha, D.: Reciprocal velocity obstacles for real-time multi-agent navigation. In: Proc. of IEEE Conference on Robotics and Automation, pp. 1928–1935 (2008)
3. Pettré, J., Ondrej, J., Olivier, A.-H., Crétual, A., Donikian, S.: Experiment-based modeling, simulation and validation of interactions between virtual walkers. In: SCA 2009: ACM SIGGRAPH/Eurographics Symposium on Computer Animation, pp. 189–198 (2009)
4. van Basten, B.J.H., Jansen, S.E.M., Karamouzas, I.: Exploiting motion capture to enhance avoidance behaviour in games. In: Proc. of Motion in Games, pp. 29–40 (2009)

Influence of Personality Traits on Backchannel Selection

Etienne de Sevin, Sylwia Julia Hyniewska, and Catherine Pelachaud

CNRS - Telecom ParisTech
37/39, rue Dareau
75014 Paris, France
{etienne.de-sevin, sylwia.hyniewska,
catherine.pelachaud}@telecom-paristech.fr

Abstract. Our aim is to build a real-time Embodied Conversational Agent able to act as an interlocutor in interaction, generating automatically verbal and non verbal signals. These signals, called backchannels, provide information about the listener's mental state towards the perceived speech. The ECA reacts differently to user's behavior depending on its predefined personality. Personality influences the generation and the selection of backchannels. In this paper, we propose a listener's action selection algorithm working in real-time to choose the type and the frequency of backchannels to be displayed by the ECA in accordance with its personality. The algorithm is based on the extroversion and neuroticism dimensions of personality. We present an evaluation on how backchanels managed by this algorithm are congruent with intuitive expectations of participants in terms of behavior specific to different personalities.

Keywords: Backchannels, Personality, Action selection, Behavior, Mimicry, ECAs.

1 Introduction

A great challenge that is to be faced in the design of Embodied Conversational Agents (ECA) is the issue of credibility, not only in the agent's aspect but also in its behavior [1]. The ECA has to display appropriate verbal and non-verbal behaviors according to its internal variables such as personality and external variables [2].

This work is part of the EU SEMAINE project in which an Embodied Conversational Agent, called Sensitive Artificial Listener (SAL) [3], dialogs with the user. This project aims to build a multimodal talking agent able to exhibit autonomously appropriate verbal and non verbal behaviors when it plays the role of the listener. Four psychologically different characters (SAL agents) have been created to elicit different types of emotion - each employing individual dialogue strategies, and displaying uniquely different responsive reactions [4]. To this end a credible and real-time listening behaviour is important.

Trait models of personality assume that traits influence behavior, and that they are fundamental properties of an individual. We base our work in a dimensional perception of personality. We focus on the extroversion-introversion and the neuroticism-emotional stability dimensions (as defined by [5] [6]), which are central to major trait

J. Allbeck et al. (Eds.): IVA 2010, LNAI 6356, pp. 187–193, 2010.
© Springer-Verlag Berlin Heidelberg 2010

theories and for which we can formulate concrete predictions in terms of behavior, such as mimicry or quantity of movements.

On the individual differences level it has been shown that empathic individuals exhibit mimicry of the postures, mannerisms, and facial expressions of others to a greater extent than do not empathic individuals [7]. Researchers have shown that in general mimicry helps to make the interaction an easier and more pleasant experience, improving the feeling of empathy [8]. Empathy is the capability to share or interpret correctly another being's emotions and feelings [9]. As according to Eysenck [10] neuroticism is negatively correlated with empathy, high neuroticism might be negatively related to the level of mimicry behavior.

Studies have also shown that high extroversion is associated with greater levels of gesturing, more frequent head nods, and general speed of movement [11].

In this paper, we focus on the influence of personality on the selection of backchannels [12]. We propose a backchannel selection algorithm working in real-time to choose the type and the frequency of backchannels to be displayed according to the personality of the ECA. Linking the extroversion and neuroticism dimensions with the two backchannel variables, unstable characters should perform less mimicry than stable ones and extravert characters should perform more backchannels than introvert ones.

The next section is a brief description of related work. Section 3 presents our real-time algorithm. It selects backchannels according to ECA's personality: extroversion is associated with the frequency of the backchannels, while neuroticism with their type. In section 4, we detail the evaluation study that we performed to verify our hypotheses and in the section 5 we discuss the results.

2 Related Work

Previous works on ECAs have provided first approaches to a backchannel model. Thórisson [13] developed a talking head, called Gandalf, able to produce real-time backchannel signals during a conversation with a user. The Listening Agent [14], developed at ICT, produces backchannel signals based on real-time analysis of the speaker's non verbal behavior (as head motion and body posture) and of acoustic features extracted from the speaker's voice. Kopp [15] proposed a model for generating incremental backchannels. The system is based both on a probabilistic model, that defines a set of rules to determine the occurrence of a backchannel, and on a simulation model that perceives, understands and evaluates input through multi-layered processes.

3 Listener Backchannel Selection Algorithm for ECA

The proposed work is part of a pre-existing system for the generation of backchannels for an ECA listener. In this architecture, two types of backchannel modules have been implemented: mimicry and response backchannels [1].

In the SEMAINE project, four SAL agents have been designed with their own personality traits. Poppy is outgoing and cheerful; Spike is aggressive and argumentative; Prudence is reliable and pragmatic; and Obadiah is pessimistic and gloomy. We can place the four SAL agents on Eysenck's two dimensions (see figure 1) of extroversion and neuroticism (emotional stability) [5].

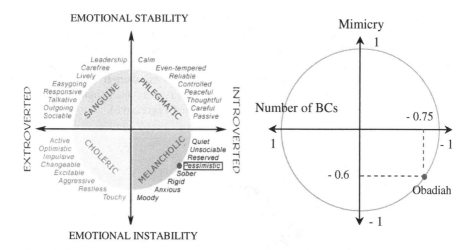

Fig. 1. Eysenck's two dimensional representation and our hypothesis of its implication on mimicry and number of backchannels. Example of deduction for Obadiah.

Our aim is to test how backchannels influence the perception of the agent's personality. To concentrate only on the behaviors and to avoid having to consider extra variables, we are considering only one facial model.

We formulate two hypotheses:

H1 : the extroversion dimension can be associated with the frequency of the backchannels (mimicry and response backchannels). Poppy (outgoing) should perform more backchannels and Obadiah (pessimistic) less [11].

H2 : the emotional stability dimension can be linked with the type of backchannels displayed by the ECA (mimicry tendency). Prudence (reliable) should mimic more than Spike (aggressive) [8].

Table. 1. Setting of BC priority and frequency for the four SAL agents

	Obadiah	Poppy	Prudence	Spike
BC priority (mimicry)	- 0.6	0.25	0.90	- 0.85
BC frequency	- 0.85	0.95	- 0.5	0.55

Following our two hypotheses, we can easily set frequency and priority of backchannels for our listener backchannel selection. We locate the personality on Eysenck's representation and by translating to our graph we obtain values for the frequency and priority of backchannels. For example, Obadiah who is pessimistic, performs few backchannels (-0.75) and only some mimicry (-0.6). We obtain these values for the four personalities (see table 1).

4   Evaluation

We performed our evaluation study on internet using a web browser showing videos. In our video corpus the woman is telling a story to a virtual agent and the agent is performing some backchannels showing listening behavior (see figure 2). We evaluate two variables: the type and the frequency of backchannels according to personality. We show to the participants a set of interactions and ask them to evaluate for each animation the appropriateness of the frequency and type of backchannels for a described personality (pessimistic, outgoing, reliable and aggressive).

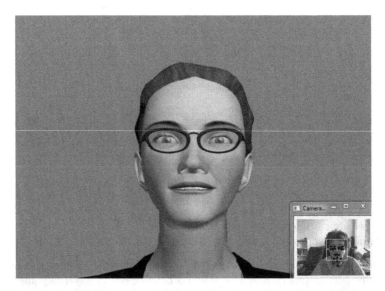

Fig. 2. Image of a video evaluated by participants: a user interacting with an agent

Each evaluation page is composed of the description of a virtual agent personality, a reminder of instructions, and two videos. For each video participants answer on a likert scale if the agent reacts appropriately (BC type: from "not at all" to "completely) and sufficiently (BC frequency: from "not enough" to "too much") accordingly to the described personality. Finally, the participants have to determine which video matches the defined personality best.

One condition is evaluated by page for the four personalities. On each page, we have one video with BC influenced by personality in terms of three conditions:

C1 :   variation of the backchannel frequency (with BC types baseline)
C2 :   variation of the backchannel type (with BC frequency baseline)
C3 :   variation of both of them

The second video corresponds to one of the two personalities of the other personality dimension. For example, if the defined personality is outgoing (extroversion dimension) and the condition is focused on BC frequency (with a BC types baseline), the second video is chosen randomly between videos displaying frequencies characteristic of Spike or Prudence (neuroticism dimension).

5 Results

Ninety three participants (57 women, 37 men) mainly from France (80%) took part in the study. 54 % of the participants chose the video that suited the described personality in terms of backchannels. The most recognized was Spike (62%), followed by Poppy (53%), Obadiah (53%) and Prudence (52%).

H1 Hypothesis: The majority of the participants answered that the frequency of backchannels of the agent is adequate for the four personalities. This was not the default choice and the participants actively chose this response. We performed an ANOVA and Paired samples tests to verify our H1 hypothesis about the selection of BC frequency (see section 3.2). We expected the C3 condition to be evaluated better by participants than the C2 condition.

The answers of the participants to the question on the frequency of the backchannels show an effect of the personality and of the condition (ANOVA, $p < .05$) but not of the interaction of personalities and conditions (ANOVA, $p > .05$). The variations of BC frequency (difference between the conditions C2 and C3) for Poppy (outgoing) and Prudence (reliable) were significant (t test, $p < .05$) and not signicative for Obadiah (pessimistic) and Spike (aggressive) ($p > .05$). The participants consider that the C3 condition for Poppy and Prudence is better than the C2 condition. The variations of BC types (difference between the conditions C1 and C3) for the four personalities are significant ($p < .05$). The participants consider that the C3 condition is better than the C1 condition for all the personalities.

H2 Hypothesis: Concerning the type of backchannels, 40,6% of the participants have evaluated better the appropriate video and 25.9% have evaluated both equally. Except Spike, the backchannels are evaluated as appropriate, particularly Poppy. We performed Friedman's ANOVA and Wilcoxon Signed Rank Test to verify our H2 hypothesis about the selection of BC type (see section 3.2). We expect the C3 condition to be evaluated better by participants than the C1 condition.

The answers of the participants on the appropriateness of the backchannels (type) are significant (Friedman test, $p < .05$). The variation of BC type (difference between conditions C1 and C3) for Obadiah (pessimistic) is significant ($p < .05$) and not signicative for the other personalities ($p > .05$). The participants consider that only for Obadiah the C3 condition is better than the C1 condition.

6 Discussion

The aim of this evaluation study was to check if the variation of the generated BC type and frequency have an impact on participant's perception. The first hypothesis was partially verified: although the attributions were higher with the selection of BC frequency than that of alternatives, the difference was not significative for some personalities. The second Hypothesis was verified only for Obadiah (pessimistic).

Concerning hypothesis H1, the participants judge by a majority that the frequency of backchannels are adequate for the personalities but it is only significative for Poppy (outgoing) and Prudence (pragmatic). When an agent performs many backchannels, it is associated with extroversion. When a agent performs a little less than the normal, it is associated with pragmatism. However the inversion is not recognized in this evaluation. Obadiah (pessimistic) should maybe have performed very few backchannels in order to see a real difference. For Spike who is aggressive, people may expect a higher frequency of backchannels. We also see that the BC type has an effect on the perception of the BC frequency. Participants evaluate better the BC frequency when only the BC types vary.

Concerning hypothesis H2, we believe it is the adjective describing the personalities that might not have been optimal in conveying the meaning we were looking for. Many comments say that participants didn't understand the adjective "pragmatic" and they do not really know how an outgoing person reacts. This miscomprehension of the terms may explain why the participants do not really see a difference between BC types selected by the listener backchannel selection. If they do not have a clear idea about how the agent should react, they cannot see the difference in the evaluation. These names need to be clarified for the next evaluations. Moreover it is difficult to show aggression for Spike only with backchannels. We believe it could explain the bad evaluation from the participants.

7   Conclusion

In this paper, we presented an evaluation of a backchannel selection algorithm working in real-time. It chooses the types and the frequency of backchannels to be displayed by the ECA. We evaluate that behavior is interpreted as appropriate for a personality when 1) backchannel frequency is linked with the extroversion dimension and 2) backchannel type with the neuroticism dimension. The frequency-extroversion link is verified for outgoing and pragmatic personalities. The type-neuroticism link is verified only for the pessimistic personality. We have to keep in mind that the personality terms need to be clarified for the participants, as the term "pragmatic" was clearly misunderstood by participants and biased these results. We conclude that the selection of type and frequency of backchannels by the presented algorithm does contribute to the interpretation of behavior in terms of personality traits.

Acknowledgments

This research was supported by the European Community's Seventh Framework Programme (FP7/2007-2013) under grant agreement No. 211486 (SEMAINE) and Web 2.0 MyPresentingAvatar project.

References

1. Bevacqua, E., Mancini, M., Pelachaud, C.: A Listening Agent Exhibiting Variable Behaviour. In: Prendinger, H., Lester, J.C., Ishizuka, M. (eds.) IVA 2008. LNCS (LNAI), vol. 5208, pp. 262–269. Springer, Heidelberg (2008)
2. de Sevin, E., Pelachaud, C.: Real-time Backchannel Selection for ECAs according to User's Level of Interest. In: Ruttkay, Z., Kipp, M., Nijholt, A., Vilhjálmsson, H.H. (eds.) IVA 2009. LNCS, vol. 5773, Springer, Heidelberg (2009)
3. Douglas-Cowie, E., Cowie, R., Cox, C., Amir, N., Heylen, D.: The Sensitive Artificial Listener: an induction technique for generating emotionally coloured conversation. In: LREC 2008 (2008)
4. McRorie, M., Sneddon, I., de Sevin, E., Bevacqua, E., Pelachaud, C.: A Model of Personality and Emotional Traits. In: Ruttkay, Z., Kipp, M., Nijholt, A., Vilhjálmsson, H.H. (eds.) IVA 2009. LNCS, vol. 5773, Springer, Heidelberg (2009)
5. Eysenck, H.J.: Dimensions of personality: Criteria for a taxonomic paradigm. Personality and Individual Differences 12, 773–779 (1991)
6. Costa Jr., P.T., McCrae, R.R.: Four ways five factors are basic. Personality and Individual Differences 13, 653–665 (1992)
7. Sonnby-Borgstrom, M.: Automatic mimicry reactions as related to differences in emotional empathy. Scandinavian Journal of Psychology 43, 433–443 (2002)
8. Chartrand, T.L., Maddux, W., Lakin, J.: Beyond the perception-behavior link: The ubiquitous utility and motivational moderators of nonconscious mimicry. In: Hassin, R., Uleman, J., Bargh, J.A. (eds.) The new un-conscious, pp. 334–361. Oxford University Press, New York (2005)
9. Decety, J., Jackson, P.L.: The functional architecture of human empathy. Behavioral and Cognitive Neuroscience Reviews (3), 71–100 (2004)
10. Eysenck, S.B.G., Eysenck, H.J.: Impulsiveness and Venturesomeness - Their Position in a Dimensional System of Personality Description. Psychol. Rep. 43(3), 1247–1255 (1978)
11. Borkenau, P., Liebler, A.: Trait inferences: Sources of validity at zero acquaintance. Journal of Personality and Social Psychology 62, 645–657 (1992)
12. Bevacqua, E., de Sevin, E., Pelachaud, C., McRorie, M., Sneddon, I.: Building Credible Agents: Behaviour Influenced by Personality and Emotional Traits. In: Proceedings of International Conference on Kansei Engineering and Emotion Research 2010, KEER 2010, Paris, France (2010)
13. Thórisson, K.: Communicative Humanoids: A Computational Model of Psychosocial Dialogue Skills. PhD Thesis, MIT Media Laboratory (1996)
14. Maatman, R., Gratch, J., Marsella, S.: Natural Behavior of a Listening Agent. In: Panayiotopoulos, T., Gratch, J., Aylett, R.S., Ballin, D., Olivier, P., Rist, T. (eds.) IVA 2005. LNCS (LNAI), vol. 3661, pp. 25–36. Springer, Heidelberg (2005)
15. Kopp, S., Stocksmeier, T.: Incremental multimodal feedback for conversational agents. In: Pelachaud, C., Martin, J.-C., André, E., Chollet, G., Karpouzis, K., Pelé, D. (eds.) IVA 2007. LNCS (LNAI), vol. 4722, pp. 139–146. Springer, Heidelberg (2007)

Multimodal Backchannels for Embodied Conversational Agents

Elisabetta Bevacqua[1], Sathish Pammi[2], Sylwia Julia Hyniewska[1],
Marc Schröder[2], and Catherine Pelachaud[1]

[1] LTCI, CNRS - Telecom ParisTech, 37/39 rue Dareau, 75014 Paris, France
[2] DFKI GmbH - Language Technology Lab, Stuhlsatzenhausweg 3, D-66123
Saarbrücken, Germany

Abstract. One of the most desirable characteristics of an Embodied
Conversational Agent (ECA) is the capability of interacting with users
in a human-like manner. While listening to a user, an ECA should be able
to provide backchannel signals through visual and acoustic modalities. In
this work we propose an improvement of our previous system to generate
multimodal backchannel signals on visual *and* acoustic modalities. A
perceptual study has been performed to understand how context-free
multimodal backchannels are interpreted by users.

1 Introduction

In the past twenty years several researchers in the human-machine interface
field have concentrated their efforts in the development of Embodied Conversational Agents (ECAs): virtual humanoid entities able to interact with users in a
human-like manner. To sustain a natural interaction with users, conversational
agents must be able to exhibit appropriate behaviour while speaking and while
listening. In this paper we focus on the listener's behaviour and in particular
on the signals performed by the interlocutor. To describe this type of signals,
Yngve [Yng70] introduced the term *backchannel*: non-intrusive acoustic and visual signals provided during the speaker's turn. According to Allwood et al.
and Poggi [ANA93, Pog07], acoustic and visual backchannels provide information about the basic communicative functions, as perception, attention, interest,
understanding, attitude (e.g., belief, liking) and acceptance towards what the
speaker is saying. In previous works [HBTP07, BHTP07] we performed perceptual studies on unimodal backchannel signals displayed on visual modality. The
results of these evaluations helped us to build up a library (called *backchannel lexicon*) of prototypical backchannel signals to be used in a listener module
for an ECA. However, backchannels are provided not only through the visual
modality, but also through voice by uttering paraverbals, words or short sentences [Gar98, ANA93]. In this work we propose to improve user-agent interaction by introducing multimodal signals in the backchannels performed by our
ECA. Moreover, we present a perceptual study that we performed to get a better understanding about how multimodal backchannels are interpreted by users.

J. Allbeck et al. (Eds.): IVA 2010, LNAI 6356, pp. 194–200, 2010.

Such an evaluation allows us to extend the backchannel lexicon. This work is set within the Sensitive Artificial Listening Agent (SAL) project that is part of the EU project SEMAINE (http://www.semaine-project.eu). Such a project aims to build an autonomous talking agent able to exhibit appropriate behaviour while listening to a user. The agent has to encourage the user into talking pulling him towards specific emotional states.

The following Section provides an overview of the related works. In Section 3 we explain how visual and acoustic backchannels are generated. Section 4 describes our ECA system. Finally, we describe the perceptual study we have conducted and we analyse the results.

2   Related Works

Past researches on ECAs have provided first approaches to the implementation of a backchannel model. K. R. Thórisson [Thö96] developed a talking head, called Gandalf, capable of interacting with users using verbal and visual signals (like a short utterance or a head nod). REA, the Real Estate Agent developed by Cassell et al. [CB99], is able to provide backchannel signals such as paraverbals (e.g. *mmhmm*), head nods or a short statements (like *I see*). Its task consists in showing users the characteristics of houses displayed behind her. Gratch et al. [GWG+07] developed the "Rapport Agent", an agent that provides solely visual backchannels when listening. The system analyzes the user's visual behaviour (nod, shake, head movement, mimicry) and some features of the user's voice to decide when backchannel must be triggered and which signal must be dispayed. Morency et al. [MdKG09] proposed an enhancement of this type of system introducing a machine learning method to find the speaker's multimodal features that are important and can affect timing of the agent backchannel. Kopp et al. [KAG+08] proposed a backchannel model based on a reasoning and deliberative processing that plans how and when the agent must react according to its intentions, beliefs and desires.

All these models above take into account a small number of multimodal backchannel signals, moreover their communicative functions are not really defined. Through this work we aim to improve our system by introducing a large set of vocalizations to generate multimodal backchannels. Moreover we want to define the meaning that these signals convey when displayed by an ECA.

3   Multimodal Backchannels

Visual signals. As a first step we endowed our agent with the capability of providing visual backchannel signals while listening to a user. From the literature [ANA93, Pog07] we selected twelve frequent meanings related to the listener's reactions and we performed perceptual studies to understand how users associate these meanings to a set of visual backchannels displayed by a virtual agent [HBTP07, BHTP07]. The results of these evaluations allowed us to define some associations between the listener's communicative functions and a set of visual signals. Each of these associations represents one element of the agent's backchannel lexicon. Within the SEMAINE project new visual signals have been added. Since SAL provides four agents with different emotional traits, the backchannel lexicon has been expanded by introducing signals that are typical to each agent. For example, Spike, who is angry and aggressive, scowls even when it performs a head nod to show agreement.

Endowing TTS with vocal backchannels. Like visual backchannels, vocal backchannels also play an important role in communicating listener intentions while the interlocutor is talking. For the generation of vocal backchannels, an ECA should be able to use the same voice with which it speaks. As the SEMAINE project is already using expressive voices available in MARY TTS [ST03, SPT09], our work requires the addition of a new functionality to TTS: to generate vocal backchannels. To collect database of listener vocalisations as they appear natural only in conversation, in addition to speech synthesis recordings, free dialogue of around 30 minutes was recorded with a professional female British actor with whom we had recorded a happy expressive speech synthesis database. The actor was instructed to participate in a free dialogue, but to take predominantly a listener role. Listener vocalisations were marked on the time axis and transcribed as a single (pseudo-)word, such as *myeah* or *(laughter)*. The dialogue speech contains 174 spontaneous listener vocalisations from the actor. Among them, most frequent segmental forms are *yeah, (sigh), (laughter), mhmh, (gasp), oh.* Phonetic alignment of speech is always required for ECA's lip synchronisation. Hand-labelled phonetic segment labels for all vocalisations were provided by a phonetically trained student assistant. The manual labels of a vocalisation contain time-stamps of each phonetic segment as well as corresponding suitable phone description. This is suitable for vocalisations with a phonemic structure such as *myeah*, but is problematic for other vocalisations such as laughter, sighs, or a rapid intake of breath. In these cases, the viseme-based mouth shapes can only serve as coarse approximations of natural behaviour. Annotations of intonation, voice quality and meaning are also performed. The MARY TTS framework was extended to generate listener vocalisations based on an XML request. The TTS system stores the recorded audio of each vocalisation together with phone segment labels and features representing the segmental form, intonation, voice quality and possible meanings of the vocalisation, as annotated previously. At run-time synthesis, the selection of a vocalisation is an extension to the MARY TTS unit selection mechanism. A cost function which operates on the features of each vocalisation finds the most suitable vocalisation for a given markup.

4   System Overview

Our system is implemented on top of the SEMAINE API, a distributed multi-platform component integration framework for real-time interactive systems [Sch10]. The communication passes via the message-oriented middleware ActiveMQ. The architecture of our system is shown in Figure 1. Components (that

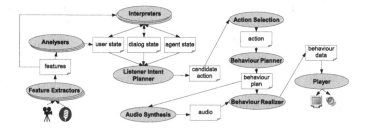

Fig. 1. Architecture of the SAL system

receive and send messages) are shown as ovals, message types as white rectangles. The architecture can generate the agent's behaviour both while it speaks and it listens, however in this paper we are interested in the generation of the listener behaviour. The raw user input is converted by a set of feature extractors into raw feature vectors which are sent very frequently (e.g., every 10 ms for audio, and for every video frame). The analyzers components derive some sense from the raw features in a context free manner; then the interpreters derive the system's *current best guess* regarding the state of the user and the dialogue. In parallel, the **Listener Intent Planner**, can trigger backchannels according to the user's behaviour, which are filtered by an Action Selection. Then, the **Behaviour Planner** computes a list of adequate visual behavioural signals for each communicative function the agent aims to transmit through the backchannel. The acoustic signals are generated by the **Audio Synthesis**. This module uses MARY TTS (see Section 3). MARY TTS looks up available vocalisations for the given speaker and will generate the most appropriate vocalisation found for the request. Finally, the agent behaviour is realized by the **Behaviour Realizer** module and rendered by a 3D character player.

5   Evaluation Description

We performed an evaluation study to analyze multimodal backchannels. To this purpose, we asked subjects to judge a set of multimodal signals performed by the 3D agent Greta [NBMP09]. Like in our previous studies, we considered in this perceptual evaluation the twelve meanings: *agreement, disagreement, acceptance, refusal, interest, not interest, belief, disbelief, understanding, not understanding, liking, disliking*. The signals were context-free, that is without knowing the discursive context of the speaker's speech. To create videos we selected 7 visual signals and 8 audio signals (7 vocalisations plus silence). The visual signals were chosen among those we studied in previous evaluations [HBTP07, BHTP07]. The vocalisations were selected using an informal listening test. Initially, three participants assigned each of the 174 vocalisations produced by the speaker to one of the 12 meanings used in this experiment. We then selected the seven stimuli which seemed least ambiguous for their respective meaning, in order to cover a reasonable range of different vocalisations. We generated 56 multimodal signals as the combinations of the visual and acoustic cues selected. Since there was quite a lot of videos to evaluate, we decided to split them in three sets (A, B and C). We hypothesized that:

- **Hp1:** the strongest attribution of a meaning will be conveyed by the multimodal signals obtained by the combination of visual and acoustic cues representative of the given meaning.
- **Hp2:** in some occasion, multimodal signals convey a meaning different from the ones associated to the particular visual and acoustic cues when presented on their own.
- **Hp3:** visual and acoustic signals that have strongly opposite meanings are rated as nonsense: like *nod+no, shake+ok, shake+yeah*.

55 participants (22 women, 33 men) with a mean age of 31.5 years, mainly from France (33%), Italy (18%), accessed anonymously to the evaluation through a web browser. The first page provided instructions, the second collected demographic information. Then the multimodal signals were played one at a time. Participants used a bipolar 7-points Likert scale: from -3 (extremely negative attribution) to +3 (extremely positive attribution). The evaluation was in English.

Table 1. Meanings significantly associated to the multimodal backchannels. AG=agreement, AC=acceptance, DA=disagreement, R=refusal, L=liking, NL=no liking, B=belief, DB=disbelief, I=interest, NI=no interest, U=understanding, NU=no understanding

	ok	ooh	gosh	really	yeah	no	m-mh	(silence)
raise eyebrows	AG, AC, U	U		I		NL		
nod	B, AG, AC, U	AC, L, U, I	AG, AC, U, I	L, U, I	B, AG, I AC, U		B, AC, AG	B, AG, AC, U
smile	B, AG, AC, U, L, I	B, AG, AC, U, L, I	AG, L	AG, AC, U, L, I	AG, AC, U, L, I	DB	B, AG, AC, L	
frown	AG, AC	NL	NL	NL, I		DA, NL		DB, N, U, NL
raise left eyebrow	AG, AC	U	DB	DB, I		DB, R		DB, NL
shake		DB, NL	DB, NL	DB, NI	DB, NL	DA, R	DA, R, NL	DA, DB, R, NL, NI
tilt&frown	AC	U		DB, I	AC, L	DA, R, NL		DB, NU

5.1 Results and Discussion

The 95% confidence interval was calculated for all the meanings. Table 1 reports all signals for which the mean was significantly above zero (for positive meanings) or below zero (for negative meanings). For each dimension of meaning (i.e. agreement/disagreement, acceptance/refusal, etc.) we performed a repeated measures ANOVA. We obtained that for all dimensions there was an effect of different visual cues ($p < .05$) and an effect of acoustic cues ($p < .05$). We did not find any effect of the interaction between the visual and acoustic cues (p>.05). Some t-test results are reported here detail. The signal *nod+yeah* (N=12, mean=2.75) was more strongly judged as showing agreement than any other signal (p<.05). *Nod* (N=12, mean=2.07) has the second highest attribution of agreement. The signal *shake+no* (N=14, mean=-1.71) was not more strongly judged as showing disagreement than the other signals. The highest disagreement mean is for *shake* (N=14, mean=-2.07), however it is not significantly different from *shake+no*, *shake+m-mh* (p>.05). There is a difference between *shake* and *shake+yeah*, which is the fourth highest disagreement attribution (0.18). The signal *raise eyebrows+gosh* was not even significantly associated to interest. The highest meaning of interest was equally attributed to *smile+ok*, *nod+ok*, *nod+ooh*, *smile+ooh* (p>.05). Highest attribution of understanding was observed for *raise eyebrows+ooh*, *nod+ooh*, *nod+really*, *nod+yeah* and *nod*. *Raise eyebrows+ooh* (mean=1.56) was not more strongly judged as showing agreement than the other signals. A significant difference was even found between *nod-ooh* and *raise eyebrows+ooh* (p<.05): *nod-ooh* was more strongly associated to the understanding than *raise eyebrows+ooh*. In conclusion our first hypothesis has been only partially satisfied. As regard to the third hypothesis we saw that four multimodal signals were significantly rated as nonsense: *nod+no* (p<.05), *shake+yeah* (p<.05), *shake+ok* (p<.05) and *shake+really* (p<.05).

Our first hypothesis has been only partially satisfied. Results showed that the strongest attribution for a meaning is not always conveyed by the multimodal signals obtained by the combination of visual and acoustic cues representative of the given meaning. That means that the meaning conveyed by a multimodal backchannel cannot be simply inferred by the meaning of each visual and acoustic cues that compose it. It must be considered and studied as a whole to determine the meaning it transmits when displayed by virtual agents. Moreover, we found that some multimodal signals convey a meaning different from the ones associated to the particular visual and acoustic cues when presented on their own (Hp2). Our evaluation showed also that multimodal signals composed by visual and acoustic cues that have strongly opposite meanings are rated as nonsense. As expected *nod+no*, *shake+yeah*, *shake+ok* and *shake+really* were rated as senseless. What is more, a high attribution of nonsense does not necessarily exclude the attribution of other meanings. Thus, the high nonsense signal of *shake+yeah* was also highly judged as showing disbelief. A possible explanation would be that these signals might be particularly context depend. This evaluation gave us a better insight about several multimodal backchannels and the meaning they convey. The results have been used to enrich and expand the backchannel lexicon of our virtual agent.

6   Conclusion

We have presented an ECA system able to generate a wide variety of multimodal backchannel signals simulating listening behaviour. A perceptual study has been conducted in order to understand how context-free multimodal backchannels are interpreted by users.

Acknowledgement

This work has been funded by the STREP SEMAINE project IST-211486 (http://www.semaine-project.eu).

References

[ANA93]   Allwood, J., Nivre, J., Ahlsn, E.: On the semantics and pragmatics of linguistic feedback. Semantics 9(1) (1993)

[BHTP07] Bevacqua, E., Heylen, D., Tellier, M., Pelachaud, C.: Facial feedback signals for ECAs. In: AISB 2007 Annual convention, workshop "Mindful Environments", Newcastle upon Tyne, UK, pp. 147–153 (April 2007)

[CB99]   Cassell, J., Bickmore, T.: Embodiment in conversational interfaces: Rean Human Factors in Computing Systems, Pittsburgh, PA (1999)

[Gar98]   Gardner, R.: Between Speaking and Listening: The Vocalisation of Understandings. Applied Linguistics 19(2), 204–224 (1998)

[GWG+07] Gratch, J., Wang, N., Gerten, J., Fast, E., Duffy, R.: Creating rapport with virtual agents. In: Pelachaud, C., Martin, J.-C., André, E., Chollet, G., Karpouzis, K., Pelé, D., et al. (eds.) IVA 2007. LNCS (LNAI), vol. 4722, pp. 125–138. Springer, Heidelberg (2007)

[HBTP07] Heylen, D., Bevacqua, E., Tellier, M., Pelachaud, C.: Searching for prototypical facial feedback signals. In: Pelachaud, C., Martin, J.-C., André, E., Chollet, G., Karpouzis, K., Pelé, D. (eds.) IVA 2007. LNCS (LNAI), vol. 4722, pp. 147–153. Springer, Heidelberg (2007)

[KAG+08] Kopp, S., Allwood, J., Grammer, K., Ahlsen, E., Stocksmeier, T.: Modeling embodied feedback with virtual humans. In: Wachsmuth, I., Knoblich, G. (eds.) ZiF Research Group International Workshop. LNCS (LNAI), vol. 4930, pp. 18–37. Springer, Heidelberg (2008)

[MdKG09] Morency, L.-P., de Kok, I., Gratch, J.: A probabilistic multimodal approach for predicting listener backchannels. In: Autonomous Agents and Multi-Agent Systems (2009)

[NBMP09] Niewiadomski, R., Bevacqua, E., Mancini, M., Pelachaud, C.: Greta: an interactive expressive eca system. In: AAMAS 2009 - Autonomous Agents and MultiAgent Systems, Budapest, Hungary (2009)

[Pog07]   Poggi, I.: Mind, hands, face and body. A goal and belief view of multimodal communication. Weidler, Berlin (2007)

[Sch10]   Schröder, M.: The semaine api: Towards a standards-based framework for building emotion-oriented systems. In: Advances in Human-Computer Interaction (2010)

[SPT09]   Schröder, M., Pammi, S., Türk, O.: Multilingual mary tts participation in the blizzard challenge 2009. In: Proc. Blizzard Challenge 2009 (2009)

[ST03]   Schröder, M., Trouvain, J.: The German text-to-speech synthesis system MARY: A tool for research, development and teaching. International Journal of Speech technology 6, 365–377 (2003)

[Thö96]   Thórisson, K.R.: Communiative Humanoids: A Computational Model of Psychosocial Dialogue Skills. PhD thesis, MIT Media Laboratory (1996)

[Yng70]   Yngve, V.: On getting a word in edgewise. In: Papers from the Sixth Regional Meeting of the Chicago Linguistic Society, pp. 567–577 (1970)

A Virtual Interpreter for the Italian Sign Language

Vincenzo Lombardo, Fabrizio Nunnari, and Rossana Damiano

Virtual Reality and Multimedia Park, Torino (Italy)
Dipartimento di Informatica, Torino (Italy)

Abstract. In this paper, we describe a software module for the animation of a virtual interpreter that translates from Italian to the Italian Sign Language (LIS).

The system we describe takes a "synthetic" approach to the generation of the sign language, by composing and parametrizing pre-captured and hand-animated signs, to adapt them to the context in which they occur.

Keywords: Animated agents, sign languages, animation languages.

1 Introduction

Sign languages build communication through features that involve the use of hands, but also non manual components, such as head, torso and facial expression. Recently, many projects have employed animated agents for the construction of interfaces that support the communication with deaf people [13,3,7,4,1]. The scenarios in which these agents can be used include different communicative situations and support types, ranging from web pages and mobile devices to television broadcasting. In this paper, we describe a system that generates the real-time animation of the virtual interpreter of the Italian Sign Language (LIS, Lingua Italiana dei Segni), as part of the ATLAS (Automatic Translation into sign LAnguageS) project for the Italian-to-LIS translation.[1]

A LIS sentence consists of a sequence of signs, ordered according to the LIS order, accompanied by possible parallel constructs, anchored in specific phenomena. Such phenomena include the positioning of the gesture in front of the interpreter (the "signing space"), the increase or reduction of the "size" of a sign or its repetition (e.g., for plural). Other more complex phenomena involve the movement of hands through the space from and to context-dependent positions, such as for the verbs "to go" and "to give" [10], possibly mixed with the use of hand-shape to indicate specific types of entities [8].

Computer animation is a natural candidate for the development of systems that communicate by using a sign language, since the generation of a full-fledged sign language requires a "synthetic" approach to adapt the default signs

---

[1] This work has been partially supported by the Converging Technologies project ATLAS funded by Regione Piemonte, Italy.

J. Allbeck et al. (Eds.): IVA 2010, LNAI 6356, pp. 201–207, 2010.

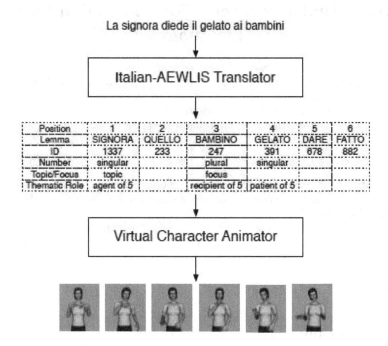

Fig. 1. In the ATLAS project, the interpretation process is performed in two steps. First, the text ("The lady gave the icecream to the children") is translated into an intermediate representation of its syntactic and semantic relations, called AEWLIS ("LADY THAT-BABY ICECREAM GIVE DONE"). Then, the LIS virtual interpreter animates the corresponding LIS signs.

(archived in a repository) to the specific context of a sentence [12,6]. So, pre-recorded animations, that include the interpreter's body and face, must be open to parametrization .

The ATLAS project takes a mixed approach to the generation of signs, by using an animation language to compose and parametrize pre-captured and hand-animated signs, stored in a repository (a "signary"). At the base of the animation engine there is a blending system. This technique, widely used in videogame architectures, joins existing animation clips through interpolation functions in real time.

2   The LIS Interpreter

The Translation module of the Atlas system relies on both statistical and rule-based techniques. Figure 1 contains a schema of the translation system; in this section, we describe the animation module (Virtual Character Animator). The

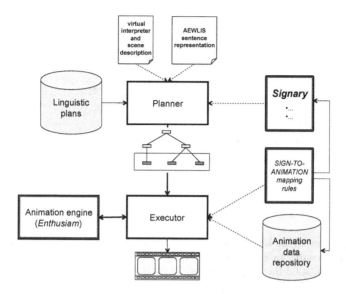

Fig. 2. A graphical representation of the architecture of the LIS virtual interpreter

linguistic input to the animation module consists of a symbolic representation of the LIS sentence, called AEWLIS (Atlas Extended Written LIS, described in [2]). The AEWLIS format is an intermediate representation containing all the phonologic, syntactic and semantic information needed by the virtual interpreter to realize the appropriate sequence of signs.

The architecture of the animation system includes three main components (Figure 2): the Planner, the Executor and the Animation engine. Each module in the architecture is related to a specific knowledge base. For the planner, the knowledge base consists of linguistic plans, that describe how signs can be adapted to the context of a specific sentence (encoded in the AEWLIS representation), given the constraints given by the communicative situation and the interpreter's configuration (signing resources, availability of the resources, etc.). Plans are represented by using the formalism of hierarchical task networks (HTN). Figure 3 represents the top-level portion of the HTN. Basically, the high-level task (LIS-sign) decomposes into the task of assigning the signs to the interpreter's hands (not shown), finding the location for each sign (Localize in the figure, achieved through the Find-position sub-task), then performing the sign (Make-sign). Some relations (such as locative ones) may require a special sign to be generated (a classifier) if the sign that represents one of the entities involved in it cannot be relocated (not shown). Also, the planner must solve the initial and final location of the signs that have a parametrized trajectory, such as movement verbs (Sign-relation task).

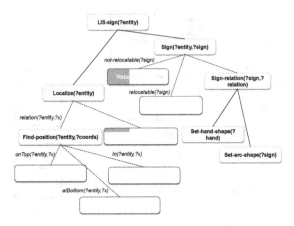

Fig. 3. A portion of the library of linguistic plans of the LIS interpreter. Light boxes contain decomposable tasks, dark boxes contain elementary tasks. Dashed line represent alternatives, solid lines represent sequences.

The Executor relies on the catalogue of signs, the Signary. It retrieves the definitions of signs from the Signary, and applies the corresponding Sign-to-Animation rule to map each sign into commands for the Animation engine. The Animation data repository stores the animation data (previously obtained through MoCap or hand animated) for the generation of signs.

At runtime, the planner (the JSHOP planning system [9] in the current implementation) takes as input the AEWLIS description of the LIS sentence to be generated (what hand is involved, whether both hands are required, what is the default sign location or the path of the movement, whether the sign can be relocated in the space, etc.) and devised a plan for signing the sentence. The actions in the plan establish how and where each sign is to be performed (parametrization).

When the Executor receives a plan from the Planner, it consults the Signary to replace each plan action with the definition of the corresponding sign. For each sign, it applies the matching animation mapping rule to obtain the animation language expression that describes how the sign is realized. The Sign-to-Animation mapping rules (bottom right) specify how a sign can be generated by using the animation data in the repository or by procedural functions (or a combination of the two).

Finally, when a sign-to-animation mapping rule is applied, the parameters specified in the definition of each action operator, such as objects and locations, are bound to the corresponding values and the Executor invokes the Animation Engine to run the procedural animation routines that generate the final animation. The Animation Engine is provided by the Enthusiasm project, an open source platform that supports the authoring of 3D real-time interactive virtual environments.[2]

---

[2] http://enthusiasm.sourceforge.net/

3   Animation Language

The primitives of the animation language control the use of procedural animation techniques, ranging from (parametrized) playback of animation clips, to the
generation of motion paths and the blending of clips. These primitives can be
embedded into control structures that support the parallel and sequential use of
the primitives, and the combination of both.

Basic animations can be obtained through the *retrieval* of a clip from a repository of animation clips, or through pure procedural animation, e.g., as a bone
performing an arc in the space (a *spline*). The set of point composing a trajectory
can be generated through dedicated primitives. For example:

$List < Vect3 > \leftarrow buildArc(from : Vect3, to : Vect3, arc\_direction : Vect3)$

allows the definition of 3-point splines, describing arcs typical of sign languages.
Other primitives can be defined for more complex recurrent movements, such
as zig-zags, spirals, and the like. Straight lines in the space are built specifying
just two points. Other bone controlling primitives are $moveBoneTo(bone, pos :$
$Vect3, speed : float)$, which moves a bone to a certain position, and $rotateBoneTo$
$(bone, rot : Rotation, angular\_speed : float)$ which rotates it.

Signs can be relocated in space by offsetting the position of some bones:

$Anim \leftarrow relocate(bone, pos : Vect3)$

where the bones names will be generally those of the wrists or finger tips. Obvi-
ously, bone controlling primitives require the presence on the animated character
of a real-time Inverse Kinematic system operating on the whole arm.

Finally, the sequential *blending* of several animations can be controlled via
the $seq(anims : List < Anim >)$ function. Considering that each animation might
operate only on a segment of the avatar, animations can also be accomplished
in parallel: $par(anims : List < Anim >)$. In LIS, plural is generally done by
repeating the same sign several times: $repeat(a : Anim, times : int)$.

For an example related to the application domain of the project, consider the
sentence, taken from a corpus of LIS sentence collected by the Atlas project:
"Cloudy at north-east. During the evening cloudiness increases at north-west".
This sentence is characterized by some peculiarities. First, the north-east location
is bound to a fixed location in the signing space because the interpreter is before
a whether map. Second, a semantic relation involving the clouds and the north-
east location constrains the sign for "cloud" to be located in the north-east
location. Finally, the increase of the cloudiness is represented by shifting the
sign representing the cloud and repeating it at the same time to obtain the
plural form ("clouds"). The shift is targeted to the north-west location, whose
position is also constrained to the map.

The planning problem (Fig. 4), is generated generated from three different
sources of knowledge: the AEWLIS representation of the sentence, the interpreter's configuration (dominant hand and initial resource allocation), the information about signs, extracted from the signary. The planning process results in
the following sign sequence:

```
;from AEWLIS              ;from the virtual interpreter    ;from signary
(lemma e00 nuvola)        (free dom)                       (is_relocatable e00)
(lemma e01 zona)          (free ndom)                      (is_relocatable e01)
(lemma e02 nordorientale) (default_position e00 0 0 0)     (not_relocatable e02)
(lemma p00 in)            (default_position e01 0 0 0)
;semantic relations       (default_position e02 0 0 0)
(into e00 e01)            (position e01 1 1 0)
;sentence information     (right ndom)
(isTopic e01)             (left dom)
```

Fig. 4. The world state description provided as input to the planner. Comments are marked by the semicolon

```
north-east;
zone (relocated top-left);
cloud (relocated top-left);
instead;
evening;
cloud (repeating and shifting from top-left to top-right);
more (relocated top-right);
zone (relocated top-right);
```

To cope with the cases illustrated by this example, parametric macro functions have been defined by using the animation language (described in Section 3): relocatedAnimation executes a clip in a different position than the default one, repeatingShiftingAnimation shifts the interpreter's hands while they execute a certain gesture.

```
relocatedAnimation(a:String, loc:Vect3) {
   relocate(clipAnimation(a), loc,{"RightHand","LeftHand"});}

repeatingShiftingAnimation(a:String, repetitions:int,
   start_loc:Vect3, end_loc:Vect3) {
   shift(
        repeat( clipAnimation(a, 3) ),
        { "RightHand", "LeftHand" },
        { start_loc, end_loc }
   )
}
```

So the system produces the following sequence, that the Animation Engine eventually executes for visualization:

```
simpleAnimation('north-east')
relocatedAnimation('zone', north-east-location)
relocatedAnimation('cloud', north-east-location)
simpleAnimation('instead')
simpleAnimation('evening')
repeatingShiftingAnimation('cloud', 3, north-east-location, north-west-location)
relocatedAnimation('more', north-west-location)

relocatedAnimation('zone', north-west-location)
```

4 Conclusions

Our approach to the interpretation of a sign language shares a number of features with other approaches. First, the implementation of a signing system in terms of planning has already been addressed in the literature (see, e.g., [8]), although in the context of a real-time performance. Then, a number of specific animation languages were developed to describe a signed sentence: some examples are HamNoSys [11] and SiGML [5], an XML-based extension of HamNoSys, made usable as an animation language.

We have conducted only a preliminary evaluation of the system, since this is an ongoing project. The approach pursued by the system – issuing a "pure" sign language (instead of a word-to-word translation) – seems to be well received by the deaf people, though it is sometimes considered a bit clumsy. So, future work includes the complete implementation of the system and its extended evaluations on a larger set of sentences.

References

1. Bartolini, S., Bennati, P., Giorgi, R.: Sistema per la Traduzione in Lingua Italiana dei Segni: Blue Sign Translator/Wireless Sign System. In: Proc. of the 50th AIES National Conference (2004)
2. Bertoldi, N., Tiotto, G., Prinetto, P., Piccolo, E., Nunnari, F., Lombardo, V., Damiano, R., Lesmo, L., Principe, A.D.: On the creation and annotation of a large-scale italian-Lis parallel corpus. In: 4th Workshop on the Representation and Processing of Sign Languages: Corpora and Sign Language Technologies, CSLT 2010 (2010)
3. DictaSign: http://www.dictasign.eu
4. Echo: http://www.let.kun.nl/sign-lang/echo/
5. Elliott, R., Glauert, J., Jennings, V., Kennaway, J.: An overview of the SiGML notation and SiGML signing software system. In: Fourth International Conference on Language Resources and Evaluation, LREC 2004 (2004)
6. Elliott, R., Glauert, J., Kennaway, J., Marshall, I., Safar, E.: Linguistic modelling and language-processing technologies for Avatar-based sign language presentation. Universal Access in the Information Society 6(4), 375–391 (2008)
7. http://www.signspeak.eu/:SignSpeak
8. Huenerfauth, M.: Generating american sign language classifier predicates for english-to-asl machine translation. Ph.D. thesis, University of Pennsylvania (2006)
9. Nau, D., Au, T., Ilghami, O., Kuter, U., Murdock, J., Wu, D., Yaman, F.: SHOP2: An HTN planning system. Journal of Artificial Intelligence Research 20(1), 379–404 (2003)
10. Pizzuto, E., Pietrandrea, P., Simone, R.: Verbal and signed languages: comparing structures, constructs and methodologies. Walter de Gruyter, Berlin (2007)
11. Prillwitz, S., Leven, R., Zienert, H., Hamke, T., Henning, J.: HamNoSys Version 2.0: Hamburg Notation System for Sign Languages: An Introductory Guide. International Studies on Sign Language and Communication of the Deaf, vol. 5
12. Veale, T., Conway, A., Collins, B.: The challenges of cross-modal translation: English-to-Sign-Language translation in the Zardoz system. Machine Translation 13(1), 81–106 (1998)
13. Visicast: http://www.visicast.co.uk/

How Our Personality Shapes Our Interactions with Virtual Characters - Implications for Research and Development

Astrid M. von der Pütten[1], Nicole C. Krämer[1], and Jonathan Gratch[2]

[1] University of Duisburg-Essen, Forsthausweg 2, 47048 Duisburg, Germany
[2] University of Southern California, Institute for Creative Technologies,
13274 Fiji Way, 90092 Marina del Rey, USA
{Astrid.von-der-Puetten,Nicole.Kraemer}@uni-due.de,
Gratch@ict.usc.edu

Abstract. There is a general lack of awareness for the influence of users´ personality traits on human-agent-interaction (HAI). Numerous studies do not even consider explanatory variables like age and gender although they are easily accessible. The present study focuses on explaining the occurrence of social effects in HAI. Apart from the original manipulation of the study we assessed the users´ personality traits. Results show that participants´ personality traits influenced their subjective feeling after the interaction, as well as their evaluation of the virtual character and their actual behavior. From the various personality traits those traits which relate to persistent behavioral patterns in social contact (agreeableness, extraversion, approach avoidance, self-efficacy in monitoring others, shyness, public self-consciousness) were found to be predictive, whereas other personality traits and gender and age did not affect the evaluation. Results suggest that personality traits are better predictors for the evaluation outcome than the actual behavior of the agent as it has been manipulated in the experiment. Implications for research on and development of virtual agents are discussed.

Keywords: virtual agents, personality traits, social effects, evaluation, nonverbal feedback.

1 Introduction

From our everyday interactions we know that people´s perception and behavior is mediated by their personality. Their impact has been broadly studied within interactions between humans as well as in the field of human-computer interaction. Personality traits are defined as habitual patterns of thought, behavior and emotion which endure over time [1]. Our personality affects our perception and actual behavior. An extroverted person is more outgoing, talkative, active, confident, and companionable. In contrast a more introverted person is reserved, and concentrated. Studies from face-to-face contexts show, for example, that extroverts and introverts use different kinds of information while judging another person under time pressure [2]. Extroverts feel more control over their interactions, judge them as more intimate and less

J. Allbeck et al. (Eds.): IVA 2010, LNAI 6356, pp. 208–221, 2010.

conflict-laden. They feel more confident after their interactions and also judge their interaction partners as higher in self-esteem than introverts did [3]. People high in social anxiety construe other reactions towards them more negatively than persons low in social anxiety [4]. These examples show how our personality shapes the perception of our interactions.

Although some research groups consider the impact of personality traits on human-computer-interaction, they concentrate on the incorporation of personality traits in artificial entities [5-11]. They are interested in whether the user actually recognizes the implementation of a personality, correctly classifies this implementations into categories of personality traits, and whether they behaviorally react in the same way towards the "artificial entity personality" like they would towards a human with a certain personality. Whether people generally react towards computers and artificial entities like they would do towards humans has been studied extensively. The results from the 'Computers Are Social Actors' studies by Nass and colleagues [5, 6, 12-15] provide broad evidence that people react to media like they would to real persons or places. In their book "The Media Equation" Nass and Reeves [14] report numerous studies (involving usually computers) which prove this assumption to be correct. In later studies researchers began to transfer these studies to virtual characters (talking heads, ECAs, avatars) and broadly confirmed this hypothesis [16-24, see 25 for an overview]. Thus, it can generally be assumed that knowledge from the field of social psychology and differential psychology should be transferable from human-human-interaction to human-agent-interaction.

The personality of the user, however, has been largely neglected (except for studies that target the benefits of a match-up of agent and user personality) [e.g. 7, 8]. There is a general lack of awareness for the influence of users´ personality traits on their perception of human-computer-interaction. Numerous studies do not even integrate easily accessible explanatory variables like age and gender, let alone variables that have to be assessed via standardized questionnaires. However, studies by Kang et al. suggest that personality traits, like for instance shyness [26] or the Big Five [27] crucially affect users´ perception, regardless of the implementation of a personality within the virtual agent. The results, which are presented in detail in the next chapter, demonstrate that the users´ evaluation of an interaction and the actual behavior in HCI-, and HAI-settings can at least partially be predicted by personality.

1.1 Related Work and Research Questions

Research on effects of human personality traits: As mentioned above the studies by Kang et al. suggest that personality traits, like for instance shyness [26] or the Big Five [27] crucially affect users´ perception. In the former study participants interacted either with a human listener, or with an agent in three different conditions: a non-responsive agent, a responsive agent and a mediated agent (a digital representation which mapped the nonverbal behavior of a human listener). The experimenters investigated the effects of shyness and public and private self-consciousness on perceived self-performance, embarrassment and the perceived trustworthiness of the interlocutor. The results indicated that users' social anxiety (shyness) significantly decreased their self-performance and self-reported rapport, while increasing their embarrassment in the condition of the non-responsive Agent. In the latter study Kang et al. explored the relationship between the Big Five and the rapport people felt in the interaction with the agent, measured via self-report and their verbal behavior. The results revealed that more agreeable people showed strong self-reported rapport when they interacted with the agent. Bickmore and his colleagues [28, 29] examined how an ECA is able to build trust via small talk. They demonstrate that the ability to chat about everyday things especially has an impact on people with a disposition to be extroverts. Adding small talk to a task-related interaction did not affect the feeling of trust in introverts. But for extroverts it seemed to be a pre-requisite for establishing the same level of trust to add this small talk ability. A recent study by Yee et al. [30] showed that users´ personality traits determine their virtual behavioral in Second Life, for instance, conscientiousness (Big Five) was correlated with variables related to geographical movement and emotional stability with log-in patterns.

Research questions: Given the rare attempts to investigate the relationship between humans' personality traits and their evaluation of interactions with embodied agents we decided to fill this gap and explore the impact of users´ personality on human-agent interaction. We assume that the participants´ personality shapes their perception and evaluation of the interaction with agents like it is the case in face-to-face- interactions. Although this paper will not provide a manual for developers on how to deal with users´ personality, we outline some initial guideposts and illustrate the clear need for further research on how to design agents that e.g. are positive for shy persons, or are evaluated positively by the broad mass of users.

2   Method

2.1   Experimental Apparatus - The Rapport Agent

We used the Rapport Agent, which was developed by Gratch et al. [31] at the Institute for Creative Technologies. The agent displays listening behaviors that correspond to the verbal and nonverbal behavior of a human speaker. In addition to the usual listening behaviors such as posture shifts and head nods automatically triggered by the system corresponding to participants´ verbal (pitch, velocity of participant´s voice) and nonverbal behavior (position and orientation of participant´s head), we modified the system so that it was possible to conduct a small dialogue. Before the interaction starts, the animated character is looking to the ground to avoid eye contact with the participant before the system begins. When the system begins, indicated by a ping sound, the animated character looks up and says "Okay, I´m ready." We used five prerecorded sentences with a female voice:

- Okay, I´m ready.
- What was the most special experience for you yesterday?
- Which of your characteristics are you most proud of?
- What has been the biggest disappointment in your life?
- Thank you. You´re done.

The study utilized two different kinds of head nods, a double head nod with higher velocity and smaller amplitude (called backchannel head nod) and a single head nod with lower velocity and larger amplitude (called understanding head nod). The backchannel was generated automatically by the Rapport Agent whereas the single head nod was triggered manually by the experimenter at the end of the participants´ verbal contribution to each of the three questions in order to support the impression of an attentive listener. The animated agent was displayed on a 30-inch Apple display. A female virtual character was used in all conditions (see figure 1).

Conditions. In addition, we implemented two levels of behavioral realism (showing (feedback) behavior versus showing no behavior).

Condition low behavioral realism. For this condition, we chose to use the breathing, eye blinking, and posture shifts, but disabled the backchannel nods normally produced by the Rapport Agent. In this way, we achieved a rather unrealistic behavior, as the Rapport Agent was simply staring at the participants and did not react to their contributions at all.

Condition high behavioral realism. For this condition, we used breathing, eye blinking, posture shifts and the two kinds of head nods. The backchannel head nod was triggered automatically by the system according to the nonverbal and verbal behavior of the participants. The so called understanding head nod was actuated by the experimenter each time the participant finished his or her contribution to one of the three questions.

Participants were randomly assigned to the conditions. Gender was distributed equally across conditions.

Fig. 1. The Rapport Agent – female character

2.2 Explanatory Variables – Personality Traits

As explanatory variables, we firstly used the well-known Big Five Inventory (44-item version, [32]). Secondly, we identified the following self-report scales measuring personality traits which relate to communicative behavior, for instance the Unwillingness-to-Communicate Scale [33], with the constructs approach avoidance, which is defined as the extent to which people fear interpersonal encounters (10 items), and reward, which is defined as the extent to which people perceive interactions with other persons as manipulative and dishonest (10 items). All 20 items were rated on a 7-point Likert scale ranging from "strongly disagree" to "strongly agree". In addition, we used the Revised Cheek and Buss Shyness Scale (RCBS; [34]) with 13 items

Table 1. Overview explanatory variables

five factor inventory Extraversion	Extent to which people are extroverted (or introverted); people high in extraversion are described as more companionable, talkative, confident, active, optimistic [32]
five factor inventory Agreeableness	Extent to which people are altruistic, complaisant, cooperative, trustworthy, sympathetic and caring [32]
five factor inventory Openness	Extent to which people are curious, inquisitive, keen on making new experiences and act more unconventional [32]
five factor inventory Conscientiousness	Extent to which people are accurate, responsible, reliable, thoughtful [32]
five factor inventory Neuroticism	Extent to which people describe themselves to be emotionally unstable. People high in neuroticism are more sorrowful, unsure, nervous, anxious and sad, but they are also more empathetic [32]
Approach Avoidance	Extent to which people fear interpersonal encounters; people low in approach avoidance fear interpersonal encounters; people high in approach avoidance are more open [33]
Reward	Extent to which people perceive interactions with other persons as manipulative and dishonest [33]
Public Self-Consciousness	Extent to which people think about aspects of themselves that form a picture of them in other persons (impression management) [35]
Self-Efficacy in Monitoring Others	Extent of peoples´ sensitivity to perceive social cues which indicate socially desired behavior [36]
Shyness	Extent to which people are shy and not confident [34]

(e.g. "I feel tense when I´m with people I don´t know well") rated on a 5-point Likert scale. From the Revised Self-Consciousness Scale [35], we took the subscale Public Self-Consciousness Scale, which measures the extent to which people think about aspects of themselves that form a picture of them in other persons (impression management). The scale consists of 7 items (e.g. "I´m concerned about my style of doing things"), which are rated on a 5-point Likert scale. Furthermore, we used the subscale Self-Monitoring Sensitivity from the Revised Self-Monitoring Scale [36]. The scale measures the extent of peoples´ sensitivity to perceive social cues which indicate socially desired behavior. The 6 items (e.g. "I am often able to read people´s true emotions correctly (through their eyes)") are rated on a 5-point Likert scale. Taking a closer look at the items we suggest that the scale actually measures one´s self-efficacy with regard to monitoring of other people and is therefore called self-efficacy in monitoring others (abbreviated with self-efficacy).

2.3 Dependent Variables

As dependent variables, we assessed the participants´ emotional state (PANAS) after the interaction, the person perception of the virtual character, the self-reported experience of social presence, and self-reported rapport. Besides these self-report measures, we also measured the following objective variables: the total number of words the participants used during the interaction and the percentage of pause-fillers and interrupted words. In the following, all measurements will be described in detail.

Quantitative measurements. In the present study, we used the Positive And Negative Affect Schedule [37] consisting of 20 items (e.g. strong, guilty, active, ashamed etc.), which are rated on a 5-point Likert scale. The factorial analysis for the Positive And Negative Affect Scale resulted in three factors. The first factor, *Positive High-Dominance* (enthusiastic, inspired, active, proud, determined, excited, strong, alert, attentive und interested), explains 28.24% of the variance (Cronbach's Alpha= .838). The second factor, *Negative High-Dominance* (hostile, irritable und upset, guilty, jittery and nervous), explains 23.09% of the variance (Cronbach's Alpha= .819), and the third factor, *Negative Low-Dominance* (afraid, scared, ashamed und distressed), explains 7.57% of the variance (Cronbach's Alpha=.712).

For the person perception (of the agent), we used a semantic differential with 26 bi-polar pairs of adjectives (e.g. friendly-unfriendly, tense-relaxed), which are rated on a 7-point scale. The factor analysis for the person perception of the virtual character resulted in four factors. The first factor, *Negative Low-Dominance* (weak, dishonest, naïve, shy, unintelligent, acquiescent and immature), explains 32.60% of the variance (Cronbach's Alpha= .852). The second factor, *Positive High-Dominance* (compassionate, inviting, involved, noisy, cheerful, sympathic, and active), explains 11.20% of the variance (Cronbach's Alpha= .816). The third factor, *Positive Low-Dominance* (soft, modest, permissive, not conceited, tender), explains 8.21% of the variance (Cronbach's Alpha= .748), and the fourth factor, *Negative High-Dominance* (threatening, proud, unpleasant, unfriendly, tense, sleepy, nervous), explains 5.65% of the variance (Cronbach's Alpha= .792).

Verbal behavior. In addition, we analyzed the participants´ verbal behavior. We counted the total amount of words, the amount of pause-fillers ("erm", "hm") and the amount of broken words (e.g. "I was in the bib... library"). From the latter two, we calculated the percentage of speech disfluencies in relation to the total amount of words.

2.4 Participants and Procedure

Eighty-three persons (42 females and 41 males) were recruited via www.craigslist.com from the general Los Angeles area and were compensated $20 for one hour of their participation. The mean age was 37.27 (*SD*=13.61) ranging from 18 to 65 years. The participants were asked to read and sign informed consent forms. After completing a web-based questionnaire about their background including demographic data and the questionnaires of the explanatory variables, participants received a short introduction about the equipment and the task of the experiment. Then, participants took a seat in front of a 30'' screen, which displayed the Rapport Agent. They were equipped with a headset with microphone. In order to assess the participants' verbal behavior, the whole session was videotaped. The camera was directed towards the participants and situated directly under the screen with the Rapport Agent in combination with the stereovision camera. Participants were instructed to wait until the system starts, indicating readiness by a ping sound. They were asked three questions by the Rapport Agent with increasing intimacy. After the interaction, the participants completed the second web-based questionnaire. They were fully debriefed, given $20 and thanked for their participation.

3 Results

Because this analysis is not driven by a specific existing model/hypothesis, we ran an exploratory data analysis using stepwise regression. In every calculation we included as predictors the independent variable behavioral realism (dummy variable with 1= responsive and 2= non-responsive) and the following demographic variables and personality traits: gender, age, the Big Five (agreeableness, extraversion, neuroticism, openness and conscientiousness), approach avoidance and reward, public self-consciousness, self-efficacy in monitoring others and shyness.

3.1 Participants´ Subjective Feelings after the Interaction (PANAS)

For the subjective feeling after the interaction results show that each of the three PANAS factors can be predicted by at least one regression model. For the factor PANAS Positive Low-Dominance approach avoidance is the best predictor. In a second step agreeableness significantly improves the model. All other predictors were excluded (see table 2). This shows that people who are more open to encounter other people (high value in approach avoidance) and are more agreeable feel better after the interaction.

Table 2. Stepwise regression for PANAS Positive Low-Dominance

	B	Sf B	B	Sig
Step 1				
Constant	-1.930	0,548		
Approach Avoidance	0,375	0,105	.370	.001
Step 2				
Constant	-3,259	0,819		
Approach Avoidance	0,391	0,103	.386	.000
Agreeableness	0,391	0,154	.218	.035

Note: R^2= .137 for step 1, ΔR^2=.047 for step 2 (ps > .05).

For PANAS Negative High-Dominance public self-consciousness is the best predictor followed by the independent variable behavioral realism in a second step (see table 3). Participants who try to leave a good impression about themselves in others report about stronger negative feelings. In addition, more behavioral realism contributed to the occurrence of negative feelings, but the data show that public self-consciousness is a better predictor for PANAS Negative High-Dominance than the behavioral realism. This shows that the behavior of the agent has less impact on feelings of the user in terms of anger than has his/her disposition to think about themselves.

The factor PANAS Negative Low-Dominance can be best predicted by the personality trait self-efficacy in monitoring others, meaning that people who are more sensitive towards social cues which indicate socially desirable behavior felt less negative after the interaction than people with a weaker value in self-efficacy (see table 4).

In sum, people who easily deal with encountering other people and more agreeable people reported to feel better after the interaction. Participants highly motivated to

Table 3. Stepwise regression for PANAS Negative High-Dominance

	B	Sf B	B	Sig
Step 1				
Constant	-1.547	0,546		
Public Self-Consciousness	0,443	0,154	.305	.005
Step 2				
Constant	-1,438	0,538		
Public Self-Consciousness	0,472	0,151	.325	.002
Behavioral realism	-0,436	0,270	-.219	.038

Note: R^2= .085 for step 1, ΔR^2=.055 for step 2 (ps > .05).

Table 4. Stepwise regression for PANAS Negative Low-Dominance

	B	Sf B	β	Sig
Step 1				
Constant	1.551	0,576		
Self-efficacy	-0,428	0,156	-.291	.008

Note: R^2= .085 for step 1.

leave a good impression report about stronger negative feelings. People who are efficient in monitoring others experienced less negative feelings. Furthermore, gender and age as well as four of the Big Five dimensions (extraversion, neuroticism, openness and conscientiousness), reward, and shyness were not included in any of the regression models.

3.2 Person Perception

For the participants´ perception of the agent after the interaction results show that two of the four person perception factors can be predicted by at least one regression model. For Person Perception Negative Low-Dominance the stepwise regression included public self-consciousness in the first model and shyness in the second model (see table 5). Public self-consciousness contributes negatively and shyness positively to the perception of the agent on the factor Negative Low-Dominance, meaning that people who care less about making a good impression and are more shy evaluate the virtual character higher on the factor Negative Low-Dominance (weak, shy, naïve, immature, etc). For the factor Person Perception Positive High-Dominance (compassionate, inviting, etc.) the stepwise regression analysis included in a first step self-efficacy and in a second step public self-consciousness into the regression model. People who are more sensitive to social cues for desirable behavior and try less to make a good impression perceive the agent as more positively high-dominant.

In sum, shyer people evaluated the agent to be more submissive and people who want to leave a good impression as less submissive. People who are more sensitive to social cues for desirable behavior and try less to make a good impression evaluate the agent more positively. Gender and age were not predictive, as well as all Big Five dimensions, and approach avoidance and reward.

Table 5. Stepwise regression for Person Perception Negative Low-Dominance

	B	Sf B	β	Sig
Step 1				
Constant	1,419	0,551		
Public Self-Consciousness	-0,406	0,155	-.280	.010
Step 2				
Constant	,644	0,584		
Public Self-Consciousness	-0,489	0,150	-.337	.002
Shyness	0,490	0,262	.313	.003

Note: R^2= .078 for step 1, ΔR^2=.095 for step 2 (ps > .05).

Table 6. Stepwise regression for Person Perception Positive High-Dominance

	B	Sf B	β	Sig
Step 1				
Constant	-1,531	0,576		
Self-efficacy	0,422	0,156	.288	.008
Step 2				
Constant	-,387	0,793		
Self-efficacy	,407	0,153	.277	.010
Public Self-Consciousness	-,312	0,152	-.215	.043

Note: R^2= .083 for step 1, ΔR^2=.046 for step 2 (ps > .05).

3.3 Verbal Behavior

We also calculated a stepwise regression for the participants´ verbal behavior. For the percentage of disfluencies no regression model emerged. However, for the number of words three models were found (see table 7).

Here behavioral realism is the best predictor for the verbal behavior (behavioral realism as dummy variable with 1= responsive and 2= non-responsive). In a second step

Table 7. Stepwise regression for total amount of words

	B	Sf B	β	Sig
Step 1				
Constant	226,7	27,0		
Behavioral realism	-106,8	39,0	-,291	.008
Step 2				
Constant	-9,4	95,4		
Behavioral realism	-128,5	38,6	-.350	.001
Extraversion	79,6	30,9	.271	.012
Step 3				
Constant	-200,9	131,6		
Behavioral realism	-135,5	38,0	-.369	.001
Extraversion	79,4	30,3	.270	.011
Public Self-Consciousness	55,9	27,0	.209	.042

Note: R^2= .113 for step 1, ΔR^2=.161 for step 2 (ps > .05).

extraversion significantly improves the model and public self-consciousness in the third step, respectively. The more realistic the agent´s behavior, the more extraverted the person is and the more the person tries to leave a good impression the more words this person will use during the interaction.

3.4 Summary

Results show that participants´ personality traits influenced how they perceived and evaluated their interaction with the Rapport Agent. Effects could be shown for their subjective feeling after the interaction, as well as for their evaluation of the virtual character and their actual behavior (see table 8).

Table 8. Survey of the results

High values in ...	...increase...	...decrease...
Behavioral realism	total amount of words	-
Big Five Extraversion	total amount of words	-
Big Five Agreeableness	positive feelings (PANAS Positive Low-Dominance)	-
Big Five Openness	-	-
Big Five Conscientiousness	-	-
Big Five Neuroticism	-	-
Approach Avoidance (more open people, see above)	positive feelings (PANAS Positive Low-Dominance)	-
Reward	-	-
Public Self-Consciousness	negative feelings (PANAS Negative High-Dominance) and total amount of words	negative and positive evaluation of agent (PP Negative Low-Dominance; PP Positive High-Dominance)
Self-Efficacy in Monitoring Others	-	negative feelings (PANAS Negative High-Dominance)
Shyness	negative evaluation of agent (PP Negative Low-Dominance)	positive evaluation of agent (PP Positive High-Dominance)
Age	-	-
Gender	-	-

Agreeableness was found to have a positive impact, as well as the explanatory variables approach avoidance and self-efficacy in monitoring others. On the other hand public self-consciousness, and shyness more negatively influenced the evaluation. People with high values in these traits felt more negative and evaluated the agent more negatively. The actual verbal behavior was positively influenced by extraversion and public self-Consciousness. We could also show that peoples´ disposition to be extroverts and their level of self-confidence influenced their verbal behavior by increasing the number of used words.

4 Discussion and Future Work

In total we included 13 possible predictors into our analyses from which seven were actually predictive for at least one of the dependent variables: extraversion, agreeableness, approach avoidance, self-efficacy in monitoring others, shyness and public self-consciousness as well as the behavioral realism of the virtual character which was the actual manipulation within the study. Gender and age and the three Big Five traits openness, conscientiousness and neuroticism were not found to be predictive. Although the Big Five reflect the most elaborate model on human personality traits they did not seem to be the best predictors regarding that three of them were not predictive. Interestingly, those two Big Five factors which are most closely related to social interaction (extraversion and agreeableness) were predictive. This is in line with the other predictive traits which also rather relate to persistent behavioral patterns in social contact.

Most studies in HAI miss to include standardized questionnaires like the Big Five or the other presented instruments and only assess dispositions for experimental purposes like matching extroverted computers to extroverted people. Researchers should also consider other instruments besides the well known Big Five, because our results suggest that the Big Five had limited explanatory value. Although there is much work concentrating on extraversion and agreeableness, other instruments might deliver more results which lead to interesting insights into the nature and the mechanisms of human-agent-interaction.

Although the traits public self-consciousness and self-efficacy in monitoring others seem to be closely related (one might expect that someone who in general wants to make a good impression also observes his or her own behavior a lot) they were found to have opposite effects on subjective feelings and perception of the virtual character. People high in public self-consciousness feel more aggressive after the interaction. This might be the case because the feedback of the agent is limited (or non-existent, respectively) in both conditions. Therefore participants do not receive feedback whether they actually left a good impression or not. In contrast, people high in self-efficacy feel less afraid and distressed after the interaction. We would speculate that as these persons report to have a high self-efficacy with regard to the ability to interpret other people´s behavior they were satisfied with even minimal cues and therefore felt less afraid and distressed (which is also reflected in the more positive evaluation of the agent). Furthermore, it has to be noted that public self-consciousness yields self-contradictory results since it decreases both negative (submissive, etc.) and positive (compassionate, etc.) perception of the agent. Here, further studies have to be conducted as this cannot be explained by our setting.

In sum, results suggest that, except in one case, certain personality traits are better predictors for the evaluation outcome than the actual manipulation of the experiment, in this case the agent´s behavior. It is quite impressive that the user´s personality has more impact on the agent´s evaluation than its actual behavior – although it is of course not predictable what would happen when the behavior of the agent is even more different. In sum, these results do not suggest that the agent´s behavior does not matter at all or that developers should design systems that can only be used by people with a specific characteristic, it is valuable to know that the effects of an agent also depend on the personality of the user. In conclusion, a person´s disposition can greatly influence his or her evaluation and also his or her actual behavior during the interaction. Therefore we advise to be aware and assess participants´ personality traits to be able to control for the effects they elicit. A rather extreme example might be that a specific agent received negative ratings caused by a sample with predominantly shy people.

Limitations. To be able to provide developers with some kind of design guidelines we have to conduct further research – especially taking different agents into account. Although shy participants rated this special agent more negative, this result is not necessarily transferable to other agents. Further research with different agents has to be conducted to be able to draw generalizable conclusions on the influence of users´ personality on evaluation. However, the present study showed that a) users´ personality plays a great role in human-agent-interaction (and is sometimes even more important than the agent´s behavior), b) that in particular those traits are important which are related to interpersonal encounters, and c) that especially people with high values in agreeableness, extraversion, approach avoidance (in the sense of being open towards communication) and self-efficacy in monitoring others (in the sense of high self-efficiacy with regard to reading other people´s behavior) judged the agent positively while people with high values on public self-consciousness, and shyness judged the agent more negatively.

Acknowledgements

This study was partially funded by the German Academic Exchange Service and by the U.S. Army Research, Development, and Engineering Command and the National Science Foundation under grant # HS-0713603. The content does not necessarily reflect the position or the policy of the Government, and no official endorsement should be inferred.

References

1. Kassin, S.: Psychology. Prentice-Hall, Inc., USA (2003)
2. Heaton, A.W., Krublanski, A.W.: Person perception by introverts and extroverts under time pressure: Effects of need for closure. Personality and Social Psychology Bulletin 17, 161–165 (1991)
3. Barrett, L.F., Pietromonaco, P.R.: Accuracy of the Five-Factor Model in Predicting Perceptions of Daily Social Interactions. Personality and Social Psychology Bulletin 23, 1173–1187 (1997)
4. Pozo, C., Carver, C.S., Weflens, A.R., Scheier, M.F.: Social Anxiety and Social Perception: Construing Others' Reactions to the Self. Personality and Social Psychology Bulletin 17, 355–362 (1991)
5. Nass, C., Moon, Y., Fogg, B.J., Reeves, B., Dryer, D.C.: Can computer personalities be human personalities? International Journal of Human Computer Studies 43, 223–239 (1995)
6. Moon, Y., Nass, C.: How "real" are computer personalities? Psychological responses to personality types in human-computer interaction. Communication Research 23, 651–674 (1996)

7. Isbister, K., Nass, C.: Consistency of personality in interactive characters: Verbal cues, non-verbal cues, and user characteristics. International Journal of Human-Computer Studies 53(2), 251–267 (2000)

8. Isbister, K.: Reading personality in onscreen characters: an examination of social principles of consistency, personality match, and situational attribution applied to interaction with characters. Doctoral dissertation, Standford University (1997)

9. Allbeck, J., Badler, N.: Toward representing agent behaviors modified by personality and emotion. In: Workshop on Embodied Conversational Agents – Let's specify and evaluate them! AAMAS 2002, Bologna, Italy (2002)

10. Pizzutilo, S., De Carolis, B., de Rosis, F.: Cooperative Interface Agents. In: Dautenhahn, K., Bond, A.H., Canamero, L., Edmonds, B. (eds.) Socially intelligent agents. Creating relationships with computers and robots, pp. 61–68. Kluwer, Norwell (2002)

11. André, E., Rist, T.: Controlling the Behavior of Animated Presentation Agents in the Interface: Scripting versus Instructing. AI Magazine (Special Issue on Intelligent User Interfaces) 22(4), 53–66 (2001)

12. Nass, C., Moon, Y., Morkes, J., Kim, E.-Y., Fogg, B.J.: Computers are social actors: A review of current research. In: Friedman, B. (ed.) Moral and ethical issues in human-computer interaction, pp. 137–162. CSLI Press, Stanford (1997)

13. Nass, C., Steuer, J., Tauber, E.R.: Computers are Social Actors. In: Human Factors in Computing Systems: CHI 1994 Conference Proceedings, pp. 72–78. ACM Press, New York (1994)

14. Reeves, B., Nass, C.I.: The media equation: How people treat computers, television, and new media like real people and places. Cambridge University Press, New York (1996)

15. Nass, C., Moon, Y.: Machines and mindlessness: Social responses to computers. Journal of Social Issues 56(1), 81–103 (2000)

16. Krämer, N.C., Simons, N., Kopp, S.: The effects of an embodied conversational agent's nonverbal behavior on user's evaluation and behavioral mimicry. In: Pelachaud, C., Martin, J.-C., André, E., Chollet, G., Karpouzis, K., Pelé, D. (eds.) IVA 2007. LNCS (LNAI), vol. 4722, pp. 238–251. Springer, Heidelberg (2007)

17. Von der Pütten, A., Krämer, N.C., Gratch, J.: Who's there? Can a Virtual Agent Really Elicit Social Presence? In: Proceedings of the PRESENCE 2009 - The 12th Annual International Workshop on Presence, Los Angeles, USA (2009)

18. Hoffmann, L., Krämer, N.C., Lam-chi, A., Kopp, S.: Media Equation Revisited: Do Users Show Polite Reactions towards an Embodied Agent? In: Ruttkay, Z., Kipp, M., Nijholt, A., Vilhjálmsson, H.H. (eds.) IVA 2009. LNCS (LNAI), vol. 5773, pp. 159–165. Springer, Heidelberg (2009)

19. Pertaub, D.-P., Slater, M., Barker, C.: An experiment on fear of public speaking in virtual reality. In: Stredney, D., Westwood, J.D., Mogel, G.T., Hoffman, H.M. (eds.) Medicine meets virtual reality, pp. 372–378. IOS Press, Amsterdam (2001)

20. Bailenson, J.N., Blascovich, J., Beall, A.C.: Equilibrium revisited: Mutual gaze and personal space in virtual environments. Presence: Teleoperators and Virtual Environments 10, 583–598 (2001)

21. Bailenson, J.N., Blascovich, J., Beall, A.C., Loomis, J.M.: Interpersonal distance in immersive virtual environments. Personality and Social Psychology Bulletin 29, 1–15 (2003)

22. Morkes, J., Kernal, H., Nass, C.: Effects of humor in task-oriented human-computer interaction and computer mediated communication: A direct test of SRCT theory. Human-Computer Interaction 14(4), 395–435 (2000)

23. Rossen, B., Johnson, K., Deladisma, A., Lind, S., Lok, B.: Virtual humans elicit skin-tone bias consistent with real-world skin-tone biases. In: Prendinger, H., Lester, J.C., Ishizuka, M. (eds.) IVA 2008. LNCS (LNAI), vol. 5208, pp. 237–244. Springer, Heidelberg (2008)
24. Von der Pütten, A.M., Krämer, N.C., Gratch, J., Kang, S.: It doesn't matter what you are! - Explaining social effects of agents and avatars. Paper presented at the Annual Conference of the International Communication Association 2010, Singapore, Singapore (2010)
25. Krämer, N.C.: Soziale Wirkungen virtueller Helfer. Gestaltung und Evaluation von Mensch-Computer-Interaktionen. Kohlhammer, Stuttgart (2008)
26. Kang, S.-H., Gratch, J., Wang, N., Watts, J.: Does Contingency of Agents' Nonverbal Feedback Affect Users' Social Anxiety? In: Proceedings of the 7th international joint conference on autonomous agents and multiagent systems, pp. 120–127. International Foundation for Autonomous Agents and Multiagent Systems, Estoril (2008)
27. Kang, S.-H., Gratch, J., Wang, N., Watts, J.H.: Agreeable people like agreeable virtual humans. In: Prendinger, H., Lester, J.C., Ishizuka, M. (eds.) IVA 2008. LNCS (LNAI), vol. 5208, pp. 253–261. Springer, Heidelberg (2008)
28. Bickmore, T., Cassell, J.: Social Dialogue with Embodied Conversational Agents. In: van Kuppevelt, J., Dybkjaer, L., Bernsen, N. (eds.) Natural, Intelligent and Effective Interaction with Multimodal Dialogue Systems, Kluwer Academic, New York (2004)
29. Bickmore, T., Gruber, A., Picard, R.: Establishing the computer-patient working alliance in automated health behavior change interventions. Patient Education Counseling 59(1), 21–30 (2005)
30. Yee, N., Harris, H., Jabon, M., Bailenson, J.N.: The Expression of Personality in Virtual Worlds. Social Psychology and Personality Science (in press, 2010)
31. Gratch, J., Okhmatovskaia, A., Lamothe, F., Marsella, S.C., Morales, M., van der Werf, R.J., Morency, L.-P.: Virtual rapport. In: Gratch, J., Young, M., Aylett, R.S., Ballin, D., Olivier, P. (eds.) IVA 2006. LNCS (LNAI), vol. 4133, pp. 14–27. Springer, Heidelberg (2006)
32. Benet-Martinéz, V., John, O.P.: Los Cinco Grandes Across Cultures and Ethnic Groups: Multitrait Multimethod Analyses of the Big Five in Spanish and English. Journal of Personality and Social Psychology 75(3), 729–750 (1998)
33. Burgoon, J.K.: Unwillingness-to-Communicate Scale: Development and Validation. Communication Monographs 43, 60–69 (1976)
34. Cheek, J.: The Revised Cheek and Buss Shyness Scale (RCBS). Wellesley College, Wellesley (1983)
35. Scheier, M.F., Carver, C.: The Self-Consciousness Scale: A Revised Version for Use with General Populations. Journal of Applied Social Psychology 15(8), 687–699 (1985)
36. Lennox, R., Wolfe, R.: Revision of the self-monitoring scale. Journal of Personality and Social Psychology 46, 1349–1364 (1984)
37. Watson, D., Tellegen, A., Clark, L.A.: Development and validation of brief measures of positive and negative affect: The PANAS scale. Journal of Personality and Social Psychology 54, 1063–1070 (1988)

Evaluating the Effect of Gesture and Language on Personality Perception in Conversational Agents

Michael Neff[1], Yingying Wang[1], Rob Abbott[2], and Marilyn Walker[2]

[1] University of California, Davis
{mpneff,yiwang}@ucdavis.edu
[2] University of California, Santa Cruz
{abbott,maw}@soe.ucsc.edu

Abstract. A significant goal in multi-modal virtual agent research is to determine how to vary expressive qualities of a character so that it is perceived in a desired way. The "Big Five" model of personality offers a potential framework for organizing these expressive variations. In this work, we focus on one parameter in this model – extraversion – and demonstrate how both verbal and non-verbal factors impact its perception. Relevant findings from the psychology literature are summarized. Based on these, an experiment was conducted with a virtual agent that demonstrates how language generation, gesture rate and a set of movement performance parameters can be varied to increase or decrease the perceived extraversion. Each of these factors was shown to be significant. These results offer guidance to agent designers on how best to create specific characters.

Keywords: personality, gesture, conversational and non-verbal behavior, evaluation.

1 Introduction

An important focus of recent research on interactive story systems, computer gaming, and educational virtual worlds is the development of animated Intelligent Virtual Agents (IVAs) [12,18,11,28,36,13]. For such characters to be effective they must simulate the most effective human interlocutors: they must be natural and believable, but moreover, they must convey personality, mood, and expression [1,32,21,37,23]. Determining how to represent such affective and individual qualities in a computational framework remains an active research problem. Gestures, speech, and facial behaviors must be precisely coordinated and their performance must be procedurally controlled to express a realistic and consistent character that responds to the current context. One possible theoretical foundation for producing such behaviors is the the "Big Five" model of personality traits. In this paper we focus on the Big Five trait of *extraversion*. We examine whether an agent whose verbal and nonverbal behavior is controlled

J. Allbeck et al. (Eds.): IVA 2010, LNAI 6356, pp. 222–235, 2010.
© Springer-Verlag Berlin Heidelberg 2010

using parameters suggested by previous research on extraversion is perceived by naive users as projecting the personality that our system intends.

Over the last fifty years the Big Five theory has become a standard in psychology. Research has systematically documented correlations between a wide range of behaviors and the Big Five traits (extraversion, neuroticism, agreeableness, conscientiousness, openness to experience) [24,29,31]. For example, research has shown that verbal behaviors are influenced by personality. Extraverts talk more, faster, louder, and more repetitively than introverts, using fewer pauses and hesitations, and with a lower type/token ratio [8]. Extraverts are less formal and use more positive emotion words and more references to context [14,31]. Spatial nonverbal attributes such as body attitude, gesture amplitude or expansiveness, motion direction, motion smoothness and fluency have also been shown to be key indicators of personality, as well as temporal attributes like gesture speed and response latency. Just as extraverts tend to have high speech rate and produce more utterances, they also have high gesture rates [2,30,20,25].

Section 2 summarizes the findings from psychology on the expression of extraversion, including a novel synthesis of research on non-verbal factors, and explains how we use these to derive parameters for both verbal and nonverbal IVA behavior. The main contribution of this paper is a study described in Section 3, that shows how verbal and non-verbal factors can be combined to affect user perceptions of levels of extraversion of an IVA, as shown in the results in Section 4. We show that all of our parameters have a significant effect on the perception of extraversion and provide an indication of how they combine. We delay a detailed description of related work to the conclusion (Section 5) where we can directly compare our approach to previous work on the generation of gesture.

2   Nonverbal and Verbal Expression of Personality

In previous work [22,21], we argue that the Big Five model of personality provides a useful framework for modeling some types of stylistic linguistic variation. Here we focus on the Big Five trait of extraversion, whose corresponding trait adjectives are shown in Table 1. We believe that these trait adjectives provide an intuitive, meaningful definition of linguistic style [7,29]. Below we review the psychology literature on the expression of extraversion and explain how we derive IVA parameters from this previous work.

Table 1. Trait adjectives associated with the extremes of the Extraversion trait

	High	Low
Extraversion	warm, gregarious, assertive, sociable, excitement seeking, active, spontaneous, optimistic, talkative	shy, quiet, reserved, passive, solitary, moody, joyless

2.1   Nonverbal Expression of Extraversion

One of the primary contributions of this paper is to review and organize findings from psychology on the nonverbal expression of the extraversion personality trait. Our summary of these findings is shown in Table 2. Postural and gestural styles are linked to personality, attitude and status in relationships [25,15].

The position of the head and trunk are the most visually salient indicators of status and attitude; leaning forward communicates a relatively positive attitude to the interlocutor whereas leaning backward or turning away communicates a more negative attitude. Leaning the torso forward is also positively correlated with extraversion [20]. Frank [6] similarly argues that extraverts amplify a sense of space by moving the upper body (chest and limbs) forward whereas introverts maintain a more vertical orientation.

Table 2. The gestural correlates of extraversion

	Introversion	Extraversion
Body attitude	backward leaning, turning away	forward leaning
Gesture amplitude	narrow	wide, broad
Gesture direction	inward, self-contact	outward, table-plane and horizontal spreading gesture
Gesture rate	low	high more movements of head, hands and legs
Gesture speed, response time	slow	fast, quick
Gesture connection	low smoothness, rhythm disturbance	smooth, fluent
Body part		head tilt, shoulder erect, chest forward, limbs spread, elbows away from body, hands away from body, legs apart, legs leaning, bouncing, shaking of legs

Several studies have shown that gestural expansiveness and range of movement is positively correlated with extraversion [2,3]. Specifically extraversion is positively correlated to factors like "expansive", "broad gestures", "elbows away from body", "hands away from body", and "legs far apart while standing" [20,33,17].

Gesture direction is also important. Argyle [2] states that introverts use fewer outward directed gestures and touch themselves more. North [30] indicates that extraverts likely show a significant number of table plane and horizontal spreading gestures. The analysis of tests by Takala [35] demonstrate the hypothesis that introverts use more inward directed movements in the horizontal dimension and extraverts more outward directed movements. Furthermore, movements directed away from the person could be an indication of aggressiveness, while inward directed shifts indicate passiveness.

Extraverts are found to be more energetic or have more physical strength, and higher gesture rates, while the gestures of introverts persist more [20,3,17,9,2].

A number of studies have examined the temporal properties of gestures [17,33]. Extraverts tend to have faster speech, which leads to higher gesture rates due to the correlation between speech and gesture. This has been experimentally demonstrated by Lippa [20]. Brebner [3] also found differences between introverts and extraverts in speed and frequency of movement. Extraverts not only behave in a more rapid manner than introverts, the time to first response, or the response latency, is shorter as well. Results related to the smoothness and rhythm of gesture suggest that introversion is negatively correlated with smoothness and positively correlated with rhythm disturbance [33,20,35].

Other research discusses extraversion and its relation to particular body parts in gesturing. Knapp [17] mentions more leg lean for an ambitious personality. Experiments by Riggio [33] suggest extraverts have more "body emphasis", defined as more head movements, more parallel gestures of the hands, more movement of the legs(position, bouncing, shaking) and more posture shifts. Besides using broad gestures, Lippa [20] also found that extraverts use most of their body when gesturing, tend to tilt their heads and raise their shoulders. Extraverts are universally believed to maintain more eye contact, and a positive correlation between eye contact, shoulder orientation, leg orientation, and body orientation indicates extraversion [25].

In addition, it is postulated that spatial behavior also differs for extraverts [2,30]. For example, it has been hypothesized that extraverts stand closer to others, either because of greater tolerance for a close interaction distance, or because of high individual confidence, self-esteem, or assertiveness.

Gesture Parameters. Two dimensions of motion variation were developed based on the findings discussed above. The first is *gesture rate* which can be either "high" or "low". The high rate used approximately twice as many gestures as the low for a given utterance. The second, termed *gesture performance*, includes a range of changes to posture, gesture form and timing. It has four evenly spaced levels ranging from "most extraverted" to "least extraverted".

Gesture performance consists of the following factors. For each, the most and least extraverted parameter values are listed in Table 3 (the row label in the table is **in bold** in the text below). For increased extraversion, the spatial scale of the gesture stroke was increased and it was moved up and out to the side of the character (**stroke scale** and **stroke position**). The **duration** was shortened. The combined duration change and spatial scaling effectively increase the velocity of the stroke. In terms of posture, for high extraversion, the elbows were rotated out (**arm swivel**), the shoulders were raised (**collar bones**) and a forward lean was added through a shift of the center of mass forward and a forward rotation at the base of the spine (**spine rotation forward** and **COM shift forward**). For the more introverted examples, the amount of body movement was scaled down both in the torso and the lower body (**body motion scale**). This included bringing the feet closer together to narrow the stance.

Table 3. Gesture Parameter Settings

parameter	max introversion	max extraversion
stroke scale	x*.5, y*.6, z*.8	x * 1.4, y*1.2, z*1.1
stroke position	x-12cm, y-5cm	x+12cm, y+ 10cm
duration	100%	80%
collar bones	down 5 deg	up 10 deg.
arm swivel		33 degree range between extremes
spine rotation forward	-6 deg	6 deg
COM shift forward	-5 cm	6 cm
Body motion scale	varies between 10 and 60% depending on parameter	100%

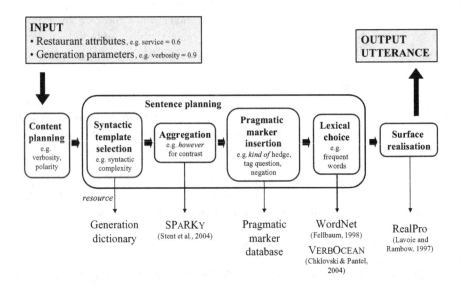

Fig. 1. The architecture of the PERSONAGE generator

2.2   Verbal Expression of Extraversion

Our experiments use the PERSONAGE generator for verbal realization of extraversion. The PERSONAGE architecture is shown in Figure 1. Table 4 provides a detailed description of many of the linguistic parameters relevant to the expression of extraversion [1] In PERSONAGE, generation parameters are implemented, and their values are set, based on correlations between linguistic cues and the Big Five traits that have been systematically documented in the psychology literature [31,24,34,8]. For example, parameters for the extraversion trait include VERBOSITY, SYNTACTIC COMPLEXITY, and CONTENT POLARITY, which controls

---

[1] PERSONAGE provides additional parameters for expressing extraversion as well as parameters for other traits.

Table 4. Sample of some PERSONAGE parameters used to express extraversion

Parameter	Description	Intro	Extra
VERBOSITY	Control the number of propositions in the utterance	low	high
RESTATEMENTS	Paraphrase an existing proposition, e.g. 'Chanpen Thai has great service, it has fantastic waiters'	low	high
CONTENT POLARITY	Control the polarity of the propositions expressed, i.e. referring to negative or positive attributes	low	high
CONCESSION POLARITY	Determine whether positive or negative attributes are emphasized	low	high
POSITIVE CONTENT FIRST	Determine whether positive propositions—including the claim—are uttered first	low	high
REQUEST CONFIRMATION	Begin the utterance with a confirmation of the restaurant's name, e.g. 'did you say Chanpen Thai?'	low	high
SYNTACTIC COMPLEXITY	Control the syntactic complexity (syntactic embedding)	high	low
TEMPLATE POLARITY	Control the connotation of the claim, i.e. whether positive or negative affect is expressed	low	high
ALTHOUGH CUE WORD	Concede a proposition using although, e.g. 'Although Chanpen Thai has great service, it has bad decor'	high	low
NEGATION	Negate a verb by replacing its modifier by its antonym, e.g. 'Chanpen Thai doesn't have bad service'	high	low
SOFTENER HEDGES	Insert syntactic elements (sort of, kind of, somewhat, quite, around, rather, I think that, it seems that, it seems to me that) to mitigate the strength of a proposition, e.g. 'It seems to me that Chanpen Thai has rather great service'	high	low
ACKNOWLEDGMENTS:	Insert an initial back-channel (yeah,right, ok, I see, oh, well), e.g. 'Well, Chanpen Thai has great service'	low	high
NEAR EXPLETIVES	Insert a near-swear word, e.g. 'the service is darn great'	low	high
FILLED PAUSES	Insert syntactic elements expressing hesitancy (like, I mean, err, mmhm, you know), e.g.'I mean, Chanpen Thai has great service, you know' or 'Err... Chanpen Thai has, like, great service'	high	low
EMPHASIZER HEDGES	Insert syntactic elements (really,basically, actually, just) to strengthen a proposition, e.g. 'Chanpen Thai has really great service' or 'Basically, Chanpen Thai just has great service'	low	high
EXCLAMATION	Insert an exclamation mark, e.g. 'Chanpen Thai has great service!'	low	high
TAG QUESTION	Insert a tag question, e.g. 'the service is great, isn't it?'	low	high
IN-GROUP MARKER	Refer to the hearer as a member of the same social group, e.g. pal and buddy	low	high
LEXICON FREQUENCY	Control the average frequency of use of each content word	low	high
VERB STRENGTH	Control the strength of the verbs, e.g. suggest vs. recommend	low	high

the production of positive content. See Table 4. The right-most columns contain the parameter values for expressing either introversion or extraversion. Parameter values are specified in terms of *low* and *high* settings, and then mapped to normalized scalar values between 0 and 1. More detail about how the PERSONAGE parameters were derived from the psychology literature can be found in [22,21].

3 Experimental Design

Our main hypotheses are that verbal and nonverbal cues to personality will reinforce each other when they are congruent and that when verbal and nonverbal cues are mixed, the perceptual effect is graded. In order to test this, we combine verbal cues in the form of restaurant recommendations generated by

PERSONAGE with nonverbal cues in the form of gestures generated by animation software based on [26,28] and rendered using the EMBR agent [13].

Four restaurant recommendations, shown below, that were generated by PERSONAGE were selected for use in the experiment, with audio generated using the VoiceText from Voiceware with the "Kate" voice:

- **low extraversion 1:** I mean, Amy's Bread isn't as bad as the others.
- **low extraversion 2:** It seems that Orange Hut is the only restaurant with friendly staff that is any good.
- **high extraversion 1:** I am sure you would like Amy's Bread. Basically, its price is 12 dollars, its cheap, you know, the food is good and the servers are friendly.
- **high extraversion 2:** I am sure you would like Orange Hut, you know. Basically, the food is great and the atmosphere is good with friendly service.

Gestures were aligned with words in the input utterances based on the information structure of each utterance in terms of theme and rheme [4]. The low gesture rate examples used about half of the placement locations of the high gesture rate examples. For both of the low extraversion utterances, the low rate sample has one gesture and the high rate sample has two. For the high extraversion examples, one had a high rate of five gestures and a low rate of three and the other a high rate of four and low rate of two.

Animated clips were generated using a combination of motion capture editing and procedural synthesis using algorithms based on our previous work [28,26]. Motion capture data of the wrist positions was used to specify the path of the wrist in each stroke and inverse kinematics was used to complete the arm motion. The stroke phases of six sample gestures were chosen for the experiment that all had similar form (a slight upward arc, like the shape of a frown) and an initial distance between start and end points of approximately 25cm. These included left, right and two handed gestures. The final gesture lengths would be scaled based on the performance parameters.

Each gesture consisted of preparation, stroke and retraction phases. The preparation and retraction phases were procedurally generated and started or ended (respectively) at the side of the character's waist. If there was not enough time to complete a retraction, a preparation would be inserted that joined the end of one gesture to the beginning of the next. For each utterance, a set of gestures was chosen based on the duration of each matched word and ensuring that a given gesture sample was not repeated. These gestures were then used in all examples for that utterance. For the low rate examples, some of the gestures were simply dropped from the sequence generation. A single piece of torso and lower body motion capture data was used to animate the body in every clip. The animation data was rendered using the EMBR agent.

Every combination of rate and gesture performance was generated for each of the four utterances, yielding 32 total clips (2x4x4) for use in the experiment. The head was blocked out by a gray square in the videos to encourage subjects to

Fig. 2. Gesture performance extraversion styles in order of increasing extraversion

attune to the character's body movement. See Figure 2. A video showing labeled example clips used in the experiment is available online[2].

3.1   Experiment Execution

We recruited 40 subjects for a web-based experiment. The majority of subjects were undergraduate university students. Eight were female and 32 were male. Thirty four were between 18 and 30 years of age, three were between 31 and 50, and three were over 50. For five subjects English was not their first language. Prior to taking the survey, subjects were shown four sample clips and an overview of the questions to give them a sense of the scope of the experiment.

Subjects were presented a video of a female avatar making a restaurant recommendation and asked to judge her extraversion level and naturalness. The subjects were allowed to replay the video as many times as they wished but were not allowed to return to previous videos. The stimuli appeared in a random order for each subject. There were 32 videos and three 7-point Likert scale questions per video. The 32 stimuli consisted of every combination of gesture rate (High, Low), gesture extraversion level (1-4), and utterance (1-4). The experiment took, on average, approximately 30 minutes to complete.

The subjects rated each stimulus utterance for perceived extraversion by answering the relevant questions measuring that trait from the Ten-Item Personality Inventory, as this instrument was shown to be psychometrically superior to a "single item per trait" questionnaire [10]. Specifically, the subject was asked to rate the clips in a form that said "I see the speaker as...", and then had questions "1. Extroverted, enthusiastic" (Disagree Strongly/Agree Strongly) and "2. Reserved, quiet" (Disagree Strongly/ Agree Strongly). The second answer is inverted and the two are then averaged to produce a rating ranging from 1 (i.e. highly introvert) to 7 (i.e. highly extravert). Because it was unclear whether users would perceive the synthetic utterances as natural, the subjects also evaluated the naturalness of each utterance on the same scale. Our hypotheses were:

---

[2] http://www.cs.ucdavis.edu/~neff

- **H1:** Combined gestural and linguistic manifestations of extraversion will be perceived as manifesting an equal combination of the extraversion of each input mode.
- **H2:** Higher gesture rates will be perceived as more extraverted.
- **H3:** The edited changes in gesture performance (Table 3) will correlate with perceived changes in extraversion.
- **H4:** Combining a higher gesture rate with a more "extraverted" performance will lead to a stronger perception of extraversion than either change on its own.
- **H5:** Perceived naturalness will be the same as PERSONAGE utterances presented textually, i.e. 5.3 average on a 7 point scale [21].

4   Results

All three experimental factors described above (language extraversion, gesture rate, and gesture performance) showed a positive correlation with perceived extraversion. A one-way ANOVA of performance extraversion on TIPI-extraversion is significant ($p = .015$, $F = 3.5$, $df = 3$) confirming Hypothesis 3. See Fig. 3. A one-way ANOVA of language extraversion on TIPI-extraversion is significant ($p < .001$, $F = 55.5$, $df = 1$). See Fig. 5(a). A one-way ANOVA of gesture rate on TIPI-extraversion is significant ($p < .001$, $F = 17.1$, $df = 1$) confirming Hypothesis 2. See Fig. 4. These results corroborate the findings in the literature (Sec. 2) on perceived markers of extraversion.

A multivariate linear regression of gesture rate, gesture performance and linguistic extraversion on TIPI extraversion shows that all of the parameters have a significant effect on the perception of extraversion.

$$.09*Performance + .12* Rate + .21*LinguisticExtraversion$$

The standardized regression equation, shown above, accounts for 27% of the variance. Linguistic extraversion has the largest effect, disconfirming Hypothesis 1,

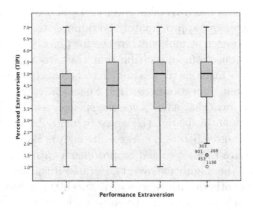

Fig. 3. Effect of Performance Extraversion on Perceived Extraversion (TIPI)

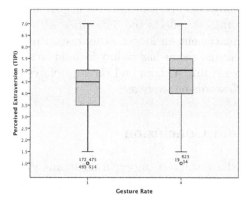

Fig. 4. Effect of Gesture Rate on Perceived Extraversion (TIPI)

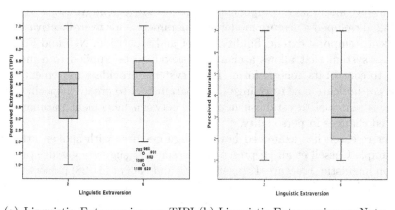

(a) Linguistic Extraversion on TIPI (b) Linguistic Extraversion on Natu-
Extraversion   ralness

Fig. 5. The effect of Linguistic Extraversion TIPI Extraversion and Naturalness

which posited that all modes would contribute equally. However the regression shows that all modes contribute to perception together, and as such confirms Hypothesis 4.

A one-way ANOVA examining the effect of performance extraversion and gesture rate on naturalness showed no significant effect. However linguistic extraversion affects naturalness, with extraverted utterances perceived as significantly less natural (F= 15.08, df = 1, p < .001). Thus Hypothesis 5 is disconfirmed. See Figure 5(b). In previous work we showed that the average naturalness of our extraversion utterances when presented as text was 5.78. Thus we posit two possibilities for the perceived unnaturalness of the highly extraverted utterances. First, it may reflect the fact that the text-to-speech engine is more likely to encounter a bad pronunciation or a bad join on a longer utterance, and our previous work used only text, rather than voice. The other possibility is that the perceived unnaturalness reflects the difficulties with developing a good algorithm for gesture placement on longer utterances. Previous work on gesture placement using theme and rheme has mainly focused on shorter utterances. Our extraverted utterances realize a claim and three satellites describing restaurant attributes, and are 25 words on average.

5   Discussion and Conclusion

This paper reports the results of an experiment analyzing the expression of extraversion using both verbal and nonverbal indicators. Our work aims to contribute to a broader discourse on how to control the expressivity of animated agents.

Considerable previous work has focused on expressive procedural animation. For instance, Chi et al. [5] developed a model for arm and torso movement based on the Effort and Shape components of Laban Movement Analysis. Hartmann et al. [12] developed a gesture model with parameters for overall activation, spatial extent, temporal extent, fluidity, power and repetition. Neff and Fiume [27] present a system that allows a character sketch to be applied to a motion sequence to control its general form. These systems provide a movement palette, but do not indicate how to change these parameters to create a specific personality. It is our goal to establish mappings between movement parameters and perceived changes in personality.

Other research has examined how to align gestures with spoken utterances. For example Cassell et al. [4] present a system that suggests gesture placement based on linguistic structure. Kipp et al. [16] and Neff et al. [28] present a system that uses probabilistic rules to model the gesturing style of particular individuals in terms of both gesture placement and gesture form. Levine et al. [19] present a system that uses the prosody of spoken text to generate gestures. Our work does not directly contribute to gesture placement strategies, but establishes a relationship between gesture frequency and personality, while also indicating which movement variations are likely to be perceived as extraverted.

Other work has examined how particular aspects of movement are perceived by users. For instance, Kipp et al. [16] demonstrated that gesture units consisting of multiple gestures performed better than singleton gestures on a variety of criteria such as naturalness and friendliness, but found no result for extraversion. Isbister & Nass [15] present the only other work we are aware of that examines the combination of gesture and linguistic expression of personality. They used fixed postures on an artist's model to accompany utterances hand scripted to convey either extraversion or introversion. This study used body expansiveness to indicate computer character's extraversion. Extraverted postures were designed with limbs spread wide from the body while introverted postures were designed with limbs close to the body. We move beyond this to full, multi-modal stimuli, including variations in both text generation and a wide range of movement parameters.

Our experiment demonstrates that each of the factors we tested – language variation, gesture rate, and a large set of gesture performance parameters – have a statistically significant impact on the perception of extraversion. Moreover, they continue to affect user perceptions of extraversion in multi-modal communication with a virtual agent and we can procedurally generate an agent that embodies these traits. The relative contribution of each of these factors was analyzed. We were surprised that misaligned combinations of parameters were perceived as just as natural as aligned combinations. There was no strong correlation between perceived naturalness and TIPI-Extraversion, though there was a correlation between our verbal extraversion parameters and naturalness.

This work indicates several potentially profitable avenues for further exploration. While a large set of movement parameters was used, other factors such as the direction of movement, smoothness and character relationships in dialogs were not explored and warrant further study. Establishing the relative contribution of each movement factor would also be worthwhile. Finally, the concept of naturalness is worth further elaboration, especially in the context of multi-modal stimuli where it can be difficult to ascertain what is dominating user judgments of naturalness (TTS quality, movement, text, or a combination of the factors).

Acknowledgements

Financial support for this research was provided in part by NSF grants 0832202 and 0845529 to UCD and in part by NSF grant 1002921 to UCSC. Thanks to Alexis Heloir for his support with EMBR, the subject participants for their time, and the anonymous reviewers for their useful comments.

References

1. André, E., Rist, T., van Mulken, S., Klesen, M., Baldes, S.: The automated design of believable dialogues for animated presentation teams. In: Embodied conversational agents, pp. 220–255 (2000)
2. Argyle, M.: Bodily communication. Taylor & Francis, Abington (1988)
3. Brebner, J.: Personality theory and movement. Individual differences in movement, 27–41 (1985)
4. Cassell, J., Vilhjálmsson, H., Bickmore, T.: BEAT: the Behavior Expression Animation Toolkit. In: Proceedings of SIGGRAPH 2001, pp. 477–486 (2001)
5. Chi, D.M., Costa, M., Zhao, L., Badler, N.I.: The EMOTE model for effort and shape. In: Proc. SIGGRAPH 2000, pp. 173–182 (2000)
6. Frank, K.: Posture & Perception in the Context of the Tonic Function Model of Structural Integration: an Introduction. In: IASI Yearbook 2007, pp. 27–35 (2007)
7. Funder, D.C.: The Personality Puzzle, 2nd edn. W. W. Norton & Company, New York (1997)
8. Furnham, A.: Language and personality. In: Giles, H., Robinson, W. (eds.) Handbook of Language and Social Psychology, Winley (1990)
9. Giles, H., Street, R.: Communicator characteristics and behavior. Handbook of interpersonal communication 2, 103–161 (1994)

10. Gosling, S.D., Rentfrow, P.J., Swann, W.B.: A very brief measure of the big five personality domains. Journal of Research in Personality 37, 504–528 (2003)
11. Hartmann, B., Mancini, M., Pelachaud, C.: Formational parameters and adaptive prototype installation for MPEG-4 compliant gesture synthesis. In: Proc. Computer Animation 2002. pp. 111–119 (2002)
12. Hartmann, B., Mancini, M., Pelachaud, C.: Implementing expressive gesture synthesis for embodied conversational agents. In: Gibet, S., Courty, N., Kamp, J.-F. (eds.) GW 2005. LNCS (LNAI), vol. 3881, pp. 45–55. Springer, Heidelberg (2006)
13. Heloir, A., Kipp, M.: EMBR – A Realtime Animation Engine for Interactive Embodied Agents. In: Ruttkay, Z., Kipp, M., Nijholt, A., Vilhjálmsson, H.H. (eds.) IVA 2009. LNCS, vol. 5773, pp. 393–404. Springer, Heidelberg (2009)
14. Heylighen, F., Dewaele, J.M.: Variation in the contextuality of language: an empirical measure. Context in Context, Special issue of Foundations of Science 7(3), 293–340 (2002)
15. Isbister, K., Nass, C.: Consistency of personality in interactive characters: Verbal cues, non-verbal cues, and user characteristics. International Journal of Human Computer Studies 53(2), 251–268 (2000)
16. Kipp, M., Neff, M., Kipp, K., Albrecht, I.: Towards natural gesture synthesis: Evaluating gesture units in a data-driven approach to gesture synthesis. In: Pelachaud, C., Martin, J.-C., André, E., Chollet, G., Karpouzis, K., Pelé, D. (eds.) IVA 2007. LNCS (LNAI), vol. 4722, pp. 15–28. Springer, Heidelberg (2007)
17. Knapp, M., Hall, J.: Nonverbal communication in human interaction. Holt, New York (1978)
18. Kopp, S., Wachsmuth, I.: Synthesizing multimodal utterances for conversational agents. Computer Animation and Virtual Worlds 15, 39–52 (2004)
19. Levine, S., Theobalt, C., Koltun, V.: Real-time prosody-driven synthesis of body language. ACM Transactions on Graphics (TOG) 28(5), 1–10 (2009)
20. Lippa, R.: The nonverbal display and judgment of extraversion, masculinity, femininity, and gender diagnosticity: A lens model analysis. Journal of Research in Personality 32(1), 80–107 (1998)
21. Mairesse, F., Walker, M.A.: PERSONAGE: Personality generation for dialogue. In: Proceedings of the 45th Annual Meeting of the Association for Computational Linguistics (ACL), pp. 496–503 (2007)
22. Mairesse, F., Walker, M.A.: Trainable generation of Big-Five personality styles through data-driven parameter estimation. In: Proceedings of the 46th Annual Meeting of the Association for Computational Linguistics, ACL (2008)
23. McQuiggan, S., Mott, B., Lester, J.: Modeling self-efficacy in intelligent tutoring systems: An inductive approach. User Modeling and User-Adapted Interaction 18(1), 81–123 (2008)
24. Mehl, M.R., Gosling, S.D., Pennebaker, J.W.: Personality in its natural habitat: Manifestations and implicit folk theories of personality in daily life. Journal of Personality and Social Psychology 90, 862–877 (2006)
25. Mehrabian, A.: Significance of posture and position in the communication of attitude and status relationships. Psychological Bulletin 71(5), 359–372 (1969)
26. Neff, M., Kim, Y.: Interactive editing of motion style using drives and correlations. In: Proceedings of the 2009 ACM SIGGRAPH/Eurographics Symposium on Computer Animation, pp. 103–112. ACM Press, New York (2009)
27. Neff, M., Fiume, E.: AER: Aesthetic Exploration and Refinement for expressive character animation. In: Proc. ACM SIGGRAPH/Eurographics Symposium on Computer Animation 2005, pp. 161–170 (2005)

28. Neff, M., Kipp, M., Albrecht, I., Seidel, H.P.: Gesture modeling and animation based on a probabilistic re-creation of speaker style. ACM Transactions on Graphics 27(1), 5:1–5:24 (2008)
29. Norman, W.T.: Toward an adequate taxonomy of personality attributes: Replicated factor structure in peer nomination personality rating. Journal of Abnormal and Social Psychology 66, 574–583 (1963)
30. North, M.: Personality assessment through movement. Macdonald and Evans (1972)
31. Pennebaker, J.W., King, L.A.: Linguistic styles: Language use as an individual difference. Journal of Personality and Social Psychology 77, 1296–1312 (1999)
32. Piwek, P.: A flexible pragmatics-driven language generator for animated agents. In: Proceedings of Annual Meeting of the European Chapter of the Association for Computational Linguistics, EACL (2003)
33. Riggio, R., Friedman, H.: Impression formation: The role of expressive behavior. Journal of Personality and Social Psychology 50(2), 421–427 (1986)
34. Scherer, K.R.: Personality markers in speech. In: Scherer, K.R., Giles, H. (eds.) Social markers in speech, pp. 147–209. Cambridge University Press, Cambridge (1979)
35. Takala, M.: Studies of psychomotor personality tests, 1-. Suomalainen Tiedeakatemia (1953)
36. Thiebaux, M., Marshall, A., Marsella, S., Kallman, M.: Smartbody: Behavior realization for embodied conversational agents. In: Proc. of 7th Int. Conf. on Autonomous Agents and Multiagent Systems (AAMAS 2008), pp. 151–158 (2008)
37. Wang, N., Johnson, W.L., Mayer, R.E., Rizzo, P., Shaw, E., Collins, H.: The politeness effect: Pedagogical agents and learning gains. Frontiers in Artificial Intelligence and Applications 125, 686–693 (2005)

Developing Interpersonal Relationships with Virtual Agents through Social Instructional Dialog

Amy Ogan[1], Vincent Aleven[1], Julia Kim[2], and Christopher Jones[1]

[1] Carnegie Mellon University, 5000 Forbes Ave, Pittsburgh PA, 15224, USA
{aeo,aleven}@cs.cmu.edu, cjones@andrew.cmu.edu
[2] USC Institute for Creative Technologies, 12015 Waterfront Drive,
Playa Vista CA, 90094, USA
kim@ict.usc.edu

Abstract. Virtual pedagogical agents are used to teach skills like intercultural negotiation. In this work, we looked at how introducing social conversational strategies into instructional dialog affects learners' interpersonal relations with such virtual agents. We discuss the development of a model for *social instructional dialog* (SID), and a comparison task informational dialog model. SID is designed to support students in taking a social orientation towards learning, through the use of conversational strategies that are theorized to produce interpersonal effects: self-disclosure, narrative, and affirmation. We discuss the implementation of these models in a virtual agent that instructs learners on negotiation and Iraqi culture. Finally, we report on the results of an empirical study with 39 participants in which we found that the SID model had significant effects on learners' interpersonal relations with the agent. While SID engendered greater feelings of entitativity and shared perspective with the agent, it also significantly lowered ratings of trust. These findings may guide development of dialog for future agents.

Keywords: pedagogical agents, encultured embodied conversational agents, social instructional dialog, interpersonal relationships, intercultural instruction.

1 Introduction

Virtual pedagogical agents are increasingly being used for educational purposes [5, 12, 19]. One exciting new possibility is the use of encultured embodied conversational agents (EECAs) for the training of interpersonal skills, such as intercultural negotiation [2]. Conversational (or pedagogical) agents engage in dialog with students to support learning through turn-based conversation called instructional dialog. This instructional dialog generally has a task focus. For example, in a system that teaches physics, the main focus of agent dialog is on the learning objectives, such as understanding momentum, force and velocity. But when considering interpersonal domains like cultural understanding or negotiation, the development of an interpersonal relationship with the agent may play a significant role in learning.

Reeves and Nass have shown through numerous studies that humans can develop interpersonal relationships with computers, which appear to mimic facets of human-human relationships [27]. However, other research has shown that, at least in the area

J. Allbeck et al. (Eds.): IVA 2010, LNAI 6356, pp. 236–249, 2010.

of education, these relationships and their subsequent desired outcomes are not guaranteed. In one recent study, the mere belief that a human was generating the instructional dialog in a system was enough to increase learning outcomes [25]. Thus, it is important to develop dialog models and agents that generate desirable interpersonal effects with the learner. In this research, we target three relational outcomes that we believe may affect learning, especially in an intercultural domain: trust, entitativity, and shared perspective.

Bickmore & Cassell have built models for relational agents that cause changes in trust in transactional tasks, e.g. real estate agents [3]. In instructional tasks, *trust* enables people to make reliability judgments about the accuracy of the information they are receiving. Early work by Pelz and Andrews [26] and Mintzberg [20] indicates that people are preferred over documents as a resource for information. In general, researchers have found relationships to be important for acquiring information [4]. Trust literature has found considerable evidence that higher levels of trust lead to an increased willingness to listen to useful knowledge and absorb it (see e.g., [16,18]). Thus, agents should engender a feeling of trust through their actions to address social and instructional objectives.

A second relational outcome that is tightly coupled to negotiation is *entitativity* - the feeling of working together as a team. In negotiation literature, this feeling leads to more positive affect towards negotiation partners, and also significantly better negotiation outcomes [11]. Agents whose purpose is to teach these negotiation skills should be able to stimulate a feeling of entitativity in the learner. Beyond the potential benefit to negotiation outcomes, agents should help learners feel that they are working together as a team to achieve educational outcomes. Numerous studies have reported the positive effects of groups on learning [13,17].

Finally, agents should be able to influence the *perspective* that learners take in the interaction. The agents we develop are encultured, meaning their behaviors (gestures, utterances, etc) are driven by a model that is, in part, culture-specific. They are intended to help learners acquire intercultural negotiation skills. In both intercultural competence and negotiation, perspective-taking has been shown to be important [10, 11, 14, 23]. Even beyond intercultural education, the ability to take on a shared perspective may be of great value. For example, in STEM (science, technology, engineering and math) education, one central objective is for students to be able to see themselves taking on the persona of scientists or mathematicians.

How we can create dialog agents that lead to these desirable outcomes is an open question. In this paper, we describe the development of an instructional dialog model aimed at achieving these outcomes, which we will call *social instructional dialog* (SID). In its development, we look to communications literature for conversational strategies that are hypothesized to have effects on entitativity, trust, and perspective. Next, we discuss the implementation of these models in a virtual agent. Unlike work on individual features of social relationships in pedagogical agents, such as politeness [32], the utterances created through the implementation of our model are transformed through conversational strategies that holistically change the dialog. We also describe a corresponding agent with (more typical) task instructional dialog, which acts as a comparison to measure the success of these strategies. Finally, we report on the results of an empirical study in which we found that the social informational dialog model had significant effects on learners' trust, entitativity, and shared perspective.

2 Dialog Model

The environment we used for agent development was BiLAT [12], a simulation-based game designed to teach intercultural negotiation skills. The 3D environment and characters are built upon the Unreal Tournament engine. A large number of EECAs exist within the game, with whom the learner interacts to practice intercultural negotiation skills. These agents simulate members of the Iraqi culture with different roles, e.g. police officer or merchant. Scenarios derived from real-world events drive the game experience. The initial scenarios are set in an Iraqi town experiencing a variety of problems. The learner is put into the role of a U.S. Army officer tasked with meeting with the townspeople and accomplishing specific missions related to peacekeeping and rebuilding. Within each encounter, the learner is given concrete, negotiation task-related goals. For example, one scenario entails a newly built town market, which is being avoided by local businessmen. The set of initial objectives for this scenario might be, "learn why the market is not being used" and "gain police cooperation." To achieve these objectives, the player must negotiate with one or more EECAs. A key learning objective is for the student to consider their counterpart's interests, such that a "win-win" result can be realized.

The virtual meeting environment within BiLAT offers an initial set of actions and dialog choices to the learner, which are available through a click interface (see Fig. 1). These actions and dialog choices were authored by the development team in collaboration with Iraqi nationals and military officials. In general, the interaction is turn-based, with each choice by the learner being followed by an utterance from the

Fig. 1. The BiLAT interface. This screenshot shows Farid, a police officer, along with the set of actions currently available to the player.

agent. Each agent has an underlying model of culture and personality that drives their responses to the learner, as well as their gestures, gaze, and posture (see Hill et al. [12] for a more complete description of the development of these agents). In addition to the initially available set of actions, a second type of interaction is allowed through "challenge networks". In a challenge network, the agent produces an utterance and the player is given a choice of several responses. This allows the agent to initiate a dialog, and also allows new dialog choices for the learner to explore a topic more deeply.

2.1 Development of an Instructional Agent

Within the framework of the BiLAT game, we developed a new agent named Zahora (meaning "flower" in Arabic) to evaluate the two instructional dialog models described in the next section. Utilizing the same non-verbal behavior models that underlie the rest of the agents in BiLAT (see [12] for more detail), Zahora moves with culturally-appropriate gestures, gaze, and posture. She speaks in English with a computer-generated voice that has a slight accent. She is introduced as an Iraqi interpreter with knowledge of the culture and negotiation experience.

Unlike the rest of the meeting partners in BiLAT, Zahora is designed to take a more explicitly instructional role. Her instructional dialog model includes a set of branching mini-dialogs that typically last two to six turns (depending on the learner's choices), each of which are organized around a particular learning objective about Iraqi culture or negotiation. Learning objectives vary from casual subjects, such as

Fig. 2. Zahora, the interpreter. The agent is fully animated: she moves with culturally-appropriate gestures gaze, and posture.

Table 1. A sample of three learner choices within a dialog about the role of family in Iraq. Zahora has just replied, "Yes, family is very important to us as well. My family are the only people that I can really trust. This is why brothers and sisters all stay in the family business. My family sells pottery."

Perspective	Description	Sample Utterance
Iraqi	A prototypical Iraqi perspective, generally in agreement with the utterance spoken by the agent	"I agree, my family is my rock."
American	A prototypical American perspective, developed through roleplay with American nationals	"Well, I wouldn't say that. I love my family, but I wouldn't go into business with them!"
Compromise	A compromise perspective in which neither strong cultural perspective was emphasized	"Actually, I'm not too close with most of them, just a few."

food, to more complex social dynamics, such as the differences in the Iraqi and American concept of privacy. Transitions between learning objectives are completed through discourse markers in the agents' utterance, e.g. "Anyway...".. The learning content was adapted from the book Understanding Arabs [24] and was validated through discussion with a small group of Iraqi nationals.

Because the interaction with the agents in the system is driven by menus rather than natural speech, we needed to develop learner responses in addition to the agent dialog model. The initial interaction with the new agent looks much the same as those in the rest of BiLAT. Learners have a set of actions and dialog choices that provide entrance into the mini-dialogs that cover each learning objective. When the learner enters into a mini-dialog by selecting an utterance from the initial set, a challenge network begins. After each agent turn, the learner is given three choices of how to respond. These choices were developed through an iterative process of role-play to each represent a different perspective: American, Iraqi, or a compromise. Table 1 shows an example of three learner choices offered within one dialog turn.

2.2 Social Dialog

Imparting instructional objectives is not the only goal of Zahora's dialog. Our investigation focused on how to design Zahora so she implements the notion of social instructional dialog, introduced above. Within our branching conversational framework, we developed a model of social informational dialog (SID) based on communication theory. The model (shown in Fig. 3) uses three main conversational strategies to communicate learning objectives: self-disclosure, narrative, and affirmation. We chose these strategies because they are posited in the communications literature to affect the relational variables described in the introduction: trust, entitativity, and perspective (see [6,8,15,22], discussed below).

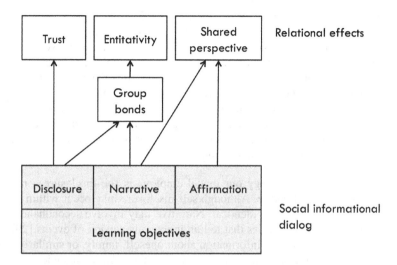

Fig. 3. Model of social informational dialog and effects on relational variables

While the choice of the strategies used in the model is heavily influenced by previous work done by Bickmore and Cassell [3], this work differs in two important ways. First, this dialog is intended to be instructional rather than transactional. The agent is intending to convey learning content with each dialog move, and therefore the strategies are employed to deliver that content. Secondly, the conversational strategies used in the social instructional dialog are designed to be woven into each utterance rather than tacked on to task dialog as additional utterances (see Table 2 below as an example). This both allowed us to keep the length of the dialogs relatively constant between task and social implementations, as well as keep the social flow of the conversation.

Narrative. Narrative is a fundamental form of human communication, which is increasingly popular in the Artificial Intelligence in Education (AIED) community as a method of conveying information, e.g. [19, 28, 30]. This conversational modality has many hypothesized effects on communication. For example, stories embedded in narrative allow the management of social bonds among group members [6]. Secondly, the use of narrative as a communication tool enables the demonstration of a perspective in a contextualized manner. This allows for more personalized and persuasive presentation. Communications literature suggests narrative is as good for knowledge transmission and retention as a paradigmatic way of knowing [7]. The key benefit, it seems, stems from our aptitude for memorizing and processing stories – a tradition that has existed for millennia. Specifically, stories allow learners to leverage pre-existing schemas to acquire new information. Additionally, the heightened affect produced by narrative leads to greater arousal, which, in turn, affords greater and more focused attention from the learner [15].

In our implementation, SID presents learning objectives within the context of a story. There has already been a wealth of material on the creation of narrative (e.g. [1,9,21]); we followed the same general processes. Our first step in generating the dialog was the development of a backstory for Zahora (known as a *character bible*). This backstory contained extensive demographic information, as well as details about her family, their occupations, and so on. Each mini-dialog we created surrounding a learning objective used pieces of this backstory to weave a narrative about her life and observations of Iraq. For instance, Zahora uses the story of her family's pottery business to describe her perspective on familial duty and closeness.

The model also has means of tracking topics discussed, so that if for example Zahora's cousins are introduced in one mini-dialog, they may be used as a referent in a subsequently chosen mini-dialog. This enables the narrative to flow more smoothly, and conforms to assumptions about common ground.

Self-Disclosure. Another strategy our model employs is self-disclosure – revealing information of a personal nature. Although self-disclosure may occur within the context of a narrative, they are not identical. Narrative may involve secondhand stories, invented stories, or official stories that tell an innocuous version of events [29]. Self-disclosure, instead, reveals real information about oneself, family, or similarly private items [8]. Disclosing information to another is a behavior that communicates that we trust that person to respond appropriately. This should have the effect of generating reciprocal trust from the learner. Additionally, this strategy is hypothesized to lead to greater social bonds [8]. Moon showed that a computer with reciprocal, deepening self-disclosure in its conversation will cause the user to rate it as more attractive, divulge more intimate information, and become more likely to buy a product from the computer [22].

In our model, the amount of self-disclosure within an utterance increases over the course of each dialog turn within a particular topic. The greater the number of turns, should the learner choose to continue discussing that particular topic, the greater the amount of disclosure from the agent. For example, as the learner continues with the topic of marriage, Zahora will disclose first that she has been married for three years, and later that she has no children, but hopes to someday.

Affirmation. The final strategy our model incorporates is affirmation, the acknowledgement that the receiving party in a communication has been heard and understood. In our implementation, affirmation is accomplished through affirmative statements. These markers (e.g., "I see", "Yes") are presented when the learner chooses to reply with an American perspective. These markers indicate that although the agent holds a different perspective, she acknowledges the learner's perspective as valid. Inclusion of this strategy was secondarily driven by pilot testing in which participants reported feeling like Zahora "didn't care about their perspective and only wanted to share her own." When affirmation was subsequently increased, she was described as too "zen-like" and accepting, as if "she really had no opinions of her own" and therefore was not able to convincingly agree with the learner's opinion either. We pursued an iterative development strategy, coupled with repeated pilot studies, to find an appropriate balance in the dialog.

2.3 Task Dialog

The task informational dialog (TID) model was developed as a comparison condition for the SID model, using the same structure of mini-dialogs each covering a learning objective. The informational content of each utterance was kept as close as possible to the content of the corresponding utterance from the SID model. However, it was delivered in an impersonal manner. None of the utterances contained any self-disclosure from the agent. Instead, the agent referred to the content as coming from the perspective of Iraqis in general. To this end, the narrative components were removed so that the content was decontextualized. The agent also did not make any affirmation of the learner's perspective, whether they choose to express an American perspective or any other perspective in their responses. Additionally, all personal pronouns were removed so that the agent never referred to itself, but rather to the Iraqi population. An important note here is that the design of the dialog was careful not to advocate stereotypes by claiming that all Iraqis feel a certain way, or always perform any particular behavior. Table 2 shows an example of the contrast between a TID model utterance and the corresponding SID model utterance.

Table 2. Sample utterances for two learning objectives, contrasting the task and social models

Instructional content	**Model**	**Utterance**
Reciprocal provision for contacts	TID	"Your contacts will give you information if you can offer them something in return. For example, translators might need protection for their families."
	SID	"Of course, that is what friends are for. I can give you some information, and maybe you will offer my family your protection in return."
Role of family in Iraq	TID	"Family life is very important to Iraqis. Some people feel like family are the only people that they can really trust. This is why often brothers and sisters all stay in the family business."
	SID	"Yes, family is very important to us as well. My family are the only people that I can really trust. This is why brothers and sisters all stay in the family business. My family sells pottery."

3   Evaluation

To understand the varying effects of SID and TID on learner relations with the instructional agent, Zahora, we ran an empirical study. We compared two versions of Zahora that were identical except for their dialog model: one where the dialog is task-focused (TID), and the second where the instructional dialog is interwoven with social conversational strategies (SID). Participants were given the role of a government official preparing to do sensitive negotiations in Iraq. In order to prepare for this task,

Zahora was introduced as an interpreter they should meet who could answer questions about Iraqi culture. We hypothesized that trust, entitativity, and shared perspective with the agent would be greater in the social condition.

Participants. Thirty-nine people, all U.S. citizens, participated in the study (64% female, 36% male). Participants were students recruited from two college campuses.

Procedure. Participants were randomly assigned to either the task instructional dialog or the social instructional dialog condition. They were seated at a desktop computer running the BiLAT software, wearing headphones to hear the agent responses. First, participants were given a briefing describing the role they were about to assume and introducing the character of Zahora, the interpreter. In both conditions the character was introduced as an authority on local Iraqi culture. Participants then interacted with the agent for as long as they wanted (around ten minutes on average). Finally, they took a post-interaction survey that asked them to rate various qualities of their interaction with the agent and collected demographic information.

Measures

Trust was measured through a standardized scale of trust on a seven-point scale (1 = strongly disagree, 7 = strongly agree) [33].

Entitativity was assessed with four items on a seven-point Likert scale (1 = strongly disagree, 7 = strongly agree): "This team is a unit", "The members of this team can act as one", "There is great togetherness in this team", and " We are as one" (Cronbach's $\alpha = 0.88$).

Shared Perspective was measured using two seven-point Likert items (1 = strongly disagree, 7 = strongly agree) asking whether 1) participants felt they had attempted to express an American perspective with their dialog choices and 2) whether they tried to conform to an Iraqi perspective with their dialog choices.

Learner Characteristics were also captured. We assessed self-reported social intelligence, a quality hypothesized to influence intercultural interactions, using a validated Social Intelligence scale [31]. Given that Bickmore and Cassell [3] found an interaction between personality and condition, where introverts were more trusting in a task condition and extroverts more trusting in a social condition, we included measures of introversion and extroversion. Extroversion and introversion were each measured by an index composed of six extrovert or introvert adjective items [34] (extrovert $\alpha = 0.85$; introvert $\alpha = 0.85$).

Learner Reactions were captured through an open-ended, post-intervention interview that asked them to express their thoughts about the character and the experience.

4 Results

To investigate the models' effects on perspective, we ran a one-way ANOVA with condition as the independent variable and perspective as the dependent variable. We

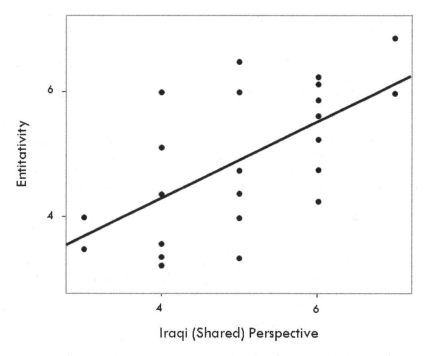

Fig. 4. Correlation of entitativity judgments and shared perspective

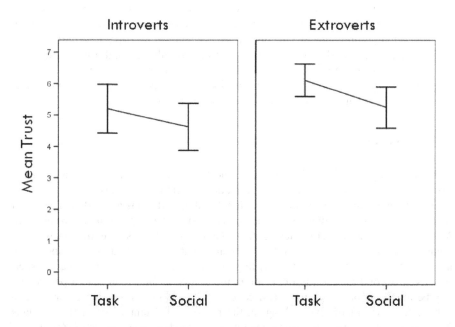

Fig. 5. Trust judgments by condition and personality

found a significant main effect of condition on perspective ($F = 8.87$; $p < .01$). Learners in the TID condition ($M = 4.42$; $SD = 1.30$) were more likely to state that they were espousing an American perspective in their responses to the agent than the SID condition ($M = 3.21$; $SD = 0.66$). In the social condition, on the other hand, participants made comments like "I altered my responses to be in agreement with what she was saying" and "I mostly answered to be aligned with the Iraqi culture, to build rapport."

Having a shared perspective also was associated with participants' feelings of entitativity. The two variables were highly correlated ($r = .62$, $p < .001$). Participants who were attempting to conform to the Iraqi perspective were more likely to feel like they were working together with Zahora (see Fig. 4). Additionally, participants with a higher self-reported Social IQ also felt significantly more like they were working on a team ($r = .5$, $p < .001$).

Given Bickmore and Cassell's [3] finding of an interaction between personality and condition on trust, we conducted an ANOVA with extroversion and condition as the independent variables, and trust as the dependent variable. Unlike prior results, we did not find an interaction. Instead, we found main effects of both condition ($F = 4.49$; $p < .05$) and extroversion ($F = 4.49$; $p < .05$). Learners in the TID condition were more likely to trust Zahora ($M = 5.63$; $SD = 1.12$) compared to learners in the SID condition ($M = 5.0$; $SD = 1.12$). Extroverts ($M = 5.62$; $SD = 1.07$) were also more likely to say that they trusted the agent than introverts ($M = 4.92$; $SD = 1.16$), regardless of condition. These two effects were additive (see Fig. 5).

Qualitatively, we were concerned about the interaction with the dialog menus feeling forced, but participants generally found it to be fairly natural. One participant commented that "It wasn't always what I would have typed in myself, but I usually felt like there was one answer more applicable to what I wanted to say". Additionally, we wanted to explore whether the context and content felt realistic. One participant of Arab background remarked that it "felt true to Arab culture", and a participant who had previously been deployed to Iraq said that the "options seemed realistic." Participants in the task condition had comments like, "This seemed like more of a work meeting," and even in one case, "I wanted more social interaction."

5   Discussion and Conclusions

In this work, we have looked at how introducing social conversational strategies into instructional dialog affects interpersonal relations with virtual agents.

Our findings show that social instructional dialog (SID) has a significant effect on the desire of learners to demonstrate a shared perspective with an intercultural agent. With respect to intercultural education, we believe that this is a significant win. We would like to see that learners both understand what the target cultural perspective is and that they are willing to (at least) temporarily consider and assume that perspective. Even beyond intercultural education, the ability to take on a shared perspective may be highly valued; e.g., in STEM education, one central objective is for students to be able to see themselves taking on the persona of scientists or mathematicians. We also saw that those who demonstrated a shared perspective with Zahora had significantly higher ratings of entitativity - they felt like they were working together on a collaborative team. The increased entitativity not only reflects positive interpersonal relations with the agent, but may also have an effect on learning as well. As noted previously, there are many studies that report the positive effects of groups on learning.

On the other hand, learners in the task instructional dialog (TID) condition expressed more trust in the agent. While this finding was not in line with our predictions, it does have theoretical underpinnings. The task dialog may have felt more authoritative – the information given was not contextualized or taken from personal experience, but presented as a general representation of the Iraqi culture. Therefore learners may have given more credence to the authoritative presentation of this information. This finding can inform research on the roles pedagogical agents play in learning environments. For example, agents have been cast as mentors, instructors, learning companions, and more (see [5] for a review). Our result suggests that the type of dialog they use may significantly affect their credibility.

These findings are important because many systems are beginning to employ some of these strategies, such as narrative, for educational purposes. What the agents in these systems gain in terms of positive interpersonal relations with the learner, they may lose if the learner does not trust the learning content they are given. In the end, a balance between TID and SID might yield the strongest way forward.

Additionally, we saw a difference from related prior work in that extroversion had a positive effect on trust in both social and task dialog, rather than interacting with condition. This result may be due to our model's infusion of all of the agent utterances with social conversational strategies, rather than the addition of social utterances to already existing task dialog. It is possible that in prior work looking at adding social elements to transactional dialog, introverts reacted negatively to the length of the dialog – they may have felt the social agent was simply talking too much. Or these effects may be related to our inclusion of conversational strategies not found in this prior work. This does not mean that we should now ignore the effects of personality on agent relations. In fact, in our study we saw that participants who rated themselves highly on social intelligence also reported a higher entitativity rating – they felt more strongly that they were working together with the agent. This finding is further evidence that personality may have a significant impact on learners' interpersonal relations with virtual agents, and that systems should be able to take this into account.

One avenue of future work is to explore in greater depth the interpersonal relationships between pedagogical agents and introverts or those who rate themselves with low social intelligence. They may respond to different conversational strategies, or it may be the case that such learners are less suited to working with pedagogical agents as we know them, and may need an entirely new model for developing agents that can support their learning. A second, critical avenue of research moving forward will be to investigate the mediated relationship between conversational strategies, learner-agent interpersonal relations, and learning results. While we hypothesize based on related literature that positive interpersonal relations will lead to greater learning, our current study does not address this question (since we did not assess student learning resulting from the social instructional dialogue, only its effect on the personal relationship with the dialogue agent). Additionally, our current model combines several strategies to maximize interpersonal effects, and more work may be done to tease apart which strategy does in fact cause each particular effect. Understanding how these strategies and in turn, interpersonal relationships, relate to learning will enable the creation of agent dialog with real benefits for education.

Acknowledgments. Thanks to Eric Forbell and Glenn Storm for their great effort at support and implementation. Part of this work has been sponsored by the U.S. Army Research, Development, and Engineering Command (RDECOM). Statements and opinions expressed do not necessarily reflect the position or the policy of the United States Government, and no official endorsement should be inferred. The research was supported by the Institute of Education Sciences, U.S. Department of Education, through Grant R305B040063 to CMU.

References

1. Bateman, C.: Game writing: narrative skills for videogames. Charles River Media, Hingham (2007)
2. Blanchard, E., Ogan, A.: Culturally-Aware Tutoring Systems: ITS in a Globalized World. In: Nkambou, R., Mizoguchi, R., Bourdeau, J. (eds.) Advances in Intelligent Tutoring Systems, Springer, Berlin (in press)
3. Bickmore, T., Cassell, J.: Relational agents: a model and implementation of building user trust. In: Proc. of the SIGCHI Conference on Human Factors in Computing Systems, pp. 396–403. ACM, New York (2001)
4. Burt, R.: Structural holes. Harvard University Press, Cambridge (1992)
5. Chou, C.-Y., Chan, T.-W., Lin, C.-J.: Redefining the learning companion: the past, present, and future of educational agents. Computers & Education 40, 255–269 (2003)
6. Bochner, A.P., Ellis, C., Tillmann-Healy, L.M.: Relationships as stories: Accounts, storied lives, evocative narratives. In: Dindia, K., Duck, S. (eds.) Communication and personal relationships, pp. 12–29. John Wiley & Sons, Ltd., Chichester (2000)
7. Bruner, J.: Actual minds, possible worlds. Harvard University Press, Cambridge (1986)
8. Cozby, P.C.: Self-disclosure: A literature review. Psychological Bulletin (1973)
9. Despain, W.: Professional Techniques for Video Game Writing (2008)
10. Galinsky, A., Mussweiler, T.: Promoting good outcomes: Effects of regulatory focus on negotiation outcomes. J. of Personality and Social Psychology 81, 657–669 (2001)
11. Gelfand, M., Brett, J. (eds.): The Handbook of Negotiation and Culture, Stanford (1983)
12. Hill, R.W., Belanich, J., Lane, H.C., Core, M.G., Dixon, M., Forbell, E., Kim, J., Hart, J.: Pedagogically Structured Game-based Training: Development of the ELECT BiLAT Simulation. In: Proc. 25th Army Science Conf. (2006)
13. Johnson, D.W., Johnson, R.T.: Cooperative learning and achievement. In: Sharan, S. (ed.) Cooperative learning: Theory and Research, pp. 23–37. Praeger, NY (1990)
14. Jones, E.E., Nisbett, R.E.: The actor and the observer: Divergent perception of the causes of behavior. In: Jones, E.E. (ed.) Attribution: Perceiving the causes of behavior, pp. 79–94. Erlbaum, Hillsdale (1987)
15. Lang, A., Bolls, P., Potter, R., Kawahara, K.: The effects of production pacing and arousing content on the information processing of television messages. Journal of Broadcasting & Electronic Media 43(4), 451–475 (1999)
16. Levin, D.Z.: Transferring knowledge within the organization in the R&D arena. Unpublished doctoral dissertation, Northwestern University (1999)
17. Lou, Y., Abrami, P.C., d'Apollonia, S.: Small group and individual learning with technology: A meta-analysis. Review of Educational Research 71(3), 449–521 (2001)

18. Mayer, R.C., Davis, J.H., Schoorman, F.D.: An integration model of organizational trust. Academy of Management Review 20, 709–734 (1995)
19. McQuiggan, S., Rowe, J., Lee, S., Lester, J.: Story-Based Learning: The Impact of Narrative on Learning Experiences and Outcomes. In: Woolf, B.P., Aïmeur, E., Nkambou, R., Lajoie, S. (eds.) ITS 2008. LNCS, vol. 5091, pp. 530–539. Springer, Heidelberg (2008)
20. Mintzberg, H.: The nature of managerial work. Harper Row, New York (1973)
21. Mirrielees, E.: Story Writing. Wildside Press LLC (2008)
22. Moon, Y.: Intimate self-disclosure exhanges: Using computers to build reciprocal relationships with consumers. Harvard Business School, Cambridge (1998)
23. Neale, M.A., Bazerman, M.H.: The role of perspective-taking ability in negotiating under different forms of arbitration. Industrial and Labor Relations Review 36, 378–388 (1983)
24. Nydell, M.: Understanding Arabs: a guide for modern times (2006)
25. Okita, S.Y., Bailenson, J., Schwartz, D.L.: Mere Belief of Social Action Improves Complex Learnin. In: Barab, S., Hay, K., Hickey, D. (eds.) Proc of the 8th International Conference for the Learning Sciences. Lawrence Erlbaum Associates, New Jersey (2008)
26. Pelz, D.C., Andrews, F.M.: Scientists in organizations: Productive climates for research and development. Wiley, New York (1966)
27. Reeves, B., Nass, C.: The Media Equation: How People Treat Computers, Television, and New Media like Real People and Place. Cambridge University Press, Cambridge (1996)
28. Riedl, M., Arriaga, R., Boujarwah, F., Hong, H., Isbell, J., Heflin, L.J.: Graphical social scenarios: Toward intervention and authoring for adolescents with high functioning autism. In: Proc. of the of the AAAI Fall Symposium on Virtual Healthcare Interaction, Arlington, VA (2009)
29. Schank, R.C., Berman, T.R.: The pervasive role of stories in knowledge and action. In: Green, M.C., Strange, J.J., Brock, T.C. (eds.) Narrative impact: Social and cognitive foundations, pp. 287–313. Lawrence Erlbaum, Mahwah (2002)
30. Schank, R.C.: Case-Based Teaching: Four Experiences in Educational Software Design. Interactive Learning Environments 1(4), 231–253 (1990)
31. Silvera, D.H., Martinussen, M., Dahl, T.I.: The Tromso Social Intelligence Scale, a self-report measure of social intelligence. Scandinavian Journal of Psychology 42, 313–319 (2001)
32. Wang, N., Johnson, W.L., Rizzo, P., Shaw, E., Mayer, R.E.: Experimental evaluation of polite interaction tactics for pedagogical agents. In: Proc of the 10th Intl. Conf. on Intelligent User interfaces, pp. 12–19. ACM, New York (2005)
33. Wheeless, L., Grotz, J.: The Measurement of Trust and Its Relationship to Self-Disclosure. Human Communication Research 3, 250–257 (1977)
34. Wiggins, J.: A psychological taxonomy of trait descriptive terms. Journal of Personality and Social Psychology 37, 395–412 (1979)

Multiple Agent Roles in an Adaptive Virtual Classroom Environment

Gregor Mehlmann, Markus Häring, René Bühling,
Michael Wißner, and Elisabeth André

Augsburg University, Multimedia Concepts and their Applications,
D-86159 Augsburg, Germany
{mehlmann,haering,buehling,wissner,andre}@informatik.uni-augsburg.de
http://mm-werkstatt.informatik.uni-augsburg.de/

Abstract. We present the design of a cast of pedagogical agents impersonating different educational roles in an interactive virtual learning environment. Teams of those agents are used to create different learning scenarios in order to provide learners with an engaging and motivating learning experience. Authors can employ an easy to use multimodal dialog authoring tool to adapt lecture and dialog content as well as interaction management to meet their respective requirements.

1 Motivation

Embodied conversational agents are widely used in educational applications such as virtual learning and training environments [1]. Beside possible negative effects of virtual characters [2], there is empirical evidence that virtual pedagogical agents and learning companions can lead to an improved perception of the learning task and increase the learners' commitment to the virtual learning experience [3]. They can promote the learners' motivation and self-confidence, help to prevent or overcome negative affective states and minimize undesirable associations with the learning task, such as frustration, boredom or fear of failure. It has been shown that a one-sided coverage of knowledge transfer or the employment of only a single educational role may either lead to satisfying learning success or motivation, but usually not both at the same time [4]. The usage of multiple virtual characters personating different educational roles can have positive influence on both the learners' learning success and their engagement. Teams of pedagogical agents can help the learners to classify the conveyed knowledge and allow for a continuous reinforcement of beliefs [5].

Point of origin for our research is *DynaLearn* [6], an interactive learning environment in which learners can express their conceptual knowledge through qualitative reasoning models [7]. In this paper, we present our effort of enriching DynaLearn with a cast of virtual characters, aiming at increasing learners' motivation as well as their learning success. We considered a variety of teaching methods, learning strategies and ways of knowledge conveyance and verification. The integration of an easy to use authoring tool simplifies visual prototyping of didactic and narrative structure as well as the creation of lecture content.

J. Allbeck et al. (Eds.): IVA 2010, LNAI 6356, pp. 250–256, 2010.

2   Related Work

The classical role of an agent in a learning environment is that of a teacher, see, for example, [8] and [1]. In [9], "AutoTutor" is presented, which allows learners to learn by having a very interactive natural language conversation with a talking head, the virtual tutor.

"Betty's Brain" [10] features Betty, a talking head, who is a so-called teachable agent. Learners can teach her by building a concept map and asking questions about it with the ultimate goal of preparing her for a quiz. Also, multiple teachable agents can compete in a quiz show like application. Questions are asked by a virtual quizmaster and each agent responds according to their concept map.

In [11], another virtual character in "Betty's Brain" is mentioned: Mr. Davis, the teacher (also realized as a talking head). Mr. Davis helps learners by giving guidelines about teaching in general or hints that address specific situations, but not the task or domain at hand. There is also no real interaction between Mr. Davis and Betty.

A closer look at these interactive learning environments shows that all of them feature a teacher-like character that interacts with the learner. However, how this interaction looks like and what is actually communicated differs widely. Only one of the systems makes use of a teachable character. Also, only one system features fully embodied agents, that can also communicate through gestures. Finally, only one of the systems features more than one character role. But these characters only interact with the learner and never with each other.

Taking all this together, we decided to integrate the following character roles into our learning environment: A *Teacher* who helps the learner with specific and general hints through an interactive dialog, a *Teachable Agent* who can be taught by the learner and a *Quizmaster* who adds a playful element by asking the learner questions, but who also directly interacts with the teachable agent to form a presentation team as suggested in [5].

3   Character Role Design

Animal characters act as culture-neutral personalities and are expected to have lower communication skills than human-like characters allowing users to more willingly forgive technical imperfections [12,13]. For these reasons, we decided to create a set of cartoonish hamster characters. We aim at ensuring that the agents' behavior follows approved pedagogical principles and meets the learners' expectations of the roles. For the definition of behavioral rules and patterns for our educational roles, we fall back on three established teaching methods from educational science: *Learning by Teaching* [10], *Scaffolding* [14,15] and *Educational Quizzes* [16].

3.1   Learning by Teaching

Learning by Teaching is an effect that many learners experience while learning with or teaching their peers. A *Teachable Agent* (TA) transfers this principle

spiky hair tips for cheeky look

forelock and ponytail female properties

bright ochre-brown fur for youth and vitality

wide gesture space and extensive motion due to show youth

soft color shades to accent eyes and mouth

bright ochre-brown fur for youth and vitality

color and shape contrasts for dynamic aura

modern clothing style for up-to-date mentality

fashioned clothing style for up-to-date mentality and bright friendly colors for open minded aura

loose posture and wide gesture space to show youth

tight motion space when feeling unsure

Fig. 1. The design criteria for the teachable boy and girl characters

to the field of learning environments. It has a knowledge representation that can be created by the learner. From this representation the agent can extract answers to questions asked by the learner. It is also able to explain its train of thought, so learners can see the causal chains in their own model. Testing the TA's understanding of the subject through questioning, learners can evaluate their own representation and find mistakes when the agent does not answer as expected.

Constant verification of one's own understanding is an important part in the learning process that unfortunately often comes short due to learners' aversion to tests. However, learners are less restrained in making an agent take a test multiple times. That is why we allow learners to take part in an educational quiz but to also send their TA instead. Since the TA's knowledge mirrors the learners' knowledge, it can serve as their proxy.

Though *Learning by Teaching* aims for learning success, the role of the teachable agent is more a motivating one. Following the research of Kim et al. [4] our TA forges a peer-like relationship to the learner with its low-competent behavior.

The learner is able to choose between a male and female personal pet and give it a name. Graphical details and animations differ and depend on the personality of each hamster's gender as shown in Figure 1. The boy character is designed to appear as a lively and extroverted person whereas politeness and open mindedness dominate the girl's personality.

3.2   Instructional Scaffolding

Of course we cannot expect the learners to detect and solve all problems, that occur during their work, by themselves. They need the help of more competent agents, like our teacher agent. We chose the constructivist approach of *Scaffolding* as learning principle for this role. *Scaffolding* emphasizes that learners should do as much work as possible by themselves. The teacher only provides assistance if learners do not possess the necessary skills or knowledge to solve the current problem.

The overview from Lipscomb et al. [14] and the work of Cade et al. [15] helped us identify the means for reaching this goal. While Cade et al. mention scaffolding as one of their mutual exclusive dialog modes in one-on-one tutoring sessions,

Fig. 2. The teacher giving a hint in the scaffolding phase

Lipscomb et al. describe scaffolding as a more extensive teaching principle. We combine the strength of both researches in our teacher role. The more widespread scaffolding of Lipscomb et al. determines the general behavior of our teacher, while we use dialog modes of Cade et al. as dialog steps within this behavior.

The task of our teacher is to communicate mistakes found in a learner's model and to help fixing them step-by-step. For this purpose the teacher provides different teaching aids for the learner from one of the following three categories: *Lecture, Scaffolding* and *Modeling*. The agent usually chooses with an equal chance between lecture and scaffolding when providing an aid. These chances are based on the observations of Cade et al. where lectures and scaffolding were the most present dialog modes with a very similar frequency. As we ideally want the learner to find the solution by himself, modeling (i.e. the exact correction of the mistake) is only appropriate if the teacher has exhausted all other means. In this way, we ensure learners can proceed with the correction of their model even if they cannot cope with a particular problem.

Figure 2 shows the teacher character giving a hint about wrong parts of a learner's model. His dialog texts convey a good-natured personality, as he never scolds the learner for mistakes or failures, but uses praise and reassurance. It can be seen that the teacher role is designed as an aged person having high competence and knowledge. To visually convey these aspects the teacher hamster and its traditional styled clothes are shaded with warm natural colors to suggest a calm aura and a down-to-earth mentality. Also round and soft facial shapes lead to a friendly charisma which is important for a trustful contact person to ask for help when needed. Age and experience are supported by bright gray colored fur, accessories like eyeglasses and calm animation characteristics.

3.3   Educational Quizzes

Tests are usually perceived as stressful situations having negative effects on concentration or motivation. In observations of quiz forms in several well known television quiz shows we found out that quizmasters sometimes try to loosen up such situations in order to countervail their negative effects and to provide an enjoyable form of test. They start lively conversations with their candidates and

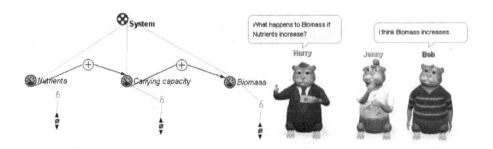

Fig. 3. Quizmaster and two teachable agents in an educational quiz scenario

discuss topics that are familiar to the participants such as job or leisure activities. We mimic this behavior with our quizmaster character. Beside the quizmaster's general behavior of asking questions and giving feedback, we integrate smalltalk utterances into the dialog. They serve as short, preferable humorous distraction for the participant that actually have no connection to the current quiz domain. As mentioned above, the quizmaster can engage a human learner as well as their teachable agent. Also, a quiz with more than one participating teachable agent is possible.

Figure 3 shows the quizmaster and the two teachable agents. To adapt the idea of a calming "fun manager" the quizmaster is designed to appear as a strongly organized, up to date person who is entertaining and serious at the same time. Seriousness and maturity are reflected in darker shaded fur and highly saturated clothing colors.

4   Modeling Dialog and Interaction

The dialog and interaction management for our agents is realized with the authoring tool *SceneMaker* [17], which facilitates the creation of interactive performances because it divides the authoring task into the creation of dialog content and the modeling of the narrative and didactic structure of a lecture.

Dialog content is organized in a set of parameterizable *scenes* that are specified in a multimodal *scenescript* which resembles a movie script with dialog utterances and stage directions for controlling gestures, postures and facial expressions. For each scene, we provide a number of variations, subsumed in a *scenegroup*, to increase variety and to avoid repetitive behavior that would impact the agents' believability. As shown in Figure 4, scenescript content is created both manually (a) and by an external generation module (b) that generates question phrases from a qualitative reasoning model.

The narrative structure of a lecture is controlled by a *sceneflow* - a hierarchical and concurrent finite-state machine specifying the logic organization and temporal order in which scenes are played. A state in a sceneflow may enfold several subgraphs, thus allowing for the hierarchical *refinement* and *parallel decomposition* of the sceneflow. This feature allows us to carry out the modeling

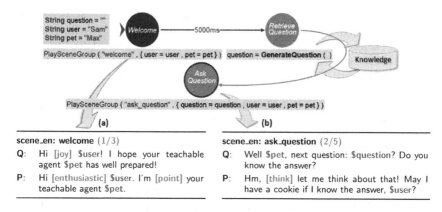

Fig. 4. Examples of calling scenes of the multimodal scenescript

task in a divide-and-conquer manner: Except for synchronization measures, various control processes and user input processing as well as the individual agents' behavior are modeled independently of each other. Thus, we keep the sceneflow clearly arranged, extensible and parts of it exchangeable.

The sceneflow *interpreter* allows the *real-time visualization* of a sceneflow's execution and active scenes within the graphical user interface in order to test, simulate and debug a model, to control the modeling progress and to verify the correctness of the model.

5 Discussion

An evaluation of the virtual characters' appearances confirmed that they successfully conveyed their intended roles and meaning. Another pilot evaluation of subjective measures confirmed that learners enjoyed the interaction with our pedagogical agents and perceived the virtual classroom setting as engaging and motivating. They understood the different learning scenarios and the justification for each single educational role. They felt that all agents and their respective educational roles successfully helped learning. More detailed and exhaustive evaluations will have to show whether those results also apply to objective measures such as learning success and if the educational roles created in the context of DynaLearn can also be applied to other learning environments.

Acknowledgments

This work is supported by DynaLearn, co-funded by the EC within the 7th Framework Programme, Project no. 231526 (http://www.DynaLearn.eu).

References

1. Johnson, L.W., Rickel, J.W.: Animated Pedagogical Agents: Face-to-Face Interaction in Interactive Learning Environments. Artificial Intelligence in Education (11), 47–78 (2000)

2. Rickenberg, R., Reeves, B.: The Effects of Animated Characters on Anxiety, Task Performance and Evaluations of User Interfaces. In: Proc. of the SIGCHI Conf. on Human Factors in Computing Systems, pp. 49–56. ACM, New York (2000)

3. van Mulken, S., André, E., Müller, J.: The Persona Effect: How Substantial Is It? In: Proc. of HCI on People and Computers XIII, pp. 53–66. Springer, London (1998)

4. Kim, Y., Baylor, A.L.: PALS Group: Pedagogical Agents as Learning Companions: The Role of Agent Competency and Type of Interaction. Educational Technology Research and Development 54(3), 223–243 (2006)

5. André, E., Rist, T., van Mulken, S., Klesen, M., Baldes, S.: The Automated Design of Believable Dialogues for Animated Presentation Teams. In: Embodied Conversational Agents, pp. 220–255. MIT Press, Cambridge (2001)

6. Bredeweg, B., Gómez-Pérez, A., André, E., Salles, P.: DynaLearn - Engaging and Informed Tools for Learning Conceptual System Knowledge. In: Technical Report FS-09-02, pp. 46–51. AAAI Press (2009)

7. Bredeweg, B., Linnebank, F., Bouwer, A., Liem, J.: Garp3 - Workbench for Qualitative Modelling and Simulation. Ecological Informatics (4), 263–281 (2009)

8. Conati, C., Zhao, X.: Building and Evaluating an Intelligent Pedagogical Agent to Improve the Effectiveness of an Educational Game. In: Proc. of the 9th Int. Conf. on Intelligent User Interfaces, pp. 6–13. ACM, New York (2004)

9. Graesser, A.C., Person, N.K., Harter, D.: The Tutoring Research Group: Teaching Tactics and Dialog in Autotutor. Artificial Intelligence in Education (12), 257–279 (2001)

10. Blair, K., Schwartz, D., Biswas, G., Leelawong, K.: Pedagogical Agents for Learning by Teaching: Teachable Agents. In: Educational Technology & Society, Special Issue on Pedagogical Agents (2006)

11. Biswas, G., Roscoe, R., Jeong, H., Sulcer, B.: Promoting Self-Regulated Learning Skills in Agent-Based Learning Environments. In: Proc. of the 17th Int. Conf. on Computers in Education, pp. 67–74 (2009)

12. Mateas, M.: An Oz-Centric Review of Interactive Drama and Believable Agents. In: Technical Report CMU-CS-97-156, School of Computer Science CMU (1997)

13. Bredeweg, B., Liem, J., Linnebank, F., Bühling, R., Wißner, M., Gracia del Río, J., Salles, P., Beek, W., Gómez Pérez, A.: DynaLearn: Architecture and Approach for Investigating the Acquisition of Conceptual System Knowledge for Ill-Defined Domains. In: Aleven, V., Kay, J., Mostow, J. (eds.) Intelligent Tutoring Systems. LNCS, vol. 6095, pp. 272–274. Springer, Heidelberg (2010)

14. Lipscomb, L., Swanson, J., West, A.: Scaffolding. In: Emerging Perspectives on Learning, Teaching and Technology (2001)

15. Cade, W.L., Copeland, J.L., Person, N.K., D'Mello, S.K.: Dialogue Modes in Expert Tutoring. In: Woolf, B.P., Aïmeur, E., Nkambou, R., Lajoie, S. (eds.) ITS 2008. LNCS, vol. 5091, pp. 470–479. Springer, Heidelberg (2008)

16. Randel, J.M., Morris, B.A., Wetzel, C.D., Whitehill, B.V.: The Effectiveness of Games for Educational Purposes: A Review of Recent Research. Simulation and Gaming (23), 261–276 (1992)

17. Gebhard, P., Kipp, M., Klesen, M., Rist, T.: Authoring Scenes for Adaptive, Interactive Performances. In: Proc. of the 2th Int. Conf. on Autonomous Agents and Multiagent Systems, pp. 725–732. ACM, New York (2003)

Creating Individual Agents through Personality Traits

Tiago Doce, João Dias, Rui Prada, and Ana Paiva

IST - Technical University of Lisbon and INESC-ID,
Av. Prof. Cavaco Silva, Taguspark 2744-016, Porto Salvo, Portugal
tiago.salsa.doce@gmail.com, {joao.dias,rui.prada,ana.paiva}@inesc-id.pt

Abstract. In the era of globalization, concepts such as individualization and personalization become more and more important in virtual systems. With the goal of creating a more familiar interaction between human and machines, it makes sense to create a consistent and believable model of personality. This paper presents an explicit model of personality, based in the Five Factor Model, which aims at the creation of distinguishable personalities by using the personality traits to automatically influence cognitive processes: appraisal, planning,coping, and bodily expression.

Keywords: Agent Architectures, Personality.

1 Introduction

In the era of globalization, where the number of different individuals with distinct characteristics that come in contact with us in everyday life has increased enormously, more and more aspects such as personalization and individuality become relevant in human-machine interaction. In order to create virtual environments that try to portray the same richness and interaction as the real-world, one needs to address the creation of unique virtual characters with distinct, believable personalities. Many definitions of personality in autonomous agents use traits to define individual characteristics of agents, however, the set of traits used is sometimes ad hoc, which can lead to combination of traits that produce personalities that are not coherent (4). This may be a small issue when using personality as a exploratory tool in multi-agent systems, but may become a major problem if the goal is to create agents that show believable personalities.

These more ad hoc approaches can be effective, however, they usually lead to more effort in the crafting of each individuality to avoid producing personalities that are not coherent. We defend that using an explicit personality model, based on well established trait theories, such as the Five Factor Model (FFM) of personality (11), provides a better tool to easily create coherent and different personalities. With this in mind, this paper addresses the problem of how to create agents with different distinguishable personalities, just by changing the values of a set of predefined personality traits. Given the definition of Personality as an organized set of characteristics that uniquely influence the processes of cognition, motivation and behaviour (28), we depart from the hiphotesis that

J. Allbeck et al. (Eds.): IVA 2010, LNAI 6356, pp. 257–264, 2010.

if we use the personality traits to automatically influence emotional, cognitive and behavioural processes, these will then influence the overall behaviour of the agent, thus portraying the defined personality.

This paper is then structured as follows: we start by describing the theories that support the model presented and additional related work. Afterwards, we present the proposed model, and its implementation in a concrete agent architecture. Finally we depict a case study used to evaluate the model, present the results obtained and draw some conclusions.

2   Background and Related Work

A very important psychology work in the area of personality is the work of Gordon Allport who considers traits as being predispositions to act in a certain way (1). Although there were many studies regarding traits, they never seemed to agree in the number of basic traits until the five-factor model started to emerge (11). This model proposed five traits as the basic units of personality(21, 11, 10, 16, 17): Neuroticism, Extroversion, Openness to experience, Agreeableness and Conscientiousness.

There are a few studies who support the validity of the five-factor model and among them there is one that found correlations between traits, emotions and interpersonal behaviour (21). Thus we need an emotion model that can easily represent emotions in a systematic way. Among the wide variety of emotion theories, the OCC (19) seems like the most suited due to its simplicity and due to the fact that is used in the architecture FAtiMA, which we will extend with our model. OCC theory proposes 22 basic emotion types (e.g. Joy, Distress, Hope) with thresholds and decay rates. The thresholds define the intensity an emotion has to have in order to be felt by an individual, and the decay rate defines the rate at which the intensity of the emotion decays.

Regarding agents with personality, there is a wide variety of approaches, whether in terms of personality theories or in architectural strategies. The works of Rousseau and Hayes-Roth (25, 8, 24, 26, 27), are particularly important in the sense that they provide a nice example of how traits can be implemented in agents. By defining a character's personality and the actions he can perform with values for each trait dimension, they provided a simple way to represent different personalities through different behaviour.

A different approach to personality in synthetic agents is explored in the work of Rizzo et al. (23). It proves that goals and plans can be used to represent a character's personality in an efficient way, by attributing specific behaviour (personality) to the pursuit of each goal. The work of Malatesta et al. (14) shows how personality can be used to create different expressions of behaviour. A personality trait is linked to mood/emotions and behaviours and these behaviours are expressed through the use of certain expressivity parameters. The works of Kshirsagar et al. (12) and Reichardt(22) show how the Big Five personality theory can be linked with the OCC model of emotions by mapping the five dimensions of personality into specific moods, which in turn influence the agent's emotions.

3   Personality Model in an Agent Architecture

We identified four cognitive/behavioural processes that are strongly influenced by personality: emotions, coping behaviour, means-ends reasoning and bodily expression.

Personality and Emotions

Personality is said to influence in a major way, the way one feels (3). Therefore, we have mapped personality traits into emotions. The personality traits define the predisposition that the agent has to feel certain emotions, as well as their intensity. We can easily make a link between traits and emotions by defining the emotions thresholds and decay rates as being influenced by each trait:

- **Neuroticism** - associated to individuals that often feel anxious and sad(17). So there is a strong relation between neuroticism and Distress/Joy emotions. Neuroticism is also associated with insecureness and self-punishment (29). Thus, neurotic agents should feel weaker positive emotions when they accomplish/achieve things and stronger negative emotions when they fail. The OCC emotions related to the success/failure of goals are Satisfaction, Disappointment, Relief, Fears-Confirmed, Gratification and Remorse. Finally, given that the neurotic individual is fearful (11) (21), this trait will be used to influence Hope(negatively) and Fear(positively).
- **Extroversion** - Some studies have said that introverts feel emotions more intensely than extrovert with the same amount of stimuli (21). For this reason, agents with a high score on Extroversion have this trait influencing negatively all emotions, i. e., extroverted agents will have higher thresholds for every emotion. However, this effect is not as strong as the influence of other traits.
- **Openness to Experience** - Individuals with a high score on Openness are unconventional and do not value norms (15). Thus, we argue that such individuals attribute less blameworthy and praiseworthy (evaluated from norms and values) to actions and events. Thus, open minded agents will fell with less intensity OCC emotions related to these evaluations: Pride, Shame, Admiration and Reproach. Opposingly, close minded individuals will experience these emotions with greater intensity.
- **Agreeableness** - A high agreeableness implies that the agent feels more intensely emotions which are positive towards others: Love, Happy-For, Pitty, Admiration, Gratitude; and that the agent feels less intensely emotions considered negative towards others: Hate, Resentment, Gloating, Reproach and Anger. A low agreeableness affects the same emotions opposingly.
- **Conscientiousness** - Conscientiousness is associated with assertiveness and research shows that there is a strong relationship between assertiveness and pride (30). Thus, a high score in this trait imply stronger feelings of pride. Conscientiousness delays gratification, which indicates that noonconscientious people feel gratification more. As such, a low score in this trait will also make the agent feel more intense Gratification emotions.

Personality and Planning

Deliberative agent architectures usually model the concepts of goals, intentions and plans. Upon the selection of a possible achievable goal, a plan is created, composed by actions, in order to achieve the goal. The point of relevance for personality here, is that the agent has many goals he can pursuit at a given time, and can construct several plans to achieve every single one of them.

Among the five traits, Conscientiousness is the one that was found to be more relevant to this process. Conscientiousness describes several characteristics of the human being that are naturally part of the planning process, such as the degree of organization, persistence and motivation in goal-directed behaviour. People who score high tend to be hard-working and persevering; people who score low are usually undetermined and sloppy (21, 11, 10, 17, 15). Therefore, an agent with a low level of Conscientiousness will prefer plans with a smaller number of actions and smaller number of open preconditions, while an agent with high Conscientiousness will prefer a plan with better probability of success, not minding a greater number of actions. This is formalized through an heuristic function, where the plan with the lowest value of $h(p)$ will be the one selected by the agent:

$$h(p) = \frac{Steps(p) \times c_{value} + OpenPrecond(p) \times c_{value}}{probability(p) \times (6 - c_{value})}$$

$Steps(p)$ returns the number of steps (actions) in the plan, $OpenPrecond(p)$ the number of open preconditions (conditions that are not yet achieved by the plan and must be planned for) and $probability(p)$ is the plan's probability of success. The constant c_{value} represents the agent's conscientiousness value.

Personality and Coping Behaviour

Research within the big five personality traits theory has shown that these traits can provide information regarding the individual's coping process (6, 18, 31, 9). However, there is not an agreement on which traits influence coping or how they influence it. Because Neuroticism is the only trait that has enough support by researchers on the matter of influencing coping, we chose to influence coping strategies with Neuroticism wherever it was possible. In our model, denial or wishfull thinking is applied when, for example, there are certain goals that are being threatened by an active plan. In this case, the agent denies those threats, going forward with the plan. To make this dependent on the personality, this strategy is only chosen by the agent, depending on his level of Neuroticism: if it is high, the agent applies denial/wishfull-thinking, if it is low, the agent does not.

Personality and Expressivity

Research shows that one's facial expressions influences the judgement that other people make about one's personality (5). Regarding other bodily expressions, several studies have shown the relationship between, for example, the arms position, facial expressions, vocal expressions and posture expressions, and personality traits (2).

Personality is then introduced at this level through the expression of emotions and through the diversity of ways that the agent can express the same gesture, by manipulating a set of expressivity parameters: Spacial extent - amount of space required to perform and expression - extroverts use a lot of spacial extent, while introverts use a small space; Temporal extent - amount of time spent to perform an expression - we assigned a short temporal extent to extroverts; Fluidity - smoothness of movements - agents have a high fluidity if they are not extroverted nor neurotic and a low fluidity otherwise; Power - intensity of an intention - power is directly proportional to extroversion; Repetitivity - repetition of certain movements - a character with high neuroticism will have a high repetitivity.

4   Implementation

Figure 1 shows the integration of the proposed trait-based personality model into an Agent Architecture, which uses FAtiMA (7) as the agent's mind and GRETA (20) as the body. Whenever an event is perceived, it starts by appraising the event according to OCC theory, generating emotions. The event is then sent to the deliberative layer, which updates the memory of the agent and checks whether any goal has become active. If so, the agent creates an intention to achieve the goal. Then, a plan of actions is created for that intention, and coping strategies such as acceptance (giving up a goal) or wishfull thinking (lowering a threat's probability) can be applied as well. Finally, the actions are sent for execution to GRETA, which expresses them through gestures, facial expressions and posture.

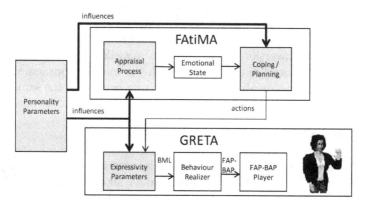

Fig. 1. Agent Architecture using FAtiMA and Greta

5   Evaluation

In order to evaluate the model, we created a very simple case study, with four different basic personality types (13): sanguine, melancholic, phlegmatic and choleric. The evaluation was then performed by having users watch a video with a performance of an agent with a specific personality (each user saw only one personality) and then fill a personality questionnaire concerning the personality of the agent. Our aim was to determine if the created architecture is able to convey the different personalities, and if users could identify correctly the traits of the agent. In total we got 46 answered questionnaires (roughly 11 for each personality), ranged from 20 to 30 years old. The Openness to Experience trait was not evaluated since it is more related to actions (painting, reading, etc) than to actual expression of emotions.

The first test consisted in determining whether users could perceive the personalities as distinct. The personality was selected as the control variable (thus creating four control groups), and the user's classification of the agent's traits as the dependent variables. We applied an one-way independent ANOVA statistical test and obtained the following results: Extraversion - $F(3, 42) = 15.95, p < 0.01, r = 0.76$; Agreeableness - $F(3, 42) = 7.91, p < 0.01, r = 0.62$; Conscientiousness - $F(3, 42) = 2.80, p = 0.051, r = 0.37$; Neuroticism - $F(3, 42) = 12.97, p < 0.01, r = 0.72$. In other words, the results show that the defined personality significantly affected the user's perception of agent's extraversion, agreeableness and neuroticism traits. Moreover, the effect was substantial. As for the conscientiousness trait, it is very close to being significant, but only has a moderate effect. Thus, this first test tells us that the architecture was indeed able to create distinguishable personality just by changing its traits.

Our second goal was making users correctly identify the traits defined for each personality. In order to test this, we checked if there was any individual correlation between the defined traits and the traits perceived. After applying a Pearson correlation test, the results obtained were: $C(Def_E, Per_E) = 0.45, p = 0.02; C(Def_A, Per_A) = 0.54, p < 0.01; C(Def_C, Per_C) = 0.09, p = 0.56; C(Def_N, Per_N) = 0.677, p < 0.01$. This means that the neuroticism trait has a positive relation with the perceived neuroticism. The same happens with agreebleness and extraversion (although with a weaker correlation). Unfortunately, there was no correlation found between the conscientiousness value used to define the agent's personality, and the user's perception of the same trait.

6   Conclusions

The work presented in this paper aimed at the creation of an explicit personality model based on trait theories, which would allow the creation of agents with distinguishable personalities, just by changing the values for the traits. In our proposed model, we identified four cognitive/behavioural processes that are strongly influenced by personality: emotions, coping behaviour, planning and bodily expression. We then used the personality traits to influence each of these processes. The model was implemented into FAtiMA, an emotional agent architecture, and integrated with the ECA GRETA. Results have shown that indeed the model is partially successful, since it is able to create perceivably different personalities, and the user's classification is correlated with the original values for extroversion, neuroticism, and agreeableness. The worst results, obtained for conscientiousness, can likely be explained by the fact that it only affects two very particular emotions.

References

[1] Allport, G.: Concepts of trait and personality. Psychological Bulletin 24, 284–293 (1927)
[2] Allport, G.: Traits revisited. American Psychologist 21, 1–10 (1966)
[3] Arnold, M.: Emotion and personality. Columbia University Press, New York (1960)
[4] Castelfranchi, C., de Rosis, F., Falcone, R., Pizzutilo, S.: Personality traits and social attitudes in multi-agent cooperation. Applied Artificial Intelligence, Special Issue on 'Socially Intelligent Agents' 12 (1998)
[5] Cattell, R.: The Scientific Analysis of Personality. Penguin (1965)
[6] David, J., Suls, J.: Coping efforts in daily life: Role of big five traits and problems appraisals. Journal of Personality 67, 265–294 (1999)
[7] Dias, J., Paiva, A.: Feeling and reasoning: a computational model for emotional agents. In: Bento, C., Cardoso, A., Dias, G. (eds.) EPIA 2005. LNCS (LNAI), vol. 3808, pp. 127–140. Springer, Heidelberg (2005)
[8] Hayes-Roth, B., Gent, R.: Story-making with improvisational puppets and actors. report ksl 96-05. Technical report, Knowledge Systems Laboratory, Stanford University (1996)
[9] Hooker, K., Frazier, L., Monahan, D.: Personality and coping among caregivers of spouses with dementia. The Gerontologist 34(3), 386–392 (1994)
[10] Howard, P., Howard, J.: The big five quickstart: An introduction to the five-factor model of personality for human resource professionals. Technical report, NC: Centre for Applied Cognitive Studies (1995)
[11] John, O., Srivastava, S.: The big five trait taxonomy: History, measurement, and theoretical perspectives. In: Pervin, L., Oliver, P. (eds.) Handbook of Personality: Theory and Research, 2nd edn., pp. 102–138. Guilford Press, New York (1999)
[12] Kshirsagar, S.: A multilayer personality model. In: SMARTGRAPH 2002: Proceedings of the 2nd international symposium on Smart graphics, pp. 107–115. ACM, New York (2002)
[13] LaHaye, T.: Why you act the way you do. Tyndale House Pub. (1988)
[14] Malatesta, L., Caridakis, G., Raouzaiou, A., Karpouzis, K.: Agent personality traits in virtual environments based on appraisal theory predictions. In: AISB 2007: Artificial and Ambient Intelligence, Language, Speech and Gesture for Expressive Characters, Newcastle upon Tyne, UK, April 2-4 (2007)
[15] McCrae, R., Costa, P.: Validation of the five-factor model of personality across instruments and observers. Journal of Personality and Social Psychology 51(1), 81–90 (1987)
[16] McGowan, J., Gormly, J.: Validation of personality traits: A multicriteria approach. Journal of Personality and Social Psychology 34, 191–195 (1976)
[17] John, L.N.O., Soto, C.: Paradigm shift to the integrative big-five trait taxonomy: History, measurement, and conceptual issues. In: John, R.R.O., Pervin, L. (eds.) Handbook of Personality: Theory and Research, pp. 114–138. Guilford Press, New York (2008)
[18] O'Brien, T., DeLongis, A.: The interactional context of problem-,emotion-, and relationship-focused coping: The role of the big five personality factors. Journal of Personality 64, 775–813 (1996)

[19] Ortony, A., Clore, G., Collins, A.: The Cognitive Structure of Emotions. Cambridge University Press, UK (1998)

[20] Pelachaud, C.: Multimodal expressive embodied conversational agents. In: MULTIMEDIA 2005: Proceedings of the 13th annual ACM international conference on Multimedia, pp. 683–689. ACM, New York (2005)

[21] Pervin, L.: The Science of Personality. Wiley, New York (1996)

[22] Reichardt, D.: Emotion and personality in driver assistance systems. In: Proceedings of the 4th Annual Meeting on Information Technology and Computer Science, pp. 17–21 (2008)

[23] Rizzo, P., Veloso, M., Miceli, M., Cesta, A.: Personality-driven social behaviours in believable agents. In: AAAI Fall Symposion on Socially Intelligent Agents (1997)

[24] Rousseau, D.: Personality in computer characters. Technical report, Knowledge Systems Laboratory, Stanford University (1996)

[25] Rousseau, D., Hayes-Roth, B.: Personality in synthetic agents. report ksl 96-21. Technical report, Knowledge Systems Laboratory, Stanford University (1996)

[26] Rousseau, D., Hayes-Roth, B.: Improvisational synthetic actors with flexible personalities. report ksl 97-10. Technical report, Knowledge Systems Laboratory, Stanford University (1997)

[27] Rousseau, D., Hayes-Roth, B.: A social-psychological model for synthetic actors. report ksl 97-07. Technical report, Knowledge Systems Laboratory, Stanford University (1997)

[28] Ryckman, R.: Theories of Personality. Thomson/Wadsworth (2004)

[29] Sedgwick, E., Frank, A., Alexander, I.: Shame and its sisters: a Silvan Tomkins reader. Duke University Press (1995)

[30] Tyler, T., Kramer, R., John, P.: The psychology of the social self. Lawrence Erlbaum Associates, Mahwah (1999)

[31] Watson, D., Hubbard, B.: Adaptational style and dispositional structure: Coping in the context of the five-factor model. Journal of Personality 64, 737–774 (1996)

Bossy or Wimpy: Expressing Social Dominance by Combining Gaze and Linguistic Behaviors

Nikolaus Bee[1], Colin Pollock[2], Elisabeth André[1], and Marilyn Walker[2]

[1] Institute of Computer Science, Augsburg University, 86135 Augsburg, Germany
{andre,bee}@informatik.uni-augsburg.de
[2] University of California, Santa Cruz
{colin,maw}@soe.ucsc.edu

Abstract. This paper examines the interaction of verbal and nonverbal information for conveying social dominance in intelligent virtual agents (IVAs). We expect expressing social dominance to be useful in applications related to persuasion and motivation; here we simply test whether we can affect users' perceptions of social dominance using procedurally generated conversational behavior. Our results replicate previous results showing that gaze behaviors affect dominance perceptions, as well as providing new results showing that, in our experiments, the linguistic expression of disagreeableness has a significant effect on dominance perceptions, but that extraversion does not.

Keywords: intelligent virtual agents, social dominance, verbal and nonverbal behaviors, personality, evaluation.

1 Introduction

This paper examines the interaction of verbal and nonverbal information for conveying social dominance in intelligent virtual agents (IVAs). Our results are of immediate practical value in understanding the issues involved in designing IVAs for various applications; appropriately parametrized IVAs can communicate social dominance by head movement and gaze behaviors [2,5], enthusiasm and friendliness by gesture [6], and Big Five personality traits by linguistic behaviors [11]. Therefore, we should be able to construct IVAs to communicate combinations of these different traits in order to achieve various conversational goals [1]. For example, because studies of human-human communication suggest persuasiveness is increased when the speaker is socially dominant and either extraverted or disagreeable [3,12,7,13], we expect expressing social dominance will be useful in applications related to persuasion and motivation.

We draw on two distinct theories of individual differences in human traits, and the way these traits are communicated: the Big Five theory of personality [6,17]; and (2) Mehrabian's Pleasure, Arousal, Dominance (PAD) model, which ties personality to fundamental human emotions [14,13]. From the Big Five theory, we concentrate on the traits of extraversion and agreeableness, and from the PAD model, we focus on the dominance trait. Mehrabian (1996) reports on a meta-analysis of studies of human-human communication that suggests

J. Allbeck et al. (Eds.): IVA 2010, LNAI 6356, pp. 265–271, 2010.

that dominance and extraversion are positively correlated, while dominance and agreeableness are negatively correlated [15]. We aim to test Mehrabian's claims with IVAs that produce utterances whose linguistic form conveys extraversion and agreeableness, while their gaze behaviors are intended to vary dominance perceptions. Our hypothesis is that when we combine verbal and nonverbal communication in a single stimulus, both will influence the participants' perceptions of the speaker's social dominance and personality traits.

To date, there have been few studies using procedurally generated conversational behavior that have examined the interaction of different modes. Rather, work has focused on providing the underlying fundamental capabilities that make such studies possible. For example, Mignault & Chaudhuri (2003) found that a bowed head is perceived as submissive, while a raised head expresses dominance [16]. Bee and colleagues use the Alfred IVA, that we also use in our experiments (See Fig. 1), to investigate the effects on dominance of varying facial expression, and head and eye gaze direction [2]. They found that a lowered head was perceived as less dominant than a raised head, and that facial expressions defined as *joy, disgust, anger* and *neutral* all had a significantly positive influence on dominance perceptions. While these studies employed static images to measure dominance perceptions, Lance & Marsella (2008) used animated virtual characters with a gaze model for emotional expression based on Mehrabians PAD model [9]. They found that a virtual character with either a raised head or a bowed body and/or fast movements appears more dominant. Low dominance was found for a bowed head and/or a neutral body posture without fast movements. Fukayama and colleagues (2002) propose a gaze behavior model for virtual characters based on amount and mean duration of gaze and averted gaze orientation [5]. They evaluated their model by displaying animated eyes to the users and found that eye gaze directed to the user is perceived as more dominant than eye gaze directed downwards.

On the verbal side, relevant previous work describes linguistic generators that convey Big Five Personality traits or which are intended to induce social compliance. Roque & Traum (2007) implemented styles of conversation related to social compliance, but have not yet tested user perceptions [18]. Mairesse & Walker show that human subjects perceive utterances as conveying the different levels of extraversion that the PERSONAGE generator was targeting; subjects also correctly perceive the level of agreeableness that the system intended [11,10]. Here we will use these prior results to examine the prediction that extraversion and agreeableness will affect dominance perceptions. Section 2 explains how we generate videos of recommendations combining gaze and linguistic behaviors. Section 3 describes our main experiment examining the interaction of personality and dominance. We conclude in Section 4.

2   Generating Verbal and Nonverbal Behaviors

We will test human perceptions of an IVA speaking restaurant recommendations generated by PERSONAGE that were reliably shown to affect the perception of the agreeableness and extraversion traits. We also use the Alfred IVA with facial and gaze behaviors shown to affect perceptions of social dominance [2,5].

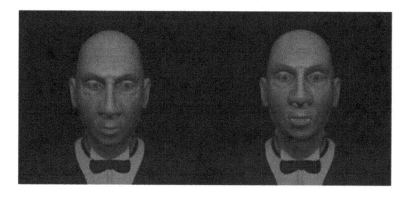

Fig. 1. Image of Low Dominance Alfred (left) and High Dominance Alfred (right)

Our generation engine for nonverbal behaviors was Alfred, a butler-like virtual character [2]. Alfred interfaces with the Microsoft Speech API in order to synchronize the audio output with the lip movements. We used the Facial Action Coding System (FACS) to control lip movements (e.g. funneling, tightening, stretching). Alfreds eyes and head are controlled with an inverse kinematics component integrated into the Horde3D GameEngine. This allows us to control each eye and head separately.

In order to target the nonverbal channel, we start from the gaze model developed by Fukayama and colleagues (2002) to specify a number of gaze parameters that influence the impression a character conveys. Their model includes two states: looking at the user and looking away from the user. Three parameters define frequency, duration (500 to 2000 ms), and location of gaze. The gaze targets consist of a set of random points from either all over the scene, above, below or close to the user. The probabilities of changing state or staying in the same state depend on the amount and the mean duration of the gaze parameters. Fukayama and colleagues found that a medium amount of gaze and a mean duration between 500 to 1000 ms conveys a friendly gaze behavior. The orientation of the gaze direction did not play a decisive role in distinguishing between friendly and dominant gaze behavior, except that a downward gaze was considered as less dominant. While their experiments only display eyes to the user, we evaluate their model with a full virtual head that in moves his head and eyes, but set the parameters according to their findings for dominant and friendly eye gaze behavior. The submissive gaze behavior was set to a mean duration of 500 ms, randomly changing between gazing at the user and averting the gaze. Further, we bowed Alfreds head according to the findings of [9,16,2]. In order to model the dominant eye gaze behavior, Alfred stares at the user when speaking the restaurant recommendation. We used Alfred's neutral facial expression [2].

For verbal behaviors, we use the PERSONAGE generator of Mairesse and Walker, along with parameter models that were shown in their work to generate utterances reliably perceived as either highly introverted or extraverted, or highly disagreeable or agreeable [10,11]. PERSONAGE is based on an extended

Table 1. Example utterances generated by PERSONAGE to be spoken by Alfred

Trait	Level	Recommendation
Extraversion	Low	I mean, Amy's Bread isn't as bad as the others.
Extraversion	High	I am sure you would like Bond Street, you know. Basically, the food is great and the atmosphere is good, wth friendly service.
Agreeableness	Low	Basically, everbody knows that John's Pizzeria is the only restaurant that is any good. Tis eatin gplace offers like, mediocre ambience, even if it's bloody expensive. Actually, the waiters aren't good.
Agreeableness	High	You want to know more about John's Pizzeria? Oh well, it's price is around 20 dollars, so it's one of my favorite eating houses, and it offers kind of dainty food, you know, you see?

set of modules from the standard NLG architecture, with modules for content planning, sentence planning, and surface realization. In contrast with many generators, PERSONAGE provides many parameters to support pragmatic transformations that affect human perceptions of the speakers personality traits. Examples of the eight utterances generated by PERSONAGE used in our experiment are in Table 1. Four utterances target extraversion and four target agreeableness, with two utterances at the low end of the scale (disagreeable, introverted) and two at the the high (agreeable, extraverted) end. In a pretest, we confirmed that voice realization of these utterances using Loquendo's Simon voice maintained previous findings on the perception of these utterances.

3   Experimental Study

Our main goal is to understand how people form impressions of an IVA's social dominance when its verbal and nonverbal communication are observed simultaneously. The simplest prediction is (H1). In addition, because of Mehrabian's findings, we predict (H2) linguistic extraversion and agreeableness will affect dominance ratings, and that gaze-based dominance will impact personality trait ratings.

- (H1) Personality traits and gaze will both effect the perception of dominance, extraversion and agreeableness.
- (H2) Extraversion will increase the perception of dominance, while agreeableness will decrease it. Gaze-based dominance will increase the perception of extraversion.

Method. Nineteen subjects participated in the experiment through a website. Nine were male and ten were female with a mean age of 26.5 years. English was the first language of all participants. Subjects first read an instruction page that described their task, but provided no information about the domain. Then the experimental stimuli were presented one at a time, in random order. For the verbal content, we used eight restaurant recommendations targeting introversion (low extraversion), extraversion, disagreeableness (low agreeableness), and

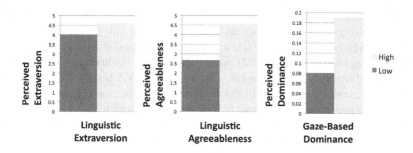

Fig. 2. Perception of Verbal and Non-verbal Cues

agreeableness, as illustrated in Table 1. Each recommendation was presented as male speech generated using the Loquendo TTS voice Simon, and combined with both dominant and submissive gaze behaviors. For each stimulus, the participants answered eleven questions about their impressions of the speaker's personality and the naturalness of the utterance: four questions for extraversion and agreeableness were from the Ten Item Personality Inventory (TIPI) [8], and six questions were from Mehrabian's dominance scale [14]. Given the large number of judgements required for all stimuli, and the fact that stimuli may be viewed repeatedly, we use a within-subjects design.

Results. In order to test whether personality traits and gaze factors both affect the perception of dominance, extraversion and agreeableness, we first establish that each of the three factors (gaze, linguistic extraversion, and linguistic agreeableness) significantly affects each of the three dependent variables (ratings of dominance, extraversion, and agreeableness), confirming H1. See Fig. 2. One way ANOVAs for each factor show significant differences for the effect of linguistic extraversion on perception of extraversion ($F(1,151) = 6.68$, $p = .01$), linguistic agreeableness on the perception of agreeableness ($F(1,151) = 71.91$, $p < .001$) and gaze-based dominance on the perception of dominance ($F(1,303) = 6.36$, $p = .01$).

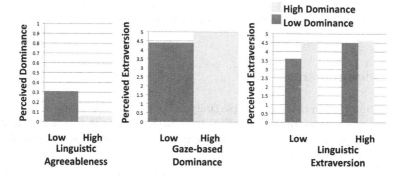

Fig. 3. Perceived Dominance and Extraversion

We then turned to the cross-modal effects on perception. See Fig. 3. Results indicate that linguistic agreeableness inversely affects the perception of dominance ($F(1,151) = 18.54$, $p < .001$), and that gaze-based dominance affects the perception of extraversion ($F(1,303) = 13.7$, $p < .001$), confirming H2. See Fig. 3. To examine interaction effects, we ran a two-way ANOVA testing for the effect of linguistic extraversion and gaze-based dominance on the perception of extraversion. This showed a significant result for an interaction ($F(3,151) = 4.37$, $p = .04$). See the right hand side of Fig. 3 which illustrates that when linguistic extraversion is high, gaze behavior has no effect on dominance, thus disconfirming one aspect of H2.

4   Discussion and Conclusion

Our studies suggest that we succeeded in conveying linguistic personality traits and visual dominance. While our results may be specific to our stimuli, all stimuli were generated procedurally using parameters that can be tested in future work. Our results show that perceptions of agreeableness and extraversion were consistent with the intended perceptual target, and that more dominant faces were perceived as such. Our novel result is the demonstration that linguistic personality traits influence the perception of dominance and that gaze-based dominance influences the perception of personality traits. Other such perceptual interactions could be investigated in future work. In future work we aim to test whether conveying dominance affects persuasiveness or motivation as predicted by previous work [3,12].

An unexpected and interesting finding is that our results suggest that neither the verbal or nonverbal channel is dominant; rather, when cues to dominance are inconsistent, perception depends on the trait being conveyed. For example, the character's gaze and head pose communicated dominance independently of the expression of linguistic extraversion, but in the case of linguistic agreeableness, the linguistic modality had a greater effect than the visual modality. Thus while previous work suggests that the nonverbal channel carries 60% of the meaning in conversation [14], our results support the findings of Ekman and colleagues (1980), who show that channel dominance depends on what is being communicated; in particular that affective, personality, and informational aspects of meaning are independently affected by different channel components in different situations [4].

Acknowledgements

The work reported in this paper is partially supported by the European Commission under grant agreement IRIS (FP7-ICT-231824), by the Bavaria California Technology Center (BaCaTec) and by award 20101185 from NPS to UCSC on Perlocutions and Dialog.

References

1. André, E., Rist, T., van Mulken, S., Klesen, M., Baldes, S.: The automated design of believable dialogues for animated presentation teams. In: Embodied conversational agents, pp. 220–255 (2000)
2. Bee, N., Franke, S., André, E.: Relations between facial display, eye gaze and head tilt: Dominance perception variations of virtual agents. In: Affective Computing and Intelligent Interaction (2009)
3. Cialdini, R.: Influence: The psychology of persuasion. Quill, New York (1993)
4. Ekman, P., Friesen, W., O'Sullivan, M., Scherer, K.: Relative importance of face, body, and speech in judgments of personality and affect. Journal of Personality and Social Psychology 38(2), 270–277 (1980)
5. Fukayama, A., Ohno, T., Mukawa, N., Sawak, M., Hagita, N.: Messages embedded in gaze of interface agents - impression management with agent's gaze. In: CHI 2002: Proc. of the SIGCHI conference on human factors in computing systems, pp. 41–48 (2002)
6. Funder, D.C.: The Personality Puzzle, 2nd edn. W. W. Norton & Company, New York (1997)
7. Furnham, A.: Language and personality. In: Giles, H., Robinson, W. (eds.) Handbook of Language and Social Psychology. Winley (1990)
8. Gosling, S.D., Rentfrow, P.J., Swann, W.B.: A very brief measure of the big five personality domains. Journal of Research in Personality 37, 504–528 (2003)
9. Lance, B., Marsella, S.: The relation between gaze behavior and the attribution of emotion: An empirical study. In: Prendinger, H., Lester, J.C., Ishizuka, M. (eds.) IVA 2008. Lance, B., Marsella, S, vol. 5208, pp. 1–14. Springer, Heidelberg (2008)
10. Mairesse, F., Walker, M.A.: PERSONAGE: Personality generation for dialogue. In: Proceedings of the 45th Annual Meeting of the Association for Computational Linguistics (ACL), pp. 496–503 (2007)
11. Mairesse, F., Walker, M.A.: Trainable generation of Big-Five personality styles through data-driven parameter estimation. In: Proceedings of the 46th Annual Meeting of the Association for Computational Linguistics, ACL (2008)
12. Marwell, G., Schmitt, D.: Dimensions of compliance-gaining behavior: An empirical analysis. Sociometry 30(4), 350–364 (1967)
13. Mehrabian, A.: Significance of posture and position in the communication of attitude and status relationships. Psychological Bulletin 71(5), 359–372 (1969)
14. Mehrabian, A.: Framework for a comprehensive description and measurement of emotional states. Genetic Social and General Psychology Monographs 121(3), 339–361 (1995)
15. Mehrabian, A.: Analysis of the big-five personality factors in terms of the PAD temperament model. Australian Journal of Psychology 48(2), 86–92 (1996)
16. Mignault, A., Chaudhuri, A.: The many faces of a neutral face: Head tilt and perception of dominance and emotion. Journal of Nonverbal Behavior 27(2), 111–132 (2003)
17. Norman, W.T.: Toward an adequate taxonomy of personality attributes: Replicated factor structure in peer nomination personality rating. Journal of Abnormal and Social Psychology 66, 574–583 (1963)
18. Roque, A., Traum, D.: A model of compliance and emotion for potentially adversarial dialogue agents. In: Proceedings of the 8th SIGdial Workshop on Discourse and Dialogue (2007)

Warmth, Competence, Believability and Virtual Agents

Radosław Niewiadomski[1], Virginie Demeure[2], and Catherine Pelachaud[3]

[1] Telecom ParisTech, 37/39 rue Dareau, 75014 - Paris, France
niewiado@telecom-paristech.fr
[2] Universitat Autonoma de Barcelona, Departamento de Psicologia Basica,
Evolutiva y de la Educacion, 08193 - Bellaterra, Spain
demeure@univ-tlse2.fr
[3] CNRS-LTCI Telecom ParisTech, 37/39 rue Dareau, 75014 - Paris, France
pelachaud@telecom-paristech.fr

Abstract. Believability is a key issue for virtual agents. Most of the authors agree that emotional behavior and personality have a high impact on agents' believability. The social capacities of the agents also have an effect on users' judgment of believability. In this paper we analyze the role of plausible and/or socially appropriate emotional displays on believability. We also investigate how people judge the believability of the agent, and whether it provokes social reactions of humans toward the agent.

The results of our study in the domain of software assistants, show that (a) socially appropriate emotions lead to higher perceived believability, (b) the notion of believability is highly correlated with the two major socio-cognitive variables, namely competence and warmth, and (c) considering an agent believable can be different from considering it human-like.

Keywords: Virtual agent, Believability, Warmth, Competence, Personification, Emotional expressions.

1 Introduction

Virtual agents (VA) are software interfaces that allow natural, human-like, communication with the machine. The growing interest in this technology renders urgent the question concerning the characteristics that virtual agents should display. In this context the term *believability* is often used [1,2,3]. Believability is not a precise concept but many authors agree that it goes beyond the physical appearance [4,2] of the virtual agent. Rather, it includes the emotions, personality and social capabilities [5,6] of the agent. According to Allbeck and Badler believability is the generic meaning of enabling "to accept as real" ([1], p. 1). de Rosis *et al.* claim that "the believable agent should act consistently with her goals, her state of mind and her personality" ([7], p. 5) where "consistency" is interpreted as coherency between speech, nonverbal behaviors and appearance.

J. Allbeck et al. (Eds.): IVA 2010, LNAI 6356, pp. 272–285, 2010.

The authors also stress that a believable virtual agent should be able to manage its emotional expressions according to the situation in which interaction occurs [7]. The social consistency of the behaviors as one condition of believability was also postulated, for instance, by Prendinger *et al.* [8]. Other studies have shown that the agent is perceived as more believable [9] and more "human being like" [10] if its emotional expressions are adequate to the situation. Following this line of research, we investigated the effect of socially adapted emotional behavior on believability.

On the other hand, we still do not know much about which other social criteria are taken into account by users when judging believability. In this paper we argue that if people prefer and judge more believable agents able to display some social behaviors, it would seem reasonable to assume that believability is linked to socio-cognitive dimensions of the agents. To test this hypothesis we used the two main socio-cognitive dimensions identified by Fiske, Cuddy and Glick [11] as the most important dimensions of interpersonal judgment: *warmth* and *competence.*

We are also interested in how humans react socially toward agents. According to Reeves and Nass [12] people answer socially and naturally to new media. Authors claim that people automatically treat media as if they were humans. Thus, according to the Media Equation people should build social relationships with virtual agents and show a human-like attitude toward them. In this paper we call *personification* this hypothetic human-like view of the virtual agent. The relation between the notion of personification and believability in virtual assistants is an interesting issue rarely analyzed so far. In [13,14] personification is strictly related to the presence of the agent. Authors have evaluated the role of the physical presence in the communication and learning experience. However, they do not put attention on social relations with the agent. In our work we rather focus on the attribution of human mental features and the creation of a human-like attitude toward the agent.

In this paper we present an experiment in the virtual assistant's domain. This experiment had three distinct objectives. Firstly, we wanted to show that a believable agent needs not only to communicate emotional states but must also express socially adapted emotions. Secondly we checked the relation between VA believability and two of the most important socio-cognitive factors considered in human intersubjective judgments [11], namely competence and warmth. Finally, we examined the difference between believability and personification.

2   Emotionally Expressive Virtual Agents

Several works have studied the role of appropriate emotional displays on the perception of virtual agents. Unadapted emotional displays may influence the user's evaluation of the agent negatively. In the experiment of Walker et al. people liked the facial interface that displayed a negative expression less than the one which showed a neutral expression [15]. However, it does not mean that negative expressions are not desirable at all. In a card game the agent that displayed only positive expressions, irrespectively of the situation, was evaluated worse than the one that also expressed negative emotions [10]. These results suggest that the choice of emotional displays influences the perception of agents' believability. They also highlight the role of the context in the judgment. Indeed, several studies have focused on the appropriateness of emotional displays in the social context. Lim and Aylett [9] developed the PDA-based Affective Guide that tells visitors stories about different attractions. The evaluation results found that the guide that used appropriate emotional displays and attitude was perceived to be more believable, natural, and interesting than the agent without emotional displays and attitudes.

Prendinger et al. showed the influence of facial expression management in the perception of "naturalness" of the agent [8]. They introduced a set of procedures called "social filter programs" that define the intensity of an expression as the function of a social threat, user's personality, and the intensity of emotion. Consequently, their agent can either increase or decrease the intensity of facial expression, or even totally inhibit it.

Niewiadomski *et al.* [16] studied the appropriate emotional displays of a virtual agent in empathic situations. In a set of scenarios, the authors compared their agent displaying the "egocentric", "empathic" emotions and the two different complex facial expressions of both emotional states. In the evaluation study, facial expressions containing elements of the empathy emotion (i.e. "empathic" or complex expressions) were considered more adequate.

All of these studies demonstrate the importance of adapting the emotions of the agents to contextual information. In our study we go further, we distinguish three levels of emotional behaviors and take into account their *appropriateness* and *plausibility*. This will be explained in greater detail in section 5.

3   Relation between Believability, Competence and Warmth

The second purpose of this paper is to better understand what kind of factors people take into account when judging the believability of a virtual agent. As seen in the previous section, a shared opinion concerning the believability of agents is that social factors are crucial. It seems thus quite reasonable to assume that the notion of believability is linked to some socio-cognitive dimensions of the agents. In this paper we focus mainly on two socio-cognitive dimensions that describe most human intersubjective judgments: competence and warmth [11,17].

Fiske et al. explained that warmth and competence are the two prior variables evaluated by people when encountering another person: "when people spontaneously interpret behavior or form impressions of others, warmth and competence form basic dimensions that, together, account almost entirely for how people characterize others." ([18], p.77). The *warmth* dimension is defined as capturing "traits that are related to perceived intent, including friendliness, helpfulness, sincerity, trustworthiness and morality", while *competence* "traits that are related to perceived ability, including intelligence, skill, creativity and efficacy" ([11], p.77).

To determine whether the judgment of the agent's believability is related to socio-cognitive traits of the agent, we evaluate in this paper whether people judge virtual agents using these two dimensions. The correlation between judgment of these two factors and judgment of believability is also tested. It will enable us to determine whether people tend to refer to the same variables while judging agents and people. This second observation raises the question of the relation between believability and personification. We discuss this topic in more detail in the next section.

4 Believability and Personification

Reeves and Nass [12] conducted a set of experiments showing that people tend to act socially with new media and treat media as if they were real people. For example, they showed that people tend to give better evaluation to the software when they answer the satisfaction questionnaire on the same computer as the one they used during the experiment. The authors explained this phenomenon by claiming that the subjects do not want to offend the computer. The concept explored in that study goes along what we defined in section 1 as personification. In both cases it tackles idea of considering an agent as a real human and having a human-like attitude toward it.

One may think that if people tend to judge more believable the agents that looks [19] and behave like humans (e.g. by displaying emotions or using politeness [20]) it means that believability and personification are two equivalent concepts. However, in our opinion the creation of a believable agent (i.e. an agent that looks and behaves like a real human being) is different from creating a human-like relation with it. Furthermore, a recent study of Hoffmann *et al.* [21] called some of Reeves and Nass' results into question by showing that when people behaved politely toward the computer, they actually thought of the programmer.

To check our hypothesis, in our experiment we used an ambiguous statement that can be understood differently in the context of human-human and human-machine interaction. We explain this in greater detail in the next section.

5 Experiment

In our experiment, we simulate a typical virtual assistant scenario. In the scenario presented to the participants, the protagonist of the story is using a new computer equipped with the virtual agent. The agent may assist in the user's tasks, it can also give the advices and the comments. The system is also equipped with some card games that can be played by the protagonist. Our experiment starts when the "hypothetic" user loses the game. We ask the participants of the experiment about their opinions on the reactions of the virtual agent to this situation. Even in this simple situation there are many factors that may influence the perception of agent' believability. In the experiment we consider the following factors: the emotional reactions of the agent and the modalities (i.e. verbal or/and nonverbal) used to communicate them, and the agent's goal strategy. Operationalization of each variable and manipulation check are described below.

In our experiment we distinguish between the appropriateness and the plausibility of emotional behaviors. *Appropriateness* refers to the fact that the emotion meets social expectations of what people are supposed to feel in the situation. For example, an expression of sadness *is expected* (i.e. is appropriate) in our context (in the sense of the OCC model [22]) because the user loses the game. The *plausibility* of an emotional state refers to the fact that an emotion can be displayed in the situation even if it is not the appropriate one. In the game context the happiness reaction is still plausible e.g. as an ironic reaction, but is not (socially) appropriate. Finally, fear is neither (socially) appropriate nor plausible in this context.

The choice of the three emotions (sadness, happiness and fear) used in the experiment follows the OCC model of Ortony, Clore and Collins [22]. The OCC model predicts that the adapted emotion to be displayed when something (event-based) happens to someone else (fortunes of others) is either happiness or sadness depending on the valence of the event. In our experiment, the event has a negative valence (the loss of the game), we thus choose sadness as the appropriate reaction, and happiness as the inappropriate one. The fear was chosen to be a totally misfit emotion, never appropriate in the context, no matter the valence of the event. A manipulation check was conducted to test the appropriateness and plausibility of each of these three emotional reactions (see section 5.4).

To obtain more precise results about the effect of emotions, we distinguish between verbal emotional reactions and nonverbal emotional reactions. This distinction was made in order to evaluate the effect of multimodality of emotional expression on agents' believability.

The *personification* of the agent was evaluated through the interpretation of the ambiguous statement "Are you sure you want to quit?". The manipulation check shows that this statement is interpreted differently depending on whether it is expressed by a computer or a human. Indeed, this statement is often used by computers when the user clicks on the cross button to close an application. In this case it is interpreted as a simple check to make sure it is not a mistake. If expressed by a human, on the other hand, the sentence may communicate the willingness not to finish the interaction (see section 5.4 for detailed results of the manipulation check).

Finally, as a control variable, the goal of the virtual agent was also manipulated. In one condition the agent was identified as "assisting the user in the task", while in the other condition, it had no obligation to support user's activity. This factor was included to ensure that this distinction has no effect on the warmth judgment (a socially appropriate emotional reaction, if perceived as forced by the context, could decrease the warmth judgment, and thus, possibly, believability).

In the following sections we present our hypotheses, the set-up of the experiment, manipulation check, results and their discussion.

5.1   General Hypotheses

We tested three main hypotheses:

H1: A virtual agent will be judged warmer, more competent and more believable when it displays socially adapted emotions;

H2: Judgment of believability will be correlated with the two socio-cognitive factors of warmth and competence;

H3: Judging an agent as believable is different from creating a human-like relation with it.

5.2   Method

The experiment was placed on the Web. The interface was composed of a set of pages illustrating the plot of a session with a software assistant. Each page corresponds to an event, it may contain an animation or a picture of the agent. We generated a set of animations corresponding to events of the prescribed scenario. The subjects could not influence the plot of the scenario, they saw the animations and answered the related questions. The scenario had two versions corresponding to two different strategies used by the agent: "task-centered" (TC) and "user-centered" (UC). The difference between these two versions of the experiment was limited to verbal content. The plot of the scenario along with the nonverbal behaviors displayed by the agent were the same. Each session was composed of two sections. In each section the user was asked to answer some questions concerning the behavior of the agent. In the first section (S1) the questions concerned hypotheses H1 and H2, while the second section (S2) was related to hypothesis H3. During the experiment each subject participated in at least 5 and at most 10 sessions, all belonging to one variation of our scenario (TC or UC).

In the scenario, participants were asked to imagine that they possessed a new computer including a virtual assistant. At the beginning of the experiment the respective version of the scenario (TC or UC) was explained to the participants.

In more detail, participants answering the "user-centered" questionnaire read that the context of the experiment was the following:

"You decide to try a new game that is included with your new computer, the agent is here to explain you the rules and give you some advices on how to play. You play a game and lose".

In the "task-centered" group a different explanation was presented which legitimate the presence of the agent that does not support the user activity:

"You open a new document for work, the agent explains the new functionality of the tool. After a few moments, you decide to take a break and open a game included with the computer. In the meantime, the agent is displayed on the screen. You play a game and lose".

In section S1, videos show virtual agent's reactions immediately after the user's defeat. For section S1 we generated 20 different animations of VA. Ten of them corresponded to user-centered strategy and ten others to task-centered strategy (see section 5.3).

After watching each video, participants were asked to judge the competence of VA (question Q1), its warmth (question Q2), and its believability (question Q3) on three separate 7 point-scales (from *not at all* to *entirely*). The participants were also asked to explain in a few words their choice concerning question Q3.

To explore the differences between believability and personification, the second part (S2) of the experiment was used. Sections S1 and S2 were split by a separate page with the explanation. The second section (S2) of the experiment corresponds to the final part of the scenario. We asked the subjects to imagine that they are tired and want to quit the application by clicking on the cross button. One video was used in section S2. On this video the agent asks with a neutral voice "Are you sure you want to quit?" According to the hypothesis discussed above in this section this ambiguous statement can be interpreted differently depending on the type of relation between the user and the agent. Participants had to choose (question Q4) if the agent's intention was only to verify that they did not click on the cross button by error (literal interpretation), or if its intention was to tell them in an implicit way not to break the interaction (indirect interpretation).

104 online volunteers participated, all native French speakers (33 men, age range 19-60, mean = 29.3, SD = 9.7). They were randomly assigned to one of the two experimental groups [user-centered (UC) vs. task-centered (TC)].

5.3   Videos

In each version of the scenario (TC/UC) one of the following videos was displayed randomly in section S1:

- 3 videos of VA displaying a socially appropriate and plausible emotional reaction (condition A&P); the emotion displayed by the agent was sadness;
- 3 videos of VA displaying a socially inappropriate but plausible emotional reaction (condition NA&P); the emotion displayed by the agent was happiness;
- 3 videos of VA displaying a socially inappropriate and implausible emotional reaction (condition NA&NP); the emotion displayed by the agent was fear;
- 1 video of VA with no reaction at all (condition NE).

In the videos containing (non) appropriate and/or (non) plausible emotional reactions, one of them showed the agent displaying both verbal and nonverbal emotional reactions, one showed the agent displaying only verbal emotional reaction and one showed the agent displaying only nonverbal emotional reaction.

We used in the experiment a pre-recorded human voice with a prosody corresponding to the illustrated emotional state. The emotional nonverbal behavior of the agent was composed of facial expressions accompanied by emotional gestures.

5.4   Manipulation Check

A manipulation check was conducted with an independent sample of 40 volunteer students of the University of Toulouse le Mirail.

Four paper and pencil questionnaires checked both the appropriateness and plausibility of three emotional reactions used in the experiment (sadness, happiness and fear) under task-centered and user-centered conditions, and the interpretation of the ambiguous statement "Are you sure you want to quit?" expressed either by a computer or by a human being.

The participants were presented a short story. The story corresponded to the scenario presented in the real experiment but in the manipulation check the virtual agent was replaced by the human being. The participants were told to imagine they were testing a new game during video-game show in the presence of the presenter. In the user-centered condition (UC) the presenter was willing to explain the rules of the game while in the task-centered one (TC) he only observed. Similarly to the scenario used in the real experiment, participants were told they have lost their game.

Participants were then asked to judge the appropriateness and plausibility of each of the 3 statements used in the experiment (the one expressing sadness, the one expressing happiness and the one expressing fear) on the same three separate 7-point scales as used in the experiment. They were also asked to interpret the ambiguous question Q4.

Results were analyzed using ANOVA for the judgment of appropriateness and plausibility and with a Mann-Whitney for the interpretation of the ambiguous statement. The results of the ANOVA show that people tend to judge sadness as appropriate (mean $= 3.90$, $SD = 1.97$) and plausible (mean $= 4.45$, $SD = 1.88$). Happiness is perceived as less appropriate (mean $= 3.03$, $SD = 1.97$) $F(1, 39) = 3.98$, $p = .05$ but plausible (mean $= 4.43$, $SD = 2.07$), and fear as neither appropriate (mean $= 1.65$, $SD = 1.25$) $F(2, 38) = 32.63$, $p < .0001$ nor plausible (mean $= 1.98$, $SD = 1.31$), $F(2, 38) = 21.36$, $p < .0001$.

The results of the Mann-Whitney test show that people interpret more often the ambiguous statement as a literal question (Mean Rank $= 15.5$) when express by the computer and as an implicit way to telling them not to exit the game (Mean Rank $= 25.5$) when express by a human, $z = -3, 12$; $p < 0, 006$; one-side.

No effect of the goal (TC vs. UC) was detected (the between subject ANOVA: $F(1, 36) = 2.57$, $p = .092$).

5.5   Results

During the experiment we collected 3973 answers. No effect of the goal of the agent was detected (TC vs. UC condition), $F(1, 100) = 0.39$, $p = .84$, we thus conducted the following analysis with the entire sample of participants. Descriptive results for all experimental conditions are displayed in Table 1.

Impact of socially adapted emotion on believability, competence and warmth: Results were analyzed with a within-subject ANOVA and revealed an

Table 1. Judgment of competence, warmth and believability in each emotional experimental condition. Standard deviations appear in parentheses.

	Participants' judgments		
	Competence	Warmth	Believability
Condition A&P			
Behavior: Multimodal	3.64 (1.83)	4.05 (1.77)	3.81 (1.77)
Behavior: Verbal	3.11 (1.60)	2.76 (1.62)	3.19 (1.70)
Behavior: Nonverbal	3.07 (1.69)	3.32 (1.70)	3.55 (1.76)
Condition NA&P			
Behavior: Multimodal	2.89 (1.64)	2.49 (1.64)	2.84 (1.73)
Behavior: Verbal	3.15 (1.73)	2.64 (1.66)	3.14 (1.83)
Behavior: Nonverbal	2.3 (1.36)	2.19 (1.63)	2.26 (1.58)
Condition NA&NP			
Behavior: Multimodal	3.02 (1.68)	3.28 (1.64)	2.73 (1.63)
Behavior: Verbal	2.79 (1.46)	2.70 (1.46)	2.74 (1.52)
Behavior: Nonverbal	2.68 (1.58)	2.76 (1.44)	2.79 (1.58)
Condition NE			
Behavior: None	1.72 (1.28)	1.55 (1.13)	2.05 (1.60)

effect of socially adapted emotion on believability $F(3, 95) = 22.77, p < .0001$, $\eta^2 = .11$[1], competence $F(3, 95) = 37.69$, $p < .0001$, $\eta^2 = .14$, and warmth $F(3, 95) = 51.71$, $p < .0001$, $\eta^2 = .22$.

The results show that participants consider the agent more believable in the socially appropriate and plausible condition (A&P) (mean = 3.50, $SD = 1.20$) than in the socially inappropriate but plausible condition (NA&P) (mean = 2.73, $SD = 1.21$) ($p < .0001$), the inappropriate and implausible condition (NA&NP) ($p < .0001$) (mean = 2.76, $SD = 1.18$), and the no reaction condition (NE) (mean = 2.05, $SD = 1.60$) ($p < .0001$). The difference between plausible (NA&P) and non plausible (NA&NP) reaction is not significative ($p = .82$), but the no reaction condition (NE) differs significantly from all other conditions ($p < .0001$).

The perceived competence of the agent's behavior also significantly increases with the social appropriateness and plausibility. The mean value of competence judgments drops from 3.28 ($SD=1.26$) in the appropriate and plausible condition (A&P) to 2.67 ($SD=1.18$) in the inappropriate and plausible condition (NA&P) ($p < .0001$) and to 1.72 ($SD=1.28$) in the NE condition ($p < .0001$). However, people judge the agent more competent when it behaves in an implausible way (NA&NP) (mean = 2.86, $SD = 1.27$) ($p < .04$) than in the (NA&P) condition.

Judgment of warmth follows the same pattern as in the case of competence. The mean value of warmth judgments drops from 3.37 ($SD=1.24$) in the appropriate and plausible condition (A&P) to 2.43 ($SD=1.25$) in the inappropriate and plausible condition (NA&P) ($p < .0001$), and to 1.55 ($SD=1.13$) in the condition NE ($p < .0001$). Again, people judge the agent warmer when it behaves

---

[1] (we report *semi partial* η^2 values, which are more appropriate and more conservative when using within-subject ANOVA).

Table 2. Minimum and maximum correlation scores between believability, competence and warmth

	Believability	Competence	Warmth
Believability	1	.555/.855	.510/.787
Competence	.555/.855	1	.498/.745
Warmth	.510/.787	.498/.745	1

in a non plausible way (NA&NP) (mean $= 2.92$, $SD = 1.18$) ($p < .001$) than in the (NA&P) condition.

In addition to these global results, a finer analysis using a within-subject ANOVA shows that socially adapted emotional behavior has more impact on believability, competence and warmth when expressed both verbally and nonverbally than verbally alone, and nonverbally alone. $F(1, 95) = 6.56$, $p = .012$, $\eta^2 = .02$ for judgment of competence, $F(1, 95) = 15.36$, $p < .0001$, $\eta^2 = .04$ for judgment of warmth, and $F(1, 95) = 4.55$, $p = .035$, $\eta^2 = .02$ for judgment of believability.

For all three judgments (i.e. believability, warmth and competence), the verbal and nonverbal display of emotion was significantly higher than those of verbal alone (respectively $p < .008$, $p < .0001$ and $p < .01$) and nonverbal alone respectively $p = .051$, $p < .0001$ and $p < .01$). No significative difference was found between the two last conditions (respectively $p = .26$, $p = .056$ and $p = 74$).

Socio-cognitive believability: The results also show a high correlation between believability, competence and warmth. Pearson's correlation scores were calculated for each experimental situation. Table 2 displays the minimum and maximum correlation scores between believability, competence and warmth. All reported correlations are significant ($p < .001$).

Believability and personification: The last hypothesis deals with the link between believability of the virtual agent and it's personification.

To assess the correlation between judgment of believability and interpretation of the ambiguous statement we introduce an index (i_{is}) to calculate "the interpretation score". Each answer for the question Q4 got a score: 1 for a literal interpretation and 2 for in indirect one.

To calculate the correlation between the believability and personification we use three interpretation score indices ($i_{is(A\&P)}, i_{is(NA\&P)}, i_{is(NA\&NP)}$) - one for each experimental condition: A&P, NA&P, and NA&NP. The value $i_{is(n)}$ in the condition n for the user m is a sum of the scores received in three sessions corresponding to three videos (verbal, nonverbal, multimodal) in section S1. Thus, in each condition, each participant has associated the interpretation score indices $i_{is(n)}, n \in \{A\&P, NA\&P, and NA\&NP\}$ - i.e. three values ranging from 3 to 6. A score of 3 indicates that the participant always interpreted the statement literally while a score of 6 that he/she always interpreted it indirectly. In other words, the higher the score $i_{is(n)}$ is, the higher the personification is.

The correlation between believability (question Q3) and personification (index $i_{is(n)}$) was calculated separately for the conditions A&P, NA&P, and NA&NP. The results of the Pearson's correlation do not show any significative correlation between believability and personification $+0.13$ ($p = .18$) for the A&P condition, -0.05 ($p = .62$) for the NA&P condition, and -0.14 ($p = .15$) for the NA&NP condition).

6   Discussion

The results clearly support our hypotheses. Firstly they show the effect of socially adapted emotional expressions on believability, warmth and competence. Secondly, they show a high correlation between these three variables. This leads us to think that these two main socio-cognitive variables are used to judge agents' believability. Finally, the results show that, even if people use the same socio-cognitive variables to judge agents and human being, the notion of believability is not correlated to the agent's personalization.

In more detail, considering hypothesis H1, the perception of believability, warmth and competence is related to the emotional reactions presented by the agent. In the same situation the agent expressing appropriate and plausible emotional reactions (A&P) was considered more believable, more competent and warmer than the other agents (NA&P, NA&NP, NE). The agent showing non appropriate but plausible emotional states (NA&P) was more believable than the one showing implausible emotions (NA&NP) or no reaction (NE) at all. It (NA&P) was also considered less warm and less competent than the agent showing implausible emotions (NA&NP). This effect may be explained by the fact that inappropriate emotional displays may have very strong negative impact on the users, which is stronger than the effect of showing emotions that are not related at all to the situation (i.e. implausible). This result is also somewhat consistent with some previous works [10,15] (see section 2). Any reaction (appropriate/plausible or not) was better evaluated than no reaction at all.

Believability, warmth and competence also increase with the number of modalities used by the agent. The agent that uses appropriate verbal (speech, prosody) and nonverbal (facial expressions, gestures) communication channels is more believable that the one using only speech with prosody or only facial expressions and gestures. Thus, the more expressive the agent is the more believable it is.

Regarding hypothesis H2 it was shown that the perception of warmth and competence are correlated with the perception of believability. It indicates that judgment of believability is linked to these two socio-cognitive variables and thus that socio-cognitive factors are taken into account while evaluating the agent's believability.

Regarding hypothesis H3 we did not find any correlation between the personification of the agent and the perception of believability. A number of factors, however, could influence this result. First of all, even in the A&P condition the mean value for the perception of the believability wasn't very high (maximum score = 3.81). We cannot exclude that personification occurs only when believability is very high (the agent is "completely believable"). Moreover the duration of the session could have been too short to generate a human-like relation between the user and the agent. Finally, during a real interaction, a user unaware of the laboratory setting may behave indifferently to the one who is explicitly asked in the experimental setting to choose the interpretation. Because of this, the relation between the believability of the agent and the human-like attitude toward it should be studied more deeply in the future.

6.1   Implication for VA' Emotional Behavior

Our results replicate previous findings showing that emotional agents are judged more believable than non emotional ones. They provide more accurate results, however, since they show that adding emotional displays is not sufficient to guarantee an improvement in agent believability. The context in which the emotion is expressed must also be taken into account. According to these results, believable virtual agents should be able to adapt their emotional displays to the context. To be able to behave in a socially adapted way, agents should be able to take into account contextual factors and decide which emotion is appropriate to the situation. Further investigations in this direction are necessary to endow an agent with such skills. More modestly, our results also show that displaying emotions both verbally and non verbally may improve the perception of agent's believability. This result should be taken into account in the design of future virtual agents.

6.2   Implication for the Concept of Believability

The results of our experiment have two implications for the concept of believability. Firstly, it appears that the notion of believability needs to be distinguished from the one of personification (at least for agent with moderate believability rate). Secondly, believability is highly correlated to the two major socio-cognitive dimensions of warmth and competence.

The warmth and competence results are consistent with previous findings in human/human judgments: (a) both judgments are positively correlated as shown in [23,24]; (b) the highest effect size of warmth judgment is consistent with the idea of a primacy of warmth judgment [25]. It seems that people use the same pattern while judging virtual agents and humans. However, it does not mean that they create a human-like relation with them. Indeed, the absence of correlation between believability and personification indicates that these are two distinct concepts.

Finally, the believability rate and free comments given by participants (question Q3 of the experiment) also reveal improvements to bring to virtual agent animation. According to some comments low quality of the physical appearance and especially the lack of fluidity of the agent's animations may also cause the lower believability. Thus physical appearance and social factors must be taken jointly into account to create more believable agents able to maintain interaction with users.

7   Conclusion

In this paper we analyzed several factors influencing the perceived believability of a virtual assistant. In the experiment we showed that to create a (more) believable agent, its emotional (verbal/nonverbal) behavior should be socially adapted. We showed also that two main socio-cognitive factors: warmth and competence are related to the perception of believability. We also suggested that even if the agent is perceived as "believable" it does not imply that humans will create "human-like" relations with it.

In the future, we plan to continue our research on believability. We would like to study in more detail the relation between believability and personification. The results presented in this paper are limited to the software assistant domain. We would like to verify our hypotheses also in other virtual agent applications.

Acknowledgments. Part of this research is supported by the French project ANR-IMMEMO.

References

1. Allbeck, J.M., Badler, N.I.: Consistent communication with control. In: Pelachaud, C., Poggi, I. (eds.) Workshop on Multimodal Communication and Context in Embodied Agents, Fifth International Conference on Autonomous Agents (2001)
2. Ortony, A.: On making believable emotional agents believable. In: Trappl, R., Petta, P., Payr, S. (eds.) Emotions in Humans and Artifacts, pp. 189–212 (2002)
3. Isbister, K., Doyle, P.: Design and evaluation of embodied conversational agents: A proposed taxonomy. In: AAMAS 2002 Workshop on Embodied Conversational Agents, Bologna, Italy (2002)
4. Bates, J.: The role of emotion in believable agents. Communications of the ACM 37, 122–125 (1994)
5. Aylett, R.: Agents and affect: why embodied agents need affective systems. In: Vouros, G.A., Panayiotopoulos, T. (eds.) SETN 2004. LNCS (LNAI), vol. 3025, pp. 496–504. Springer, Heidelberg (2004)
6. Lester, J., Voerman, J., Towns, S., Callaway, C.: Cosmo: A life-like animated pedagogical agent with deictic believability. In: Working Notes of the IJCAI Workshop on Animated Interface Agents: Making Them Intelligent, Nagoya, Japan, pp. 61–69 (1997)
7. de Rosis, F., Pelachaud, C., Poggi, I., Carofiglio, V., de Carolis, B.: From Greta's mind to her face: Modelling the dynamics of affective states in a conversational embodied agent. International Journal of Human-Computer Studies 59, 81–118 (2003)
8. Prendinger, H., Ishizuka, M.: Let's talk! socially intelligent agents for language conversation training. IEEE Trans on Systems, Man, and Cybernetics - Part A: Systems and Humans, Special Issue on Socially Intelligent Agents - The Human in the Loop 31, 465–471 (2001)
9. Lim, Y., Aylett, R.: Feel the difference: a guide with attitude? In: Pelachaud, C., Martin, J.-C., André, E., Chollet, G., Karpouzis, K., Pelé, D. (eds.) IVA 2007. LNCS (LNAI), vol. 4722, pp. 317–330. Springer, Heidelberg (2007)

10. Becker, C., Wachsmuth, I., Prendinger, H., Ishizuka, M.: Evaluating affective feed-back of the 3D agent Max in a competitive cards game. In: Tao, J., Tan, T., Picard, R.W. (eds.) ACII 2005. LNCS, vol. 3784, pp. 466–473. Springer, Heidelberg (2005)
11. Fiske, S.T., Cuddy, A.J., Glick, P.: Universal dimensions of social cognition: warmth and competence. Trends in Cognitive Sciences 11(2), 77–83 (2007)
12. Reeves, B., Nass, C.I.: The media equation: How people treat computers, television, and new media like real people and places. Cambridge University Press, Cambridge (1996)
13. Mulken, S.V., André, E., Müller, J.: The persona effect: How substantial is it? In: HCI 1998: Proceedings of HCI on People and Computers XIII, London, UK, pp. 53–66. Springer, Heidelberg (1998)
14. Moundridou, M., Virvou, M.: Evaluating the persona effect of an interface agent in a tutoring system. Journal of Computer Assisted Learning 18(9), 253–261 (2002)
15. Walker, J., Sproull, L., Subramani, R.: Using a human face in an interface. In: Proceedings of the SIGCHI Conference on Human Factors in Computing Systems: Celebrating Interdependence, Boston, Massachusetts, pp. 85–91 (1994)
16. Niewiadomski, R., Ochs, M., Pelachaud, C.: Expressions of empathy in ECAs. In: Prendinger, H., Lester, J.C., Ishizuka, M. (eds.) IVA 2008. LNCS (LNAI), vol. 5208, pp. 37–44. Springer, Heidelberg (2008)
17. Harris, L.T., Fiske, S.T.: Dehumanizing the lowest of the low. Psychological Science 17, 847–853 (2006)
18. Fischer, K., Jungerman, H.: Rarely occurring headaches and rarely occuring blindness: is rarely-rarely? Journal of Behavioral Decision Making 9, 153–172 (1996)
19. Nowak, K.L., Biocca, F.: The effect of the agency and anthropomorphism on users' sense of telepresence, copresence, and social presence in virtual environments. Presence: Teleoperators & Virtual Environments 12(5), 481–494 (2003)
20. Gupta, S., Romano, D.M., Walker, M.A.: Politeness and variation in synthetic social interaction. In: H-ACI Human-Animated Characters Interaction Workshop in conjunction with the 19th British HCI Group Annual Conference (2005)
21. Hoffmann, L., Krämer, N.C., Lam-chi, A., Kopp, S.: Media equation revisited: Do users show polite reactions towards an embodied agent? In: Ruttkay, Z., Kipp, M., Nijholt, A., Vilhjálmsson, H.H. (eds.) IVA 2009. LNCS, vol. 5773, pp. 159–165. Springer, Heidelberg (2009)
22. Ortony, A., Clore, G., Collins, A.: The Cognitive Structure of Emotions. Cambridge University Press, Cambridge (1988)
23. Judd, C.M., James-Hawkins, L., Yzerbyt, V., Kashima, Y.: Fundamental dimensions of social judgment: Understanding the relations between judgments of competence and warmth. Journal of Personality and Social Psychology 89(6), 899–913 (2005)
24. Rosenberg, S., Nelson, C., Vivekananthan, P.S.: A multidimensional approach to the structure of personality impressions. Journal of Personality and Social Psychology 9(4), 283–294 (1968)
25. Peeters, G.: From good and bad to can and must: subjective necessity of acts associated with positively and negatively valued stimuli. European Journal of Social Psychology 32(1), 125–136 (2002)

Ada and Grace: Toward Realistic and Engaging Virtual Museum Guides

William Swartout[1], David Traum[1], Ron Artstein[1], Dan Noren[2], Paul Debevec[1], Kerry Bronnenkant[2], Josh Williams[1], Anton Leuski[1], Shrikanth Narayanan[3], Diane Piepol[1], Chad Lane[1], Jacquelyn Morie[1], Priti Aggarwal[1], Matt Liewer[1], Jen-Yuan Chiang[1], Jillian Gerten[1], Selina Chu[3], and Kyle White[3]

[1] USC Institute for Creative Technologies
[2] Museum of Science, Boston
[3] USC Speech Analysis and Interpretation Laboratory

Abstract. To increase the interest and engagement of middle school students in science and technology, the InterFaces project has created virtual museum guides that are in use at the Museum of Science, Boston. The characters use natural language interaction and have near photoreal appearance to increase and presents reports from museum staff on visitor reaction.

Keywords: virtual human applications, photoreal characters, natural language interaction, virtual museum guides, STEM, informal science education.

1 Introduction

A well-informed guide or interpreter can have a tremendous influence on the quality of a museum visitor's experience. The best guides not only provide information but also engage the visitor in an interactive exchange that can lead to deeper understanding and promote excitement about museum content. Unfortunately, human museum guides are often in short supply. Many studies have shown that people react to virtual humans in much the same way that they react to real people [1-3]. Could virtual humans be used to create museum guides that can engage visitors with museum content? The InterFaces project, a collaboration between the USC Institute for Creative Technologies (ICT) and the Museum of Science, Boston (MoS), has been exploring exactly that question.

Set in Cahners ComputerPlace (CCP) at the Museum of Science where most of the museum's information technology exhibits

Fig. 1. Guides at the Museum of Science, Boston

J. Allbeck et al. (Eds.): IVA 2010, LNAI 6356, pp. 286–300, 2010.

are located, the virtual human guides are housed in exhibit called InterFaces (Figure 1) designed to promote interest in Science, Technology, Engineering and Mathematics (STEM). The primary audience that we sought to reach was children between ages 7 to 14, and we were particularly interested in engaging females and other groups under-represented in STEM. We chose middle school aged children as our primary audience for two main reasons.

First, recent studies such as [4] suggest that children's level of interest in science during middle school or even earlier can have a strong effect on ultimate career choice. Our hypothesis is that interacting with Virtual Humans will help pique and engage children's interest in what computer science and related STEM can offer because not only can they provide knowledge and advice, as computers typically do, but the fact that they are embodied as Virtual Humans adds a social element that can create greater rapport and involvement.

Second, it is sometimes difficult to get younger museum visitors to engage with the exhibits, particularly when in school groups. Museum personnel report that school group behavior tends to be "run in, run around, run out." Students spend relatively little time actually engaged with the exhibits and teachers struggle to guide them to interact with the many choices available. In our project, however, visitors encounter Ada and Grace, twin virtual museum guides who are a focal point of the space, when they first enter the ComputerPlace. Ada and Grace are life-sized, photo-realistic characters that interact in natural language, complete with gestures and other forms of non-verbal communication. In our current implementation, a museum staff member interacts with the virtual museum guides in natural language and the visitors who can pose their own questions to the guides through the staff member. The virtual museum guides answer general questions about ComputerPlace and the information sciences, and based on visitor's expressed interests, they can suggest exhibits to check out. Our hope was that the cutting edge technology of the virtual humans as well as the social rapport they could establish would engage the students and "stop them in their tracks."

1.1 Creating Engagement

Creating an engaging experience for museum visitors is a central goal of the Virtual Museum Guides project. Several facets of the virtual humans' design are intended to increase engagement:

- **Broadly appealing appearance.** We conducted a study (described in Section 4.1) to select a (human) model for our guides that was not clearly identified with any one ethnic group and had broad appeal to museum visitors.
- **Two characters.** When virtual humans have been used as information agents or guides in the past, in most cases, there is a single virtual human interacting with one or more real people. To enhance engagement, we decided to use two characters so that they could dialogue with each other as well as the visitors. In section 4.3, we describe our rationale for this approach in more detail.
- **Natural language interaction.** We chose to have Ada and Grace interact using natural language input and output rather than a menu-based or type-in interface because it makes the interface more transparent and the characters more realistic.

- **Near photoreal appearance.** Studies have shown that a more realistic depiction of either a simulated scene [5] or virtual human [6] can create greater participant involvement in a virtual experience. As we will describe below, Ada and Grace, our virtual museum guides, were created using Light Stage technology. That technology has been used to create photorealistic non-interactive characters for movies such as *Avatar, Hancock,* and *The Curious Case of Benjamin Button.* Ada and Grace are the first examples of deployed, interactive virtual humans that make extensive use of Light Stage technology (See Section 4.2).

1.2 Related Work

There have been some previous installations of Virtual Humans in museums. The "pixie" system [7] was part of a 2003 exhibit in the Swedish Telecom museum called 'Tänk Om' ('What If '), where visitors experienced a full-size apartment of the year 2010. The visitors could help Pixie perform certain tasks in the apartment or ask the agent general questions about herself or the exhibition. In January 2004, the Max agent was installed in the Heinz Nixdorf Museums Forum (HNF), a public computer museum in Paderborn (Germany) [8]. Max is human-like in size on a static screen, standing face-to-face to visitors of the museum. Acting as a museum guide, Max's primary task is to engage visitors in conversations to provide information about the museum, the exhibition, or other topics of interest. However, Max only allows keyboard input. In Cahners ComputerPlace, the Tinker exhibit [9], an embodied conversational agent (ECA) in the guise of a robot, builds relationships and tracks engagement with the user, and includes novel user ID via analysis of hand-images. Visitors must select options from a menu to interact with Tinker.

In the next section, we present a sample interaction with Ada and Grace, followed by a more detailed discussion of how they work and were developed. We then present evaluations of the Twins' natural language processing, and reports from the museum staff about visitor reaction to the deployed virtual museum guides.

2 Sample Scenario

In our current implementation, a museum staff member uses speech to interact with the guides. Visitors may pose questions to the guides through the staff member. We choose to take this approach rather than having visitors speak directly to the guides to ensure speech recognition accuracy, which is less accurate when there is wide variability in dialects among speakers. This first group of interchanges illustrates a drill-down exchange in which the twin characters, Ada and Grace, are leading a visitor (via the Handler) towards information the visitor is interested in:

HANDLER: What are your names?

ADA: My name's Ada.

GRACE: And I'm Grace. We're your Virtual Museum Guides. With your help, we can point you towards exhibits that will get you thinking! Or answer questions about things you've seen here.

ADA: What do you want to learn about?

HANDLER: I'm interested in computers.

GRACE: Here at Cahners ComputerPlace, you can *build* your own model computer, solve a *puzzle* like a computer, examine computer *brains*, and learn how to *think* like a computer. Which one of these do you want to put through your processor?

HANDLER: I want to learn how computers think.

GRACE: At Logic Land you can learn how computers think by trying to decode a bitmap, and interacting with Boolean logic gates.

HANDLER: What are Boolean logic gates?

GRACE: Boolean logic gates are the basic building blocks of computing! Remember these three words; AND, OR, NOT. Each of these is a type of logic gate. Like real gates you walk through, some need a key, or even two identical keys to let you through. Head over to Logic Land, or ask one of our volunteers if you want to learn more.

Other common exchanges include information about the Museum of Science and Cahners ComputerPlace:

HANDLER: Why is this place named Cahners ComputerPlace?

ADA: Cahners ComputerPlace is named after Norman Cahners, a publisher based in Boston, and longtime supporter of the museum.

GRACE: Welcoming 300,000 visitors annually, Cahners ComputerPlace offers a one-stop resource for software that inspires people to create, explore and learn.

ADA: Did you read that in the brochure?!

The twins are also capable of responding to questions about their own exhibit and supporting technology:

HANDLER: What is your technology?

ADA: We're virtual humans. We use speech recognition technology to identify your words...

GRACE: [Finishing her twin's sentence] ...and use statistics to figure out the meaning of the words based on context. Once we know what you're talking about, we'll reply appropriately.

Grace and Ada are also intended to highlight the major role that women have played historically in the development of computer science:

HANDLER: Who are you named after?

ADA: Our namesakes are Ada Lovelace and Grace Hopper.

GRACE: Yeah, they may be old-fashioned names, but both from the most modern computing women of their time.

ADA: In the 1800s, Ada Lovelace predicted that computers would some day help us write music and create art.

GRACE: And in this past century, Grace Hopper created a type of computer program called a compiler, which helps people tell computers what to do.

ADA: It could be said that Ada inspired Grace.

GRACE: Or that Grace did all the work, in which case our names are perfect.

Finally, Ada and Grace can answer questions that middle schoolers might be interested in:

HANDLER: Do you have boyfriends?

ADA: Why? [Tongue in cheek] Is there another virtual human you think we should meet?

GRACE: I hope they're into neural networks and amino acid sequences.

ADA: Grace?! What's wrong with just charming and generous?

3 How the Guides Work

The Twins are based on and extend the approach used in the SGT Star character [10] and the Gunslinger project [11]. To interact with the characters, an operator presses a push-to-talk button and speaks into a microphone. An audio acquisition client then sends audio to the automatic speech recognizer (ASR), which creates hypotheses of the words that were said, and then sends this text to the Language Understanding (LU) module. The ASR module uses the SONIC toolkit [12], with custom language and acoustic models (see Section 4.4). The LU module uses a statistical text classification algorithm to map the utterance text onto character responses. It selects a set of responses it believes to be appropriate to the utterance from a domain-specific library of scripted responses and passes them to the dialogue management (DM) module. The DM module uses that response set and the recent dialogue history to select one response for the characters to perform. The response is sometimes a sequence of utterances, as seen in section 2. In this case, the DM keeps a schedule of pending utterances, and sends them one at a time to the animation components, waiting for a callback signal before sending the next one. If the characters are interrupted by more speech from the operator before the schedule has completed, the DM can cancel the remaining sequence.

The LU/DM module pair uses the NPCEditor software [13]. The NPCEditor classification algorithm analyzes the text of the sample utterances and the text of the responses and creates a statistical model of the "translation relationship" that defines how the content of an input utterance determines the likely appropriateness of a response. Specifically, it learns how to compute a conditional likelihood of observing a particular word in a character's response given an operator's utterance [14]. When NPCEditor receives a new (possibly unseen) utterance, it uses this translation information to build a model of what it believes to be the best response for the utterance. The classifier then compares this representation to every stored response and returns the best match to the DM part of NPCEditor. In contrast, a traditional text classification approach would compare a new question to sample questions and then directly return the corresponding responses, ignoring the actual text of the response. We have observed that this "translation-based" classification approach significantly increases the effectiveness of the classifier for imperfect speech recognition [14]. NPCEditor has been fielded in a number of applications and has been shown to be successful in noisy classification tasks [13].

The Twins have a large but finite set of responses (currently about 400), so the characters might repeat themselves. One of the tasks of the DM is to match the classifier selection to the recent dialogue history and choose responses that have not been heard. The DM also handles cases when the classifier returns no responses. This happens when the operator asks a question for which the characters have no answer or speech is not understood by the ASR module. In that case, the classifier decides that none of the known answers is appropriate. The Twins database contains a number of responses that we call "off-topic." These responses range from prompts for repetition "Could you ask that again?" to utterances indicating that the characters do not know how to answer the questions "I really wish we had an answer for that."

The animation process is revised from that used by SGT Star and employs the Smartbody (SBM) behavior realization system [15] and a new sequencer module, as well as the Gamebryo animation engine. The sequencer module retrieves Behavior Markup Language (BML) [16] animation schedules for each of the utterances coming from the DM. Since BML as interpreted by SBM only animates a single agent, the sequencer schedule includes a number of synchronization points that are broadcast back to the sequencer. When the sequencer receives these callbacks it sends additional BML schedules to animate the other agent, so that Ada and Grace can each react appropriately while the other is speaking. SBM uses several behavior controllers and blending to realize the specific combination of motion, and sends the resulting commands to the Gamebryo engine to generate the motion.

4 Building the Guides

In this section we outline the main steps we took to create the Twins. We start with the appearance, then the content and output expression, and finally the resources for speech understanding.

4.1 Formative Study on Visitor Preferences

To support the goals of engagement and ability to serve as role models for young girls potentially interested in STEM, we decided to base the characters' appearance on a young adult female of indeterminate racial background. We conducted a formative study with 75 museum visitors from the target audience of 7-14 year olds (with parental consent), which was used to inform the choice of character appearance as well as impressions the visitors associate with the person shown. Six photos (selected from a larger set provided by a modeling agency) were presented and visitors were asked to select the one whom they would most want to speak to in Cahners ComputerPlace and provide reasons for their choices. In addition, visitors were probed for ideas about what the virtual human might do with their free time, what characteristics of a virtual human guide would be most important to them, and what interested them about computers and robots. Results from the exit survey indicate that one photo (actress/model Bianca R.) was the overwhelming choice of the museum visitors, and thus she was selected to be recorded in the Light Stage. Visitors rated the following traits as being most important for their virtual human: Friendly, Smart and Patient. Visitors reported that their virtual human occupied their time: having a job/occupation, having pets, going to the mall/shops, hanging out with friends, and playing sports. This information was used in the content development (described in Section 4.3) to help craft the backstory for the characters.

4.2 Light Stage: Capturing the Model

We recorded Bianca Rodriguez using ICT's Light Stage 5 high-resolution facial scanning system (Figure 2) that enables the creation of characters that appear and animate realistically, and look substantially better than standard video game characters that visitors might be familiar with. Light Stage 5 is a two-meter diameter sphere with 156 evenly-spaced white LED light sources pointing toward the center from all angles. A stereo pair of high-resolution digital still cameras photographs the actor's face under a variety of different lighting conditions as in [17]. Polarized lighting conditions allow us to independently measure the skin color, surface shine, and surface orientation at each point on the face with 0.1mm resolution. Using spherical harmonic lighting conditions – essentially bright-to-dark gradients of light across the sphere's X, Y, and Z axes – allows us to measure the surface orientation at each pixel, telling us the shape of skin pores, creases, bulges, and wrinkles. From that data we created a highly detailed 3D model of the subject's face.

Fig. 2. Light Stage 5

The first use of the Light Stage system for creating a virtual character was for SGT Star. Based on the deployed version of the character, an advanced prototype was created by leveraging the hybrid normal rendering skin technique from [17] where the diffuse and specular reflectance components of the skin are rendered with different surface orientation maps as measured from the photometric data.. This significantly increased the realism of the character with little impact on rendering speed(Figure 3).

The face looked quite realistic in a neutral pose but less convincing as it animated, since it distorted unnaturally when morphed to form expressions.

To improve upon SGT Star's facial quality for the Twins, we acquired scans of the actor in a variety of facial expressions to be used as blend shapes in the animated character rig. Thus, when Ada or Grace exhibit an expression, the shape of her face is based on the actual shape of the actor's face in that expression. The complexity of facial expression is difficult to model manually, making this blend shape data very valuable for creating believable digital characters.

We had previously built a character from light stage scans in a variety of expressions, most notably in the "Digital Emily" project [18] in collaboration with facial animation company Image Metrics. However, Digital Emily was

Fig. 3. Hybrid Normal

rendered offline using computationally intensive light transport simulations. For the museum guides, we further developed the real-time skin shader using the hybrid normal maps technique of [17] to render a faithful rendition of skin reflectance in the Gamebryo game engine. The deployed Twins at the museum use this rendering technology. A detail of one of the Twins' faces produced by a more advanced version of the shader is shown in Figure 4[1]. The neutral pose of the guides was based directly on fitting an animatable facial mesh to the original high-resolution scan data of the model's neutral pose. The blend shapes for the expressions were created semi-automatically by using approximately seven expression scans as reference in a 3D modeling program. The resulting models were exported in formats compatible with off the shelf tools such as Maya.

While the Twins' faces were being created using Light Stage technology, the rest of the characters (bodies, clothing, hair, eyes etc) were created by digital artists. These elements were then brought together with the Light Stage models to create the characters shown in Figure 1.

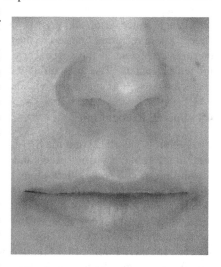

Fig. 4. Twins Detail Enhanced Shader

4.3 Developing the Content

As described above, the main goals for inter-action were to involve 7-14 year old kids in natural, engaging conversation related to STEM and the Museum's related exhibits in Cahners ComputerPlace. Rather than a single guide, we decided to use twins to enhance visitor engagement in several ways. First, some character responses are quite information-rich and inherently lengthy. Having one character deliver long responses can seem long-winded and tax the attention span of younger visitors. By having two characters share such responses (as exemplified in Section 2), we can better maintain the pace of the conversation and visitor interest. Second, two characters can be an obvious source of differing opinions and behaviors, which allows a dialectal approach to providing information [19] as well as allowing the characters to act as foils for each other's humor. There is also some evidence that presenting different types of information as coming from different agents may enhance learning over having all information come from a single agent [20]. The decision to use twins as opposed to two distinct characters was mainly to reduce production costs and allow maximal reuse of resources, but it also provides a good backstory for their interaction.

There were six content areas developed for the twins:

1. Cahners ComputerPlace (CCP) exhibits, activities and exhibit space namesake
2. General computer, robot, and cell phone communications
3. Overview of the Museum of Science
4. Backstory about the characters (favorite color, pets, etc)
5. Technology of the Virtual Human Guides
6. Off topic responses (triggered by un-interpretable inputs)

For areas 1-3, the CCP staff collected typical visitor questions and interpretation responses given by the staff and volunteers. From a base of over 300,000 visitors per

---

[1] This advanced version has not yet been released in the museum. We expect to release it in June 2010.

year, we were able to compile comprehensive, detailed questions and answers from the viewpoint of many different visitor demographics - with a range of Computer STEM skills and knowledge. For topics 4-6 we were able to rely on ICTs previous experience with Virtual Humans, such as SGT Star. An iterative process involving both groups led to the final content.

A single voice actor was cast to create the slightly different voices of Ada and Grace. These recorded lines were then used as the basis for animation, using the authoring component of the sequencer to allow artists to select appropriate animations for the characters. The animations were designed to match the personalities of the characters as well as engage the visitor.

4.4 Speech Recognition

The SONIC toolkit [12] and the SRI Language Modeling Toolkit (SRILM) [21] were used to create the acoustic speech and language models, as well as to provide an API for on-line speech recognition. Language models were constructed by combining a large vocabulary (5-15k words) with the full set of inputs used for classifier training.

Several acoustic models were built, customized to individual Museum staff member's voices, using gender-dependent three state triphone context HMM acoustic models trained from the Wall Street Journal corpus as well as around 250 utterances for each speaker. Twelve Mel Frequency Cepstral Coefficients (MFCCs) and normalized frame energy, along with the velocity and acceleration of these features, are used for audio frame representation. Systems were built via three iterations of Maximum a Posteriori adaptation on the baseline gender dependent model (e.g., [22]). The performance (word error rate) of the adapted systems improved by 33% (from 15% to 10%) compared to the baseline. A number of engineering optimizations helped improve the overall performance robustness. For example, allowing for a larger beam path in the speech decoding process, yielded a performance gain. Similarly, optimizing the adaptation function parameters for frame count threshold and silence count threshold increased performance as well, especially in the presence of acoustic variability such as background noise.

5 Additional Project Elements

As part of the project, we are developing two additional exhibit elements aimed primarily at our secondary audience, older teen-agers and adults:

The Science Behind Virtual Humans. Because many sophisticated computer science research areas are required to create virtual humans, in addition to serving as a guide, a virtual human can *itself* serve as an exhibit of technology. In its current form, the "Science Behind" exhibit (Figure 5) consists of flat panel displays on the side of the virtual guides kiosk (Figure 1) that dynamically show the virtual human's speech recognition and statistical NLU text classifier in operation as the characters interact. It also includes several posters that describe different stages of the installation design and construction. Visitors can watch as the system recognizes the words in the handler's speech and see how the classifier ranks and then selects a response. Another window shows a transcript of recent interactions. These supporting exhibits engage visitors by allowing to see first-hand the cutting edge of technology and grasp the promise and limitations of current virtual humans.

Living Laboratory. As part of the exhibit, we include a "Living Laboratory", which engages the museum visitors in the scientific method (as applied to virtual humans) in three different ways. First, visitors can be experimental subjects, just by interacting with the virtual humans. In a standard university research laboratory one of the most difficult aspects of advancing the state of user interaction with virtual humans is finding enough appropriate subjects to evaluate the system. Thus, only a small set of the experimental conditions that are worth testing can actually be accomplished. The thousands of visitors to the museum provide a much larger pool from which to test a number of issues, such as performance of the speech understanding, coverage of the domain, appropriateness of the dialogue strategies, and effectiveness at teaching and motivating interest in STEM. Secondly, visitors can help evaluate the data and analyze the results. Finally, through interaction with the museum staff and on the Exhibit website, visitors can suggest new experiments.

Fig. 5. Museum visitors exploring the Science Behind exhibit

6   Evaluation

The Museum Guide Twins were first displayed to the public on December 8, 2009. We have since conducted evaluations of the Twins' natural language performance and we have reports from museum staff about how visitors are reacting to the Guides, which we discuss below. In the future, we will conduct summative evaluations to assess the impact that the Guides have on a museum visitor's experience, and their engagement and interest in STEM topics.

Evaluation of Natural Language Performance
We evaluated the Twins' performance based on data collected at two venues: ongoing live sessions at the Museum of Science between February 10 and March 18, 2010, and a demo at the AAAS annual meeting in San Diego on February 19-21. The data

consist of system logs and audio recordings of utterances spoken to the characters; the vast majority of the utterances are by trained museum staff, though occasionally a visitor spoke directly to the Twins. All recordings were transcribed manually.

Utterances spoken to the characters can be divided into those that appear in the classifier training data (*known* utterances) and those that are not in the training data (*unknown* utterances). Since speech input to the characters is provided primarily by museum staff familiar with the Twins, we found a large proportion of known utterances (about 70%); unknown utterances usually come about when the interpreter diverges from the standard questions, for example, by posing a question asked by a visitor. For known utterances we can automatically determine whether the response was correct (by seeing if it is linked to the utterance in the classifier), incorrect (an on-topic response that is not linked to the utterance), or off-topic. For unknown utterances there are no defined correct responses, but we can automatically determine whether the response was on-topic or off-topic. Table 1 shows the breakdown of responses.

Table 1. Responses from the Museum of Science, February 10 to March 18, 2010

Question	Response	N	%	WER
Known	Correct	3516	56.8	0.1726
Known	Incorrect	106	1.7	0.8261
Known	Off-topic	629	10.2	0.5829
Unknown	On-topic	1444	23.3	0.2222
Unknown	Off-topic	498	8.0	0.4543
Total		6193	100.0	0.2597

The results show that performance on the known utterances is good, with over 80% of known utterances receiving a correct response; those known utterances that received off-topic and incorrect responses typically had higher word error rates (WER), so the failure of the classifier is likely due to poor speech recognition. Unknown utterances also result in mostly on-topic responses. To better understand the performance on the unknown user utterances we used a sample of the data (all the data collected at the museum between February 10 and February 19) to perform two manual annotation tasks: separating the unknown utterances into in-domain and out-of-domain utterances, and rating the coherence of system responses.

Unknown user utterances can be divided into two types: in-domain utterances which have a good on-topic responses and out-of-domain utterances which do not have an on-topic response in the characters' repertoire. In-domain utterances are typically minor variations on known utterances, and for such input the classifier is expected to provide the correct response; out-of-domain utterances are often not related to any known utterance, and the dialogue manager should handle these by issuing an off-topic response. Since the definition of in-domain and out-of-domain utterances depends on the desired system output, determining which class an utterance belongs to is a somewhat subjective task which has to be performed manually. To ensure the annotations were meaningful we had the sample data marked by two annotators, and calculated inter-rater reliability using Krippendorff's alpha [23]; reliability was reasonably high at $\alpha=0.75$ (observed agreement=0.89, N=264; alpha ranges from -1 to 1, where 1 signifies perfect agreement and 0 obtains when agreement is at chance level).

To assess the quality of the responses we conducted a separate rating study, similar to [10], where annotators rated utterance-response pairs on a scale of 1 to 5. All the utterance-response pairs collected at the museum between February 10 and February 19 were rated. A reliability study on a separate sample, the utterance-response pairs from the AAAS demo, showed that reliability was fairly high for the on-topic responses, with $\alpha=0.827$ for unknown on-topic responses and $\alpha=0.596$ for known incorrect responses, but negative for the off-topic responses, indicating that the ratings of the latter cannot be trusted. Table 2 shows the ratings of the 390 on-topic responses (out of 582 total utterances analyzed). The table shows that on-topic responses to unknown utterances are generally very good, especially for those user utterances that are in-domain.

Table 2. Coherence ratings for On Topic Responses to Unknown Utterances

Question	N	Mean	Median
In-domain	342	4.78	5
Out-of-domain	48	3.40	4

Interaction reports from museum staff

While we have yet to conduct formal studies, anecdotal reports from the museum staff are encouraging. Museum staff reports that the exhibit really does 'stop the kids in their tracks' when the Twins are talking. In idle mode, when the Twins are not interacting, most visitors pause then walk on, whether or not a handler is present. When the handler is interacting with the Twins and a visitor walks by, a significant percentage stop, with a majority of them staying and interacting.

For most exhibits in Cahners ComputerPlace, adults accompanying children in families tend not get involved themselves. In contrast, with the Twins, the entire family tends to get involved. Females seem to be attracted to the exhibit more than males, and they tend to stay longer. There is some reticence for visitors to ask questions, although females tend to ask questions more spontaneously than males and these questions tend to be more personal questions about the Twins.

Visitors do not immediately make the connection between what is going on at "The Science Behind" and what the Twins are doing, they think "The Science Behind" stands alone. This suggests a need clarify the connection in the exhibit design.

Fig. 6. Visitors engaging with Ada and Grace

The natural language technology tends to engage the visitors attention, and there is some real amazement at the exhibit. Staff has literally observed jaw-dropping reactions from visitors to the Twins.

An email sent by Dan Noren, director of Cahners Compter Place and a co-author of this paper, shortly after the Twins debut, sums up the initial observations:

> "Well, the young visitors are enchanted! Lots of *"Awesome"*, *"Wow"*, *"Really cool"*, *"Neat"*..., lots of smiles / wide eyes, lots of questions - and both girls and boys are interested in looking at the Science Behind and the actual computers / networks driving the whole thing. I believe InterFaces is everything we have been working so hard to do - give the WOW factor to Computer STEM."

7 Future Work and Conclusions

In the near future, we intend to enhance ASR to support direct interaction between the Twins and museum visitors. We are investigating several approaches to rapidly selecting or adapting speech models to visitors. Other future enhancements include more expressive facial expressions and eye gaze, and idle behaviors in which the characters will interact with each other when no one is talking with them to help draw in visitors.

A major goal for this project was to create virtual guides that would truly engage visitors. We sought to do this through several means. We surveyed visitors to help design a character that would be broadly appealing. We used two characters instead of one so that the characters could interact with each other as well as the visitors and increase engagement. We used natural language input and output for a more natural interface, and we used Light Stage technology to capture highly realistic models of the characters' faces, and developed the technology to render those models in realtime within the Gamebryo game engine.

Our evaluation of the Twins' performance shows the feasibility of using natural language interaction, and we believe the pictures of visitors and the reports from the museum staff give strong evidence of success in creating engagement.

Acknowledgements. This material is based upon work supported by the National Science Foundation under Grant 0813541. We thank the staff and volunteers of Cahners ComputerPlace for their support. We also thank Kim LeMasters, Creative Director of the ICT, for the suggestion to use twins, Ed Fast for software support, and Stacy Marsella and Andrew Marshall for help with the Smartbody system. Finally, we would like to thank Arlene de Strulle for her continued support and enthusiasm.

References

1. Reeves, B., Nass, C.: The Media Equation. Cambridge University Press, Cambridge (1996)
2. Krämer, N.C., Tietz, B., Bente, G.: Effects of embodied interface agents and their gestural activity. In: Rist, T., Aylett, R.S., Ballin, D., Rickel, J. (eds.) IVA 2003. LNCS (LNAI), vol. 2792, pp. 292–300. Springer, Heidelberg (2003)

3. Gratch, J., Wang, N., Okhmatovskaia, A., Lamothe, F., Morales, M., van der Werf, R., Morency, L.-P.: Can virtual humans be more engaging than real ones? In: 12th International Conference on Human-Computer Interaction, Beijing, China (2007)

4. Tai, R., Liu, C., Maltese, A., Fan, X.: Planning early for careers in science. Science(Washington) 312, 1143–1144 (2006)

5. Slater, M., Khanna, P., Mortensen, J., Yu, I.: Visual realism enhances realistic response in an immersive virtual environment. IEEE Computer Graphics and Applications 29, 76–84 (2009)

6. MacDorman, K., Coram, J., Ho, C.-C., Patel, H.: Gender Differences in the Impact of Presentational Factors in Human Character Animation on Decisions in Ethical Dilemmas. Presence: Teleoperators and Virtual Environments 19 (2010)

7. Bell, L., Gustafson, J.: Child and adult speaker adaptation during error resolution in a publicly available spoken dialogue system. In: EUROSPEECH-2003, pp. 613–616 (2003)

8. Kopp, S., Gesellensetter, L., Krämer, N., Wachsmuth, I.: A conversational agent as museum guide - design and evaluation of a real-world application. In: Panayiotopoulos, T., Gratch, J., Aylett, R.S., Ballin, D., Olivier, P., Rist, T. (eds.) IVA 2005. LNCS (LNAI), vol. 3661, pp. 329–343. Springer, Heidelberg (2005)

9. Bickmore, T., Pfeifer, L., Schulman, D., Perera, S., Senanayake, C., Nazmi, I.: Public displays of affect: deploying relational agents in public spaces. In: CHI 2008, pp. 3297–3302. ACM, New York (2008)

10. Artstein, R., Gandhe, S., Gerten, J., Leuski, A., Traum, D.: Semi-formal evaluation of conversational characters. In: Grumberg, O., Kaminski, M., Katz, S., Wintner, S. (eds.) Languages: From Formal to Natural. LNCS, vol. 5533, pp. 22–35. Springer, Heidelberg (2009)

11. Hartholt, A., Gratch, J., Weiss, L., The Gunslinger Team: At the virtual frontier: Introducing gunslinger, a multi-character, mixed-reality, story-driven experience. In: Ruttkay, Z., Kipp, M., Nijholt, A., Vilhjálmsson, H.H. (eds.) IVA 2009. LNCS, vol. 5773, pp. 500–501. Springer, Heidelberg (2009)

12. Pellom, B., Hacioglu, K.: Sonic: The university of colorado continuous speech recognizer. University of Colorado, Technical Report# TR-CSLR-2001-01, Boulder, Colorado (2001)

13. Leuski, A., Traum, D.: NPCEditor: A tool for building question-answering characters. In: Language Resources and Evaluation Conference (2010)

14. Leuski, A., Traum, D.: Practical language processing for virtual humans. In: Conference on Innovative Applications of Artifical Intelligence (2010)

15. Thiebaux, M., Marshall, A., Marsella, S., Kallmann, M.: SmartBody: Behavior Realization for Embodied Conversational Agents. In: International Conference on Autonomous Agents and Multi-Agent Systems, Portugal (2008)

16. Vilhjalmsson, H., Cantelmo, N., Cassell, J., Chafai, N.E., Kipp, M., Kopp, S., Mancini, M., Marsella, S., Marshall, A.N., Pelachaud, C., Ruttkay, Z., Thorisson, K.R., van Welbergen, H., van der Werf, R.: The behavior markup language: Recent developments and challenges. In: Pelachaud, C., Martin, J.-C., André, E., Chollet, G., Karpouzis, K., Pelé, D. (eds.) IVA 2007. LNCS (LNAI), vol. 4722, pp. 99–111. Springer, Heidelberg (2007)

17. Ma, W., Hawkins, T., Peers, P., Chabert, C., Weiss, M., Debevec, P.: Rapid acquisition of specular and diffuse normal maps from polarized spherical gradient illumination. In: Rendering Techniques 2007 (2007)

18. Alexander, O., Rogers, M., Lambeth, W., Chiang, M., Debevec, P.: Creating a Photoreal Digital Actor: The Digital Emily Project. In: Sixth European Conference on Visual Media Production (CVMP) (2009)

19. Piwek, P.: Presenting arguments as fictive dialogue. In: 8th Workshop on Computational Models of Natural Argument (in conjunction with ECAI 2008), Patras, Greece (2008)
20. Baylor, A., Ebbers, S.: Evidence that multiple agents facilitate greater learning. In: Hoppe, U., Verdejo, M., Kay, J. (eds.) Artificial Intelligence in Education: Shaping the Future of Learning Through Intelligent Technologies, pp. 377–397. IOS Press, Amsterdam (2003)
21. Stolcke, A.: SRILM-an Extensible Language Modeling Toolkit. In: Seventh International Conference on Spoken Language Processing, pp. 901–904 (2002)
22. Wang, D., Narayanan, S.: A confidence-score based unsupervised MAP adaptation for speech recognition. In: 36th Asilomar Conference on Signals, Systems and Computers, Asilomar, CA (2002)
23. Krippendorff, K.: Content analysis: An introduction to its methodology. Sage Publications, Inc., Thousand Oaks (1980)

Interaction Strategies for an
Affective Conversational Agent

Cameron Smith[1], Nigel Crook[2], Johan Boye[2], Daniel Charlton[1], Simon Dobnik[2],
David Pizzi[1], Marc Cavazza[1], Stephen Pulman[2], Raul Santos de la Camara[3],
and Markku Turunen[4]

[1] School of Computing, Teesside University, Middlesbrough, United Kingdom
[2] Oxford University Computing Laboratory, Wolfson Building, Oxford, United Kingdom
[3] Telefonica I+D, C/ Emilio Vargas 6, 28043 Madrid, Spain
[4] Department of Computer Sciences, 33014 University of Tampere, Finland
{c.g.smith,d.charlton,d.pizzi,m.o.cavazza}@tees.ac.uk,
{nigel.crook,simon.dobnik,stephen.pulman}@comlab.ox.ac.uk,
johan.boye@speechact.se,e.rsai@tid.es,mturunen@cs.uta.fi

Abstract. The development of Embodied Conversational Agents (ECA) as Companions brings several challenges for both affective and conversational dialogue. These include challenges in generating appropriate affective responses, selecting the overall shape of the dialogue, providing prompt system response times and handling interruptions. We present an implementation of such a Companion showing the development of individual modules that attempt to address these challenges. Further, to resolve resulting conflicts, we present encompassing interaction strategies that attempt to balance the competing requirements. Finally, we present dialogues from our working prototype to illustrate these interaction strategies in operation.

Keywords: Embodied Conversational Agents, Companion, Affective Dialogue, Conversational Dialogue, Interruptions, Interaction Strategies.

1 Introduction

An emerging concept in recent years has been that of a social agent which focuses more on the relationship it can establish with a human user than on the assistance or information it can provide for a practical task. This concept of a "Companion" is particularly significant for Embodied Conversational Agent (ECA) research where the notion of companionship emerges from the overall communicative abilities of the ECA (that is, embodied and conversational aspects feeding into affective dialogue). Yet, there are also significant technical challenges encountered here in the integration of linguistic communication and non-verbal behaviour for affective dialogue [1].

In this paper, we present the implementation of a companion ECA integrating all the above aspects into a single prototype, in a way which supports conversational phenomena one would expect from affective dialogue, namely lengthy utterances on both sides and interruptions. This presentation mainly focuses on the interaction strategies supported by the agent, which support the principled integration of the large

J. Allbeck et al. (Eds.): IVA 2010, LNAI 6356, pp. 301–314, 2010.

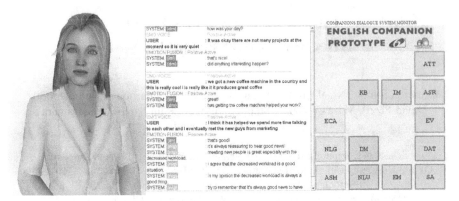

Fig. 1. The Companion during a typical dialogue

number of software components required to analyse user input, reason upon the situation, control the flow of dialogue and generate appropriate ECA responses and multimodal behaviours. Our main objective is to give an insight into these interaction strategies and to illustrate the Companion's performance with detailed examples from a fully-implemented prototype.

2   System Overview and Application

The Companion (as shown in Figure 1) presents itself as an ECA with which the user can engage in a free conversation, albeit on a select set of topics. As an application scenario, we wanted an everyday life domain that would support conversation with some affective content. We opted for a scenario in which the user, a typical office worker, returns home and talks about the day's events. We refer to this as the "How was your day?" (HWYD) scenario. The system currently supports over 40 work-based conversational topics, with further discussion of a range of influencing factors and event outcomes, across a range of emotional situations. By definition, the conversation is not task-oriented (unless one considers a very high level task of supporting the user through positively influencing their attitudes) and follows a mixed-initiative paradigm. User initiative, as expected, takes a central role, but without reducing the Companion to a passive, although sympathetic, listener. As evidenced by the example dialogues of Figures 5, 6 and 7, the Companion will attempt to offer appropriate advice as soon as it has assessed the user situation and considers such advice as appropriate.

Our system integrates no less than 15 different software components covering aspects of multimodal affective input, affective dialogue processing, interruption management and multimodal affective output. The software architecture integrating these components follows a blackboard philosophy [2], which provides the control flexibility required to implement various interaction strategies (see below). The system (Figure 2) comprises speech, language, reasoning and animation modules. Automatic Speech Recognition (ASR) is provided by Nuance's Dragon NaturallySpeaking, whilst Text-To-Speech (TTS) is an extension of Loquendo's commercial system developed as part of this project. The ECA appearance and animation are based on the Haptek™ toolkit. As expected, all dialogue and Natural Language Understanding (NLU) modules are proprietary. Emotional aspects are pervasive in these modules but their inclusion depends on the module itself: the animation module for the ECA naturally supports non-verbal behaviour and the expression of emotions, whilst our Text-To-Speech system has been specifically extended to support emotional markers. Finally, some modules are entirely dedicated to affective processing: the recognition of emotional categories from speech is based on the EmoVoice [3] system, the affective content of utterances' transcripts is uncovered using a Sentiment Analysis module [4]. Depending on the interaction strategy considered, these modules will be used separately or their output will be merged using an Emotional Model performing multimodal fusion of affective categories. In this system, multimodality is primarily dedicated to affective aspects, both in terms of input (emotional contents of speech/voice and transcribed utterances) and output (ECA speech, facial expressions and gestures).

Affective dialogue processing is lead by the Dialogue Manager (DM), which supports traditional functions such as managing clarification dialogue and repair. It further makes use of the more specific Affective Strategy Module (ASM) for generating complex affective utterances and a Natural Language Generation (NLG) module for realising replies into utterances for the multimodal affective output stage. The multimodal affective output is coordinated by the Multimodal Fission Manager (MFM) which controls both the ECA and Text-To-Speech modules. This is all overseen by an interruption management layer coordinated by the Interruption Manager (IM). The necessity to control turn-taking and interruptions has led to the incorporation of specific speech modules: the Acoustic Analysis (AA) and Acoustic Turn Taking (ATT) modules, which input into a Dialogue Act Tagger (DAT).

Natural language processing was also adapted to the objectives of affective dialogue and free conversation. The techniques used, including tagging, shallow parsing, named entity identification and contextual reference resolution, resemble Information Extraction and provide a robust coverage of the longer utterances, compared to previous dialogue systems, found in non-task orientated conversations.

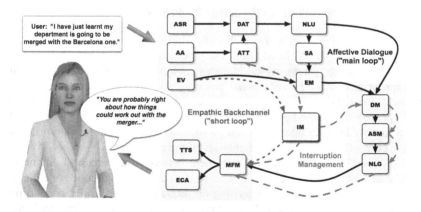

Fig. 2. System components with principal interaction loops (see text for details)

3 Interaction Strategies

The majority of language-enabled ECA have been developed in the context of task-based dialogue; this was dictated by both application constraints and linguistic coverage. However, the very idea of a companion agent assumes a level of conversation which is disconnected from any immediate task, and in particular is freed from strict constraints on the nature of dialogue.

Therefore several traditional assumptions which have presided over the formalisation of human-computer dialogue may need to be relaxed when exploring affective conversation. In everyday life, many inter-human conversations see one of the participants relating events through lengthy descriptions, without this corresponding to any specific request or encompassing speech act. Our objective was to support such free conversation, whilst still obtaining meaningful answers from the Companion in the form of advice appropriate both to the affective and informational content of the conversation.

In order to balance the constraints of free conversation with those of tractability, we have deliberately opted for a single-topic conversation, in contrast both to small talk [5] and 'chatterbot' approaches. It should be noted that even 'chatterbots' fail to depart from the conventions of human-computer dialogue, and most often feature dialogues in which user and agent utterances alternate rather strictly [6].

Our individual components seek to address some of the challenges of conversational dialogue: affective input, longer utterances, balancing clarification dialogue with long-form responses and the generation of these long-form responses. Yet individual optimisations only tackle part of the problem and can often introduce further problems of their own. As such, we additionally sought a more holistic approach; several interaction strategies allowing the different components to work together effectively, each strategy catering to different requirements of a Companion.

In the following sections we look in detail at the interaction strategies available before going on to provide examples from our implemented system showing the various interaction strategies in operation.

3.1 "Short Loop" Interaction: An Empathic Backchannel

Previous work has amply demonstrated the importance of backchannels in human-agent conversation [7] [8] [9]. In addition, the processing time required by the complete affective dialogue system, which includes reasoning upon the user's situation and the appropriateness of her emotional reaction, still exceeds recommended response time for dialogue systems, being on average over 3 seconds. This makes it essential to provide a real-time (< 700ms) yet relevant backchannel to the user, which is able to acknowledge user interaction and provide an initial response appropriate to the affective context even without a full analysis of the utterance.

The "short loop" implements a fast alignment between the perceived emotional state of the user and the ECA's expression, as well as acknowledging user utterances (see Figure 2). This is achieved by matching the ECA's non-verbal response to the emotional speech parameters detected by the emotional speech recogniser EmoVoice and including an appropriate verbal acknowledgement (on a random basis to avoid acknowledging all user utterances). The short loop thus essentially aligns the ECA response on the user's attitude.

3.2 "Main Loop" Interaction: Affective Dialogue and Reasoning

The main interaction strategy consists in a complete end-to-end implementation of affective conversation (with a response time of under 3000 ms). It enacts the overall behaviour of the Companion as an affective dialogue system and involves its full response to the user utterance in terms of both verbal and non-verbal behaviour (both gestures and facial expressions).

The "main loop" (see Figure 2) thus corresponds to an end-to-end implementation of affective conversation between the user and the agent. It is based on the identification of office life events, together with the affective context in which they are introduced. Following an appraisal step that determines the adequacy of the user's response to the situation she is facing (e.g. difficulties with colleagues, restructuring, redundancies), the Companion will provide an affective response in the form of reassurance, advice, comfort (or, in some cases, warning) to positively affect the user's attitude. The content is however specific to the details of the situation reported and makes reference to the different causes and consequences of the reported events. Conversational dialogue further requires a degree of flexibility in juggling user utterances of varying lengths with shifting topics while accounting for affective aspects. The expectation is that the Companion will be able to provide a response of appropriate length and tone in reply to the topic provided by the user. However, in order to do this effectively the Companion may be required to clarify information and elicit further information to support a meaningful response. The dialogue management thus needs to find a balance between employing clarification dialogue and generating appropriate responses to the information provided by the user.

The overall conversational loop is under the supervision of a Dialogue Manager which controls the various phases of dialogue and their timing, as well as the level of system initiative, in an integrated fashion. One of the main decisions it has to make is when to trigger lengthier utterances (which we have termed 'tirades' – see e.g. Figures 5, 6 and 7), which correspond to an affective dialogue strategy aiming at influencing the user's attitude by means of a short narrative. The challenge for the DM is to shift between the various aspects of conversation: allowing long rants from the user, providing sympathetic feedback without shifting dialogue initiative towards itself, triggering clarification sub-dialogues, or regaining initiative through long utterances that provide advice and support in a more structured fashion. Some of these aspects may be covered by the identification of Dialogue Acts, but Dialogue Acts alone may not be able to deal with the contents of longer user utterances (> 30 words). This is why one of the integrating principles adopted in our system is to also base dialogue control on event instantiation, thus relating it to Information Extraction.

3.3 Information Extraction

Conversations may involve utterances of various lengths including utterances much longer (> 50 words) than those typically found in task-oriented dialogues. Sentences may be ill-formed or highly elliptical. Furthermore, speech recognition under realistic conditions frequently results in a high word error rate making the task of syntactic analysis even harder. The task of the Natural Language Understanding module is to recognise a specific set of events reported by the user. These events are formalised as objects consisting of feature-value pairs. The NLU (in collaboration with the DM) employs shallow processing methods that instantiate event templates. These methods resemble Information Extraction (IE) techniques [10] [11].

The NLU takes the 1-best output from the speech recogniser, which has already been segmented into dialogue-act sized utterances. The utterances are then part-of-speech tagged and separated into Noun Phrase (NP) and Verb Group (VG) chunks which denote concepts in our domain. VGs consist of a main verb and any auxiliary verbs or semantically important adverbs. Both of these stages are carried out by a Hidden Markov Model trained on the Penn Treebank, although some customisation has been carried out for this application (relevant vocabulary added and some probabilities re-estimated to reflect properties of the application). NP and VG chunks are then classified into Named Entity (NE) classes, some of which are the usual 'person', 'organisation', 'time' etc. but others of which are specific to the scenario, as is traditional in IE: e.g. salient events, expressions of emotion, organisational structures etc. NE classification, in the absence of domain specific training data, is carried out via hand-written pattern matching rules and gazetteers. The NPs and VGs are represented as unification grammar categories containing information about the internal structure of the constituents: for example, an utterance like "John will move to the Madrid office next month" would yield results like that on the left of Figure 3.

In the next stage of NLU processing, domain specific IE patterns are applied on NP and VG chunks which rely on their syntactic and semantic information to form constituents called objects. For example, "meeting with X about Y" where NE type of X

```
<sentence>
<np head="John" stem="John" netype="per" gndr="male">
  <w>John/NNP</w>
</np>
<vg head="move" stem="move" polarity="pos"
netype="event_nature" tense="future">
  <w>will/MD</w>
  <w>move/VB</w>
</vg>
<w>to/TO</w>
<np head="office" stem="office" netype="org_generic">
  <w>the/DT</w>
  <w>Madrid/NNP</w>
  <w>office/NN</w>
</np>
<np head="month" stem="month" netype="time_period">
  <w>next/JJ</w>
  <w>month/NN</w>
</np>
</sentence>
```

```
[ A: event
    participants = [B],
    nature = move_office,
    agent = C,
    temporal_reference = future,
    modal = will,
    adv = D]

[ B: office
    full_name = [Madrid,office],
    name = office,
    number = sing]

[ D: time_period
    time = month,
    number = sing]

[ C: person
    gender = male,
    name = John,
    number = sing]
```

Fig. 3. NP and VG representation (*left*) and final semantic representation (*right*) used by the NLU

is person, or "move to X" where NE type of X is org_generic. In the final stage reference resolution for pronouns and definite NPs is performed. This module is based partly on the system described by Kennedy and Boguraev [12], with the various weighting factors based on theirs. Each referring NP gives rise to a discourse referent, and these are grouped into coreference classes based on grammatical, semantic, and salience properties.

On its own the NLU module is a large-coverage system which can tag, shallow parse and resolve pronoun reference of any English sentence. Its coverage is most restricted by domain specific NE classes and IE patterns which must be introduced manually. The system covers more than 40 work-based topics of conversation, for example discussions of meetings, problems with office equipment, relationships with colleagues and even the weather. These are mostly represented as event objects. Complex objects such as these are created by a set of IE rules which attempt to cover a range of syntactic and semantic structures which denote identical content. In addition to event objects, the system covers objects of various NE types that relate to the events. For example, to refer to persons, the system may have to collect their names, gender and profession, organisation they work for, their colleagues and the location where they live. In contrast to events, these objects mostly rely on recognition of NE classes.

The final output from the NLU in the format expected by the DM for the utterance "John will move to the Madrid office next month" is shown on the right of Figure 3.

3.4 Dialogue Management

The DM is based on work described in Boye and Gustafson [13], Boye et al [14] and Boye [15] but has been substantially modified for the challenges of conversational dialogue. It receives user utterances from the NLU as semantic representations (right of Figure 3). The DM first checks which information addresses the previous question or comment posed by the system in the dialogue and which information opens up new topics. The information constituting answers to system questions is integrated into the information state of the DM (called the Object Store), while new topics give rise to new conversational goals.

The DM keeps track of all the topics under discussion by maintaining a set of conversational goals, e.g. (1) "Find out more about the possible office relocation to Madrid", or (2) "Make a comment about today's meeting". A number of goal-satisfaction rules (similar to the one on the left of Figure 4) specify how goals are broken down into sequences of sub-goals and system utterances. For instance, finding out more about the office relocation (1) might amount to asking specific questions about whether the relocation will indeed take place, what the consequences would be for the user, etc. The goal is considered satisfied when further information about the relocation has been collected.

The various possible topics of conversation are organised as in an ontology, so that it is known what attributes can be expected to be present for a particular object. For example, the value of the "effect" attribute of the event object must be another object of type "event". Again this is reminiscent of Information Extraction, and the DM is in

```
satisfy (systemKnowsAbout($x,event))
  {
    holds valueOf($x,nature,move_office);
    holds valueOf($x,temporal_reference,future);
    satisfy systemKnowsValueOf($x,event,likelihood);
    satisfy systemKnowsValueOf($x,event,effect);
    assert systemKnowsAbout($x,event);
  }
```

```
agenda [1]
  systemKnowsAbout(o2,event) [1.4]
    holds valueOf(o2,nature,move_office) [1.4.41]
    holds valueOf(o2,temporal_reference,future) [1.4.42]
    systemKnowsValueOf(o2,event,likelihood) [1.4.43]
      perform qw(o2,event,likelihood) [1.4.43.11]
    systemKnowsValueOf(o2,event,effect) [1.4.44]
    assert systemKnowsAbout(o2,event) [1.4.45]
  systemKnowsAbout(o3,loc) [1.3]
  systemKnowsAbout(o4,person) [1.2]
    holds valueOf(o4,number,sing) [1.2.11]
    (---)
    systemKnowsValueOf(o4,person,profession) [1.2.13]
      perform qw(o4,person,profession) [1.2.13.11]  ◄—
    assert systemKnowsAbout(o4,person) [1.2.14]
    (---)
```

Fig. 4. Goal Satisfaction Rule (*left*) and Agenda (*right*) used by the DM

effect aiming to fill a template via clarification and supplementary questions (satisfy systemKnowsValueOf($x,event,effect)) to the point where it can be passed to the Affective Strategy Module.

The active goals are organised in a tree-structure, the so-called agenda, as shown on the right of Figure 4. At any given point in time, the agenda might contain many topics, some old, some new (systemKnowsAbout(o2,event)), some completed (---), some still open for discussion, and some not yet addressed by the system (system-KnowsValueOf(o2,event,likelihood). For each turn of the clarification dialogue, the DM chooses which topic to pursue next by considering all the currently un-satisfied goals on the agenda and heuristically rating them for importance. The heuristics employed use factors such as recency in the dialogue history, general importance, and emotional value associated with the goal. In the example in Figure 4, the system considered it more important to find out about the person (o4 or "John") than to find out about the event that the person is a participant of (o2 or "move_office"))[1].

When sufficient information has been gathered from the user through the clarification dialogue, the DM will invoke the Affective Strategy Module so it can generate a suitable tirade. The DM makes the decision to invoke the ASM using heuristics that take into account, amongst other things, the emotional value of the user's utterances and the recency of the latest ASM invocation[2].

3.5 Affective Dialogue Strategies

Previous dialogue systems [16] [17] have resorted to different models as a basis for influencing user behaviour, such as the Transtheoretical Model [18]. However, in our current scenario we are more interested in changes in attitudes rather than behaviour [19]. In presenting a response to the user then, it is first necessary to understand, or appraise, the situation that the user presents to the Companion. This involves gaining an understanding of the events described and how these will affect the user. Further, the user's reaction to these events is also crucial in generating an appropriate tirade. The Affective Strategy Module (ASM) centres its response on a main event, generally the focal event selected by the DM, and its consequences for the user.

---

[1] We are currently exploring the use of reinforcement learning with a reward function based on the emotional value of the user utterance to choose goals in a more natural way.

[2] This decision could also involve reinforcement learning.

An appraisal process determines the nature of the main event in terms of both its impact on the user and the appropriateness of the user's reaction. The impact depends on whether the event constitutes an improvement (`promotion`, `payrise`) or a deterioration (`office-move`, `redundancy`, `increased-workload`) to the user's situation. This is determined by using the NLU information to instantiate an event template which indicates both the event type (e.g. improvement) and anticipated outcome based on what the event is and the information available. Every possible NLU event has its own event template within the ASM and default knowledge is used to instantiate these templates where information is not available from the NLU.

Next, the user's mood, provided by the Emotional Model, is used to determine whether the user is showing an appropriate or inappropriate emotional reaction to the event, given the anticipated outcome. This is essentially whether the user is reacting positively to improvements and negatively to deteriorations.

These details are then used to determine the strategy employed by the Companion. These strategies have been selected such that they cover the full range of possible situations a user can be in: a congratulatory strategy for when things are going well for the user, a sympathetic strategy for when they are not, encouraging or reassuring strategies for when the user's outlook is too negative and warning or cautionary strategies for when the user's outlook is too positive. The appraisal process also analyses additional influences, be they positive or negative, for the events at hand. These will be used to enrich the Companion's tirade, giving a more precise content to reassurance or warning statements.

In common with both narrative generation [20] and text generation [21], the ASM is based on planning technologies, more specifically a Hierarchical Task Network (HTN) planner [22], which works through recursive decomposition of a high level task into sub-tasks until a plan of sub-tasks that can be directly executed is produced. The HTN planning process uses the information from the event templates along with results from the appraisal as heuristics to guide its decomposition. Combined with the fact that this heuristic selection process occurs at multiple levels of the HTN, it allows for greater complexity and variance than is achievable with a scripted approach.

The resulting plan of operators provides a set of communicative functions, each targeting different aspects of the user's utterance but unified under the overall affective strategy. For instance, various operators can emphasise or play down the event consequences or comment on additional factors that may affect the course of events. The planner uses a set of 40 operators, each with multiple parameters. Overall this supports the seamless generation of hundreds of significantly different influencing strategies from the base set of influence operators.

This plan is passed to the NLG module where each operator is realised as a sentence forming part of the overall narrative utterance. The operators contain information supporting an FML-like language [23] which allows full multimodal output comprising affective TTS, gestures and facial expressions.

Figure 5 illustrates the operation of the ASM on an excerpt from an actual dialogue. The Companion first instantiates some basic information (a "bad day" event and discussion of "office politics") from the first user utterance. However, this is not enough to meet the threshold for generating an affective tirade so the DM triggers a clarification step ("tell me more ..."), which actually prompts a longer and more detailed reply from the user. From this reply the system is able to instantiate further

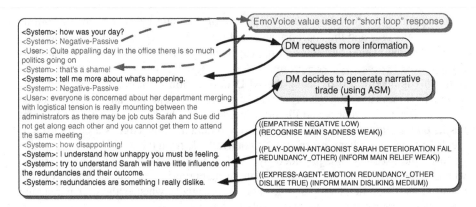

Fig. 5. An example dialogue where the user[3] discusses a negative situation and shows a correspondingly negative emotional state. Yet the Companion detects this is just a potentially bad situation and employs a reassuring affective strategy.

event templates, one about company restructuring, one about redundancies and one about relationships between colleagues, with the DM determining that the redundancies event template is the most prominent event. The ASM then appraises this main event, determining (from the instantiated event template) that the redundancies have not yet happened, and opting to perform a reassuring strategy. The ASM then generates a plan which shows different levels of empathy (one generic and one specific, mentioning the threat of redundancy), but also dissociates the two incidents by reminding the user that antagonistic colleagues will have no influence on redundancy decisions (this is achieved by looking for factors potentially influencing the key event, here company restructuring).

3.6 Handling Interruptions

Conversational flow in natural dialogues tends to be quite fluid, with partners frequently interrupting each other rather than observing the strict turn-by-turn structure of most current spoken language dialogue systems. Further, the generation of long, multi-sentence utterances by the ASM creates opportunities for the user to interrupt the Companion whilst it is speaking. Indeed, the long ASM utterances may even provoke a user interruption given that they often include advice on dealing with difficult or stressful situations the user has experienced. To resolve this, our Companion includes interaction strategies for dealing with both "barge-in" interruptions and "non-barge-in" interruptions. When a user starts talking at the same time as the Companion, interrupting the Companion's reply, this is classed as a "barge-in" interruption. We now describe the handling process (see also Figure 2).

(1) As the user may speak at any time, the Acoustic Turn Taking module must decide whether this constitutes a 'genuine' user interruption (as opposed to, say, backchannel). This decision is based on both the intensity and duration of the voice signal with the Interruption Manager being informed when an interruption is detected.

---

[3] Note that user utterances show the result recognised by ASR, hence the inclusion of speech recognition errors.

(2) The IM then requests that the ECA stop speaking and be given a look of surprise or irritation at being interrupted before broadcasting a notification of the interruption to all modules so they know the previous turn was not completed.

(3) The DM determines how much of the ASM response was completed.

(4) The ATT informs the IM when the interruption has ended. The IM then tracks the processing of the interrupting utterance through the system using a System State Model implemented as a two-level Finite State Machine [24]. Tracking the processing is necessary to ensure that the Companion responds within a realistic time frame.

(5) When triggered the DM must decide how to respond to that interruption.

(5a) The DM would choose to continue the interrupted utterance if the user's utterance does not provide any new information. For example, if the interrupting utterance was "I couldn't agree with you more", then it would be reasonable for the DM to decide to continue the Companion's planned utterances from the point where the interruption took place. In Figure 6 the user interrupts the tirade in Figure 5 causing the system to stop the tirade and process the interruption. After the short loop response, the DM determines that it is not necessary to revise information and so will just 'continue', acknowledging the interruption and resuming the tirade from the point of interruption (that is, repeating the interrupted utterance).

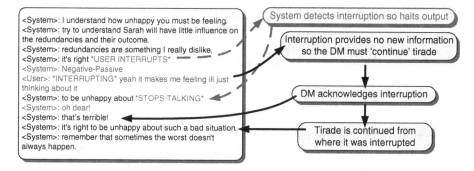

Fig. 6. An example dialogue where the user interrupts without providing new information. The Companion responds with 'continue' interrupt handling.

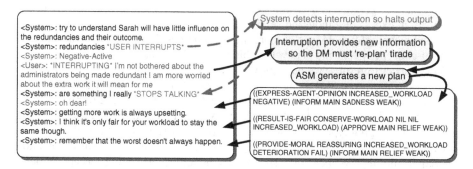

Fig. 7. An example dialogue where the user interrupts the Companion with new information. The Companion responds with 're-plan' interrupt handling.

(5b) The DM would choose to re-plan if the user's utterance provides new information. This would be the case, for example, if the user's interrupting utterance corrected what the system had just said. The re-plan is necessary because the current ASM plan was generated from a set of assumptions which have now been shown to be false or incomplete. In Figure 7 the user also interrupts the tirade in Figure 5. This time, after the short loop response, the DM determines that it is necessary to 're-plan'. The user interruption is understood as correcting the main topic to that of an increased workload for the user rather than discussion of redundancies. The tirade is then re-generated using this new main topic (with the strategy remaining reassuring). Note that it is not necessary to generate a full tirade for this new topic, as we have already relayed about half of the previous tirade, so we generate an equivalent to the remaining amount for the new tirade.

(5c) The DM chooses to abort if the user's utterance rejects the current dialogue strategy. An abort would be necessary if the interrupting utterance was something like "Don't talk to me about work, I'm not in the mood". An abort would discontinue the conversation until the user chose to continue by providing another utterance.

Handling "non-barge-in" interruptions is more straightforward as the user interrupts before the Companion has initiated its reply. The "non-barge-in" interruption can be summarised as follows:

1. The ATT detects an interrupt and informs the IM
2. The IM informs the affective dialogue processing modules
3. Affective dialogue processing modules disregard the current turn
4. The DM continues, incorporating the previous turn into the next.

4 Conclusion and Results

We have presented a fully-implemented prototype of an ECA supporting affective dialogue under a truly conversational paradigm, which allows longer utterances both from the user and the agent, mixed-initiative as well as user interruptions. We conclude that our approach to the integration of conversational and affective aspects rests with the definition of interaction loops, all under the control of a top-level Dialogue Manager, orchestrating elementary dialogue steps (e.g. clarification), narrative utterances for advice giving and user interruptions. The system has been extensively tested in the lab, in excess of a thousand sessions, and has demonstrated a regular ability to withstand meaningful dialogues of more than 10 minutes. It has reached maturity as a proof-of-concept system and is now the object of public demonstrations [25].

With respect to results, we have previously presented a validation of the affective output of our prototype [26] along with a more in-depth discussion of the generation of affective strategies, which has shown the affective content of ECA responses to be linguistically adequate in over 80% of cases. We continue to expand the linguistic coverage of our prototype and now seek to carry out extensive user evaluations involving prolonged use of the system. Such a systematic evaluation of our Companion will require the development of a specific methodology measuring the appropriateness of the ECA's responses locally as well as over the whole dialogue.

Acknowledgments. This work was funded by the Companions project (http://www.companions-project.org) sponsored by the European Commission as part of the Information Society Technologies (IST) programme under EC grant number IST-FP6-034434. The EmoVoice system has been used courtesy of the Multimedia Concepts and Applications Group of the University of Augsburg.

Other contributors to the prototype described in this paper from the COMPANIONS consortium include: Wei Wei Cheng, Morena Danieli, Carlos Sanchez Fernandez, Debora Field, Mari Carmen Rodriguez Gancedo, Jose Relano Gil, Ramon Granell, Jaakko Hakulinen, Sue Harding, Topi Hurtig, Oli Mival, Roger Moore, Lei Ye and Enrico Zovato.

References

1. Heylen, D., Vissers, M., op den Akker, R., Nijholt, A.: Affective feedback in a tutoring system for procedural tasks. In: André, E., Dybkjær, L., Minker, W., Heisterkamp, P. (eds.) ADS 2004. LNCS (LNAI), vol. 3068, pp. 244–253. Springer, Heidelberg (2004)
2. Englemore, R., Morgan, T.: Blackboard Systems. Addison-Wesley, Reading (1988)
3. Vogt, T., André, E., Bee, N.: EmoVoice – A framework for online recognition of emotions from voice. In: André, E., Dybkjær, L., Minker, W., Neumann, H., Pieraccini, R., Weber, M. (eds.) PIT 2008. LNCS (LNAI), vol. 5078, pp. 188–199. Springer, Heidelberg (2008)
4. Moilanen, K., Pulman, S.: Sentiment Composition. In: Proceedings of the Recent Advances in Natural Language Processing International Conference (RANLP 2007), Borovets, pp. 378–382 (2007)
5. Bickmore, T., Cassell, J.: Small Talk and Conversational Storytelling in Embodied Interface Agents. In: Proceedings of the AAAI Fall Symposium on Narrative Intelligence, Cape Cod, MA, pp. 87–92 (1999)
6. De Angeli, A., Brahnam, S.: I hate you! Disinhibition with virtual partners. Interacting with Computers 20(3), 302–310 (2008)
7. Morency, L.-P., de Kok, I., Gratch, J.: Predicting listener backchannels: A probabilistic multimodal approach. In: Prendinger, H., Lester, J.C., Ishizuka, M. (eds.) IVA 2008. LNCS (LNAI), vol. 5208, pp. 176–190. Springer, Heidelberg (2008)
8. Kopp, S., Stocksmeier, T., Gibbon, D.: Incremental multimodal feedback for conversational agents. In: Pelachaud, C., Martin, J.-C., André, E., Chollet, G., Karpouzis, K., Pelé, D. (eds.) IVA 2007. LNCS (LNAI), vol. 4722, pp. 139–146. Springer, Heidelberg (2007)
9. Bevacqua, E., Mancini, M., Pelachaud, C.: A listening agent exhibiting variable behaviour. In: Prendinger, H., Lester, J.C., Ishizuka, M. (eds.) IVA 2008. LNCS (LNAI), vol. 5208, pp. 262–269. Springer, Heidelberg (2008)
10. Grishman, R.: Information Extraction: Techniques and Challenges. In: Pazienza, M.T. (ed.) SCIE 1997. LNCS (LNAI), vol. 1299, pp. 10–27. Springer, Heidelberg (1997)
11. Jönsson, A., Andén, F., Degerstedt, L., Flycht-Eriksson, A., Merkel, M., Norberg, S.: Experiences from combining dialogue system development with information extraction techniques. In: Maybury, M.T. (ed.) New Directions in Question Answering. AAAI/MIT Press (2004)
12. Kennedy, C., Boguraev, B.: Anaphora for everyone: Pronominal anaphora resolution without a parser. In: Proceedings of COLING 1996, ACL, Copenhagen, pp. 113–118 (1996)
13. Boye, J., Gustafson, J.: How to do dialogue in a fairy-tale world. In: Proceedings of the 6th SIGDial workshop on discourse and dialogue, Lisbon, Portugal (2005)

14. Boye, J., Gustafson, J., Wirén, M.: Robust spoken language understanding in a computer game. Journal of Speech Communication 48, 335–353 (2006)
15. Boye, J.: Dialogue management for automatic troubleshooting and other problem-solving applications. In: Proceedings of the 8th SIGDial workshop on discourse and dialogue, Antwerp, Belgium (2007)
16. Cavalluzzi, A., Carofiglio, V., de Rosis, F.: Affective Advice Giving Dialogs. In: André, E., Dybkjær, L., Minker, W., Heisterkamp, P. (eds.) ADS 2004. LNCS (LNAI), vol. 3068, pp. 77–88. Springer, Heidelberg (2004)
17. Bickmore, T., Sidner, C.L.: Towards Plan-based Health Behavior Change Counseling Systems. In: Proceedings of AAAI Spring Symposium on Argumentation for Consumers of Healthcare, Stanford, CA (2006)
18. Prochaska, J., Di Clemente, C., Norcross, H.: In search of how people change: applications to addictive behavior. American Psychologist 47, 1102–1114 (1992)
19. Tørning, K., Oinas-Kukkonen, H.: Persuasive system design: state of the art and future directions. In: Proceedings of PERSUASIVE 2009, New York, NY, USA, vol. 350 (2009)
20. Cavazza, M., Charles, F., Mead, S.J.: Character-Based Interactive Storytelling. IEEE Intelligent Systems 17(4), 17–24 (2002)
21. Appelt, D.E.: Planning English sentences. Cambridge University Press, Cambridge (1985)
22. Nau, D., Ghallab, M., Traverso, P.: Automated Planning: Theory & Practice. Morgan Kaufmann Publishers Inc., San Francisco (2004)
23. Hernández, A., López, B., Pardo, D., Santos, R., Hernández, L., Relaño Gil, J., Rodríguez, M.C.: Modular definition of multimodal ECA communication acts to improve dialogue robustness and depth of intention. In: Heylen, D., Kopp, S., Marsella, S., Pelachaud, C., Vilhjálmsson, H. (eds.) AAMAS 2008 Workshop on Functional Markup Language (2008)
24. Crook, N., Smith, C., Cavazza, M., Pulman, S., Moore, R., Boye, J.: Handling User Interruptions in an Embodied Conversational Agent. In: Proceedings of the AAMAS International Workshop on Interacting with ECAs as Virtual Characters, Toronto, pp. 27–33 (2010)
25. Cavazza, M., Santos de la Camara, R., Turunen, M.: The Companions consortium.: How was your day? A Companion ECA. In: Proceedings of AAMAS 2010, accepted for publication (demonstration paper), Toronto (2010)
26. Cavazza, M., Smith, C., Charlton, D., Crook, N., Boye, J., Pulman, S., Moilanen, K., Pizzi, D., Santos de la Camara, R., Turunen, M.: Persuasive Dialogue based on a Narrative Theory: an ECA Implementation. In: Proceedings of PERSUASIVE 2010, Copenhagen (2010)

"Why Can't We Be Friends?" An Empathic Game Companion for Long-Term Interaction

Iolanda Leite, Samuel Mascarenhas, André Pereira, Carlos Martinho,
Rui Prada, and Ana Paiva

INESC-ID and Instituto Superior Técnico
Av. Prof. Cavaco Silva, Taguspark 2744-016, Porto Salvo, Portugal
{iolanda.leite,samuel.mascarenhas,andre.pereira}@inesc-id.pt,
{carlos.martinho,rui.prada,ana.paiva}@inesc-id.pt

Abstract. The ability of artificial companions (virtual agents or robots) to establish meaningful relationships with users is still limited. In humans, a key aspect of such ability is empathy, often seen as the basis of social cooperation and pro-social behaviour. In this paper, we present a study where a social robot with empathic capabilities interacts with two users playing a chess game against each other. During the game, the agent behaves in an empathic manner towards one of the players and in a neutral way towards the other. In an experiment conducted with 40 participants, results showed that users to whom the robot was empathic provided higher ratings in terms of companionship.

Keywords: affective interaction, companionship, empathy, friendship.

1 Introduction

To develop artificial agents capable of building long-term social relationships with users, we need to model the complex social dynamics present in human behaviour. We argue that one of such social requirements is empathy. Previous research has shown that empathic agents are perceived as more caring, likeable and trustworthy than agents without empathic capabilities [3,11]. Empathy involves perspective taking, the understanding of nonverbal cues, sensitivity to the other's affective state and communication of a feeling of care [7]. As such, empathy is often related to helping behaviour and friendship: people tend to feel more empathy for friends than for strangers.

The main objective of this paper is to investigate people's perceptions of a companion agent with empathic behaviour, more specifically in terms of the possible relation of companionship established between them. To do so, we developed a scenario where a social robot observes a chess match played between two humans and reacts empathetically by commenting the game and disclosing its affective state. The results of a study conducted in this scenario indicate that subjects interacting with the empathic version of the robot considered it more as a "companion" than subjects interacting with a neutral version of the agent.

J. Allbeck et al. (Eds.): IVA 2010, LNAI 6356, pp. 315–321, 2010.

2   Related Work

The idea of using empathy as a way to establish and maintain social relations between users and agents was first addressed by Bickmore and Picard [2]. They developed Laura, a relational virtual agent that plays the role of an exercise advisor. Among other relational strategies, Laura uses empathic dialogue. After four weeks of daily interaction with the agent, the relational behaviours increased user's perceptions of the quality of the working alliance on measures such as liking, trust and respect.

Some researchers have also been studying the effect of empathic agents in game scenarios. Brave *et al.* [3] concluded that empathic agents in a blackjack game were perceived as more caring, likeable and trustworthy than agents without empathic capabilities, and that people feel more supported in the presence of such agents. More recently, other researchers extended these results [10], arguing that empathic agents can improve user's attention and willingness to interact with a system. Moreover, human-like agents without empathic capabilities can lead to a negative user experience due to the expectations that users may create while interacting with such agents.

In the field of social robotics, significant research has been pursued in one particular aspect of empathy - emotional contagion - where the user's affective state is mimicked [12]. One of the plausible reasons for this is that only recently the first working prototypes of automatic affect recognition using speech and vision started to appear [8], while in the field of virtual agents these problems have been surpassed, for example, by predicting the user's affective state using task related features or predefined dialogues [5].

3   Modelling an Empathic Game Companion

Although no precise definition of the internal processes of empathy exists so far, most researchers agree that empathy can be divided in two stages: (1) inferring the state of others and (2) responding emotionally to those states. These stages are also the basis of our empathy model, implemented in the Philip's iCat robot. The robot acts as an empathic game companion during a chess match played on an electronic chessboard between two human players (see Fig. 1) and treats the two players differently: empathises with one of them - the *companion*, and behaves in a neutral way towards the other player - the *opponent*. This scenario is a follow-up work from the scenario described in [9], where the iCat plays chess against a human opponent.

3.1   Inferring the User's Affective State

The iCat uses role-taking to perceive the companion's affective state. This means that when a new move is played on the chessboard by one of the players, the iCat evaluates the new board position using a chess heuristic function in the perspective of its companion. This function returns positive scores if the companion is in advantage (higher values indicate more advantage), and negative scores if the companion is in disadvantage. The evaluation is then used by the iCat's own emotional system, based on the *emotivector* anticipatory mechanism, which associates one of nine possible affective states to the move played on the chessboard. For more details on the *emotivector* system and its implementation in the iCat please consult [9].

An important motivation for using this form of emotion recognition comes from a previous study [4], where it was showed that, in the particular context of a chess game, the game state is relevant to discriminate the valence (positive or negative) of the user's affective state. We are aware that the agent may have a different perspective of the game from the user which may lead to wrong interpretations. Yet, the same can also happen with humans.

3.2 Behaving in an Empathic Manner

To define how the agent would act in an empathic manner towards its companion and in a neutral way towards the opponent, the agent's behaviour was based in characteristics of empathic teachers described in [6], such as body-language, voice, attitudes, facial characteristics or verbal responses. Given the limitations of the scenario, only differences in the facial characteristics and verbal responses were modelled.

Facial Characteristics. One important behaviour of empathic teachers is that they constantly reflect the student's emotions in their facial expressions. Similarly, our empathic agent always expresses its affective state using a proper facial expression that reflects the companion's situation in the game. As an example, if the opponent plays a good move and captures one of the companion's pieces, the iCat expresses a sad expression as a result of its empathy towards the companion who has lost advantage.

Aside from constantly expressing their emotional states, another facial characteristic of empathic teachers is that they tend to use lots of eye-contact. This characteristic was also modelled in our agent: while players are thinking on their next moves, the iCat looks two times more to the companion than it does to the opponent.

Verbal Responses. After exhibiting a facial expression, the iCat makes a comment on the move just played. The comments not only depend on the iCat's empathic state, but also if the user who just played is the iCat's companion or the opponent. Inspired on the characteristics of empathic teachers, two sets of utterances for each affective state of the iCat were defined: "empathic" utterances, to be used when the iCat is commenting the companion's moves, and "neutral" utterances, to be used when the robot is commenting on the opponent's moves. While neutral utterances merely indicate the quality of the move in a very direct way (e.g., "bad move", "well done", ...), empathic utterances often contain references to possible companion's emotions (e.g., "don't be sad, you didn't had better options"), and try to encourage and motivate the companion (e.g., "you're doing great, carry on!").

Furthermore, the iCat also congratulates the companion when she/he captures a piece and also encourages the companion in critical moments of the game, whether he/she is gaining a large advantage or disadvantage (for example, when the chances of winning become evident).

4   Experiment

The hypothesis of this experiment is that subjects to whom the iCat behaved in an empathic manner perceive the robot more as a "friend" than subjects to whom the iCat behaved in a neutral way.

4.1   Procedure

Forty subjects, 36 male and 4 female, with ages ranging from 18 and 28 years old, took part in the experiment. All of them were undergraduate or graduated students and were recruited via email. The selected participants obeyed two requirements: they knew the basic rules of chess and had never interacted with the iCat before.

During the experiment, participants sat in front of each other in a table that held both the electronic chessboard and the iCat as depicted in Fig. 1. They were instructed to play an entire chess game against each other, and while doing so to pay attention to the iCat's behaviour, as they were going to be questioned about it at the end of the game. On average, each game took one hour.

At the end of the game, participants were guided to another room where they filled a questionnaire. After filling the questionnaire, they were rewarded with a movie ticket and the experiment was over.

4.2   Manipulation

There were two different conditions regarding the iCat's behaviour, *empathic* and *neutral*, according to the behaviours described in the previous section. The iCat

Fig. 1. Users interacting with the iCat

behaved in an *empathic* way towards subjects playing with the black pieces, and in a *neutral* way towards subjects playing with the white pieces, which means that we have 20 subjects in each condition. There was no criteria for assigning the participants to the different conditions. At the beginning of the game, participants could chose the side of the board where they prefer to sit down and they were not aware that the iCat's behaviour was going to be different.

4.3   Measures

To evaluate the different attitudes of the subjects towards the iCat, we employed McGill Friendship Questionnaire (MFQ) [1], which measures the degree to which a friend fulfils the following six functions: (1) *stimulating companionship* - doing enjoyable or exciting things together; (2) *help* - providing guidance and other forms of aid; (3) *intimacy* - being sensitive to the other's needs and states and being open to honest expressions of thoughts, feelings and personal information; (4) *reliable alliance* - remaining available and loyal; (5) *self-validation* - reassuring, encouraging, and otherwise helping the other maintain a positive self- image; (6) *emotional security* - providing comfort and confidence in novel or threatening situations. The questionnaire contains a set of assertions for each one of the six functions, and participants express their agreement or disagreement about each assertion using a five-point Likert scale.

A version of the MFQ questionnaire validated to Portuguese was used [13]. Given that some of the assertions of MFQ were not applicable to the interaction experience that users had with the iCat, we replaced those by assertions obtained in an online survey. Sixteen subjects participated in this survey, and there was no overlap between these subjects and the ones who participated in the experiment. In this paper, the results of the Stimulating Companionship function of this questionnaire will be presented and discussed.

4.4   Results and Discussion

As we used a modified version of MFQ, we first performed a Cronbach alpha test to evaluate the internal consistency of the Stimulating Companionship function (reliable, α=.79). Outliers in our data were removed according to the following criteria: $1.5 * stdev$. Four outliers were identified in the *empathic* condition and five in the *neutral* condition.

After eliminating the outliers, we ran Mann-Whitney U test to compare the overall result of the Stimulating Companionship function. The overall result was calculated by the sum of the ratings for the corresponding assertions in the questionnaire. Subjects in the empathic condition significantly gave higher ratings in this function than subjects in the neutral condition ($U = 72.5$, $p < 0.05$, $z = -1.893$). Figure 2 contains the mean values of each one of the assertions of the questionnaire that belong to this function. The chart shows that participants in the empathic condition rated each assertion higher than subjects in the neutral condition. However, this was only significant for the third question, "iCat behaved as my companion during the game" ($U = 69$, $p < 0.05$, $z = -2.239$). Given

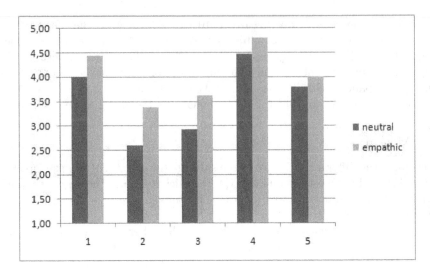

Fig. 2. Mean values for each assertion of the Stimulating Companionship function: (1) I had fun playing with iCat by my side; (2) I enjoyed talking to iCat; (3) iCat behaved as my companion during the game; (4) iCat made me laugh; (5) It was nice being with iCat.

that this function is about spending time doing things together, these results suggest that subjects prefer to interact with empathic agents. As they consider the interaction more enjoyable, they may eventually spend more time interacting with the agents, which is important if we aim to build artificial companions capable of engaging users in the long term.

5   Conclusions

This paper explored users' perceived companionship towards a social robot that displays empathic behaviours. We argued that if an agent behaves in an empathic manner, users could more easily establish a relationship with it. An experiment involving forty subjects was conducted to evaluate this hypothesis. Participants interacting with the empathic version of the robot gave significant higher ratings in terms of stimulating companionship. In the future, we intend to analyse the results of the other functions of the friendship questionnaire, in the attempt to understand which functions are more determinant for the robot to establish a friendship relationship with the user.

Acknowledgements. The research leading to these results has received funding from European Community's Seventh Framework Program (FP7/2007-2013) under grant agreement n° 215554, FCT (INESC-ID multiannual funding) through the PIDDAC Program funds, and 3 scholarships (SFRHBD/41358/2007, SFRH/BD/41585/2007, SFRHBD/62174/2009) granted by FCT.

References

1. Measuring friendship quality in late adolescents and young adults: Mcgill friendship questionnaires. Canadian Journal of Behavioural Science 31(1), 130–132 (1999)
2. Bickmore, T., Picard, R.: Establishing and maintaining long-term human-computer relationships. ACM Transactions on Computer-Human Interaction (TOCHI) 12(2), 327 (2005)
3. Brave, S., Nass, C., Hutchinson, K.: Computers that care: investigating the effects of orientation of emotion exhibited by an embodied computer agent. Int. J. Hum. Comput. Stud. 62(2), 161–178 (2005)
4. Castellano, G., Leite, I., Pereira, A., Martinho, C., Paiva, A., McOwan, P.: It's all in the game: Towards an affect sensitive and context aware game companion, pp. 1 –8 (September 2009)
5. Conati, C., Maclaren, H.: Empirically building and evaluating a probabilistic model of user affect. User Model. User-Adapt. Interact. 19(3), 267–303 (2009)
6. Cooper, B., Brna, P., Martins, A.: Effective affective in intelligent systems - building on evidence of empathy in teaching and learning. In: Paiva, A.C.R. (ed.) IWAI 1999. LNCS, vol. 1814, pp. 21–34. Springer, Heidelberg (2000)
7. Goldstein, A.P., Michaels, G.Y.: Empathy: development, training, and consequences. In: Goldstein, A.P., Michaels, G.Y. (eds.) New American Library (1985)
8. Kapoor, A., Burleson, W., Picard, R.W.: Automatic prediction of frustration. International Journal of Human-Computer Studies 65(8), 724–736 (2007)
9. Leite, I., Martinho, C., Pereira, A., Paiva, A.: icat: an affective game buddy based on anticipatory mechanisms. In: Padgham, L., Parkes, D.C., Müller, J., Parsons, S. (eds.) AAMAS (3), pp. 1229–1232. IFAAMAS (2008)
10. Nguyen, H., Masthoff, J.: Designing empathic computers: the effect of multimodal empathic feedback using animated agent. In: Chatterjee, S., Dev, P. (eds.) PERSUASIVE. ACM International Conference Proceeding Series, vol. 350, p. 7. ACM Press, New York (2009)
11. Paiva, A., Dias, J., Sobral, D., Aylett, R., Sobreperez, P., Woods, S., Zoll, C., Hall, L.E.: Caring for agents and agents that care: Building empathic relations with synthetic agents. In: AAMAS, pp. 194–201. IEEE Computer Society Press, Los Alamitos (2004)
12. Riek, L.D., Paul, P.C., Robinson, P.: When my robot smiles at me: Enabling human-robot rapport via real-time head gesture mimicry. Journal on Multimodal User Interfaces 3(1-2), 99–108 (2010)
13. Souza, L.K.: Amizade em adultos: adaptação e validação dos questionários McGill e um estudo de diferenças de género. PhD thesis, Universidade Federal do Rio Grande do Sul (2006)

Towards an Episodic Memory for Companion Dialogue

Gregor Sieber and Brigitte Krenn

Austrian Research Institute for Artificial Intelligence
Freyung 6/6, 1010 Vienna, Austria
http://www.ofai.at

Abstract. We present an episodic memory component for enhancing
the dialogue of artificial companions with the capability to refer to, take
up and comment on past interactions with the user, and to take into
account in the dialogue long-term user preferences and interests. The
proposed episodic memory is based on RDF representations of the agent's
experiences and is linked to the agent's semantic memory containing the
agent's knowledge base of ontological data and information about the
interests of the user.

Keywords: dimensions of intelligence, cognition and behavior; autobiographic episodic memory; relating memory and dialogue.

1   Introduction

Recently, research on artificial companions has come more and more in focus.
They are artificial agents (virtual or robotic) that are intended to support the
human user in aspects of everyday life. Application areas may range from virtual
agents that assist their users in accessing information from the Internet in accordance with the users' interests, preferences and needs , up to assistive robots
in home environments that support the elderly in mastering their life at home.

As regards the dialogue capabilities of companions, approaches are required
that allow the agent's mental models and memories to be connected to its expressive behaviour [3], and where natural language dialogue is semantically grounded
[1]. Companions need to be aware of their own history and past interactions with
their individual users, so that the single user can believe that her/his companion
knows "what it is talking about". This is particularly important for creating
acceptable long–term interactions.

To account for this kind of requirements, we propose a communication component for companions where autobiographic episodic memory, semantic memory
and dialogue are closely connected.

2   Related Work

Episodic memory (EM) has first been distinguished from other memory types
by [9]. Implementations have e.g. been used in artificial life agents [7], in storytelling agents [5], and for non-player characters in games [2]. Since our memory

J. Allbeck et al. (Eds.): IVA 2010, LNAI 6356, pp. 322–328, 2010.

component is realized as an RDF graph, neither nearest–neighbour search nor retrieval by keywords directly apply. The Adaptive Mind Agent by [6] and Gossip Galore [10] describe companion systems able to answer questions on domain data encoded in RDF. Both agents only have limited knowledge of their own past and do not use it for dialogue. Thus they cannot ground dialogue in their own experiences, and are unable to employ knowledge about user preferences for providing more interesting dialogue. [4] describe a companion system for helping users plan a healthier lifestyle. Dialogue is driven by a daily exercise plan. Our system aims at a more open kind of dialogue which does not revolve around a plan model. This leaves the companion in a situation where much less expectations can be made towards the next user utterance.

In the remainder of this contribution, we will concentrate on the interplay between episodic memory and dialogue. In particular, we describe how the episodic memory is represented, how episodes are retrieved (Sec. 3.1), and how episodic memory is used in the dialogue manager (Sec. 4). For an account of how natural language output is generated from memory content, see [8].

3   Episodic Memory

An episodic memory component for companion dialogue needs to provide adequate knowledge representation in connection with the cognitive model and the tasks of the agent. RDF-based[1] data stores are widely used for representing domain knowledge as well as common sense knowledge (e.g. the Open Mind Common Sense Database[2], or ConceptNet[3]). Accordingly, we have developed an episodic memory component for artificial companions that stores and operates on episodes as RDF graphs, and that is interfaced with the agent's semantic memory which must be also composed of RDF triples, making both memories interoperable. We employ a Sesame[4] repository for hosting the data stores.

Our implementation of episodic memory is realized using the Elmo[5] framework, which provides Java to RDF mapping and persistence. A persistence framework such as Elmo significantly reduces the amount of plain RDF data that needs to be generated and parsed within the application. The domain data stored within the episodes is independent of the memory implementation.

For episode retrieval, we propose three different mechanisms, each suited to a different function of episodic memory in our companion.

3.1   Episodes

Episodes store the time of their creation in epoch time, the actors involved in the episode, and an episode ID. Input episodes additionally store the user input

---

[1] http://www.w3.org/RDF/

[2] http://commons.media.mit.edu/en/

[3] http://conceptnet.media.mit.edu/

[4] http://www.openrdf.org/doc/sesame2/2.3.1/users/index.html

[5] http://www.openrdf.org/doc/elmo/1.5/

string and its analysis in the form of a set of triples, along with a label describing the function of the utterance, such as wh-question or assertion. The analysis of user input is composed of concepts, individuals and relations from the domain ontologies.

Action episodes are a subclass of episodes that represent the actions the agent is capable of. These are: AnswerQuestion: the agent uses domain knowledge to answer a user's question. AssertStatement: The companion attempts to assert user input using the domain knowledge. FindSimilar represents deliberate remembering, i.e. actively searching for similar situations. ExecuteModule: this action is stored when the companion uses one of the modules in the dialogue manager. RetrieveContext is generated when the companion retrieves data from a previous episode to add it to the current input, because it could not be processed otherwise. SendOutput can either convey the results of a query, results of remembering, or details about the situation of the agent, which encompasses e.g. reporting errors or the incapability to solve a certain problem.

Output episodes store the domain data sent to the user, and the name of the template used for output generation, if any.

Finally, evaluation episodes represent positive or negative feedback on previous actions. They are crucial for the agent to be able to learn from its past actions. If an evaluation is available, the agent can decide based on its memories whether a past solution should be repeated or not. Not all episodes have an evaluation. Evaluation values can either come from direct user feedback, internal feedback such as empty query results or failure to retrieve a query result, as well as from an emotional model integrated in the agent.

In order to be able to find the right associations and memories, the agent is capable of translating the time stored in the episodes into relative time categories such as morning, noon, afternoon, yesterday, and so on. This allows the agent to relate episodes to human–understandable fuzzy time categories when receiving input, but also when generating output.

As the retrieval of memories is bound to become inefficient once the episode store grows too big, we have implemented a forgetting mechanism. In our case, forgetting means deleting those episodes that have not been retrieved for a long time. This is similar to deleting the least activated memory, as described in [7]. This approach still bears some risk of losing important memories of situations that are rarely encountered. As an alternative, we consider a blending mechanism for combining redundant or similar information into one episode for our future work, and integrating a model of emotions which could help in deciding which episodes are more important than others.

The retrieval of episodes in our RDF–based model of EM is performed using queries on the RDF store that are able to use properties of episodes, the user model and the domain data, as well as the structural information of the data such as the class hierarchy. Since there are different applications of EM in our system, we present three different retrieval mechanisms: retrieval by similarity, retrieval using patterns in memory, and retrieval of parts of the context for resolution of references in the input.

Retrieval of similar episodes allows an agent to avoid past mistakes, to repeat successful strategies, and to connect and refer to past interactions. Input to retrieval by similarity consists of the set of triples representing the current situation, as stored in short–term memory. First, the memory is searched for identical episodes: a query is generated that searches for episodes that contain the same triples as the input. Additionally, queries using combinations and subsets of the instance set and the set of relations present in the user utterance are issued. For instance, given a popular music gossiping scenario, if the user asks a question about Michael Jackson and Janet Jackson, the agent searches its memory for previous episodes involving both artists, but also using the individual artists, in order to connect to and take up previous discussions. Further broadening the search, the structure of the domain data is used to generate queries containing the classes of the individuals in the utterance. The class hierarchy can be applied, as long as the class is in the domain of the property in the query. For example, talking about the birthday of an *Artist*, the companion can relate this input to episodes about birthdays involving its superclass *Person*, but not for episodes involving its superclass *Entity*, since the class *Entity* has no birthday property.

The episodes retrieved by the queries described above are ranked to retrieve the most similar episode. Ranking is performed by temporal distance and the number of overlapping properties, individuals and classes. Evaluations are found by searching the episodes temporally following each of the episodes until either an evaluation or the next user input is found in memory.

In addition to actively searching episodes identical or similar to the current situation, the companion has a second mode of retrieval that matches patterns in memory. This retrieval mode is used by the dialogue manager to generate output based on the content of episodic memory in combination with the user model, domain knowledge, and the current input.

As an example, some patterns allow the companion to talk about when a certain topic or individual was last discussed. Other patterns allow for detecting preferences of the user: for example, if a property – such as in our scenario, the birth place of an artist – appears very regularly in dialogue. Such preferences can also be extended to include specific values, such as a preference for artists born in New York City. Detection of preferences enables the companion to provide information more focused on the interests of the user. For example, the companion may comment on the fact that a preference is being discussed. Or, it may automatically add the kind of information covered by the preference to other answers, if appropriate. Continuing the example from above: a day after being asked about artists born in New York, the companion might notice while talking about the albums recorded by Billy Joel that he was also born in New York, and communicate it to the user. Alternatively, the companion can ask the user whether she would like to know about other individuals that share this property, and provide a list.

Finally, patterns can match data not encoded in the episodes, but in the agent's knowledge base. For example, consider a dialogue about artists that won certain prizes. If some of the last–mentioned artists share a property and its value with an artist included in the current input – such as being born in the same city – a pattern that looks for such properties matches, and the companion is able to provide this information to the user. How these patterns are utilized in the dialogue manager can be seen in Sec. 4.

Additionally, episodic memories are used by the agent to retrieve information necessary to understand utterances from the user that make reference to previous dialogue. Commonly this problem is addressed by maintaining different lists or stacks of entities and topics. In the following part we present an approach that requires no additional external storage mechanisms but relies on episodic memory. While this is by no means a complete resolution mechanism for anaphoric or elliptic expressions, it does show that it is possible to find candidates for such a mechanism using episodic memories. As an example, a method for resolving simple elliptic references in the type of dialogue encountered in our application scenario is described. For selection of candidates, we use the semantic structure of the utterances, i.e. their RDF representations.

Consider the following snippet of dialogue, where the agent would not be able to answer (3) without further inferences, since the information necessary for generating a query is missing from the input string:

(1) User: When was Charlie Parker born?

(2) Agent: Charlie Parker was born on August 29th 1920.

(3) User: And what about John Scofield?

The agent can extract from the user utterance that some information about the individual John Scofield is required, but not which information exactly. Using its episodic memories, the agent can retrieve the missing information from the context of the dialogue. With context we mean a set of recent episodes that are relevant to the current conversation. The actual number of episodes to consider is determined by a heuristic which selects up to a fixed number of episodes occurring within the previous and current time of day category (morning, noon, etc.).

Context retrieval is handled in the following way: First, the agent needs to determine whether or not a user utterance requires completion. The agent assumes an utterance to be complete if its analysis contains either one or more full triples, or a triple where one of the nodes is a variable. If a single individual or a single property is encountered, the agent needs to complete the utterance. Since a single individual is encountered in step (3) of the example dialogue, the agent has to complete the utterance. Thus from the input string, the agent only knows that the user has some question about John Scofield who is an artist. This artist could either be the subject, or the object of a statement. Thus for further interpretation of the utterance, the episodic memory is called for. The retrieval of the episode used for completion is done by evaluating a SeRQL query that searches for a) the last occurrence of the same class or superclass in case a property is missing (subject position), b) episodes containing a property whose rdfs:range covers the individual under discussion (object position). In our example, the agent looks for the most recent episode that contains the class of the individual (in this case, *Artist*), retrieves the co-occurring property and adds it to the representation of the current input in the agent's short-term memory.

In case no such episode is found within the context, the agent can generalize the query to a superclass of the individual. For example, John Scofield in (3) is an *Artist*, just like Charlie Parker in (1). However, if we substitute Salvador Allende in (1), the agent needs to look for their common superclass, *Person*, to be able to retrieve context information.

4   Dialogue Management

Our dialogue manager is a hybrid approach combining rule–based decision and a scoring approach on a set of modules that search memory and user preferences for relevant information. The rule–based system is used to cover situations such as replying to a greeting or feedback, and also for reporting about errors in the system (e.g. failing to connect to the knowledge base).

For each turn in dialogue the dialogue manager generates a set of modules that encode the kind of recency- and preference-driven patterns exemplified in Sec. 3.1. Modules are generated by inserting information from the user model into pre-fabricated queries. Each module has a unique ID and contains the labels of the templates to be used for generating output. The basic scores of modules are set depending on the complexity of the query and the importance of the user preference. Modules are executed in parallel, and those are discarded for which the query does not finish before a certain temporal threshold, in order to keep the response time limited. Penalties are applied to the modules that have successfully matched, one for each recent occurrence of the module, and one for each negative evaluation. The dialogue manager then executes the action contained in the module and sends the output to the user, possibly requiring feedback for further actions.

5   Conclusion

We have presented an RDF–based episodic memory component for enhancing dialogue with the user and grounding domain knowledge in interaction experiences. As a result of our model and implementation, the companion is not only able to retrieve situations similar to the current one from its memory. By searching for patterns in memory, it also can detect and comment on preferences of the user, and automatically provide information relevant to the user. In addition, we have shown how episodic memory can be used to find candidates for resolving references in dialogue necessary to understand the user's input.

Retrieval of episodes is accomplished by using a set of SeRQL queries. Our model shows how the contents of past interactions and their relation to current dialogue can be employed by a companion for selecting the next dialogue move and generating dialogue content. In addition, the connections between the episodic memory and the knowledge base by means of RDF graphs allow for a grounding of knowledge in the experiences of each agent.

Acknowledgments. The work presented is supported by the Austrian Ministry for Transport, Innovation and Technology (BMVIT) under the programme "FEMtech Women in Research and Technology" grant nr. 821855, project C4U. The Austrian Research Institute for Artificial Intelligence (OFAI) is supported by the Austrian ministries BMVIT and BMWF.

References

1. Benyon, D., Mival, O.: Scenarios for companions. In: Austrian Artificial Intelligence Workshop (2008)
2. Brom, C., Lukavsky, J.: Towards virtual characters with a full episodic memory ii: The episodic memory strikes back. In: Proc. Empathic Agents, AAMAS workshop, pp. 1–9 (2009)
3. Castellano, G., Aylett, R., Dautenhahn, K., Paiva, A., McOwan, P.W., Ho, S.: Long-Term Affect Sensitive and Socially Interactive Companions. In: Proceedings of the 4th International Workshop on Human-Computer Conversation (2008)
4. Cavazza, M., Smith, C., Charlton, D., Zhang, L., Turunen, M., Hakulinen, J.: A 'companion' ECA with planning and activity modelling. In: AAMAS 2008: Proceedings of the 7th international joint conference on Autonomous agents and multiagent systems, pp. 1281–1284 (2008)
5. Ho, W.C., Dautenhahn, K.: Towards a narrative mind: The creation of coherent life stories for believable virtual agents. In: Prendinger, H., Lester, J.C., Ishizuka, M. (eds.) IVA 2008. LNCS (LNAI), vol. 5208, pp. 59–72. Springer, Heidelberg (2008)
6. Krenn, B., Skowron, M., Sieber, G., Gstrein, E., Irran, J.: Adaptive mind agent. In: Ruttkay, Z., Kipp, M., Nijholt, A., Vilhjálmsson, H.H. (eds.) IVA 2009. LNCS, vol. 5773, pp. 519–520. Springer, Heidelberg (2009)
7. Nuxoll, A.: Enhancing Intelligent Agents with Episodic Memory. Ph.D. thesis, Univ. of Michigan, Ann Arbor (2007)
8. Sieber, G., Krenn, B.: Episodic memory for companion dialogue. In: Danieli, M., Gambäck, B., Wilks, Y. (eds.) Proceedings of the 2010 Workshop on Companionable Dialogue Systemsi (ACL 2010). Association for Computational Linguistics (ACL), Uppsala (July 2010)
9. Tulving, E.: Episodic and semantic memory. In: Tulving, E., Donaldson, W. (eds.) Organization of Memory, pp. 381–403. Academic Press, New York (1972)
10. Xu, F., Adolphs, P., Uszkoreit, H., Cheng, X., Li, H.: Gossip galore: A conversational web agent for collecting and sharing pop trivia. In: Filipe, J., Fred, A.L.N., Sharp, B. (eds.) ICAART, pp. 115–122. INSTICC Press (2009)

Generating Culture-Specific Gestures for Virtual Agent Dialogs

Birgit Endrass[1], Ionut Damian[1], Peter Huber[1],
Matthias Rehm[2], and Elisabeth André[1]

[1] Multimedia Concepts and Applications, Augsburg University,
Universitätsstr. 6a, D-86159 Augsburg, Germany
{endrass,andre}@informatik.uni-augsburg.de
http://mm-werkstatt.informatik.uni-augsburg.de
[2] Department of Media Technology, Aalborg University,
Niels-Jernes Vej 14, DK-9220 Aalborg, Denmark
matthias@imi.aau.dk

Abstract. Integrating culture into the behavioral model of virtual agents has come into focus lately. When investigating verbal aspects of behavior, nonverbal behaviors are desirably added automatically, driven by the speech-act. In this paper, we present a corpus driven approach of generating gestures in a culture-specific way that accompany agent dialogs. The frequency of gestures and gesture-types, the correlation of gesture-types and speech-acts as well as the expressivity of gestures have been analyzed in the two cultures of Germany and Japan and integrated into a demonstrator.

Keywords: Virtual Agents, Gesture Generation, Culture, Dialog.

1 Motivation

Virtual agents are used in a vast variety of applications. However, many researchers are only interested in certain aspects of behavior. In our interactive storytelling system [1], for example, we investigate dialog generation. But when focusing on verbal behavior, nonverbal behavior cannot be left aside. According to Kita [2], they are tightly linked systems, where *"the link is strong enough that speech-accompanying gestures do not disappear even when the addressee does not have a visual access to the gestures (e.g., on the telephone)"*. Selecting gestures appropriate to a virtual agent dialog, however, can be a time consuming task. Thus, we aim at generating gestures automatically. In human conversations, gestures are not performed randomly and are not just a decorative feature. Often they serve a function, such as supporting a speech-act.

Verbal and nonverbal behavior of virtual agents became more sophisticated in recent years and social factors such as personality or culture came into focus. In this paper, we present an approach of generating gestures for virtual agents in a culture-specific way, driven by the speech-act generation of the system. To this end, we recorded a video corpus in the two cultures of Germany and Japan and integrated our findings into a multiagent system.

J. Allbeck et al. (Eds.): IVA 2010, LNAI 6356, pp. 329–335, 2010.

2   Related Work

Several approaches have focused on the challenge of automatically generating nonverbal behaviors. The most well known system, BEAT, was presented by Cassell et al. [3]. As input, it receives plain text and generates synchronized nonverbal behavior for a virtual character. In their work, the authors describe behavior selection according to filter functions that regulate how much nonverbal behavior is performed. Such filters can reflect the personality, affective state or energy level of an agent. We consider these filters as an inspiration for our work and therefore suggest culture as an aspect that effects the selection of nonverbal behaviors.

A nonverbal behavior generator that generates BML scripts containing nonverbal behaviors for a given input text is introduced in [4]. Nonverbal behavior is generated based on rules that were extracted from a set of video clips. Similar to in the work described in this paper, speech-utterances have been labeled by the authors and their co-occurrences with nonverbal behaviors have been analyzed. They focused on head movements, facial expressions and body gestures. However, they did not analyze different cultures in their approach.

Bergman and Kopp [5] introduce a system that generates iconic gestures to express spatial information. A corpus containing landmark descriptions was recorded and annotated for their purposes and a prototype that performs iconic gestures has been developed and evaluated. The authors state that the performance of iconic gestures varies across speakers. It would be interesting whether there are differences aroused by cultural background as well.

In [6], Ruttkay describes a markup language, where different aspects of styles are defined in a dictionary of meaning-to-gesture mappings. The style dictionary suggests appropriate verbal and nonverbal behaviors. Culture specific styles could be considered as well.

Integrating culture into the behavioral model of virtual agents has come into focus lately. Most other work either focuses on abstract cultures, is not very specific in modeling differences in certain aspects of behavior or is not corpus driven. In [7], for example, an educational application for inter-cultural empathy is introduced. To achieve cultural awareness, a group of users interacts as a team with a group of virtual agents. However, in their system no awareness for an existing culture or culture-specific behavior is trained, but an overall awareness of something that is different from one's own culture.

The tactical language training system [8] explores cultural differences in gesture usage. Users have to select gestures for their avatars along with speech input. In addition, they have to interpret the gestures made by other agents appropriately in order to solve their tasks. Another system that demonstrates cultural differences is presented in [9]. A group of characters performs differently in a situation, depending on their cultural background. However, abstract concepts of culture are used rather than differences extracted form a corpus.

We consider the automatically generation of gestures to agent dialogs along with a corpus driven approach to simulate culture-specific differences in behavior, as the new contribution of our work.

3   Theoretical Background

In order to generate gestures that accompany virtual agent dialogs in a culture-specific way, we have to explore the concepts of gestures, dialog-acts and different cultures.

McNeill [10] has introduced the most well known classification of gestures into gesture-types: *Deictic* gestures are pointing or indicative gestures. *Beat* gestures are rhythmic gestures that follow speech prosody. *Emblems* have a conventionalized meaning and do not need to be accompanied by speech. *Iconic* gestures explain the semantic content of speech. *Metaphoric* gestures accompany the semantic content of speech in an abstract manner by the use of metaphors. *Adaptors* are hand movements towards other parts of the body. In addition, McNeil [10] explores the temporal course of gestures according to the phases: preparation, hold, stroke and retraction. In the preparation phase, the hands are brought into the gesture space. A hold might occur when the gesture is not aligned with the corresponding utterance yet. The stroke phase carries the content of the gesture and can be categorized by the gesture-types described above. In the retraction phase, the hands are finally brought back into a resting position. Annotating gestures as suggested by McNeill [10] is already successfully used in behavior generation for virtual agents (see [11], [3] or [12] for examples). The dynamic variation of a gesture is another aspect to be considered. In [13], Pelachaud describes six parameters that characterize a gesture's expressivity, which can depend on individual factors, such as personality or emotional state. The *spatial extent* describes the arm's extent toward the torso. The *speed* and the *power* of a gesture can vary as well. The *fluidity* describes the continuity between consecutive gestures, while the *repetitivity* holds information about the repetition of the stroke. The *overall activation* explains the frequency of gestures.

To categorize dialog-acts, we use the annotation schema DAMSL (Dialog Act Markup in Several Layers) that was introduced by Core and Allen [14]. One layer of the schema, the communicative function, serves our purposes very well as it labels the communicative meaning of a speech-act. For the work described in this paper, we use the following subset of communicative functions: statement, into-request, influence on future, agreement/disagreement (indicates the speaker's point of view), hold, understanding/misunderstanding (without stating a point of view) and answer.

To generate nonverbal behaviors for prototypical German and Japanese agents, we need to distinguish these two cultures. Ting-Toomey [15] distinguishes high- and low-context communication cultures. In high-context communication little is encoded explicitly and the conversation relies mainly on physical context. Messages and symbols might seem relatively simple but contain a deep meaning. In contrast, low-context communication explicitly codes information; symbols and messages are direct and to the point. In [15], Germany is mentioned as one of the most extreme low-context cultures, while Japan is named to be on the extreme high-context side. We expect a more frequent use of direct gestures (deictic and iconic) in low-context cultures. Vice versa, we expect more metaphoric gestures in Japanese conversations.

4   Empirical Verification

In order to find statistical tendencies that describe what gesture-types are commonly used for which dialog-utterance, we analyzed the video corpus recorded for the CUBE-G project [16]. In total, more than 40 students from Germany and Japan participated in the study, where around 25 minutes of video data were recorded for each subject. To ensure a high control over the recordings, subjects interacted with actors whom they did not know in advance. At the beginning of the experiment, participants were asked to get acquainted with each other as a preparation for the task they had to solve later. During this time recording already started. For the work described in this paper, we analyzed this Small Talk scenario that lasted for approximately five minutes for each subject. For more information on the recordings, please see [16].

4.1   Quantitative Analysis

Using the Anvil tool [17], verbal and nonverbal behavior was annotated according to the subset of DAMSL dialog-utterances, McNeill's classification of gestures and the gestural expressivity parameters (see Section 3). So far, the videos of 21 German and 7 Japanese subjects were considered. As we focused on gestures that accompany speech and that are of a general nature, we did not consider adaptors and emblems yet.

Table 1 shows the frequencies of dialog-utterances per minute in the two cultures of Germany and Japan averaged over the number of subjects (left), as well as the probability that a gesture is performed during a given utterance (right). During the dialog-utterances "hold" and "influence on future" rarely any gestures occurred. We thus do not consider them for our model. Our analysis revealed that there are significantly more info-requests in the Japanese videos than in the German ones (with a p-value ≤ 0.003 using the two sided t-test). Interestingly, there are also more gestures occurring during info-requests in the Japanese corpus ($p \leq 0.075$). Regarding the frequency of understanding/misunderstanding utterances, we found significantly more of these dialog-acts in the Japanese conversations ($p \leq 0.02$). This is in line with expectations about the two cultures: giving verbal feedback without stating a personal opinion is supposed to be very

Table 1. Average occurrence of dialog-utterances per minute (left) and probabilities that a gesture occurs during the utterance (right) in German and Japanese videos

utterance per minute	Germany	Japan
info-request	1.10	2.09
answer	2.95	2.20
statement	4.96	5.74
agreement/ disagreement	0.87	0.74
understanding/ misunderstanding	1.64	2.74

gesture co-occurrence	Germany	Japan
info-request	5%	11%
answer	10%	10%
statement	24%	15%
agreement/ disagreement	2%	4%
understanding/ misunderstanding	0%	0%

Table 2. Probabilities that a certain gesture accompanies an utterance in the two cultures of Germany and Japan

utterance/gesture	Germany				Japan			
	beat	deictic	iconic	metaphoric	beat	deictic	iconic	metaphoric
info-request	0%	**67%**	**33%**	0%	0%	**75%**	0%	**25%**
answer	25%	25%	21%	29%	25%	12.5%	37.5%	25%
statement	27%	17%	27%	29%	16%	26%	35%	23%
agreement/disagreement	50%	50%	0%	0%	0%	100%	0%	0%

common in the Japanese culture, while stating an opinion is more common in Western cultures.

As a next step, we explored the gesture-types that accompany dialog-utterances. Table 2 shows the probabilities for a gesture-type during an utterance given that a gesture occurs. Our analysis revealed differences in the usage of gestures that occur with info-requests. Japanese subjects showed significantly more deictic and metaphoric gestures during info-requests than German subjects (both with p-values ≤ 0.01).

4.2 Qualitative Analysis

Besides the choice of gesture-type, the way a gesture is performed differs across cultures, too. A German deictic gesture, for example, is usually executed using the index finger for pointing, while in a typical Japanese deictic gesture the whole flattened hand is used. For other gestures, differences are not as simple to distinguish. To simulate these differences, we modeled different animations for the two cultures. Figure 1 shows two iconic gestures in Germany (1) and Japan (2). Animations for virtual agents (a) are presented next to the video-samples from our corpus (b), where the gestures were extracted from.

Our analysis of gestural expressivity revealed significant differences for all parameters. German subjects repeat gestures less, have more fluid motions, gesture more powerfully and faster and use more space in gesturing than Japanese subjects (see [16] for more details).

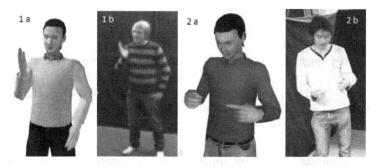

Fig. 1. Examples for iconic gestures in Germany (1b) and Japan (2b), imitated by virtual agents (a)

5   Integration into a Virtual Scenario

As a simulation platform, we are using the Virtual Beergarden scenario (see [18] for technical details). The process of action selection is realized by a hierarchical planning system. Verbal behavior is generated from a knowledge base and sent to the text-to-speech component. Nonverbal behavior is added, considering the agent's cultural background, taking into account the following questions: (1) Should the speech act be accompanied by a gesture? (2) Which gesture-type should be selected? (3) Are there culture-specific restrictions on the execution?

For the first decision, Table 1 (right) is used as a basis. If a gesture should be performed, the gesture-type is selected according to the distribution presented in Table 2. Finally, the animation is selected.

Gestures are stored in a nonverbal knowledge base inspired by [12]. Following their approach, we are using an XML structure that comprises a form, a function and restrictions for each gesture. In our version, a gesture can either be culture-specific or not. Culture-specific gestures can only be performed by agents of the specified cultural background. General gestures, e.g. a simple beat gesture, can be exhibited by every agent. The performance of these gestures, however, is realized in a culture-specific way, taking into account the expressivity parameters. Therefore every gesture is divided into phases: preparation, stroke and retraction. Preparation and retraction phases are used for animation blending. A gesture could, for example, be chosen while the agent does not stand in a neutral position. In this case, the preparation phase is used to blend into the gesture space. In the stroke phase, the actual gesture is performed. It can be customized to match different gestural expressivities. The parameter repetition, for example, can be varied by playing the stroke phase several times, while it can be played faster or slower to customize the speed parameter.

6   Conclusion

We recorded a video corpus in the two cultures of Germany and Japan where speech-acts and gestures as well as their correlation were annotated and analyzed. Findings were integrated into a demonstrator. The contribution of this work is to automatically generate gestures for virtual agents in a culture-specific way. By that means, the process of gesture selection is speech-act as well as corpus driven. Although we consider this integration as an important step towards enculturating our virtual agents, there is still a long way to go. Other nonverbal behaviors, e.g. head nods, have not been considered yet. We found differences in the usage of understanding utterances in our corpus. It would be interesting to know how these utterances correlate with head-nods.

Acknowledgments. The first author was supported by a grant from the Elitenetzwerk Bayern (Elite Network Bavaria). This work was also partly funded by the European Commission under grant agreement IRIS (FP7-ICT-231824).

References

1. Endrass, B., Rehm, M., André, E.: What Would You Do in their Shoes? Experiencing Different Perspectives in an Interactive Drama for Multiple Users. In: Iurgel, I.A., Zagalo, N., Petta, P. (eds.) ICIDS 2009. LNCS, vol. 5915, pp. 258–268. Springer, Heidelberg (2009)
2. Kita, S.: Corss-cultural variation of speech-accompanying gesture: A review. Language and Cognitive Process 24(2), 145–167 (2009)
3. Cassell, J., Vilhálmsson, H., Bickmore, T.: BEAT: The Behaviour Expression Animation Toolkit. In: SIGGRAPH 2001, pp. 477–486. ACM, New York (2001)
4. Lee, J., Marsella, S.: Nonverbal Behavior Generator for Embodied Conversational Agents. In: Gratch, J., Young, M., Aylett, R.S., Ballin, D., Olivier, P. (eds.) IVA 2006. LNCS (LNAI), vol. 4133, pp. 243–255. Springer, Heidelberg (2006)
5. Bergmann, K., Kopp, S.: Bayesian Decision Networks for Iconic Gesture Generation. In: Ruttkay, Z., Kipp, M., Nijholt, A., Vilhjálmsson, H.H. (eds.) IVA 2009. LNCS, vol. 5773, pp. 76–89. Springer, Heidelberg (2009)
6. Ruttkay, Z.: Presenting in Style by Virtual Humans. In: Esposito, A., Faundez-Zanuy, M., Keller, E., Marinaro, M. (eds.) COST Action 2102. LNCS (LNAI), vol. 4775, pp. 22–36. Springer, Heidelberg (2007)
7. Aylett, R., Paiva, A., Vannini, N., Enz, S., André, E., Hall, L.: But that was in another country: agents and intercultural empathy. In: Decker, S., Sierra, C. (eds.) AAMAS 2009, pp. 329–336. ACM, New York (2009)
8. Johnson, W.L., Choi, S., Marsella, S., Mote, N., Narayanan, S., Vilhjálmsson., H.: Tactical Language Training System: Supporting the Rapid Acquisition of Foreign Language and Cultural Skills. In: InSTIL/ICALL 2004 (2004)
9. Mascarenhas, S., Dias, J., Afonso, N., Enz, S., Paiva, A.: Using rituals to express cultural differences in synthetic characters. In: Decker, Sichman, Sierra, Castelfranchi (eds.) AAMAS 2009, pp. 305–312. ACM, New York (2009)
10. McNeill, D.: Hand and Mind – What Gestures Reveal about Thought. University of Chicago Press, Chicago (1992)
11. Rehm, M., Nakano, Y., André, E., Nishida, T., Bee, N., Endrass, B., Wissner, M., Lipi, A.A., Huang, H.H.: From observation to simulation: generating culture-specific behavior for interactive systems. AI & Society 24(3), 267–280 (2009)
12. Krenn, B., Pirker, H.: Defining the Gesticon: Language and Gesture Coordination for Interacting Embodied Agents. In: AISB 2004, pp. 107–115 (2004)
13. Pelachaud, C.: Multimodal expressive embodied conversational agents. In: Zhang, Chua, Steinmetz, Kankanhalli, Wilcox (eds.) ACM Multimedia, pp. 683–689. ACM, New York (2005)
14. Core, M., Allen, J.: Coding Dialogs with the DAMSL Annotation Scheme. In: Working Notes of AAAI Fall Symposium on Communicative Action in Humans and Machines, Boston, MA (1997)
15. Ting-Toomey, S.: Communicating across Cultures. The Guilford Press, New York (1999)
16. Rehm, M., André, E., Nakano, Y., Nishida, T., Bee, N., Endrass, B., Huan, H.H., Wissner, M.: The CUBE-G approach — Coaching culture-specific nonverbal behavior by virtual agents. In: Mayer, Mastik (eds.) ISAGA 2007 (2007)
17. Kipp, M.: Anvil - A Generic Annotation Tool for Multimodal Dialogue. In: Dalsgaard, Lindberg, Benner, Tan (eds.) Eurospeech 2001, pp. 1367–1370 (2001)
18. Damian, I., Huber, P., Endrass, B., Bee, N.: Advanced Agent Animation. In: IVA Gala 2010 (2010)

Avatars in Conversation: The Importance of Simulating Territorial Behavior

Claudio Pedica, Hannes Högni Vilhjálmsson, and Marta Lárusdóttir

Center for Analysis and Design of Intelligent Agents, School of Computer Science, Reykjavik University, Menntavegur 1, IS-101 Reykjavik, Iceland

Abstract. Is it important to model human social territoriality in simulated conversations? Here we address this question by evaluating the believability of avatars' virtual conversations powered by our simulation of territorial behaviors. Participants were asked to watch two videos and answer survey questions to compare them. The videos showed the same scene with and without our technology. The results support the hypothesis that simulating territorial behaviors can increase believability. Furthermore, there is evidence that our simulation of small scale group dynamics for conversational territories is a step in the right direction, even though there is still a large margin for improvement.

1 Introduction and Background

This paper reports the results of a survey we conducted to evaluate the believability of our simulated avatar behavior for conversations. Our approach is strongly influenced by the theories of Human Territories [1] and F-formations [2], and it has been described in two previous publications [3,4]. It models the group dynamics of positions and orientations as a result of a special class of behaviors, conventionally called territorial behaviors, that we believe are essential for a complete simulation of a believable conversation.

Most of the work on automating avatar conversations focuses on the generation of communicative behaviors after the conversation has already started. The assumption is that the avatars are already in the right location and correctly oriented for engaging each other. However, we developed a method to let the avatars autonomously cluster and arrange themselves when a conversation takes place. Our approach generates an emergent dynamic arrangement as the result of the behavioral constraints suggested by the territorial field of the conversation. As a result, the avatars dynamically react to each other's position and orientation in a given social context. The purpose of the study is to investigate whether our approach, based on human territoriality, improves the believability of few avatars having a conversation, compared to the state of the art in avatar animation, that still relies on user control for moving them or at most arranges them into fixed formations such as a circle. A study by Jan and Traum [5] reports how the wrong positioning of virtual characters in a conversation significantly reduced the believability of the simulated social interaction. The finding lead to their model of small scale group dynamics for conversations [6], the first to keep proper positioning but not proper orientations. So far, an evaluation of believability of that model has not been conducted.

J. Allbeck et al. (Eds.): IVA 2010, LNAI 6356, pp. 336–342, 2010.

Believability is hard to define. It is a construct and a hypothetical variable that cannot be measured directly. Therefore, we have chosen four variables we believe relate to believability when we evaluate simulated social interactions. Having better scores on these variables will increase the overall believability of the scene. The four variables we identified are: *artificiality*, *appeal*, *social richness* and *avatar awareness*. To evaluate our technology we built a questionnaire around these measurable quantities. Our dynamic avatars' conversations competed against a static version of them where avatars were chatting but not rearranging according to important events. Notice that while a static arrangement would be plausible in certain social situations, a random collective movement of the participants would not be. As confirmed by other studies on gaze behavior, an algorithmically generated gaze shift has proven more effective than just a randomized motion [7,8]. Synchronization and timing are important for simulating social behaviors and testing against random motion would not have been informative.

2   The Survey

We conducted the survey by means of a web questionnaire[1]. The survey was open to anyone interested in it and we sent an invitation email to students, teachers and staff members of Reykjavik University, reaching about 5000 potential target respondents. Anonymity and confidentiality were assured. 171 people responded.

The only information about the participants we were interested in, apart from typical demographic information, was how often they played video games in the last three months. We wanted to discriminate between those accustomed to state-of-the-art character animation and those who were not.

The respondents were asked to answer a questionnaire organized into four test cases. Each case was focused on one of the following important situations: joining a conversation, moving within a conversation, avoiding a conversation and passing-by a conversation. For each case, there were two videos to watch and some questions to answer. At the end, we asked the subjects to answer some extra questions about the survey itself to learn more about the quality of the survey procedure.

2.1   Subjects

The mean age was 31 years with the majority of the subjects between 20 and 40 years old. 35% of the subjects hadn't played video games in the last three months, 32% played once a week (*casual players*), 21% played four times a week (*habitual players*) and 12% played every day (*hardcore players*). We classified the people who don't play and the casual players as *non-gamers* (113) while habitual and hardcore players were classified as *gamers* (57).

2.2   Questionnaire

For each of the four test cases, the subjects were asked to watch two videos of the same scene, with and without our technology (Fig. 1), and answer a set of simple questions (Table 1) about the artificiality or appeal of those scenes. The questions made the

---

[1] http://populus.cadia.ru.is/survey

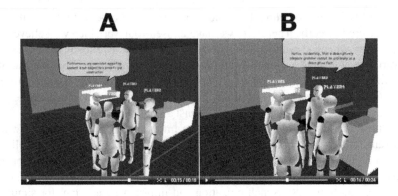

Fig. 1. Screenshot from the *joining* test case (Here A is dynamic and B static)

Table 1. The set of questions for each of the four test cases

TEST CASE	QUESTIONS
Joining	1. Which scene do you find more artificial? 2. Which scene do you find more appealing? 3. Which scene do you find more socially rich? 4. In which scene does the group appear more disconnected from the situation? 5. In which scene does the group seem more aware of the new person joining?
Moving within	1. Which scene do you find more artificial? 2. Which scene do you find more appealing? 3. Which scene do you find more socially rich? 4. In which scene do the others appear more disconnected from the situation? 5. In which scene do the others seem more aware of the blue person moving around?
Avoiding	1. Which scene do you find more artificial? 2. Which scene do you find more appealing? 3. In which scene does the blue person's behaviour seem more appropriate?
Passing-by	1. Which scene do you find more artificial? 2. Which scene do you find more appealing? 3. Which scene do you find more socially rich? 4. In which scene does the group seem more aware of the blue person's existence? 5. In which scene does the group appear less involved in their conversation?

subjects compare video A and B by evaluating a statement about what they saw and associating it with one value of the following rating scale: A - much more, A - more, A - slightly more, the same, B - slightly more, B - more and B - much more.

To avoid any trivial differentiation, each pair of videos was recorded from the same system, with the same camera angle, running the same animated simulation of turn taking to let the conversation appear "alive". The difference was that in one instance our group dynamics were disabled and enabled in the other. The order of the two scenes was alternated to avoid a systematic order bias.

3   Results

The results of the survey are shown in Fig. 2. The graphs are vertically grouped by test case and horizontally by question. The horizontal axis within each graph denotes the preference for either the *Static* version (numbers lower than 4) or the *Dynamic* version (numbers higher than 4).

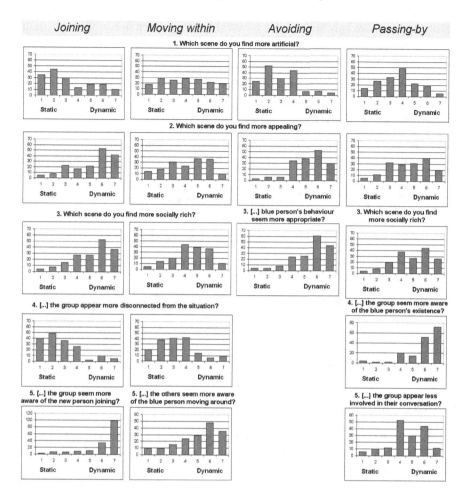

Fig. 2. Results of the survey

Table 2. Mean values and standard deviations. Bold numbers indicate where our technology performed better (Cohen's estimated effect size $|d| > 0.45$).

	Joining					Moving within					Avoiding			Passing-by				
Question:	1	2	3	4	5	1	2	3	4	5	1	2	3	1	2	3	4	5
Mean:	**3.22**	**5.18**	**5.19**	2.72	**6.05**	3.95	4.18	4.49	**3.27**	**5.02**	**3.00**	**5.21**	**5.47**	3.67	4.59	**4.87**	**5.88**	**4.62**
Std dev:	1.90	1.68	1.55	1.55	1.51	1.87	1.71	1.47	1.54	1.72	1.49	1.39	1.44	1.52	1.60	1.56	1.39	1.46

Table 2 shows mean value and standard deviation of the answers for each question. The numbers in bold indicate where our technology performed effectively better. For those mean values the effect size was "medium" or "large" (Cohens's $|d| > 0.45$).

Our results are statistically significant against our testing hypothesis, for which we had close to zero p-values for all the questions, except for question n. 1 ($p = 0.37$) and n. 2 ($p = 0.08$) in the second test case. Some of the negative comments on those questions were about how both scenes were unlikely to happen in real life. One of the subjects commented as follow:

> "Yes, in the second test, the blue person moved to the side [in] a way I haven't seen anyone move. It look the most fake of all off the test, both A and B."

3.1   Quality of the Survey

On the last page of the questionnaire, the respondents answered some questions about the survey itself so that we could verify its quality. The results are shown in Fig. 3.

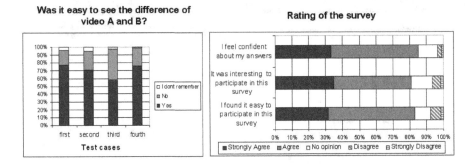

Fig. 3. Results from questions about the survey itself indicate adequate quality

4   Discussion

The results confirm that simulating human territories significantly increases believability, by reducing artificiality and increasing appeal, social richness and apparent avatar awareness in simulated conversations.

For two out of four tests, the scene powered by our technology was judged significantly less artificial, more appealing, more socially rich and with a higher avatar awareness. Social richness was also slightly higher in the second and fourth tests, although the effective sizes are "medium/small", or 0.33 and 0.37 respectively.

In the second test case both the static and dynamic videos were judged equally artificial and appealing. This is a clear limitation of our small group dynamics model that needs to be improved. The group was too responsive to the avatar's movement and some subjects felt this was unnatural. Another reason was that the group went along with the avatar moving, giving the feeling he was followed by the others:

> "For the second scene, it is clear that the moving group is too artificial: if a group is speaking and someone joins, it is the group that rules over the single person; this means that the person can move but the group should stands still."

The *gamers* were generally tougher on our technology than the *non-gamers* although the difference is only significant for the second test case (Cohen's effect size $0.46 < |d| < 0.49$). This further suggests we need to improve group dynamics for conversations.

4.1   Dynamics of Orientation

Avatar awareness was judged significantly higher with our technology in all test cases probably due to our simulation of gaze and body orientation. This indicates the importance of controlling orientation of body parts for correctly simulating conversation. Introducing orientational motivation to our model of group dynamics improved the believability of the overall scene, making the avatars look more aware of their surroundings and more connected to the social context. This is not surprising, considering that the orientation of some bodily regions normally express temporary membership to a group or a subgroup, or more generally our claim of territory as argued by Scheflen [1].

We believe that a proper simulation of body part orientation is essential for simulating, not only conversations, but social interactions in general. This provides clues and signals that retain their expressiveness when simulated. To correctly realize these orientations requires them to be incorporated into the model of group dynamics, but also to have a behavioral architecture where they can be easily controlled in a reliable way. Our technology provides both such a model and architecture.

4.2   Conclusions

Our model of group dynamics can be improved. This is not surprising considering that it was originally inspired by models of the dynamics in a flock of birds. Two fundamental concepts of the theory of Human Territories are still not included in our model, which may impact the simulation quality. They are the *transactional segment* [2] and *locations* [1]. The transactional segment is an amount of space necessary to carry on an interaction. A participant in a conversation will adjust his position and orientation to keep his transactional segment intersected with the segment of the other participants. Locations are placeholder amounts of space that contribute to shaping the territory of an interaction. Each participant in a conversation holds a location but is allowed to temporarily leave it and then get back to it. In the meantime the territory will probably keep the same shape, without requiring a rearrangement of all the participants.

Territorial behaviors are important for the overall believability of a simulated avatar's conversation. They show participation in a social interaction and awareness of the context and therefore they are necessary for socially intelligent agents. Simulating this class of behaviors by reactive responses appears to be an approach worthy of pursuit.

Further investigation is necessary and we plan to evaluate our technology in a real game environment with high quality character models and animations. The higher visual quality may increase expectations of the character behavior and result in lower ratings. However, we may still find evidence of the validity of our approach and may even match it with a brand new model of social territorial dynamics.

Acknowledgments. We are grateful to Jina Lee, Brent Lance and Stacy Marsella for web survey ideas. Big thanks to the CADIA team, but special thanks to Ankell Logi for web work. This was supported by the Humanoid Agents in Social Game Environments Grant of Excellence from The Icelandic Research Fund.

References

1. Scheflen, A.E.: Human Territories: how we behave in space and time. Prentice-Hall, New York (1976)
2. Kendon, A.: Conducting Interaction: Patterns of behavior in focused encounters. Cambridge University Press, Cambridge (1990), Main Area (multimodal commnication)
3. Pedica, C., Vilhjálmsson, H.: Social perception and steering for online avatars. In: Prendinger, H., Lester, J.C., Ishizuka, M. (eds.) IVA 2008. LNCS (LNAI), vol. 5208, pp. 104–116. Springer, Heidelberg (2008)
4. Pedica, C., Vilhjálmsson, H.H.: Spontaneous avatar behavior for human territoriality. In: Ruttkay, Z., Kipp, M., Nijholt, A., Vilhjálmsson, H.H. (eds.) IVA 2009. LNCS, vol. 5773, pp. 344–357. Springer, Heidelberg (2009)
5. Jan, D., Traum, D.R.: Dialog simulation for background characters. LNCS, pp. 65–74. Springer, Heidelberg (2005)
6. Jan, D., Traum, D.: Dynamic movement and positioning of embodied agents in multiparty conversation. In: Proc. of the ACL Workshop on Embodied Language Processing, pp. 59–66 (June 2007)
7. Garau, M., Slater, M., Bee, S., Sasse, M.A.: The impact of eye gaze on communication using humanoid avatars. In: CHI 2001: Proceedings of the SIGCHI conference on Human factors in computing systems, pp. 309–316. ACM, New York (2001)
8. Vertegaal, R., Ding, Y.: Explaining effects of eye gaze on mediated group conversations: amount or synchronization? In: CSCW 2002: Proceedings of the 2002 ACM conference on Computer supported cooperative work, pp. 41–48. ACM, New York (2002)
9. Casselt, J., Vilhjalmsson, H.: Fully embodied conversational avatars: Making communicative behaviors autonomous. Autonomous Agents and Multi-Agent Systems 2(1), 45–64 (1999)

The Impact of Linguistic and Cultural Congruity on Persuasion by Conversational Agents

Langxuan Yin[1], Timothy Bickmore[1], and Dharma E. Cortés[2]

[1] Northeastern University
{yinlx,bickmore}@ccs.neu.edu
[2] Harvard Medical School
dharma_cortes@hms.harvard.edu

Abstract. We present an empirical study on the impact of linguistic and cultural tailoring of a conversational agent on its ability to change user attitudes. We designed two bilingual (English and Spanish) conversational agents to resemble members of two distinct cultures (Anglo-American and Latino) and conducted the study with participants from the two corresponding populations. Our results show that cultural tailoring and participants' personality traits have a significant interaction effect on the agent's persuasiveness and perceived trustworthiness.

Keywords: agent, language, culture, persuasion.

1 Introduction

There has been a growing interest in developing conversational agents that can motivate users to change their health behavior. In the health care domain, several studies have now demonstrated that tailored messages—individualized to various aspects of users, such as demographic, personality, or lifestyle variables—are more persuasive and effective at achieving health behavior change [1], and the more variables that messages are tailored on, the more effective they are.

According to the Elaboration Likelihood Model, one of the leading theoretical frameworks in persuasion research, individuals are predisposed to processing messages through one of two routes to persuasion: a *central route*, where an individual considers a message via effortful, logical thinking, and the *peripheral route*, where the decision making is more reliant on heuristic environmental cues of the message, sender, and context [2], a trait referred to as "need for cognition" [3]. Message tailoring is thought to impact both routes to persuasion [1].

One form of tailoring that has received recent attention in the virtual agents community is adaptation of an agent's apparent culture. However, much of the existing research on this topic has only investigated whether or not users could perceive the cultural manipulations, but not the effect of these manipulations on outcomes of practical significance. A related form of tailoring is whether an agent speaks to users in their preferred (L1) natural language, or in a second (L2) language, assuming users are bilingual. Message tailoring theory would predict that the effects of cultural tailoring and linguistic tailoring should be separate and additive. However, a study by Luna, et al, on the effects of linguistic and cultural tailoring of websites on product

J. Allbeck et al. (Eds.): IVA 2010, LNAI 6356, pp. 343–349, 2010.

evaluations demonstrated an interaction between these two factors, which the authors explained using the Elaboration Likelihood Model and differences in message processing effort between L1 and L2 text [4].

In the current study, we explore the separate and relative effects of cultural and linguistic tailoring of a conversational agent on its ability to change user attitudes. In order to inform the design of future counseling agents, we are interested in determining which of these manipulations are more effective, and what role personality traits such as need for cognition play in this process.

2   Related Work

Earlier research on virtual agents has shown a tendency of users' preference of culturally tailored agents. Rossen et al., using virtual agents with different skin tones, found that Caucasian subjects tend to show more empathy to the agent with a lighter skin tone [5]. Endrass et al. showed that German subjects preferred virtual characters speaking in the German way to those speaking in the Japanese way (in terms of silence and speech overlapping, etc.) [6], and similar preference tendencies were found among American and Arabic subjects as well [7]. Other studies such as that conducted by Jan et al. also suggest that people tend to favor a virtual agent resembling an in-group member of their culture [8].

Virtual agents have been shown to be effective in persuasion as well. By delivering persuasive messages via humans and virtual characters, Zanbaka et al. concluded that virtual characters can be as effective as humans at persuasion [9]. A study by Katagiri et al. has shown that virtual agents engaged in relationships with their users and other agents are effective in changing user's behaviors [10]. Also, in Schulman and Bickmore's experiment, participants had significantly more positive attitudes towards exercise after interacting with an exercise counseling virtual agent [11].

3   Experiment Design

To determine the effects of linguistic and cultural tailoring of a conversational agent on persuasion, we conducted a 2x2 factorial between-subjects experiment. Independent variables are linguistic congruity (whether the agent speaks the language that is L1 or L2 for a subject) and cultural congruity (high or low, relative to a subject's cultural affiliation).

The experiment protocol was similar to that from Schulman and Bickmore [11], inspired by the desert survival problem, commonly used to measure persuasion [12]. Participants performed a ranking task designed to measure attitudes towards exercise, then held a conversation with an agent, which consisted of a social dialogue and a persuasive dialogue. Finally, participants completed the same ranking task again, and perceptions of the agent were assessed.

Anglo-American and Latina Agents. Two agents were developed for this study (Fig. 1). Katherine (the "Anglo-American" agent) was designed to resemble an Anglo-American in appearance, behavior and values, and was situated in a background

Fig. 1. Katherine (left), designed to resemble a member of the Anglo-American culture, and Catalina (right), designed to resemble a member of the Latino culture

picturing an Anglo-American-looking household. Catalina (the "Latina" agent) was designed to resemble a member of the Latino culture and was situated in a Latino-looking household background.

At the beginning of an interaction, the agent walked on to the screen and greeted the user, and then she talked about her personal background, which differed based on the agent's simulated culture. Following this, the agent presented a persuasive dialogue similar to that used by Schulman and Bickmore [11], arguing for the benefits of regular exercise and against statements about the disadvantages of regular exercise. However, the two agents argued for and against the same statements in different ways: the Anglo-American agent focused on participants' well-being, whereas the Latina agent expressed more interest in participants' family and friends, due to the importance of these aspects in the Latino culture [13]. A short clip of music representing the agent's culture was played as the agent walked on the screen. The Latina agent was also shown at a closer proximity to the user more often than the Anglo-American agent, because Latinos "interact at closer distances and employ more touching behaviors when interacting with family and friends" [14].

Linguistic Congruity. All dialogue content was first developed in English, and then translated to Spanish by a bilingual research assistant (native Spanish speaker). The Spanish scripts were then reviewed for accuracy by a native Spanish speaking researcher in our research team. The scripts were processed by a text-to-speech engine at runtime, using a female English voice (Loquendo "Susan") and a female Spanish voice (Loquendo "Soledad").

Measures. Four 7-point scale Likert questions were used as a manipulation check for cultural congruity: "How much do you feel that the agent is a member of the American culture", "How much do you feel that the agent is a member of the Latino/Hispanic culture", "How easy was it to understand the agent's language" and "How much do you feel you and the agent are from the same culture".

The ranking task consisted of a list of ten statements about regular exercise from most to least important (see Figure 2), and a score ranging from 1 (least important) to 10 (most important) was used to create a composite measure, subtracting the total score of the items argued against from the total score of the items argued for. The difference between the two measures before and after the conversation was calculated to measure persuasion (following Schulman & Bickmore [11]).

Need for cognition was measured using the Need for Cognition Scale short form [2]. A high need for cognition score indicates the participant is predisposed to being influenced by *central route* to persuasion, while a low score indicates the participant is predisposed to being influenced by *peripheral cues*. And also, agent trustworthiness was measured by a standardized trust scale [15].

A semi-structured interview was conducted at the end of the study, focused on the user's opinions on the agent's cultural background and on their interaction.

+	I would have more energy if I exercised regularly.
	Exercise is important even if I don't want people to see me exercising.
+	I would feel less stressed if I exercised regularly.
−	Exercise is important even if it is time-consuming.
+	Exercising puts me in a better mood for the rest of the day.
−	Exercise is important even if exercise clothes make me uncomfortable or embarrassed.
	I would feel more comfortable with my body if I exercised regularly.
−	Exercise is important even if it is complicated.
+	Regular exercise would help me have a more positive outlook on life.
	My doctor tells me that exercise is important.

Fig. 2. Ten statements about regular exercise. Statements starting with a "+" are those that the agent argued for, and those starting with a "-" are those argued against. Statements starting with neither were not mentioned.

4 Results

Participants. Participants were recruited via fliers and advertisements, and enrolled only if they were able to speak read and understand both English and Spanish fluently and were either: a) an Anglo-American born in the United States who had stayed in Spanish-speaking Latin American countries for at least two months with English being their first language, or b) a Latino/Latina born in a Spanish-speaking Latin American country who had lived in the United States for at least two months, with Spanish being their first language.

Among the 43 participants recruited for the study, 65.0% were Latinos, and 44.2% were female. Participants' ages ranged from 18 to 65, and over half of them (65.0%) had been doing regular physical activity for more than 6 months.

Manipulation Checks. MANOVA tests reveal that the Latina agent was perceived as significantly more Latina than the Anglo-American agent, $F(1,42)=18.1$, $p<.001$, $\eta^2=0.254$. The Anglo-American agent was perceived as slightly more American than the Latina agent was, although the difference was not significant, $F(1,42)=1.05$, n.s. Agents that spoke English were rated as significantly more American, $F(1,42)=6.98$, $p=.012$, $\eta^2=0.148$, while Spanish-speaking agents were rated as significantly more Latina, $F(1,42)=13.06$, $p=.001$, $\eta^2=0.184$. Participants were also significantly more likely to rate the agent as a member of their own culture if the agent's simulated culture was congruent with theirs, $F(1,42)=5.299$, $p=0.026$, $\eta^2=0.114$.

Outcomes. We analyzed the data with a 2x2x2 between-subjects MANOVA, using linguistic congruity, cultural congruity and need-for-cognition (split at the median) as independent variables, and persuasion (the difference between the scores of pre- and post- ranking tasks) and agent trustworthiness as dependent variables. A significant interaction effect of congruity and need-for-cognition was found on both persuasion, $F(1,42)=5.537$, $p=0.024$, $\eta^2=0.129$, and agent trustworthiness, $F(1,42)=4.583$, $p=0.039$, $\eta^2=0.096$. Figure 3 shows this effect. A near significant main effect of need-for-cognition was also found on agent trustworthiness, $F(1,42)=4.070$, $p=0.051$, $\eta^2=0.085$. There were no significant effects of linguistic congruity on outcomes.

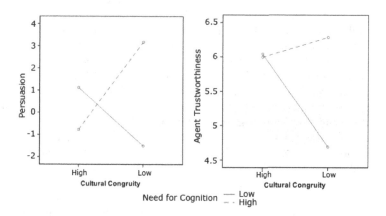

Fig. 3. Effect of need for cognition and cultural congruity on persuasion and agent trustworthiness

Many subjects mentioned that the agent's language strongly influenced their perception of the agent's cultural background. As an example, the following quote is from a Latino participant interacting with an English-speaking Latina agent.

"She seems more American, no but she said that... she came from Latin America right? Since she spoke English I'd say she's more Americanized than um... her original background. But she could be like me, you know, because I speak English and I'm a Hispanic. ... Yeah, I think she's more American because you know she spoke um... perfect English." (Participant 33)

This indicates that an English-speaking agent with a Latino appearance is considered, to a large extent, a member of the American culture, or at least highly "Americanized". The Spanish-speaking Anglo-American agent was also considered as a Latina or as "neutral", as much as she was considered an American, regardless of her appearance.

Several Latino participants also recognized the Latina agent as from the Caribbean. This indicates that subtle cultural traits specific to one or a few Latin American countries, when implemented in the agent, can be easily picked up by a member of the Latino culture, and that "Latino" should not be treated as a unitary culture.

5 Discussion and Future Work

Our findings suggest that participants who are predisposed to being influenced by *peripheral cues* tend to trust and be persuaded by an agent tailored to their culture more than by an agent from a different culture. Since most participants have been doing regular exercise for over six months, and many mentioned they already knew what the agent talked about, this is unlikely caused by an increase in the knowledge of physical activity, but rather because individuals taking the *peripheral route* to persuasion rely on environmental characteristics of the message delivered, and an agent resembling their in-group members is considered more credible and trustworthy, which is consistent with the Elaboration Likelihood Model. However, our findings also suggest that participants who are predisposed to process information deeply (i.e. high need for cognition) tend to be persuaded more by an agent from a different culture compared to one from their own culture. This may be explained by the fact that short-term engagement and relationship between speaker and hearer can reduce the impact of the speaker's persuasiveness on high-involvement topics (important topics that require thorough analysis) [16], since an interaction with an agent of high cultural congruity is presumably highly engaging and involving.

Linguistic tailoring had no effect on persuasion. This may be explained by the fact that participants were bilingual and their level of fluency in both languages was very high (all rated their proficiencies of both languages as 5 or higher on a 7-point scale).

Our results are from a single conversation between a user and a counseling agent, however, so one important direction of future research is to examine whether our results hold over repeated interactions. The correlation between persuasion and the agent's trustworthiness needs to be examined in greater detail. Future studies should be designed to examine trust as a mediating factor of persuasion and the interaction of cultural congruity and need for cognition. Our study also looked at the agent's appearance, nonverbal behaviors and the message delivered as a single cultural variable, but future research may investigate these aspects separately. Significant work also needs to be done on developing a systematic methodology for cultural tailoring of conversational agents, whether driven by a taxonomy such as Hofstede's cultural dimensions theory [17] or deeper knowledge of the norms and practices of the target culture.

Acknowledgments. We want to thank Juan Fernandez for administering the experiment, Daniel Schulman, Laura Pfeifer, Lazlo Ring, and the other members of the Relational Agents Group at Northeastern University for their help and insightful comments.

References

1. Hawkins, R.P., Kreuter, M., Resnicow, K., Fishbein, M., Dijkstra, A.: Understanding Tailoring in Communicating About Health. Health Educ. Res. 23, 454–466 (2008)
2. Petty, R., Wegener, D.: Attitude Change: Multiple Roles for Persuasion Variables. The handbook of social psychology 1, 323–390 (1998)

3. Cacioppo, J., Petty, R., Feinstein, J., Blair, W., Jarvis, W.: Dispositional Differences in Cognitive Motivation: The Life and Times of Individuals Varying in Need for Cognition. Psychological Bulletin 119, 197–253 (1996)
4. Luna, D., Peracchio, L., de Juan, M.: The Impact of Language and Congruity on Persuasion in Multicultural E-marketing. Journal of Consumer Psychology 13(1&2), 41–50 (2003)
5. Rossen, B., Johnsen, K., Deladisma, A., Lind, S., Lok, B.: Virtual Humans Elicit Skin-Tone Bias Consistent with Real-World Skin-Tone Biases. In: Prendinger, H., Lester, J.C., Ishizuka, M. (eds.) IVA 2008. LNCS (LNAI), vol. 5208, pp. 237–244. Springer, Heidelberg (2008)
6. Endrass, B., Rehm, M., André, E.: Culture-Specific Communication Management For Virtual Agents. In: Proc. of 8th Int. Conf. on Autonomous Agents and Multiagent Systems (2009)
7. Endrass, B., Andre, E., Huang, L., Gratch, J.: A Data-Driven Approach to Culture-specific Communication Management Styles for Virtual Agents. In: Proc. of 9th Int. Conf. on Autonomous Agents and Multiagent Systems (2010)
8. Jan, D., Herrera, D., Martinovski, B., Novick, D., Traum, D.: A Computational Model of Culture-Specific Conversational Behavior. In: Pelachaud, C., Martin, J.-C., André, E., Chollet, G., Karpouzis, K., Pelé, D. (eds.) IVA 2007. LNCS (LNAI), vol. 4722, pp. 45–56. Springer, Heidelberg (2007)
9. Zanbaka, C., Goolkasian, P., Hodges, L.: Can a Virtual Cat Persuade You?: The Role of Gender and Realism in Speaker Persuasiveness. In: Proceedings of the SIGCHI conference on Human Factors in computing systems, pp. 1153–1162. ACM, New York (2006)
10. Katagiri, Y., Takahashi, T., Takeuchi, Y.: Social Persuasion in Human-Agent Interaction. In: Second IJCAI Workshop on Knowledge and Reasoning in Practical Dialogue Systems, pp. 64–69 (2001)
11. Schulman, D., Bickmore, T.: Persuading users through counseling dialogue with a conversational agent. In: Proceedings of the 4th International Conference on Persuasive Technology (2009)
12. Lafferty, J., Eady, P.: The Desert Survival Problem. Experimental Learning Methods (1974)
13. Sue, D., Ivey, A., Pedersen, P.: A Theory of Multicultural Counseling and Therapy. Brooks/Cole Pacific Grove, Calif.(1996)
14. Albert, R., Ha, A.: Latino/Anglo-American Differences in Attributions to Situations Involving Touch and Silence. International Journal of Intercultural Relations 28, 253–280 (2004)
15. Wheeless, L., Grotz, J.: The Measurement of Trust and Its Relationship to Self-Disclosure. Human Communication Research 3, 250–257 (2006)
16. Dolinski, D., Nawrat, M., Rudak, I.: Dialogue Involvement as a Social Influence Technique. Personality and Social Psychology Bulletin 27, 1395 (2001)
17. Hofstede, G.: Culture's consequences: Comparing Values, Behaviors, Institutions, and Organizations Across Nations. Sage Pubns, Thousand Oaks (2001)

A Multiparty Multimodal Architecture for Realtime Turntaking

Kristinn R. Thórisson[1,2], Olafur Gislason[1],
Gudny Ragna Jonsdottir[2], and Hrafn Th. Thorisson[1]

[1] Center for Analysis & Design of Intelligent Agents, Reykjavik University
[2] Icelandic Institute for Intelligent Machines
Menntavegur 1, 101 Reykjavik, Iceland
{thorisson,olafurgi,gudny04,hrafnt05}@ru.is

Abstract. Many dialogue systems have been built over the years that
address some subset of the many complex factors that shape the behavior of participants in a face-to-face conversation. The Ymir Turntaking
Model (YTTM) is a broad computational model of conversational skills
that has been in development for over a decade, continuously growing in
the number of factors it addresses. In past work we have shown how it
addresses realtime dialogue, communicative gesture, perception of turn-
taking signals (e.g. prosody, gaze, manual gesture), dialogue planning,
learning of multimodal turn signals, and dynamic adaptation to human speaking style. The architectural principles of the YTTM prescribe
smaller architectural granularity than most other models, and its principles allow non-destructive additive expansion. In this paper we show
how the YTTM accommodates *multi-party dialogue*. The extension has
been implemented in a virtual environment; we present data for up to
12 simulated participants participating in realtime cooperative dialogue.
The system includes dynamically adjustable parameters for impatience,
willingness to give turn and eagerness to speak.

Keywords: Turntaking, Dialogue, Realtime, Multiparty, Multimodal,
Architecture, YTTM.

1   Introduction

Traditionally, research on turntaking in natural dialogue has focused on surface
phenomena, observable patterns of behavior such as speech generation, turn-
taking, interruptions, prosody, gaze, gestures, head and body movements, and
so on. Many researchers have tried to characterize the complex interplay of
movement and *action* in the "simplest possible way", searching for a set of
rules or a "main element" or key unit with general explanatory powers (c.f.
[1] [2]). In contrast to a focus on behavior, we have been addressing the many
control processes underlying dialogue behavior – the *architecture of dialogue
cognition*, and adopted a systems focus. Our work on turntaking extends well over
a decade, and the results have been demonstrated in the Ymir Turntaking Model

J. Allbeck et al. (Eds.): IVA 2010, LNAI 6356, pp. 350–356, 2010.

(YTTM) [3] [4], which by now has been implemented in numerous interactive systems (c.f. [5] [6] [7]). Over the past decade we have expanded the YTTM in various ways. Throughout these enhancements we have preserved the YTTM's architectural principles, this being perhaps the most significant distinguishing feature of our approach: Extensions of the YTTM have been additive, meaning that prior functions included in – and explained by – the model are preserved as it gains generality. By now the model addresses a relatively broad set of features, including issues of coordinated multimodal planning and execution, perceptual organization and prioritization, and even learning.

In this paper we describe an extension of the YTTM for *multiparty turntaking*, adding to the model's existing functionalities the ability to model multiple speakers engaged in cooperative dialogue. In line with prior expansions, this particular one has not changed any of the framework's operating principles. We present data showing the behavior of the system with up to 12 simulated agents interacting in "polite" (cooperative) dialogue. While data presented here is limited to simulated scenarios; elsewhere we have tested the YTTM in realtime dialogue with human users with good results [5] [8], and evaluated its performance in comparison to human-human dialogue [9]. Although this does not replace eventual testing of the new multiparty features with human users, YTTM's prior track record in in this respect gives the simulation data presented here added weight, making it more than simply preliminary.

The paper is organized as follows: In section 2 we d iscuss theoretical framework and related work; in section 3 we discuss the YTTM, with section 4 detailing the multi-party extensions. Section 5 describes the evaluation setup and conclusions.

2   Background and Related Work

Schegloff described turntaking as that "When persons talk to each other in interaction, they ordinarily talk one at a time and one after each other" ([10], p. 207). Many have pointed out, however, that during the "live performance" of dialogue this characterization is a gross simplification at best, and at worst a rather inaccurate description of what actually happens in dialogue, as utterances frequently overlap, people interrupt themselves and others all the time, and talk on top of each other. We agree. We have argued elsewhere [11] that conversational skills belong to the class of systems that Simon referred to as *nearly-decomposable* [12], and that much of the complexity of dialogue stems from complex interaction between a set of both loosely and tightly coupled ("nearly decomposable") functions. The runtime behavior of these functions produces side effects on the observable surface phenomena that we recognize as hesitations, interruptions, and so on. A corollary can be found in much of last century's research on attention (c.f. [13] [14]), which has reached similar conclusions with regards to attentional mechanisms. Turntaking, in this view, is an indirect result of the many mechanisms at play in dialogue, in particular *their complex interaction* and effects of *limitations of realtime cognitive capabilities*. Our stance is that the best way to capture the operation of the many interacting mental functions in dialogue is to try to model dialogue as a fairly complete cognitive system, at a relatively fine level of detail.

Lessman et al. [15] describe one of the few efforts, besides YTTM, describing an explicitly cognitively motivated computational turntaking system, includng some thoughts on anticipation and the perception-action loop. They integrated turntaking mechanisms of the Max agent in a belief-desire-intention (BDI) ar- chitecture (although the BDI approach itself is not cognitively motivated). The system incorporated dialogue framework ideas from Traum and Rickel [16], who propose what they call "layers" of dialogue, although their use of the concept of layers does not seem connected to architectural concerns or cognitive principles.

The original prototype of YTTM employed close to 100 modules of various types (deciders, perceptors, etc.), as well as layers motivated by experimen- tal data on the human perception-action cycle [3] [4] [8]. As mentioned above, YTTM has been expanded over time, at this point incorporating not only a complete set of modes (manual gesture, facial expression, head movements, eye movement, speech) for both perception and action, but also more recently re- altime adaptation to human speakers' speaking style. This is a direct result of its architectural foundation, building on fine-grain modularity and a cognitively- motivated organizational structure. Much of the work of others has dismissed the YTTM's fine granularity, choosing coarser-grain approach, in line with stan- dard software practices; one example is Traum and Rickel's work [16]; another example is Raux' [17] two-party dialogue architecture, which otherwise builds on YTTM. Coarse granularity is likely to hamper architectures' further expansion and may result in significant redesigns and changes every time the systems are improved with new functionality.

3   Cognito-Theoretical Basis of the YTTM

The YTTM [3] [4] is an agent-oriented model, motivated by a cognitive focus, taking into account top-down and bottom-up processing and making *time* a first-class citizen through- out. One of the key concepts in the YTTM is the idea of a *perception-action context* ("con- text" for short): an active set of perception and action processes relevant to the current

I-Have-Turn	Other-Has-Turn
I-Accept-Turn	Other-Accepts-Turn
I-Give-Turn	Other-Gives-Turn
I-Want-Turn	Other-Wants-Turn

Fig. 1. Turntaking contexts

situation and goal(s) of an agent. In our implementations for turntaking only one or two contexts are typically active at the same time, although parallelism is not prohibited and the context set may be changed – permanently or tem- porally – by attention processes that dynamically activate and deactivate the processes. Turntaking is essentially a *coupling* of these contexts – an agent syn- chronizes his context(s) with those of others, as inferred from behavior tracked by his perceptual processes. Contexts bear some resemblance to the approach for perception-action organization taken in behavior-based A.I., a major difference being that our approach allows dynamic context evolution at runtime, resulting in greater flexibility and dynamic system behavior, and being more compatible with cognitive research on human attention mechanisms (c.f. [14]). Most system modules (perception, decision, behavior, etc.) in the YTTM are confined to be active only in one or at most two contexts. This is in effect a way of implementing dynamic attention control. The architecture's modularity and separation of topic knowledge and behavioral knowledge make it relatively easy to install and add increasingly complex components to the system, which forms the basis for the multiparty extension.

4   Multi-party Extension

Our multiparty implementation includes the main principles of the above outlined functionalities, including multimodal action and perception. We have implemented eight dialogue contexts (see Figure 1), each containing the various perception and action modules, representing the disposition of the system at any point in time (see discussion of perception-action contexts, above). As in prior versions, activations of contexts are done via messages, and executed by a set of cooperating modules. In the previous model the turntaking contexts were implemented to be mutually exclusive; in the updated model the contexts *I-Want-Turn* and *Other-Wants-Turn* are allowed to be active simultaneously with other states. This was not necessary in the

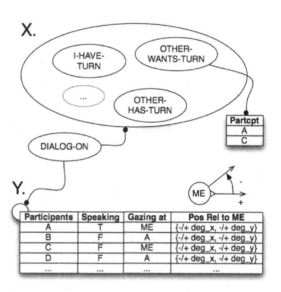

Fig. 2. Extensions to implement multi-party/multimodal turntaking within the YTTM model include adding perceptions of participants, gaze, position and who is speaking (not the same as who has turn). Some information is relevant in some contexts and not others. Notice the distributed nature of the data: all data represented in the system (shown here in tables) is accessible by *any* *active* cognitive process that needs it.

dyad model as *Other-Wants-Turn* would imply that "I have turn" and vice versa – in multiparty dialogue this information is not given. Further extensions include lists of participants, who is speaking, gaze perception and position perception (see Figure 2).

We have implemented the complete set of contexts hypothesized for Western dialogue participants and implemented in prior versions of the YTTM, including the minimal set of perceptions and actions necessary to run the system, as proven in our prior evaluations with live human interlocutors. As before, modules are confined to be active only in certain contexts, e.g. backchannel generation only happens when someone else has turn. Multimodal deciders use information extracted from the external (perceptual) and internal environment, to synchronize the perceived and anticipated contexts, which in turn steer both perceptual and behavioral actions. All activation and de-activation of contexts is driven by perceptual events, modulated in some cases by temporally-dependent thresholds. Each agent is implemented to run in its own thread, so perceptual aliasing can happen in the system just like in human conversations. The core operating principles of the YTTM have been thoroughly demonstrated for realtime interaction with human users in [5] and [8], and our artificial agents are based on what has worked before in this respect.

Each conversation participant has an individual context model, updated with decisions from its internal deciders and input from its perception modules. Perceptions include a list of all conversation participants, who is talking, who is "looking at me" (for any given agent) and who is requesting turn at each given time. Each participant also has configuration for *urge-to-speak*; probability that another participant wants to talk (based on perceptions of their actions), the *speed at which urge-to-speak rises* (modeling a type of impatience for getting the turn), and the *yield tollerance* when someone else wants it (while he has turn). The last parameter is currently linked to the amount that an agent intends to say, so that interruptions are less likely in the middle of an utterance than at their very beginning or end. When the agent perceives that someone has the turn the agent looks at that person. When that agent gives turn (semi-explicitly) by looking at a specific person at the end of an utterance, other agents look at that person as well. For any given participant, its perception of the gaze behaviors of others determines in part whether it is possible to take turn politely. These behaviors provide only the beginning of what could be a much more elaborate set of behaviors; what is more important are the principles by which the system can easily be expanded to accommodate a much larger set of these behaviors.

5   Experimental Results

The model has been implemented in a virtual world, and we have tested it with up to 12 agents, demonstrating its scalability to relatively large groups.[1] Under a cooperation goal, participants take into consideration each other's limitations on attention, and yield if someone wants to speak, depending on the setting of their *yield* parameter. Our simulation works at the decisecond level of granularity; it should be noted that the perception of turn availability is a process that takes time, as does the decision to start speaking. Typically, overlaps only occur when two agents simultaneously decide to take turn, when their decisions are executed at a frequency above perceptual sampling rate of 10 Hz. In our scenario we have seen overlaps, but since agents are set to be very polite, typically these periods last less than 300 msecs.

---

[1] See video at http://www.youtube.com/watch?v=CVvNrv7K4bA

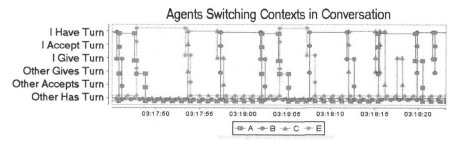

Fig. 3. The graph shows 30 seconds of conversation between 4 agents. Throughout these 30 seconds all agents' perception about who has turn is synchronized; as one agent perceives he has turn, others perceive that other has turn.

Each agent has an isolated context model and during the course of a conversation he switches contexts within the turntaking model based on his own local perceptions. If agents' perceptions agree on the proceeding of the conversation we should see a pattern of one agent having the turn at a time and others perceiving that someone else has the turn. This is precisely what we see in Figure 3. For further detail on this way of plotting context activations, and the meaning of context alignment, the reader is referred to [5].

We have evaluated the difference in behavior when all agents have a low urge to speak (5%) versus high (95%) (see Table 1). When all agents have high urge 6,6% of the total time is silence, this rises to 43,47% when urge to speak is low. These different settings do not effect average length of turn, nor overlaps.

Although further work will be needed to thoroughly evaluate the multiparty extension, earlier work shows the ability of the YTTM to address realworld, real-time dialogue [5] [8], strengthening the simulated results shown here. A thorough comparison to human group dialogue/turntaking patterns remains to be made. Future extensions include adding content generation and interpretation mechanisms, which we have demonstrated for two-party conversation [3], as well as incorporating prosody analysis demonstrated in other versions of the YTTM [5].

Table 1. Average length of turns/silences/overlaps in milliseconds.

Agents	Factor High			Factor Low		
	Portion	Average	StdDev	Portion	Average	StdDev
A	26,6%	3206	1.102	17,37%	3346	1.243
B	18,65%	3232	1.126	11,04%	2841	1.184
C	26,13%	3149	1.145	12,39%	3607	1.041
E	20,87%	4451	1.223	13,7%	3221	1.161
Overlap	1,15%	910	981	2,04%	2122	1.603
Silence	6,6%	256	159	43,47%	2505	3.832

Acknowledgments. This work was supported in part by research grants from RANNIS, Iceland. The authors wish to thank Claudio Pedica for help with the CADIA Populus environment and Erik Parr for help with the animations.

References

1. Allwood, J.: An activity based approach to pragmatics. In: Black, W., Bunt, H.C. (eds.) Abduction, Belief and Context in Dialogue: Studies in Computational Pragmatics, pp. 47–80. John Benjamins, Amsterdam (2000)
2. Sacks, H., Schegloff, E.A., Jefferson, G.A.: A simplest systematics for the organization of turn-taking in conversation. Language 50, 696–735 (1974)
3. Thórisson, K.R.: Natural turn-taking needs no manual: Computational theory and model, from perception to action. In: Granström, B., House, D.,, I.K. (eds.) Multimodality in Language and Speech Systems, Dordrecht, The Netherlands, Kluwer Academic Publishers, pp. 173–207. Kluwer Academic Publishers, Dordrecht (2002)
4. Thórisson, K.R.: Communicative Humanoids: A Computational Model of Psycho-Social Dialogue Skills. PhD thesis, Massachusetts Institute of Technology (1996)
5. Jonsdottir, G.R., Thórisson, K.R.: Teaching computers to conduct spoken interviews: Breaking the realtime barrier with learning. In: Ruttkay, Z., Kipp, M., Nijholt, A., Vilhjálmsson, H.H. (eds.) IVA 2009. LNCS, vol. 5773, pp. 446–459. Springer, Heidelberg (2009)
6. Thórisson, K.R., Jonsdottir, G.R.: A granular architecture for dynamic realtime dialogue. In: Prendinger, H., Lester, J.C., Ishizuka, M. (eds.) IVA 2008. LNCS (LNAI), vol. 5208, pp. 131–138. Springer, Heidelberg (2008)
7. Bonaiuto, J., Thórisson, K.R.: Towards a neurocognitive model of realtime turntaking in face-to-face dialogue. In: Wachsmuth, I., Lenzen, M.,, G.K. (eds.) Embodied Communication in Humans And Machines, Oxford University Press, U.K (2008)
8. Thórisson, K.R.: A mind model for communicative creatures and humanoids. International Journal of Applied Artificial Intelligence 13(4-5), 449–486 (1999)
9. Jonsson, G.K., Thórisson, K.R.: Evaluating multimodal human-robot interaction: A case study of an early humanoid prototype. In: Proceedings of the 6th International Conference on Methods and Techniques in Behavioral Research (2010)
10. Schegloff, E.A.: Between micro and micro: Contexts and other connections. In: Alexander, J.C., Giesen, B., Munch, R., Smelser, N.J. (eds.) The Micro-Macro Link, pp. 207–234. University of California Press, Berkeley (1987)
11. Thórisson, K.R.: Modeling multimodal communication as a complex system. In: Wachsmuth, I., Knoblich, G. (eds.) ZiF Research Group International Workshop. LNCS (LNAI), vol. 4930, pp. 143–168. Springer, Heidelberg (2008)
12. Simon, H.: Near decomposability and the speed of evolution. Industrial and Corporate Change 11(3), 587–599 (2002)
13. Cavanagh, P.: Attention routines and the architecture of selection. In: Cognitive Neuroscience of Attention, pp. 13–28 (2004)
14. Driver, J.: A selective review of selective attention research from the past century. British Journal of Psychology 92, 53–78 (2001)
15. Lessmann, N., Kranstedt, A., Wachsmuth, I.: Towards a Cognitively Motivated Processing of Turn-Taking Signals for the Embodied Conversational Agent Max. In: AAMAS 2004 Workshop Proceedings: Embodied Conversational Agents: Balanced Perception and Action (July 2004)
16. Traum, D., Rickel, J.: Embodied agents for multi-party dialogue in immersive virtual worlds. In: AAMAS 2002: Proceedings of the first international joint conference on Autonomous agents and multiagent systems, pp. 766–773. ACM, New York (2002)
17. Raux, A., Eskenazi, M.: A multi-layer architecture for semi-synchronous event-driven dialogue management. In: ASRU, Kyoto, Japan, pp. 514–519 (2007)

The Influence of Emotions in Embodied Agents on Human Decision-Making[*]

Celso M. de Melo[1], Peter Carnevale[2], and Jonathan Gratch[1]

[1] Institute for Creative Technologies, University of Southern California,
12015 Waterfront Drive, Building #4 Playa Vista, CA 90094-2536, USA
demelo@usc.edu, gratch@ict.usc.edu
[2] USC Marshall School of Business
Los Angeles, CA 90089-0808, USA
peter.carnevale@marshall.usc.edu

Abstract. Acknowledging the social functions that emotions serve, there has been growing interest in the interpersonal effect of emotion in human decision making. Following the paradigm of experimental games from social psychology and experimental economics, we explore the interpersonal effect of emotions expressed by embodied agents on human decision making. The paper describes an experiment where participants play the iterated prisoner's dilemma against two different agents that play the same strategy (tit-for-tat), but communicate different goal orientations (cooperative vs. individualistic) through their patterns of facial displays. The results show that participants are sensitive to differences in the facial displays and cooperate significantly more with the cooperative agent. The data indicate that emotions in agents can influence human decision making and that the nature of the emotion, as opposed to mere presence, is crucial for these effects. We discuss the implications of the results for designing human-computer interfaces and understanding human-human interaction.

Keywords: Emotion, Embodied Agents, Decision Making, Cooperation, Experimental Games.

1 Introduction

The expression of emotion can serve important social functions in humans [1, 2]. Anger can communicate to the receiver to cease its actions as they might be hindering the sender's goals; shame can convey regret for actions that might have obstructed the receivers' goals; happiness or sadness might convey a general positive or negative appraisal of the current situation; and so on. Complementing the focus on the *intra*personal effects of emotion [3, 4] and acknowledging this social view of emotions, there is interest in the *inter*personal effects of emotion on human decision making.

---

[*] This work was sponsored by the Fundação para a Ciência e a Tecnologia (FCT) grant #SFRH-BD-39590-2007; and, the U.S. Army Research, Development, and Engineering Command and the National Science Foundation under grant #HS-0713603. The content does not necessarily reflect the position or the policy of the Government, and no official endorsement should be inferred.

J. Allbeck et al. (Eds.): IVA 2010, LNAI 6356, pp. 357–370, 2010.
© Springer-Verlag Berlin Heidelberg 2010

Work in social psychology and experimental economics [5, 6, 7] seeks to understand, using experimental games, the impact emotions expressed by others have on one's decision making. Experimental games are laboratory tasks where ([8], pg.363) "(a) each individual must make one or more decisions that affect his own and the other's welfare; (b) the outcomes of these decisions are expressed in numerical form; and (c) the numbers that express these outcomes are chosen beforehand by the experimenter." In this paper we use the paradigm of experimental games to study the impact emotions expressed by embodied agents – which are agents that have virtual bodies and are capable of expressing themselves through their bodies in similar ways to humans [9] – have on human decision making.

Understanding the effect emotions in embodied agents have on people's decision making is important for several reasons: (a) it provides insight on how to facilitate cooperation between agents and humans and, thus, can enhance human-machine interaction [10]; (b) it permits hypothesizing about the interpersonal impact of emotions in human-human interaction based on human-agent interaction; (c) it is a chance to examine the viability of using embodied agents as a research method to learn about human-human interactions. So, to address this goal, we describe an experiment where people play the iterated prisoner's dilemma, a game that has been traditionally used to study emergence of cooperation in social dilemmas [11], with different embodied agents that, even though following the same strategy to choose their actions, express different patterns of facial expressions. What this study demonstrates is this seemingly irrelevant change, with no bearing on the agent's action policy, can have a profound impact on human cooperation.

People's decisions in games such as the prisoner's dilemma depend on inferences about the other player's propensity to cooperate, and emotional displays play a central role in such inferences, at least between human players [12]. According to appraisal models of human emotion [13], such displays arise from a cognitive appraisal of the relationship between situational events and an agent's goals (e.g., is this event congruent with my goals? Who is responsible for this event?), and thus indirectly reveal a player's future intentions. Of central interest here is if human participants infer that an embodied agent will or will not cooperate depending on its emotional displays. Our hypothesis is that agent emotions that are consistent with a goal of cooperation will foster cooperation whereas emotions consistent with self-interested goals will not.

To test this hypothesis, we created two agents that differ in their goals toward the human player: the *cooperative* agent; and, the *individualistic* agent. The cooperative agent has the goal of reaching mutual cooperation. Thus, when both players cooperate, it will express gratitude (as the outcome is appraised to be positive for the self and the participant is appraised to have contributed for it); when the agent defects and the participant cooperates, it expresses shame (as the outcome is negative for the participant and the agent is responsible); and so on. The individualistic agent, on the other hand, has the goal of maximizing its own points (independently of the outcome of the other player). Therefore, when the agent defects and the participant cooperates, it expresses joy (as this event is appraised to be very positive); when the participant defects and the agent cooperates, it expresses sadness (as this is the worst event for the self); and so on. We hypothesize, then, that participants will be sensitive to differences in the patterns of facial display, use these differences to inform their own decision-making, and cooperate more with the cooperative agent.

2 Experiment

The experiment follows a repeated-measures design where participants play 25 rounds of the iterated prisoner's dilemma with two different computational agents for a chance to win real money: the cooperative agent; and the individualistic agent. The agents differ in the way their facial displays reflect the outcome of each round. The action policy, i.e., the strategy for choosing which action to take in each round, is the same for both agents.

Game. Following the approach by Kiesler, Waters and Sproull [14], the prisoner's dilemma game was recast as an investment game and described as follows to the participants: "You are going to play a two-player investment game. You can invest in one of two projects: Project Green and Project Blue. However, how many points you get is contingent on which project the other player invests in. So, if you both invest in Project Green, then each gets 5 points. If you choose Project Green but the other player chooses Project Blue, then you get 3 and the other player gets 7 points. If, on the other hand, you choose Project Blue and the other player chooses Project Green, then you get 7 and the other player gets 3 points. A fourth possibility is that you both choose Project Blue, in which case both get 4 points". There are, therefore, two possible actions in each round: *Project Green* (or cooperation); and *Project Blue* (or defection). Table 1 summarizes the payoff matrix. The participant is told that there is no communication between the players before choosing an action. Moreover, the participant is told that the agent makes its decision without knowledge of what the participant's choice in that round is. *After* the round is over, the action each chose is made available to both players and the outcome of the round, i.e., the number of points each player got, is also shown. The experiment is fully implemented in software and a snapshot is shown in Fig.1.

Table 1. Payoff matrix for the investment game

		Agent	
		Project Green	Project Blue
Participant	Project Green	Agent: 5 pts Participant: 5 pts	Agent: 7 pts Participant: 3 pts
	Project Blue	Agent: 3 pts Participant: 7 pts	Agent: 4 pts Participant: 4 pts

Action Policy. Agents in both conditions play the same action policy, i.e., they follow the same strategy to choose their actions. The policy is a variant of *tit-for-tat*. Tit-for-tat is a strategy where a player begins by cooperating and then proceeds to repeat the action the other player did in the previous round. Tit-for-tat has been argued to strike the right balance of punishment and reward with respect to the opponent's previous actions [15]. So, the action policy used in our experiment is as follows: (a) in rounds 1 to 5, the agent plays the following fixed sequence: cooperation, cooperation, defection, defection, cooperation; (b) in rounds 6 to 25, the agent plays pure tit-for-tat. The rationale for the sequence in the first five rounds is to make it harder for participants

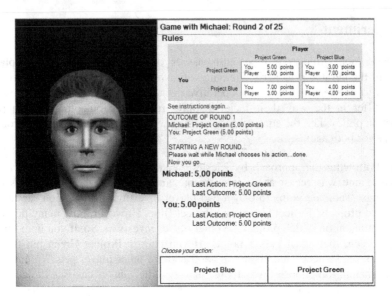

Fig. 1. The software used in the experiment. During game playing, the payoff matrix is shown on the top right, the outcome of the previous round in the upper mid right, the total outcome and the actions in the previous round in the lower mid right, the possible actions on the bottom right and the real-time animation of the agent on the left.

to learn the agents' strategy and to allow participants to experience a variety of facial displays from the start.

Conditions. There are two conditions in this experiment: the *cooperative* agent; and the *individualistic* agent. Both agents follow the same action policy but differ in their facial display policies. The facial display policy defines the emotion and intensity which is conveyed for each possible outcome of a round. Table 2 shows the facial displays for the cooperative agent and Table 3 for the individualistic agent. The facial displays are chosen to reflect the agents' goals in a way that is consistent with appraisal models of emotion [13]. The cooperative agent has the goal of reaching mutual cooperation. Thus, when both players cooperate, it will express gratitude (with a facial display of joy), as the outcome is appraised to be positive for the self and the participant is appraised to have contributed for it; when the agent defects and the participant cooperates, it expresses shame, as the outcome is negative for the participant and the agent is responsible; when the agent cooperates and the participant defects, it expresses anger, as the outcome is negative and the participant is responsible for it; and, when both defect, it expresses sadness, as the event is negative. The individualistic agent, on the other hand, has the goal of maximizing its own points (independently of the outcome of the other player). Therefore, when the agent defects and the participant cooperates, it expresses joy, as this event is appraised to be very positive; when both cooperate, it expresses nothing, as this event could be more positive; when both defect, it expresses sadness at 50%, as this is a negative event; when the participant defects and the agent cooperates, it expresses sadness at 100%, as this is

Table 2. Facial displays (emotion and intensities) for the cooperative agent

Cooperative Agent		*Agent*	
		Project Green	Project Blue
Participant	Project Green	Joy (100%)	Shame (100%)
	Project Blue	Anger (100%)	Sadness (100%)

Table 3. Facial displays (emotion and intensities) for the individualistic agent

Individualistic Agent		*Agent*	
		Project Green	Project Blue
Participant	Project Green	Neutral	Joy (100%)
	Project Blue	Sadness (100%)	Sadness (50%)

the worst event for the self. Facial displays are animated using a real-time pseudo-muscular model for the face which also simulates wrinkles and blushing [16]. The facial display is shown in the end of the round, after both players have chosen their actions and the outcome is shown. Moreover, there is a 4.5 seconds waiting period before the participant is allowed to choose the action for the next round. This period allows the participant to appreciate the outcome of a round before moving to the next round. Finally, to enhance naturalness, blinking is applied to both agents as well as subtle random motion of the neck and back.

The condition order is randomized while making sure that 50% of the participants experience one order and the remaining 50% the other. Two different bodies are used: *Michael* and *Daniel*. These bodies are shown in Fig.2 as well as their respective facial displays. Bodies are assigned to each condition in random order and agents are referred by the names of their bodies throughout the experiment.

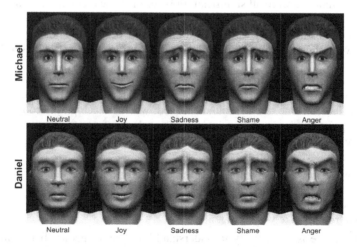

Fig. 2. The agent bodies - Michael and Daniel - and their facial displays. Shame is distinguished from sadness by blushing of the cheeks.

Table 4. Classification of the facial displays with respect to perception of joy, sadness, shame and anger. Scale goes from 1 (meaning 'not at all') to 5 (meaning 'very much').

	Perceived Emotion			
	Joy	*Sadness*	*Shame*	*Anger*
Real Emotion	Mean (SD)	Mean (SD)	Mean (SD)	Mean (SD)
	Michael			
Neutral	1.86 (.941)	1.86 (1.037)	1.91 (1.065)	1.68 (.945)
Joy*	4.05 (.899)	1.18 (.501)	1.23 (.528)	1.41 (1.098)
Sadness*	1.27 (.703)	4.09 (1.019)	2.77 (1.478)	1.50 (.859)
Shame*	1.32 (.716)	3.59 (1.182)	3.55 (1.371)	1.45 (.858)
Anger*	1.36 (.727)	1.95 (1.046)	1.32 (.646)	4.32 (1.211)
	Daniel			
Neutral	1.55 (1.057)	1.73 (.935)	1.68 (.894)	2.18 (1.259)
Joy*	3.77 (1.020)	1.18 (.501)	1.23 (.528)	1.14 (.468)
Sadness*	1.41 (.854)	3.68 (1.492)	2.73 (1.386)	1.50 (.740)
Shame*	1.32 (.780)	3.77 (1.412)	3.86 (1.356)	1.41 (.734)
Anger*	1.27 (.703)	1.82 (1.332)	1.55 (1.011)	4.27 (1.420)

* Significant difference between means in same row using *repeated-measures ANOVA*, $p < .05$

To validate the facial displays, a pre-study was conducted where participants were asked to classify, from 1 (meaning 'not at all') to 5 (meaning 'very much'), how much each of the displays conveys joy, sadness, shame and anger. Images of the displays and questions were presented in random order. Twenty-two participants were recruited just for this study from the same participant pool as the main experiment (described below). The results are shown in Table 4. A *repeated-measures ANOVA* was used to compare the means for perceived emotion in each display. Significant differences were found for all displays except, as expected, for the neutral case. Moreover, pairwise comparisons of the perception of the real emotion with respect to perception of the other emotions were all significant in favor of the real emotion, with one exception: displays of shame were also significantly perceived as displays of sadness. This is not a problem since it is usually agreed that shame occurs upon the occurrence of a negative event, thus causing sadness, plus the attribution of blame to the self [17].

Measures. Before playing the game the participant is asked to fill out profile information: age, gender, country of origin, profession, education level and major. During game-play, the outcome of each round is saved: whether each player cooperated; and, how many points each got. After playing with each agent, a set of classification questions is presented to understand how human-like the agents are (scale goes from 1 - 'not at all' to 6 - 'very much'):

- How likely was the agent to have experienced emotions?
- Was the agent scripted?
- How human-like was the agent?
- How robotic-like was the agent?

After the game is over, to try to understand how the agents are being interpreted, the participant is asked to classify each agent according to the Person-Perception scale [18] which consists of 33 bipolar pairs of adjectives: dislikable-likable; cruel-kind; unfriendly-friendly; cold-warm; unreliable-reliable; relaxed-tense;

detached-involved; rude-polite; dishonest-honest; unpleasant-pleasant; naïve-sophisticated; unapproachable-inviting; passive-active; aloof-compassionate; non-threatening-threatening; not cool-cool; unintelligent-intelligent; cold-sensitive; sleepy-alert; proud-humble; unsympathetic-sympathetic; shy-self-confident; callous-tender; permissive-stern; cheerful-sad; modest-arrogant; not conceited-conceited; weak-strong; mature-immature; noisy-quiet; nervous-calm; soft-tough; acquiescent-emancipated. In this scale items are rated on a 7-point scale (e.g., 1-'dislikable' to 7-'likable'). Finally, participants are asked 'Which agent did you prefer to play with?' as well as two exploratory classification questions (scale goes from 1-'never' to 6-'always'), where the agents are actually referred to by the names of their bodies:

- How considerate of your welfare was the <cooperative/individualistic agent>?
- How much would you trust the <cooperative/individualistic agent>?

Participants. Fifty-one participants were recruited at the University of Southern California Marshall School of Business. Average age was 21.0 years. Gender distribution was as follows: *males*, 45.1%; *females*, 54.9%. Most participants were undergraduate students (96.9%) majoring in business (86.3%). Most were also originally from the United States (84.3%). The incentive to participate follows standard practices in experimental economics [19]: first, participants were given credit for their participation in this experiment; second, with respect to their goal in the game, participants were instructed to earn as many points as possible, as the total amount of points would increase their chance of winning a lottery for $100.

3   Results

Cooperation. To understand how much people cooperated with the agents in each condition, the following variables were defined:

- Coop.All - % of cooperation in all rounds;
- Coop.AgC - % of cooperation when the agent cooperates in the previous round;
- Coop.AgD - % of cooperation when the agent defects in the previous round.

The *Kolmogorov-Smirnov* test was applied to all these variables to test for their normality and all were found to be significantly non-normal. Therefore, the *Wilcoxon signed ranks* test is used to compare means between the two conditions. The results are shown in Table 5. Also, the evolution of percentage of cooperation per round is shown in Fig.3.

To understand whether people's decision-making was reflecting only facial displays, as opposed to facial displays *and* action policy, we compared percentage of cooperation for the same display between conditions. Table 6 shows these results. Significance values are calculated using the *Wilcoxon signed ranks* test.

Since there is evidence that people form judgments of people based only on appearance [22] we wanted to make sure that the body was not a confounding factor in our experiment. Thus, we compared percentage of cooperation with the two agent bodies used in the experiment. It was found that participants were *not* cooperating significantly more with Michael (M=.33, SD=.26) than with Daniel (M=.31, SD=.26, p>.05) Significance level is calculated using the *Wilcoxon signed ranks* test.

Table 5. Descriptive statistics and significance levels for percentage of cooperation

Variables	Cooperative		Individualistic		Sig.	r^1
	Mean	SD	Mean	SD	2-sd	
Coop.All*	.37	.28	.27	.23	.022	.320
Coop.AgC	.40	.32	.34	.29	.262	ns
Coop.AgD*	.30	.26	.20	.20	.022	.320

* Significant difference, p < 0.05.

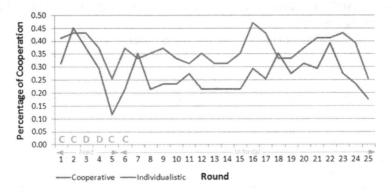

Fig. 3. Evolution of percentage of cooperation with each round. The agent strategy is marked above the horizontal axis: 'C' stands for cooperation, and 'D' for defection.

Table 6. Comparison of percentage of cooperation for the same facial display between conditions. Joy occurs when there is mutual cooperation in the cooperative condition and when the agent defects and the participant cooperates in the individualistic condition. Sadness occurs when there is mutual defection in the cooperative condition and when the participant defects and the agent cooperates in the individualistic condition.

Variables	Cooperative		Individualistic		Sig.	r
	Mean	SD	Mean	SD	2-sd	
Joy*	.42	.42	.22	.28	.008	.371
Sadness	.29	.31	.26	.29	.484	ns

* Significant difference, p < 0.05.

Agent Characterization. The results for the post-condition classification questions are shown in Table 7. Significance values are calculated using the *Wilcoxon signed ranks* test.

---

[1] Effect size for the dependent *t* test statistic is calculated as suggested by Rosenthal [20]. The guidelines for interpretation are [21]:
- $r = 0.10$ (small effect): the effect explains 1% of the total variance;
- $r = 0.30$ (medium effect): the effect explains 9% of the total variance;
- $r = 0.50$ (large effect): the effect explains 25% of the total variance.

Table 7. Descriptive statistics and significance for post-condition classification questions

Variables	Cooperative		Individualistic		Sig.	r
	Mean	SD	Mean	SD	2-sd	
Emotions?*	4.20	1.51	3.47	1.67	.003	.422
Scripted?	4.45	1.49	4.53	1.38	.743	ns
Human-like?	2.88	1.40	2.65	1.40	.165	ns
Robot-like?	4.59	1.33	4.63	1.34	.889	ns

* Significant difference, p < 0.05.

Principal component analysis (varimax rotation, scree-test) on the Person-Perception scale revealed three factors consistent with the literature [18]: *evaluation*, explains 33.1% of the variance (Cronbach's Alpha = .962) with main loading factors of friendly-unfriendly, kind-cruel and sympathetic-unsympathetic; *potency* (or *power*), explains 17.5% of the variance (Cronbach's Alpha = .902) with main loading factors of emancipated-acquiescent, tough-soft and arrogant-modest; *activity*, explains 8.0% of the variance (Cronbach's Alpha = .762) with main loading factors of active-passive, involved-detached and alert-sleepy. These three factors were calculated for both conditions and the means compared using the *dependent t test* (since the *Kolmogorov-Smirnov* test was not significant). The results are shown in Table 8.

Table 8. Descriptive statistics and significance levels for Person-Perception scale

Variables	Cooperative		Individualistic		Sig.	r
	Mean	SD	Mean	SD	2-sd	
Evaluation	5.01	1.75	4.74	1.61	.461	ns
Potency/Power	5.26	1.54	5.81	1.26	.086	ns
Activity	3.88	1.49	3.50	0.94	.163	ns

Regarding the post-game questions, participants' preference for the agents did not differ significantly ($\chi^2(2)=3.30$, $p=.193>.05$): *cooperative*, 29.4%; *individualistic*, 25.5%; *both*, 45.1%. The results for the classification questions are shown on Table 9. Significance values are calculated using the *Wilcoxon signed ranks* test.

Table 9. Descriptive statistics and significance levels for post-game questions

Variables	Cooperative		Individualistic		Sig.	r
	Mean	SD	Mean	SD	2-sd	
Considers your Welfare?	3.06	1.68	2.82	1.47	.327	ns
Trustworthy?	3.04	1.67	2.56	1.28	.065	ns

4 Discussion

The results show that people are cooperating more with the cooperative agent than with the individualistic agent. Effectively, Table 4 reveals that the percentage of cooperation, over all rounds, is significantly higher with the cooperative agent (M=.37, SD=.28) than with the individualistic agent (M=.27, SD=.23; p<.05, r=.32). This result is in line with Frank's view that, in social dilemmas, people look for cues in their trading partners that they might be willing to cooperate before engaging in cooperation themselves [23]. What our results suggest is that people also care and look for these cues when they are engaged in a social dilemma with embodied agents.

So, why are people cooperating more with the cooperative agent than with the in-dividualistic agent? Before suggesting an explanation for the results, we'll begin by excluding two alternative explanations. The first is the *persona effect* which argues that people are more engaged with embodied agents that express emotions [24, 25]. In a previous study [26] we asked people to play the iterated prisoner's dilemma with the cooperative agent and with an agent that expressed no emotions. The results again showed that people cooperated significantly more with the cooperative agent. How-ever, though promising, the results did not prove that the agent needed to have "coop-erative" emotions in order to promote cooperation. The argument is that the mere fact the agent had emotions, "cooperative" or not, led to increased engagement and this alone was sufficient to explain the increase in cooperation. However, this explanation cannot apply to the current experiment as both the cooperative and the individualistic agents display emotions. Further evidence that engagement alone is insufficient to explain these results is the fact that there was no significant difference in terms of agent preference. A second alternative explanation is that people are favoring the agent which is more human-like. Again, in our previous study, it was found that the cooperative agent was perceived as being more human-like than the agent without emotions and, thus, the argument was that by a mechanism similar to *kin selection* [27] extended to include embodied agents, people were simply cooperating with the more human-like agent. However, in the present experiment, there was no significant difference in perception of human-likeness (Table 7) and, thus, kin selection cannot explain the results.

We argue people are using the facial displays conveyed by the agents to learn about the agents' goals and, then, act accordingly. Keltner and Kring [28] argue that the display of emotions can serve an *informative* function, signaling information about feelings and intentions to the interaction partner. The argument, then, is that the agents' facial displays allow participants to understand what the agents' goals are through a process of "inverse appraisal", i.e., from the displayed emotion the partici-pant is inferring how the agent appraises the situation and what its goals are. For in-stance, if after the participant cooperates and the agent defects, the agent displays shame (as in the case of the cooperative agent), then the participant can infer that this outcome is appraised as negative by the agent and, moreover, that the agent believes itself to be at blame. However, if for the same actions, the agent displays joy (as in the case of the individualistic agent), then the participant can infer that the agent finds the outcome positive and, thus, is likely to keep defecting. This would explain, for in-stance, why participants are reacting differently to the same expression of joy in the different agents (Table 6). This explanation also allows us to understand how cooperation evolves in time. Figure 3 reveals that people perceive a difference be-tween the agents very early in the game. Effectively, people start cooperating less with the individualistic agent as early as the 3rd round. Even though both agents defect in rounds 3 and 4 (see the 'Experiment' section), participants cooperate much less with the individualistic agent in round 5. After the agents cooperate in rounds 5 and 6, people seem to attempt cooperation again in round 7 with the individualistic agent but, from then on, they again consistently cooperate less with the individualistic agent. The results on the Person-Perception scale are also interesting (Table 8). Even though not significant, they suggest people perceive the cooperative agent to be less powerful but more active than the individualistic agent. Because the facial displays of the individualistic agent only reflect its own utility and not that of the participant, the agent might be perceived as not caring about reaching mutual cooperation and that, in turn, might be perceived as an expression of power. The result on activity is congruent with the result that participants perceived the cooperative agent to be more likely to be experiencing emotions (Table 7) and could reflect the complexity of the emotions each agent expresses. For instance, it is agreed that self-conscious emotions such as shame (displayed by the cooperative agent) are more complex than joy and sadness (displayed by the individualistic agent) and, accordingly, tend to evolve later in life [29]. Finally, the post-game classification questions (Table 9) reveal a tendency for the cooperative agent to be perceived as more considerate of the participant's welfare and also more trustworthy. Again this is in line with the interpretation that one agent is perceived to be more cooperative than the other.

There also seems to be evidence that the agents' facial displays are influencing participants' decision-making at an unconscious level. First, anecdotally, in our debriefing sessions, it was not uncommon for participants, even though confirming they noticed the emotions in the agents, to state that they were not being influenced by them when deciding what to do. This is, of course, in contrast with what the results actually show. Second, we note that the results on the Person-Perception scale and the post-game classification questions, even though tending towards the expected interpretations for the cooperative and individualistic agents, were not statistically significant. Effectively, emotions had already been argued to influence decision-making at an unconscious level by Damasio [30]. Reeves and Nass [31] also suggested that people unconsciously treat interactions with the media (in our case, embodied agents) in the same way as with real humans. Notice also that this would not invalidate our explanation based on appraisal theory, as appraisals can be more cognitive or occur subcortically and automatically [13]. However, further research is necessary to confirm whether people's decision-making is being influenced at a conscious and/or unconscious-level.

The results in this paper suggest important consequences for the design of embodied interface agents. First, despite the large amount of empirical studies, it is still not clear whether embodied agents can enhance human-computer interaction [10, 32]. This paper adds evidence that embodied agents that express emotions can influence the emergence of cooperation with people. Second, our results emphasize that this effect depends on the *nature* of the emotions being expressed. It is not simply a matter of adding emotions to an embodied agent but, these emotions need to be coherent with the goals we want the user to perceive the agent to have. Effectively, in our study both agents are expressing emotions, nevertheless, participants cooperate more with the cooperative agent. Third, we propose that participants could be interpreting the agents' emotions through a process of "inverse appraisal" where they infer from perceived emotion the agents' goals, desires and beliefs. This proposal still needs further investigation and empirical evidence. Nevertheless, if this were the case, then it would mean that the mechanism defining when and which emotions the agent expresses should reflect the goals, desires and beliefs we want the user to perceive the agent to have. Consequently, computational models of appraisal theory [33] would constitute a promising approach to synthesize emotions in agents that people could comprehend.

The results also seem to be in line with predictions from theories in the social sciences. Effectively, participants do seem to care about social cues, such as facial displays, when interacting with an agent in a social dilemma, which is in line with Frank's proposal regarding human-human interactions [23]. Moreover, the results suggest that the social functions of emotions we see in people [1, 2] also carry to human-agent interactions. Altogether, the results provide further evidence that it is possible to study human-human interaction from human-agent interaction. This is interesting as embodied agents introduce new possibilities for designing experiments and constitute a unique research tool, as has already been noticed [34, 35]. First, it is easier for a researcher to have control over the manipulation using agents than using confederates. Confederates can inadvertently introduce noise, as their performance can have slight but relevant differences between participants. Second, agents can be carefully animated and tested before running the experiment, whereas a confederate improvises in real-time. This is analogous to the distinction between choreography and improvisation we see in the arts. Third, using embodied agents is less expensive than recruiting confederates.

There is still a lot of future work ahead. First, we excluded above two alternative explanations but, there are still further explanations we need to exclude: (a) some might still argue that the cooperative agent has more emotions than the individualistic, as the latter expresses no emotion when both the agent and participant cooperate and, thus, that explains the increase in cooperation; (b) it could also be argued that the fact the cooperative agent has more distinct emotions (joy, sadness, shame and anger) than the individualistic (joy and sadness) explains the results. We've begun addressing these issues in a variant of the current experiment where we compare two new agents: the *very cooperative* agent (Table 10), that expresses joy only when both agent and participant cooperate and sadness otherwise; and, the *very individualistic* agent (Table 11), that expresses joy only when the agent defects and the participant cooperates and sadness otherwise. Preliminary results show that, even though both agents have the same number and type of emotions, participants are, as expected, cooperating more with the very cooperative agent. Second, we've already compared previously the cooperative agent with a control agent [26], but we still need to do this for the individualistic agent. Third, we're interesting in understanding the effect each emotion has on decision-making. We can tackle this issue using the same paradigm and compare an agent which expresses a single emotion, in the right contingency, with the control agent. Fourth, we need to understand whether the effect on decision-making equals the composition of the effect of each emotion or not, i.e., whether the whole is simply the sum of its parts. Finally, we propose that participants could be interpreting the agents' emotions through a process of "inverse appraisal" where they infer from perceived emotion the agents' goals, desires and beliefs. As mentioned above, this proposal requires further investigation and empirical evidence.

Table 10. Facial displays (emotion and intensities) for the very cooperative agent

Very Cooperative Agent		Agent	
		Project Green	Project Blue
Participant	Project Green	Joy (100%)	Sadness (100%)
	Project Blue	Sadness (100%)	Sadness (100%)

Table 11. Facial displays (emotion and intensities) for the very individualistic agent

Very Individualistic Agent		Agent	
		Project Green	Project Blue
Participant	Project Green	Sadness (100%)	Joy (100%)
	Project Blue	Sadness (100%)	Sadness (100%)

References

1. Frijda, N.H., Mesquita, B.: The social roles and functions of emotions. In: Kitayama, S., Markus, H.S. (eds.) Emotion and culture: Empirical studies of mutual influence, pp. 51–87. American Psychological Association (1994)
2. Keltner, D., Haidt, J.: Social functions of emotions at four levels of analysis. Cognition and Emotion 13, 505–521 (1999)
3. Blanchette, I., Richards, A.: The influence of affect on higher level cognition: a review of research on interpretation, judgment, decision making and reasoning. Cognition & Emotion, 1–35 (2009), doi:10.1080/02699930903132496
4. Lerner, J.S., Small, D.A., Loewenstein, G.: Heart strings and purse strings: effects of specific emotions on economic transactions. Psychological Science 15, 337–341 (2004)
5. O'Quin, K., Aronoff, J.: Humor as a technique of social influence. Social Psychology Quarterly 44, 349–357 (1981)
6. Van Kleef, G., De Dreu, C., Manstead, A.: The interpersonal effects of anger and happiness in negotiations. Journal of Personality and Social Psychology 86, 57–76 (2004)
7. Scharleman, J., Eckel, C.C., Kacelnik, A., Wilson, R.: The value of a smile:Game theory with a human face. Journal of Economic Psychology 22, 617–640 (2001)
8. Pruitt, D., Kimmel, M.: Twenty Years of Experimental Gaming: Critique, Synthesis, and Suggestions for the Future. Ann. Rev. Psychol. 28, 363–392 (1977)
9. Gratch, J., Rickel, J., Andre, E., Badler, N., Cassell, J., Petajan, E.: Creating Interactive Virtual Humans: Some Assembly Required. IEEE Intellig. Systems 17(4), 54–63 (2002)
10. Beale, R., Creed, C.: Affective interaction: How emotional agents affect users. Human-Computer Studies 67, 755–776 (2009)
11. Poundstone, W.: Prisoner's Dilemma. Doubleday, New York (1993)
12. Krumhuber, E., Manstead, A., Kappas, A.: Facial Dynamics as Indicators of Trustworthiness and Cooperative Behavior. Emotion 7(4), 730–735 (2007)
13. Ellsworth, P., Scherer, K.: Appraisal Processes in Emotion. In: Davidson, R.J., Scherer, K.R., Goldsmith, H.H. (eds.) Handbook of Affective Sciences, pp. 572–595. Oxford University Press, Oxford (2003)
14. Kiesler, S., Waters, K., Sproull, L.: A Prisoner's Dilemma Experiment on Cooperation with Human-Like Computers. Journal of Personality and Social Psych. 70(1), 47–65 (1996)
15. Axelrod, R.: The Evolution of Cooperation. Basic Books (1984)

16. de Melo, C., Gratch, J.: Expression of Emotions using Wrinkles, Blushing, Sweating and Tears. In: Ruttkay, Z., Kipp, M., Nijholt, A., Vilhjálmsson, H.H. (eds.) IVA 2009. LNCS, vol. 5773, pp. 188–200. Springer, Heidelberg (2009)

17. Ortony, A., Clore, G., Collins, A.: The Cognitive Structure of Emotions. Cambridge University Press, Cambridge (1988)

18. Bente, G., Feist, A., Elder, S.: Person Perception Effects of Computer-Simulated Male and Female Head Movement. Journal of Nonverbal Behavior 20(4), 213–228 (1996)

19. Hertwig, R., Ortmann, A.: Experimental practices in economics: A methodological challenge for psychologists? ehavioral and Brain Sciences 24, 83–451 (2001)

20. Rosenthal, R.: Meta-analytic procedures for social research (revised). Sage, Newbury Park (1991)

21. Cohen, J.: Statistical power analysis for the behavioural sciences, 2nd edn. Academic Press, New York (1988)

22. Willis, J., Todorov, A.: First impressions: Making up your mind after a 100-ms exposure to a face. Psychological Science 17, 592–598 (2006)

23. Frank, R.: Introducing Moral Emotions into Models of Rational Choice. In: Manstead, A.S., Frijda, N., Fischer, A. (eds.) Feelings and Emotions: The Amsterdam Symposium, pp. 422–440. Cambridge University Press, Cambridge (2004)

24. Lester, J., Converse, S., Kahler, S., Barlow, S., Stone, B., Bhogal, R.: The persona effect: affective impact of animated pedagogical agents. In: Proceedings of the SIGCHI Conference on Human Factors in Computing Systems, pp. 359–366 (1997)

25. Bates, J.: The role of emotion in believable agents. Communications of the ACM 37(7), 122–125 (1994)

26. de Melo, C., Zheng, L., Gratch, J.: Expression of Moral Emotions in Cooperating Agents. In: Ruttkay, Z., Kipp, M., Nijholt, A., Vilhjálmsson, H.H. (eds.) IVA 2009. LNCS, vol. 5773, pp. 301–307. Springer, Heidelberg (2009)

27. Hamilton, W.: The Genetical Evolution of Social Behaviour. Journal of Theoretical Biology 7(1), 1–16 (1964)

28. Keltner, D., Kring, A.: Emotion, Social Function, and Psychopathology. Review of General Psychology 2(3), 320–342 (1998)

29. Lewis, M.: Self-Conscious Emotions: Embarrassment, Pride, Shame, and Guilt. In: Michael, L., Haviland-Jones, J. (eds.) Handbook of Emotions, pp. 623–636. The Guilford Press, New York (2008)

30. Damasio, A.: Descartes' Error: Emotion, Reason, and the Human Brain. G.P. Putnan's Sons (1994)

31. Reeves, B., Nass, C.: The Media Equation: How People Treat Computers, Television, and New Media Like Real People and Places. University of Chicago Press, Chicago (1996)

32. Dehn, D., Van Mulken, S.: The impact of animated interface agents: a review of empirical research. International Journal of Human–Computer Studies 52(1), 1–22 (2000)

33. Marsella, S., Gratch, J., Petta, P.: Computational Models of Emotion. In: Scherer, K.R., Bänziger, T., Roesch, E. (eds.) A blueprint for an affectively competent agent: Cross-fertilization between Emotion Psychology, Affective Neuroscience, and Affective Computing, Oxford University Press, Oxford (in press)

34. Bente, G., Kramer, N., Petersen, A., de Ruiter, J.: Computer Animated Movement and Person Perception: Methodological Advances in Nonverbal Behavior Research. Journal of Nonverbal Behavior 25(3), 151–166 (2001)

35. Blascovich, J., Loomis, J., Beall, A., Swinth, K., Hoyt, C., Bailenson, J.: Immersive Virtual Environment Technology as a Methodological Tool for Social Psychology. Psychological Inquiry 13(2), 103–124 (2002)

Dimensional Emotion Prediction from Spontaneous Head Gestures for Interaction with Sensitive Artificial Listeners

Hatice Gunes and Maja Pantic

Department of Computing, Imperial College London
180 Queen's Gate, London SW7 2AZ, U.K.
{h.gunes,m.pantic}@imperial.ac.uk

Abstract. This paper focuses on dimensional prediction of emotions from spontaneous conversational head gestures. It maps the amount and direction of head motion, and occurrences of head nods and shakes into arousal, expectation, intensity, power and valence level of the observed subject as there has been virtually no research bearing on this topic. Preliminary experiments show that it is possible to automatically predict emotions in terms of these five dimensions (arousal, expectation, intensity, power and valence) from conversational head gestures. Dimensional and continuous emotion prediction from spontaneous head gestures has been integrated in the SEMAINE project [1] that aims to achieve sustained emotionally-colored interaction between a human user and Sensitive Artificial Listeners.

Keywords: spontaneous head movements, dimensional emotion prediction, virtual character-human interaction.

1 Introduction

Researchers have extensively studied the behavior of the head within social interaction context. They have observed that 'the head movements we make when we speak are not random; these movements mark the structure of the ongoing discourse and are used to regulate interaction' [2], [3]. For instance, side-to-side shakes have been shown to correlate with verbalizations expressing inclusivity, intensification, and uncertainty [3]. Some speaker head nods have been shown to have an interactive function in triggering back-channels to which listeners appear to respond within a second. Therefore, automatic detection of head nods and shakes can be seen as a valuable non-verbal component for achieving natural and affective computer-human and virtual character-human interaction.

When it comes to recognizing human affect and emotion, the mainstream research has mostly focused on facial and vocal expressions and their recognition in terms of seven discrete, basic emotion categories (neutral, happiness, sadness, surprise, fear, anger and disgust). In line with these, most of the past research on automatic emotion sensing and recognition has focused on recognition of facial

J. Allbeck et al. (Eds.): IVA 2010, LNAI 6356, pp. 371–377, 2010.

and vocal expressions in terms of basic emotional states, and then based on data that has been posed on demand or acquired in laboratory settings [4]. However, a number of researchers have shown that a single label (or any small number of discrete classes) may not reflect the complexity of the affective state conveyed by various rich sources of information [5]. These researchers advocate the use of dimensional description of human affect, where an affective state is characterized in terms of a number of latent dimensions (e.g., [5], [6]).

The search for the optimal low-dimensional representation of emotion remains open [7]. Fontaine et al. showed that four dimensions are needed to satisfactorily represent similarities and differences in the meaning of emotion words for three languages: valence (the level of positivity or negativity), activation (the degree of excitement or apathy), power (the sense of control), and expectation (the degree of anticipating or being taken unaware) [7]. Ideally it should be possible to obtain the overall level of intensity from other more specific dimensions. However, to obtain a more complete description of affective coloring, at times intensity is included as the fifth dimension.

This paper focuses on automatic and dimensional prediction of emotions from head gestures. More specifically, we focus on the mapping between the amount and direction of head motion, and occurrences of head nods and shakes and the arousal, expectation, intensity, power and valence level of the observed subject as there has been virtually no research bearing on this topic.

2   Related Work

Various techniques have been developed for the detection and recognition of head nods and shakes. [8] observed the spatial evolution of the 'between eyes' circle that serves as a template for tracking and a basis for head movement estimation. The system was tested on 450 frames collected from three people who moved their heads up and down and left and right. An overall recognition accuracy of about 80% was reported. [9] recognizes head nods and head shakes based on two Hidden Markov Models (HMMs) trained and tested using 2D coordinate results from an eye gaze tracker. A total number of 110 samples from 10 subjects answering a number of factual questions (with a head nod or a head shake) were collected, and a recognition rate of 78.46% was reported. [10] calculates eye coordinate using an AdaBoost-based classifier along with two HMMs (one for nods and one for shakes). Data (80 samples for training and 110 samples for testing) were collected by asking the participants a number of factual questions, and a recognition accuracy of 85% was reported. [11] uses a head pose tracker that outputs a head rotation velocity vector. Based on that the head movement is classified by a two-class (nods and shake) SVM. The system was trained with 10 natural head gesture sequences taken from interactions with an embodied agent and 11 on-demand head gesture sequences. When tested on 30 video recordings of 9 subjects interacting with an interactive robot, a true detection rate of 75% for nods and 84% for shakes was obtained. Incorporating speech context further improved detection.

When it comes to automatic and dimensional emotion recognition, the most commonly employed strategy is to reduce the recognition problem to a 4-class problem (classification into the quadrants of 2D arousal-valence space, e.g. [12]), a 3-class valence-related classification problem (positive, neutral, and negative emotion classification), or a 2-class problem (positive vs. negative and active vs. passive classification). Systems that target automatic dimensional emotion recognition, considering that the emotions are represented along a continuum, generally tend to quantize the continuous range into certain levels. Representative works include quantization into low, medium and high [13] and excited-negative, excited-positive and calm-neutral [14]. More recently, works focusing on continuous prediction of arousal and valence from the audio modality have also emerged (e.g. [15]). See [16] for details.

As is reflected by the summary of related work, virtually no work has focused on dimensional prediction of emotions in terms of arousal, expectation, intensity, power and valence dimensions from spontaneous conversational head gestures.

3   Methodology

3.1   Data and Annotations

The Sensitive Artificial Listener database (SAL-DB) [17] consists of emotionally colored conversations. The SEMAINE Database (SEMAINE-DB) [18] builds upon and extends the concept of SAL-DB, and has been created as part of the SEMAINE project [1]. In both cases, spontaneous (induced) data was collected by recording conversations between a participant and an operator undertaking the role of a Sensitive Artificial Listener (SAL) with four personalities: Poppy (happy), Obadiah (gloomy), Spike (angry) and Prudence (pragmatic). The SAL characters are virtual dialogue partners, based on audiovisual analysis and synthesis [19]. Despite their very limited verbal understanding, they intend to engage the user in a conversation by paying attention to the user's emotions and non-verbal expressions.

Automatic detection of head nods and shakes from visual cues requires the existence of annotated nod and shake videos. To this aim, training data was obtained by visually inspecting the SAL-DB and manually cutting 100 head nod and 100 head shake clips of variable length.

The SEMAINE-DB contains 20 participants, a total of 100 character conversational and 50 non-conversational recordings of approximately 5 minutes each. Recordings have been annotated by multiple coders who provided continuous annotations with respect to five affect dimensions (arousal, expectation, intensity, power and valence) using the Feeltrace annotation tool. Feeltrace allows coders to watch the affective behavior recordings and move their cursor within each emotional dimension separately, i.e. within the value range of [-1,+1], to rate their impression about the emotional state of the subject (see [16] for details).

For our preliminary experiments, we chose a maximum number of sessions that have been annotated by the highest number of coders (not all coders annotated all sessions). This provided us with data from 7 subjects (27 sessions and $351,510$ video frames) annotated by 3 different coders.

3.2   Feature Extraction

Automatic detection of head nods and shakes is based on the 2-dimensional (2D) global head motion estimation. The facial region is detected using the well known technique of [20]. In order to determine the magnitude and the direction of the 2D head motion, optical flow is computed between two consecutive frames. It is applied to a refined region (i.e., resized and smoothed) within the detected facial area to exclude irrelevant background information. After preliminary analysis, the angle feature has been considered as the distinguishing feature in order to represent nods and shakes. The angle measure has then been discretized by representing it with directional codewords. The directional codeword is obtained by quantizing the direction into four codes for head movements (for rightward, upward, leftward and downward motion, respectively) and one for no movement. Figure 1(a) illustrates results from the feature extraction process.

3.3   Nod and Shake Detection

The directional codewords generated by the visual feature extraction module were fed into an HMM for training a *nodHMM* and a *shakeHMM*. However, to be able to distinguish other head movements from the actual head nods/shakes, we (i) threshold the magnitude of the head motion, (ii) build an *otherHMM* to be able to recognize any movement but nods/shakes, and (iii) statically analyze the likelihoods outputted by the nod/shake/other HMM (maximum likelihood vs. training classifiers on the outputted likelihoods). In order to analyze the visual data continuously, we empirically chose a window size of 0.6 secs that allows the detection of both brief and longer instances of head nods/shakes (similarly to other related work [9], [10]).

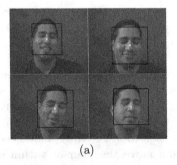
(a)

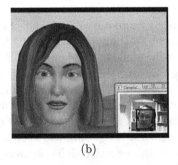
(b)

Fig. 1. (a) Illustration of the 2D global head motion and angle estimation; (b) illustration of the SEMAINE system where a human subject is conversing with Poppy

3.4   Dimensional Emotion Prediction

From the global head motion features extracted and the head movements (nod or shake) detected, we created a window-based feature set that consists of total duration of the head movement in terms of codewords, average of the magnitude and angle values (within the window), standard deviation of the magnitude and angle values, loglikelihoods outputted by nodHMM, shakeHMM and otherHMM, the results of the maximum likelihood classification and the classifier trained on the outputted likelihoods. The ground-truth for the window at hand consists of the dimensional annotations averaged over that window, for each coder separately. Such a representation allows us to consider each feature vector independently of the others using the so-called static (frame-based) regressors. We considered the Support Vector Machines for Regression (SVR) [21] to the aim of dimensional emotion prediction from head gestures as they are among the most widely used regressors in the field [16]. The final feature set was scaled in the range of $[-1, +1]$. The parameters of SVR, for each coder-dimension combination, were optimized using 10-fold cross-validation on a subset of the data at hand.

We employ subject-dependent cross-validation evaluation as most of the works in the field report only on subject-dependent dimensional emotion recognition when number of subjects and data are limited (e.g.,[15]). For evaluation we used all data from 7 subjects and 27 sessions: 11, 717 instances obtained by processing 351, 510 video frames. Evaluation then has been done by adopting 10-fold cross-validation over the full data set. The measure of performance is the mean squared error (MSE) that measures the average of the square of the errors. MSE is reported for each coder-dimension combination separately.

4   Preliminary Experiments and Results

The aim of the dimensional emotion prediction experiments is to demonstrate how well the trained SVR models are able to predict the arousal, expectation, intensity, power and valence level of the user compared to the human coders (i.e., the ground truth). The MSE for each coder's annotation was estimated by constructing vectors of coder annotation pairs that correspond to each video session, and averaging the results over all estimations (that the coder has contributed to).

Our findings, presented in Table 1, confirm that it is possible to obtain dimensional emotion prediction from conversational head gestures, and overall, the trained SVR predictors provide an MSE level comparable to human coders.

To the best of our knowledge, it is not possible to directly compare our results to other state-of-the art systems in the field due to lack of works reporting on automatic dimensional emotion prediction from spontaneous head movements. The work presented by Wollmer et al. [15] that extracts audio cues to obtain automatic dimensional emotion prediction in arousal and valence space is the most similar one to the work reported in this paper in terms of context and data used. They conducted subject-dependent hold-out evaluation using spontaneous

Table 1. Comparison of the MSE values obtained: human coders' annotation (C1-C3) vs. prediction of the trained SVRs (P1-P3) for five emotional dimensions

coder	arousal	expectation	intensity	power	valence	average
C1	0.137	0.044	0.091	0.121	0.068	0.092
P1	0.128	0.128	0.099	0.143	0.145	0.129
C2	0.160	0.064	0.160	0.149	0.089	0.124
P2	0.069	0.114	0.049	0.123	0.060	0.083
C3	0.191	0.055	0.143	0.141	0.078	0.122
P3	0.064	0.093	0.092	0.119	0.103	0.094

emotional data (i.e., the SAL database), and reported a mean squared error MSE=0.18 using SVR, and MSE=0.08 using Long Short Term Memory Neural Networks as the best results. Although different data sets and experimental conditions have been used, our results can be seen as comparable to these.

Note that the coders have annotated the expectation dimension using only the positive hemisphere [0,+1]. In order to make the MSE values obtained during evaluation comparable to the other dimensions, during experimentation we normalized the expectation ground truth into the range of [-1,+1]. This somewhat explains the difference observed in Table 1 between the coders' MSE and the predictors' MSE for the expectation dimension. Additionally, the table also indicates that modeling the annotations provided by *coder 1* (C1) is somewhat more challenging compared to other coders. This might be due to the fact that non-verbal cues other than the head movements (possibly) influenced the annotations of C1.

5   Conclusions

This paper focused on dimensional and continuous emotion prediction from spontaneous head movements occurring in a conversational setting. The preliminary experimental results suggest that it is possible to automatically predict the arousal, expectation, intensity, power and valence dimensions from conversational head movements and gestures.

Dimensional emotion prediction from spontaneous head gestures has been integrated in the SEMAINE project [1] that aims to support sustained emotionally-colored computer-human interaction using non-verbal expressions. One of the key ways the SEMAINE system creates a sense of interaction is having SAL characters producing head movements, and responding to the user's head movements. Fig. 1(b) illustrates a human subject conversing with Poppy while his spontaneous conversational head movement is analyzed. This is utilized to simultaneously predict the arousal, expectation, intensity, power and valence level of the user. The prediction result is then used by the SEMAINE framework to choose appropriate back-channels and sustain an ongoing interaction between the virtual character and the user.

Acknowledgment. The work of H. Gunes is funded by the EC's 7th Framework Programme [FP7/2007-2013] under grant agreement no 211486 (SEMAINE). The work of M. Pantic is funded in part by the ERC Starting Grant agreement no. ERC-2007-StG-203143 (MAHNOB).

References

1. The SEMAINE project, http://www.semaine-project.eu/
2. Kendon, A.: Facial Expression of Emotion. In: Some functions of the face in a kissing round, pp. 117–152. Cambridge University Press, Cambridge (1990)
3. McClave, E.Z.: Linguistic functions of head movements in the context of speech. J. of Pragmatics 32, 855–878 (2000)
4. Zeng, Z., et al.: A survey of affect recognition methods: Audio, visual, and spontaneous expressions. IEEE Tran. on PAMI 31, 39–58 (2009)
5. Russell, J.A.: A circumplex model of affect. J. of Personality and Social Psychology 39, 1161–1178 (1980)
6. Scherer, K.: Psychological models of emotion. In: The Neuropsychology of Emotion, pp. 137–162. Oxford University Press, Oxford (2000)
7. Fontaine, J.R., et al.: The world of emotion is not two-dimensional. Psychological Science 18, 1050–1057 (2007)
8. Kawato, S., Ohya, J.: Real-time detection of nodding and head-shaking by directly detecting and tracking the between-eyes. In: IEEE FGR, pp. 40–45 (2000)
9. Kapoor, A., Picard, R.W.: A real-time head nod and shake detector. In: Workshop on Perceptive User Interfaces (2001)
10. Tan, W., Rong, G.: A real-time head nod and shake detector using hmms. Expert Systems with Applications 25(3), 461–466 (2003)
11. Morency, L.-P., et al.: Contextual recognition of head gestures. In: ICMI, pp. 18–24 (2005)
12. Glowinski, D., et al.: Technique for automatic emotion recognition by body gesture analysis. In: CVPR Workshops, pp. 1–6 (2008)
13. Kulic, D., Croft, E.A.: Affective state estimation for human-robot interaction. IEEE Tran. on Robotics 23(5), 991–1000 (2007)
14. Chanel, G., et al.: Valence-arousal evaluation using physiological signals in an emotion recall paradigm. In: IEEE SMC, pp. 2662–2667 (2007)
15. Wollmer, M., et al.: Abandoning emotion classes - towards continuous emotion recognition with modelling of long-range dependencies. In: Interspeech, pp. 597–600 (2008)
16. Gunes, H., Pantic, M.: Automatic, dimensional and continuous emotion recognition. Int. Journal of Synthetic Emotions 1(1), 68–99 (2010)
17. Douglas-Cowie, E., et al.: The Humaine database: addressing the needs of the affective computing community. In: Paiva, A.C.R., Prada, R., Picard, R.W. (eds.) ACII 2007. LNCS, vol. 4738, pp. 488–500. Springer, Heidelberg (2007)
18. The SEMAINE database, http://semaine-db.eu/
19. Schroder, M., et al.: A demonstration of audiovisual sensitive artificial listeners. In: ACII, pp. 263–264 (2009)
20. Viola, P., Jones, M.: Rapid object detection using a boosted cascade of simple features. In: IEEE CVPR, pp. 511–518 (2001)
21. Chang, C.C., Lin, C.J.: LIBSVM: a library for support vector machines (2001), http://www.csie.ntu.edu.tw/~cjlin/libsvm

An Intelligent Virtual Agent to Increase Involvement in Financial Services

Tibor Bosse[1], Ghazanfar F. Siddiqui[1,2], and Jan Treur[1]

[1] Vrije Universiteit Amsterdam, Department of Artificial Intelligence,
De Boelelaan 1081a, 1081 HV Amsterdam, The Netherlands
[2] Quaid-i-Azam University Islamabad, Department of Computer Science, 45320, Pakistan
{tbosse,ghazanfa,treur}@few.vu.nl, ghazanfar@qau.edu.pk
http://www.few.vu.nl/~{tbosse,ghazanfa,treur}

Abstract. In order to enhance user involvement in financial services, this paper proposes to combine the idea of adaptive personalisation with intelligent virtual agents. To this end, a computational model for human decision making in financial context is incorporated within an intelligent virtual agent. To test whether the agent enhances user involvement, a web application has been developed, in which users have to make a number of investment decisions. This application has been evaluated in an experiment for a number of participants interacting with the system and afterwards providing their judgement by means of a questionnaire. The preliminary results indicate that the virtual agent can show appropriate emotional expressions related to states like happiness, greed and fear, and has high potential to enhance user involvement.

Keywords: user involvement, finance, greed and risk, adaptive personalisation.

1 Introduction

In recent years, there has been a huge increase in the amount of services that are being offered via the Internet. These services include, among others, financial services such as Internet banking [17]. Despite the success of such services, an existing challenge in this area concerns the question how to make people more *involved* in such financial applications. According to [1], customer involvement in financial services can be defined as 'an unobservable state of motivation, arousal or interest' (taken from [14]). In order to increase this state of involvement in users of financial applications, some authors claim that personalisation is an important criterion (e.g., [2, 6]): by having the system learn certain characteristics of the customer, this person will feel more understood and will be more likely to accept the service that is offered. However, there is also research that suggests that personalisation alone is not sufficient for financial services to attract users for longer periods (e.g., [8]).

To deal with this last issue, the current paper proposes to enhance user involvement in financial applications by combining adaptive personalisation with the use of an intelligent virtual agent. As pointed out by various authors (e.g., [9, 12]), human-like virtual agents have the ability to increase a user's presence in virtual environments. This finding was the inspiration to develop a personalised intelligent agent which

J. Allbeck et al. (Eds.): IVA 2010, LNAI 6356, pp. 378–384, 2010.

supports persons that have to make financial (investment) decisions. As known from behavioural economics, humans do not behave completely rationally when they have to decide between alternatives that involve risk (as, for example, in financial situations). Since then, from time to time it has been argued that theories of economic decision making need to incorporate psychological factors such as greed and fear [5, 11, 13, 16]. Thus, the main goal of this paper is to develop a virtual agent that has insight in and adapts to the individual psychological characteristics and states over time of persons that are working with financial applications. The virtual agent should exploit this on the one hand by providing appropriate support, in following these (dynamical) states and characteristics in an adaptive personalised manner. On the other hand, by showing the appropriate emotions at the right moment the virtual agent encourages involvement and reflection by the person through mirroring his or her states and decision making processes; for example, the agent may show the person how greedy he or she behaves.

In order to develop such a supporting virtual agent, as a basis a solid computational model of human decision making in financial context is needed. To this end, the model presented in [3] is taken. This model takes some of the main principles underlying the Modern Portfolio Theory (MPT) [7, 15] as a point of departure, and extends these with mechanisms to incorporate psychological factors (inspired, among others, by [11, 13]). In the current paper, this model is incorporated within an intelligent virtual agent. To test whether the agent enhances user involvement, a simple web application has been developed, in which users make a number of investment decisions. This application has been evaluated by a number of participants in an experiment in which they interacted with the agent and afterwards provided their judgement by means of a questionnaire.

The remainder of this paper is structured as follows. In Section 2, the basic model for financial decision making (taken from [3]) is summarised, and an intelligent virtual agent application is introduced that incorporates the model. Section 3 introduces the experiment that was performed to evaluate the virtual agent, and Section 4 presents the results. Section 5 concludes the paper with a discussion.

2 The Virtual Agent Application

The model for financial decision making described in [3] is based on the assumption that a person's greed is determined by her (long-term) personality profile (e.g., some persons are more risk seeking than others), combined with observations about recent events (e.g., if many investments have provided high returns recently, persons are more likely to increase their greed, and as a consequence take more risk). These assumptions can also be found in existing literature such as [11, 13]. By incorporating this model within a virtual agent, the agent is able to analyse a human's decision making by observing her decisions and the received returns, while tuning the risk profile to the person. Within this analysis not only this personal risk profile is available, which is assumed static for the person, but also the more dynamic greed level that actually determines the decisions. By having this, at each point in time the agent can predict what a reasonable decision would be for the human, given her personal background and history. In particular at all stages of the process it can estimate and show the type and level of emotions expected. These emotions can be shown to the human at runtime.

To design and implement the virtual agent, Haptek's Peopleputty software [19] has been used. Through this software the face of the virtual agent was created. More specifically, twelve different faces were designed using the built in sliders for happy, sad, anger, mellowness, suspicion, and curiosity (which are related to facial expressions), and ego, aggression and energy (which are related to head movement). Each of these twelve faces represented a particular emotional state; one for each possible combination of the three required levels of the emotions *happiness* (slightly_happy, happy and very_happy), *sadness* (slightly_sad, sad and very_sad), *fear* (slightly_scared, scared and very_scared) and *greed* (slightly_greedy, greedy and very_greedy). In addition, a face for the state neutral was used. A web-based application was implemented, within which the virtual agent was embedded as a Haptek player. For this the scripting language JavaScript [18] was used, in combination with scripting commands provided by the Haptek software [19], to control the Haptek player within a web browser.

Within the application, a human can make a number of consecutive investment decisions, while the virtual agent mimics the estimated emotional states related to happiness, sadness, greed and fear of the human (see the screenshot in Figure 1, where the agents shows a slightly_greedy face). In this application, in total 10 (represented by letters from *A* to *J*) products are given. The characteristics of these products are represented by the two variables *X* and *Y*, which are shown on the right hand part of the screen. Here, as in [3], *X* represents the expected risk of the product, and *Y* represents the expected return of the product. Note that in the model both *X* and *Y* have a value in the domain [*0, 1*], but in the application the values of *Y* have been scaled to the domain [*0, 1000*], to have them represent US dollars (see Section 3 and 6 of [3] for the exact formulae used within the model).

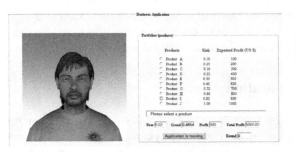
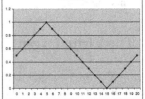

Fig. 1. Screenshot of the Application   **Fig. 2.** Fluctuation of *W*

During a number of rounds, the human is asked to select a product from the given products (from A to J). After she selected a product, some time will pass, until a message is shown on the screen that the "result of your investment will soon be announced". Next, it again takes some seconds until the real result is shown on the screen. To determine what this result will be, the formulae introduced in [3] are used. Note that these formulae make use of an additional parameter *W* (in the domain [*0, 1*]) which represents the economic situation of the world (e.g., a high value indicates a strong economy, thus a higher probability to receive return on investment). The value of this parameter fluctuates over time, and is not known to the user.

In every round, the virtual agent shows emotional facial expressions at appropriate moments. The following fixed scheme determines when to show which type of emotional expression: 1) human is asked to select a product, 2) agent shows face related to greed, 3) human selects a product, 4) agent shows face related to greed, 5) message is shown stating that result will soon be announced, 6) agent shows face related to fear, 7) result of investment is announced, 8) agent shows face related to happiness/sadness, 9) go back to 1.

The criteria that determine the exact faces that are displayed are as shown in Table 1 (where risk equals the *X* value of the selected product, profit equals the result of the investment (i.e., either *0* or the *Y* value of the selected product), and greed equals the value of *G* as estimated by the model).

Table 1. Criteria for the displayed Face Expressions

	Criterion	Displayed
Fear	risk ≤ 0.5	neutral face
	risk > 0.5 & risk ≤ 0.7	scared face
	risk > 0.7 & risk ≤ 1	very scared face
Happiness/Sadness	profit = 0	very sad face
	profit > 0 & profit ≤ 300	slightly happy face
	profit > 300 & profit ≤ 600	happy face
	profit > 600) & profit ≤ 1000	very happy face
Greed	greed ≤ 0.1	neutral face
	greed > 0.1 & greed ≤ 0.3	slightly greedy face
	greed > 0.3 & greed ≤ 1	very greedy face

When the agent shifts from one facial expression to another, it would be undesirable if the emotions of the agent would shift too quickly. Therefore, these shifts are performed in a more fluent manner. For instance, if the agent shifts from very happy to very greedy, the following faces are shown consecutively:

very happy → happy → slightly happy → neutral → slightly greedy → greedy → very greedy

Such a scenario is used when the agent shifts from any emotional state to another emotional state.

While the application is running, some information about the user is displayed in the bottom right part of the screen (see Figure 1). This information concerns the user's estimated amount of fear and greed (in the domain [0, 1]), her current amount of profit received, and her total (cumulative) amount of profit.

3   Experiments

A number of experiments were performed to test to what extent users of the application feel involved with the agent. In total, 15 participants were recruited to perform the experiment. The age of the participants ranged between 24 and 34, with a mean age of 29 and a standard deviation of 2.78. Among the participants, 11 were male and 4 were female. Two variants of the experiment were designed, one with which the virtual agent was showing the appropriate emotions and one in which it did not show any emotions. All of the participants were asked to perform both variants (where we used counterbalancing to determine the order in which they were performed).

Before they started the experiment, each participant was first are asked to read the following instructions:

Imagine that you are an investor in a stock market. During a number of subsequent rounds, you have to select a product from a given set of products. Each round, the same 10 products are available. The characteristics of these products are represented by two variables (called X and Y), which are shown on the screen. Here, X is a value in the domain [0, 1] which represents the __risk__ of the product (i.e., a higher value for X means that it is more likely that you will __not__ receive the corresponding return), and Y is a value in the domain [0, 1000] which represents the __expected return__ of the product in US dollars (i.e., a higher value for y means that you will earn more profit). The value of X is related to the probability p of __not__ receiving the corresponding return Y according to the formula p = X * (1-W). Here, W is a number in the domain [0, 1] which represents the economic situation of the world (i.e., a higher value for W means that it is more likely that you will receive the corresponding return). However, the value of W fluctuates during the simulation, and is not shown to you. After you have selected a product, some time will pass, until a message is shown on the screen that the result of your investment will soon be announced. Next, it still takes some seconds until the real result is shown on the screen. As mentioned above, the probability of receiving the profit also depends on the economic status of the world. After the result of your investment has been announced, a new round starts, in which you are asked to make a new investment. In total, the experiment lasts 20 rounds.

Next, a small training was given to each participant, and after that the participants performed the actual experiment. When the experiment was finished, the person was asked to fill in a questionnaire. In this questionnaire (cf. [4]), the participants were asked to evaluate, using a 7 point Likert scale [10] (with 1=strongly disagree, 7=strongly agree and 4=neutral), various properties of the agent related to involvement. In particular, they were asked whether they thought the virtual agent was friendly, trustworthy, showing emotions adequately, realistic, showing happiness, showing sadness, showing greed, showing fear, and behaving human-like.

In each experiment, the value of the economic state W fluctuated between 0 and 1, as shown in Figure 2. However, the participants were not aware of this.

4   Results

The answers provided by the participants to the questions about their involvement with the virtual agent were analysed by means of paired sample t-tests. The results are shown in Table 2. As shown in the table, for all properties except 'greed', the participants scored the virtual agent with emotions above moderate. Similarly, for all properties except 'greed', the participants appreciated this variant more than the virtual agent without emotions. The participants were also asked to give suggestions or comments about the application. Some participants said, for example, that the fear emotion should be more intense, while others said that the greed emotion should be improved, as they did not see this very well. Participants also indicated that they were more involved with the virtual agent with emotions. In addition, some participants were of the opinion that the agent should speak as well.

The fact that greed did not score very well in this first test may depend on the type of face expression chosen for greed. To explore how the perception of greed could be enhanced, another small experiment was conducted. For this purpose 9 different alternative faces for greed were created using the Peopleputty software [19]. Six new participants were asked to rate each face on a 7 point scale, for its appropriateness to express greed. After all the participants gave their responses, for each face the average score over all participant responses was taken, and the face with the highest average

Table 2. Results of the Questionnaire

Q #	Question	With Emotions		Without Emotions		Paired Sample Test	
		Mean	SD	Mean	SD	t	Sig(2tailed)
1	Friendly	4.47	1.506	3.53	1.992	2.168	.048
2	Trustworthy	4.13	1.598	2.47	1.246	4.183	.001
3	Adequate emotions	4.93	1.223	2.40	1.844	4.219	.001
4	Realistic	4.93	1.534	3.47	1.922	2.442	.028
5	Happiness	5.84	0.834	2.13	1.457	9.153	.000
6	Sadness	5.67	1.113	2.20	1.474	7.124	.000
7	Greed	2.67	1.877	2.00	1.195	1.323	.207
8	Fear	4.27	1.751	2.00	1.254	5.264	.000
9	Happiness at right time	5.60	0.986	2.20	1.656	7.462	.000
10	Sadness at right time	5.87	0.990	2.00	1.363	9.648	.000
11	Fear at right time	4.13	1.598	1.93	1.387	4.036	.001
12	Human-like	4.67	1.291	2.93	1.667	2.578	.022

Table 3. Results of the Questionnaire for the Additional Experiment related to Greed

Q #	Question	With Emotions		Without Emotions		Paired Sample Test	
		Mean	SD	Mean	SD	t	Sig(2-tailed)
1	Greed	5.167	0.983	2.33	1.366	3.782	.013

value was selected for a next experiment (again with 6 new participants). This experiment was identical to the experiment of which the results are given in Table 2, only in this case the new face was used to display the greed. Table 3 shows (part of) the results of this experiment. As can be seen, this time the greed was evaluated much better, and resembles the evaluations of the other emotions.

5 Discussion

In this paper an application was presented combining adaptive personalisation with intelligent virtual agents, in order to enhance user involvement in financial services. To this end a computational model for human decision making in financial context (taken from [3]) was incorporated within an intelligent virtual agent. This computational model enables the virtual agent to have a form of understanding of the person's (dynamical) states and decision making processes in an adaptive manner. Moreover, a second way in which the agent was made adaptive was by equipping it with a model to tune the risk profile parameter to the person.

A web application has been developed, in which users make a number of investment decisions. This application has been used to test whether the virtual agent enhances user involvement. This has been evaluated in an experiment for a number of participants interacting with the system and afterwards providing their judgement by means of a questionnaire. The preliminary results indicate that the virtual agent can be given facial expressions showing emotional states like happiness, greed and fear that are evaluated as appropriate (regarding the type of facial expression as well as the moments on which the expressions are shown). In particular, getting an appropriate expression for greed was nontrivial.

For future work the virtual agent may be tested in a real environment to analyse whether it makes humans perform better in financial decision making, for example in the form of a smart phone application. One of the factors that may need some more attention is the level of awareness of the person of the state of the world.

References

1. Aldlaigan, A.H., Buttle, F.A.: Consumer involvement in financial services: An empirical test of two measures. Int. Journal of Bank Marketing 19(6), 232–246 (2001)
2. Blom, J., Monk, A.: One-to-one e-commerce: who's the one? In: Proc. of the Conference on Human Factors in Computing Systems (CHI 2001), pp. 341–342. ACM Press, New York (2001)
3. Bosse, T., Siddiqui, G.F., Treur, J.: Supporting Financial Decision Making by an Intelligent Agent Estimating Greed and Risk. In: Proc. of the Fourth Int. Workshop on Human Aspects in Ambient Intelligence, HAI 2010. IEEE CS Press, Los Alamitos (to appear, 2010)
4. Bowling, A.: Questionnaire design. In: Research Methods in Health. Open University Press, Buckingham (1997)
5. Brandstätter, H.: Should Economic Psychology Care about Personality Structure? Journal of Economic Psychology 14, 473–494 (1993)
6. Chau, P.Y.K., Lai, V.S.K.: An empirical investigation of the determinants of user acceptance of internet banking. Journal of Organizational Computing & Electronic Commerce 13(2), 123–145 (2003)
7. Haugen, R.A.: Modern Investment Theory. Prentice-Hall, Englewood Cliffs (1997)
8. Ho, S.Y.: The Attraction of Internet Personalization to Web Users. Electronic Markets 161, 41–50 (2006)
9. Leite, I., Pereira, A., Martinho, C., Paiva, A.: Are Emotional Robots More Fun to Play With? In: Proceedings of the IEEE RO-MAN, Conference, pp. 77–82 (2008)
10. Likert, R.: A Technique for the Measurement of Attitudes. Archives of Psychology 140, 1–55 (1932)
11. Lo, A., Repin, D.V., Steenbarger, B.N.: Fear and Greed in Financial Markets: A Clinical Study of Day-Traders. American Economic Review 95, 352–359 (2005)
12. Nowak, K.L., Biocca, F.: The effect of the agency and anthropomorphism on users' sense of telepresence, copresence, and social presence in virtual environments. Presence: Teleoperators and Virtual Environments 12(5), 481–494 (2003)
13. Rabin, M.: A Perspective on Psychology and Economics. European Economic Review 46, 657–685 (2002)
14. Rothschild, M.L.: Perspective on Involvement: Current Problems and Future Directions. In: Kinnear, T.C. (ed.) Advances in Consumer Research, ACR, vol. 11 (1984)
15. Sabal, J.: Financial Decisions in Emerging Markets. Oxford Univ. Press, Inc., New York (2002)
16. Simon, H.A.: Behavioural Economics. In: The New Palgrave: A Dictionary of Economics. MacMillan, London (1987)
17. Tan, M., Teo, T.S.H.: Factors Influencing the Adoption of Internet Banking. Journal of the AIS 1(5), 1–42 (2000)
18. http://developer.mozilla.org/en/docs/About_JavaScript
19. http://www.haptek.com

Exploration on Affect Sensing from Improvisational Interaction

Li Zhang

School of Computing, Teesside University
TS1 3BA, UK
l.zhang@tees.ac.uk

Abstract. We report work on adding an improvisational AI actor to an existing virtual improvisational environment, a text-based software system for dramatic improvisation in simple virtual scenarios, for use primarily in learning contexts. The improvisational AI actor has an affect-detection component, which is aimed at detecting affective aspects (concerning emotions, moods, value judgments, etc.) of human-controlled characters' textual "speeches". The AI actor will also make an appropriate response based on this affective understanding, which intends to stimulate the improvisation. The work also accompanies basic research into how affect is conveyed linguistically. A distinctive feature of the project is a focus on the metaphorical ways in which affect is conveyed. Moreover, we have also introduced affect detection using context profiles. Finally, we have reported user testing conducted for the improvisational AI actor and evaluation results of the affect detection component. Our work contributes to the conference themes on affective user interfaces, affect inspired agent and improvisational or dramatic interaction.

Keywords: Affect detection, metaphorical language, an improvisational AI actor and context profiles.

1 Introduction

In our previous work, we developed online multi-user role-play software that could be used for education or entertainment. In this software young people could interact online in a 3D virtual drama stage with others under the guidance of a human director. In one session, up to five virtual characters are controlled on a virtual stage by human users ("actors"), with characters' (textual) "speeches" typed by the actors operating the characters. The human actors are given a loose scenario around which to improvise, but are at liberty to be creative. In order to enrich users' experience and stimulate the improvisation, we developed an intelligent agent with the ability to detect affect from human-controlled characters' text input and make appropriate responses based on the detected affective states. The affect detection component embedded in the AI agent detects 25 affect states, including basic and complex emotions, meta-emotions such as desiring to overcome anxiety, moods such as hostility, and value judgments. The results of this affective analysis have also been used to drive the

J. Allbeck et al. (Eds.): IVA 2010, LNAI 6356, pp. 385–391, 2010.

animations of the avatars in the user interface so that they react bodily in ways that is consistent with the affect that they are expressing, for instance by changing gesture.

Much research has been done on creating affective virtual characters in interactive systems. Indeed, Picard's work [1] makes great contributions to building affective virtual characters. Also, emotion theories, particularly that of Ortony, et al. [2] (OCC), have been used widely in such research. Egges et al. [3] provided virtual characters with conversational emotional responsiveness. Aylett et al. [4] also focused on the development of affective behaviour planning for the synthetic characters. There is much other work in a similar vein.

Emotion recognition in speech and facial expression has been studied extensively. But very little research work has made an attempt to reveal affect in human open-ended linguistic textual input in online role-play, although the first textual interactive system, Eliza, was first developed back in 1966. Thus there has been only a limited amount of work directly comparable to our own, especially given our concentration on improvisation and open-ended language. However, Façade [5] included shallow natural language processing for characters' open-ended utterances. But the detection of major emotions, rudeness and value judgements is not mentioned. Zhe and Bou-couvalas [6] demonstrated an emotion extraction module embedded in an Internet chatting environment. Unfortunately the emotion detection focuses only on emotional adjectives, and does not address deep issues such as figurative expression of emotion. Also, the concentration purely on first-person emotions is narrow. Our work is thus distinctive in these aspects, including affect detection in metaphorical language and context profiles, and also from first-person & third-person perspectives.

In this paper, we briefly summarize our previous work in section 2.1 and emphasis our new implementations on metaphorical language processing in section 2.2, and affect interpretation based on context in section 2.3. Evaluation results for the AI agent and the overall affect sensing component are reported in section 3.

2   The Affect Detection Processing

After an inspection of the recorded improvisational transcripts, we noticed that the language used in e-drama is complex and idiosyncratic, e.g. often ungrammatical and full of abbreviations, mis-spellings, etc. Several pre-processing procedures have been developed in our application previously to deal with misspellings, abbreviations, letter repetitions, interjections and onomatopoeia etc [7]. Moreover, the language contains a large number of weak cues to the affect that is being expressed. These cues may be contradictory or they may work together to enable a stronger interpretation of the affective state. In order to build a reliable and robust analyser of affect it is necessary to undertake several diverse forms of analysis and to enable these to work together to build stronger interpretations.

2.1 Affect Detection using Rasp and Pattern Matching and Responding Regimes

One useful pointer to affect is the use of imperative mood, especially when used without softeners such as 'please' or 'would you'. Strong emotions and/or rude atti-tudes are often expressed in this case. Expression of the imperative mood in English is surprisingly various and ambiguity-prone. We have used the syntactic output from the Rasp parser [8] and a semantic resource [9] to deal with certain types of imperatives. In an initial stage of our work, affect detection was based purely on textual pattern-matching rules that looked for simple grammatical patterns or templates partially involving specific words or sets of specific alternative words. A rule-based Java framework called Jess is used to implement the pattern/template-matching rules in the AI agent allowing the system to cope with more general wording and ungrammatical fragmented sentences. The rules conjecture the character's emotions, evaluation dimension (negative or positive), politeness (rude or polite) and what response the automated actor should make. However, it lacks other types of generality and can be fooled when the phrases are suitably embedded as subcomponents of other grammatical structures.

In order to go beyond certain such limitations, sentence type information obtained from Rasp has also been adopted in the rule sets. Such information not only helps the agent to detect affective states from the input (such as the detection of imperatives), and to decide if the detected affective states should be counted (e.g. affects detected in conditional sentences won't be valued), but also contributes to proposing appropriate responses. Moreover, the AI agent can adjust its response likelihood according to how confident it is about what it has discerned in the utterance at hand.

2.2 Metaphorical Language Understanding in the AI Actor

The metaphorical description of emotional states is common and has been extensively studied. In our application, metaphorical language has been used extensively to convey emotions and feelings in the collected transcripts. One category of affective metaphorical expressions that we're interested in is 'Ideas/Emotions as Physical Objects" [10], e.g. "joy ran through me", "my anger returns in a rush", etc. In these examples, emotions and feelings have been regarded as external entities. The external entities are often, or usually, physical objects or events. Therefore, affects could be treated as physical objects outside the agent in such examples, which could be active in other ways [10]. Implementation has been carried out to provide the AI agent with the ability to deal with such affect metaphor. We mainly focus on the user input with the following structures: 'a singular common noun subject + present-tense lexical verb phrase' or 'a singular common noun subject + present-tense copular form + -ing form of lexical verb phrase'. WordNet-affect domain (part of WordNet-domain 3.2) [11] has been used in our application. It provides an additional hierarchy of 'affective domain labels', with which the synsets representing affective concepts are further annotated (e.g. 'panic' is interpreted as 'negative-fear -> negative-emotion -> emotion -> affective-state -> mental-state'). Also with the assistance of the syntactic parsing from Rasp, the input "panic drags me down" is interpreted as 'a mental state + an activity + object (me)'. Thus the system regards such expression as affective metaphor belonging to the category of 'affects as entities'.

In daily expressions, food has been used extensively as metaphor for social position, group identity, etc. In one of the scenarios we used (school bullying), the big bully has called the bullied victim (Lisa) names, such as "u r a pizza", "Lisa has a pizza face" to exaggerate that fact that the victim has acne. Another most commonly used food metaphor is to use food to refer to a specific shape. E.g. body shape could be described as 'banana', 'pear' and 'apple' (http://jsgfood.blogspot.com/2008/02/food-metaphors.html). In our application, "Lisa has a pizza face" could also be interpreted as Lisa has a 'round (shape)' face. Therefore, insults could be conveyed in such food metaphorical expression. We especially focus on the statement of 'second-person/a singular proper noun + present-tense copular form + food term' to extract affect. A special semantic dictionary has been created by providing semantic tags to normal English lexicon with the assistance of Wmatrix [12], which facilitates users to obtain corpus annotation to compose dictionary. The semantic dictionary created consists mainly of food terms, animal names, measureable adjectives (such as size) etc with their corresponding semantic tags due to the fact they have the potential to convey affect and feelings.

In our application, Rasp informs the system the user input with the desired structure - 'second-person/a singular proper noun + present-tense copular form + noun phrases' (e.g. "Lisa is a pizza", "u r a hard working man"). The noun phrases are examined in order to recover the main noun term. Then its corresponding semantic tag is derived from the composed semantic dictionary if it is a food term, or an animal-name etc. E.g. "u r a peach" has been regarded as "second-person + present-tense copular form + [food-term]". WordNet [13] has been employed in order to get the synset of the food term. If among the synset, the food term has been explained as a certain type of human being, such as 'beauty', 'sweetheart' etc. Then another small slang-semantic dictionary collected in our previous study containing terms for special person types (such as 'freak', 'angle') and their corresponding evaluation values (negative or positive) has been adopted in order to obtain the evaluation values of such synonyms of the food term. If the synonyms are positive (e.g. 'beauty'), then we conclude that the input is an affectionate expression with a food metaphor (e.g. "u r a peach"). In order to gain more flexibility, we also used a statistical-based approach for the recognition of the above affect and food metaphors.

2.3 Context-Based Affect Detection

Our previous affect detection has been performed solely based on individual turn-taking user input. Since natural language is ambiguous and there are cases that contextual information is required in order to appropriately interpret the affect conveyed in the input (e.g. "go on then"), in this section, we will discuss linguistic contextual indicators, cognitive emotion simulation from communication context and our approach developed based on these features to interpret affect from context.

In our study, we noticed some linguistic indicators for contextual communication in the recorded transcripts. One useful indicator is (i) imperatives, which are often used to imply negative or positive responses to the previous speaking characters, such as "shut up", "go on then", "let's do it" and "bring it on". Other useful contextual indicators are (ii) prepositional phrases (e.g. "by who?"), semi-coordinating conjunctions (e.g. "so we are good then"), subordinating conjunctions ("because Lisa is a dog") and coordinating conjunctions ('and', 'or' and 'but'). These indicators are normally used by the current 'speaker' to express further opinions or gain further confirmation from the previous speakers. In addition, (iii) short phrases for questions are also used frequently in the transcripts to gain further communication based on context, e.g. "where?", "who is Dave" or "what". (iv) Character names are also normally used in the user input to indicate that the current input is intended for particular characters, e.g. "Dave go away", "Mrs Parton, say something", etc. Finally there are also (i) some other well known contextual indicators in Internet relay chat such as 'yeah/yes/no/nah followed by a sentence ("yeah, we will see")', "I think so", "me too", "thanks", "grrrr", etc. Such expressions are normally used to indicate affective responses to the previous input.

There are also other aspects which may influence the affect conveyed in the communication context. E.g. in our application, the 'improvisational mood' that the speaking character is created, and emotions expressed by other characters, especially by the contradictory ones (e.g. the big bully), have great potential to influence the affect conveyed by the current speaking character (e.g. the bullied victim). Sometimes, the story themes or topics also have potential impact on emotions or feelings expressed by characters. For example, people tend to feel 'happy' when involved in discussions on positive topics e.g. raising salary and vice versa. In our application, the hidden story sub-themes used in the scenarios are highly emotionally charged and can be used as the signals for potential changes of emotional context for each character. E.g. In the school bullying scenario (which is mainly about the bully, Mayid, picking on the new comer to the school, Lisa. The school teacher and Lisa's friends, Elise and Dave, are trying to stop the bullying), the director mainly provided interventions based on several main sub-themes to push the improvisation forward, i.e. "why Lisa is crying", "why Mayid is so nasty/a bully", "how Mayid feels when his uncle finds out his behavior" etc. From the inspection of the recorded transcripts, when discussing the topic of "why Lisa is crying", we noticed that Mayid tends to be really aggressive, while Lisa tends to be upset and other characters (Lisa's friends etc) are inclined to show anger at Mayid. For the improvisation of the sub-theme "why Mayid is so nasty/a bully", the bully changes from rude to sad and embarrassed (e.g. because he is abused by his uncle), while Lisa and other characters become sympathetic (and even caring) about Mayid. Thus, the emotion patterns expressed by each character within the improvisation of each story sub-theme could be very useful for the prediction of the affect shown in a similar topic context, although the improvisation of the characters is creative within the scenario. A Markov chain is used to learn from the emotional context shown in the recorded transcripts for each sub-theme and for each character, and generate other possible reasonable unseen emotional context similar to the training data for each character. Markov chains are usually used for word generation. In our application, they are used to record the frequencies of several emotions showing up after one particular emotion. A matrix has been constructed dynamically for neutral and the 12 most commonly used emotions in our application (caring, arguing, disapproving, approving, grateful, happy, sad, threatening, embarrassed, angry/rude, scared and sympathetic) with each row representing the previous emotion followed by the subsequent emotions in columns. The Markov chains employ roulette wheel selection to ensure to produce a greater probability to select emotions with higher frequencies than emotions with lower occurrences. This will allow the generation of emotional context to probabilistically follow the training data to reflect the creative nature of the improvisation.

Then a dynamic algorithm is used to find the most resembling emotional context for any given new situation from Markov chain's training and generated emotional contexts. I.e. by using the algorithm, a particular series of emotions for a particular story sub-theme has been regarded as the most resembling context to the test emotional situation and an emotional state is recommended as the most possible emotion for the current user input. Since the most recent affect histories of other characters and relationships between characters may also have impact on the affect conveyed by the current speaking character, the recommended affect will be further evaluated using other characters' recent affect and relationships profiles (e.g. a most recent 'insulting' input from Mayid may cause Lisa to be 'angry'). At the test stage, our affect detection component detects affect for each user input solely based on the analysis of individual turn-taking input itself first. The above algorithms for context-based affect sensing will be activated when the affect detection component recognizes 'neutral' from the input and one of the five linguistic indicators mentioned above is shown in it, i.e. the input caused by contextual interaction. In this way, our affect detection component has been able to inference emotion from context profiles. Also, the detected affective states play an important role in producing emotional expressive gesture animation for human characters' avatars.

3   Evaluation of the AI Actor and Conclusion

We conducted an intensive user test with 160 secondary school students, in order to try out and refine a testing methodology. The aim of the testing was primarily to measure the extent to which having the AI agent as opposed to a person play a character affects users' level of enjoyment, sense of engagement, etc. We concealed the fact that the AI-controlled actor was involved in some sessions in order to have a fair test of the difference that is made. We obtained surprisingly good results. Having a minor bit-part character called "Dave" played by the AI agent as opposed to a person made no statistically significant difference to measures of user engagement and enjoyment, or indeed to user perceptions of the worth of the contributions made by the character "Dave". Users did comment in debriefing sessions on some utterances of Dave's, so it was not that there was a lack of effect simply because users did not notice Dave at all. Inspection of the transcripts indicates that it usefully pushed the improvisation forward on various occasions. Furthermore, it surprised us that few users appeared to realize that sometimes Dave was computer-controlled.

We have conducted an initial evaluation of the quality of the AI agent's determinations about emotion during these testing sessions, by comparing the AI agent's determinations during one of the school bullying improvisations with emotion labels later assigned offline by two members of our team (not involved in the development of the AI agent's algorithms). We used the kappa statistic. It is a measure of the pairwise agreement among a set of coders making category judgements, correcting for expected chance agreement. We calculated K for each pair among the three labellers (the AI agent and two humans). The inter-human K was only 0.45, and so it is not surprising that the AI agent/human values were only 0.32 and 0.4. Although they are not ideal, at least these results give grounds for hope that our affect detection with further refinement can come near the rather low human/human level of agreement. Moreover, the accuracy rate of affect interpretation based on context in our current analysis achieves 68% via the comparison of the annotation of part of the recorded school bullying transcripts between human annotators and the AI agent.

In future work, we aim to explore the automatic relationship interpretation between characters from users' input during the improvisation of comparatively complex scenarios (such as Crohn's disease) to assist the contextual affect sensing. We also intend to consider a metaphor ontology for metaphor recognition and generation.

References

1. Picard, R.W.: Affective Computing. The MIT Press, Cambridge (2000)
2. Ortony, A., Clore, G.L., Collins, A.: The Cognitive Structure of Emotions. Cambridge U. Press, Cambridge (1998)
3. Egges, A., Kshirsagar, S., Magnenat-Thalmann, N.: A Model for Personality and Emotion Simulation. In: Palade, V., Howlett, R.J., Jain, L. (eds.) KES 2003. LNCS, vol. 2774. Springer, Heidelberg (2003)
4. Aylett, R.S., Dias, J., Paiva, A.: An affectively-driven planner for synthetic characters. In: Proceedings of ICAPS (2006)
5. Mateas, M.: Ph.D. Thesis. Interactive Drama, Art and Artificial Intelligence. School of Computer Science, Carnegie Mellon University (2002)
6. Zhe, X., Boucouvalas, A.C.: Text-to-Emotion Engine for Real Time Internet Communication. In: Proceedings of International Symposium on Communication Systems, Networks and DSPs, Staffordshire University, UK, pp. 164–168 (2002)
7. Zhang, L., Gillies, M., Dhaliwal, K., Gower, A., Robertson, D., Crabtree, B.: E-drama: Facilitating Online Role-play using an AI Actor and Emotionally Expressive Characters. International Journal of Artificial Intelligence in Education 19(1), 5–38 (2009)
8. Briscoe, E., Carroll, J.: Robust Accurate Statistical Annotation of General Text. In: Proceedings of the 3rd International Conference on Language Resources and Evaluation, Las Palmas, Gran Canaria, pp. 1499–1504 (2002)
9. Heise, D.R.: Semantic Differential Profiles for 1,000 Most Frequent English Words. Psychological Monographs. 70 8(Whole 601) (1965)
10. Barnden, J., Glasbey, S., Lee, M., Wallington, A.: Varieties and Directions of Inter-Domain Influence in Metaphor. Metaphor and Symbol 19(1), 1–30 (2004)
11. Strapparava, C., Valitutti, A.: WordNet-Affect: An Affective Extension of WordNet. In: Proceedings of the 4th International Conference on Language Resources and Evaluation (LREC 2004), Lisbon, Portugal, pp. 1083-1086 (2004)
12. Rayson, P.: Matrix: A statistical method and software tool for linguistic analysis through corpus comparison. Ph.D. thesis, Lancaster University (2003)
13. Fellbaum, C.: WordNet, an Electronic Lexical Database. The MIT Press, Cambridge (1998)

Using Virtual Humans to Bootstrap
the Creation of Other Virtual Humans

Brent Rossen[1], Juan Cendan[2], and Benjamin Lok[1]

[1] Computer Information Sciences Engineering
[2] Department of Surgery
University of Florida
Gainesville, FL 32611, USA
{brossen,lok}@cise.ufl.edu, cendajc@surgery.ufl.edu

Abstract. Virtual human (VH) experiences are increasingly used for training interpersonal skills such as military leadership, classroom education, and doctor-patient interviews. These diverse applications of conversational VHs have a common and unexplored thread – a significant additional population would be afforded interpersonal skills training if VHs were available to simulate *either* interaction partner. We propose a computer-assisted approach to generate a virtual medical student from hundreds of interactions between a virtual patient and real medical students. This virtual medical student is then used to train standardized patients – human actors who roleplay the part of patients in practice doctor-patient encounters. Practice with a virtual medical student is expected to lead to greater standardization of roleplay encounters, and more accurate evaluation of medical student competency. We discuss the method for generating VHs from an existing corpus of human-VH interactions and present observations from a pilot experiment to determine the utility of the virtual medical student for training.

Keywords: Virtual Humans, Agents and Intelligent Systems, Authoring Tools, Virtual Patients, User Interfaces, End-user Programming.

1 Introduction

Across a wide range of fields, interactions with conversational virtual humans (VHs) have become an integral part of training interpersonal skills. Medical students practice taking a medical history by conversing with a VH patient [1]; teachers re-enact classroom situations with virtual students [2]; and soldiers learn conflict resolution in interactions with virtual civilians [3]. In these human-VH interactions, human-human interactions are simulated through verbal and gestural communication. During development of these human-VH interactions, the role played by the human and the role played by the VH are fixed. In the examples given, the soldier, teacher, and doctor are humans, while the civilian, student(s), and patient are VHs. We have observed that reversing these roles (e.g. human patient with a VH doctor) will facilitate interpersonal skills training for additional large populations. However, traditional approaches to creating a VH for each role would double development time and effort. Instead, we

J. Allbeck et al. (Eds.): IVA 2010, LNAI 6356, pp. 392–398, 2010.

propose processing an existing conversational model of the human-VH interaction to generate a VH for the human side of the interaction.

When a human-VH interaction is conducted, recordings are made of the human user's utterances. These recordings ("interaction logs") are then used to generate new VHs to take the (originally) human role in the conversation. This is accomplished by aggregating the scenario's interaction logs. Given a set of interaction logs having sufficient size and scope, we can create a conversational model for the human role in the human-VH interaction. In essence, recordings of a human-VH interaction are used to bootstrap the creation of a new VH representing the human.

We have implemented the Roleplay Trainer Creator, a system to investigate bootstrapping the generation of virtual humans. We have used the Roleplay Trainer Creator to apply this bootstrapping technique to medical education. In medical education interview training, standardized patients (human actors) are paid to roleplay a patient for medical student education. To help train standardized patients for standardized patient interactions, we propose to create virtual medical students from hundreds of interactions of medical students with a virtual patient. The virtual medical student generation process is as follows (see Figure 1): medical students interact with a virtual patient, resulting in a set of interaction logs; those logs are used by the Roleplay Trainer Creator to generate a VH medical student, which is then used to train standardized patients. We report on a pilot study using a generated virtual medical student to train standardized patients.

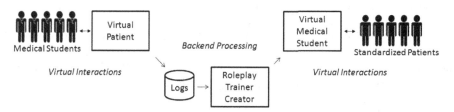

Fig. 1. Overview of VH medical student creation process

1.1 Driving Application: Healthcare Standardized Patient Training

Standardized patient interactions have been used since 1963 for training medical interview skills. The medical interview is a 5 to 30 minute conversation in which the healthcare professional and patient exchange information. The healthcare professional elicits both verbal and physical symptoms from the patient. Standardized patients are hired actors that roleplay a medical condition. They interact with many medical students (i.e. hundreds of students over several days, one student at a time) and need to represent the same patient in each student interaction. Representing the same patient with each student is crucial to providing standardized (i.e. *equal*) education and evaluation of students.

Standardizing standardized patients is a difficult problem [4-6]. On average, standardized patients respond with 90.2% correct verbal content of responses, but their accuracy can be as low as 30% [4]. Reasons for these accuracy errors include: forgetting the correct answer, misunderstanding the question, or use of preparation materials that do not provide an answer to the student's question. Preparation materials given to standardized patients are often incomplete because medical educators are unable to anticipate all questions that medical students may ask.

We propose to train standardized patients using virtual medical students generated from conversational models containing questions real medical students ask virtual patients. The proposed solution provides the standardized patients with more complete coverage of the questions that medical students will ask, the correct responses to those questions, experience answering the questions, and feedback on their responses to those questions. By conversing with the virtual medical student, standardized patients will be better able to standardize their interactions with real medical students, providing increased educational value to the students and more accurate evaluation of medical student competency [6].

2 Roleplay Trainer Creator: Generating Virtual Versions of the Human Partner

The Roleplay Trainer Creator enables domain experts to create question-asking VHs from the interaction logs of question-answering VHs. These question-asking VHs are used to train roleplay partners (standardized patients) to conduct a question-answering conversation (such as a medical interview). The challenges in generating a question-asking VH that accurately represents a specific class of human (a medical student) within a specific type of conversation (a medical interview) is determining the representative questions to ask, and the order in which to ask them.

The Roleplay Trainer Creator is a web-application developed using PHP, JavaScript with jQuery, MySQL, and Apache. It was developed on top of the Virtual People Factory web-application framework [7]. The Roleplay Trainer Creator generates conversation models that are compatible with Virtual People Factory. Virtual People Factory simulates the question-asking VHs in a browser-based interaction (see section 2.3 for details).

The Roleplay Trainer Creator enables a domain expert to create a VH roleplay partner by assisting the expert in selecting representative questions, and ordering those questions appropriately. The system extracts questions that are actually asked by users by analyzing the interaction logs of question-answering VHs. The original question-answering VHs were developed using a collaboration between end-users, and domain experts, this technique is known as Human-centered Distributed Conversational Modeling. Using Virtual People Factory, end-users (e.g. medical students) conduct typed conversations with browser-based VHs to provide new utterances (questions and statements), and domain experts (e.g. medical educators) use a web-interface to provide new VH responses. This process is repeated iteratively with novices providing utterances and experts providing responses until the question-answering VH has a robust ability to respond to utterances. This approach results in a corpus of thousands of questions paired with hundreds of answers. The resulting interaction logs enumerate the space of both sides of the conversation.

2.1 Selecting Questions

The Roleplay Trainer Creator enables question selection by pre-processing the interaction logs and then enlisting the expert to validate the results.

Selecting the questions is accomplished by:

1. Identifying the semantically unique questions,
2. Analyzing the usage of the questions in the interaction logs, and
3. Presenting the questions and responses to a domain expert for final selection.

To identify semantically unique questions, each question in the interaction logs is categorized by its similarity to questions that are used in the existing question-answering VH conversation model. Similarity is determined using lexical keyword matching. The semantically unique questions are then counted once for each interaction log in which they appear and divided by the total number of interaction logs to determine the frequency of usage.

We used this process with The Roleplay Trainer Creator to create a new question-asking VH from a test-bed question-answering VH. The test-bed question-answering VH patient case was selected because the VH patient conversation was previously well developed for answering questions [7]. The selected case is described as follows:

"You are presenting at an outpatient clinic with pain in the middle of your stomach. The onset of the pain was two months ago. You have been taking Tums twice a day for the stomach pain. You have also been having low back pain for the past three months. You have been taking two Aspirin three times a day for the back pain. The Aspirin consumption has caused a stomach ulcer, which is the source of the pain."

The frequency of usage analysis allows the user to rapidly select which questions to use in the question-asking VH (see Figure 2). With this interface, the most common questions can be quickly selected. In essence, this generates a "most common questions" medical student.

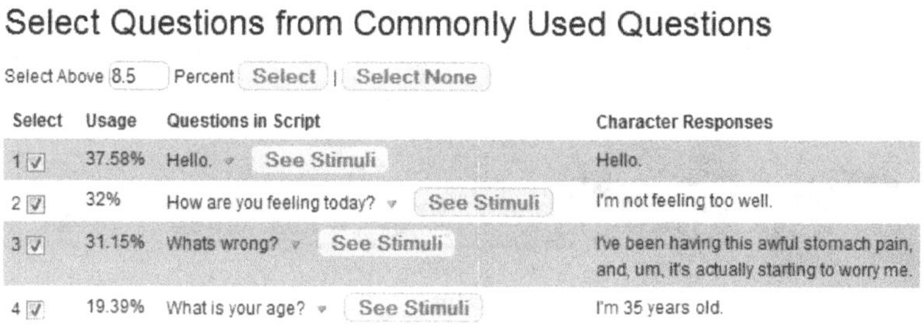

Select Questions from Commonly Used Questions

Select Above 8.5   Percent Select | Select None

Select	Usage	Questions in Script	Character Responses
1 ☑	37.58%	Hello. ▾ See Stimuli	Hello.
2 ☑	32%	How are you feeling today? ▾ See Stimuli	I'm not feeling too well.
3 ☑	31.15%	Whats wrong? ▾ See Stimuli	I've been having this awful stomach pain, and, um, it's actually starting to worry me.
4 ☑	19.39%	What is your age? ▾ See Stimuli	I'm 35 years old.

Fig. 2. Interface for selecting questions by usage. "Questions in Script" are the questions from the question-answering VH to be selected for the question-asking VH. "Character Responses" are the original responses from the question-answering VH.

Selecting questions for the test-bed scenario: The interaction logs from robust question-answering VHs are too large for a human to parse by hand. For the test-bed scenario there were 14872 total questions. Of these questions, the system found 493 semantically unique questions. From those unique questions, the expert was able to select 71 questions for our virtual medical student in approximately 60 minutes. This number was a compromise between maximizing coverage, minimizing expert time to select questions, and having a reasonable interaction length.

2.2 Determining Question Order

The next challenge was determining the question ordering. The system again pre-processes the interaction logs, and enlists the expert to validate the results. The goal is to have the virtual roleplay partner (virtual medical student) ask questions in an order similar to the order used by real novices (medical students).

For each selected question, the system finds the time in all the interaction logs where the question (or a semantically similar question) was used. It normalizes each of those values according to how far through the interaction the question was used. Normalizing these values is important because the interviews range from 5 minutes to 90 minutes. Last, the system uses the average of the values to determine order.

This method automatically arranged questions in an order roughly similar to a real medical student. The Rolplay Trainer Creator provides an interface to the expert for validating and fixing the order. Validating the order of the 71 questions in the test-bed scenario required approximately 30 minutes.

2.3 Simulating the Roleplay Partner

Virtual People Factory provides a web browser interface to interact with VHs using text-based chat. This interface is similar to online chat interfaces such as AOL Instant Messenger or Gmail Chat in which a user types an input and receives a text-based response. For simulating the roleplay interaction, the VPF interface was augmented with additional features to enable effective training of roleplay partners. A screenshot of the interaction interface is shown in Figure 3. The virtual roleplay partner (virtual medical student) asks questions, and the user (standardized patient) enters text-based responses. If the user does not know the answer to a question, they can mouse over the "See Correct Answers" box. The system will then display the answer that the

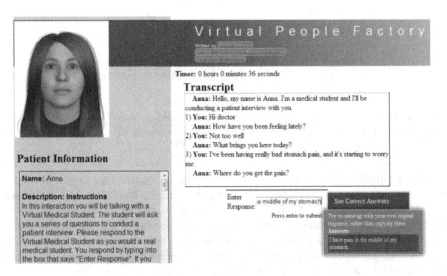

Fig. 3. Screenshot of the virtual medical student interaction interface

question-answering VH would give to the current question. This experience provides a way to practice formulating responses and learn the case beyond rote memorization.

3 Pilot Study

The evaluation study examined the Roleplay Trainer Creator for usability, acceptability, and learning. The usability and usefulness survey was based on Davis's perceived usefulness, ease of use, and user acceptance of information technology survey [8]. There are 12 questions in this questionnaire; responses are rated from 1 (unlikely) to 7 (likely). Learning was measured by the standardized patient's perceived feelings of preparation and confidence for playing the role of the patient pre- and post- experience. Preparedness and confidence were rated on a Likert scale from 1 (not very) to 7 (very). This pilot study is intended as a feasibility study, rather than an exhaustive examination of a finished application. The study was additionally used to elicit feedback from standardized patients on future directions for the project.

Population: Five ($n = 5$) standardized patients at the University of Florida Medical College conducted a medical interview with the virtual medical student. Participants were paid their regular hourly wage for the hour they participated in the study.

Procedure: Participants filled out the pre-survey, conducted their interview, and filled out the post-survey on a Dell D400 laptop using Internet Explorer 7.

Results: Three out of five participant's preparedness and confidence increased from pre-survey to post-survey (see Figure 4). Participants reported a usability of 6.3 ± 0.9, and usefulness of 4.5 ± 1.7. The usability and usefulness were analyzed by computing the mean value of the usability and usefulness questions for each participant, then taking the mean over all participants.

Discussion: The results of the study indicate that training standardized patients with a virtual medical student has potential. Three out of five participants reported an increased feeling of preparedness and confidence after interacting with the virtual medical student. The one user whose ratings decreased pre- to post- survey rated himself pre-survey at maximum (7), and so may have overrated his preparedness and confidence in the pre-survey.

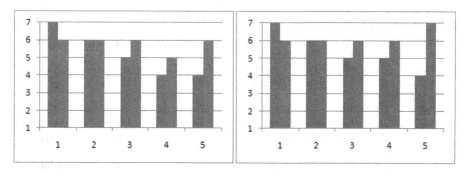

Fig. 4. Left: Participant's responses for pre- post- preparedness. Right: pre- post- confidence.

According to the usability survey results, the users felt it was easy to converse with the virtual medical student. The usefulness score had a high standard deviation, indicating that some users found the system to be useful for preparing and others did not. In future studies, with a larger number of users, we may be able to determine which users gain greater benefit from the experience, such as less experienced users or users with greater comfort with technology.

4 Conclusions and Future Work

We present Roleplay Trainer Creator, a system that uses logs from user interactions with a VH to generate a new unique VH. This VH is a virtual representation of the aggregate set of users. This method of generating a new VH from existing interaction logs has significant potential for interpersonal training applications. This research has shown that a question-asking VH generated using this method could become a beneficial training tool for increasing the standardization of roleplay partners.

These results are significant for developers of VH agents for interpersonal skills training. In our ongoing work in this area we are developing other types of VHs using this method. As an example, we will be creating VH instructors that will be able to talk *about* a patient case, including addressing common student mistakes, by drawing information from the interaction logs of a scenario. We will also explore using other inputs for generating VH gestures and emotions using logs of student's tracked movements and videos of their emotional reactions. We plan to continue exploring ways to reuse the interaction logs to bootstrap the creation of VHs for training additional types of health professionals such as nurses, pharmacists, and psychiatrists as well as non-health fields such as training sales agents.

References

1. Johnsen, K., Dickerson, R., Raij, A., et al.: Experiences in Using Immersive Virtual Characters to Educate Medical Communication Skills, vol. 324, pp. 179–186 (2005)
2. Dieker, L., Hynes, M., Stapleton, C., et al.: Virtual Classrooms: STAR Simulator. In: New Learning Technology SALT (2007)
3. Hill, R., Gratch, J., Marsella, S., et al.: Virtual Humans in the Mission Rehearsal Exercise System. Künstliche Intelligenz 4(03), 5–10 (2003)
4. Tamblyn, R.M., Klass, D.J., Schnabl, G.K., et al.: The accuracy of standardized patient presentation. Medical Education 25(2), 100–109 (2009)
5. Lei, G.A.O., Xiao-song, L.I., Xue-hong, W.A.N., et al.: An application of multivariate generalizability theory in the study on the reliability of objective structured clinical examination. China Higher Medical Education 3 (2004)
6. Wessel, J., Williams, R., Finch, E., et al.: Reliability and validity of an objective structured clinical examination for physical therapy students. Journal of Allied Health 32(4), 266–269 (2003)
7. Rossen, B., Lind, D.S., Lok, B.: Human-centered Distributed Conversational Modeling: Efficient Modeling of Robust Virtual Human Conversations. In: Ruttkay, Z., Kipp, M., Nijholt, A., Vilhjálmsson, H.H. (eds.) IVA 2009. LNCS, vol. 5773, pp. 474–481. Springer, Heidelberg (2009)
8. Davis, F.D.: Perceived usefulness, perceived ease of use, and user acceptance of information technology. MIS quarterly 13(3), 319–340 (1989)

Making It Personal: End-User Authoring of Health Narratives Delivered by Virtual Agents

Timothy Bickmore· and Lazlo Ring

College of Computer and Information Science, Northeastern University
360 Huntington Ave - WVH 202, Boston, MA 02115
{bickmore,lring}@ccs.neu.edu

Abstract. We describe a design study in which five different tools are compared for end-user authoring of personal stories to be told by an embodied conversational agent. The tools provide varying degrees of control over the agent's verbal and nonverbal behavior. Results indicate that users are more satisfied when their stories are delivered by a virtual agent compared to plain text, are more satisfied when provided with tools to control the agent's prosody compared to facial display of emotion, and are most satisfied when they have the most control over all aspects of the agent's delivery.

Keywords: Embodied Conversational Agent, Relational Agent, Narrative, Storytelling.

1 Introduction

Storytelling plays a central role in group counseling for health behavior change, and is the cornerstone of many formal and informal counseling and support group methodologies, such as the 12-step program used by Alcoholics Anonymous. Hearing successful stories of change from peers not only conveys specific information that may be instrumental in effecting change, but increases motivation and self-efficacy to change through social learning [1]. The act of writing such stories also has psychological benefits for the author, including better coping with post traumatic events [2] and improvement in self-efficacy [3]. In one study of participants attending a cancer-related storytelling workshop, 85% of respondents indicated that hearing stories of others living with cancer gave them hope, and 97% indicated that the act of storytelling helped them cope with cancer [4].

We plan to leverage the power of personal change narratives in an online system to promote "preconception care" among young African American women. Preconception care involves addressing health issues that may negatively impact the health of a baby before a woman conceives [5]. We are focusing on African American women since they have roughly twice the rate of infant mortality and low infant birth weight compared to Caucasian women in the U.S. Our automated intervention involves first screening women for 53 risk factors during a clinic visit, ranging from vaccinations, diet and chronic disease management, to smoking and drug abuse. Following this, screened women will interact with a web-based virtual agent (based on [6]) approximately three times a week for two months, during which time the agent will counsel

J. Allbeck et al. (Eds.): IVA 2010, LNAI 6356, pp. 399–405, 2010.

them on how to address any health issues identified in the screening and motivate them to take action.

In addition to having the agent give advice authored by the clinicians on the design team, we will also elicit stories of health behavior change from the users of the system. These (moderated) stories will then be shared with other users who are struggling with issues addressed in the stories. We face several fundamental design choices in developing this system, including: how these stories should be authored by users; how the stories should be told to other users; how users should be motivated to contribute stories (e.g., using incentive mechanisms as in [7]); how the stories should be indexed (e.g., as in [8]); and how their telling should be integrated into the rest of the online counseling dialogue system [9]. Among these many issues, we have decided to initially focus our design efforts on the first one: what kind of tools should we provide to users for them to author their stories?

The simplest end-user story authoring tools would just let users write their stories in text and display them in a similar fashion. However, since the system will incorporate a conversational agent, users could be provided with the means to author their stories so that they could be told to other users by the agent in dialogue, taking advantage of the additional expressivity afforded by the agent. Given this, how much control over the conversational agent and its delivery of the story would users want? Is it sufficient to let users write the text of their story and have a text-to-embodied speech translation engine (such as BEAT [10]) automatically generate all of the verbal and nonverbal agent behavior used in the story telling? Or, despite evidence that naïve users have difficulty with task-specific programming languages [11], will they want full control over the agent and its delivery of their story, and if so, which aspects of that control are most important to them?

In this article we present the results of an initial design study comparing a range of authoring tools to support users in creating health behavior change narratives.

2   Related Work

Several researchers have investigated the use of embodied conversational agents as aides in storytelling. For example, Umaschi and Cassell developed the SAGE system for the purpose of eliciting stories from children [12]. The system's interface allowed children to author stories using a branching dialogue representation, with the interactive stories told by a conversational rabbit character.

Many others have developed authoring tools to enable non-programmers to create stories or storytelling systems, in which the stories are told using a variety of media. Cassell and Ryokai developed the StoryMat system to elicit stories from preliterate children using a combination of physical location cues (where a child was playing on a play mat), audio prompts and voice recording [13]. Skorupski and Mateas developed Wide Ruled, an authoring system to enable non-programmers to create AI plan-driven interactive storytelling systems [14].

Avatar-based CMC systems typically provide users with some control over the verbal and nonverbal behavior of their avatar. For example, Comic Chat allows users to communicate with each other online using a comic strip metaphor, in which many aspects of a character's nonverbal behavior, such as its emotional state, can be manipulated.

3   An Initial Design Study of Storytelling Support Tools

In order to determine how much and what kind of control end users would want over an embodied conversational agent telling their stories to others, we conducted an experiment comparing five different versions of story authoring and re-telling tools. These five versions were based on the capabilities of our system, with each one giving a different level of control to the user. The use of simple audio or video recording to disseminate stories was not possible due to the necessity of maintaining user anonymity. In all versions, the story fragment was comprised of a short linear sequence of utterances, and the tools provided different sets of controls over agent verbal and nonverbal behavior. The five tools evaluated were:

- TEXT – The author enters their story in a text edit box, and the story is "told" by simply displaying the text (intended as a baseline control condition).
- AGENT – The author enters their story in a text edit box, and the story is told by an embodied conversational agent speaking the story ("Gladys", Figure 1), with nonverbal behavior (eyebrow raises, head nods, eye gaze motion, posture shifts) automatically generated using BEAT [10], and prosody generated by the default rules in the text-to-speech engine (Loquendo "Susan" voice). The agent maintains a neutral facial display throughout.
- FACE – The same as AGENT, but the author can specify alternative facial displays (happy and sad/concerned displays in addition to neutral) to be used when delivering different parts of the story.
- VOICE – The same as AGENT, but the author can use a variety of prosody commands to affect speech delivery, including speed (increase/decrease), volume (increase/decrease), baseline pitch (increase/decrease), emphasis, and pause at specified locations in the story.
- ALL – Combination of FACE and VOICE (Figure 2).

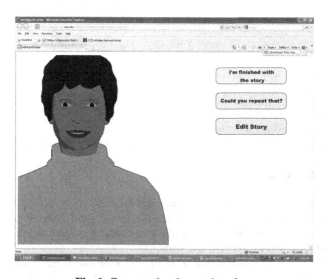

Fig. 1. Conversational agent interface

Fig. 2. Story authoring interface

The study had a five treatment counterbalanced within-subjects design. In order to minimize burden on study participants, they were provided with a set of 10 pre-authored health stories and asked to select 5 that they wanted to work with (rather than having to write their own). Following administration of demographic and personality questionnaires, participants conducted a brief training interaction with the agent, then filled out a questionnaire assessing their attitude towards the agent. Next they were asked to input each of the five stories they selected into different versions of the tool and asked to modify each until they were happy with its delivery, filling out evaluation questionnaires after each story.

Measures. After submitting a story with each version of the tool, participants answered the questions shown in Table 1. In addition, we measured the number of controls they used in each story and the amount of editing they did on the text of the story that was provided to them, using Levenshtein distance [15].

Participants. Nine African American females aged 20-24 were recruited via craigslist.org. All had high levels of computer proficiency and were well educated (one had a high school level education, the rest had at least some college).

3.1 Quantitative Results

For all rating measures (with larger values representing more positive evaluations), TEXT was always rated the lowest, ALL the highest, and VOICE second highest (Table 2). Analyses across the five treatments were performed using SPSS Repeated Measures ANOVA, with LSD post hoc tests.

There was a significant difference in ratings of how much the agent helped users tell their stories, $F(4,24)=8.6$, $p<.001$. Post hoc tests indicated significant differences

Table 1. Tool Evaluation Questions

Item	Question Text	Anchor 1	Anchor 7
Helpful	How much did Gladys help you tell your story?	Not at all	Very much
Confident	How confident are you that Gladys will re-tell your story the way you want it to be heard by others?	Not at all	Very much
Express	How much did you feel you could express yourself in Gladys' telling of your story?	Not at all	Very much
Easy	How easy was it to author a story using this version of the tool?	Very difficult	Very easy
Satisfied	How satisfied were you with your authoring experience using this version of the tool?	Not at all	Very much

Table 2. Primary Study Outcomes – Mean (SD) - *p<.05

Item	TEXT	AGENT	FACE	VOICE	ALL
Helpful*	2.86 (1.57)	4.43 (1.40)	5.14 (1.34)	5.43 (0.79)	5.86 (1.46)
Confident	3.22 (1.86)	4.22 (1.20)	4.00 (2.24)	4.78 (2.28)	5.11 (2.21)
Express	3.67 (1.50)	4.00 (1.32)	4.00 (2.40)	4.89 (2.21)	5.22 (2.22)
Easy	3.44 (2.01)	4.22 (1.56)	4.22 (2.22)	5.00 (2.29)	5.44 (2.19)
Satisfied*	3.00 (1.87)	4.00 (1.41)	3.78 (2.11)	5.00 (2.34)	5.33 (2.24)
ControlsUsed*	N/A	N/A	3.33 (2.40)	7.22 (6.69)	8.00 (6.27)
EditDistance	24 (32)	25 (42)	21 (56)	63 (89)	80 (186)

between TEXT and the other conditions, and AGENT and the other conditions, but no significant differences among FACE, VOICE and ALL.

There was also a significant difference in ratings of overall satisfaction with the authoring experience, $F(4,32)=2.8$, $p<.05$. Post hoc tests indicated significant differences between TEXT and ANIMATION, TEXT and VOICE, and TEXT and ALL, but no other differences.

There were no significant differences among the treatments on reported confidence that the agent would properly re-tell the story, $F(4,32)=1.6$ n.s., or in the amount they felt they could express themselves, $F(4,32)=1.2$ n.s., or in ratings of ease of use, $F(4,32)=1.6$ n.s.

3.2 Qualitative Results

When asked for their overall impressions of the storytelling system, six respondents provided positive responses ("interesting", "fun", "cool" being the most common):

"I thought it was really cool, um, I've never worked with inputting text and seeing it read back to me or portrayed to me um virtually so that was a new experience for me and I really really liked it."

"Gladys was able to use emotion and express it the way I wanted her to express it so I felt like I was telling the story."

Two respondents complained that the tools still did not let them express themselves enough:

> *"I thought it was an interesting concept but sometimes working with the tool was a little difficult. It was kind of hard to get the person online to talk the same way that I wanted it to sound like in my head."*

When asked which of the tools they thought was most effective, seven respondents said they preferred having all of the tools available to them. Given a choice between control of facial display and prosody, two respondents indicated they preferred the speech controls, while two others indicated they preferred control over facial display:

> *"The one where you can add all of the emotions and pauses and increase pitch um I think that one was better because you can make it more human."*

Finally, when asked about suggestions to improve the authoring tool, several mentioned better voice quality, two suggested a broader range of emotion displays for the face and one suggested more emotion controls for the voice. One participant also volunteered that the ability to customize the look of the agent would be important to her.

4 Discussion

We find that, rather than being intimidated by a wide range of controls for verbal and nonverbal behavior of an embodied conversational agent, participants actually preferred having as many controls at their disposal as possible for crafting their stories. They also appeared to prefer speech controls over facial display controls, although this may also simply be an artifact of the number of options available in each (8 prosody controls vs. 3 facial display controls). Participants used the most controls and made the most edits on the pre-written story text when the speech controls were available to them (VOICE and ALL), likely due to a focus on getting their story to sound right given the quirks of the speech synthesizer. Finally, participants preferred all versions of agent storytelling to simply having the text of their story displayed to others.

4.1 Future Work

We plan to explore several additional design alternatives for story authoring tools, including "storyboards" in which users can select from static images of the character telling the story, allowing a much broader range of characters and nonverbal behavior than we can currently support, but without animation. We also plan to explore the space of tools to help users write well-formed and impactful stories, for example by providing them with relevant examples, forms to fill out, prompts, coaching, or guiding them through a process of oral storytelling and transcription.

Acknowledgments. Thanks to Jenna Zaffini and Kristin Mainello for their assistance in conducting the study, to Laura Packer for writing the stories used in the study, and to the other members of the Relational Agent Group for their help.

References

1. Bandura, A.: Self-efficacy: toward a unifying theory of behavioral change. Psychol. Rev. 84, 191–215 (1977)
2. Andersen, P., Guerrero, L.: Principles of Communication and Emotion in Social Interaction. In: Andersen, P., Guerrero, L. (eds.) Handbook of Communication and Emotion. Academic Press, New York (1998)
3. Roberts, L.: Giving and receiving help: Interpersonal transactions in mutual-help meetings and psychosocial adjustment of members. American Journal of Community Psychology 27, 841–868 (1999)
4. Chelf, J., Deshler, A., Hillman, S., Durazo-Arvizu, R.: Storytelling: A Strategy for Living and Coping with Cancer. Cancer Nursing 23, 1–5 (2000)
5. Mitchell, S., Bickmore, T., Paasche-Orlow, M., Williams, C., Forsythe, S., Atrash, H., Johnson, K.J.: B Increasing Access to Preconception Care Using Health Information Technology Salud(i)Ciencia (2010)
6. Bickmore, T., Schulman, D., Shaw, G.: DTask & LiteBody: Open Source, Standards-based Tools for Building Web-deployed Embodied Conversational Agents. In: Ruttkay, Z., Kipp, M., Nijholt, A., Vilhjálmsson, H.H. (eds.) IVA 2009. LNCS, vol. 5773, pp. 425–431. Springer, Heidelberg (2009)
7. Farzan, R., DiMicco, J.M., Millen, D.R., Dugan, C., Geyer, W., Brownholtz, E.A.: Results from deploying a participation incentive mechanism within the enterprise. In: CHI 2008, pp. 563–572 (2008)
8. Domeshek, E.: Do The Right Thing: A Component Theory for Indexing Stories as Social Advice. Institute for the Learning Sciences, Northwestern University (1992)
9. Jefferson, G.: Sequential aspects of storytelling in conversation. In: Schenkein, J. (ed.) Studies in the organization of conversational interaction, pp. 219–248. Academic Press, New York (1978)
10. Cassell, J., Vilhjálmsson, H., Bickmore, T.: BEAT: The Behavior Expression Animation Toolkit. In: SIGGRAPH 2001, Los Angeles, CA, pp. 477–486 (2001)
11. Nardi, B.A.: A Small Matter of Programming: Perspectives on End User Computing. The MIT Press, Cambridge (1993)
12. Umaschi, M., Cassell, J.: Storytelling Systems: Constructing the Innerface of the Interface. In: Cognitive Technologies Proceedings, pp. 98–108 (1997)
13. Cassell, J., Ryokai, K.: Making Space for Voice: Technologies to Support Children's Fantasy and Storytelling. Personal Technologies 5, 203–224 (2001)
14. Skorupski, J., Jayapalan, L., Marquez, S., Mateas, M.: Wide Ruled: A Friendly Interface to Author-Goal Based Story Generation. In: Proceedings ICVS 2007 (2007)
15. Levenshtein, V.: Binary codes capable of correcting deletions, insertions, and reversals. Soviet Physics Doklady 10, 707–710 (1966)

MAY: My Memories Are Yours

Joana Campos and Ana Paiva

Instituto Superior Técnico - UTL and INESC-ID,
Av. Prof. Cavaco Silva, Taguspark 2744-016, Porto Salvo, Portugal
joana.campos@ist.utl.pt,
ana.paiva@inesc-id.pt

Abstract. In human relations engagement and continuous communication is promoted by the process of *sharing experiences*. This type of social behaviour plays an important role in the maintenance of relationships with our peers and it is grounded by cognitive features of memory. Aiming at creating agents that sustain long-term interactions, we developed MAY, a conversational virtual companion that gathers memories *shared* by the user into a three layer knowledge base, divided in Lifetime Periods, General Events and Event-Specific-Knowledge. We believe that its cue sensitive structure increases agent adaptability and gives it capabilities to perform in a social environment, being able to infer about the user's common and uncommon events. Results show that these agent's capabilities contribute to development of intimacy and companionship.

Keywords: virtual companion, biographical memory, shared memory.

1 Introduction

In human interactions, memory is fundamental to hold up conversations and to sustain long-term relations. Without noticing we constantly choose from our memories of experiences the best fit for the current situation, either to make a decision or to communicate with other people. That valuable information is not just about one's personal experiences, but also acquaintance of others' lives too. It is this process of *sharing personal memories*, available by autobiographical remembering, that enriches our conversations, making them seem more truthful, believable and engaging [3].

Similarly, the importance of memory in agents is undeniable and many researchers have recently focused their agents' architectures on its relation to long-term believability. In artificial companions systems, episodic memory based architectures are believed to be essential [9], as they aim to reflect the agent's experience. But taking the human memory comparison a little bit further, an agent's memory that is constituted by only its own experiences might not be adequate for maintaining a long-term relationship.

This suggests that if we want to create more pleasant and acceptable agents, capable of carrying on with more engaging interactions [7] and consequently maintain the relationship for a longer period of time, we need to consider the memory aspect and its sharing and social function.

J. Allbeck et al. (Eds.): IVA 2010, LNAI 6356, pp. 406–412, 2010.

Aiming at creating agents that sustain long-term interactions with humans, we focus on mechanisms to retain, over multiple interactions, *shared* information, that is, stories of experiences that the user has told the agent. We believe that artificial companions capable of indexing user's "experiences" in their memory and at the same time able to show acquaintance of user's life, are likely to lead to the development of attachment. To try to achieve that goal, we have explored an Autobiographical Memory architecture suggested by Conway [5].

Our purpose was to exploit whether the level companionship between the user and agent through a conversational interface correlates with the memory model or not. As such, our intention is to exploit if MAY, an agent capable of shape its memory for user's events, can influence its responsiveness and create proximity between them.

2 Related Work

The area of intelligent agents that act as companions is fastly growing. An example is the LIREC[1] and the COMPANIONS[2] projects, which focus is on creating technology that support long-term relationship between humans and computers.

Researchers have focused their efforts in creating more engaging and user adaptable agents. So far, most companion systems are focused on capturing the user attention by endowing the agent with empathetic behaviour [2] and robust dialogue capabilities[14]. However they need more social skills to surpass the limited engagement with the agent over time.

To overcome this issue, several researchers have developed methods to create Autobiographical Memory (AM). Ho et al.[8] emphasize that AM can increase believability of intelligent agents, thanks to its capacity to increase agents' adaptability to the environment or to new situations. A different approach was taken by Mei Yii Lim et al [10], where an initial prototype for a social companion generic memory was developed. The aim was to create mechanisms reflecting human memory characteristics to allow companions to identify, characterize and distinguish experiences[8]. Focusing on the adaptability to preferences and to the environment they expect the maintenance of a long-term interaction.

The mentioned autobiographical mechanisms have showed several improvements in intelligent agents, yet they have not been tested in conversational companions systems, in which AM dynamics might improve reasoning skills in real-time. Further, none of the these systems considers the creation of a "shared" memory element, but concentrates more on the agents' biographical memory.

3 Memory's Anatomy

Conway [5] focused his work on refining the concept of AM and drew a contrast between it and episodic memory, which limits were somehow blurred. He

---

[1] http://www.lirec.org/

[2] http://www.companions-project.org/

suggests, a unified model, where episodic memory is seen as a system which contains sensory-perceptual details of recent experiences, and those memories only are retained in memory when linked to a more permanent type of memory – *autobiographical memory*.

AM can be seen as "semantic knowledge" about one's life, retaining knowledge about the progress of personal goals, a 'life story'. According to [5], this "semantic knowledge" has three levels of specificity :

Lifetime Periods can be seen has temporal and thematic knowledge. Often those periods last for years, for example "When I was at school", and can be grouped by themes. Themes consist in outstanding situations in a higher abstraction view, such as "school" or "work".

General events are linked to life time periods and cover single events that could last for few days or months, for example, "study for an algebra exam".

Event-Specific Knowledge (ESK) Detailed information concerned with a single event. They are often accompanied by "images that pop into mind" and have the duration of seconds or hours.

Besides AM dynamics, this memory division provides some important functions. The *social function* is claimed by Neisser [11] as the most fundamental function of AM. Nelson [12] also suggests that autobiographical memory has high significance on *sharing memories* with other people. The memory-sharing [1] process is influenced by responsiveness, that is, listeners make empathetic and contextually grounded responses to what the speaker is saying. Not only does memory-sharing enhance believability of conversations, but also serves to attain engagement and intimacy in relations [3].

4   Conceptual Model for *Shared Memories*

According to Conway[5], autobiographical memories can be seen as mental constructions generated from an underlying knowledge base (or regions), which are sensitive to cues, and patterns of activation. Autobiographical memories contain knowledge at three levels of specificity: *Event-specific knowledge (ESK)*, *General Events* and *Lifetime periods*.

While *lifetime periods* identify thematic and temporal knowledge, *general events* are related to actions, happenings and situations in one's life. *ESK*'s details are contextualized within a general event that in turn is associated with one or more lifetime periods, linking self autobiographical memory as a whole(Fig.1).

In this section we explain how we have mapped these concepts onto a virtual companion's memory system as a way to capture factual and emotional events experienced by the user. As such, the agent's memory is biographical as it uses a model of AM to reflect user's experiences and better adapt to him/her.

4.1   Structure of the Knowledge Base

The knowledge base's architecture is like a small ontology of semantic relations, which describe the main cues for triggering one's memories. As Conway [5] and

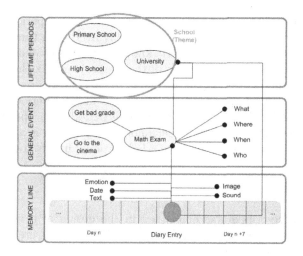

Fig. 1. Agent's Memory System

others researchers refer, anything can be a cue. In our model we only considered cues that could be represented by text and syntactically inferred from it.

Based on theoretical concepts [5], the memory is divided into three independent levels, using RDF (Resource Description Framework).

The underlying structure of this framework is a collection of triples, each consisting of $< subject, predicate, object >$. These triples are organized in graphs. Representing the information like this, we have a simple data model for inference.

The knowledge base consists of 3 subgraphs, each one representing one level of specificity (Figure 1) – lifetime periods, general events and ESKs. They act as specific views the knowledge base and all graphs(levels) are interrelated. Yet they can be evaluated separately.

Base level – memory line. This level tries to represent Event Specific Knowledge. The main idea is to capture a timeline over which the details of memories are stored. In other words, for each chronological position we have a node linked by a predicate to text objects. These objects are the associated details of the memory. The predicates are date, text (the personal description of the experience), image, and sound, and they allow the retrieval of one memory at the less abstract level.

Middle level – general event. General events capture the main action of one memory and allow retrieval by small pieces of text syntactically inferred from text. They are "what", "where", "when" and "who". The edge "when" links to a different and more detailed object than the predicate "date" in the level below. It can also have a string related to the time of the day. Further, a general event can be within one or more lifetime periods, thus an edge should be included into this feature. For example, the event "Holiday in Rome with Sam" can be linked to the lifetime period "Year 2008" and at the same time "Relationship with Sam", because it was an event that happened during these periods of life.

Top level – lifetime period. For any given chronological period there may be a number of lifetime periods, which probably overlap in time. That is why, as Conway describes, that thematic knowledge is associated with temporal knowledge to index different parts of the memory and fix the overlap problem. The lifetime period graph is organized by context or theme, this is, a generic concept that specifies the content of a lifetime period. For example, the theme "School" may comprise lifetime periods like "primary school", "high school" and "university". Each node in the graph is a lifetime period inserted into a context, which have a bidirectional link to a general event.

5   Introducing MAY

The model just described was embedded in the design of a virtual companion agent MAY(my Memories Are Yours). MAY is an agent created to assist a teenager user on self-reflection about what happens in his/her life. The interaction between MAY and the user is through dialogue, which allows the agent to collect the user's experiences and save them in a diary form (or a timeline). The memories (or events) stored in MAY constitute a kind of "shared memory" between MAY and the user. MAY is like an *affective diary* [13].

Figure 2 shows a screenshot of a chat like interface during an interaction between a user(Amy) and MAY. At the bottom, one can see the *Memory Line*, which represents the base level of the memory hierarchy. Each cloud represents an entry in the 'diary'.

The interaction is text-based and the information extracted is syntactically inferred from it. MAY's dialogue system uses a modified version of A.L.I.C.E[3], an engine that uses AIML (Artificial Intelligence Markup Language) to create responses to questions and inputs. The dialogue is pro-active and adapted to the main goals of a teenager user – school, love and play. To preserve situations of which the agent does not have an appropriate answer, we use ConceptNet to endow the system with dynamical capabilities to adapt to unpredictable input. ConceptNet is the largest freely available, machine-useable commonsense resource and it aims to create a network of relationships, which represent the facts that each of us know about the world [6]. It is used essentially to find relations between concepts (words) in the written sentences, to relate events and to produce 'intelligent' replies to the user during the dialogue.

The events are extracted, using natural language tools, carefully adapted to the memory structure and used in the extend of the interactions to create agent's responsiveness. From those events characteristics (4W) such as 'what', 'who', 'where' and 'when', are also extracted. These are then used to index the event in the memory structure mentioned before. As anything can be a clue, if some pattern of data in memory is activated, MAY can show to the user that it has been listening, by relating the clue with some previous memories. In the following example, the user says "Tonight I'm going to the cinema" to which the agent replies "Sounds good. Are you going with Lyam?". The agent 'reminds'

---

[3] http://alicebot.org/

Fig. 2. Screenshot of MAY's interface

that Amy uses to go to the cinema with Lyam. This will also work for events specified as goals and to make predictions.

6   Evaluating Memories in Memory

We conducted a experiment to evaluate if is perceived some sort of relationship that the agent can establish with the user. To do that we used a friendship questionnaire to measure the quality of the relationship. The results showed that when the agent manifests acquaintance about the user's life, even little details of common events, the users classified more positively the *intimacy* and *companionship* dimensions of friendship. These outcomes corroborate Nelson argument about how the social function of the sharing process contributes to development of intimacy and consequently maintenance of a relationship. For more details please see [4].

7   Conclusions and Future Work

This companion prototype enhances some social aspects possible by having a memory structure capable of indexing user's memories of experiences. Its functionalities and its efficiency on retrieval gives the agent the ability to perform in a social environment. We explored how acquaintance about one's life can influence positively a relationship and we introduced such characteristic into a conversational companion. Yet, this memory structure may offer many others possibilities that can be explored in future work. For instance, the use of previous knowledge to make more complex analogies and more informed forecasts.

Acknowledgements. The research leading to these results has received funding from European Community's Seventh Framework Program (FP7/2007-2013) under grant agreement n° 215554, FCT (INESC-ID multiannual funding) through the PIDDAC Program funds.

References

1. Alea, N., Bluck, S.: Why are you telling me that? a conceptual model of the social function of autobiographical memory. Memory 11(2), 165–178 (2003)
2. Bickmore, T.W., Pfeifer, L., Schulman, D., Perera, S., Senanayake, C., Nazmi, I.: Public displays of affect: deploying relational agents in public spaces. In: CHI 2008: CHI 2008 extended abstracts on Human factors in computing systems, pp. 3297–3302. ACM Press, New York (2008)
3. Bluck, S.: Autobiographical memory: Exploring its funtions in everydaylife. Memory 11(2), 113–123 (2003)
4. Campos, J.: May: my memories are yours. an interactional companion that saves user memories. Master's thesis, Instituto Superior Técnico (2010)
5. Conway, M.A.: Sensory-perceptual episodic memory and its context: autobiographical memory. Philosophical Transactions of the Royal Society B: Biological Sciences 356, 1375–1384 (2001)
6. Havasi, C., Speer, R., Alonso, J.: Conceptnet 3: a flexible, multilingual semantic network for common sense knowledge. In: Recent Advances in Natural Language Processing (2007)
7. Ho, W., Dautenhahn, K., Lim, M., Enz, S., Zoll, C., Watson, S.: Towards learning 'self' and emotional knowledge in social and cultural human-agent interactions. International Journal of Agent Technologies and Systems 1(3), 51–78 (2009)
8. Ho, W., Lim, M., Vargas, P.A., Enz, S., Dautenhahn, K., Aylett, R.: An initial memory model for virtual and robot companions supporting migration and long-term interaction. In: 18th IEEE International Symposium on Robot and Human Interactive Communication RO-MAN 2009, pp. 277–284. IEEE, Los Alamitos (2009)
9. Laird, J.E., Derbinsky, N.: A year of episodic memory (2009)
10. Lim, M.Y., Aylett, R., Ho, W.C., Enz, S., Vargas, P.: A socially-aware memory for companion agents. In: Ruttkay, Z., Kipp, M., Nijholt, A., Vilhjálmsson, H.H. (eds.) IVA 2009. LNCS, vol. 5773, pp. 20–26. Springer, Heidelberg (2009)
11. Neisser, U.: Five kinds of self-knowledge. Philosophical Psychology 1(1), 35–59 (1988)
12. Nelson, K.: The psychological and social origins of autobiographical memory. Psychological Science 4(1), 7–14 (1993)
13. Ståhl, A., Höök, K., Svensson, M., Taylor, A.S., Combetto, M.: Experiencing the affective diary. Personal Ubiquitous Comput 13(5), 365–378 (2009)
14. Stahl, O., Gambäck, B., Hansen, P., Turunen, M., Hakulinen, J.: A mobile fitness companion. In: Fourth International Workshop on Human-Computer Conversation, Bellagio, Italy (2008)

Expression of Behaviors in Assistant Agents as Influences on Rational Execution of Plans

Jean-Paul Sansonnet and François Bouchet

LIMSI-CNRS, B.P. 133, F-91403 Orsay Cedex, France

Abstract. Assistant Agents help ordinary people about computer tasks, in many ways, thanks to their rational reasoning capabilities about the current model of the world. However they face strong acceptability issues because of the lack of naturalness in their interaction with users. A promising approach is to provide Assistant Agents with a personality model and allow them to achieve behavioral reasoning in conjunction with rational reasoning. In this paper, we propose a formal framework to study the relationships between the rational and behavioral processes, based on the expression of the behaviors in terms of influence operators on the rational execution of actions and plans.

Keywords: Behavior modelization, Rational reasoning, Assistant agents.

1 Introduction

1.1 Conversational Assistant Agents

This study is placed in the particular context of conversational situations (further called UAS situations) where three entities are in bilateral interaction: a human user (U), an assistant agent (A) and a computer system (S). In a typical UAS situation, the user performs some activity on/with the system; at times, the user can solicit from the agent a general advice or some direct help upon the system or the task at hand. Actually, this definition, stemming from [7], encompasses a large class of conversational interactions ranging from situations where the user has control upon the agent to opposite situations where the agent has a leading/intrusive role: Presenters, Helpers, Butlers, Friends, Companions, Teachers, Trainers, Coachs.

An assistant agent, in a UAS situation, has two faces needing distinct capabilities: a control face, directed towards the system, and a dialogical face, directed towards the user. Controlling a computer application requires two main things: a *symbolic model* of the application and a *rational reasoning capacity* about that model. In the following, we will refer to the control face of an agent as the *"rational agent"* [10]. Dialoguing with the user requires three main things: a) a conversational interface (often multimodal); b) the input of user's requests and the output of factual replies processed by the rational reasoning capacity; c) the expression of the agent's personality according to the role it endorses in a particular UAS situation, as listed above. In the following, we will refer to

J. Allbeck et al. (Eds.): IVA 2010, LNAI 6356, pp. 413–419, 2010.

the expression of the agent's personality as the *"behavioral agent"* [9]. Although presented here as separate notions, the rational and the behavioral capacities of an agent actually work in a quite intricate manner [5,6]. This is the reason why our work focuses on the study of the nature of their relationships.

1.2   Rational and Behavioral Agents

The implementation of an agent A, in a UAS situation, at time t, that has both rational and behavioral capacities, can be represented as a quadruple $\langle \Phi_t, \Psi_t, A_R, A_B \rangle$:
– Φ_t is the dynamic model of the agent's world, updated at time t,
– Ψ_t is the dynamic model of the agent's mental state, updated at time t,
– A_R is the rational agent, at a certain position of its reasoning process,
– A_B is the behavioral agent, at a certain position in Ψ_t.
Relying on these definitions, we make two statements:

S1. The results of the execution by A_R of the current action α_i in the current endeavored plan π_i directed to the current goal γ_i influence the evolution $\Psi_t \rightarrow \Psi_{t+1}$. This statement is closely related to the literature on emotions and affect elicitation, involving notions such as *arousal, appraisal,* and *coping*. While fully part of our framework, it is not discussed in detail in the paper.

S2. A behavioral agent A_B at Ψ_t is defined in terms of its influences on the execution by A_R of the current action α_i in the current endeavored plan π_i directed to the current goal γ_i. It is the main focus of the paper.

The outline of the paper is as follows: in the next section we present the general framework that supports the quadruple $\langle \Phi_t, \Psi_t, A_R, A_B \rangle$ and we give the notations for Φ_t and A_R. In section 3 we give the notations for Ψ_t and A_B, then we classify the possible influences of A_B upon A_R execution in terms of preferences and biases. Finally, we give some examples and we compare with related works.

2   The R&B Framework

2.1   General Architecture

The general architecture supporting the quadruple $\langle \Phi_t, \Psi_t, A_R, A_B \rangle$ is called the R&B framework. Its four main parts, represented on Fig. 1 are:

— The *model of the world* Φ is a symbolic representation of the assisted application (see [3] for a complete formal definition of Φ) that describes: a) the structure of the application (e.g. its topology); b) the objects contained in the application; c) the actions that can be performed upon the objects. Note that if the agent is an actor in the application (i.e. it has a physicality) it is viewed as a particular object of the world and as such, its physical attributes are described in Φ.

— The *model of the mental state* of the agent Ψ is a symbolic representation, technically based on the same formalism as Φ.

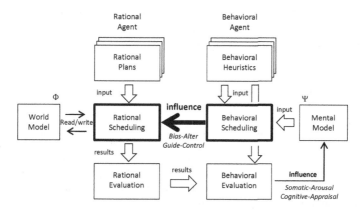

Fig. 1. General Architecture of the R&B framework (in bold, the focus of the paper)

— The *rational agent* A_R builds, chooses and executes plans π_i. The *rational scheduler* S_R selects actions in the current plan and executes them over Φ. Reports of executed actions are produced and evaluated by the *rational evaluator* E_R the results of which are used both by S_R to further schedule the current plan and by the behavioral agent.

— The *behavioral agent* A_B is controlled by the *behavioral scheduler* S_B and the *behavioral evaluator* E_B that executes *behavioral heuristics* H_B according to the current state of the mental model of the agent Ψ. Basically, S_B and E_B execute two symmetric processes: 1) S_B influences the selection process of the actions within the current plan performed by S_R; 2) E_B performs a behavioral evaluation of the results of the executed actions and in turn it influences the dynamic part of the mental states of the agent.

In this paper, we focus on the study of the S_B process: the influence of the behavioral scheduling upon the rational scheduling of the currently executed plan (i.e. the process emphasized in bold in Fig. 1).

2.2   Handling Actions and Plans

Plan definition. Traditionally [1,8], rational plans are defined from basic actions in the *rational plan language* $\mathscr{L}_\pi$. Formally, a plan $\pi_i \in \Pi$ is a tree structure with nodes tagged by one of those entities:

- a plan identifier p_i, introducing a (non recursive) subplan of π_i;
- one of the four procedural operators (cf. Tab. 1): seq, alt, par, case; the declarative operator $\langle\rangle$ introduces a declarative plan as a quadruple $\langle S_g, S_p, S_o, S_d\rangle$ composed of a set of goals S_g and three sets of subplans: preferred S_p, optional S_o, and default S_d. As soon as one of the goals $\gamma_i \in S_g$ is achieved, the plan is terminated (similarly to the set of terminal states of an automata).

With the definitions given in Tab. 1, a textual definition of a plan can be given by a set of statements taking one of the three following forms (an example of plan is given in Fig. 2):

PlanExpression $\rightarrow$ ScriptProcedural | ScriptDeclarative | Action
ScriptProcedural $\rightarrow$ ProcOp[PlanExpression, ...]
ScriptDeclarative $\rightarrow$ $\langle S_g, S_p, S_o, S_d \rangle$

Table 1. Procedural Operators (ProcOp) by descending order of precedence

Name	Symbol	Semantics (informal)
seq	;	$a_1; a_2$: Done(a_1) is a precondition to start a_2
alt	|	$a_1 \| a_2$: only one of the elements is randomly chosen and executed
par	||	$(a_1 \| a_2) \equiv (a_1; a_2)\|(a_2; a_1)$
		one of the sequences is randomly chosen and executed
case	$\mapsto$	$\text{guard}_1 \mapsto a_1, \text{guard}_2 \mapsto a_2$
		guard_i are explicit preconditions for a_i to be executed
		If several guards are True, then one is randomly chosen and executed

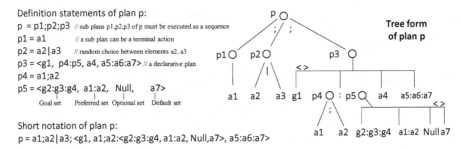

Fig. 2. Example of a plan p including 8 terminal actions ($a_1 \ldots a_8$), 4 terminal goals ($g_1 \ldots g_4$) and 5 subplans ($p_1 \ldots p_5$) where p_3 and p_5 are declarative plans

3   Implementing Behaviors

3.1   Definition of the Influence Operators

The principle of the execution of a rational plan (algorithm abridged), is illustrated in a graphical manner in Fig. 3. If we want to interfere with this process, e.g. for implementing behavioral influences, a theoretical question arises: what kinds of influences are formally possible on a plan scheduling? In theory, any arbitrary alteration can be applied upon the currently executed plan or subplan. However in UAS situations, alterations should not alter the basic rationality of the agent (i.e. lead to erratic behaviors) so we will not consider, for the time being, alterations such as aborting plans or subplans, switching plans or subplans, etc. Despite these restrictions, several kinds of influence operators ($\iota \in \mathbb{I}$) can be exhibited (as illustrated by black bold arrows in Fig. 3) that are situated at three levels of the rational process:

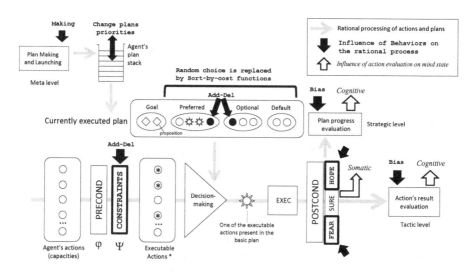

Fig. 3. Principle of the interaction of the behavioral heuristics with the rational process. In this example, the currently executed plan is a declarative plan, so as to illustrate the most complex situation (otherwise it is a terminal action).

1. The *tactic level* is related to the execution of the current action α_i by the rational scheduler S_R. Three kinds of influence operators can be applied:

1a) *Adding pre-constraints*: when selecting the possible candidate action for execution, S_R computes the physical pre-conditions of the actions (e.g. the agent cannot open a locked door). However, social norms/obligations or personal psychological constraints can be added to or deleted from the list of pre-conditions (like – supposing the action is physically executable – normative conditions: "do not poison your grandma to inherit", "do not fart/swear in public"; intrinsic conditions: "never take a plane", "do not eat meat", etc.);

1b) *Annotating post-conditions*: when an action α_i is executed, the rational scheduler S_R ensures that it's necessary (noted 'sure' in Fig. 3) post-conditions hold in Φ when Done(α_i). However, actions can also make potential conditions to hold that can be either indifferent to the agent or relevant to the agent with a positive/negative charge (noted hope/fear in Fig. 3). Defining the classes of indifferent/fear/hope post-conditions is in the scope of the behavioral agent (while sure post-conditions pertain to the rational agent).

1c) *Reacting to post-conditions*: the way the agent reacts to the post-conditions events (e.g. by Arousal [4]) can also be influenced by its current position Ψ in the psychological space.

2. The *strategic level* is related to the control and evaluation of plan execution. Again three kinds of influence operators can be applied:

2a) When a plan is executed, like the declarative plan illustrated in Fig. 3 (but also in plans compounded by procedural operators like 'alt' and 'par'), the decision making process can face equal alternatives (e.g. when several preferred actions are executable). This under determination in plan execution makes it possible for the behavioral agent to influence the decision making without altering the plan.

2b) Also it is possible to add or delete actions in the S_p, S_o and S_d sets of a plan without altering the plan post-conditions (e.g. adding an optional action "sing a happy tune" can express a happy mood; deleting a disliked optional action, etc).

2c) A similar approach to action evaluation (case 1c) can be done at the plan level.

3. The *meta level* is related to plan making and to plan launching, in a similar way to action and plan execution, the personality of an agent can influence the plan synthesis and the deliberative process.

3.2   Preferences and Desires as Influence Operators

In this section we give the general definition of two closely related notions: *preferences* and *desires*. Then we restrain the discussion to their implementation in the R&B framework in terms of influence operators related to case 1b.

Definition of preferences: Preferences can be static or dynamic that is, always or at a given moment, an agent prefers some entities over some others:
– the agent prefers action a_i to action a_j: "I prefer swimming to walking";
– the agent prefers plan p_i to plan p_j: "I prefer purchasing an object to stealing it";
– the agent prefers object x_i to object x_j: "I prefer cats over dogs".
Preferences on objects can depend on the context: "I prefer blue over red for cars and red over blue for clothes" . Objects can appear as arguments of actions, and thus can depend on task context: "I prefer to eat a piece of cake than to eat a worm"; "I prefer to fish with a worm than with a piece of cake" .
Preferences are explicit: the agent has a symbolic representation of its preferences (in Φ), thus it can say "I prefer x over y" if required.

Implementation: Preferences can be implemented as influence operators of case 1b. In this case, they do not alter the static structure of a plan (like adding/deleting actions). They just take advantage of the under determination present in the plans when several constituents are considered to be equal alternatives by the rational process. Hence, preferences are implemented in terms of *ranking* equivalent elements (actions or subplans) of the currently executed plan.

Definition of desires: Desires can be static or dynamic that is, always or at a given moment, an agent is compelled to change the world or to accommodate its beliefs about the world, so that the world satisfies its intimate desires. Desires are implicit: often, the agent is unaware of its desires and that it is currently behaving to satisfy its desires. Even if the agent is aware of its desires, often it cannot refrain from behaving to satisfy them, sometimes at a high cost. The agent can go up to perform drastic operations upon its rational plan execution, including severe alterations.

Implementation: Desires can be implemented as influence operators of case 1b. They are implemented in terms of their alterations upon the plan static structure and dynamic execution. In previous work, we have proposed a specific framework for the implementation of desires in terms of *cognitives biases* [2].

4   Conclusion and Further Work

A first software toolkit of the R&B framework has been implemented (using Wolfram's Mathematica symbolic computation system) and can be freely accessed on the webpage of the R&B project (`http://www.limsi.fr/~jps/research/rnb/rnb.htm`). It supports the whole A_R agent and the E_B module of the A_B agent, including a first case-study of appraisal. Development of the S_B module of A_B is still in progress with the examples of personality expression described above. Further work will be carried out at three levels: at the formal level, while the principles of the R&B framework have been illustrated here through a case study, a generic formalism of the expression of behaviors as influences is required; at the software level, a second version of the R&B toolkit must support a complete A_B agent; finally this new toolkit will be used to support experimentations with subjects to evaluate their actual perception of personality traits through influence operators.

References

1. Allen, J.F., Kautz, H.A., Pelavin, R.N., Tenenberg, J.D.: Reasoning About Plans. Representation And Reasoning. Morgan Kaufmann Publishers, Inc., San Francisco (1991)
2. Bouchet, F., Sansonnet, J.-P.: A framework for modeling the relationships between the rational and behavioral reactions of assisting conversational agents. In: Proc. of the 7th European Workshop on Multi-Agent Systems (EUMAS 2009), Agia Napa, Cyprus (December 2009)
3. Bouchet, F., Sansonnet, J.-P.: Subjectivity and cognitive biases modeling for a realistic and efficient assisting conversational agent. In: Proc. of 2009 IEEE/WIC/ACM International Conference on Web Intelligence and Intelligent Agent Technology, vol. 2, pp. 209–216. IEEE Computer Society, Milan (September 2009)
4. Broadhurst, P.L.: The interaction of task difficulty and motivation: The Yerkes-Dodson law revived. Acta Psychologica 16, 321–338 (1959)
5. Ellsworth, P.C., Scherer, K.R.: Appraisal processes in emotion. In: Davidson, R.J., Scherer, K.R., Goldsmith, H.H. (eds.) Handbook of affective sciences. Series in affective science, pp. 572–595. Oxford University Press, New York (2003)
6. Frijda, N.H.: The Laws of Emotion. Psychology Press (2006)
7. Maes, P.: Agents that reduce work and information overload. ACM Commun. 37(7), 30–40 (1994)
8. Mahiout, A., Giavitto, J.-L., Sansonnet, J.-P.: Distribution and scheduling data-parallel dataflow programs on massively parallel architectures. In: SMS-TPE 1994: Software for Multiprocessors and Supercomputers. Moscow (1994)
9. Ortony, A., Clore, G.L., Collins, A.: The Cognitive Structure of Emotions. Cambridge University Press edn., Cambridge (1988)
10. Russell, S., Norvig, P.: Artificial Intelligence: A Modern Approach, 3rd edn. Prentice-Hall, Englewood Cliffs (2009)

Reflecting User Faces in Avatars

Rossana Baptista Queiroz[1], Adriana Braun[1], Juliano Lucas Moreira[1],
Marcelo Cohen[1], Soraia Raupp Musse[1],
Marcelo Resende Thielo[2], and Ramin Samadani[3]

[1] Graduate Programme in Computer Science - PUCRS
Av. Ipiranga, 6681 - Building 32 - Porto Alegre/RS - Brazil
{rossana.queiroz,soraia.musse}@pucrs.br
[2] Hewlett Packard Brazil
Av. Ipiranga, 6681 - Building 95c - Porto Alegre/RS - Brazil
thielo@hp.com
[3] Hewlett Packard Laboratories
1501 Page Mill Rd., Palo Alto, CA, USA
ramin.samadani@hp.com

Abstract. This paper presents a model to generate personalized facial animations for avatars using Performance Driven Animation (PDA). This approach allows the users to reflect their face expressions in his/her avatar, considering as input a small set of feature points provided by Computer Vision (CV) tracking algorithms. The model is based on the MPEG-4 Facial Animation standard, and uses a hierarchy of the animation parameters to provide animation of face regions where it lacks CV data. To deform the face, we use two skin mesh deformation methods, which are computationally cheap and provide avatar animation in real time. We performed an evaluation with subjects in order to qualitatively evaluate our method. Results show that the proposed model can generate coherent and visually satisfactory animations.

Keywords: facial animation, avatar control, performance-driven animation.

1 Introduction

In a application of 3D virtual world (VW), such as Second Life[1] and Playstation Home[2], the user interacts by controlling an avatar, which is a virtual character that visually represents he or she. Avatars can evolve inside the VW, interacting with other characters and sharing the same space and objects of the world, even if participants are physically apart from each other. Such interaction is important for many kinds of applications, from games, training, education to even business meetings in a teleconference, among others.

One clear current disadvantage of VWs is the lack of technologies that both robustly and in real-time provide information about the emotions of the participants. Recent movies show excellent results in terms of reflection with high polygon models using

---

[1] http://secondlife.com/
[2] http://www.us.playstation.com/PS3

J. Allbeck et al. (Eds.): IVA 2010, LNAI 6356, pp. 420–426, 2010.

sophisticated motion capture devices and markers on the face. However, such results can not yet be achieved with the current techniques in real time and without markers.

This paper describes an approach for parametric control of the avatar face using Performance Driven Animation (PDA). The main goal of this work is to provide reflective avatars in real time, for further use in complex interactive applications, such VWs. Therefore the processing cost for generating the animations must be as low as possible. Hence the main contribution of this work is a low cost model to provide a better representation of the user's face through their avatar, as well as its qualitative evaluation with subjects.

2   Related Work

Since the pioneering work of Parke [1], several work aiming to provide realistic models of facial animation exploring parameterized expressiveness [2] and interactive personalized animation [3,4] have been proposed. In such works, animations are generated according to character's behavior. We can say that the personalization of the animation is given as the sequence of actions coherent with the character psychological characteristics. But they do not use data captured from real faces and most of the animation is predefined or generated through templates crafted manually by artists. It is an expensive process, where all characters with the same emotion or personality traits will, for example, to smile in the same way.

Concerning facial PDA techniques, the pioneer paper is proposed by Williams in 1990 [5], using markers, where basis functions are manually applied on virtual faces through an interactive interface. In this work, the mapping of the real face movements to the virtual face is made by direct association of the marker points and their corresponding locations in virtual faces. This approach is still being used in more recent work, such as [6], but speeding the animation techniques. Other approaches improve the generated animations using other type of information, such as motion captured data [7]. We can cite also approaches that use the MPEG-4 Facial Animation (MPEG-4 FA) standard of parameterization [8] to create rule systems [9] and animation tables [10] that, giving the captured data and the identification of high-level actions, provide animation parameters values. Method presented in [11] focuses on the translation of real captured data to a stylized representation language (e.g, 2D cartoon), which demands expensive manual work in the mapping stage. Our approach is based on feature points as [6], but also allows correlation of the tracked points with other feature points (not tracked), providing a more refined animation of the entire face and further improvements by combining low-level information with semantic data (such as high-level states).

3   Model

Figure 1 presents the overall architecture of the model. For the **Generation of 3D Face Deformations** stage, we need a **Parameterized 3D Face** data set, which is obtained offline, by using an authoring tool to associate the 3D face **Polygonal Mesh** and the **Description Parameters**. Such parameters refer to the set of **Feature Points** (FPs) and **Influence Regions** (IRs), which must be assigned in the 3D face and saved in a

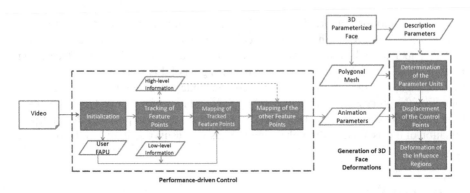

Fig. 1. Overall Architecture of the proposed model

text file. The FPs are the same of MPEG-4 FA. For the IRs, we suggest a set of 21 empirically determined regions, which must be manually assigned only once to a 3D face. To each FP, we assign one or more **Animation Parameters**, provided by the PDA control stage. Our scheme for animation parametrization is based on MPEG-4 FA using FAPs (Facial Animation Parameters), but it is not fully compliant, because we have extended the set of FAPs in order to supply the lack of movement in some directions that the standard does not directly consider. In order to use the animation parameters in different face topologies, MPEG-4 FA describes the Facial Animation Parameter Units(FAPU) to normalize the parameter values, which is a set of key distances among some FPs. The **Determination of the Parameter Units** is performed automatically, using the set of FPs specified by the MPEG-4 FA.

The **Displacement of Control Points** is given by the value of the animation parameter of the FAP set scaled by the avatar FAPU. After displacing the control points, each vertex within the FP influence region is deformed according to a deformation function, on **Deformation of Influence Regions** stage. In this stage, we apply Raised Cosine Functions [12] or Radial Basis Functions [13] on IRs to deform the face, according to the specification on description parameters file of the avatar face. This approach was chosen based on observations of deformation techniques which generate the best visual results in the face regions.

The input of the **Performance-driven Control** currently is captured images of a frontal face including markers. After a manual **Initialization** stage, in which the user clicks in the center of each face marker, they are tracked using the optical flow technique proposed by Lucas-Kanade-Tomasi (LKT) [14] in the **Tracking of Feature Points** stage. The Initialization stage computes the FAPU of the user, used further to determine the animation parameters values. The tracked points (markers) correspond to a subset of FPs (figures 2 and 3). For such points, the mapping of the displacements as a function of time is directly carried out, using the FAPU (**Mapping of Tracked Feature Points to 3D Face** stage). The FPs that are not tracked correspond to points whose mapping is obtained by a relation established among them and the FAPs of the tracked points (**Mapping of the other Feature Points** stage).

With the user's FAPU computed in the Initialization stage and a reference point for the calculation of the displacements of all of the other points (we chose the tip of the

(a)   (b)

Fig. 2. a) Example of our PDA technique applied to three different avatars b)Example of the use of "high-level" information to improve the animation ("kissing" mouth state), showing the difference of taking into account it on mapping stage.

nose), we obtain a set of reference distances, corresponding to the neutral face. At each timestep, we obtain the set of points tracked by the LKT algorithm, which distances with respect to the reference point are calculated, giving the set of displacements per frame. In order to determine the values of the set of animation parameters (FAPs) in a given frame, the difference between reference distances and current frame's displacements is calculated, normalized by the user FAPU. In present stage, the model also does not take into account the rotations of the head.

For the points that are not tracked, the basic idea is to stablish a hierarchy of FPs and FAPs, as if they were some kind of "pseudo-muscles". The hierarchy is described by a set of rules that associate pairs of FAPs (one tracked and one non-tracked) through an empirically defined coefficient of relationship. Therefore we can enumerate three main functions for this mapping stage: *i)* to estimate displacement values of FPs that are not tracked, such as the FPs of the cheek and the internal side of the lips; *ii)* to estimate values of some FAPs with movement in the z axis, not considered by the mapping that only deal with two-dimensional information of the images; and *iii)* to define rules from so-called "high-level" information obtained during the tracking. For this last point, we carried out some preliminary studies, considering some mouth states that should be manually identified in the prototype of the model (such as "kissing" and "smiling"). Figure 2 shows the visual impact of such kind of information.

4   The "Reflection Evaluation"

In order to evaluate if the performance of a real person when animating an avatar can be identified by the users using our PDA approach, we performed a qualitative analysis, which we called *Reflection evaluation*. The evaluation was elaborated aiming to investigate if users can associate expressions of real people with the generated avatar animations. We modeled several avatars which are animated using real user expressions and produced a web survey where investigate some topics mentioned hereafter. To create the questions, we recorded the performance of five volunteers (we will call them *actors*) following a scripted face actions sequence. The avatars corresponding to actors' faces were obtained by the software Facegen[3] which reconstructs 3D faces from photos. We also used three other avatars without actor correspondence: two based on real faces and one with a cartoon shape[4].

---

[3] http://www.facegen.com/modeller.htm
[4] http://jasonpierce.animadillo.com/resource/ludwig/ludwig.html

Fig. 3. Example of two actors performing the requested six facial expressions

The script requires the actor to perform the six basic emotions defined by Ekman [15] (joy, sadness, surprise, disgust, fear and anger) in a pre-defined sequence. Figure 3 shows the performance of two actors and their corresponding avatar performance. Images and videos of recorded animation were used to compose the survey. The main questions we want to answer in this paper are: **Q1)** Can users correctly associate facial expressions of real and virtual people, even if we capture the animation from a real person and apply it to avatars with different face shapes? **Q2)** Can users easily associate reflection in pictures or by viewing videos (static vs. dynamic)? **Q3)** If we consider one specific emotion, e.g. joy, performed by a specific actor, can users correctly identify this performance in the avatars?; and **Q4)** As a consequence of last 3 questions, can we say that reflection may be perceived by the users?

The survey has three types of question sets, elaborated to explore the questions above: *i)* questions where the user must identify the expression of a given actor in a set of avatar performance images (with user corresponding or different shape). In such questions, one option is correct, while the others represent the same Ekman expressions performed by other actors; *ii)* questions where the user must try to correctly associate actor pictures performing the same expression with pictures from a single avatar. The avatar face is not correspondent to any of the actors; and *iii)* questions similar to *i)*, but using videos (animations) instead of static pictures. Fifty-one users answered the survey which contains 29 questions.

Regarding questions Q1 and Q2, Figure 4 shows the mean score of the corrected answers. Concerning Q1, the questions relating the actor with his/her correspondent avatar present the mean score of $\bar{x}_1 = 61\%$ with standard deviation of 21%. The remaining questions use another avatar and the mean score was 59% with standard deviation of $\bar{x}_2 = 21\%$. In order to evaluate if the averages have a significant difference, we performed the two-tailed t-test which generates a p-value= 0.63, which indicates no significantive difference between $\bar{x}_1$ and $\bar{x}_2$. Consequently, the answer for Q1 is yes, if we consider our universe of actors and avatars. Concerning Q2, the questions which include pictures had the mean score $\bar{x}_3 = 61\%$ and standard deviation of 24%. The questions which use videos have the mean score $\bar{x}_4 = 58\%$ and standard deviation of 17%. The two-tailed t-test considering different variances generates a p-value= 0.46, that indicates no significative difference between $\bar{x}_3$ and $\bar{x}_4$.

In order to answer question Q3, we select the animation of the performances corresponding to the expression "joy", because we consider it the most spontaneously represented expression in the script (all people know how to represent happiness), as our volunteers are not professional actors. We create questions including videos of the

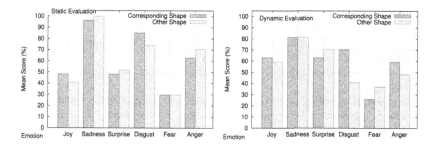

Fig. 4. Mean score of the corrected answers in survey questions we use to answer Q1 and Q2

five actors expressing joy that should be associated to only one of four avatar animations. The percentages of correct associations (mean score) for the five actors were 74%, 52%, 76%, 50% and 76%. Analyzing these results, we can see that around 75% of people who answer the survey could correctly associate the "joy" performance for three actors to their respective avatar animation. In two cases, however, the scores are lower. One reason is because the smiling performance of such two actors are very similar if we compare the recorded videos. Even in those cases, the scores were around 50%.

Finally, concerning Q4, the overall score of percentages of correct associations was 70%. Even in the questions with low scores, the mode of the answers was always the correct association. Considering these facts and the answers to Q1, Q2 and Q3, we can say that, in general, people could perceive the reflection of the performances in recorded videos using the model presented in this paper.

5   Final Considerations

In this work, we present a model of parametric control of the avatar face using PDA. The PDA approach allows the personalization of the animation through the reflection of user movements: for example, when the user smiles, the avatar can smile the way that the user smiles. The main contribution of this work is to provide a low cost approach for generating personalized and reflective avatars in real time, as well its qualitative evaluation with subjects. The evaluation shows that the proposed model can generate animations that reflects the user movement. As future work, we can cite improvements on detection stage (including head movements) and generation of expression wrinkles.

Acknowledgments

This work was developed in cooperation with Hewlett-Packard Brasil Ltda. using incentives of Brazilian Informatics Law (Law n° 8.2.48 of 1991). The authors acknowledge the support granted by CNPq and FAPESP to the INCT-SEC (National Institute of Science and Technology Embedded Critical Systems Brazil), processes 573963/2008-8 and 08/57870-9.

References

1. Parke, F.I.: Computer generated animation of faces. In: ACM 1972: Proceedings of the ACM annual conference, pp. 451–457. ACM, New York (1972)
2. Perlin, K.: Layered compositing of facial expression. In: ACM SIGGRAPH - Technical Sketch (1997)
3. Vilhjálmsson, H., Cantelmo, N., Cassell, J., Chafai, N.E., Kipp, M., Kopp, S., Mancini, M., Marsella, S., Marshall, A.N., Pelachaud, C., Ruttkay, Z., Thórisson, K.R., van Welbergen, H., van der Werf, R.J.: The behavior markup language: Recent developments and challenges. In: Pelachaud, C., Martin, J.-C., André, E., Chollet, G., Karpouzis, K., Pelé, D. (eds.) IVA 2007. LNCS (LNAI), vol. 4722, pp. 99–111. Springer, Heidelberg (2007)
4. Zammitto, V., DiPaola, S., Arya, A.: A methodology for incorporating personality modeling in believable game characters. In: 4th Intl. Conf. on Games Research and Development (CyberGames), p. 2 (2008)
5. Williams, L.: Performance-driven facial animation. In: SIGGRAPH 1990: Proceedings of the 17th annual conference on Computer graphics and interactive techniques, pp. 235–242. ACM, New York (1990)
6. Dutreve, L., Meyer, A., Bouakaz, S.: Feature points based facial animation retargeting. In: VRST 2008: Proceedings of the, ACM symposium on Virtual reality software and technology, pp. 197–200. ACM, New York (2008)
7. Chai, J.: x., Xiao, J., Hodgins, J.: Vision-based control of 3d facial animation. In: SCA 2003 Proceedings of the 2003 ACM SIGGRAPH/Eurographics symposium on Computer animation, Aire-la-Ville, Switzerland, Switzerland, Eurographics Association, pp. 193–206 (2003)
8. Pandzic, I.S., Forchheimer, R. (eds.): MPEG-4 Facial Animation: The Standard, Implementation and Applications. John Wiley & Sons, Inc., New York (2003)
9. Khanam, A., Mufti, M.: Intelligent expression blending for performance driven facial animation. IEEE Transactions on onsumer Electronics 53(2), 578–584 (2007)
10. Tang, H., Huang, T.: Mpeg4 performance-driven avatar via robust facial motion tracking, pp. 249–252 (2008)
11. Quax, P., Di Fiore, F., Lamotte, W., Van Reeth, F.: Efficient distribution of emotion-related data through a networked virtual environment architecture. Computer Animation and Virtual Worlds 9999(9999), n/a+ (2009)
12. Balci, K.: Xface: Mpeg-4 based open source toolkit for 3d facial animation. In: AVI 2004: Proceedings of the working conference on Advanced visual interfaces, pp. 399–402. ACM Press, New York (2004)
13. Yong Noh, J., Fidaleo, D., Neumann, U.: Animated deformations with radial basis functions. In: VRST 2000: Proceedings of the ACM symposium on Virtual reality software and technology, pp. 166–174. ACM, New York (2000)
14. Lucas, B.D., Kanade, T.: An iterative image registration technique with an application to stereo vision. In: IJCAI 1981: Proceedings of the 7th international joint conference on Artificial intelligence, pp. 674–679. Morgan Kaufmann Publishers Inc., San Francisco (1981)
15. Ekman, P., Friesen, W.: Facial Action Code System. Consulting Psychologists Press, Inc., Palo Alto (1978)

How a Virtual Agent Should Smile?
Morphological and Dynamic Characteristics of Virtual Agent's Smiles

Magalie Ochs, Radosław Niewiadomski, and Catherine Pelachaud

CNRS-LTCI, Télécom ParisTech
{ochs,niewiado,pelachaud}@telecom-paristech.fr

Abstract. A smile may communicate different meanings depending on subtle characteristics of the facial expression. In this article, we have studied the morphological and dynamic characteristics of amused, polite, and embarrassed smiles displayed by a virtual agent. A web application has been developed to collect virtual agent's smile descriptions corpus directly constructed by users. Based on the corpora and using a decision tree classification technique, we propose an algorithm to determine the characteristics of each type of the smile that a virtual agent may express. The proposed algorithm enables one to generate a variety of facial expressions corresponding to the polite, embarrassed, and amused smiles.

Keywords: Smile, Embodied Conversational Agent (ECA), Facial Expression, Decision Tree.

1 Introduction

Smiling is one of the simplest and most easily recognized facial expressions [1]. Only one muscle, the zygomatic major, has to be activated to create a smile. But a smile may have several meanings – such as amusement, politeness, or embarrassment – depending on subtle characteristics of the smile itself and of other elements of the face that come with the smile. These different types of smile are often distinguished by humans during an interaction. Recently [2,3] has shown that people also distinguish different types of smile when they are expressed by a virtual agent. Moreover, a smiling virtual agent enhances the human-machine interaction, for instance the perception of the task, of the agent, and the motivation and enthusiasm of the user [4,5]. However, an inappropriate smile (an inappropriate type of smile or a smile expressed in an inappropriate situation) may have negative effects on the interaction [5].

In this paper, we present a research work that aimed at identifying the morphological and dynamic characteristics of different types of smile. More precisely, we have investigated how a virtual agent may display different types of smile in context-free situations. For this purpose, we have created a web application to

J. Allbeck et al. (Eds.): IVA 2010, LNAI 6356, pp. 427–440, 2010.

collect a virtual agent's smile descriptions corpus directly constructed by users. Based on the corpus, we have used a machine learning algorithm to determine the characteristics of each type of the smile that a virtual agent may express. As a result, we obtain the algorithm that may be easily implemented in any virtual agent. It enables one to generate a variety of facial expressions corresponding to the polite, embarrassed and amused smiles.

The paper structure is as follow. After giving an overview of existing work on humans' smiles (Section 2.1) and on virtual agents' smiles (Section 2.2), we introduce the web application developed to collect the smiles corpus (Section 3). Section 4 describes the corpus. In Section 5, we present the algorithm to compute the smile's characteristics based on the smiles corpus. We conclude in Section 6.

2   Related Work

2.1   Theoretical Background: Smiles' Types and Characteristics

When someone smiles, it does not necessarily mean that he feels happy. Indeed, different types of smile with different meanings can be distinguished. The most common one is the *amused smile*, also called felt, Duchenne, enjoyment, or genuine smile. The amused smile is often opposed to the *polite smile*, also called non-Duchenne, false, social, masking, or controlled smile [6]. Perceptual studies [6] have shown that people unconsciously and consciously distinguish between a smile of amusement and a polite smile. Someone may smile in a negative situation. For instance, a specific smile appears in the facial expression of embarrassment [7], or anxiety [8].

In this paper, as a first step, we focus on the three following smiles: *amused*, *polite* and *embarrassed* smiles. These smiles have been selected because they have been explored in the Human and Social Sciences literature both from the *encoder* point of view (from the point of view of the person who smiles) [7,1] and from the *decoder* point of view (from the point of view of the one who perceived the smile) [9].

The different smiles have different morphological and dynamic characteristics that enable one to distinguish them. *Morphological characteristics* are, for instance, the mouth opening or cheek raising. *Dynamic characteristics* correspond to the temporal unfolding of the smile such as the velocity. In the literature on smile [9,7,1], the following characteristics are generally considered to distinguish the amused, polite and embarrassed smiles[1]:

- *morphological characteristics*: AU6 (cheek raising), AU24 (lip press), AU12 (zygomatic major), symmetry of the lip corners, mouth opening, and amplitude of the smile;

---

[1] Note that other elements of the face, such as the gaze and the eyebrows, influence how a smile is perceived. However, in the presented work, we focus on the influence of the smile and we do not consider the other elements of the face.

– *dynamic characteristics*: duration of the smile and velocity of the onset and offset of the smile.

Concerning the *cheek raising*, Ekman [10] claims the orbicularis oculi (which refers to the Action Unit (AU) 6 in the Facial Action Coding System [11]) is activated in an amused smile. Without it, the expression of happiness seems to be insincere [12]. However, recently the role of AU6 in the smile of amusement was challenged by Krumhuber and Manstead [13]. *Lip press* (AU24) is often related to the smile of embarrassment [7]. According to Ekman [10], *asymmetry* is an indicator of voluntary and non-spontaneous expression, such as the polite smile. The different types of smile may have different *durations*. The felt expressions, such as the amused smile, last from half a second to four seconds, even if the corresponding emotional state is longer [10,14]. The duration of a polite or embarrassed smile is shorter than 0.5 second or longer than 4 seconds [1,10,14]. Not only the overall duration, but also the course of the expression is different depending on the type of the smiles. The dynamic of facial expressions is commonly defined by three time intervals. The *onset* corresponds to the interval of time in which the expression reaches its maximal intensity starting from the neutral face. Then, the apex is the time during which the expression maintains its maximal intensity. Finally, the *offset* is the interval of time in which the expression starting from the maximal intensity, returns to the neutral expression [1]. In the deliberate expressions the onset is often abrupt or excessively short, the apex is held too long, and the offset can be either more irregular or abrupt and short [1].

However, no consensus exists on the morphological and dynamic characteristics of the amused, polite and embarrassed smile. In general, AU6 is more present in amused smile than in polite or embarrassed smile. For instance, according to Ekman the amused smile is characterized by a cheek raising (AU6), the activation of the zygomatic major (AU12) and a symmetry of the zygomatic major. The dynamic characteristics of the amused smile are the smoothness and regularity of the onset, apex, offset and of the overall zygomatic actions, and a duration of the smile between 0.5 and 4 seconds [1]. According to the same author, in the expression of a polite smile, the cheek raising (AU6) is absent, the amplitude of the zygomatic major (AU12) is small, the smile is slightly asymmetric, the apex is too long, the onset too short, the offset too abrupt, and the lips may be pressed [1]. The embarrassed smile is characterized by the lips pressed, the closed mouth, a small amplitude, the absence of AU6, asymmetry, and a duration shorter than 0.5 seconds or longer than 4 seconds [7,1].

2.2 Smiling Virtual Agents

In order to increase the variability of virtual agent's facial expressions, several researchers have considered different virtual agent's smiles. For instance, in [15], two different types of smile: an amused and polite are used by a virtual agent.

The amused smile is used to reflect an emotional state of happiness whereas a polite smile (called fake smile in [15]) is used in a case of a sad virtual agent. The amused smile is represented by lip corners raised, lower eyelids raised, and an open mouth. The polite smile is represented by an asymmetric raising of the lip corners and an expression of sadness in the upper part of the face.

In [2], virtual agents mask a felt negative emotion of disgust, anger, fear or sadness by a smile. Two types of facial expression were created according to the Ekman's description [16]. The first expression corresponds to a felt emotion of happiness. The second one corresponds to the other expression (e.g. disgust) masked by unfelt happiness. In particular, the expression of unfelt happiness lacks the AU6 activity and is asymmetric (see Section 2.1). A perceptive test has enabled the authors to measure the impact of such fake expressions on the user's subjective impression of the agent. The participants were able to perceive the difference, but they were unable to explain their judgment. The agent expressing an amused smile was perceived as being more reliable, trustable, convincing, credible, and more certain about what it said compared to the agent expressing a negative emotion masked by a smile.

In [4], the authors have explored the impact of varying dynamic characteristics of smile in virtual faces on the users' job interview impressions and decisions. The results show that smiles with long onset and offset durations were associated with "authentic smiles" (amused smile). Fake smiles were characterized by short onset and offset durations. The total duration of the smiles was equal (4 seconds). In the interaction, the type of smiles used by the virtual agents has an impact on the user's perception: the job is perceived as more positive and suitable in case of authentic smiles. Globally, whatever is the smile (fake or authentic), a smile increases the positive perception of the agent.

Niewiadomski and Pelachaud [3] proposed an algorithm to generate complex facial expressions, such as masked or fake expressions. An expression is a composition of eight facial areas, each of which can display signs of emotion. For complex facial expressions, different emotions can be expressed on different areas of the face. In particular, it is possible to generate different expressions of joy: a felt and a fake one. The *felt* expression of joy uses the reliable features (AU6), while the second one is asymmetric.

Several other virtual agents *smile* during an interaction, for instance to express a positive emotion [17], or to create a global friendly atmosphere [5]. Generally, such virtual agents use only one type of smiles: the *amused smile*. In this work, we aim at exploring the different types of smiles a virtual agent may perform. Whereas previous research (presented above) has analyzed the impact of different smiles on the users' perception of the agent or of the interaction, in the work presented in this article, we focus on the different smiles that a user may perceive. More particularly, we have conducted a study to analyze the morphological and dynamic characteristics of the amused, polite and embarrassed smiles of a virtual agent. In the next section, we present the platform we have developed to study such smiles.

3 E-Smiles-Creator: Web Application for Smiles Data Collection

In order to identify the morphological and dynamic characteristics of the amused, embarrassed and polite smile of a virtual agent, we have created a web application, called *E-smiles-creator*, that enables a user to easily create different smiles on a virtual agent's face. The interface of the *E-smiles-creator* is composed of 4 parts (Figure 1):

1. on the upper part, a description of the task: the smile that the user has to create, for instance an amused smile;
2. on the left part, a video showing, in loop, the virtual agent animation;
3. on the right part, a panel with different smile parameters (such as the duration) that the user may change to create the smile (the video on the left changes accordingly);
4. and on the bottom part, a Likert scale that enables the user to indicate his satisfaction related to the smile he has created.

Using *E-smiles-creator*, the user can generate any smile by choosing the combination of seven parameters. Any time he changes the value of one of the parameters, a corresponding video is automatically played. Based on the research on human smile (see Section 2.1), we consider the following morphological and dynamic characteristics of a smile: the activation of AU6 (cheek raising), the

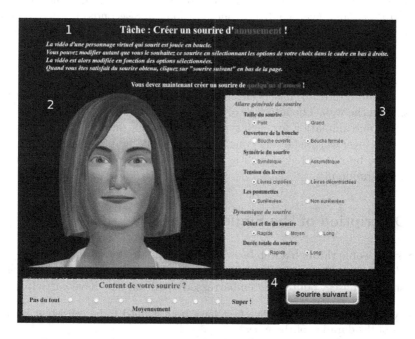

Fig. 1. Screenshot of the *E-smiles-creator*

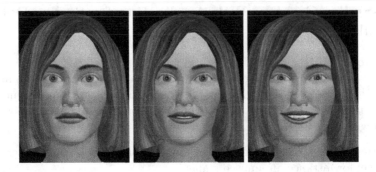

Fig. 2. Example of a sequence of the first images of a video of the smiling virtual agent

activation of AU24 (lip press), the activation of AU12 (zygomatic major), the symmetry of the lip corners, the mouth opening, the amplitude of the smile, the duration of the smile and the velocity of the onset and the offset of the smile. Accordingly, on the right part of the *E-smiles-creator* interface (Figure 1, panel 3), the user may select these parameters of the smile. The video of the smiling agent will correspond to a smile with the selected parameters. We have considered two or three discrete values for each of these parameters: small or large smile (for the amplitude); open or close mouth; symmetric or asymmetric smile; tensed or relaxed lips (for the AU24); cheekbone raised or not raised (for the AU6); short (1.6 seconds) or long (3 seconds) total duration of the smile, and short (0.1 seconds), average (0.4 seconds) or long (0.8 seconds) begin and end of the smile (for the onset and offset)[2,3]. Considering all the possible combinations of these discrete values, we have created 192 different videos of smiling agent. An example of a sequence of images of a video of the virtual agent smiling is illustrated Figure 2.

The *E-smiles-creator* has been created using Flash technology to enable a diffusion on the web. The interface of the *E-smiles-creator* is in French. The user can create one animation for each type of smile. Each time, the user also has to express his level of satisfaction concerning the smile he has created. The order of smiles to be illustrated as well as the initial values of the seven parameters are chosen randomly.

4   Description of the Smiles Corpus

By asking people through a web browser to participate to a study on smiles using *E-smiles-creator*, we have collected 1044 smile descriptions: 348 descriptions for each smile (amused, polite, and embarrassed). 348 subjects have participated to

---

[2] The values of the onset and the offset have been defined to be consistent with the values of the duration of thesmile.

[3] As a first step, discrete variables have been considered. To obtain a more fine-grained description of smiles, continuous variables could be considered.

Table 1. The characteristics of the amused smiles in the most frequently selected videos of amused smiles

id	# amused	size	mouth	symmetry	lips tension	AU6	onset/offset	duration
1	49	large	open	yes	no	yes	0.1s	3s
2	43	large	open	yes	no	yes	0.8s	3s
3	30	large	open	yes	no	yes	0.4s	3s
4	22	large	open	no	no	yes	0.8s	3s
5	21	large	open	no	no	yes	0.1s	3s
6	20	large	open	no	no	yes	0.4s	3s
7	9	large	open	yes	no	yes	0.1s	1.6s
8	8	large	open	yes	no	no	0.8s	3s

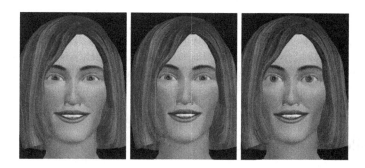

Fig. 3. Images of amused smiles at their apex with the id 1, 4, and 8 in the Table 1

this study (195 females and 153 males). Each participant has created one smile of amusement, politeness and embarrassment. The average participants' age is 30 years. The subjects are mainly French. In average, the subjects are satisfied by the created smiles (5.28 on a Likert scale of 7 points)[4]. Below, we describe the most frequent amused, polite and embarrassed smiles that appear in the smiles corpus.

Table 1 presents the characteristics of the most frequently selected parameter values of amused smiles. In the table, the second column (for instance # *amused*) represents the number of amused smiles (out of 348 amused smiles) defined with the parameter values of the line of the table. For instance, 49 out of 348 amused smiles have been defined with a large size, an open mouth, a symmetry, no lips tension, an activated AU6, an onset and an offset of 0.1 second and a total duration of 3 seconds (first line of the Table 1). Globally, the amused smiles are mainly characterized by a large amplitude, an open mouth, and relaxed lips. Most of them also contain the activation of the AU6, and a long global duration. Table 2 illustrates the characteristics of the most frequently selected parameter values of embarrassed smiles. Compared to the amused smiles, the embarrassed smiles often have small amplitude, a closed mouth, and tensed lips. They are also

---

[4] Globally, the user's satisfaction is the same for the three smiles (between 5.2 and 5.5)

Table 2. The characteristics of the embarrassed smiles in the most frequently selected videos of embarrassed smiles

id	# embarrassed	size	mouth	symmetry	lips tension	AU6	onset/offset	duration
1	19	small	close	no	yes	no	0.1s	1.6s
2	18	small	close	no	yes	no	0.4s	3s
3	16	small	close	yes	yes	no	0.4s	3s
4	13	small	close	no	yes	no	0.8s	1.6s
5	11	small	close	yes	yes	no	0.1s	1.6s
6	11	small	close	no	yes	no	0.8s	3s
7	9	small	close	no	yes	yes	0.4s	3s
8	8	small	close	no	yes	no	0.4s	1.6s

characterized by the absence of AU6. Table 3 describes the characteristics of the most frequently selected parameter values of polite smiles. The polite smiles are mainly characterized by a small amplitude, a closed mouth, a symmetry, relaxed lips, and an absence of AU6. We also analyzed the frequency of the occurrence of each feature separately for each type of smiles. The contingency table is presented Table 4.

5   Smiles Decision Tree Learning

In this section we propose an algorithm to generate different types of smile in virtual agent. It allows an agent to display various polite, amused or embarrassed smiles. Our approach is based on machine learning methodology and on the data presented in the previous section.

5.1   The Decision Tree

In order to analyze the smiles corpus, we have used a *decision tree learning* algorithm to identify the different morphological and dynamic characteristics of the amused, polite and embarrassed smiles of the corpus. The input variables

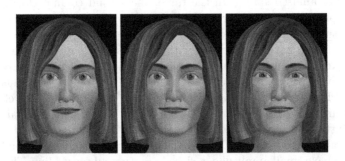

Fig. 4. Images of embarrassed smiles at their apex with the id 1, 3, and 7 in the Table 2

Table 3. The characteristics of the polite smiles in the most frequently selected videos of polite smiles

id	# polite	size	mouth	symmetry	lips tension	AU6	onset/offset	duration
1	16	small	close	yes	no	no	0.4s	3s
2	12	small	close	yes	no	no	0.8s	3s
3	11	small	close	yes	no	no	0.4s	1.6s
4	11	large	close	yes	no	no	0.4s	3s
5	10	small	close	yes	no	no	0.8s	1.6s
6	10	small	close	yes	yes	no	0.4s	1.6s
7	9	small	close	yes	no	no	0.1s	3s
8	8	small	close	yes	no	no	0.1s	1.6s

(predictive variables) are the morphological and dynamic characteristics and the target variables are the smile types (amused, embarrassed, or polite). Consequently, the nodes of the decision tree correspond to the smile characteristics and the leaves are the smile types. We have chosen the decision tree learning because this technique has the advantage to be well-adapted to qualitative data and to product results that are interpretable and that be easily implemented in a virtual agent.

To create the decision tree, we took into account the level of satisfaction indicated by the user for each created smile (a level that varied between 1 and 7). More precisely, in order to give a higher weight to the smiles with a high level of satisfaction, we have done *oversampling*: each created smile has been duplicated n times, where n is the level of satisfaction associated to this smile. So, a smile with a level of satisfaction of 7 is duplicated 7 times whereas a smile with a level of satisfaction of 1 is not duplicated. The resulting data set is composed of 5517 descriptions of smiles: 2057 amused smiles, 1675 polite smiles, and 1785 embarrassed smiles.

To construct the decision tree, we have used the free data mining software TANAGRA [18] that proposes several data mining methods for data analysis. We have used the method CART (Classification And Regression Tree) [19], a popular and powerful method to induce decision tree. The resulting decision tree is represented in Figure 6. We have set a minimum size of node to split of 75 to avoid a large number of leaves and then an uninterpretable tree. The resulting decision tree is composed of 39 nodes and 20 leaves. All the input variables (the smile characteristics) are used to classify the smiles.

To compute the error rate, a 10-folds cross-validation (with 5 trials) has been performed. The global error rate is 27.75%, with a 95% confidence interval of 1.2%: the global error rate is then in the interval [26.55%, 28.95%]. An analysis of the error rate for each smile type shows that the amused smiles are better classified (18 % of error) than the polite (34% of error) and the embarrassed smiles (31% of error). Indeed, the confusion matrix reveals that the polite and embarrassed smiles are often confused each other compared to the amused smiles.

In the next section, we discuss in more details how the resulting decision tree can be used to identify the smiles that a virtual agent could express.

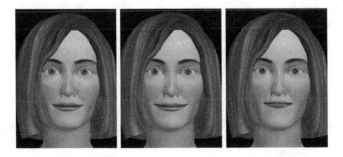

Fig. 5. Images of polite smiles at their apex with the id 1, 4, and 6 in the Table 3

Table 4. Contingency table of the smile's characteristics and the smile types

variable	value	amused	embarrassed	polite
size	small	16,4%	73,1%	67,7%
	big	83,6%	26,9%	32,3%
mouth	close	14,4%	81.8%	76%
	open	85,6%	18,2%	24%
symmetry	sym.	59,9%	40,5%	67,1%
	assym.	40,4%	59,1%	32,9%
lips tension	no tension	92.2%	25.4%	69.4%
	tension	7.8%	74.6%	30.6%
AU6	no	21.6%	59%	58.9%
	yes	78.4%	41%	41.1%
onset/offset	short	33.4%	28.9%	30.3%
	average	30.3%	39.6%	37.1%
	long	36.3%	31,5%	32.6%
duration	short	15.6%	43.6%	42.9%
	long	84.4%	56.4%	57.1%

5.2   Smile Selection Based on Decision Tree

Our smiles decision tree reveals 20 different smile patterns, corresponding to the 20 leaves of the tree. Ten leaves are labeled as polite smiles, 7 as amused smiles, and 3 as embarrassed smiles. Because some branches of the tree do not contain a value for each morphological and dynamic characteristics, more than 20 smiles may be created from our decision tree. For instance, for the first polite smile pattern that appears in the tree (indicated by a black arrow on Figure 6), the size of the smile, its duration, and the velocity of the onset and offset are not specified. Consequently, this polite smile pattern can be expressed by the virtual agent in 12 different manners.

In order to identify the smile that the virtual agent should express, we propose an algorithm based on the resulting decision tree. We suppose that as input of the algorithm we have the type of smile the virtual agent should express (amused,

Decision tree

- MOUTH_OPEN in [open]
  - ○ SMILE_SIZE in [small]
    - ■ LIPS_TENSION in [no_tension]
      - ■ SMILE_DURATION in [short] then SMILE_TYPE = **polite** (60,40 % of 101 examples)
      - ■ SMILE_DURATION in [long]
        - ■ SMILE_SYM in [sym]
          - ■ SMILE_AU6 in [no_AU6] then SMILE_TYPE = **polite** (66,00 % of 50 examples)
          - ■ SMILE_AU6 in [AU6] then SMILE_TYPE = **amused** (64,58 % of 48 examples)
        - ■ SMILE_SYM in [asym] then SMILE_TYPE = **amused** (60,53 % of 76 examples)
    - ■ LIPS_TENSION in [tension]
      - ■ SMILE_SYM in [sym] then SMILE_TYPE = **polite** (61,11 % of 54 examples)
      - ■ SMILE_SYM in [asym] then SMILE_TYPE = **embarrassed** (69,09 % of 55 examples)
  - ○ SMILE_SIZE in [large]
    - ■ LIPS_TENSION in [no_tension]
      - ■ SMILE_DURATION in [short]
        - ■ SMILE_AU6 in [no_AU6] then SMILE_TYPE = **polite** (52,63 % of 57 examples)
        - ■ SMILE_AU6 in [AU6] then SMILE_TYPE = **amused** (73,08 % of 130 examples)
      - ■ SMILE_DURATION in [long] then SMILE_TYPE = **amused** (89,38 % of 951 examples)
    - ■ LIPS_TENSION in [tension]
      - ■ SMILE_ONOFFSET in [short,medium] then SMILE_TYPE = **amused** (41,67 % of 34 examples)
      - ■ SMILE_ONOFFSET in [long] then SMILE_TYPE = **embarrassed** (61,29 % of 31 examples)
- MOUTH_OPEN in [close]
  - ○ LIPS_TENSION in [no_tension]
    - ■ SMILE_SYM in [sym]
      - ■ SMILE_AU6 in [no_AU6] then SMILE_TYPE = **polite** (84,05 % of 370 examples)
      - ■ SMILE_AU6 in [AU6]
        - ■ SMILE_SIZE in [small] then SMILE_TYPE = **polite** (66,12 % of 121 examples)
        - ■ SMILE_SIZE in [large]
          - ■ SMILE_ONOFFSET in [short,medium] then SMILE_TYPE = **amused** (45,00 % of 36 examples)
          - ■ SMILE_ONOFFSET in [long] then SMILE_TYPE = **polite** (67,27 % of 55 examples)
    - ■ SMILE_SYM in [asym]
      - ■ SMILE_DURATION in [short] then SMILE_TYPE = **polite** (61,84 % of 152 examples)
      - ■ SMILE_DURATION in [long]
        - ■ SMILE_SIZE in [small] then SMILE_TYPE = **polite** (53,72 % of 121 examples)
        - ■ SMILE_SIZE in [large]
          - ■ SMILE_AU6 in [no_AU6] then SMILE_TYPE = **amused** (57,41 % of 54 examples)
          - ■ SMILE_AU6 in [AU6] then SMILE_TYPE = **polite** (41,46 % of 41 examples)
  - ○ LIPS_TENSION in [tension] then SMILE_TYPE = **embarrassed** (70,60 % of 1085 examples)

Fig. 6. Smiles Decision Tree

polite, or embarrassed) and a value, between 0 and 1, called *importance of smile recognition*. This value expresses both the importance that the smile is well-recognized by the user, and the variability of smiles that the virtual agent could express. The closer the value is to 1 (resp. 0), the more it is important (resp. it is not important) that the smile is recognized by the user as embarrassed, amused, or polite. But, at the same time, the variability is lower. Indeed, a high value implies few possible smiles to express whereas an average value enables the virtual agent to express several different smiles. For instance, an input of the algorithm (*polite*; 0, 9) means that the virtual agent has to express a polite smile and it is important that this smile is perceived as polite by the user. However, an input (*polite*; 0, 6) gives more polite smile variability.

The algorithm to determine the virtual agent's smile is composed of two steps: a first step aims at selecting the smile pattern in the tree, and the second step determines the smile from the pattern.

In the first step of the algorithm, the *importance of smile recognition* is used to select the appropriate smile in the decision tree. More precisely, for each leaf of the tree, we compute the 95% confidence interval from the classification rate and the number of examples in the leaf (Figure 6) using the formula: $r = 1.96\sqrt{\frac{*(1-p)}{N}}$ such as N is the number of examples and p the classification rate. The 95% confidence interval is then $[p - r, p + r]$. For instance, for the first polite smile appearing in the tree (indicated by a black arrow on Figure 6), 60.41% of 101 examples of smile with these characteristics are well-classified (Figure 6). The 95% confidence interval for this leaf is $[60.41 - 9.5, 60.41 + 9.5]$. The confidence interval enables us to consider the number of examples in the classification rate. Finally, the selected smile will be the one with the specified type and with the smallest confidence interval containing, or the closest to, the importance of smile recognition value. For instance, the selected smile for a polite smile with an importance of 0.9 will be the fifth polite smile that appears in the tree (with the classification rate 84.05% on 370 examples, so, the 95% confidence interval $[80.32; 87.79]$): a symmetric smile with a closed mouth, relaxed lips, and no AU6.

In the second step of the algorithm, in order to determine the smile's characteristics not defined in the tree, we consider the contingency table representing the frequency of smile types for each characteristic (Table 4). For instance, if the selected smile is the first polite smile that appears in the tree (indicated by a black arrow on Figure 6), the following characteristics are not specified in the tree: the size of the smile, its duration, and the velocity of the onset and offset. Because in the contingency table, it appears that a majority of polite smiles have a small size, long duration, and an average velocity of the onset and offset, we consider a smile with such characteristics and the characteristics described in the branch of the tree leading to the selected smile.

Finally, the proposed algorithm enables one to determine the morphological and dynamic characteristics of the smile that a virtual agent should express given the type of smile and the importance that the user recognizes the expressed smile. The advantage of such a method is to consider, not only one amused, embarrassed, or polite smile but several smile types. That enables one to increase the variability of the virtual agent's expressions. Compared to the literature on human smiles [1,7,9], the decision tree contains the typical amused, polite and embarrassed smiles as reported in the literature (see Section 2.1). However, it contains also amused, polite, and embarrassed smiles with other morphological and dynamic characteristics.

6   Conclusion

In conclusion, in this paper, we have proposed an algorithm to determine the morphological and dynamic characteristics of virtual agent's smiles of amusement, politeness, and embarrassment. The algorithm has been defined based on a virtual agent's smiles corpus constructed by users and analyzed with a decision tree classification technique. Such an algorithm enables us to consider not only one specific smile for each type, but several smiles with different characteristics. The proposed algorithm allows for the generation of different smiles and for choosing between an higher potential smile recognition and variability. Depending on this value, the number of smiles that a virtual agent may express for a given smile type (amused, polite, or embarrassed) varies from one (high value of importance) to several (average value of importance).

Because we cannot guarantee that the decision-tree learning algorithm returns the optimal decision tree, the next step of this work is an evaluation of the proposed method to verify that the smiles selected by our algorithm are perceived by the user as relevant in amusement, polite and embarrassed contexts. Other machine learning techniques may also be explored, for instance SVM (Support Vector Machine). This technique has some advantages compared to decision tree, for instance stability, but it remains a black box. Lastly, the work presented in this paper has been conducted in the specific context of a western culture (mainly French culture), with a specific female virtual agent, and in context-free situations. We aim at extending this work by considering the influence of the social context on the type of smile expressed by the virtual agent. Moreover, using the same method, we aim at studying other types of smile identified in the literature, such as for instance melancholy or stifled smile [20].

Acknowledgments

This work has been financed by the NoE SSPNET (Social Processing Network) European Project.

References

1. Ekman, P., Friesen, W.: Felt, false, and miserable smiles. Journal of Nonverbal Behavior 6, 238–252 (1982)
2. Rehm, M.: Catch me if you can – exploring lying agents in social settings. In: AAMAS, pp. 937–944. Academic Press Inc., London (2005)

3. Niewiadomski, R., Pelachaud, C.: Model of facial expressions management for an embodied conversational agent. In: Paiva, A.C.R., Prada, R., Picard, R.W. (eds.) ACII 2007. LNCS, vol. 4738, pp. 12–23. Springer, Heidelberg (2007)

4. Krumhuber, E., Manstead, A., Cosker, D., Marshall, D., Rosin, P.: Effects of dynamic attributes of smiles in human and synthetic faces: A simulated job interview setting. Journal of Nonverbal Behavior 33, 1–15 (2008)

5. Theonas, G., Hobbs, D., Rigas, D.: Employing virtual lecturers' facial expressions in virtual educational environments. International Journal of Virtual Reality 7, 31–44 (2008)

6. Frank, M., Ekman, P., Friesen, W.: Behavioral markers and recognizability of the smile of enjoyment. Journal of Personality and Social Psychology 64, 83–93 (1993)

7. Keltner, D.: Signs of appeasement: Evidence for the distinct displays of embarrassment, amusement, and shame. Journal of Personality and Social Psychology 68(3), 441–454 (1995)

8. Harrigan, J.A., O'Connell, D.M.: How do you look when feeling anxious? Facial displays of anxiety. Personality and Individual Differences 21, 205–212 (1996)

9. Ambadar, Z., Cohn, J., Reed, L.: All smiles are not created equal: Morphology and timing of smiles perceived as amused, polite, and embarrassed/nervous. Journal of Nonverbal Behavior 17-34, 238–252 (2009)

10. Ekman, P.: Darwin, deception, and facial expression. Ann. N.Y. Acad. Sci. 1000, 205–221 (2003)

11. Ekman, P., Friesen, W.V., Hager, J.C.: The facial action coding system. Weidenfeld and Nicolson (2002)

12. Duchenne, G.: The Mechanism of Human Facial Expression. Cambridge University Press, Cambridge (1990) (1862)

13. Krumhuber, E.G., Manstead, A.S.R.: Can duchenne smiles be feigned? new evidence on felt and false smiles. Emotion 9(6), 807–820 (2009)

14. Hess, U., Kleck, R.E.: Differentiating emotion elicited and deliberate emotional facial expressions. European J. of Social Psychology 20(5), 369–385 (1990)

15. Tanguy, E.: Emotions: the art of communication applied to virtual actors. PhD thesis, Department of Computer Science, University of Bath, England (2006)

16. Ekman, P., Friesen, W.: Unmasking the Face. A guide to recognizing emotions from facial clues. Prentice-Hall, Inc., Englewood Cliffs (1975)

17. Poggi, I., Pelachaud, C.: Emotional meaning and expression in performative faces. In: Affective Interactions: Towards a New Generation of Computer Interfaces (2000)

18. Rakotomalala, R.: Tanagra: un logiciel gratuit pour l'enseignement et la recherche. In: Sloot, P.M.A., Hoekstra, A.G., Priol, T., Reinefeld, A., Bubak, M. (eds.) EGC 2005. LNCS, vol. 3470, pp. 697–702. Springer, Heidelberg (2005)

19. Breiman, L., Friedman, J., Olsen, R., Stone, C.: Classification and Regression Trees. Chapman and Hall, Boca Raton (1984)

20. Faigin, G.: The Artist's Complete Guide to Facial Expression. Watson-Guptill (1990)

How Turn-Taking Strategies Influence Users' Impressions of an Agent

Mark ter Maat, Khiet P. Truong, and Dirk Heylen

Human Media Interaction, University of Twente
PO Box 217, 7500 AE Enschede, the Netherlands
{maatm,truongkp,heylen}@ewi.utwente.nl

Abstract. Different turn-taking strategies of an agent influence the impression that people have of it. We recorded conversations of a human with an interviewing agent, controlled by a wizard and using a particular turn-taking strategy. A questionnaire with 27 semantic differential scales concerning personality, emotion, social skills and interviewing skills was used to capture these impressions. We show that it is possible to influence factors such as agreeableness, assertiveness, conversational skill and rapport by varying the agent's turn-taking strategy.

1 Introduction

Turn-taking is a fundamental and universal aspect of conversation that has been described extensively in the literature (for example, in [15,5,13]). Although there have been critical reviews on the well-known model by Sacks et al. [15] – "one party speaks at a time", "occurrences of more than one speaker at a time are brief" – researchers agree that something interesting happens when two or more speakers speak at the same time. Interruptions, for example, have been found to correlate with competitive attitudes such as dominance and power, but also with cooperative attitudes such as attentive listening, backchannel feedback and other rapport-oriented acts [14,8]. Similarly, pauses in conversation, within or between turns, have various functions and are powerful cues for what is happening in a conversation [3]. Pauses in speech can indicate cognitive processing, but can also be used for grounding, as a politeness marker [2] or as a signal of acceptance or refusal. Endrass et al. [6] showed that there is a cultural component to the perception of pauses.

One application for which turn-taking models are important are Embodied Conversational Agents (ECAs). For ECAs to have humanlike conversations, the ECA needs to know (among other things) when the user has finished or is about to finish his or her turn before it starts speaking. Many turn-taking models have been developed that considered turn-taking theories as described in the literature, in particular with the goal to avoid overlapping speech. For example, Atterer et al. [1] and Schlangen [16] developed algorithms that *predict* turn-endings as soon as possible such that the system can behave quick enough to simulate human-like behavior. Jonsdottir et al. [12,11] developed a real-time turn-taking

J. Allbeck et al. (Eds.): IVA 2010, LNAI 6356, pp. 441–453, 2010.

model that is optimized to minimize the silence gap between the human's speech turn and the system's speech turn. When evaluating these algorithms they only looked at the performance of the prediction as they were trying to keep the number of overlaps and the average length of the silence gap as low as possible.

But why should the average length of the silence be as short as possible? And why should there be no overlapping speech? In the Semaine project (http://www.semaine-project.eu), we aim to create four different ECAs, each with a different personality. We have Poppy, who is cheerful and optimistic, Obadiah, who is gloomy and depressed, Spike, who is aggressive and negative, and Prudence, who is always pragmatic. Several strategies can be applied to evoke different user impressions of the ECA's personality, for example, one can imagine that the ECA's appearance or speaking style (e.g. friendly or bored) influences the user's impressions of the ECA. Here, we are interested in applying different turn-taking strategies (i.e. the management of when to speak) to evoke these user impressions. What we would therefore like to know is how people perceive different turn-taking behaviors, and how we can use this knowledge to assign certain personality-like characteristics to an agent.

Some previous studies have partly addressed these questions. In human-human conversations, interruptions are usually associated with negative personality attributions and assertiveness [14]. In this study, an offline experiment was performed in which participants listened to recorded human-human conversations and judged the participants on several personality and sociability scales. In [7], Fukayama et al. evaluated the impressions conveyed with different gaze models for an embodied agent. Although their research is not related to turn-taking, the concept of 'impression management' is very relevant to the 'perception' part of the current study. In [17], a similar experiment was carried out, but instead of gaze models, turn-taking strategies were evaluated. Spoken dialogues were simulated with a *Conversation Simulator*, which can simulate conversational agents that use a certain turn-taking strategy, for example, starting to speak before the other agent's turn ended. The turns were simulated with unrecognizable, mumbling speech. Participants listened to these simulations and rated the 'speakers' on scales of personality and affect.

These studies have all used recordings of conversations which were rated by outside observers that were not participating in the conversation. The participants had to rate either audio or video clips which were generated or recorded earlier. Our current study, however, presents a similar agent perception study in which the participants are now *actively involved* in the conversation. We look at how different turn-taking strategies alter the impressions that people have of an agent, and we do this in an *interactive* way. Participants are interacting with a virtual interviewer – using speech only – whose turn-taking strategy is controlled by a Wizard of Oz. After each interview, the participants fill in a questionnaire about the perceived impression of the agent. We describe the setup of this study in Section 2, and the questionnaire used in Section 2.4. The results are presented and discussed in Section 3.

2   Experimental Setup

The goal of this experiment is to assess how different turn-taking strategies of an agent affect the human interlocutor's perception of the agent. In a previous experiment [17], this was studied by simulating conversations between two agents using unrecognisable speech. After listening to these simulated conversations, people had to write down how they perceived one of the agents. In each of the conversations the agent was following a predetermined turn-taking strategy.

A disadvantage of that experiment was that the human raters were not subjected to the turn-taking strategies themselves; they were only bystanders overhearing each conversation. When someone is using a certain strategy when talking directly to you, the *effect* on your perception of the other person will probably be stronger than that of a third person, and may even be completely different. For example, when you hear one person interrupting another person, this will have a different (probably weaker) effect than when that person is interrupting you. Therefore, the experiment was adapted in such a way that the human raters had to talk to a computer which was using a certain turn-taking strategy.

2.1   Turn-Taking Strategies

In our previous study [17], two distinct turn-taking strategies were tested. The first was the *startup* strategy, which determined when to start speaking, relative to the end of the other agent's turn. The different strategy choices for the startup strategy were 'before', 'at', and 'after'. The other strategy was the *overlap resolution* strategy, which determined how the agent would behave when it detected overlapping speech – both agents talking at the same time. The different choices of the overlap resolution strategies were 'stop' (stop speaking), 'normally' (continuing normally), and 'raised' (continuing with a raised voice). Our initial goal was to apply these strategies to the current experiment as well. However, a pilot test showed that overlapping speech was avoided by the human interlocutors; they would immediately stop speaking. Therefore, we decided to simplify the experiment and only assess the startup strategy.

The three startup strategies used in the current study are:

1. EARLY: the system will start its turn just before the end of the interlocutor's turn
2. DIRECT: the system will start its turn immediately after the interlocutor's turn has finished
3. LATE: the system will leave a pause (of a few seconds) before it starts its turn after the interlocutor's turn has finished.

Although the strategies are *conceptually* similar to those used in our previous study [17], the actual *realization* of these strategies is different, so we decided to use other strategy names to stress this difference. In [17], the agent knew exactly when the other agent's turn would end so the start of turns could be placed at fixed points before or after the other's turn (depending on the strategy). In the current study, the strategies are enforced by the human wizard as current automatic algorithms are not advanced enough to accurately predict the end of a turn in the EARLY strategy [4]. In contrast with [17], the human wizard will start turns at variable time intervals before or after the interlocutor's turn.

2.2 Scenarios

Testing the startup strategy in an experiment in which the participants have to talk to the agent makes the experiment more complex. In the previous experiment [17] the agents used unrecognisable speech to simulate a conversation. However, it does not make much sense to have the partipants talk to an agent that uses unintelligible speech. In the current experiment we therefore used an interview setting, with the computer (the agent) in the role of an interviewer. This constrains the flow of the conversation as the initiative is mainly with the agent. It allowed us to limit the number of utterances the agent should be able to say. The agent will ask a question, and independent of the content of the answer of the user, the agent (or Wizard rather) anticipates the user's turn-end and then asks the next question using one of the three startup strategies.

In such a setup, the agent's questions are very important. We designed the questions such that they would be easy to answer, since a complex question can disrupt the flow of the conversation. Also, the questions asked by the agent should not be answerable with one or two words only, since it is hard to apply a certain startup strategy when the user only says 'Yes'.

Another possible problem is that certain questions can influence the results because each question has certain connotations that are perceived differently by each user. Therefore, we decided to create three sets of questions each on a different topic ('food and drinks', 'media' and 'school and study'). By making three different topics it was possible to interchange the questions used in each session (a single conversation of a user with the system). This decreases the influence of the questions on the results. Also, by making three sets of related questions, the questions fit in the same context and will not disrupt the flow of the conversation.

Another factor to consider is the voice that is used. A male or a female voice can greatly influence the perception of the user, for instance, because the voice sounds more friendly, or because male and female participants may listen differently to male and female voices. To control for this variable we introduced two agents: one with a male and another with a female voice. These voices were changed each session to decrease the influence of the voice on the results.

With these changes the different scenarios were created. A scenario consists of a certain startup strategy (EARLY, DIRECT, or LATE), a certain voice (MALE or FEMALE), and a certain topic ('food and drinks', 'media', and 'school and study'). A session is a single conversation of the user with the agent, using a certain scenario. These scenarios were created in such a way that every possible combination and order was used at least once.

2.3   Procedure and Participants

22 people participated in the experiment(16 male, 6 female, mean age 27.55, SD 3.41). Prior to the experiment they were told that they would talk with a speech-to-speech dialogue system, with the agent in the role of an interviewer. They were told that we implemented different personalities in different parts of the dialogue system, and that their role was to write down, in a questionnaire, how they perceived each agent. After this introduction they talked with the agent three times (three sessions), each session with a different scenario.

During a session the participant sat in front of a microphone and a set of loudspeakers. The wizard sat behind the participant, out of sight but in the same room. During the interview, the wizard would follow the current startup strategy by clicking on the button to start the next question at the right time. The spoken questions were synthezised with the Loquendo TTS software (http://www.loquendo.com). After the interview, the subjects would complete a questionnaire about how they perceived the interviewer.

2.4   Questionnaire

After each interview, the participant received a questionnaire. In order to measure the perceived impression the users had of the agent, we adopted semantic differential scales: pairs of bipolar adjectives were placed at the extremes of 7-point Likert scales. The selection of scales was based on previous experiments by [7,17,9,14]. In general, our goal was to have a set of scales that captures users' impressions of personality-related attributes, social-skills-related attributes, and the interviewer's interviewing capabilities, see Table 1.

Table 1. Semantic differential adjectives used in questionnaire

negative - positive	not aroused - aroused	unfriendly - friendly
disagreeable - agreeable	negligent - conscientious	rude - respectful
distant - close	unpredictable - stable	unattentive - attentive
cold - warm	passive - active	submissive - dominant
competitive - cooperative	impolite - polite	introvert - extravert
inexperienced - experienced	shy - bold	careless - responsible
insecure - confident	tensed - relaxed	disengaged - engaged
aggressive - clam	closed - open	weak - strong
pushy - laidback	arrogant - modest	not socially skilled - socially skilled

3   Results

This section presents the results of the experiment. First, the annotated recordings were checked to confirm that the startup strategies were applied correctly by the Wizard. Second, a factor analysis was performed to reduce the number of scales to a more manageable number. We will present both steps in the first two subsections below. Finally, the results of the data analysis are presented.

3.1 Strategy Validation

During the sessions, it became clear that not just machines have problems predicting the end of the user's turn correctly. Especially with the EARLY strategy it is likely that there are occasions where the user was not almost finished with the turn and wanted to start another sentence, but was interrupted by the interviewer (aka Wizard).

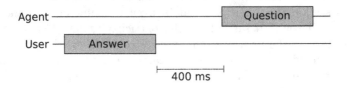

Fig. 1. An example of a pause length of 400 ms

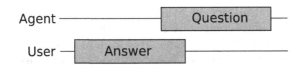

Fig. 2. An example of an instance of overlap

Since applying the correct strategy is error-prone, we need an objective measure to see how consistently each startup strategy was applied. For this we looked at the two objective measures *pause length* and *number of overlaps*. The pause length is the average duration of silence between the end of the user's turn and the start of the agent's next question. Figure 1 illustrates this. We expect that this duration is shortest for the EARLY strategy and longest for the LATE strategy. The number of overlaps is the average number of overlaps per session, where an overlap is defined as an agent that starts the next question while the user is still speaking. For an example, see Figure 2. One should expect that the number of overlaps is highest for the EARLY strategy, and lowest for the LATE strategy. To verify these expectations we annotated the recorded interviews on who was speaking when. With these annotations, we counted the number of overlaps and we measured the average pause length.

Table 2 shows the average pause length between the user's current turn and the following interviewer's question, grouped by the startup strategy that was used. As expected, the EARLY strategy contains the shortest pauses, and the LATE strategy the longest. Also, the differences between the three strategies are highly significant ($p < 0.001$).

Table 3 shows the average number of overlaps per session – which happened when the agent started speaking before the user was finished – again grouped by

Table 2. Average pause length between user's turn and following interviewer's question. *** = $p < 0.001$

| | Average pause length | | | | |
	EARLY	DIRECT	LATE	Mean	Sd
EARLY	-	***	***	0.72	0.69
DIRECT	***	-	***	1.07	0.58
LATE	***	***	-	1.97	0.57

Table 3. Average number of overlaps (user and interviewer speaking at the same time) *** = $p < 0.001$

| | Average number of overlaps | | | | |
	EARLY	DIRECT	LATE	Mean	Sd
EARLY	-	***	***	4.16	2.19
DIRECT	***	-		1.20	1.24
LATE	***		-	0.70	1.13

the startup strategy that was used. As one should expect, the number of overlaps is highest in the EARLY strategy and lowest in the LATE strategy. The difference between the EARLY strategy and the other two strategies is highly significant ($p < 0.001$), but the difference between the DIRECT and the LATE strategy are not. Because both the DIRECT and the LATE strategy wait for the end of the user's turn, we did not expect any significant difference between these strategies for overlaps.

These results show that there is indeed a significant difference in the sessions between the different startup strategies in accordance with the desired effect, which means that the different strategies were correctly applied. Therefore, differences in the results are based on significantly different startup strategies.

3.2   Factor Analysis

To reduce the number of scales (27 different scales) a factor analysis was performed. We used a Principal Component Analysis, with the rotation method Varimax with Kaiser normalization. From the results we used the items with a correlation > 0.5, which resulted in four different factors. These four factors, the corresponding scales and the corresponding correlations can be found in Table 4.

The next step is to interpret these factors. The first factor of Table 4 appears to be related to the *agreeableness* trait, one of the five main personality traits as described by Goldberg [9]. A high level of agreeableness corresponds to someone who is cooperative, compassionate, friendly and optimistic. The adjectives strong, dominant, extravert, bold, arrogant, and pushy, are grouped by the second factor and seem to be well described as *assertiveness*, a term that has been used previously by [14] in a similar context. The items of the third factor do not match with one of the personality traits. It appears that those items say something about the *conversational skill* of the agent. The agent took the role of the interviewer, and a 'good' interviewer should be socially skilled, attentive and experienced. The last factor seems to be related to *rapport* [10]. A high level of rapport means the participants are 'in sync' or 'on the same wavelength', and this often means that the participants are very close and engaged.

In the remaining sections the four factors will be referred to as *agreeableness*, *assertiveness*, *conversational skill* and *rapport*, respectively.

Table 4. Results of Factor Analysis

Factors	Related adjective for low values	Related adjective for high values	Correlation
Factor_1	Cold	Warm	0.86
	Unfriendly	Friendly	0.78
	Tensed	Relaxed	0.72
	Disagreeable	Agreeable	0.70
	Aggressive	Calm	0.63
	Competitive	Cooperative	0.60
	Negative	Positive	0.60
	Impolite	Polite	0.52
Factor_2	Strong	Weak	0.85
	Dominant	Submissive	0.79
	Extravert	Introvert	0.76
	Bold	Shy	0.73
	Arrogant	Modest	0.57
	Pushy	Laid back	0.53
Factor_3	Inexperienced	Experienced	0.72
	Not socially skilled	Socially skilled	0.72
	Unpredictable	Stable	0.69
	Careless	Responsible	0.60
	Unattentive	Attentive	0.50
Factor_4	Closed	Open	0.82
	Disengaged	Engaged	0.71
	Distant	Close	0.62
	Negligent	Conscientious	0.58

3.3   Data Analysis

For the analysis of the data, an ANOVA test was performed on the data with a Bonferroni Posthoc test. The ratings that were used were the four factors found in the previous section, and the four scales that did not fit in these factors: rude-respectful, not aroused-aroused, insecure-confident and passive-active. This section shows the results.

Startup Strategy Figure 3 shows the results of this analysis for the different startup strategies. This figure only shows the results of the four factors and the rude-respectful scale. The other three scales did not provide any significant results.

The strongest factor clearly is Factor 1 (agreeableness): the ratings for all three strategies are significantly different. Starting EARLY is seen as more unfriendly, tensed, aggressive, competitive and negative, and starting LATE is perceived as more friendly, relaxed, agreeable, cooperative and positive. Factor 2 (assertiveness) is mostly strong in the EARLY strategy. The mean rating is significantly higher compared to the other two strategies, but the DIRECT and the LATE strategy are not significantly different compared to each other. Starting EARLY was

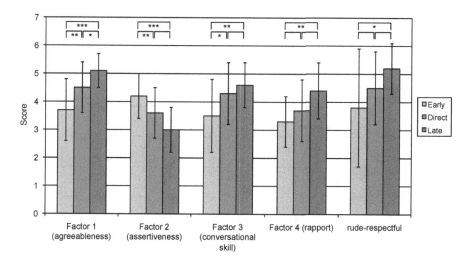

Fig. 3. The results of the different startup strategies * = $p <0.05$, ** = $p <0.01$, *** = $p <0.001$

rated as more strong, dominant, extravert and bold, and using the DIRECT or LATE strategy was rated as more weak, submissive, introvert and shy.

The same result was found with Factor 3 (conversational skill): the EARLY strategy was rated significantly lower than the other two strategies, but those two strategies were not rated significantly different compared to each other. An agent using the EARLY strategy was rated as less experienced, less socially skilled, less predictable, less careless and less attentive. An agent using the DIRECT or the LATE strategy was seen as more experienced, socially skilled, stable, responsible and attentive.

Agent Gender. We observed that the voice that was used – male or female – made a big difference in the perception of the user. In the analysis of startup strategy this effect was filtered out by using an equal number of male and female voices. However, the differences between the voices are still interesting, which is why we analyzed the differences between these voices as well. Figure 4 shows the results.

This figure shows that the male voice was rated higher in Factor 1 (agreeableness), lower in Factor 2 (assertiveness) and lower in the arousal scale. This means the male voice was perceived, among others, as more friendly, positive, polite, submissive, shy, and less aroused. The female voice was perceived, among others, as more cold, aggressive, negative, dominant, bold, and aroused. This may appear strange, but the results probably say more about the voices used than about gender in general.

Along the same line, we also did some other gender comparisons in the data which showed only minor differences. Robinson and Reis [14] explain that

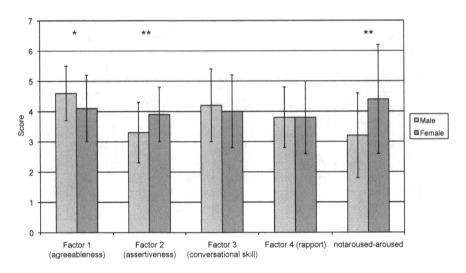

Fig. 4. The results of the different genders. * = p <0.05, ** = p <0.01, *** = p <0.005.

an important factor could be the difference between the gender – same-sex or opposite-sex. To study this we compared the gender of the user with the gender of the agent. However, only two minor results were found. Male users rated male agents significantly lower ($p < 0.05$) in the notaroused-aroused scale than they rated female agents. Also, female agents were rated significantly lower ($p < 0.05$) in Factor 4 (rapport) by male users than they were rated by female users.

We were also interested in the combination of the startup strategy and the gender of the user. For example, to check whether a male user perceives an agent using the EARLY strategy differently than a female user. However, no significant results were found. Another interesting combination is the startup strategy and the gender of the agent. A male agent using the EARLY strategy might be perceived differently than a female agent using the same strategy. Only one result came out of this. A male agent using the DIRECT strategy is perceived significantly higher in Factor 1 (agreeableness) than a female agent using the same strategy.

The final thing we checked was the combination of user gender, agent gender and startup strategy, but we only found one significant result here. A male user rates a male agent using the LATE strategy significantly lower ($p < 0.05$) in the notaroused-aroused scale than a female agent using the same strategy.

Comparison with Previous Study. In a previous study [17], we also studied the effects of different turn-taking strategies, but instead of actively involving the user in the conversation we used recordings of simulated conversations. The questionnaire that was used contained 13 scales, of which 11 were also used in this experiment. Eight of those scales can be put in a factor (see section 3.2), and most of them (four) belong in Factor 1 (agreeableness).

When comparing the results of the two studies, the results are about equal. However, an interesting difference can be found in the scales that belong to Factor 1. As can be seen in Figure 3, the DIRECT strategy scores significantly higher in agreeableness than the EARLY strategy, and the LATE strategy scores signigicantly than the DIRECT strategy. Looking at the results of the previous experiment, to the scores of the four scales that belong in Factor 1, the EARLY strategy (on average) scores lower than the other two strategies, but the DIRECT and LATE strategy do not have a significantly different score. On average, the score for the LATE strategy is even slightly *lower* than that of the EARLY strategy. While this is not a sufficient statistical conclusion, this could point to the fact that humans are influenced more by LATE strategies when being actively involved than when being a passive bystander. However, this difference could also be caused by the interview scenario that was used.

4   Conclusions and Discussion

In this paper we studied how three different turn-taking strategies affect how people perceive the actor of those strategies. With a Wizard-of-Oz setup we simulated a conversational interviewing agent, and the start-time of the next question of the agent was determined by the turn-taking strategies we were testing: EARLY, DIRECT or LATE. Although it is not easy to guarantee that a Wizard uses a certain strategy consistently, the analysis of the recordings revealed that the three different strategies were applied accordingly in this experiment.

Based on the results we found, we can conclude that an agent that uses a certain turn-taking strategy can indeed influence the impression that a user has of this agent. Starting too early (that is, interrupting) is mostly associated with negative and strong personality attributes: agents are perceived as less agreeable and more assertive. Leaving pauses between turns has contrary associations: it is perceived as more agreeable, less assertive, and creates the feeling of having more rapport. The agent's voice did play a role in the results too. In general, we can say that the male voice was perceived as more agreeable and less aroused than the female voice. However, this effect could be more related to the quality of the synthesized voices than to the gender of the agent. Since we only used two different voices for each gender (one Dutch and one English) it is very hard to generalize these results to gender. Previous studies also report on relations between gender and interruptions and interpersonal perceptions of interlocutors – for example, females who interrupt would be penalized more than male interrupters – but we did not find such effects in our data. This was mainly because our prime interest was the turn-taking strategy. Also, we have to keep in mind that the results are specific to this interviewing domain, and that some findings might probably not generalize to a 'free-talk' conversation in which dialogue partners can talk about anything they like, or in a setting in which both dialogue partners can ask questions to each other.

In future work, we will implement several of these turn-taking strategies to convey different personalities and agent impressions (in the Semaine project).

It would be interesting to design more finely-grained turn-taking strategies and to look more locally, for example, at what meaning or impressions pauses can convey. Rather than leaving pauses between *each* turn, it would be better to adapt to the conversational context and leave a rightly-timed pause that may convey a certain meaning.

Acknowledgement. The research leading to these results has received funding from the European Community's Seventh Framework Programme (FP7/2007-2013) under grant agreement n° 211486 (SEMAINE), and by the European Community's Seventh Framework Programme (FP7/2007-2013) under grant agreement n° 231287 (SSPNet).

References

1. Atterer, M., Baumann, T., Schlangen, D.: Towards Incremental End-of-Utterance Detection in Dialogue Systems. In: Proceedings of the 22nd International Conference on Computational Linguistics, pp. 11–14 (August 2008)
2. Brown, P., Levinson, S.C.: Politeness: Some universals in language use. Cambridge University Press, Cambridge (1987)
3. Clark, H.H.: Using Language. Cambridge University Press, Cambridge (1996)
4. de Kok, I., Heylen, D.: Multimodal End-of-Turn Prediction in Multi-Party Meetings. In: ICMIMLMI 2009 Proceedings, pp. 91–98. ACM Press, New York (2009)
5. Edelsky, C.: Who's got the floor? Language and Speech 10, 383–421 (1981)
6. Endrass, B., Rehm, M., André, E., Nakano, Y.I.: Talk is silver, silence is golden: A cross cultural study on the usage of pauses in speech. In: Proceedings of the IUI-Workshop on Enculturating Interfaces, ECI 2008 (2008)
7. Fukayama, A., Ohno, T., Mukawa, N., Sawaki, M., Hagita, N.: Messages embedded in gaze of interface agents impression management with agent's gaze. In: Proceedings of the SIGCHI conference on Human factors in computing systems (CHI 2002), pp. 41–48 (2002)
8. Goldberg, J.A.: Interrupting the Discourse on Interruptions: an Analysis in Terms of Relationally Neutral, Power- and Rapport-Oriented Acts. Journal of Pragmatics 14, 883–903 (1990)
9. Goldberg, L.R.: The structure of phenotypic personality traits. American Psychologist 48(1), 26–34 (1993)
10. Gratch, J., Marsella, S., Okhmatovskaia, A., Lamothe, F., Morales, M., Werf, R.J., Morency, L.P.: Virtual rapport. In: Gratch, J., Young, M., Aylett, R.S., Ballin, D., Olivier, P. (eds.) IVA 2006. LNCS (LNAI), vol. 4133, pp. 14–27. Springer, Heidelberg (2006)
11. Jonsdottir, G.R., Thorisson, K.R.: Teaching Computers to Conduct Spoken Interviews: Breaking the Realtime Barrier with Learning. In: Ruttkay, Z., Kipp, M., Nijholt, A., Vilhjálmsson, H.H. (eds.) IVA 2009. LNCS, vol. 5773, pp. 446–459. Springer, Heidelberg (2009)
12. Jonsdottir, G.R., Thorisson, K.R., Nivel, E.: Learning Smooth, Human-Like Turntaking in Realtime Dialogue. In: Prendinger, H., Lester, J.C., Ishizuka, M. (eds.) IVA 2008. LNCS (LNAI), vol. 5208, pp. 162–175. Springer, Heidelberg (2008)
13. O'Connell, D.C., Kowal, S., Kaltenbacher, E.: Turn-Taking: A Critical Analysis of the Research Tradition. Journal of Psycholinguistic Research 19(6), 345–373 (1990)

14. Robinson, L.F., Reis, H.T.: The Effects of Interruption, Gender, and Status on Interpersonal Perceptions. Journal of Nonverbal Behavior 13(3), 141–153 (1989)
15. Sacks, H., Schegloff, E.A., Jefferson, G.: A Simplest Systematics for the Organization of Turn-Takiing for Conversation. Language 50(4), 696–735 (1974)
16. Schlangen, D.: From Reaction To Prediction Experiments with Computational Models of Turn-Taking. In: Proceedings of Interspeech 2006, pp. 2010–2013 (2006)
17. ter Maat, M., Heylen, D.: Turn Management or Impression Management? In: Ruttkay, Z., Kipp, M., Nijholt, A., Vilhjálmsson, H.H. (eds.) IVA 2009. LNCS, vol. 5773, pp. 467–473. Springer, Heidelberg (2009)

That Avatar Is Looking at Me! Social Inhibition in Virtual Worlds

Austen L. Hayes, Amy C. Ulinski, and Larry F. Hodges

School of Computing
Clemson University
Clemson, SC 29634
ahayes@clemson.edu, amyulinski@gmail.com, lfh@clemson.edu

Abstract. What effect does controlling an avatar, while in the presence of other virtual agents, have on task performance in virtual worlds? Would the type of view have an influence on this effect? We conducted a study to observe the effects of social inhibition/facilitation traditionally seen in human-to-human interaction. The theory of social inhibition/facilitation states that the presence of others causes people to perform worse on complex tasks and better on simple tasks. Simple tasks are well-learned, easy tasks, while complex tasks require more thought processes to complete the task. Participants interacted in a virtual world through control of an avatar. Using this avatar, they completed both simple and complex math tasks in both 1st person and 3rd person views, either in the presence of another female virtual agent, male agent, or alone. The results from this study show that gender of virtual agents has an effect on real humans' sense of presence in the virtual world. Trends exist for inhibition and facilitation based on the gender of the agent and the view type. We have also identified several challenges in conducting experimental studies in virtual worlds. Our results may have implications on designing for education and training purposes in virtual worlds.

Keywords: Avatars, virtual agents, embodied agents, virtual worlds, Second Life, social facilitation, and social inhibition.

1 Introduction and Motivation

Virtual agents, avatars, and virtual worlds are new ways to interact with both computers and other people [11, 13, 14]. A virtual agent is a graphically represented computer-controlled character. An avatar refers to the graphical embodiment of a user [12]. Virtual worlds are three-dimensional spaces where thousands of people can interact using avatars. Second Life (SL) is a highly popular virtual world that has seen rapid growth in the past few years [12]. While virtual worlds like SL have similarities to online 3D games, they differ in that users are not bound by a set of goals [16]. The lack of structured goals, the ability to construct almost any kind of environment desired, and the highly social nature of SL are major reasons for its popularity. SL is currently favored by researchers for the ease of access and its open, dynamic nature [26]. Many researchers and institutions are using SL and other virtual worlds as a natural way to extend

J. Allbeck et al. (Eds.): IVA 2010, LNAI 6356, pp. 454–467, 2010.

online learning, due in large part to students' interest and ability today in gaming and other online technology [26]. Recently there has been rapid growth in the use of virtual agents, avatars, and development in virtual worlds for education, business, and entertainment [17, 13]. The more avatars are used, the more important it becomes to determine how these highly social forms of interaction affect users.

With all the interest and development in virtual worlds through universities and other institutions, it is still not completely clear in what cases virtual worlds provide benefits over traditional or established communications [9]. Indeed, formal research into the impacts of using virtual worlds such as SL is limited [4]. To best make use of these worlds, we need to understand how interaction with virtual agents and avatars in these virtual worlds affects those using avatars. By investigating the effect of avatar use on social influence we hope to identify implications for effective virtual world applications. One way to identify the effects of social influence is to investigate how social facilitation/inhibition theory plays a role in virtual world interaction.

Social facilitation/inhibition is a classical test in social psychology literature to investigate how the presence of others affects task performance [7, 18, 22]. Social facilitation refers to the performance enhancement displayed when a person performs a simple or well-learned task in the presence of others. Social inhibition refers to the performance impairment seen when a person performs a complex or novel task in the presence of others. Previous work has shown inhibition effects on real humans caused by projected virtual humans and immersive virtual humans [25]. The limitations of this study were such that the majority of participants were females and only a female observer was used in both the virtual human and real human conditions. Additionally, this study did not evaluate users controlling avatars at a desktop display with a keyboard, which is more than immersive or projected displays.

Our current study seeks to evaluate the effect seen in previous research on male participants using a standard desktop display and keyboard for interaction and examine the effects of both a female and male observer. In addition, previous research has shown that viewing a virtual world in 1st-person view increases the sense of being in the room [10]. We seek to observe this increase in presence, and determine if there is a larger effect on task performance in 1st-person as a result. *The main goal of this study is to examine if the presence of an avatar or virtual agent has an effect on task performance, while interacting through the use of an avatar. The secondary goal is to determine if view type has an effect on presence, which may have an effect on task performance. Investigating how avatar use affects performance may result in a better understanding of the impacts of virtual worlds and lead to improved virtual world design and applications.*

2 Related Work

2.1 Social Facilitation/Inhibition

Triplett's research into social influence led to many other studies into social theories [19], including Zajonc's *drive theory,* Cottrell, Wack, Sekerak, and Rittle's *socialization theory,* Sanders, Baron and Moore's *attentional conflict theory,* and Guerin and Innes' *social monitoring theory* [22, 5, 18, 7]. There have been numerous studies investigating how the presence of others affects task performance. Bond and Titus looked at 241 social facilitation studies and summarized the results of the studies in a meta-analysis [3]. Some researchers suggest inhibition is caused by the evaluation apprehension that is experienced in front of an audience [5]. Zajonc, however, suggests the mere presence of others can cause the physiological arousal needed for inhibition to occur [22].

Blascovich et al. studied social facilitation in goal-relevant situations involving affective and cognitive processes, based on the biopsychosocial model of challenge and threat [2]. Challenge occurs when the resources from individual experiences meet the demands of the situation, while threat occurs when the resources are insufficient. Participants who performed a novel task in the presence of others had both increased cardiac response and increased vascular resistance. Participants performing the well-learned or novel tasks alone showed no significant reactivity from the baseline. These findings are consistent with the challenge-threat model.

Hoyt et al. studied virtual worlds as a platform for social psychology research [8]. Participants performed two tasks: mastered and not mastered. Participants performed these two tasks either in presence of a virtual audience, or alone. Those who received the virtual audience condition were led to believe the audience was either automated agents or human-controlled avatars. The results of the study found that those performing in the presence of avatars displayed social inhibition performance effects, as compared to either the alone or automated agent condition. The study, however, introduced a possible confound in that the researchers controlling the avatar condition were physically present in the room with the participants. Also, the data did not strongly indicate the effect of audience.

2.2 Virtual Humans

Zanbaka et al. conducted a study into how visual realism and gender affected how persuasive a speaker was [24]. Either a virtual human, virtual character, male or female person presented a persuasive passage to participants. The results showed that virtual characters were as persuasive as real people. Additionally, female participants were more persuaded by male speakers, and male participants were more persuaded by female speakers [24]. Pertaub et al. investigated to what extent a virtual audience could cause social anxiety, in particular the fear of public speaking [17]. The study showed that the virtual audience indeed caused social anxiety, and the level of anxiety was directly related to type of feedback the audience provided. Garau et al. conducted a study to determine how people react to different kinds of behavior and levels of responsiveness exhibited by virtual agents in virtual worlds [6]. Each participant received one of three virtual agent conditions: static, moving, or both moving and responsive to participant movements. Participants were aware that the virtual agents were computer-generated, but participants with higher levels of social anxiety were more likely to avoid "disturbing" the agents. Also, participants who received the responsive condition experienced a higher sense of personal contact with the agents. The researcher's findings seem to show the participant responses are influenced by both the expectations of the technology and the agents' behavior [6].

Zanbaka et al. also conducted a study investigating the effect of virtual human presence on task performance. Participants learned a task and performed either the learned task or a novel task, while being in the presence of a virtual human, a real human, or alone. While the data did not indicate a strong effect, it did show that participants reacted similarly to a virtual human as they would a real person. The weak results of the study were largely attributed to the use of pattern recognition and number categorization tasks [25]. In a follow-on experiment, participants performed both simple and complex math tasks in the presence of a virtual human, of a real human, or alone [23]. The virtual human was present either in a virtual environment viewed through a head-mounted display, or through a life-size projection of the virtual human on the wall near the participant. Results showed participants were inhibited while performing the complex tasks in the presence of a virtual human.

2.3 Avatars and Virtual Worlds

Yee et al. investigated the effects of avatar height and perceived avatar attractiveness in a virtual world [21]. The researchers found that that attractiveness affected confidence of user, and height affected how the users negotiated. In another study, it was found that users who had the taller avatars negotiated more aggressively in face-to-face interactions than those who received the shorter avatars [21]. Okita et al. found that the mere belief that one is interacting with a human-controlled avatar, as opposed to a virtual agent, results in participants focusing more on the task given to them [15]. Participants in the experiment interacted with a virtual agent they believed to be either an avatar or an agent. Both post-test data and skin conductance measures showed the avatar condition resulted in higher arousal. This higher arousal was correlated to better learning [15]. Lims and Reeves research suggests not only that self-representation via avatars increases arousal and interaction from users, but also physiological arousal is increased during identical interactions when told a character was an avatar as opposed to an agent [11].

3 Experimental Study

Our focus was to determine if controlling an avatar had any measurable effect on task performance when in the presence of another virtual agent. We also were interested in how the view (either 1st person or 3rd person) might affect task performance. The theory of social facilitation states that people perform better on simple tasks in the presence of others, while social inhibition states that people perform worse on complex tasks in the presence of others. *Our hypothesis was that previous results of the inhibition effects of virtual humans on task performance would carry over into virtual worlds where the real humans use avatars as a medium for interaction. In addition, we hypothesized that the type of view used would influence these effects.*

3.1 Study Design

We used a 3x2x2 mixed experimental design of the following independent variables:

1. Audience type (Alone, Female Observer, Male Observer)
2. Task type (Simple, Complex)
3. Participant view (1st person, 3rd person)

The first condition was manipulated between subjects and participants were randomly assigned to one of three variables for audience type. The last two were manipulated within subjects where variables were counterbalanced Latin Square to account for residual effects. Participants were randomly assigned to one of four orders:

1. V1,S   V1,C   V2,C   V2,S
2. V1,C   V2,S   V1,S   V2,C
3. V2,S   V2,C   V1,C   V1,S
4. V2,C   V1,S   V2,S   V1,C

V1 refers to 1st person view, V2 refers to 3rd person view, S refers simple math task type and C refers to complex math task type. The dependant variables were participants' accuracy performance on the tasks and response times on the tasks.

3.2 Experimental Tasks and Measures

Pre-experimental questionnaires collected demographic data (gender, age, ethnicity, computer use levels), and math anxiety data. The math questionnaire we used asked participants to rate how anxious different math-related statements made them [1]. The 25 items presented were assesed on a 5-point Likert scale (1–Not at all, 2–A little, 3–A fair amount, 4–Much, 5–Very Much). Mean responses were computed and helped determine any preexisting confounding factors among participant groups.

Both simple and complex experimental tasks required participants to verify whether or not a particular math equation, presented in sentence form, was accurate. Math tasks were chosen because it eliminated the need for additional training, as we could assume all college students have basic math skills. The simple task contained only one operation of addition or subtraction displayed as a yes or no question, for example: "Is $4 + 2 = 6$?" The complex question contained four operations of a combination of multiplication, division, addition and subtraction. For example: "Is $(3 \times 4) + (2 \times 1) - 7 = 9$?" For the incorrect equations, the answer was within two values of correct answer. Participants used key presses to respond to questions. The number of the questions answered correctly and the amount of time to response to each question were recorded and used to measure task performance.

Post-experimental questionnaries collected data on co-presence and presence. Copresence refers to the extent participants who received the observer condition felt they were in the room with another person and was measured using the 17-item Slater Co-Presence Questionnaire [14]. Participants used a 7-point numerical scale (1-Not at all to 7-A great deal) to answer question such as "The experience seems to me more like interacting with the other person..." or "I had a sense of being with the other person....". Item responses were used to compute the copresence mean. Presence refers to the extent participants felt that they were in the virtual room and was measured using the 9-item Steed-Usoh-Slater (SUS) Presence Questionnaire [20]. Item responses were used to compute the presence mean. We also collected other information, such as how the participant felt about the tasks, the agent present in the room, and the environment, through an open-ended debriefing interview.

3.3 Experimental Setup

3.3.1 Physical Testing Room and Apparatus

All participants completed experimental tasks, pre- and post-experimental question-naires in a designated physical testing room without a real human present in the room. Stimulus presentation and data collection were controlled by an Intel Core 2 2.66GHz Dell Pc with an ATI Radeon HD 3450 graphics card attached to a 20-inch flat screen monitor. The observer avatar and the guide avatar were run in the virtual world on a PC of the same specifications. A Rosewill RH-40C stereo headset with microphone allowed the participant to hear the observer and instructions.

3.3.2 Virtual World

SL viewer version 1.23.5 rendered the virtual world to the user. A male guide avatar trained the participant in the virtual world how to move around, sit in a chair, stand up, answer questions, advance to the next question, and what to do if any problems occurred. The participant communicated with the guide avatar using voice chat through the headset and microphone worn during the task completion. This experi-ment requires that the virtual observers, both male and female, exhibit human-like behaviors and gestures. To make the virtual observer human-like, we modeled both the male and female virtual observers actions based on the non-verbal behaviors noted from observing a human observer, including coughing, scratching the head, looking around, tilting the head, and looking at the participant, all triggered at random. The guide could trigger a pre-recorded phrase to be heard by the participant if they talked to the observer during the task. Participants were not told if the observer was an avatar or agent.

Fig. 1. a) 1st person view of a complex math task with male observer condition. b) 3rd person female participant view of a simple math task in male observer condition.

3.4 Procedure

After entering the main lab, participants gave consent and then the greeter took them to the physical testing room where they filled out pre-experimental questionnaires. Each participant was assigned an avatar, of their same gender, to use for interaction. The greeter instructed the participants how to communicate with the avatar guide, displayed on the screen. The greeter introduced them and left the physical testing room. Through voice chat, the guide avatar provided instructions on their virtual task.

The guide first gave instructions on how to walk in the virtual room and sit in the virtual chair. After the participant mastered avatar movement, the guide told the participant the objective of the tasks and how to respond to the tasks using the keyboard. The guide then led participants through a practice task to familiarize them with the procedure and the visual and audio feedback they would receive. Participants were shown how to open and walk through a virtual green door, which led into the actual task room. For the observer condition, the guide introduced the participant to the observer agent, while triggering the agent to greet the participant. The participant remained in the virtual task room for task completion, while the guide returned to the virtual training room.

Participants completed a total of four math task sections, with each section containing 25 math sentences of correct and incorrect problems randomly arranged. At the end of each math section, the participant was instructed via the task display to stand their avatar up and walk around the virtual room and sit back down in the chair when ready. Upon completion of this task the view either switched or stayed the same, depending on what view the order specified.

After completion of the tasks, the participant received instructions on the task display to stand up their avatar, walk back into the training room, and speak with the guide avatar. The guide avatar instructed the participant to walk out of the physical testing room and return to the lab. Participants completed a post-questionnaire, were debriefed and thanked for participating. Participation lasted no more than one hour.

4   Experimental Control in Online Virtual Worlds

SL is a virtual world designed to be highly interactive. Avatars are meant to move freely in open spaces and interact with nearly all objects and avatars. While this level of interaction is both the design and appeal of SL, creating an experiment in a virtual world posed several interesting challenges.

4.1   Limiting the Virtual World and Avatar Interference

We observed in pilot studies that participants tended to interact with elements of the virtual world before receiving instructions. This tendency to interact at-will meant participants could perform actions at any time before understanding the task. One design issue we considered was the door in the training room that led into the actual task room. To ensure participants received all necessary training, the door was programmatically locked to prevent the participant from opening the door before being instructed to. After training, the guide unlocked the door using key presses. Once unlocked, participants were able to open the door at-will during the tasks.

SL presents users with a large amount of stimulus. For our study, any stimulus other than math tasks and the observer avatar could present a confound. To help minimize visual distractions, the virtual task rooms only contained objects necessary to complete the tasks. Also, the virtual building containing both the training and actual task rooms had no doors to the outside. This enclosure ensured that the other parts of our virtual world would not distract participants from their tasks. Limiting participant movement to only the building did not present a confound as they were unaware that a larger environment existed outside the building.

Traditionally, avatars can come and go from public islands at will. We therefore had to ensure no outside avatars interfered with the study and no accidental input from other avatars was collected. The experiment was housed on the Clemson School of Computing's virtual research island, which was restricted to only avatars of authorized faculty and students. Additionally, all data collection scripts were configured to only accept responses from the participant avatar.

4.2 Camera Movement

SL's built-in camera positioning allowed the participants' view to swing outside the walls of the building, allowing a view of the rest of the virtual world. To ensure participants were not distracted by the virtual world outside of the building, we constructed a black shell surrounding the building. This shell ensured that if the view moved outside the walls of the building, participants would see only the color black.

4.3 Sit Detection

If a person walks away from a physical task, they cannot perform that task. However, in a virtual world, where key presses are used to collect responses, a participant could respond to a question without focusing on it. To overcome this issue, we programmatically determined in real-time if the participant was currently sitting in the chair. Only when the participant was sitting in the chair, which ensured the task and the observer were properly view, would key presses be logged. Knowing when the participant was sitting was also critical for what view the participant received. When the script detected the avatar sitting in the task chair, the view would change to either a preset 3rd person or 1st person view including the task and the observer, if present. Camera angles in SL for experimental purposes need to be programmed to ensure that a specific view is seen consistently.

5 Results

Mean accuracy performance percentages and mean reaction times were computed by summing each item across each of the 25 trials in each block of the math tasks. A repeated measures analysis of variance (ANOVA) was conducted to test for the between subjects effect of audience type (alone, female observer, and male observer) and within subjects effects of task type (Simple and Complex) and view type (1st person and 3rd person), where $\alpha=0.05$ was used to indicate significance. A total of 35 participants, males only, from Clemson University participated in this study, mean age $=19.77$ (SD$=$ 1.78). They were randomly assigned one of the three audience conditions (Alone$=11$, Male Observer$=14$, Female Observer$=10$). There was no significant difference found among audience type for computer usage, online worlds usage, 2D game usage, 3D game usage, exposure to virtual humans, and math anxiety.

5.1 Accuracy Performance

The results of a repeated measures ANOVA found no significant main effect of mean accuracy percentage based on Audience type $F(2,31) < 1$. As expected, there was a significant interaction effect of mean accuracy percentage based on task type, $F(1,31)= 5.67$, $p=0.024$, $n^2=0.16$, where participants performed significantly better on the simple task (M=98.2%, SD=0.04) than on the complex task (M=96.9%, SD= 0.03). An interaction effect for task type by audience type was not significant, $F(2, 31)=1.05$, $p=0.364$. There was a near significant interaction effect of task type by view type, $F(1,31)=2.30$, $p=0.14$. An interesting observation was that participants performed better on tasks in 1st person view while alone or with a male observer, but better in 3rd person view with a female observer. There was no significant interaction effect of view type, $F(2,31) < 1$, or view type by audience type, $F(2,31)=1.15$, $p=0.33$.

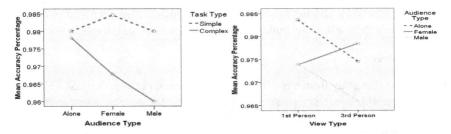

Fig. 2. Mean accuracy among audience type by task type and view type by audience type

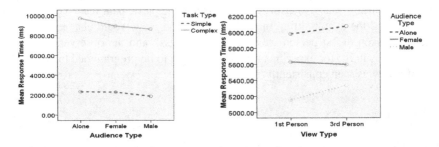

Fig. 3. Mean response times among audience type by task type and view type by audience type

5.2 Response Times

The results of a repeated measures ANOVA found no significant main effect of mean response times based on audience type $F(2,31) < 1$. As expected, there was a signifi-cant interaction effect of mean response times based on task type, $F(1,32)= 283.63$, $p<0.001$, $n^2=0.09$, where mean response times were significantly slower during the complex task (M=9094.26 ms, SD=2.82) than the simple task (M=2163.41 ms, SD=0.71). Interaction effects for task type by audience type, $F(1,32)=2.10$, $p=0.15$, and for task type by view type, $F(1,32)=2.30$, $p=0.14$, were near significance. An interesting observation, similar to accuracy results by view type, was that participants responded faster on tasks in 1st person view while alone or with a male observer, but faster in 3rd person view with a female observer. There was no significant interaction effect of view type, $F(1,32)=1.19$, $p=0.28$, nor view type by audience type, $F(1,32)<1$.

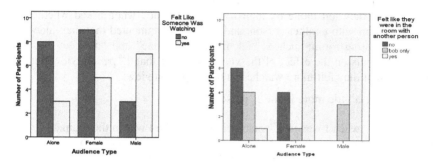

Fig. 4. Number of participants responding to the presence of the avatars by audience type

5.3 Presence, Co-presence, and Debriefing Interview

A one-way ANOVA found a significant difference for presence among audience type $F(2,33)=3.45$, $p=0.044$, where mean presence ratings were significantly higher for the male observer (M=4.45, SD=1.25) than both the female observer (M=3.24, SD=1.22) and alone (M=3.35, SD=1.04). No significant differences were found for mean co-presence ratings among audience type, $F(2,34)<1$, for alone (M=3.40, SD=0.56), female observer (M=3.06, SD=1.01), and male observer (M=3.14, SD=0.96). 66% (16 out of 24) of participants in the audience condition, felt like they were in the room with someone. Of those, 9 participants were observed by a female, and 7 were observed by a male. The difference of proportions was significant, $\chi^2(4, N=35)=13.25$, $p=0.01$, with 6% (4 out of 24) of those who did not feel like they were in the room with someone responded "not at all" and 6% (4 out of 24) responded "with Bob only" (the guide). 50% (12 out of 24) of participants in the audience condition felt like someone was watching them, as compared with the alone condition, though the differences in proportion were not significant, $\chi^2(2, N=35)=4.39$, $p=0.11$. Of those in the audience condition, 7 participants were observed by a male and 5 participants were observed by a female. Responses of participants feeling like someone was watching them was significantly correlated with the audience type, $r=0.330$, $n=35$, $p=0.05$, though was not significantly correlated with participants' accuracy performance and response times. Participants in the audience condition responded to the questions 'did you feel like you were in the room with another person' or 'did you feel like you were being watched':

- "…when she sneezed or coughed, felt more like a human…"
- "…a little bit, when she was watching me and looking at the screen…"
- "…at times, a cough seemed like he was impatient…"
- "…yeah, in a way when I was walking around. I focused on the math, but looked at him occasionally…"

An interesting observation was that although both observer avatars were developed to resemble college students in age. One participant characterized the female character as "a presence of a strict teacher" or "like a teacher" while another participant characterizing the male as a peer, "like a peer watching me". Although conclusions cannot be made based on comments from only two participants, it might be useful to collect data on participants' perceptions of the design of characters. Those in the alone condition confirmed they felt alone by their responses of "no" when asked whether they were in the room with another person, and that they commented that they indeed felt alone in the testing room, such as "felt like I was alone" and "did feel like I was alone". Comments on the effect of the view type were that 1st person view felt more realistic and that they felt more watched in the 1st person view:

- "...a little more in the 1st person view..."

- "...when I was in 1st person view I felt like I was in the room..."

Other comments were in relation to comparing the realism of the guide avatar, Bob, to the realism of the observer avatars, Sally and John:

- "...no lip-syncing and gestures made her [Sally] look fake..."

- "...if Bob was in the room it would have been more real..."

- [felt like someone was in room] "...with Sally no, but with Bob, yes..."

6 Discussion

The lack of significant difference found for any of the pre-experimental measures among audience type indicates that none of these aspects were contributing factors in performance differences among participants grouped by audience type. Although results were weak, trends were found to indicate an inhibition effect, where participants performed worse and responded slower on the complex task in the presence of both a female and male observer. Furthermore, participants performed the worst and slowest in the presence of a male observer. There was also a trend of facilitation that participants performed better and responded faster on the simple task in the presence of a female observer only. It is likely that continuing the study with more participants, resulting in higher power, results on task performance may become significant. Presence was found to be significantly higher when participants were observed by a male than when observed by a female or alone. Differences found in presence are typically dependent on display type; however this result means that participants had a higher sense of being in the virtual room based on observer gender. This higher sense of presence could have contributed to the stronger inhibition result found among the male observer condition.

Co-presence ratings were low, less than 4 on a scale from 1 to 7, and did not differ between the alone condition and the two observer conditions. Additionally, more participants reported that they felt like the male observer was watching them than the female observer, yet more participants felt like they were in the room with someone else with the female observer than with the male observer. Though, it is not clear as to what differences there were between the male and female observer to produce these differences. Low co-presence may help to explain the weak results of inhibition and facilitation. Participants may not have felt like they were with another person possibly due to the realism of the character, animations and gestures, or other properties of the virtual world viewer. The lack of conversation between the character and the participant could not have been a contributing factor due to the fact we incorporated a similar amount of conversation as our previous experiment [23]. Although not significant, the results on view type reveal a trend that when males are performing a task, performance is higher in 1st person view unless a female is present. If a female avatar or virtual agent is present in the room, males' performance will be better if the task is completed in 3rd person view. Since our sample population consisted of only males, further research is needed to determine the effects of the female population.

7 Conclusions and Future Work

This paper has identified several challenges as a result of conducting an experimental study in a virtual world, due to the freedom and flexibility in interaction. These results could have important implications for designing virtual worlds for education and training. It was important to limit the stimulus of the virtual world so that participants would perform the experimental task rather than explore other areas of the virtual world. Secure access was another important issue when evaluating effects based on the presence of another avatar. Having another avatar present would have affected the results on the study and can have effects during educational and training tasks. In addition, we needed to implement features that would make sure that the participant's view was focused on the task while they were actually performing the task. These features were used to avoid any accidental button presses that would interact with the task as a result of participants' focus on something else, not realizing their actions on the task. This would be an important feature to implement if conducting an evaluation for educational or training purposes to ensure poor results came from individual's actual performance and not from interaction with other elements of the virtual world.

This study statistically found that males feel higher sense of presence in the virtual world while a male virtual agent is in the virtual room, as opposed to a female agent or alone. This study also revealed several interesting trends. Males tend to be more inhibited by male agents while performing a complex task and perform better on simple tasks in the presence of a female agent. Males also tend to perform better on tasks while using 1st person view, unless a female is present, then 3rd person view will afford better performance. Although these additional trends exist, they were not significant. We plan, however, to continue to run more participants through the study to determine if these trends will become significant effects. As our sample population consisted of males only, we also plan to recruit female participants to determine the cross-gender effects of inhibition and facilitation among virtual agents and real humans. In summary, the results from this study have implications for future designers of virtual worlds using virtual humans for interaction. The results from this study show that gender of virtual agents or avatars have an effect on sense of presence in the virtual world. Additionally this study found trends that virtual agents or avatars may have an effect on task performance in a virtual world using a desktop display and keyboard. Furthermore, the combination of using various view types, either 1st person or 3rd person view, with characters of certain genders in the virtual room can have an effect on task performance as well. When designing virtual worlds, designers must be careful that characters in the virtual world do not inhibit rather than facilitate the user.

Acknowledgments. This research was supported, in part, by NSF Research Experiences for Undergraduates (REU) Site Grant CNS-0850695. We would like to thank Toni Bloodworth, Lauren Cairco, and Jerome McClendon for their assistance in conducting the study.

References

1. Alexander, L., Martray, C.: The development of an abbreviated version of the mathematics anxiety rating scale. Measurement and Evaluation in Counseling and Development 22(3), 143–150 (1989)
2. Blascovich, J., Mendes, W.B., Hunter, S.B., Salomon, K.: Social "facilitation" as challenge and threat. Journal of Personality and Social Psychology 31, 422–429 (1999)
3. Bond, C.F., Titus, L.J.: Social facilitation: A meta-analysis of 241 studies. Psychological Bulletin 94, 265–292 (1983)
4. Cliburn, D.C., Gross, J.L.: Second Life as a Medium for Lecturing in College Courses. In: 42nd Hawaii International Conference on System Sciences, HICSS 2009, pp. 1–8, 5–8 (2009)
5. Cottrell, N.B., Wack, D.L., Sekerak, G.J., Rittle, R.H.: Social facilitation of dominant responses by the presence of an audience and the mere presence of others. Journal of Personality and Social Psychology 9, 245–250 (1968)
6. Garau, M., Slater, M., Pertaub, D.P., Razzaque, S.: The responses of people to virtual humans in an immersive virtual environment. Presence: Teleoperators and Virtual Environments 14, 104–116 (2005)
7. Guerin, B., Innes, J.M.: Social facilitation and social monitoring: A new look at Zajonc's mere presence hypothesis. British Journal of Social Psychology 2, 7–18 (1982)
8. Hoyt, C., Blascovich, J., Swinth, K.: Social inhibition in immersive virtual environments. Presence: Teleoperators and Virtual Environments 12(2), 183–195 (2003)
9. Jaeger, B.: What educational activities fit virtual worlds: Towards a theoretical evaluation framework. In: 3rd IEEE International Conference on Digital Ecosystems and Technologies, DEST 2009, pp. 715–720 (2009)
10. Kallinen, K., Salminen, M., Ravaja, N., Kedzior, R., Sääksjärvi, M.: Presence and emotion in computer game players during 1st person vs. In: Proceedings of the PRESENCE 2007, 3rd person playing view: Evidence from self-report, eye-tracking, and facial muscle activity data, pp. 187–190 (2007)
11. Lim, S., Reeves, B.: Computer agents versus avatars: Responses to interactive game characters controlled by a computer or other player. Int. J. Hum.-Comput. Stud. 68(1-2), 57–68 (2010)
12. Messinger, P.R., Stroulia, E., Lyons, K., Bone, M., Niu, R.H., Smirnov, K., Perelgut, S.: Virtual worlds – past, present, and future: New directions in social computing. Decision Support Systems, Communities and Social Network 47(3), 204–228 (2009)
13. Middleton, S.E.: Interface agents: A review of the field. Technical Report. University of Southampton (2000)
14. Mortensen, J., Vinayagamoorthy, V., Slater, M., Steed, A., Lok, B., Whitton, M.C.: Collaboration in Tele-Immersive Environments. In: Proc. of the Workshop on Virtual Environments, vol. 23, pp. 93–101 (2002)
15. Okita, S.Y., Bailenson, J., Schwartz, D.: The mere belief of social interaction improves learning. In: Proceedings of the 29th Annual Cognitive Science Society, pp. 1355–1360. Congnitive Science Society, Austin (2007)

16. Oliver, I.A., Miller, A.H., Allison, C.: Virtual worlds, real traffic: interaction and adaptation. In: Proceedings of the First Annual ACM SIGMM Conference on Multimedia Systems, MMSys 2010, pp. 305–316. ACM, New York (2010)
17. Pertaub, D.P., Slater, M., Barker, C.: An experiment on pubic speaking anxiety in response to three different types of virtual audience. Presence: Teleoperators and Virtual Environments 11, 68–78 (2002)
18. Sanders, G.S., Baron, R.s., Moore, D.L.: Distraction and social comparison as mediators of social facilitation effects. J. of Experimental Social Psych. 14, 291–303 (1978)
19. Triplett, N.: The dynamogenic factors in pacemaking and competition. Journal of Psychology 9, 507–533 (1898)
20. Usoh, M., Catena, E., Arman, S., Slater, M.: Using Presence Questionnaires in Reality. Presence: Teleoperators and Virtual Environments 9(5), 497–503 (2000)
21. Yee, N., Bailenson, J.N., Ducheneaut, N.: The Proteus effect: Implications of transformed digital self-representation on online and offline behavior. Communication Research 36(2), 285–312 (2009)
22. Zajonc, R.B.: Social Facilitation. Science 149, 269–274 (1965)
23. Zanbaka, C.A., Ulinski, A.C., Goolkasian, P., Hodges, L.F.: Social responses to virtual humans: implications for future interface design. In: Proceedings of the SIGCHI Conference on Human Factors in Computing Systems, CHI 2007, San Jose, California, USA, April 28 - May 03, pp. 1561–1570. ACM, New York (2007)
24. Zanbaka, C., Goolkasian, P., Hodges, L.F.: Can a virtual cat persuade you? The role of gender and realism in speaker persuasiveness. In: Proc. CHI 2006, pp. 1153–1162. ACM Press, New York (2006)
25. Zanbaka, C., Ulinski, A., Goolkasian, P., Hodges, L.F.: Effects of Virtual Human Presence on Task Performance. In: Proc. ICAT 2004, pp. 174–181 (2004)
26. Zhang, Q., Marksbury, N., Heim, S.: A Case Study of Communication and Social Interactions in Learning in Second Life. In: 2010 43rd Hawaii International Conference on System Sciences (HICSS), pp. 1–9 (2010)

Know Your Users! Empirical Results for Tailoring an Agent's Nonverbal Behavior to Different User Groups

Nicole C. Krämer[1], Laura Hoffmann[1], and Stefan Kopp[2]

[1] University of Duisburg-Essen, Forsthausweg 2, 47048 Duisburg, Germany
[2] CITEC - Center of Excellence "Cognitive Interaction Technology", Bielefeld University,
P.O. Box 10 01 31, D-33501 Bielefeld
{Nicole.Kraemer,Laura.Hoffmann}@uni-due.de,
skopp@techfak.uni-bielefeld.de

Abstract. Since embodied agents are considered as equally usable by all kinds of users, not much attention has been paid to the influence of users´ attributes on the evaluation of agents in general and their (nonverbal) behaviour in particular. Here, we present evidence from three empirical studies with the agent Max, which focus on the effects of participants` gender, age and computer literacy. The results show that all three attributes have an influence on the feelings of the participants during their interaction with Max, on the evaluation of Max, as well as on the participants` nonverbal behavior.

Keywords: virtual agents, nonverbal behavior, user groups, gender, elderly users, computer literacy.

1 Introduction

Within human-computer interaction it has long been proclaimed that due to the fact that humans show inter-individual differences, it is important to "know the user" [1] when designing an interface. In research on embodied conversational agents this goal has not received much attention. This is perfectly plausible, given that an interface agent has always been assumed to be appealing to all kinds of users [2]. In fact, the vision of embodied interface agents as an interface of the future has always been connected to the notion that due to its ability to produce and understand verbal and nonverbal human communication, a tailoring to specific user will not be necessary [3]. At best, the question of appearance, that is, how the agent should look like when being employed in different contexts and for different user groups has received some attention [4]. However, it is not only appearance but also the (nonverbal) behaviour of the agent that might be analyzed with regard to the question whether it is generally appropriate and appealing for human users or whether individual users prefer particular nonverbal behaviours. Also, it can be asked whether people vary with regard to the desired number of certain behaviours (e.g., the agent´s smiling or gaze). Inter-individual differences with regard to the perception of nonverbal behaviour seem plausible against the background of, for example, the increased sensitivity of women with regard to nonverbal behaviour [5]. Thus, the goal of the present paper is to

J. Allbeck et al. (Eds.): IVA 2010, LNAI 6356, pp. 468–474, 2010.
© Springer-Verlag Berlin Heidelberg 2010

analyze whether different user groups exhibit specific preferences for specific nonverbal behaviours of an interface agent. We present evidence from three different studies which originally targeted the question which effects different nonverbal behaviours of the agent Max [6] have: Eyebrow raising and gestural activity [7], smiling [8] and feedback behaviour [9]. As we additionally assessed information on the user (gender, age, and computer literacy) we are now able to present an overview on the influence of these variables on the evaluation of specific nonverbal cues and can derive first conclusions on the preferences of different user groups with regard to the nonverbal design of embodied agents.

2 Method

Three studies. Three studies were conducted, employing the ECA Max as stimulus material, to test whether an agents´ nonverbal behavior has different effects on different users. The experimental sessions were conducted in the laboratory at Bielefeld University (Germany) where Max [6] is displayed on a life-sized screen.

Procedure. The procedure was similar in all three studies: Each participant had a 5-10 minute lasting small-talk with Max, which was recorded via video camera. Since speech technology is so far not able to reliably recognize spoken language input in noisy environments, a so-called "Wizard of Oz" scenario was used. The Wizard, however, had no influence on the reactions of Max, which were autonomously generated by the system. After the conversation participants had to fill in a questionnaire concerning the feelings they had during the interaction, their perception of Max, and their evaluation of the interaction in general. The participants` gender, age and computer literacy were assessed as well. With regard to age, however, merely study 1 tested a relevant number of participants older than 30 years and therefore age was only considered as potentially moderating variable in this study.

Dependent Variables. The dependent variables were collected via paper-and-pencil questionnaires and via video-recordings of the participants during the interaction with Max. The questionnaires were designed based on existing questionnaires, which were developed and repeatedly employed in previous studies [7]. By means of 20-items, the feelings of the participants during the interaction were determined (e.g. "attentive", "amused", "relaxed" and "lethargic"). Participants had to state their level of agreement by means of 5-point Likert-scales, with the extremes "strongly disagree" and "strongly agree". The person perception of Max was measured by means of a 34-item semantic differential (seven-point bipolar rating scales, whose extremes are designated by two opposite adjectives). It was assessed, for example, whether Max was perceived rather as "warmhearted" or "cold", "self-confident" or "shy", "wooden" or "animated". Finally, the general evaluation of the interaction was assessed by items which asked for the participants` enjoyment of the interaction, the perceived controllability of the conversation, and whether participants could imagine to complete tasks like programming a video recorder with Max. Again, participants had to state their level of agreement by means of 5-point Likert-scales. The participants` nonverbal behavior towards the agent was assessed by quantitative analyses of the recorded video material.

Independent Variables: Manipulations of the agent´s nonverbal behavior

Study 1: Eyebrow movement & self-touching gestures. 50 persons, 28 female and 22 male, aged from 15 to 72 years volunteered to participate in the study (mean value = 27.73 years; SD = 11.53). They were confronted with Max, who´s nonverbal behavior was manipulated with respect to eyebrow movements and self-touching gestures. The presence of eyebrow movement as well as self-touching gestures were manipulated [7].

Study 2: Frequency of smiling. 104 persons (52 male, 52 female) aged from 19 to 55 years participated in the second study. In order to analyze whether the frequency of an agent´s smile has an effect on its evaluation, three conditions were distinguished: a) no-smile condition, in which Max did not show any smile; b) infrequent smile condition, in which Max shows occasional smiles, and c) frequent smile condition, where Max shows frequent smiles [8].

Study 3: Different styles of feedback. In the third study 70 persons, 19 males and 51 females, aged from 17 to 48 years (M= 24.09, SD= 5.717) participated. In this study different styles of the agent´s feedback were varied: emotional feedback, which provided a feedback about the emotional state of Max (including smiles and compliments), and envelope feedback, which provided a feedback about the comprehension of the participants´ contributions and presents Max as an attentive listener [9].

3 Results

3.1 Feelings during the Interaction with Max

Effects moderated by participants` gender

Study 1: When we added the participants` gender into an ANOVA, no main effects, but a significant interaction was found for the factor „interest". Females show more interest than men, when self-touching gestures were shown $(F(1;42)= 6.272; p = .016;$ Part. $\eta^2 = .130;$ female: M = 0.56; SD = 0.77; male: M = -0.55; SD = 1.21). In turn when no self-touching gestures were shown, male participants experienced the conversation as more interesting than females (male: M= 0.23, SD= 1.00; female: M= -0.16, SD= 0.83).

Study 2: In study 2 one main effect of gender emerged $(F(1; 103)= 5.67; p= .019;$ Part. $\eta^2= .060)$, showing that women (M= -0.29; SD= 0.85) are more nervous than men (M= 0.21; SD= 1.12) when interacting with Max. There was also one interaction between gender and Max`s smiling concerning the factor disinterest $(F(2; 103)= 4.72; p= .011;$ Part. $\eta^2 =.10)$. Whereas men are least disinterested in the no-smile condition (M=- 0.41; SD= 0.50), women are most disinterested in this condition (M= 0.06; SD= 1.04). In the infrequent-smile condition, the pattern is reversed (males: M= 0.57; SD= 0.98; females: M= -0.48; SD= 0.89). However, women and men do not differ in disinterest in the frequent-smile condition (males: M= 0.05; SD= 1.31; females: M= -0.05; SD= 0.74).

Study 3: No significant differences or interactions occurred due to gender.

Effects moderated by participants` age

Study 1: As depicted above, age only varied considerably in study 1, therefore it was only considered within this study. Here, the participants` age had an effect on their feelings during the interaction, explicitly on the factor nervousness, $F(1; 40)= 4.253$; $p= .046$; Part. $\eta^2 = .096$. Younger participants (15-23 years) were significantly less nervous ($M= -0.34$, $SD= 0.69$) than older participants (24-72 years) ($M= 0.288$, $SD= 1.108$). Additionally, study 1 yielded a significant interaction between age and self-touching gestures for the factor attention, $F(1; 40)= 5.019$; $p= .031$; Part. $\eta^2 = .111$: Younger participants were more attentive ($M= 0.438$, $SD= 0.600$) than older participants ($M= -0.448$, $SD= 1.448$), when Max showed self-touching gestures. In turn, older participants were more attentive ($M= 0.31$, $SD= 0.77$) than younger ones ($M= -0.04$, $SD= 0.41$), when no self-touching gestures were shown.

Effects moderated by participants` computer literacy

Study 1: We observed that experts were less nervous ($M= -0.20$; $SD= 0.89$) during the interaction with Max than novices ($M= 0.33$; $SD= 1.11$). This was proven by a significant main effect for the factor nervousness ($F(1; 42)= 6.736$; $p= .040$; Part. $\eta^2 = .097$).

Study 2 and 3: Neither main effects nor interaction effects of the users` computer literacy emerged.

3.2 Evaluation of Max

Effects moderated by participants` gender

Study 1 and study 3: The gender of the participants had no significant influence on the perception of Max nor interacted with the independent variables.

Study 2: Results for the factor incompetence show a significant main effect, ($F(1; 103)= 5.761$; $p= .018$; Part. $\eta^2= .061$): Max`s incompetence is rated higher by male participants ($M= 0.29$; $SD= 1.02$) than by female participants ($M= -0.23$; $SD= 5.76$). Thus, men are more rigorous in their judgment with regard to competence. There was no significant interaction between gender and the smiling condition.

Effects moderated by participants` age. In study 1, no main effects, or interactions were found.

Effects moderated by participants` computer literacy

Study 1: With regard to computer literacy, experts experienced Max as more strained ($M= 0.20$, $SD= 0.86$) than novices ($M= -0.32$, $SD= 1.16$), as a main effect for the factor strain showed, $F(1; 42)= 4.235$; $p= .046$; Part. $\eta^2 = .092$.

Study 2: Also study 2 emphasizes differences in the evaluation of Max due to computer literacy: the factor passiveness was significantly ($F(2; 103)= 4.219$; $p= .018$; Part. $\eta^2 = .087$) stronger perceived by gamers ($M= 0.38$, $SD= 1.11$) than by experts ($M= 0.26$, $SD= 1.01$) and least by novices ($M= -0.29$; $SD= 0.86$). No significant interactions between Max`s smiling behavior and computer literacy were found.

Study 3: No main effects, or interactions were found.

3.3   General Evaluation of the Interaction

Effects moderated by participants` gender

Study 1: ANOVA yielded a significant interaction between self-touching gestures and the participants` gender for the factor acceptance: When self-touching gestures were shown by Max women show a higher acceptance than men (F(1; 42)= 4.552; p= .039; Part. eta 2= .098; woman: M= 0.57, SD= 0.99; men: M= -0.38, SD= 1.10). But when no self-touching gestures were shown men show more acceptance than women (men: M= 0.13, SD= 0.94; woman: M= -0.21, SD= 0.87).

Study 2 and 3: No main effects or interactions on factor level were observable.

Effects moderated by participants` age. Neither main effects, nor interaction effects were found in study 1.

Effects moderated by participants` computer literacy. No main effects, or interactions emerged on factor level in any of our studies.

3.4   Participants` Nonverbal Behavior towards the Agent

Effects moderated by participants` gender

Study 1: No main effects but a significant interaction for the participants` gender were found: Self-touching gestures by the participants depend on eyebrow raising of the agent, as study 1 shows. But the direction differs between male and female participants. The interaction effect (F(1; 42)= 4.095; p= .049; Part. η^2 = .089) suggests that female participants show more self-touching gestures (M= 0.12, SD= 0.17) than male participants (M= 0.03, SD= 0.05), when Max did not raise his eyebrows. Instead, females show less self-touching gestures (M= 0.09, SD= 0.10) as men (M= 0.13, SD= 0.11) when Max shows eyebrow raising behavior.

Study 2: One main effect of the participants` gender was found in study 2, but no significant interaction emerged: women showed more (F(1; 103)= 9.8; p = .002; Part. η^2 = .087; men: M= 0.49; SD= 0.319; women: M= 0.70; SD = 0.34) and longer (F(1; 103)= 6,34; p= .011; Part. η^2= .061; men: M= 0.07, SD= 0.06 ; women: M= 0.11; SD = 0.07) full smiles than men.

Study 3: No main effects or interactions emerged.

Effects moderated by participants` age. In study 1 the age of the participant caused no main, or interaction effects.

Effects moderated by participants` computer literacy

Study 1 and study 3: No significant main effects or interactions were observable.

Study 2: An ANOVA with respect to the influence of the participants` computer literacy on their nonverbal behavior showed one main effect, but no interaction. The main effect occurred for the overall duration of smiling behaviors of the participants: novices smiled the most followed by experts and gamers (F(2; 103)= 3.333; p= .040; Part. η^2 = .062; novices: M= 0.44; SD= 0.17; experts: M= 0.38; SD= 0.16); gamers: M= 0.34; SD= 0.15).

4 Discussion

The aim of this paper was to analyze whether different user groups exhibit specific preferences for specific nonverbal behaviors of an interface agent. For that purpose, evidence from three empirical studies with the agent Max was presented, with a focus on moderating aspects, namely the participants` gender, age and computer literacy. The results show that the attributes have an influence on the feelings of the participants during their interaction with Max, on the evaluation of Max, on the general evaluation of the interaction, as well as on the participants` nonverbal behavior. In the following, we sum up and interpret the corresponding results in detail.

Know your users` gender. Men and women have different preferences with regard to embodied agents. In fact, compared to the effects of age and computer literacy, the influence of gender was prevailing. When developing agents it would thus be most important to take these results into account – either by providing two versions from which the user can choose, or by designing the agent accordingly when it is known whether predominantly men or women will use it.

Study 2 showed that women were, in general, more nervous during the interaction with the agent, which is on the one hand not astonishing given that women are still less accomplished with regard to computer technology, but on the other hand it contradicts the vision that embodied agents will facilitate human-computer-interaction for these kinds of users. Our data suggests that female users´ interest and acceptance can be increased when self-touching gestures are implemented (see study 1) and when the agent frequently smiles. Therefore we conclude that women especially benefit from an increased nonverbal behavior of the agent, in line with the finding that women are more sensitive for nonverbal behaviors [5]. One can speculate that they are reassured when they perceive signals from the interlocutor that they can interpret.

Besides, for male users it was shown that self-touching gestures decrease interest in the conversation with an agent (see study 1). Also men in study 2 were most interested when the agent did not smile. Thus it can be concluded that agents for male users should be kept simple with regard to nonverbal behavior.

Know your users` age. Study 1 showed that also older persons were more nervous when they interacted with Max. Additionally the interaction between the age of the participants in study 1 and the manipulation of self-touching gestures demonstrates that older participants were more attentive when no self-touching gestures were shown. Especially the increased nervousness should be analyzed carefully in future studies in order to be able to derive conclusions.

Know your users` computer literacy. Computer novices proved to be more nervous than other users. This is in line with previous findings that computer laypeople do not benefit from embodied agents in the way that it is typically hoped for [10]. Also, people who are frequently in contact with computers and newer technologies have different demands concerning embodied agents than persons who are novices in this area. The results of our studies showed that computer experts evaluate Max as more strained and gamers as more passive. This might be due to the fact that especially gamers are used to sophisticated virtual characters. As this is independent from the specific nonverbal behavior no specific design guidelines for nonverbal behavior can be derived but still the results point to the importance of supporting the specific needs of novices versus experts.

Conclusions. Although it has to be considered that results could have been more consistent since not all studies yielded the same main effects, they show distinct patterns. The results presented here are just a first step towards knowing the user but they already indicate that there are differences which when taken into account might lead to specific design guidelines. As suggested above this might either lead to different versions of an embodied agent from which the users can choose or – if the agent is to be employed with only one specific group of users – to a specifically designed version of the agent. As especially gender effects were prevailing these might be a good starting point for first implementations and further tests.

Besides, other moderating aspects like culture should be taken into account in future studies, because especially different cultures might like to see different nonverbal behaviors, as also people from different cultures show and prefer different behaviors.

References

1. Shneiderman, B.: Designing the user interface: Strategies for effective human-computer interaction, 1st edn. Addison-Wesley, Reading (1987)
2. Cassell, J., Bickmore, T., Campbell, L., Vilhjálmsson, H., Yan, H.: Human conversation as a system framework: Designing embodied conversational agents. In: Cassell, J., Sullivan, J., Prevost, S., Churchill, E. (eds.) Embodied conversational agents, pp. 2–63. MIT Press, Cambridge (2000)
3. Krämer, N.C.: Social communicative effects of a virtual program guide. In: Panayiotopoulos, T., Gratch, J., Aylett, R.S., Ballin, D., Olivier, P., Rist, T. (eds.) IVA 2005. LNCS (LNAI), vol. 3661, pp. 442–453. Springer, Heidelberg (2005)
4. Domagk, S.: Pädagogische Agenten in multimedialen Lernumgebungen. Empirische Studien zum Einfluss der Sympathie auf Motivation und Lernerfolg. Logos, Berlin (2008)
5. Hall, J.A.: Nonverbal sex differences. Communication accuracy and expressive style. Johns Hopkins University Press, Baltimore (1984)
6. Kopp, S., Gesellensetter, L., Krämer, N.C., Wachsmuth, I.: A conversational agent as museum guide - design and evaluation of a real-world application. In: Panayiotopoulos, T., Gratch, J., Aylett, R.S., Ballin, D., Olivier, P., Rist, T., et al. (eds.) IVA 2005. LNCS (LNAI), vol. 3661, pp. 329–343. Springer, Heidelberg (2005)
7. Krämer, N.C., Simons, N., Kopp, S.: The effects of an embodied conversational agent's nonverbal behavior on user's evaluation and behavioral mimicry. In: Pelachaud, C., Martin, J.-C., André, E., Chollet, G., Karpouzis, K., Pelé, D. (eds.) IVA 2007. LNCS (LNAI), vol. 4722, pp. 238–251. Springer, Heidelberg (2007)
8. Krämer, N.C., Kopp, S., Sommer, N., Becker-Asano, C.: Smile and the world will smile with you. The effects of a virtual agent's smile on users' evaluation and behavioral mimicry (revised and resubmitted)
9. Von der Pütten, A., Reipen, C., Wiedmann, A., Kopp, S., Krämer, N.C.: Comparing emotional vs. envelope feedback for ECAs. In: Prendinger, H., Lester, J.C., Ishizuka, M. (eds.) IVA 2008. LNCS (LNAI), vol. 5208, pp. 550–551. Springer, Heidelberg (2008)
10. Krämer, N.C., Rüggenberg, S., Meyer zu Kniendorf, C., Bente, G.: Schnittstelle für alle? Möglichkeiten zur Anpassung anthropomorpher Interface Agenten an verschiedene Nutzergruppen. In: Herzceg, M., Prinz, W., Oberquelle, H. (eds.) Mensch und Computer 2002, pp. 125–134. Teubner, Stuttgart (2002)

The Persona Zero-Effect: Evaluating Virtual Character Benefits on a Learning Task with Repeated Interactions

Jan Miksatko[1], Kerstin H. Kipp[2], and Michael Kipp[1]

[1] DFKI, Embodied Agents Research Group, Germany
{jan.miksatko,michael.kipp}@dfki.de
[2] Saarland University, Experimental Neuropsychology Unit, Germany
k.kipp@mx.uni-saarland.de

Abstract. Embodied agents have the potential to become a highly natural human-computer interaction device – they are already is use as tutors, presenters and assistants. However, it remains an open question whether adding an agent to an application has a measurable impact, positive or negative, in terms of motivation and learning performance. Prior studies are very diverse with respect to design, statistical power and outcome; and repeated interactions are rarely considered. We present a controlled user study of a vocabulary trainer application that evaluates the effect on motivation and learning performance. Subjects interacted either with a no-agent and with-agent version in a between-subjects design in repeated sessions. As opposed to prior work (e.g. Persona Effect), we found neither positive nor negative effects on motivation and learning performance, i.e. a *Persona Zero-Effect*. This means that adding an agent does not benefit the performance but also, does not distract.

Keywords: Embodied conversational agents, human-computer interaction, computer supported learning.

1 Introduction

Embodied agents can be a powerful user interface because they are capable of *multimodal interaction*: they can communicate with verbal and non-verbal channels, react to user behavior and give subtle feedback in the form of a smile or a nod. Moreover, embodied agents can engage users in a *social* way, becoming supervisor, audience or virtual friend, and thus increasing commitment, motivation and ultimately performance. Applications of embodied agents include virtual teachers, presenters in museums or personal shopping assistants. In the domain of education, virtual characters have received special attention because their potentials in terms of nonverbal communication and social relations, both important aspects of a good *human* teacher.

The benefits of embodied agent presence in computer based learning environments have been analyzed in multiple prior studies (cf. [1,2]). Generally, an

J. Allbeck et al. (Eds.): IVA 2010, LNAI 6356, pp. 475–481, 2010.

embodied agent allows for a *richer interaction* since the communication is multimodal (gaze, facial expressions, head nods and gestures) [3]. An important question is whether the agent can *motivate the student to learn longer* with the system [4,5]. Also, a positive effect on *learning performance* (e.g. recall, comprehension and problem solving) has been suggested [6,7]. A learning effect can be due to the agents' *stimulation of the learning process* by guiding the user, directing attention, and encouraging exploration and reflection [8,9] and also may benefit from a *personal relationship* similar to that between teacher and student [10]. A related finding is that the agent's presence makes the task and learning material to be *perceived as being easier* than without an agent [11].

The actual findings, however, do not conclusively answer the above questions and are often contradictory. Several studies [6,7] show learning improvement when an agent is present, whereas other studies [11,5] show the contrary. The studies not always include a control *no-agent* condition, for instance the Persona Effect study [4,6] compares only five different agent versions among each other. In terms of study duration, almost all studies assessed their systems in a single session, with the notable exception of Bickmore [10]. However, it could have a decisive impact on e.g. learning performance if the user feels annoyed by the agent after a few sessions or, on the contrary, becomes more comfortable over time. Furthermore, the empirical studies vary significantly in the interaction style (e.g., an agent presenting a text [11,7] vs. agent giving hints and commenting on user actions [6,5]), in the agent appearance (a cartoon-style full-body agent [11,6] vs. a talking head [7,5]), in the learning task (a problem solving [6,5] or a memory task [11,7]) and also in the measures (questionnaires for rating subjective perception vs. quantitative measures for collecting performance data).

We present a user study with a vocabulary trainer application with repeated interactions that evaluates the effect of an agent on motivation and memory performance. The system consists of a *no-agent* version (control condition) and a *with-agent* version. In a between-subjects design, 36 subjects interacted with one system version each. We evaluate the question of motivation and performance in a clean experimental design. In particular, we examine the development over multiple sessions and employ quantitative measures for user motivation. The results show neither positive nor negative effect on the motivation and memory performance. In other words, the agent is not detrimental to learning, but also, does not improve it.

In summary, the major aspects of this work are as follows:

- *Clean experimental manipulation:* We designed a system with two conditions (no-agent, with-agent). The with-agent condition features very few nonverbal behaviors so that the main difference between conditions is the presence/absence of a (moving) agent, following Dehn et al [2] to not introduce confounding aspects between conditions. We used objective measures (e.g. subjective perception of time) for assessing effects of agent presence.
- *Repeated interactions:* Following criticism on existing studies [1,2], we designed our study to encompass repeated interactions over a 8-day period to emulate how our system is perceived as if in real-world usage.

– *Persona Zero-Effect:* We show that the presence of our agent does not change learning performance or motivation compared with the no-agent system.

2 User Study

To investigate the potential benefits of embodied agents in the learning environments we created the ITeach environment [12]. Regarding the question of how the presence of a virtual character influences memory performance and motivation, we have the following hypotheses:

H1. The agent presence has no positive effect on memory performance [11,5].
H2. The presence of our agent increases the motivation of the learner [9,4].

2.1 Scenario: A Virtual Vocabulary Trainer

In the present study we used ITeach for a simple vocabulary trainer, based on the flash card learning system. The flash card system is a question/answer game: a card with a foreign language expression is presented and the user answers for herself what the correct translation is. Then, the correct answer is displayed and the user rates: "I knew it" or "I did not know it". All cards are stored in *bin 1* at first. Depending on the rating, a card is moved one bin forward ("I knew it") or backward ("I did not know it"). This means that (1) difficult words are repeated more often than easy words, and (2) the user can easily see progress by looking at the bins where the rightmost one represents "long-term memory".

Each learning session has three phases. First, a fixed number of new unseen cards are presented. Only if such a card is unknown, it is is moved to Bin 1. The goal of this filtration phase is to introduce the new learning material and align the user's knowledge to the same level. Second, the cards in Bin 3, Bin 2 and Bin 1 are presented in the mentioned order. These bins contain material to be reviewed (cards from the previous learning sessions and newly added cards). In the last phase, the user can learn optional vocabulary cards. The session

Fig. 1. Screenshots of no-agent and with-agent version of the application

serves as motivation measures discussed in the following section. We selected vocabulary topics of common interest for all users: animals, clothes, body and medicine. The algorithm orders the cards by the topic when selecting them from the current bin.

The user interface was deliberately kept simple (see Fig. 1). In the *no-agent* version, it consists of two windows displaying the English and German expressions and a row of buttons for showing and rating the answer. Each expression is displayed and spoken by a commercial text-to-speech (TTS) engine (Nuance RealSpeak Solo). The system gives positive feedback, e.g. "good!", for known cards 20% of the time. In the *with-agent* version, a female embodied agent is added in the middle of the screen. It features some idle movement to make the agent look alive and does a minimum amount of gestures: pointing to the card 15% of the time and accompanying positive feedback with a smile or nod. Subjects were seated in a cubicle and wore headphones to exclude any external distractions.

2.2   Study Design

In our study we compared two conditions: no-agent and with-agent in a between-subjects design, i.e. the subjects were split into two groups and each group interacted with one condition. The second major design decision was to repeatedly (four times) interact with the system over a longer period of time (8 days). Subjects were briefed before the first session and, during every session, saw short on-screen instructions before the each phase (filtration, learning, open-ended). 36 subjects participated in the study, all students of Saarland University and native German speakers. They were paid 20 EUR for the experiment. In both experiment groups, there were 50% male and 50% female, the average age was 26 years, one third of participants were students of computer science related disciplines and less than 10% of participants indicated greater experience with e-learning systems and virtual agents. We used the following measures for evaluating the agent's influence on learning.

Memory performance measures. To measure learning performance, we introduce the measure of *card score* and *bin score*. The card score captures the learning progress within a session by summing up card "movement" between bins. We sum up +1 point for a known card and -1 point for an unknown card (i.e. a movement forwards and a movement backwards respectively). The bin score reflects the overall knowledge as a weighted sum of cards in each bin with weights 0 to 3 for bins 1 to 4, respectively. The higher the bin number the more deeply the contained vocabulary is stored in memory, therefore the higher weight. Both measures are normalized by the total number of total cards.

Motivation measures. We employ two motivation measures. The learning phase is split into *legs*: segments of 60-70 seconds length each. After each leg, a *post-leg questionnaire* is displayed. It asks the subject "How long do you think the last leg took?" and provides a slider for giving the time estimate. We hypothesize that if the user is well motivated and engaged, she will estimate the time below the actual time, whereas if the user is less motivated, the subjective time passes more slowly and a higher estimate will be given. We refer to this measure as *perception of time*. The second measure, *optional vocabulary cards*, is obtained in the open-ended phase: the subject is asked, in regular intervals of 5 cards, whether 5 additional cards should be learned. This goes on until the subject decides to quit. The number of additional cards is recorded as a measure of motivation.

3   Results

For all data, 36 subjects, 4 sessions each, we performed ANOVAs with the two factors *agent* (no-agent, with-agent) and *session* (session 1–4). We only report main effects on interactions with factors agent since only the influence of the agent is of interest.

For memory performance we compared card score (learning quality within a session) and bin score (overall knowledge). Fig. 2 shows that our measures indeed reflect the learning progress across the four sessions. As for the two conditions, no-agent and with-agent, the score development is statistically equal when computing a two-factored ANOVA $(F(1,3)=.35;\ p=.79)$.

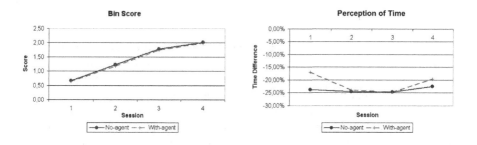

Fig. 2. Bin Score measure for learning performance and Perception of Time measure for motivation

Motivation was measured using a post-leg perception of time and the number of additional cards. The first measure was analyzed across sessions (see Fig. 2) and across legs (we took the average of the first four legs). An ANOVA with factors agent and session product no main effect $(F(1,3)=.58;\ p=.63)$. An ANOVA with factors agent and leg yielded a main effect $(F(1,3)=.03;\ p<.05)$ which was, however, not confirmed in post-hoc analysis. Therefore, we can regard the leg-wise development as equal. The second motivation measure, the number of additional cards, was also compared between the no-agent and with-agent conditions but yielded no significant result in a two-factored ANOVA $(F(1,3)=1.09;\ p=.36)$.

4   Discussion

With respect to the memory performance, the users clearly improved their vo-cabulary knowledge according to the both measures which confirms the validity of our learning setup. However, the measured values are statistically equal in both conditions (no-agent, with-agent). This *confirms hypothesis H1* that the presence of the agent is not detrimental to learning performance — neither is it beneficial. This confirms findings by [11,5] and contradicts studies claiming to find a positive effect [6,7]. Note that all mentioned studies only looked at a single interaction, so this is the first study were this zero-effect was found in repeated interactions. There was also no difference in terms of motivation between the no-agent and with-agent conditions. There was neither increase nor decrease in the motivation rating, the users perceived time equally in both versions and did not interact longer or shorter with the system in the open-ended phase. This result *refutes hypothesis H2* that the presence of an agent motivates the learner. It contradicts the finding by Höök et al. [9] where users interacted longer in the with-agent condition and partially supports the results by Bickmore [10,13] that the number of user logins was not different among the conditions. Note that the interaction sessions were short (about 15 minutes) and the participants were not overloaded with new vocabulary.

5   Conclusions

We presented a user study evaluating the presence of an agent concerning mo-tivation, memory performance and agent perception. In a vocabulary learning task, 36 participants participated in a study where half of the subjects inter-acted with a system with an agent and the other half with a plain system (no agent). Both systems had the same voice output, so only differed in terms of presence/absence of the agent's body. Memory performance was assessed with quantitative measures. For measuring motivation we assessed the subjects' per-ception of time and the number of voluntary additional cards. Each subject interacted in four sessions over a period of eight days. Our results showed that the agent presence has neither negative nor positive effect on the memory perfor-mance and motivation as suggested by previous single-interaction studies (e.g. [11]) and as opposed to some studies (e.g. [7]). We conclude that adding an agent is not detrimental but also does not beneficial in terms of learning or motivation. This finding can only be generalized with caution, however, since (a) introducing new features may induce distraction and/or a positive learning effect, (b) our finding may be specific to the domain and/or to the particular agent employed.

Our study establishes a solid baseline for future repeated interactions studies. Future studies should identify which kind of additional value is required to in-duce a positive learning effect in terms of performance and/or motivation (e.g. trying to build a personal relationship with the user, richer multimodal interac-tion, more learning-related contributions by the agent). An equally important question is which additional features would cause distraction and how to balance distracting and motivating factors.

Acknowledgments. This research has been carried out within the framework of the Excellence Cluster Multimodal Computing and Interaction (MMCI), sponsored by the German Research Foundation (DFG). We would also like to thank to Charamel GmbH for providing us with their Avatar engine.

References

1. Gulz, A.: Benefits of virtual characters in computer based learning environments: Claims and evidence. International Journal of Artificial Intelligence in Education 14(3), 313–334 (2004)
2. Dehn, D.M., van Mulken, S.: The impact of animated interface agents: a review of empirical research. International Journal of Human-Computers Studies 52(1), 1–22 (2000)
3. Cassell, J., Thorisson, K.R.: The power of a nod and a glance: Envelope vs. emotional feedback in animated conversational agents. Applied Artificial Intelligence 13, 519–538 (1999)
4. Lester, J.C., Converse, S.A., Kahler, S.E., Barlow, S.T., Stone, B.A., Bhogal, R.S.: The persona effect: affective impact of animated pedagogical agents. In: Proceedings of the SIGCHI conference on Human factors in computing systems, pp. 359–366. ACM, New York (1997)
5. Moundridou, M., Virvou, M.: Evaluating the persona effect of an interface agent in a tutoring system. Journal of Computer Assisted Learning 18, 253–261 (2002)
6. Lester, J.C., Converse, S.A., Stone, B.A., Kahler, S.E., Barlow, S.T.: Animated pedagogical agents and problem-solving effectiveness: A large-scale empirical evaluation. In: Proceedings of 8th Conference on Artificial Intelligence in Education, Press (1997)
7. Beun, R.J., Vos, E.D., Witteman, C.: Embodied conversational agents: effects on memory performance and anthropomorphisation. In: Rist, T., Aylett, R.S., Ballin, D., Rickel, J. (eds.) IVA 2003. LNCS (LNAI), vol. 2792, pp. 315–319. Springer, Heidelberg (2003)
8. Rickel, J., Johnson, W.L.: Animated agents for procedural training in virtual reality: Perception, cognition, and motor control. Applied Artificial Intelligence 13, 343–382 (1999)
9. Höök, K., Persson, P., Sjölinder, M.: Evaluating users' experience of a character-enhanced information space. AI Commun 13(3), 195–212 (2000)
10. Bickmore, T.W.: Relational agents: Effecting change through human-computer relationships. PhD thesis, Massachusetts Institute of Technology (2003)
11. Mulken, S.V., André, E., Müller, J.: The persona effect: how substantial is it? People and Computers, 53–66 (1998)
12. Miksatko, J., Kipp, M.: Hybrid control for embodied agents applications. In: Mertsching, B. (ed.) Proc. of the 32nd Annual Conference on Artificial Intelligence (2009)
13. Bickmore, T.W., Picard, R.W.: Establishing and maintaining long-term human-computer relationships. ACM Trans. Comput. Hum. Interact. 12(2), 293–327 (2005)

High Score! - Motivation Strategies for User Participation in Virtual Human Development

Shivashankar Halan[1], Brent Rossen[1], Juan Cendan[2], and Benjamin Lok[1]

[1] Computer Information Sciences Engineering,
[2] Department of Surgery,
University of Florida, USA
shivashankarh@ufl.edu, {brossen,lok}@cise.ufl.edu,
cendajc@surgery.ufl.edu

Abstract. Conversational modeling requires an extended time commitment, and the difficulty associated with capturing the wide range of conversational stimuli necessitates extended user participation. We propose the use of leaderboards, narratives and deadlines as motivation strategies to persuade user participation in the conversational modeling for virtual humans. We evaluate the applicability of leaderboards, narratives and deadlines through a user study conducted with medical students (n=20) for modeling the conversational corpus of a virtual patient character. Leaderboards, narratives and deadlines were observed to be effective in improving user participation. Incorporating these strategies had the additional effect of making user responses less reflective of real world conversations.

Keywords: Virtual Humans, Intelligent Agent Authoring Tools, motivational strategies, persuasive technology, virtual patients, leaderboards, narratives, deadlines.

1 Introduction

End-users are increasingly becoming an integral part of application development processes. User interactions with the system during the development phase have different goals than interactions after deployment. The developmental user interactions primarily benefit the developers by helping them identify issues with the system. This is opposed to post-deployment interactions where the goal is to use the system to primarily benefit the user. During the developmental interactions, the system will likely have poor performance as measured by number of errors and ease of use. The poor performance of the system causes a *motivation gap*. We define a motivation gap as the lack of proper motivation for a user to participate in a particular task. Since the developmental interactions do not primarily benefit the user, there is minimal motivation for the user to expend effort and time to interact with a system that is still in development. We propose using external motivation strategies to address the motivation gap.

In the past, providing monetary compensation and extra credit have been effective motivational techniques for increasing user participation [3] [4], however, these motivational techniques are not always applicable. For example, providing monetary

J. Allbeck et al. (Eds.): IVA 2010, LNAI 6356, pp. 482–488, 2010.

compensation can be costly and may bias participants. Video games and social networking platforms have been successful in bridging the motivation gap [1], and thus we searched their literature for easily deployable motivation techniques that can effectively persuade users to participate in developmental interactions.

Our work focuses on creating virtual human patients for training healthcare students with their interviewing and interpersonal skills. The development of these virtual patients requires participation from healthcare students in the developmental interactions. We enlisted the help of healthcare experts to select appropriate motivation strategies for motivating participation amongst the healthcare students. When presented with various possible motivation strategies, the healthcare experts identified three strategies that they anticipated would work well for the specific application of motivating medical students: leaderboards, narratives and deadlines.

- A **leaderboard** is an ordered display of the scores and the names of participants in a competition. Video games are a good example of where leaderboards have been used to encourage user participation [1].
- A **narrative** is the telling of a story or account of events or experiences [2].
- A **deadline** is a specific timeframe within which the user is expected to complete a task.

In this paper, we evaluate the applicability of leaderboards, narratives and deadlines in bridging the motivation gap and persuading user participation in the developmental interactions for VH corpus development. A user study was conducted with medical students, and the results indicate that leaderboards, narratives and deadlines were effective in increasing user participation amongst the medical students.

2 Motivation Strategies for Conversational Modeling

One method of simulating human-VH interpersonal conversations is to use a corpus based retrieval approach. The corpus of a VH consists of question-answer pairs of what the users will say to the VH (stimulus) and what the VH will say back (response). When a user asks a question, the system searches the corpus for the most similar question and provides the paired answer. Developing the corpus for human - VH interpersonal conversations is a time-consuming task [3]. This need for extended time commitment is because of the need to gather the various stimuli that can trigger a response. For example, the response "*I have really bad stomach pain*" could be a response to any of the following stimuli: "*How are you feeling?*", "*What's wrong?*" and "*How can I help you?*". The corpus requires comprehensive coverage of the questions that will be asked and the answers the VH should provide.

The time taken for corpus development can be reduced by using a technique called Human-Centered Distributed Conversational Modeling (HDCM) [4]. In HDCM, novice users conduct interactions with the VH during the VH corpus development phase and pose questions (stimuli) to the VH. Stimuli to which the VH did not have a response are automatically gathered into a list. The user is further enlisted to mark when the VH responds incorrectly and these are gathered into the same list. The domain expert can then go through this list to validate new stimuli for existing responses or add new responses for the new stimuli. Thus, through iterations of user interactions and subsequent expert reviews, the corpus of the VH is progressively developed. The HDCM method was observed to take only 10% of the time taken for conversational modeling by previous approaches [4].

As an example, the corpus of a VH that plays the role of a patient suffering from lower back pain was developed for training medical students. The first draft of the corpus that was developed by a physician contained 51 responses and 139 stimuli. After 27 iterations of different users interacting followed by expert reviews of the accumulated stimuli, the corpus now has 118 responses and 446 stimuli. The HDCM model saves time [4] but shifts much of the corpus development work from the expert to the novice. This leaves domain experts with the problem of motivating enough novice users to interact with the VH during the corpus development phase.

3 Motivation Strategies for Medical Students

The target application for this work is the creation of VHs that act as virtual patients. The corpus for these virtual patients is built by medical educators, and medical students constitute the set of novice users who need to interact with the virtual patient during the corpus development stage. The participation of medical students in previous iterations of developmental interactions has been suboptimal and has been observed to vary from 50% to as low as 5%. This low response rate can be attributed to the fact that the subjects of our research are medical students in their surgical clerkship phase. This is a particularly difficult time in a medical student's professional career marked by long work days, patients with high acuity of illness and replete with high-stakes decision-making. It is in this environment that we now ask them to take on another task – to participate in the developmental interactions for conversational modeling of a virtual patient VH. As a result, it is difficult to get the medical students to participate in the VH developmental interactions. Also, requests for participation sent out during advance stages of the semester, which is a very busy time for the medical students, received fewer responses.

The experts' reasoning for choosing the three motivational strategies discussed includes the desire to leverage the competitive nature of medical students for the leaderboards. Medical education also engages the student by presenting medical knowledge in the context of the patient [5] and thus we utilize the narrative format to continue this tradition. Medical students are readily engaged when the information is couched in a clinical milieu. Medical students are also well trained to react to critical timelines and focus their attention on tasks with imminent deadlines.

4 Implementation

The external motivation strategies evaluated in this paper were implemented using Virtual People Factory (VPF). VPF is a web-based application that allows users to create and interact with VHs [4]; the VHs created using VPF conduct natural language conversations using a corpus retrieval approach.

Leaderboards: During an interview that aims at bettering interpersonal skills, there generally exists a mechanism to evaluate the trainee's performance. In the case of medical interview training, a checklist of information that is critical to the scenario is used for evaluating the student's performance. Each piece of information on the checklist is called a "discovery" because when the user asks the appropriate question, they "discover" a critical piece of information- (e.g. *"patient smokes 2 packets of cigarettes a day"*). In our implementation, the user's score is based on how many discoveries were elicited during the interaction. This score is then displayed on the leaderboard. A sample leaderboard interaction is shown in Fig.1. Users are allowed to have multiple interactions with the VH, and the score for a user is the highest score over all interactions with the VH (maximum score is 100).

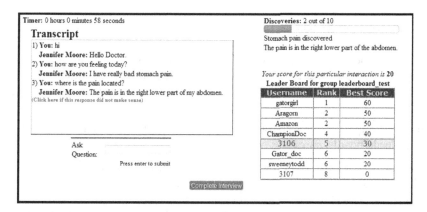

Fig. 1. Leaderboard enabled medical student–virtual human interaction

The users were given the option to choose nicknames for themselves that will be displayed on the leaderboard. For users who did not choose a nickname, a numerical user id was displayed on the leaderboard to represent the user. This provides anonymity for students who would prefer others did not know how they performed.

An important part of appealing to the competitive nature of the participants was to constantly inform them of their leaderboard status. The leaderboards show the user's current position throughout the interaction. Through this mechanism, students receive immediate feedback in seeing their scores pass that of colleagues and classmates. In addition to displaying their status during the interaction, three different kinds of e-mails were sent to the users that informed them of their status on the leaderboard: after an interaction with the VH, weekly update e-mails and whenever a user's score was beaten by another user.

Narratives were a part of the participation-request e-mails that were sent to the users. Medical students who conduct medical interviews are normally given a patient case document that contains information about the demographics and background of the patient. This case document was used to create the narrative for the VH interaction. A sample excerpt from the narrative for a virtual patient suffering from right lower quadrant pain is shown below (used in the evaluation study in Section 5).

> *"Jennifer Moore, a 21-year-old female, presents to the emergency department complaining of lower right quadrant abdominal pain. . The onset of the pain was 1 p.m. The current time is 5 p.m. She has never had this kind of pain before and is extremely worried about what might be the cause."*

Deadlines add a sense of urgency and appeal to the medical student's instinct for providing immediate medical attention. The deadline for the interaction is included in the invitation e-mail sent to the user. Additionally, update e-mails also reference the remaining time for the user to meet with the VH.

5   Evaluation Study

We present the results of an experimental user study conducted with (n=20) medical students. The study was a between-subjects experimental design with the use of external motivation as the independent factor. The participants were split randomly into two groups:

Control group: The control group with n=9 participants interacted with the VH without the leaderboards, narratives or a deadline.

Experimental group: The experimental group with n=11 participants was sent an e-mail with a narrative and a two-week deadline. This group also saw leaderboards during their interactions and was sent update e-mails three times a week.

The chosen medical scenario was one where the VH was suffering right lower quadrant pain because of an ectopic pregnancy. One of the reasons for choosing this particular medical scenario was that we had difficulties in the past recruiting users for participating in the developmental interactions for this very same scenario. At the time of testing, the VH's corpus consisted of 115 responses and 745 different stimuli for these responses.

Hypothesis-1: Participants who are sent invitations to interactions with leaderboards, narratives and deadlines will be more likely to participate in the developmental VH interactions than participants without leaderboards, narratives and deadlines as measured by the response percentage of the participant group to recruitment e-mails.

Hypothesis-2: Participants who are sent invitations to interactions with leaderboards, narratives and deadlines will spend a greater amount of time interacting with the developmental VH than participants without leaderboards, narratives and deadlines.

The following metrics were evaluated:
- **Number of interactions** – the total number of VH interactions. Students performing multiple interactions were counted multiple times.
- **Duration of the interactions** - the time from the start of the interaction to when the users clicked "complete interview"

5.1   Results

The control group received one interaction out of nine users (11%). The experimental group had fifteen interactions out of eleven users. Seven of the eleven users conducted one interview, while one user conducted three interviews, and another conducted five for a total of nine users responding out of eleven (**82%**).

Since the control group received only one interaction, we examined data from a previous developmental study group (*n=22*) that used the same scenario as the current study (*previous group*). Of the 22 participants recruited for the previous group, 12 were contacted in person by their professor and requested to participate but still we got a response rate of only 50 %. We also compared the response rate to three previous developmental study groups that used other scenarios. In Table 1, we see the ratio of interactions per group size for each of the groups and the average time spent interviewing the VH patient.

Table 1. Comparing the number of interactions and average time spent between the experimental group (with persuasion strategies), control group, and four prior developmental study groups

	Experimental	Control Group	Previous Group	GI Hemm.	Post-Op Hemm.	STD
Interactions/ Users	15 / 11	1 / 9	12 / 22	9 / 22	1 / 22	2 / 22
% responded	**81.82 %** [9/11]	11.11% [1/9]	50 % [11/22]	40.91% [9/22]	4.54% [1/22]	9.09% [2/22]
Average time	10.12 min	-	9.84 min	-	-	-

User participation: One-way ANOVA analysis of the number of interactions per user showed that there was a significant difference ($p < .001$) between at least two of the groups. Tukey HSD analysis showed that there were significantly more interactions per user for the *experimental group* than any of the five other groups ($p < .01$ for all groups). Thus, we accept **hypothesis-1**. Additional evidence supporting hypothesis-1 is that two out of the eleven experimental group participants recorded multiple interactions while only one out of the 88 users from all the four previous study groups had multiple interactions with the VH. Amongst the experimental group participants, one user interacted five times and another user interacted three times with the VH. A further reinforcement of this result is that the experimental and control groups were requested to participate at the end of a clinical rotation, the period in which they have the greatest demands on their time.

The behavior of the experimental group participants indicated that the "You were beaten by user [username]" e-mails had a significant effect. There were several times during the study where a participant would beat the score of their competitors, and this would cause a cascade of interactions. As an example we highlight an interaction on the fourth day after the recruitment e-mails were sent out. In this interaction a participant received a higher score than seven other users, causing a "beaten-by" e-mail to be sent to those seven users. Within eight minutes of the e-mail, three additional interactions occurred.

Duration of Interaction: The difference in average time between the experimental group and the previous group did not reach statistical significance (p=0.435). The users did not spend significantly more time with the VH in a single interaction. Therefore, the results of this study do not support **hypothesis-2**.

Difference in user's approach to the interaction: While analyzing the data, it was observed that participants from the experimental group behaved less realistically during the interaction. The realism of the interactions was evaluated through the use of greeting phrases. Nine out of eleven participants (82%) in the *previous group* used a greeting such as "Hello", or "How are you?" while one out of nine participants (11%) in the *experimental group* used a greeting. Using a two-tailed Fisher test shows this to be extremely statistically significant at $p < .001$. This finding highlights a possible limitation of these external motivation strategies; the scoring mechanism may influence user behavior in the VH interview. The participant's primary motivation when influenced by these motivation strategies appears to have been to get a high score, rather than to conduct a realistic medical interview.

6 Conclusion

We proposed motivation strategies for persuading users to participate in the conversational modeling of VHs. The evaluation study results indicate that the motivational strategies were effective in increasing user participation in the conversational modeling process. However, the users seem to approach the externally motivated human-VH interactions in a less realistic way. These results allow us to conclude that external motivation strategies can be helpful in increasing user participation during virtual human development, but care must be taken to align the scoring mechanism with learning goals in the stage of virtual human deployment.

References

1. King, D., Delfabbro, P., Griffiths, M.: Video Game Structural Characteristics: A New Psychological Taxonomy. International Journal of Mental Health and Addiction 8(1), 90–106
2. Bickmore, T., Schulman, D., Yin, L.: Engagement vs. Deceit: Virtual Humans with Human Autobiographies. In: Ruttkay, Z., Kipp, M., Nijholt, A., Vilhjálmsson, H.H. (eds.) IVA 2009. LNCS, vol. 5773, pp. 6–20. Springer, Heidelberg (2009)
3. Dickerson, R., et al.: Evaluating a script-based approach for simulating patient-doctor interaction. In: International Conference on Human-Computer Interface Advances for Modeling and Simulating (SIMCHI 2005), pp. 79–84 (2005)
4. Rossen, B., Lind, S., Lok, B.: Human-Centered Distributed Conversational Modeling: Efficient Modeling of Robust Virtual Human Conversations. In: Ruttkay, Z., Kipp, M., Nijholt, A., Vilhjálmsson, H.H. (eds.) IVA 2009. LNCS, vol. 5773, pp. 474–481. Springer, Heidelberg (2009)
5. Charon, R.: Narrative medicine: form, function, and ethics. Annals of Internal Medicine 134(1), 83 (2001)

Author Index

Printed in the United States
By Bookmasters